SERMONS

AUGUSTINIAN HERITAGE INSTITUTE

THE WORKS OF SAINT AUGUSTINE

A Translation for the 21st Century

Part III — Sermons

Volume 10: Sermons 341-400

The English translation of the works of Saint Augustine has been made possible with contributions from the following:

Order of Saint Augustine

> Province of Saint Thomas of Villanova (East)
> Province of Our Mother of Good Counsel (Midwest)
> Province of Saint Augustine (California)
> Province of Saint Joseph (Canada)
> Vice Province of Our Mother of Good Counsel
> Province of Our Mother of Good Counsel (Ireland)
> Province of Saint John Stone (England and Scotland)
> Province of Our Mother of Good Counsel (Australia)
> The Augustinians of the Assumption (North America)
> The Sisters of Saint Thomas of Villanova

Order of Augustinian Recollects

> Province of Saint Augustine

Mr. and Mrs. James C. Crouse
Mr. and Mrs. Paul Henkels
Mr. and Mrs. Francis E. McGill, Jr.
Mr. and Mrs. Mariano J. Rotelle

THE WORKS OF SAINT AUGUSTINE

A Translation for the 21st Century

SERMONS

III/10
(341-400)
on Various Subjects

translation and notes

Edmund Hill, O.P.

editor

John E. Rotelle, O.S.A.

New City Press

Hyde Park, New York

Published in the United States by New City Press
202 Cardinal Rd., Hyde Park, New York 12538
©1995 Augustinian Heritage Institute

Cover design by Ben D'Angio

Library of Congress Cataloging-in-Publication Data:

Augustine, Saint, Bishop of Hippo.
    The works of Saint Augustine.

    "Augustinian Heritage Institute"
    Includes bibliographical references and indexes.
    Contents: — pt. 3., v. 1. Sermons on the Old Testament, 1-19.
— pt. 3, v. 2. Sermons on the Old Testament, 20-50 — [et al.] — pt. 3,
v. 10 Sermons on various subjects, 341-400.
    1. Theology — Early church, ca. 30-600.   I. Hill,
Edmund.   II. Rotelle, John E.   III. Augustinian
Heritage Institute.   IV. Title.
BR65.A5E53   1990   270.2   89-28878
ISBN 1-56548-055-4 (series)
ISBN 1-56548-028-7 (pt. 3, v. 10)

Nihil Obstat: John E. Rotelle, O.S.A., S.T.L.
Censor Deputatus
Imprimatur: + Patrick Sheridan, D.D.
Vicar General
Archdiocese of New York, December 2, 1994

Printed in the United States

CONTENTS

Two loves fighting each other in this life, love of God and love of the world — 49; The right order of charity; God to be loved more than ones parents — 49; Christ in Gethsemane gives us an example of feeling, and overcoming, human fears — 50; Why fear the first death, Christian? What is really needed is to be redeemed from the second death — 51; The way people love this life should convince us how much we should love eternal life — 53; Losing one's life in order to find it—and finding it in order to lose it — 54; There is a life to be found which it is absolutely impossible to lose — 55

What God is — 383; The divine Trinity is one, and the divine unity is three — 383; Scriptural texts supporting the doctrine of the Trinity — 384

474; Being Moderate and Temperate in Our Pleasures — 475; the Connection Between Fasting and Our Final Goal — 475; Preserving the Unity of the Body of Christ — 476; Even the Pagans Can Teach the Schismatics a Lesson about Unity — 477; Work for Unity a Prerequisite for Evangelization — 478; the Apostles Were Fishers of Men; We Have to Be Hunters of Men — 479; the Illustration of the Old Man in a Lethargy — 480; the Lord's Inheritance Is Not to Be Divided — 481

Sermons

SERMON 341

ON THE THREE WAYS OF UNDERSTANDING CHRIST IN SCRIPTURE:
AGAINST THE ARIANS

Date:419[1]

Christ to be understood in the scriptures in three ways

1. Our Lord Jesus Christ, brothers and sisters, as far as I have been able to tune my mind to the sacred writings, can be understood and named in three ways, whether in the law and the prophets, or in the letters of the apostles, or through our confidence about his deeds, which we know about from the gospel. The first way is: as God and according to the divine nature which is coequal and coeternal with the Father before he assumed flesh. The next way is: when, after assuming flesh, he is now understood from our reading to be God who is at the same time man, and man who is at the same time God, according to that pre-eminence which is peculiar to him and in which he is not to be equated with other human beings, but is the mediator and the head of the Church. The third way is: in some manner or other as the whole Christ in the fullness of the Church, that is as head and body, according to the completeness of a certain *perfect man* (Eph 4:13), the man in whom we are each of us members.

This is what is preached to believers, and offered for their approval to the wise. In the short time available we cannot recall or expound all the innumerable testimonies of scripture, by which we could prove these three aspects of Christ. But on the other hand we cannot leave them all entirely unproved. So let me remind you of some of the testimonies, so that the rest, which lack of time does not permit us to recall, you can go on to note and discover in the scriptures for yourselves.

The first way

2. So as regards the first way of putting forward our Lord Jesus Christ the savior, the only Son of God, through whom all things were made, we have that text that is the most noble and glorious one in the gospel according to John: *In the beginning was the Word, and the Word was with God, and the Word was God; this was in the beginning with God. All things were made through him,*

and without him was made nothing. What was made was in him life; and the life was the light of men, and the light shines in the darkness, and the darkness did not comprehend it (Jn 1:1-5). These are wonderful and amazing words, and before they can be understood, they have to be wholeheartedly embraced.

If food were set before your mouths, one of you would receive that part of the food, another this part; still, the same food would reach you all, but not all the food would reach you all. So too, a kind of food and drink consisting of words is now being set before your ears; and yet all of it does reach you all. Or is it the case, perhaps, that while I'm speaking, one of you takes one syllable for himself, another a second one? Or does one get one word, another a second word? If that's how it is, I am going to utter as many words as I see people, so that at least one word may get to each of you. And in fact it's easy for me to speak more words than there are people here; but all of them reach all of you. So a human word does not have to be divided up by syllables for all to hear it; and is the Word of God to be cut up into slices, in order to be everywhere? Can we suppose, brothers and sisters, that these spoken and passing words are comparable in any respect to that unchangeably abiding Word? Or have I, by saying this, been comparing them? But I just wanted to suggest to you in any way I could, that what God provides us with in material things can help you to believe what you cannot yet see about spiritual words.

But now let's pass on to better things; because words are spoken, and fade away. Think, among all spiritual thoughts, think of justice. Someone who stays in these western regions thinking of justice; someone staying in the east thinking of justice—how is it that the first one thinks of the whole of justice, and the second one also of the whole of it? And that the first sees the whole of it and the second the whole of it? I mean if you see justice, and do something according to it, you are doing it justly. You see inwardly, act outwardly. How can you see it inwardly, if nothing is present to you? Because you are staying in one area, the thought of someone somewhere else won't reach that area.[2] But you, staying here, see the same thing in your mind as he does, though he is staying so far away, and the whole of it shines on you, the whole of it is seen by him; because things that are divine and immaterial are whole everywhere. That being the case, believe that the Word is wholly in the Father, wholly in the womb. Yes, believe this about the Word of God, who is God with God.

The second way: Christ as God and man

3. But now listen to the other proposition, the other way of proposing Christ which scripture proclaims. What I've just been saying, you see, refers to before the taking of flesh.[3] But now listen to what scripture goes on promptly to declare: *The Word*, it says, *became flesh, and dwelt among us* (Jn 1:14). He had said, you see, *In the beginning was the Word, and the Word was with God, and the Word was God; this was in the beginning with God; all things were made through him, and without him was made nothing* (Jn 1:1-3). But he would have been declaring the divinity of the Word to us in vain, if he had kept quiet about

the humanity of the Word. In order, I mean, for me to see that,[4] he deals with me down here; in order to refurbish my gaze for contemplating that, he himself comes to the aid of my weakness. By receiving from human nature the same human nature, he became man.[5] He came with the packhorse of the flesh to the one who was lying wounded on the road,[6] in order to give shape to our little faith and nurture it, and to clear our intellects from mist, so that they might see what he never lost as a result of what he took on. He began to be man, indeed, but did not cease to be God.

So that is the presentation of our Lord Jesus Christ insofar as he is the mediator, insofar as he is the head of the Church; that God is man, and man is God, since John says, *And the Word became flesh, and dwelt among us.*

The apostle presents us with Christ in both ways

4. Listen now to each way in that well-known passage from the apostle Paul: *Who while he was in the form of God,* he says, *did not think it robbery to be equal to God* (Phil 2:6). That's the same as, *In the beginning was the Word, and the Word was with God, and the Word was God* (Jn 1:1). How could the apostle say, *He did not think it robbery to be equal to God,* if he isn't equal to God? But if the Father is God, and Christ isn't God, how can he be equal?[7] So where that one says, *The Word was God,* this one says, *He did not think it robbery to be equal to God*; and where that one says, *The Word became flesh and dwelt amongst us* (Jn 1:14), this one says, *But he emptied himself, taking the form of a servant* (Phil 2:7).

Pay careful attention; so by his becoming man, by the fact that *the Word became flesh and dwelt amongst us,* he thereby *emptied himself, taking the form of a servant.* Why, in fact, did he empty himself? Not in order to lose divinity, but in order to put on humanity, appearing to human beings as what he was not before he was man. Thus it was by appearing visibly that he emptied himself, keeping back, that is to say, the dignity of his divine greatness, and presenting us with his flesh as the garment of humanity. So it was by the fact that *he emptied himself, taking the form of a servant*—not taking the form of God. When he was speaking about the form of God, he didn't say he received it, but, *While he was established in the form of God, he did not think it robbery to be equal to God*; but when it came to the form of a servant, *taking,* he said, *the form of a servant.* So it was by this that he is the mediator and the head of the Church, through whom we are reconciled to God, through the mystery of his humanity,[8] his passion and resurrection and ascension, his future coming as judge, so that those two things to come may be heard, when God has spoken only once.[9] Where are two things heard? When he renders *to each one according to his works* (Mt 16:27).

We are not to be seduced by the cunning questions of the Arians

5. So then, hold on firmly to this, and don't be taken by surprise at the problems people raise, which creep along like a cancer, as the apostle said;[10] but

guard your ears, and the virginity of your minds, as betrothed by the friend of the bridegroom to one man, to be presented *as a chaste virgin to Christ*. Your virginity, you see, is in the mind. Virginity of the body is preserved by a few in the Church; virginity of the mind is something all the faithful ought to have. It is this virginity that the serpent wishes to corrupt, about which the same apostle said, *I have betrothed you to one man, to present you as a chaste virgin to Christ; and I am afraid that, just as the serpent took in Eve by his cunning, so also your senses may be corrupted, and fall away from the chastity which is in Christ Jesus* (2 Cor 11:2-3). *Your senses*, he said; that is, your minds. This, surely, is the more suitable way of understanding it. There are, I mean, also the senses of this body, of seeing, hearing, smelling, tasting, touching. It was our minds that the apostle feared might be corrupted, where the virginity of faith is to be found. Go now, soul, preserve your virginity, later on to be made fruitful by the embrace of your bridegroom. So then, hedge your ears about, as it is written, with thorns.[11]

The weaker brethren in the Church have been troubled by the problem raised by the Arians, but thanks to the Lord's mercy, the Catholic faith has triumphed. He hasn't, after all, deserted his Church; and if he troubled it for a time, he troubled it with this intention, that it should always continue to implore his aid, by whom alone it could be kept firmly established on solid rock.[12] And the serpent is still hissing, and doesn't keep quiet. He is trying, by promising a kind of knowledge, to cast us out of the paradise of the Church, not permitting us to return to that paradise from which the first man was thrown out.

The serpent still active with his false suggestions;
in this case that the Son is less than the Father

6. Pay close attention, brothers and sisters. What was done in that paradise, is still being done in the Church. Don't let anybody seduce us out of this paradise. Let it be enough that we fell from that one; at least, now that we have experienced that, let us show that we've learned the lesson. It's the same old serpent, who is always suggesting iniquity and impiety.[13] He is sometimes promising impunity, just as he did then, saying, *Will you really die the death?* (Gn 3:4). He is still making the same sort of suggestion, so that Christians may lead bad lives now: "Is God really," he says, "going to throw away everyone? Is God really going to damn everyone?" God says, "I will damn them; I will pardon those who change their ways; let them change their deeds, I will then change my threats."

So he is also the one who whispers and hisses, and says, "Look where it is written, *The Father is greater than I* (Jn 14:28); and are you saying he is equal to the Father?"

I accept what you say;[14] but I accept each statement, because I read each statement. Why do you accept one, and not want one? Because in fact you've read each of them with me. Here we are, *The Father is greater than I*; I accept it, not from you, but from the gospel; and you, in your turn, please accept from the apostle that the Son is equal to the Father. Join them both together, let both be harmonized; because the one who spoke through John in the gospel is the same as the one who spoke through Paul in his letter. He cannot be discordant with himself; but you for your part are unwilling to understand the harmony of the gospel, seeing that you love disputing. And I, in fact, can also prove it from the gospel: *I and the Father are one* (Jn 10:30).

"How can each be true?"

In the way the apostle teaches us: *I and the Father are one: Who, since he was in the form of God, did not think it robbery to be equal to God* (Phil 2:6). Listen now to *The Father is greater than I: But he emptied himself, taking the form of a servant* (Phil 2:7).

There you are, I'm showing you why he is greater; now you show me in what respect he's not equal. After all, we read that each is the case. He is less than the Father insofar as he is the Son of man; equal to the Father insofar as he's the Son of God; because *the Word was God* (Jn 1:1). The mediator, God and man; God, equal to the Father; man, less than the Father; equal in the form of God, less in the form of a servant. So now you tell me, in what way he is both equal and less?[15] Can he be equal in one part, less in another? So there you are; apart from the taking on of the flesh, show me how he is both equal and less. I really want to see how you are going to demonstrate it.

The notion of God consisting of parts held up to ridicule

7. Notice, all of you, the stupid impiety of having ideas according to the flesh; as it's written, *Having ideas according to the flesh is death* (Rom 8:6). Take your stand here, Sir. I'm still setting aside the incarnation of our Lord Jesus Christ, the only Son of God, not yet talking about it; but as though what has already happened hadn't yet happened, I'm attending with you to *In the beginning was the Word, and the Word was with God, and the Word was God; this was in the beginning with God* (Jn 1:1-2). I'm attending with you to *Who, since he was in the form of God, did not think it robbery to be equal to God* (Phil 2:6). Precisely there, please, show me a greater and a less. What are you going to say? Are you going to divide God up by qualities, that is by certain dispositions of body and soul, in which we perceive one thing here, another there? Naturally, I can say this,[16] but whether you people too understand it like this, let God see.

So, as I had begun to say, before the taking on of the flesh, before the Word became flesh and dwelt amongst us, show how he is less, show how he is equal. Is God one thing and another thing, so that in one part the Son can be less than he, and in another his equal? As though we were to say, "They are bodies of a sort;[17] you can say to me, it's equal in length, but less in strength." We often come across such bodies, after all, such that they are equal in length but in strength one is less, the other greater. So are we going to think of God and his Son as such bodies? Are we going to think like that of the one who was wholly in Mary's womb, wholly with the Father, wholly in the flesh, wholly above the angels? May God avert the hearts of Christians from such thoughts!

Again, perhaps, you will be thinking like this, and saying, "Both in strength and length they are equal, but they are disparate in color."

Where but in bodies do you find color? There, on the other hand, is to be found the light of wisdom. Show me the color of justice. If such things have no color, you wouldn't say these things about God, if you yourself had the color of shame.

The Son cannot be equal to the Father in one quality
or attribute, and less in another

8. So what are you going to say? They are equal in power, but the Son is less in sagacity? God[18] is unjust, if he has given equal power to less sagacity. If they are equal in sagacity, but the Son is less in power, God is guilty of jealousy, for having given less power to equal sagacity. In God, though, everything that is said about him is one and the same; in God, you see, power isn't one thing and sagacity another, courage one thing and justice another, or chastity another. Whichever of these you attribute to God, it isn't to be understood as one thing and another, and none of them, in any case, is attributed to him worthily; because these are qualities of souls, upon which that divine light is shed somehow or other, so that it affects them with its own qualities—rather like when this visible light rises upon material bodies. If it is removed, all bodies have one color, or one should rather say, no color. But when it comes up to shine upon bodies, though in itself it is uniform, nonetheless, given the varying qualities of bodies, it sprinkles them with a variegated lustre or sheen. So these qualities are dispositions of souls, which have been affected and disposed in a good way by that light which is not itself affected or disposed by anything, and formed by that light which is not itself formed by anything.

Though they are not worthy of him, we say these things about God,
because we cannot find anything better to say

9. And yet we say these things about God, brothers and sisters, because we cannot find anything better to say. I call God just, because in human terms I can't find anything better; in fact, he is beyond justice. It says in the scriptures, *The Lord is just, and loves deeds of justice* (Ps 11:7). But it also says there that God repents, it also says there that God doesn't know things.[19] Is there anybody who isn't horrified at the idea? God doesn't know things, God repents? Still, scripture does descend to the salutary use of these terms which horrify you, precisely in order to save you from imagining that terms you think are fine are said about God fittingly and worthily.

And thus, if you ask, "So then, what can worthily be said about God?" someone may perhaps answer you, and say that he is just. But another person, who understands things better than this one, may tell you that even this term is overridden by God's total excellence, and even this one is not worthy to be said of him, although it is suitably said of him according to our human capacity. So when the former tries to prove his point from the scriptures, because it is written, *the Lord is just*, this other will very properly answer him that it is stated in the same scriptures that God repents; and just as he doesn't take this according to the common way of speaking, the way human beings normally repent; so too he likewise understands that what is meant by "just" doesn't fit God's super-eminence. Though scripture was indeed right to state this, so that the human spirit might be led gradually by all sorts of words to that which cannot be said at all.

Yes, you call God just; but you must understand something beyond the justice which you are in the habit of attributing to human beings.

"But the scriptures called him just."

That's why they also called him repentant and ignorant, which you now don't want to call him. So just as you realize that those things which now horrify you were said on account of your weakness;[20] in the same way these things which you value highly were said on account of a certain tougher weakness of yours.[21] But any who have risen beyond even these words, and begun to think worthily of God as far as man is permitted to, will find a silence that is to be praised, by the unutterable voice of the heart.

The argument concluded; a rule for interpreting the scriptures: any text suggesting equality is to be referred to Christ's divinity; any suggesting inequality to the form of a servant

10. So then, brothers and sisters, because in God power is identical with justice (whatever you say in him, you are saying the same thing, since in fact you are not saying anything that is worthy of him), you cannot say that the Son is equal to the Father in justice and not equal in power, or equal in power and not equal in knowledge; because if he is equal in one respect, he is equal in every respect; because all the things you say in that field are one and the same, and all have the same value. So it remains that you cannot say how the Son may be both equal and unequal,[22] unless you posit some variations in the substance of God. When you do posit them, Truth casts you out, and you forfeit all access to that inner sanctuary of God, where he can most perfectly be seen.[23] But since you cannot say he is equal in one part and unequal in another, because there are no parts in God; and you cannot say he is equal in one respect, less in another, because there are no qualities in God; it follows that as regards God you cannot say he is equal unless he is equal in every respect. So how can you say he is less, except because he took the form of a servant?

And so, brothers and sisters, this is what you must always bear in mind; if you accept a certain rule in the scriptures, that very light will make everything clear to you. Wherever you find, according to what's said, that the Son is equal to the Father, take it as being meant with respect to his divinity. But according to the form of the servant which he took, take him as less. On the one hand, according to what is said, *I am who I am*; on the other according to what is said, *I am the God of Abraham, and the God of Isaac, and the God of Jacob* (Ex 3:14-16); in this way you will hold firmly both to what is in his nature, and to what is in his mercy.[24]

I think that that is enough said also about that way[25] in which our Lord Jesus

Christ is presented to us in the scriptures as having become our savior, the head of the Church, the mediator through whom we are reconciled with God, both God and man.

The whole Christ, head and body, Christ and the Church together

11. The third way is how the whole Christ is predicated with reference to the Church, that is as head and body. For indeed head and body form one Christ. Not that he isn't complete without the body, but that he was prepared to be complete and entire together with us too, though even without us he is always complete and entire, not only insofar as he is the Word, the only-begotten Son equal to the Father, but also in the very man whom he took on, and with whom he is both God and man together. All the same, brothers and sisters, how are we his body, and he one Christ with us? Where do we find this, that head and body form one Christ, that is the body together with its head? In Isaiah the bride is speaking with the bridegroom as if in the singular; certainly it's one and the same person speaking; and see what is said: *As for a bridegroom he has bound a turban on my head, and as for a bride he has decked me out with ornaments* (Is 61:10). As bridegroom and bride; he calls one and the same person bridegroom with reference to the head, bride with reference to the body.

Otherwise, how are we the members of Christ, with the apostle saying as clearly as can be, *You are the body of Christ and its members* (1 Cor 12:27)? All of us together are the members of Christ and his body; not only those of us who are in this place, but throughout the whole world; and not only those of us who are alive at this time, but what shall I say? From Abel the just[26] right up to the end of the world, as long as people beget and are begotten, any of the just who make the passage through this life, all that now—that is, not in this place but in this life—all that are going to born after us, all constitute the one body of Christ; while they are each individually members of Christ. So if all constitute the body and are each individually members, there is of course a head, of which this is the body. *And he himself*, it says, *is the head of the body, the Church, the firstborn, himself holding the first place* (Col 1:18). And because it also says of him that *he is always the head of every principality and power* (Col 2:10), this Church which is now on its pilgrimage is joined to that heavenly Church where we have the angels as fellow citizens,[27] with whom we would be quite shameless in claiming equality after the resurrection of our bodies, unless Truth had promised us this, saying, *They shall be equal to the angels of God* (Lk 20:36); and there is achieved one Church, *the city of the great king* (Mt 5:35).

The three ways recapitulated;
Christ and the Church constitute one Christ

12. Thus it is then that sometimes in the scriptures Christ is presented in such a way that you are to understand him as the Word equal to the Father; in such a way sometimes that you are to understand him as the mediator, since *the Word*

became flesh to dwell amongst us (Jn 1:14); since that only-begotten Son, *through whom all things were made* (Jn 1:3), *did not consider it robbery to be equal to God, but emptied himself, taking the form of a servant, becoming obedient to the death, even death on the cross* (Phil 2:6-8).

Sometimes, though, in such a way that you are to understand the head and the body, with the apostle himself expounding as clearly as may be what was said about husband and wife in Genesis: *They shall be two*, it says, *in one flesh* (Gn 2:24). Notice his exposition, because I don't want to give the impression of having the nerve to say something I've cobbled up myself. *For they will be two*, he said, *in one flesh*; and he added, *This is a great sacrament*. And in case anyone should still think that this is to be found in husband and wife according to the natural joining of the sexes, and their bodily coming together,[28] *but I mean*, he went on, *in Christ and the Church* (Eph 5:31-32). So this is how we take as referring to Christ and the Church what is said elsewhere: *They shall be two in one flesh; they are not now two, but there is one flesh* (Mt 19:5-6).[29]

And just as bridegroom and bride, so also head and body, because *the head of the woman is the man* (1 Cor 11:3). So whether I say head and body, or whether I say bridegroom and bride, you must understand the same thing. And that's why the same apostle, while he was still Saul, heard the words, *Saul, Saul, why are you persecuting me?* (Acts 9:4); because the body is joined to the head. And when as a preacher of Christ he was now suffering from others what he had done himself as a persecutor, *that I may fill up*, he said, *in my flesh what is lacking from the afflictions of Christ* (Col 1:24); thus showing that what he was suffering was part and parcel of the afflictions of Christ. This can't be understood of the head, which now in heaven is not suffering any such thing; but of the body, that is the Church; the body, which with its head is the one Christ.

We must conduct ourselves as a body worthy of such a head,
as a bride worthy of such a bridegroom

13. So present yourselves to such a head as a body worthy of him, to such a bridegroom as a worthy bride. That head can only have a correspondingly worthy body; and such a great husband as that can only marry a correspondingly worthy wife. *To present himself*, it says, *with a glorious Church, not having stain or wrinkle, or any such thing* (Eph 5:27).[30] This is the bride of Christ, without stain or wrinkle. Do you wish to have no stain? Do what is written: *Wash yourselves, be clean, remove the wicked schemes from your hearts* (Is 1:16). Do you wish to have no wrinkle? Stretch yourself on the cross. You see, you don't only need to be washed, but also to be stretched, in order to be without stain or wrinkle; because by the washing sins are removed, while by the stretching a desire is created for the future life, which is what Christ was crucified for.

Listen to Paul himself, once he was washed: *Not*, he says, *because of the works of justice which we have done, but according to his own mercy he has saved us, by the washing of rebirth* (Ti 3:5). Listen to him as he is stretched: *Forgetting*, he says, *what lies behind, stretched out to what lies ahead, accord-*

ing to intention I follow after to the palm of God's calling from above in Christ Jesus (Phil 3:13-14).

NOTES

1. The date is generally agreed by the scholars to have been 12 December. They also concur in affirming that the sermon was preached in Carthage in the Restored Basilica; all this in accordance with the sermon heading in one manuscript. See O. Perler, *Les Voyages de Saint Augustin*, 359-360. It is, one must confess, a rather messy, ill-constructed sermon; but one that makes some very important doctrinal points.

2. The text makes this sentence a question. The whole argument is indeed rather labored and clumsy; but I think it makes better sense to treat this as a simple statement of fact. What someone is thinking in the east cannot reach you in the west; but if you are both thinking justice, it's one and the same justice you are thinking.

3. Though he has just said that the Word is wholly with the Father, wholly in the womb!

4. The divinity of the Word.

5. Surely we have here a very tired preacher!

6. See the parable of the good Samaritan, Lk 10:30-37.

7. He is arguing, let us remember, against the Arians, who denied that the Son or Word is true God, and hence that he is equal to the Father.

8. So several manuscripts; the published Maurist text says "humility."

9. See Ps 62:11.

10. See 2 Tm 2:17.

11. See Sir 28:24, Vulgate.

12. See Mt 7:25.

13. Iniquity—bad actions; impiety—wrong faith.

14. "You," I think, is now more the Arian than the old serpent whispering his deceptions through the Arian.

15. An odd question, it would seem, to ask an Arian, who simply denied that he is equal. But then Augustine was rubbing his nose in Phil 2:6; what he is in fact saying is, "Now it's your turn to explain that verse." And to the next question the Arian would reply, like Augustine himself, with a decisive "No," because it would be equally abhorrent to him to think of the deity as consisting of parts.

16. *Naturaliter quidem dicere possum.* I must be wrong in translating *naturaliter* as "naturally" in the colloquial English sense of "obviously," "of course." But I cannot for the life of me see what he means, or how sense can be made of translating it correctly as "according to nature."

17. Tertullian, Augustine's African predecessor as leading theologian 200 years earlier, had taken it for granted that God is a body of sorts. To suggest that the Arians, however, who were much more sophisticated natural theologians than Tertullian, entertained any such ideas, was a piece of colossal cheek on Augustine's part. But this is the absurdity to which he is aiming to reduce their opinions.

18. It is perhaps worth noting that he is throughout this argument referring to the Father simply as God. This is indeed in accordance with common New Testament usage; but I suspect he is doing it here as a kind of concession to the Arian way of talking, since for the Arians only the Father is in fact God in the strict and truest sense.

19. See, for example, Gn 6:7; also 18:21, which implies that God doesn't yet know what he is intending to find out.

20. By bringing God down to your human level; and then also to train you in your weakness to rise above the literal meaning of words; to escape from the prison of univocity—"one word, one meaning"—which indeed appears to hold in bondage the contemporary mind, dominated by science and mathematics.

21. Reading with one manuscript *pro aliqua infirmitate validiore*, where the others and the Maurist text read *pro aliqua firmitate validiore*, on account of a tougher strength of yours. But I don't think Augustine is concerned in this context to attribute any native strength to the human intellect.

22. Reading *aequalis et inaequalis*, following a suggestion of the Maurists, which was prompted by variations among the manuscripts; this instead of the single *inaequalis* of the text.

23. See Ps 73:17.

24. A strange text to choose in order to illustrate his point, because being the God of Abraham, Isaac and Jacob hardly implies the incarnation with any logical necessity. But Augustine has used the same text in a similar vein elsewhere. He would no doubt reply to our query, that while being the God of Abraham, Isaac and Jacob, the God of Israel, does not imply the incarnation with any logical necessity, it implies it with the divine necessity imposed by the divine mercy and conde-scension.

25. See section 1 for the three ways in which scripture presents Christ. We have just finished the second way, on which we embarked in section 3.

26. See Mt 23:35.

27. See Eph 2:19.

28. Is Augustine here obliquely criticizing an incipient theology of marriage as a sacrament, based on this text? It rather looks like it.

29. And is he here underplaying the literal interpretation of this passage as an absolute prohibition of divorce? Again, it could be argued that he is.

30. In his *Revisions* II, 38, commenting on his work on *Baptism,* he says about this text: "Wher-ever in these books I mentioned *the Church not having stain or wrinkle*, it is not to be taken in the sense that it is now like that, but that it is being prepared to be like that, when it will also be manifested as glorious." Whether he was fully alive to this point when he preached this sermon may be doubted. This is perhaps another telling indication of an early date for the sermon.

SERMON 341A

Date: uncertain[1]

The humility of Christ shown in the mystery of the incarnation,
the eternal God humbling himself to become a mortal man

1. I am hoping to impress upon you, dearest brothers and sisters, the humility of our Lord Jesus Christ; indeed he himself is impressing it upon us all. Just how great his humility was, let me show you. Isaiah the prophet cries out, *All flesh is grass, and all the glory of the flesh as the flowers in the grass; the grass has dried up, the flowers fallen; but the Word of the Lord abides for ever* (Is 40:6-8). With what scorn he disregarded and rejected the flesh! With what conviction he put first the Word of God and praised it! I say it again, please notice again, take a look at his disregard of the flesh: *All flesh is grass, and all the glory of the flesh as the flowers in the grass*. What does grass amount to, what do the flowers in the grass amount to? He goes on to tell us. Do you want to hear what grass amounts to? *The grass has dried up, the flowers fallen*. What about the Word of God? *It abides for ever*.

Let us see if we can recognize the Word which *abides for ever*; let us listen to the evangelist praising the Word. *In the beginning was the Word, and the Word was with God, and the Word was God; this was in the beginning with God. All things were made through him, and without him was made nothing. What was made in him is life, and the life was the light of men* (Jn 1:1-4). Great praise indeed of the eternal Word; high praise indeed of the Word of God abiding for ever. And what does the evangelist say later on? *And the Word became flesh and dwelt amongst us* (Jn 1:14). If this was all that God the Word did, to become flesh, it would be unbelievable humility; and blessed are those who believe this unbelievable thing; our faith, after all, consists of unbelievable things.[2] The Word of God became grass,[3] God was crucified, it's all incredible; because your disease had become so grave, that it needed unbelievable remedies to cure it.

And indeed that humble doctor came, he found the patient lying sick, he shared his infirmity with him, summoning him to share his own divinity; he became in his passion the slayer of passions, and dying he was hung on the tree in order to put death to death. He made a food for us, which we were to take,

30

and be cured. Where does this food come from? Having died, he rose again.[4] And whom does it nourish? Those who have imitated the Lord's humility. You won't even imitate that humility; how much more will you fail to imitate the divinity! So imitate the humility, if you can.

When? How?

He, being divine, became a human being; you, a human being, just realize that you are merely human. If only you would acknowledge what he became on your account! Acknowledge what you are on his account; see that you are merely human, and yet you are worth so much that on your account God became man. And don't make that a matter for your pride, but put it down to his mercy. The Lord our God, you see, has redeemed us with his blood, and has willed that his blood, innocent blood, should be the price of our souls.

*The difference between God and man infinitely greater
than that between man and beast*

2. Coming back to what I had started to say, brothers and sisters, if God humbled himself so much that he became man, who would dream of demanding anything more from him? You, after all, don't humble yourself to the point of becoming a brute beast; and yet where's the comparison? If you were humbled to the extent of being made into a beast from being a human being, you wouldn't be humbled to the same extent, by the same amount as God humbled himself. A human being, after all, made into an animal, would indeed be something endowed with reason made into something lacking reason; but still in each case mortal and mortal. A human being is conceived just as an animal is conceived; is fed on material nutriments and grows just like an animal. How many things the human animal has in common with brute beasts! The sole difference is that it has a mind endowed with reason, in which the image of the creator is set.[5] The God, on the other hand, who was made man, was the eternal made mortal, clothing himself with flesh from the lump of our human stock, but without sin, becoming a human being, being born, taking to himself that in which he would suffer on our behalf.

But look, he hasn't yet suffered; take a look now at what he has become for you, before he suffers. Is this a trifling act of humility? God has become man. Man, man, notice that you are just a man. It is on your account that God is a man; and you there still won't acknowledge that you are merely a man? Let's take a look, brothers and sisters, at those who won't acknowledge that they are merely human beings. Who are the ones who refuse to acknowledge that they are merely human beings? Those who justify themselves, and blame God.[6] Let people suffer something hard and harsh in this life; nothing comes so readily to their tongues as blaming God and praising themselves. They exclaim indignantly about their distress, and instead of confessing their sins they boast of their merits, and say, "God, what have I done to you? Why am I suffering all this?"

"God, what have I done to you?" says a human being to God.

God may well reply, "You're right to say 'What have I done to you?' because you haven't done anything to me, but everything to yourself."

If you did anything to God, after all, you would do what gives him pleasure; that's what doing something to him means.[7] But as it is, whatever you've done, you've done it to and for yourself, because following your own will you have ignored his authority. Assuredly, if you understand it that way, you are right to say this. What, after all, can you do to God, that you should exclaim "What have I done to you"? If you hurl a stone towards the sky, are you hurling it at the sky, or at yourself? What you've thrown doesn't stick up there, and it falls back on you. It's the same with all the blasphemies you may throw in God's direction, the same with all the insults, the same with everything that upsets that sacrilegious and godless and proud mind of yours; the more you hurl them upwards, all the heavier the weight with which they fall back on top of you.

Never try to run away anywhere from God, except to God

3. So what were you going to do to God? Now you would indeed be going to do something to, or for, him, if you acted on his word; if you did what he had commanded, you would be right to exclaim, "What have I done to you?" And yet for all that, shake out your justice, shake up your conscience, enter into your heart; don't cry outside, take a look inside, go back into the inner chambers of your heart. See if you've really done nothing bad; see if you are not suffering what you deserve for what you've done, when you find yourself in any distress. All that the sinner is owed, after all, is the scourge of eternally burning fire. You have forsaken your God and followed your own lusts. What are you suffering, when you're being scourged? It's correction, not damnation. If God scourges you in this life, it means he is not angry with you.

Don't offend him when he's scourging you, don't provoke him, and then he will spare you. You provoke him by complaining, and then he abandons you. Take refuge under the scourge of the one who is correcting you; don't flee from the scourge, but under the scourge. Where he's beating you, that's where you must run to. He certainly knows where to strike, and where to find you; and it's in vain that you wish to hide from the eyes of one who is everywhere. Do you want to run away from God in his anger? Run away to God who has been placated; nowhere away from him except to him. You thought you were running away from him when you stiffened that proud neck of yours; humble it, and run away to him. *He scourges every son whom he accepts* (Prv 3:12). But you scornfully decline to be scourged? Then scornfully decline to inherit. The good Father is training you for the inheritance; he's good when he spares you, and good when he beats you, in every case truly kind-hearted.

NOTES

1. The title in the manuscript from which this sermon is taken actually reads, *Incipit de humilitate* . . .: "It/he begins on the humility . . ." etc. This may simply be, perhaps, because the first word of the sermon is *Humilitatem*; or just possibly because the sermon came first in some collection of texts on the subject.

There is no reason to doubt that it was preached in Hippo Regius. My personal inclination would be to date it about 420-425; there are signs here and there of an old man's incoherences and slightly wandering thoughts.

2. He is here echoing, no doubt deliberately, a famous saying of Tertullian's, the doughty African apologist of 200 years earlier, *Credo quia incredibile*, I believe it because it is unbelievable. This is one of the many pieces of theological spice with which Lewis Carroll (the Rev. Charles Dodgson) flavors his masterpieces, *Alice's Adventures in Wonderland* and *Through the Looking Glass*; see the White Queen's boast, "Why, sometimes I've believed as many as six impossible things before breakfast"; *Through the Looking Glass*, chapter 5.

3. The text here adds a phrase, *mortuus resurrexit*, having died he rose again, which is surely completely out of place in this context. I tentatively insert it a few lines further down, where it reasonably answers a question he asks, that in the text as it stands is left unanswered. It could, within the bounds of possibility, have shifted its place through a series of mistakes and corrections by successive copyists.

4. Here is the place to which I transfer the phrase mentioned in note 3.

5. Augustine places the image of God in our *minds*, not in our *souls*, where most catechisms and old theology textbooks usually locate it. Animals too have souls, *animae*, which is indeed why they are called *anima-ls*.

6. How does this imply that they don't acknowledge that they are merely human beings? It shows that they think they can pass judgment on God, and so are putting themselves in a position of superiority over him; they are indeed again succumbing to that false suggestion, *You shall be like gods, knowing good and evil*, Gn 3:5.

7. It means the same as doing something *for* him. The Latin dative can be translated both ways; both meanings are conveyed by that single case.

SERMON 342

ON THE EVENING SACRIFICE, WITH AN EXPLANATION OF THE BEGINNING
OF THE GOSPEL OF JOHN

Date: uncertain[1]

The evening sacrifice is the sacrifice of the cross,
in which the priest is himself the victim

1. A sermon has to be preached about the evening sacrifice. We prayed after all as we sang, and sang as we prayed, *May my prayer rise straight up like incense in your presence; the lifting up of my hands an evening sacrifice* (Ps 141:2). In the prayer we observe the man, in the extension of the hands we recognize the cross. So this is the sign which we carry on our foreheads, the sign by which we have been saved. A sign that was mocked, in order to be honored; despised in order to be glorified. God appears in visible form, so that as man he may intercede; he remains hidden so that as man he may die. *For if they had known, they would never have crucified the Lord of glory* (1 Cor 2:8). So this sacrifice, in which the priest is also the victim, has redeemed us by the shedding of the Creator's blood.

Not that he created us with blood, but he redeemed us by blood. He created us, after all, in the beginning which was the Word,[2] *and the Word was with God, and the Word was God.* It was by this that we were created. The text goes on to make the connection: *All things were made through him, and without him was made nothing.* That's the one we were created by. Now listen to whom we were redeemed by: *What was made*, it says, *in him was life,*[3] *and the life was the light of men; and the light shines in the darkness, and the darkness did not comprehend it* (Jn 1:1.3-5). He is still God; still being called what he always remains, unchangeable; still being called what hearts are to be purified by the sight of;[4] but how they are to be purified, he doesn't yet say. *The light*, he says, *shines in the darkness, and the darkness does not comprehend it.* But that it may cease to be darkness, and be able to comprehend it—the darkness, you see, is sinners, the darkness is unbelievers; so in order that they may cease to be darkness and be able to comprehend, *the Word was made flesh and dwelt among us* (Jn 1:14).

Observe the Word, observe the Word as flesh. As regards the Word before flesh, *In the beginning was the Word, and the Word was with God, and the Word*

34

was God; all things were made through him. Where is there any blood there? There you already have your maker, but it's not yet your price. So how is it you have been redeemed? It's because *the Word was made flesh and dwelt among us.*

A comparison between John the Baptist and Christ

2. Look back a little earlier on: *The light,* he says, *shines in the darkness, and the darkness did not comprehend it* (Jn 1:5). So because the darkness did not comprehend the light, human beings needed some human testimony. They couldn't see the daylight, perhaps they would be able to tolerate a lamp. So because they were less able to see the daylight, but could nevertheless somehow or other tolerate a lamp, *there was a man sent from God, whose name was John. This man came to bear witness about the light* (Jn 1:6-7). Who about whom? John about Christ, the lamp about the daylight?[5] How was he not the light, if he was at least a lamp? First of all, observe that he was in fact a lamp. Do you want to listen to the lamp about the daylight, and the daylight about the lamp? *You people,* he says, *sent to John, and you were willing for a time to exult in his light; he was a lamp, burning and shining* (Jn 5:33.35). So what did this other John[6] see, to make him play down the lamp? *He was not the light, but to bear witness about the light.* About what light? *That was the true light, which enlightens every man coming into this world* (Jn 1:9-10). If every man, then John as well.

The one who was not yet ready to show himself as the daylight, himself lit his lamp as a witness to himself. But it was such a lamp as could be kindled from the daylight. Listen to John himself confessing: *We,* he says, *have all received from his fullness* (Jn 1:16).[7] He was thought to be the Christ, he confessed that he was merely a man; he was thought to be the Lord, he confessed that he was a servant. You do well, Lamp, to acknowledge your humble state, or else the wind of pride would blow you out. *That,* after all, *was the true light which enlightens every man coming into this world*; that is, every living creature which is capable of being enlightened; that is, every one of us human beings possessed of a mind and reason, by which we are able to be partakers of the Word.

Two ways of understanding "world"

3. So that true light which enlightens every human being possessed of a mind coming into this world—where was it? *He was in this world.* But the earth too was in this world, and the sun and the moon were in this world.[8] Listen, eye of the human mind, to what is said about your daylight. *He was in this world, and the world was made through him.* He was here in such a way as to be even before the world was, not as though he didn't have a place to be in. God, you see, contains things by dwelling in them, he is not contained by them. So it was in a marvelous and inexpressible way that he was in this world. *And the world was made through him, and the world did not know him* (Jn 1:10).

Which is the world that was made through him? *In the beginning God made heaven and earth* (Gn 1:1), because *all things were made through him* (Jn 1:3). Which *world did not know him?* There's world and world, just as there's house and house; house in the sense of the building, house in the sense of the occupants. House in the sense of a building, as "He's built a big house, he's constructed a very beautiful house." House in the sense of the occupants, as "It's a good house, may God bless it; it's a bad house, may God spare it." So, *the world was made through him*, both habitation and inhabitants; *and the world did not know him*, its inhabitants.

Those who did not receive him, and those who did

4. *He came into his own domain, and his own people did not receive him* (Jn 1:11). So why did he come—as though he did not know beforehand that his own people would not receive him? Listen to the reason he came for: *But as many as did receive him* (Jn 1:12). His own people did not receive him, and his own people did receive him; the world did not believe, and the whole world did believe. It's like our saying, "The whole tree is full of leaves"; is there no place left for the fruit? Each can be said, each understood, both that the tree is full of leaves, and that the tree is full of fruit; one and the same tree in each case, but full of leaves that are to be blown away, full of fruit that is to be picked.[9] So then, you his faithful, you his servants, his lovers, to whom the glory belongs, to whom the hope, to whom the reality belongs; when you hear, *His own people did not receive him*, don't grieve; because you are his by believing.

His own people did not receive him. Who are these? The Jews, perhaps, called out of Egypt long ago, delivered with a mighty hand, brought across through the Red Sea, escaping on dry ground, suddenly deprived of enemies in hot pursuit, fed on manna, rescued from slavery, brought through to the kingdom, bought by so many favors. There you have his own people who did not receive him; but by not receiving him they became foreigners. They were part of the olive tree; it was for their pride that they were broken off. The contemptible wild olive, to be scorned for the bitterness of its berries, was to be found throughout the world; the whole world was bristling with that wild olive of the woods; but all the same it earned the right, through humility, to be grafted in where the olive, through pride, had deservedly been lopped off.[10]

Listen to the olive being proud, and deserving to be broken off: *We were not born of slavery; we have Abraham for our father.* The answer comes, *If you were the children of Abraham, you would do the deeds of Abraham.* And in reply to their saying, *We were not born of slavery*, he says, *If the Son sets you free, you will be free indeed.* Are you boasting about being free? *Everyone who commits sin is the slave of sin.*[11] So, man, how much safer for you to have been the slave of a man, rather than of your distorted desires! They, all the same, by being so proud, did not receive the humble one.

See now a wild olive deserving to be grafted in—that centurion, not an Israelite, but a Gentile: *Lord, I am not worthy that you should enter under my roof;* and the Lord's comment, *Amen, I tell you, I have not found such great faith in Israel.* I haven't found in the olive what I have just found in the wild olive; so let the proud olive be lopped off, the humble wild olive grafted in. Observe him grafting, observe him lopping: *That is why I tell you that many shall come from the east and the west;* many wild olives to be grafted on the olive; *and shall sit down with Abraham and Isaac and Jacob in the kingdom of heaven.* You have heard how the humble wild olive is to be grafted in; listen to how the proud olive is to be lopped off: *But the sons of the kingdom shall go into the outer darkness, where there will be weeping and gnashing of teeth* (Mt 8:8-12). Why? Because *his own people did not receive him.* And why the wild olive grafted in? Because *as many as did receive him, he gave them authority to become children of God* (Jn 1:11-12).

The nature of the authority given to those who did believe in him

5. Don't be downhearted, human race; breathe in the fresh air of life and of the surest liberty. What are you hearing? What's being promised you? *He gave them authority.* What sort of authority? The sort, perhaps, which swells people's heads, to sit in judgment on human lives, in capital cases, to deliver verdicts on the innocent and the guilty? *He gave them authority,* it says, *to become children of God.* They weren't yet sons, you see, and they became sons, because the one through whom they become sons of God was himself already the Son of God, and became the Son of man. So they were already sons of men, and became sons of God.

He came down to what he was not, the one who was something else. He lifted you up to what you were not, because you were someone else. So stir up your hope. It's a great thing that has been promised you,[12] and it seems incredible, and it's generally reckoned that it's impossible for the sons of men to become sons of God. But much more was done for them, when the Son of God became a son of man. So stir up your hope, Mr. and Mrs. Man, expel disbelief from your hearts. Something more incredible has already been done for you than what has been promised you. Are you amazed that as human beings you should have eternal life? Are you amazed that as human beings you should arrive at eternal life? You should rather be amazed that God for your sake arrived at death.

So notice how he gives you every assurance, how he confirms the promise of God: *As many,* he says, *as did receive him, he gave them authority to become children of God.* Engendered in what kind of way? Not in that usual one, not in the old way, not in the fleeting or fleshly way. *It is not of the flesh,* he says, *nor of blood, nor of the will of the man, but of God that they are born* (Jn 1:13). Does that amaze you? You don't believe it? *The Word became flesh and dwelt among us* (Jn 1:13-14).

There you have what the evening sacrifice is constituted by. Let us cling fast to him; let the one who was offered for us be offered with us. In this way, you see, the old life is slain with the evening sacrifice, and the new life rises with the dawn.

NOTES

1. A curiously complicated, involuted sermon. Does it represent the excessive intellectual ebullience of the younger Augustine near the beginning of his ministry, or the occasional tendency to incoherence and wandering of the older man, 25 years or so later? I lean towards the former inference, and suggest, very tentatively of course, a date about 400. Perhaps it was preached to a more select congregation than usual at an evening service, and at a church in Carthage as likely as not.

2. There is a curious mix of references here: Gn 1:1, then Jn 8:25, where in answer to the Jews asking who he was, he replied, according to Augustine's reading of the text, "The beginning." Only after that does he enter into the text of Jn 1:1-14.

3. It seems clear that he understands the statement "what was made in him was life" to refer to the incarnation, to the Word being made flesh; and this was indeed, in all likelihood, the meaning of the author.

4. That is to say, light.

5. I here follow one manuscript. The Maurist text reads, "Who came here, about whom, to bear witness to the light?" But then that single manuscript continues: "Who, about whom? John, about Christ; therefore the lamp about the daylight. We are not doing John any injustice; but if we cannot gaze constantly on our daylight, at least let us praise him with honor. He came to bear witness about the light. He was not himself the light, but to bear witness about the light. How was he not, etc." This mostly seems redundant.

6. The evangelist.

7. All contemporary editions of the gospel treat this as comment by the evangelist, not as the words of John the Baptist. But Augustine's interpretation is perfectly reasonable.

8. "World" in the total sense of the universe or cosmos—which is indeed the word employed in the Greek text. In translation we have to stick to the familiar "world," though we don't normally use it to mean the universe.

9. This is more than an example of a manner of speaking; it is a little simile or parable, which he invariably develops when dealing with the trees of scripture, like the one in the incident of the barren fig-tree, for example. In this case the leaves represent those who did not receive him, the fruit those who did.

10. See Rom 11:17-24.

11. He is quoting snatches of Jn 8:33-39 in a very mixed up order, which readers, if they wish, can sort out for themselves.

12. Here the Maurists follow that one manuscript already referred to (note 5 above), in inserting, *sed a magno promissum est. Multum . . .*; "but it has been promised by a great person. It seems much and incredible . . ."

SERMON 343

DISCOURSE ON SUSANNA AND JOSEPH

Date: 397[1]

Susanna a splendid example of conjugal chastity and fidelity

1. May the divine readings and the holy oracles of God which have sounded in our ears make a nest for themselves in our minds. May they not fly away, mere birds of passage, or stay for a moment and then depart, but instead may they hatch out some progeny there. For if *the sparrow has found herself a house, and the turtle-dove a nest where she may lay her fledglings* (Ps 84:3), how much more the sparrow which is the word of God, and the turtle-dove which is the mercy of God! We have heard the reading about Susanna.[2] May married chastity be built up by it, and laid on such a firm foundation, and fenced about with such a wall, that it can both repel intruders, and convict false witnesses.

This woman had remained chaste, though she would have been doomed to die unless someone had been present who saw what was hidden from her judges. Her words are recorded, which she spoke *in the paradise* (Dn 13:7), that is her shrubbery; words that no human being heard, apart from the two who were lying in wait to ensnare the modesty of another man's wife, and planning to give false evidence against her if she proved unwilling. They were the only ones who heard what she said: *I am trapped on every side. For if I do this thing, it means death for me; but if I do not do it, I shall not escape your hands. But it is better for me not to slip out of your hands, than to sin in the sight of God* (Dn 13:22-23). She turned down what she heard, because she feared one whom she could not see, to whose divine eyes, however, she was herself visible. Because she couldn't see God, after all, it doesn't mean she couldn't be seen by God either. God could see what he was building, he was inspecting his work, living in his temple. He was there; he was himself replying to the trap they were setting. If the giver of chastity, I mean, had abandoned her, chastity would have been undone.

So she said, *I am trapped on every side.* But she was waiting for the one who would save her from weakness of spirit, and from the stormy attack of the false witnesses, as from adverse winds. In the midst of those winds and waves, however, chastity did not suffer shipwreck, because the Lord was at the helm. The cry was raised, people came running, proceedings began, the case came up for judgment. Susanna's household believed the lying elders against their mistress. And although the innocent and stainless life she had hitherto led would seem quite sufficient to testify in favor of her virtue, it still seemed irreligious to them not to believe the elders. No such word had ever been heard about Susanna. So there they are, false witnesses, but known to God. The household believed one thing, the Lord could see another. But what the Lord could see, human beings were ignorant of; it seemed right that the elders should be believed.[3] So she had to die.

But even if[4] the flesh were to die, chastity would be crowned. The Lord was at hand to her prayers, he heard the one whom he knew.[5] He did not abandon her to death, after having helped her to avoid adultery. *The Lord stirred up the holy spirit of Daniel* (Dn 13:45), still a stripling in age, but a sturdy oak in piety. So because there was a prophetic spirit in him, he immediately saw through the deceitfulness of the utterly depraved elders. But he had to work out how what he could discern plainly could be demonstrated to the others. *They are false witnesses*, he said. *Resume the trial* (Dn 13:49). Yes, he knew they were false, as the prophetic spirit had revealed it to him. Those who didn't know had to be convinced. So if the judges were to be convinced, the witnesses had undoubtedly to be convicted. So to convict them, concentrating on the falseness of their evidence, which he was already aware of, he ordered them to be separated from each other. He questioned them one at a time. You see, they could certainly both have one and the same lust, but they couldn't both think up one and the same plan. The first was questioned under which tree he had caught the adulterers. He replied, *Under a mastic tree* (Dn 13:55). The other was questioned. He answered, *Under a holm-oak* (Dn 13:59). The disagreement of their testimony made truth plain, set chastity free.

As death is inevitable anyway, the innocent
should not be afraid of false witnesses

2. And chastity in fact, brothers and sisters, would have been set free and crowned, even if the flesh, which was due to die some time anyway, had died in that trial. We are all going to die, after all, nor does anyone who is eager to avoid death manage to eliminate it, but only to delay it. This is a debt that all are held by. This is a debt we are all going to pay, having inherited it from Adam. And because we don't want to die, we can ask the collector of this debt for a delay, we can't be given a remittance. So Susanna, religious woman and virtuous wife that she was, would certainly be going to die some time or other. And if that some time or other had been right then and there, what damage would it have done to her virtue? Her flesh would have been laid in a tomb, her chastity given back to God and crowned by God.

I mean, do you imagine, brothers and sisters, that it is a matter of great consequence, if false witnesses do not prevail against an innocent person? It isn't of great consequence if false evidence doesn't prevail against the innocent. It would have been of great consequence if it hadn't prevailed against the Lord.

Our Lord Jesus Christ himself was crucified by the tongues of false witnesses. But while these same false witnesses did indeed prevail for a time, what harm did they do to the one who was going to rise again? And so by his example the Lord our God in his flesh, in his weakness, and in the form of a slave which he took in order to liberate the slave, to seek the fugitive, to redeem the captive, to release the prisoner from his chains, to make of the slave a brother; coming to all this in the form of a slave, he showed the slave an example not to be too horrified by false witnesses, and not to be afraid when they are believed. Yes, they can ruin your reputation, but they can't kill your conscience.

The three men were delivered from the burning fiery furnace. Their God was present, they were walking in the midst of harmless fires, which were blazing all round them and not burning them, and as they walked they sang God's praises, and came out as unscathed as when they had been thrown in.[6] So their God was present with them. Does that mean the God of the Maccabees was absent from them?[7] The former escaped unscathed, the latter were soon burned to death; both were tested. The flesh of these was consumed, the flesh of those unharmed; both were crowned. That the three men should escape the flames, it was granted to Nebuchadnezzar to believe in their God.[8] Because the one who was able to deliver them so publicly, would also have been able to crown them secretly. But if he had crowned them in secret, he would not have delivered the king who was raging against them. The saving of their bodies became the saving of his soul. They by praising God escaped—from present flames; he by believing God escaped—but from eternal gehennas. Antiochus, however, who was torturing the Maccabees, was not worthy to have such favors granted him. That's why he exulted while they were being consumed by their torments; but *whoever exalts himself shall be humbled*[9] (Lk 18:14).

The case of Mary saved from false suspicions

3. So the one who delivered Susanna, a chaste woman, a faithful wife, from the false evidence of the elders, is the same as the one who also delivered the virgin Mary from the false suspicions of her husband. So this virgin was found to be pregnant, though her husband had not approached her. Her womb, indeed, had begun to swell with child, but her virginity had remained intact. It was by faith that she had conceived the sower of faith. She had taken the Lord into her body, and he had not allowed her body to be interfered with. Her husband, however, being human, had his suspicions. He thought another must be responsible for what he knew he himself was not, and suspected adultery from some other quarter. He is put right by an angel. Why was he worthy to be put right by an angel? Because there was nothing evil-minded about his suspicions, of the sort the apostle mentions, evil-minded suspicions arising among the brotherhood.[10]

Evil-minded suspicions are nursed by scandal-mongers, right-minded suspicions can be entertained by persons responsible for others. Anyone may justifiably entertain wrong suspicions about his son, but hardly be justified in spreading scandal about his son. You suspect evil, but hope to discover good. When you suspect something in a benevolent frame of mind, you are eager to be proved wrong; you are rightly and really happy when you discover your suspicions were unfounded. Such were Joseph's suspicions about his wife, with whom he had not been coupled in the flesh, but to whom he had already plighted his troth. So the virgin too came under false suspicion. But just as the Spirit was present in Daniel to help Susanna, so also to help Mary the angel was present to Joseph: *Do not be afraid to accept Mary as your wife. For what is being born of her is of the Holy Spirit* (Mt 1:18-20).

A comparison between married and virginal chastity

4. A few moments ago married women were rejoicing over Susanna. Now it's the turn of virgins to rejoice over Mary. Let each group hold on to chastity, married chastity in the one case, virginal chastity in the other. Even if virginal chastity is the greater kind, married the lesser, still each is pleasing to God, because each is the gift of God. All sorts come through to eternal life, but in eternal life all don't obtain the same honor, the same dignity, the same merit. Eternal life and the kingdom of God will be like what, for the sake of a comparison, we say about the sky. In the sky are all the heavenly bodies; so too in the kingdom of God will be all the good faithful. Eternal life will be the same for all of them. It's not the case, I mean, that one has more life there, another less, since they are all going to have life without end. That is the tenner[11] which all the workers are going to receive, whether they have worked in the vineyard from early morning, or have come at the eleventh hour; that tenner is eternal life, which is one and the same for all. But look at the sky, remember the apostle: *Heavenly bodies are one thing, earthly ones another. The glory of the sun is one thing, the glory of the moon another, yet another the glory of the stars. For star differs from star in glory; it is the same too with the resurrection of the dead* (1 Cor 15:40-42).

So let each one of you, my brothers and sisters, fight the good fight in this life with the gift you have received, in order to rejoice in the next. Are you married? It's a lower sort of life, you can only hope for a lower sort of reward; but all the same you must not despair of the eternal kingdom.[12] You have to remember and observe the rules about marriage. What's the case, after all? Just because you have a wife, does it mean you don't have to recognize that you are just a foreign visitor in this world?[13] Shouldn't you be reflecting that you are going to die, that you are going to leave the bed of pleasure? And consider where precisely you will get to, whether the torments of ultimate disaster or the reward of eternity. Reflect carefully then, keep what you have received, carry your burden through to the end, because it is light if you love, heavy if you hate. It's not for nothing, after all, that the Lord said—or was he really, when he said this, only talking to those vowed to celibacy?—*Come to me, all you who labor and are overburdened, and I will refresh you. Take my yoke upon you and learn from me; because I am meek and humble of heart, and you will find rest for your souls*—not for your flesh, but for your souls; *for my yoke is easy, and my burden is light* (Mt 11:28-30); light for the one who loves, heavy for the one who denies.

Have you taken the Lord's yoke upon your neck? It's easy and smooth, if you pull well; rough if you show reluctance. The married life is hedged about with trials and temptations. Did this Susanna, for example, avoid being tested and tempted in her virtue, just because she was wedded to a husband? Here's Susanna, another man's wife, with her own husband; yet she was tested. She was tossed about in the storm: *I am trapped*, she said, *on every side* (Dn 13:22). She was afraid of being condemned to die, you see, by the false witnesses, but she was also afraid of being condemned definitively to die by God the true judge. By the false witnesses, I mean, she would be doomed to die in time, by the divine judge she would be punished for eternity. She weighed up the alternatives, she made her choice. First she was afraid, and weighed the alternatives. She weighed the alternatives and made her choice. She made her choice and was victorious. She had a lesson to teach religious married women. She taught them to resist the tempter, taught them to fight, taught them to struggle, taught them to implore God's help.

Susanna a model for women; what about men?

5. If scripture bears witness to such a great woman,[14] does that mean it has abandoned men? Has it really permitted them to be without a model to imitate? We were watching Susanna severely tried by men who were lusting to undermine her virtue. We were watching her engaging in the contest. That reading was a kind of theater for our minds. We were on the lookout for God's athlete, for a virtuous spirit, we saw her opponent closing with her.[15] We shared the winner's triumph over her defeated foe. Religious married women have here their edifying example,[16] have something to imitate. Let them owe to God the fidelity they keep, not to man. It's then indeed that they really keep it, when they owe it to God. It's then that they keep it when they owe it to the one who sees what they are keeping, which even the husband cannot see. The husband, after all, is often away, God is always there. And sometimes, because the husband is only human, he entertains false suspicions. Then the wife should pray for her husband who is suspecting her falsely—pray that he may be saved, not that he may be condemned. I mean, the man's false suspicions don't blinker the eyes of God. Her conscience is open to the sight of the one who creates her. He, you see, sets her free for eternity from her temporary oppression.

But let her pray for her husband, and take pains not only to lead a good life, but also to have an unblemished reputation. Her very virtue ensures the deliverance of a good wife,[17] and her not being condemned. But a good reputation contributes to the deliverance of others, who might otherwise err by entertaining false suspicions, and fall into sin, perhaps, by passing judgment on what they cannot see; as those judges did, in fact; and then Saint Daniel, or rather the Lord through Daniel, delivered the judges rather than Susanna from an inner death. He delivered her, you see, from a temporal and temporary condemnation. But he delivered them from making a bad judgment and condemning an innocent woman, and so incurring being sentenced to eternal punishment by a judge whom nobody can bribe, and from whom nobody can hide.

6. So I was saying about the men, that they haven't been left without a model either. You chaste men, men who fear God, men for whom your own wives are enough, men who don't break the promise you don't want broken to you, men who show the fidelity you require to be shown to you; come and watch, yes you too, as I remind you of it, the same sort of spectacle as your wives were watching when the reader was telling that story. The divine scriptures haven't left you without a model either. The ladies were hearing about Susanna, and rejoicing at her victory. You now pay attention to Joseph. Not the Joseph to whom the virgin Mary was betrothed when she gave birth to Christ, because he was tempted to be suspicious, and was soon cured of that by an angel. Scripture tells of another Joseph, who was tempted by a shameless woman.[18]

She loved his beauty, being unchaste herself, and of a twisted mind in which she didn't have those eyes by which spiritual beauty may be discerned. She loved him because he was beautiful, she didn't want him to be chaste. She loved him although he belonged to another, she loved her husband's slave. But she didn't love him[19] being loyal to his master. Or do you think she loved him, or rather herself? I myself don't think either him or herself. After all, if she loved him, why did she wish to destroy him? If she loved herself, why did she wish to perish?[20] She was on fire with the poison of lust, not aglow with the flame of charity. But he was able to see what she wasn't able to. He was more beautiful inwardly than outwardly, more beautiful in the light of his heart than in the skin of his body. Where that woman's eyes couldn't penetrate, he was himself enjoying his own beauty.[21] So then, as he gazed on the inner beauty of chastity, when could he ever allow it to be soiled, ever allow it to be ravished by the seduction of that woman? She was in love; but he was in love too. And what he was in love with was worth more than what she was in love with; because he could see what she couldn't.

7. If you want to see in any way at all the spiritual beauty of chastity, if you have any sort of eyes for it, let me propose something as an example; you love it in your wife. So don't hate in another man's wife what you love in your own. What in fact do you love in your wife? Her chastity, of course. Precisely what you hate in another man's wife is what you love in your own. You hate it in another man's wife, because you want to destroy her chastity by lying with her. What you love in your own wife, do you want to kill in another man's? What you love in your own, do you want to destroy in another man's? How will you be able to make the prayer of piety,[22] you murderer of chastity? Preserve, then,

in another man's wife what you wish to have preserved in your own. Love chastity itself, rather than the flesh.[23]

But perhaps you reckon you are a lover of your wife's body, not of her chastity. It's a sordid calculation indeed, but I won't leave you without an example. I, you see, do think that you love chastity in your wife more than her body. But to show you up to yourself without question as a lover of chastity; it's something you love in your daughter. What man is there who doesn't want his daughters to be chaste? What man is there who doesn't rejoice over the chastity of his daughters? Is it the flesh that you love even in this case? Do you really lust after a beautiful body, where you're shocked at the thought of its being unchaste? There you are then, I've proved you are a lover of chastity. So if I've shown you to be a lover of chastity, how have you offended yourself, so that you don't love it in yourself? There you have it in a nutshell: love in yourself what you love in your daughter. Love it in another man's wife, because your daughter too is going to be another man's wife. So love chastity also in yourself. If you love another man's wife, you won't get her straightaway. If you love the lady chastity, you will have her at once. So love chastity, so that you may have eternal felicity.

The example of Joseph recalled in more detail

8. But perhaps you'll be tempted; a shameless woman will fall in love with you. She'll find you alone somewhere, and make every effort to extract a kiss and an embrace from you. If you refuse, she will threaten to punish you by blackening your good name. That's what those false old men did to Susanna. That's what the wife of his master did to Saint Joseph. Just because there's no witness, does it mean God is not there?[24] It was his eyes that Joseph was unwilling to offend, the eyes of that Lord of his who was present. He refused to consent to the shameless woman and to unlawful intercourse with her. He repelled another person's lust, embraced his own virtue.

However, she carried out her threat. She lied to her man, she was believed by her husband. God is still patient. Joseph is thrown into prison, kept in custody as guilty,[25] though God had not been offended by him. But even there God was not absent, because Joseph was not, in fact, guilty. God was there with Joseph in his sufferings; the fact that he didn't come to his aid at once, meant that he was deferring him for greater rewards. After putting him through his paces with punishment, he rewarded him with the blessing he deserved. This holy man Joseph, you see, had rightly to suffer something for the sake of chastity, yes even something hard, which is to say bitter. If by any chance he had loved that shameless woman, he would have been prepared to suffer hardships for her sake. And she wouldn't have accepted his love for her as genuine, unless he had endured such difficulties and hardships on her account, and in that way returned her love—or rather not love but evil lust. She in turn would be burning with love for him, because she would see him on fire with such love for her, that on account of it he didn't refuse to endure any kind of punishment. If all that for a shamelessly unchaste woman, how much more for the lady chastity herself! So it's good that God sometimes puts off helping people in order to test them, in order to put them through their paces, in order that people may come to know themselves; because nothing, after all, is hidden from God.

We must put the sweetness of wisdom, the splendor of virtue,
the beauty of chastity before the vanities of this life

9. So this, brothers and sisters, is what I want to warn your graces about: that above all you should prefer to the lusts of the flesh and the joys of the world and the vain and fleeting parade of this life and its vapidity, that you should have a preference for the splendor and beauty of wisdom, a preference for the pleasant sweetness of wisdom, a preference for the splendor of virtue, the beauty of chastity. These things are all hidden away in the heavenly treasury.[26] These are precious gems, laid out openly in their dazzling brilliance before the very eyes of God. If you've got eyes for them, you can all see them too. So put these things before the whole gamut of unlawful pleasures.

And if trial and temptation comes your way, to the extent that you even suffer serious annoyance, my brothers and sisters, well, do any of you not suffer such things on account of your purses? Don't you put up with annoyances on account of your land, on account of one boundary stone on your land? If you put up with annoyances on account of these things, which you do not have under your control, however long you wish to hold onto them, and whoever you wish to leave them to—but they are often lost while we are still alive, and they often go after our death to people we hate; if for these goods (if in any case they are to be called good, since they don't make people good) people endure so many evils with unruffled composure, why are they so reluctant to endure difficulties for the sake of fidelity and truth? Why are they so timid in standing up for the heavenly treasure, for those riches which not even shipwrecks can deprive us of? The just man, you see, emerges from a shipwreck both rich and stripped of everything.

The example of Job

10. Holy Job was well endowed with these riches. He had lost everything at a single stroke, there was nothing left in his house of what a short while before had made him seem so wealthy. Suddenly reduced to beggary, sitting on his dunghill, riddled with worms from head to foot. What could be more wretched than wretchedness like that? What could be better off than such inner prosperity? He had lost everything God had given him, but he still had the one who had given him everything. *Naked*, he said, *I came out from my mother's womb, naked shall I return to the earth. The Lord has given, the Lord has taken away. As it pleased the Lord, so has it been done. Blessed be the name of the Lord* (Jb 1:21). Is he really poor? Does he really have nothing? If there's nothing left, from what treasury were these gems of praise being offered to God?[27]

Later on the tempter approached as far as the flesh was concerned.[28] Having taken everything off him, he left him his wife to tempt him. He left Eve behind—but that man wasn't Adam. And in this instance too, as what kind of man did he emerge? How did he answer his wife's suggestion that he should blaspheme? *You have spoken,* he said, *like the silly woman you are. If we have received good things from the hand of the Lord, why can we not bear with evil things?* (Jb 2:10). What a man, rotting away, yet whole and entire! Filthy, and at the same time lovely! Sorely stricken, yet in perfect health! Sitting on a dunghill, and at the same time reigning in heaven! If we love him, let us imitate him. To imitate him, let us wear ourselves out. And if in our weariness we become feebler than ever, let us beg for help.

The one who arranged the contest helps the contestant. God, you see, doesn't watch you in the ring in the same way as the populace watch a charioteer; they know how to shout, they don't know how to help. God doesn't watch you battling in the ring in the same way as the president at the games watches an athlete, and prepares a crown of leaves for the winner; he doesn't know how to give strength to the man struggling in the arena and he can't do it anyhow; after all he's a man, not God. And perhaps while he's watching, he endures more weariness sitting there than the other does as he wrestles. God, you see, when he watches his champions, helps them when they call upon him. I mean, it's the voice of his athlete in the psalm, *If I said, My foot is slipping, your mercy, Lord, came to my help* (Ps 94:18). So, my brothers and sisters, don't let's be slow about it; let us ask, let us seek, let us knock. *For everyone who asks receives, and who seeks will find, and who knocks will have the door opened* (Lk 11:10).

NOTES

1. All are agreed on this date, even on more precise dating to the week 7 to 13 May of that year; and on the sermon being preached in Carthage.

2. Daniel 13, Jerusalem Bible; Susanna, RSV Apocrypha.

3. See Dn 13:4.

4. Reading *etsi* instead of the text's *si*, if.

5. See Dn 13:42-44.

6. See Dn 3:19-27.

7. See 2 Mac 7.

8. Surely he has put it the wrong way round? Their coming unscathed from the flames was the reason and occasion for Nebuchadnezzar believing, not *vice versa*, as indeed Augustine goes on to spell out.

9. See 2 Mac 9.

10. See 1 Tm 6:4.

11. The *denarius* of Mt 20:9-10. When it has occurred in other sermons he has usually played on its connection with the number ten, which is why I translate by "tenner" there. So I keep to that translation here. The old translation "a penny" was strictly accurate, the penny being the d (*denarius*, or French *denier*) of L.s.d., pounds, shillings, and pence. But nowadays it just sounds ridiculous.

12. For a more up-to-date, less starkly stated theology of the different states of life, see Vatican II's document on The Church in the Modern World, *Gaudium et Spes*, Part II, chapter 1.

13. See 1 Cor 7:27-31; also 2 Cor 5:6.

14. Reading with the Maurists *de femina tanta*. A later edition reads *de femina tentata*, about a woman being tested.

15. As it is in the singular, *adversarius*, it presumably does not refer to the two old men directly, but to the sin they were trying to drag her into committing.

16. I here combine, and adjust, the Maurist reading, *Habent exemplum suum*, and that of the later edition, *Habent aedificium suum*, to read: *Habent ad aedificium exemplum suum*. This is something, according to the approved canons of textual criticism, one should hardly ever do. But I feel it is justified in this case, in which the fuller reading could, by simple scribal error, give rise to each of the other two alternatives. Neither of them, on the other hand, could very accountably give rise to the other.

17. The text says "of a good life," *bonam vitam*; shorthand, you could say, for the wife leading a good life. I wonder, though, if he didn't in fact say *bonam uxorem*, which an early copyist, his eye caught by *bonam vitam* in the line above, then understandably and unintentionally changed into *bonam vitam*.

18. See Gn 39:6-18.

19. Following the Maurists; the later edition reads, "But did she love him . . .?"

20. So the Maurists; from "I myself" to this point the later edition reads, "Not even him. If she loved him, why did she wish to destroy him?"

21. In fact the beauty of chastity, as he goes on to say.

22. So the Maurists; *Quomodo habetis orationem pietatis*. The later edition reads, . . .*rationem pietatis*, how will you have the essence of piety . . .

23. So the Maurists; the later edition omits "than the flesh."

24. So the Maurists; the later edition makes it a statement, beginning the sentence with *Non* instead of the Maurists' *Num*.

25. So the Maurists; the later edition simply has, "But Joseph is kept in prison as guilty." See Gn 39:13-23.

26. See Col 2:3.

27. Reading *Deo* instead of the text's *Dei*, these gems of the praise of God being offered.

28. *Usque ad carnem*, literally, "as far as the flesh." I don't know what it means. Perhaps it was a saying, like "up to the hilt," "down to the quick," "to the very limit," "the last straw."

SERMON 344

ON LOVE OF GOD AND LOVE OF THE WORLD

Date: 428[1]

Two loves fighting each other in this life,
love of God and love of the world

1. In this life there are two loves wrestling with each other in every trial and temptation: love of the world, and love of God. And whichever of these two wins, that's where it pulls the lover as by the force of gravity. It isn't, you see, on wings or on foot that we come to God, but on the power of our desires. And again, it isn't with knots and chains that we find ourselves stuck to the earth, but with contrary desires. Christ came to change our love, and to make lovers of the heavenly life out of earthly lovers; he was made man on our account, having made us men in the first place; he was God taking on a human being, in order to make human beings into gods.

This is the combat we are challenged to, this the struggle with the flesh, this the struggle with the devil, this the struggle with the world. But let us have confidence, because the one who instituted this contest does not watch his own champions[2] without helping them, nor does he encourage us to rely on our own strength. Anyone relying on his own strength, you see, is relying, being clearly a man, on the strength of a man; and *accursed is everyone who rests his hope in man* (Jer 17:5). The martyrs caught fire from the flame of this pious and holy love, and indeed burned up the straw of the flesh with the steadily burning oak logs of the mind;[3] while they themselves came through whole and entire to the one who had set them alight. However, on the flesh that despises these things[4] due honor will be bestowed in the resurrection of the dead. It is sown, you see, in disgrace, precisely in order to rise again in glory.[5]

The right order of charity; God to be loved more than ones parents

2. To those set alight by this love, or rather that they may be set alight, this is what he says: *Whoever loves father or mother above me is not worthy of me; and whoever does not take up his cross and follow me is not worthy of me* (Mt 10:37-38). He didn't abolish love of parents, wife, children, but put them in their

right order. He didn't say "Whoever loves," but *Whoever loves above me.* That's what the Church is saying in the Song of Songs: *He put charity in order for me* (Sg 2:4). Love your father, but not above your Lord; love the one who begot you, but not above the one who created you. Your father begot you, but didn't himself fashion you; because who or what would be born to him, when he sowed the seed, he himself did not know. Your father reared you, but when you were hungry he didn't provide bread for you from his own body.[6] Finally, whatever your father is keeping for you on earth, he has to pass away for you to succeed to it; he will leave space for your life by his death. But what God your Father is keeping for you, he is keeping with himself, so that you may possess the inheritance with your Father, and not, as his successor, be waiting for his demise, but rather may cleave to him who is always going to abide, and may always abide yourself in him. So love your father, but not above your God.

Love your mother, but not above the Church, who bore you to eternal life. Finally, from the love you have for your parents weigh up how much you ought to love God and the Church. After all, if those who bore you, only to die in due course, are to be loved so much, with how much charity are those to be loved who have borne you in order to enter eternity, in order to remain in eternity? Love your wife, love your children after God, in such a way that you take care they too worship God with you; when you're joined to him, you will fear no separation. The reason you ought not to love them more than God, is that you love them in a totally bad way if you neglect to bring them to God together with you. Perhaps the time for martyrdom will come. You, for your part, wish to confess Christ. When you've confessed him you will perhaps have some temporal punishment, some temporal death to endure. Father or wife or son is coaxing you not to die, and by coaxing you is insuring that you do die. If they are not to ensure that, it's because those words will come into your mind, *Whoever loves father, or mother, or wife, or children above me is not worthy of me.*[7]

Christ in Gethsemane gives us an example of feeling,
and overcoming, human fears

3. But feelings of carnal affection are easily played on by the coaxings of one's own kin. Gather in the folds of your flowing garments, gird yourself with strength. Is love of the flesh crucifying you? Pick up your cross and follow the Lord. He too, your savior, though God in the flesh, though God with flesh, still gave you a demonstration of purely human feelings, when he said, *Father, if it is possible, let this cup pass from me* (Mt 26:39). He knew that this cup could not pass from him, that it had come to him in order to be drunk. That cup was to be drunk willingly, not out of necessity. He was almighty; if he wished, it would most certainly pass from him, because he was God with the Father, and he and God the Father were one God. But in the form of a servant,[8] in the form he took from you for you, he uttered those words in the voice of a man, in the voice of the flesh. He stooped to transposing you into himself, so that you in

him might utter words of weakness, so that you in him might take a grip on decisive strength. He showed you the will through which you could be tempted; and straightaway he taught you which will you should prefer to which. *Father, he said, if it can be so, let this cup pass from me.* This is a human wish; I am wearing a man, I am speaking from the form of a servant. *Father, if it can be so, let this cup pass.* It's the voice of the flesh, not of the spirit,[9] the voice of infirmity, not of divinity. *If it can be so, let this cup pass.*

This is the wish about which Peter is told, *But when you get old, another will gird you, and take you away, and bring you where you do not wish* (Jn 21:18). So how did the martyrs too overcome? Because they put the wishes of the spirit before the wishes of the flesh. They loved this life, and they weighed it up and played it down. From it they considered how much eternal life should be loved, if this perishable life is loved like that. The man about to die doesn't want to die; and yet he will of necessity be dying some time, even though he is reluctant to die immediately. You can do nothing by just not wanting to die, achieve nothing, extort nothing, you have no power or authority to eliminate the necessity of death. It will come, what you are afraid of, even though you don't want it; it will present itself, what you are putting off, even though you refuse it. Yes, you can take steps to put death off; you can't take any, can you, to eliminate it? So if such efforts are made by the lovers of this life to delay death, how great the pains that should be taken to eliminate it! Certainly, you don't want to die. Change your kind of love, and you will be shown, not a death that will present itself to you against your will, but a death which will, if you so will, absent itself altogether.

Why fear the first death, Christian? What is really needed
is to be redeemed from the second death

4. Observe then, if love has woken up just a little bit in your heart, if just a spark has been struck from the ashes of the flesh, if some solid oak chippings in your heart have caught it and burst into flames, which not only are not put out by the wind of trial and temptation, but are even fanned by it into a bigger blaze than ever; if you are burning, not like a wick which is put out by one light breath, but burning like oak chippings, burning like coal, so that you are on the contrary stirred up by a breath of wind; observe two sorts of death, one temporal, and that's the first; the other everlasting, and that's the second. The first death is ready and waiting for all; the second only for the bad, the godless, unbelievers, blasphemers, and whatever else is opposed to sound teaching.[10] Look closely, set these two sorts of death before your eyes. If it can be avoided, you don't want to suffer both of them.

I know, you love being alive, you don't want to die; and you would like to pass from this life to the other life in such a way that you don't rise again dead, but are changed, alive, into something better. That's what you would like, that's what ordinary human feelings desire, that's what the soul itself has, in I don't know what kind of way, engraved in its deepest will and desire. Since in loving life it hates death, and since it doesn't hate its own flesh, it doesn't want what it hates to happen even to that. *For nobody ever hated his own flesh* (Eph 5:29). The apostle shows us these feelings, where he says, *We have a dwelling from God, a house not made with hands, eternal in the heavens. Indeed, we groan in this one, longing to have our dwelling from heaven put on over us, in which,* he says, *we do not wish to be stripped, but to be clothed over and above, so that what is mortal may be swallowed up by life* (2 Cor 5:1-4). You don't want to be stripped, but stripped you have to be. What you should do your best to ensure, though, is that when you have been stripped of your shirt of flesh by death, you may be found clothed with the armor of faith. That, you see, is what he goes on to add: *provided, that is, that we may be found to be clothed, not naked* (2 Cor 5:3).

The first death, I mean, is going to strip you of the flesh, to be set aside for a while, and received back again at its own proper time. This, whether you like it or not; it's not because you want to, after all, that you will rise again; or, if you don't want to, that you won't; or, if you don't believe in the resurrection, that that will be a reason for your not rising again. What's needed is that you, who are going to rise again willy-nilly, should rather do your best to ensure that you rise again in such a way that you have what you would like to have. The Lord Jesus himself, in fact, said, *The moment is coming when all who are in the tombs will hear his voice and come forth,* whether they're good, whether they're bad; *all who are in the tombs will hear his voice and come forth*; and they will be turned out of their hidden recesses. No creature will hold any of the dead against the voice of the living creator. *All,* he says, who are in the tombs will hear his voice and come forth. In saying *all,* he seems to have created some confusion, and mixed them all up. But listen to the distinction, listen to the separation: *those who have done good,* he says, *to the resurrection of life; those who have committed evil to the resurrection of judgment* (Jn 5:28-29).

This judgment, which the godless are going to rise again to undergo, is called *the second death* (Rv 20:6.14). So, Christian, why be afraid of this first one? It will come even though you don't want it to, and it will be there waiting for you, even though you reject it. You can, perhaps, ransom yourself from the barbarians and so save yourself from being killed; you can ransom yourself for a vast sum, not sparing any of your property at all, and stripping your children of their inheritance; and on being ransomed, you die the next day! It's from the devil you need to be redeemed, who is dragging you off with him to the second death, where the wicked placed on the left hand will hear, *Go, you accursed, into the eternal fire, which has been got ready for the devil and his angels* (Mt 25:41). It's from this second death you need to be ransomed.

"What with?" you will answer.

Don't go looking for goats and bulls. Don't, as a last resort, go turning out your strong box, and saying to yourself, "To ransom myself from the barbarians I had money." To ransom yourself from the second death, have justice.

It would be quite possible for the barbarian first to take your money himself, and then later on lead you away captive, so that there would be nothing with which to redeem yourself, seeing that the one who had possession of you also had possession of all your property. Justice, though, you cannot lose against your will. It's locked up in the innermost strongbox of your heart. Hold on to that, keep possession of that, that's what you can ransom yourself with from the second death. This, if you don't want it to, will not be waiting for you there, for the good reason that what you can use to redeem yourself from this death will be there if you want it to be. It is the will that obtains justice from the Lord, drinking it there as from its own proper source or spring. This is a spring nobody is forbidden to approach, if that person is worthy to do so.

Finally, consider the means you are helped by. What ransomed you from the barbarians was your silver, what redeemed you from the first death was your money; what has ransomed you from the second death is the blood of your Lord. He had the blood to redeem us with; and that's why he accepted to have blood, so that there would be something for him to shed for our redemption. The blood of your Lord, if you wish it so, was given for you; if you don't wish it so, it wasn't given for you.[11]

Yes, but perhaps you're saying, "My God had the blood to redeem me with; but he has already given it all, when he suffered. What is there left for him to give for me?"

That's the great thing about it, that he gave it once only, and gave it for all. The blood of Christ is salvation for the one who wishes it so, torment for the one who refuses it. So why hesitate, you there who don't want to die, to be delivered rather from the second death? From it you are indeed delivered, if you are ready to take up your cross and follow the Lord;[12] because he took up his cross, and sought the slave.

The way people love this life should convince us
how much we should love eternal life

5. Isn't it absolutely true, my brothers and sisters, that the ones who above all others encourage you to love eternal life, are the people who are so in love with temporal life? How many things people do, just to live a few more days! Who could count the efforts and exertions of all those who are so eager to live, and die a little while later? The things they do for the sake of those few days! What, on the same scale, are we doing for the sake of eternal life?

What do I mean by those few days they feel must be paid a ransom for, and that on this earth? By a few days, you see, I mean if the person grows old after being saved from death; I call it a few days, if a person is saved as a child and lives to a decrepit old age.[13] I don't mean that ransomed today, he may perhaps die tomorrow. Just look, with life so uncertain, merely for the sake of those few uncertain days, just look at the things people do, the things they think up! If they come, through some disease of the body, into the hands of a doctor, and every chance of recovery is despaired of by those who examine the case and give their opinion; and if there is a prospect of some other doctor who is capable of saving even desperate cases, what rewards are promised him! How much is given on a totally uncertain chance! For the sake of just a little more life, even what is needed to live on is given up. Now again, if he falls into the hands of an enemy or a brigand, to save him from being killed, even to get him ransomed if it's a father who has been taken, the sons run hither and thither and spend what would have been left to them, in order to redeem the one whom they could soon be carrying out to the grave. What expedients, what prayers, what efforts! Can anybody satisfactorily explain it?

And yet I want to tell you about something even more serious, and even more incredible, if it didn't actually happen. What am I saying, after all? That people give away all their money in order to live, that they leave themselves nothing to live on? In order to live a few days more, and those entirely uncertain, to live them in fear, live them in toil and trouble, how much they are prepared to spend! How much they give away! Alas for the human race! I've said that in order to go on living they spend what they have to live on; listen to something worse, something much more serious, something much more abominable, something quite incredible, as I said, unless it actually happened. To enable them to live a little longer, they give away even that on which they could live forever. Hear what I've said, and understand it. It's still a closed book, you see, and yet it worries many people, for whom the Lord had already opened it up when it was closed.[14] Leave aside those people who, in order to be granted a little longer life, give away and let go what they have to live on. Pay attention to those who, in order to be granted a little longer life, let go of what they could live on forever. What is that? It's called faith, it's called loyalty.[15] This is all like the money, by which eternal life is acquired.

The enemy will cut obliquely across your bows to terrify you, and he won't say to you, "Give me money, in order to go on living"; what he'll say is, "Deny Christ, in order to go on living." If you, in fact, do do that, in order to be permitted to live a little longer, you will be letting go of what would enable you to live always. Is that loving life, you there who were so afraid of death? My good man, why were you afraid of death, if not because you loved life? Christ is life. Why seek a small life, and forfeit a sure and certain one? Or perhaps you haven't let go of faith, but didn't have anything to let go of?[16] So hold onto what will enable you to live always. Look at your neighbor, and how much he does in order to go on living a little while. Look, too, at the person who has denied Christ, and see what an evil thing he has done for the sake of a few more days of life. And you, now, are not willing to despise a few days of life, in order to die on no day, and to live out the everlasting day, to be protected by your redeemer, to be made the equal of the angels in the eternal kingdom? What have you been in love with? What have you been letting go of and losing? You have never taken up your cross in order to follow the Lord.

Losing one's life in order to find it—and finding it in order to lose it

6. See how wise and thoughtful he wants you to be, the one who said to you, *Take up your cross and follow me* (Mk 8:34). *Whoever finds his life*, he said,

will lose it; and whoever loses it on my account will find it (Mt 10:39). Whoever finds will lose it; whoever loses will find it. In order to lose it, the first thing is to find it; and when you've lost it, the final thing is to find it again. There are two findings; in between there is one losing, by which you pass across.[17] None of us can lose our life for Christ's sake unless we have first found it; and none of us can find our life in Christ unless we have first lost it. Find, in order to lose; lose, in order to find.

How are you going to find it, in order to have something you can lose? When you think of yourself as being in part mortal, when you think of the one who made you and created you by breathing life into you,[18] and realize that you owe it to the one who gave it; that it's to be paid back to the one who lent it; that it is to be kept safe by the one who provided it; then you have found your life, finding it in faith. I mean, you have believed this, and found your soul, your life.[19] After all, you were lost, before you came to believe. You have found your life; you had been dead, that is, in your unbelief; you have come back to life in faith. You are just like the one about whom it can be said, *He was dead, and has come to life again; he was lost and is found* (Lk 15:32).

So you have found your life in the true faith, if you have come back to life from the death of unbelief. That is, you have found your soul. Lose it, and your soul becomes seed for you. I mean the farmer too by threshing and winnowing finds the wheat, and again by sowing it he loses the wheat. What had been lost in the sowing is found on the threshing floor. What is found in the harvest is lost in the sowing. So, *whoever finds his life will lose it.* You work so hard at gathering; why be so slow in the sowing?

There is a life to be found which it is absolutely impossible to lose

7. Notice carefully, however, how you are to find it, and why you are to lose it. What would you find it with, after all, unless a light were struck for you by the one to whom it is said, *You will light up my lamp, Lord* (Ps 18:28)? So you have already found it, with him lighting a lamp for you. Notice why you are to lose it. It's not, you see, to be lost anywhere and everywhere, something that has been found with such diligence. He didn't say, "Whoever loses it will find it," but *Whoever loses it on my account.* When you've taken a look, perhaps, at the body of a shipwrecked trader on the shore,[20] you're moved to pity and you pay him his due of tears, and say, "Alas for this man! It was for the sake of gold that he lost his life." You are right to mourn him, right to feel sorry for him. Give him his due of weeping, since you can't also give him any help. For the sake of gold, you see, he was able to lose his life, but not able, for the sake of gold, to find it. He was quite capable of suffering the loss of his life and soul, but turned out to be less capable of gaining it.

We should reflect, you see, not on what he lost but on why he lost it. If it was on account of avarice, look, that's where the flesh lies; where is what was so dear to him?[21] And yet avarice gave the command, and for the sake of gold the soul was lost, and for the sake of Christ the soul does not perish, nor can it. You fool, don't hesitate; listen to the creator's advice. He's the one who fashioned you to use your wits, the one who made you before you were there to have any wits. Listen, don't hesitate to lose your life for Christ's sake. You are in fact entrusting to a trustworthy creator what you are said to be losing. You, indeed, will lose it; but he will receive it, and for him nothing perishes and is lost. If you love life, lose it in order to find it; because when you find it, it won't any longer be the sort of thing you can lose, there won't be any reason why you should lose it. The life in fact that will be found is one that will be found to be such that it cannot ever perish or be lost at all. Because Christ too, who by his birth, death and resurrection has given himself to you as a model, *rising from the dead dies no more, and death will no longer lord it over him* (Rom 6:9).

NOTES

1. This date is suggested by the Italian edition, but with no authorities quoted. The sermon does ramble rather, and show a certain incoherence; qualities that do perhaps reveal the old man of seventy-four or so. The high probability is that it was preached in Hippo Regius; just possibly in Carthage. But if the date is correct, Augustine was not traveling anymore. See note 20 below.

2. Reading *non sine adjutorio suos spectat*, instead of the text's . . . *adjutorio suo spectat*, does not watch without his help.

3. In the Latin simply *robore mentis*, which could usually be simply translated as "strength of mind." But contrasted with the straw of the flesh, *robur* must here surely retain its basic meaning of hardwood—usually oak.

4. What things? There is no obvious antecedent for *ipsa*. He thinks he has mentioned the things to which love of the world tends, but he hasn't.

5. See 1 Cor 15:43.

6. Reading *sed non de corpore suo pater panem . . . instituit* instead of the text's *sed non de suo pater . . . .* I think there must be an allusion to the eucharist here.

7. See Mt 10:37, influenced by Lk 14:26.

8. See Phil 2:7.

9. See Mk 14:38.

10. See Tit 2:1.

11. A theologically careless way of putting it; Christ shed his blood for all, without exception. It was the later error of the Jansenists, relying on some of Augustine's more careless statements, to say that Christ only died for the elect. No, his blood was shed for you, whether you wish it or not. But if you don't wish it, you don't profit from its having been shed for you; you refuse to be ransomed or redeemed.

12. See Lk 14:27.

13. Something that had happened to Augustine himself. See *Confessions*, I, 11.

14. I think he is alluding to the text he is going to quote at the beginning of section 6.

15. *Pietas*; but "piety" will hardly suffice as a translation here.

16. Quite what turn the argument is taking here, it is hard to see. From what he immediately goes on to say, it is clear that he is not now turning to address the unbeliever. He is still addressing the believing Christian—and asking him severely if he really has any genuine faith. Then, presuming the answer to be, "Yes, he has," he goes on as before.

17. Reading *transis* instead of the text's *transit*, he/one passes across.

18. See Gn 2:7.

19. The same word, *anima*, meaning soul, and hence life. Jesus is talking about finding and losing one's soul. But to translate it so, given what English Christianity and language have done to the word "soul," would be to give an entirely wrong impression.

20. This remark indicates that he was preaching in a seaside town—and where more likely than in his home port of Hippo Regius? But it could have been Carthage, if the sermon was preached several years earlier than we are supposing.

21. An untranslatable pun: *ecce ubi jacet caro; ubi est quod erat carum?* The pronunciation of *caro*, flesh, and *carum*, dear, was probably almost identical. The question is about the gold he died for—but can also be about his soul, his "dear one," Ps 22:20.

SERMON 345

ON THE CONTEMPT OF TEMPORAL THINGS: PREACHED ON THE BIRTHDAY
OF THE WOMEN MARTYRED AT THUBURBO

Date: 411[1]

Indifference to the present age and hope for the age to come
should encourage the rich to be generous to the poor

1. The fact that today is both a feast of the martyrs and the Lord's day constrains me to speak to your graces about what concerns indifference or contempt for the present age and hopes for the age to come. If you want to know what you should be indifferent to, every holy and pious martyr has shown indifference even to the present life. If you want to know what you should hope for, today the Lord rose again.[2] If you are faltering now under the harsh realities of the present, be strong in your hopes for the future;[3] if the work makes your spirits droop, let the reward for it revive them. The first reading from the apostle, in the letter which he writes to Timothy, also reminds us of what he commanded him, in the words, *Command the rich of this world not to be haughty in their ideas, nor to have their hopes set on the uncertainty of riches, but on the living God, who bestows all things on us abundantly for our enjoyment. Let them be rich in good works, let them be ready to give things away, and to share; let them store up for themselves a good foundation for the future, so that they may lay hold of true life* (1 Tm 6:17-19).

And this reading should not strike us as having little reference to the feast of the blessed martyrs; it does, after all, suggest indifference to the world. You see, when the rich are commanded to store up for themselves a good foundation for the future, and to lay hold of true life, it undoubtedly means that this life is a false one. And the rich above all have to hear this, because when the poor look at them, they grumble, sigh, praise them, envy them, would love to be on their level, lament that they are so much below it, and among their praises of the rich they frequently say this sort of thing: "These are the only ones, these the only ones who really live." So on account of these words, with which the lower orders flatter the rich, that they really live, and are the only ones to do so; in case these words of flatterers should go to their heads, and make them think that they really are living; *Command*, he says, *the rich of this world not to be haughty in their ideas, nor to have their hopes set on the uncertainty of riches, but on the living God, who bestows all things on us abundantly for our enjoyment.* Yes, let them be rich; but in what way? In good works; let them be ready to give things away, because they don't lose what they give away; let them share with those who haven't got things. And what follows from this? *Let them store up for themselves a good foundation for the future, so that they may lay hold of true life*; not giving their assent to the flatterers, who say that they really live, and are the only ones who really live.

This life is a dream life; these riches are, as it were, flowing through our sleep. Listen to the psalm, O poorest of the poor, Mr. Rich Man: *They have slept their sleep, and have found nothing in their hands, all the men of riches* (Ps 76:5). Sometimes, too, a beggar lying on the ground, shivering with cold, but still overcome with sleep, will dream of untold wealth, and rejoice and grow proud in his sleep, and not deign to recognize his ragged old father, and until he wakes up he's rich. So when he goes to sleep, he finds something false and unreal to rejoice in; when he wakes up he finds something only too real and true to grieve over. So the rich man when he dies is like the poor man when he wakes up, after seeing untold wealth in his sleep. I mean, there was that man too, *clothed in purple and fine linen* (Lk 16:19), a certain rich man who was neither named nor fit to be named, a despiser of the poor man lying at his gate. He was clothed in purple and fine linen, as the gospel testifies, and he feasted sumptuously every day. He died, he was buried; he woke up, and found himself in the flames. So he slept his sleep, and found nothing in his hands, that man of riches, because he had done nothing good with his hands.

People prepared to pay vast sums to be redeemed from the barbarians

2. So then, riches are sought for the sake of life, not life for the sake of riches. How many there are who have come to terms with their enemies, to the effect that they should take everything, and leave them their lives! However much they possessed, they[4] gave it all, simply in order not to lose their lives.

You gave everything you had to the barbarians, brother?

"I gave everything," he says; "I am left completely bare; even if I'm naked, I'll live."

But why?

"I was all of me due to be killed; that's why I gave all of it away."

And why did this happen to you? Do you want me to tell you? Because before the barbarian arrived on the scene, you weren't helping the poor, so that through the poor man your alms might reach Christ. You didn't give Christ even a little, and you've given the barbarians everything you had, and given it with an oath. Christ begs and doesn't receive; the barbarian tortures, and takes the lot.

How much, then, is eternal life to be bought for, if this life that's going to perish is valued so highly? Give Christ something so that you may live in bliss, if you give all you have to your enemy, so that you may live a beggar. From your temporal life, which you redeem at such a vast price, in order to live a few days more—that's all they are, even if you reach a ripe old age—calculate how much the eternal life you neglect is worth.[5] All the days of a person's life, after all, from infancy to old age, are just a few days; and if Adam himself were to die today, he would only have lived for a few days, because all his days would have come to an end. So are you redeeming just a few days, and these so painfully laborious, lived in such want, amid such trials? How much for? You are willing to have nothing, in order to have just yourself.

Do you want to know how much eternal life is worth? Add yourself too to the price. There was your enemy, who had captured you, saying to you, "If you want to stay alive, give me whatever you have." And in order to stay alive, you gave him everything; redeemed today, just to die, perhaps, tomorrow; left alive by this one, to be slaughtered, perhaps, by that one. May such dangers serve to educate us, my brothers and sisters. How could people be so ignorant, and that with all God's words, and all human experience to instruct them? Look, you've given everything and gone your way rejoicing, because you're still alive, even though poor, even though in want, even though naked, even though a beggar; still, you're rejoicing, because you are alive, and the light of day is sweet.

Now let Christ appear; let him too suggest terms, not the one who captures you, but the one who was captured for your sake; not the one who seeks to kill you, but the one who was ready to be killed for your sake. The one who gave himself for you—what a price!—who made you, says to you, "Come to terms with me. You are willing to have yourself and lose everything? If you wish to have yourself, you must have me; so as to hate yourself in order to love me, and so as to find your life by losing it, in order not to lose it by clinging onto it. About these riches of yours, which you love to possess, and which all the same you are prepared to give away for the sake of your present life, I have already given you some salutary advice. If you love them too, don't lose them too; but they are going to perish with you where you are loving them now. I'm giving you some advice about them. Do you love them? Send them on ahead where you can follow them; or else, when you are loving them on earth, you either lose them while you are still alive, or leave them behind you when you're dead. About this too," he says, "I've given you advice. I haven't said 'Lose them,' but 'Keep them.' Do you want to save them up? I'm not saying, 'Don't do it,' but what I am saying is, 'Where?' Accept me as an adviser, not as a notice saying 'It is prohibited.' So where am I telling you to save them up? *Save up for yourselves treasure in heaven, where the thief cannot approach, and rust cannot spoil* (Mt 6:20)."

Salutary advice about how to keep one's riches

3. "But I can't see," you say, "what I'm depositing in heaven."

You can see, of course, what you bury in the earth? Burying in the earth gives you a nice sense of security, while handing over to the one who made heaven and earth leaves you feeling anxious? Well, keep it where you like; if you can find a better custodian than Christ, entrust it to him.

"I'm entrusting it," you say, "to my slave."

How much better to your Lord and master! The slave, very possibly, will take it and run away; and among all the great evils that have already happened, what we have to hope for is this: that the slave will just take it and run away, and not lead enemies to his master.[6] Many slaves have suddenly turned out to be the enemies of their masters, and have betrayed them with everything they have to the foe. So who are you entrusting it to?

"For the time being," you say, "I'm entrusting my gold to my slave."

Your gold to your slave; your soul to whom?

"I'm entrusting my soul," you say, "to God."

How much better to entrust your gold also to the one to whom you entrust your soul! Or perhaps he's to be trusted to keep your soul safe, and not to be trusted to keep your gold safe? The one who can keep you won't keep anything for you?

So then, trust him. The slave may guarantee not to take it; can he guarantee not to lose it? Yes, he's to be trusted entirely not to cheat you; aren't you considering his trustworthiness, without paying any attention to his weakness? He has put it away, he hasn't hidden it for himself; along comes somebody else and steals it. Now is anybody going to do that to Christ? Snap out of your lazy inertia, follow his advice; bank your treasure in heaven. And what's this I've said, "Snap out of your lazy intertia"? As though there was hard work involved in banking treasure in heaven! Even if it did involve hard work, it should still be done, and the hard work should be undertaken, and the things we value so highly deposited in a well-secured place, from which nobody could possibly steal them. Christ, though, isn't saying to you, "Bank your treasure in heaven, look for ladders, fit yourself out with wings," but "Give it to me here on earth, and I will keep it for you up there. It's on earth," he says, "that you should give it to me; that's why I came here as a poor man, so that you could be rich up there. Arrange a transfer." Are you afraid of losing it to a fraudulent middle man, are you wondering who's going to carry it to where you're moving? Christ is on hand for you at each end; he's not organizing a racket, he's arranging transport.

You will find Christ here on earth in the poor

4. "Yes," you say, "but where do I find Christ? Since my faith tells me what I've heard in the Church, this is what I have learned, what I have believed, this is what I was given at my baptism; he was buried, he rose again on the third day, after forty days he ascended into heaven before the very eyes of his disciples, he is seated at the right hand of the Father, he is going to come again at the end. When can I find him here? To whom can I give?"

Stop fretting; listen to the whole of it. Or if you've heard the whole of it, tell the whole of it. I know that this is what you have received; that Christ was hung up on the cross, taken down from the tree, placed in the tomb, rose again, ascended into heaven. You have also read that other thing, that when his Church was being persecuted by Saul in his pride and cruelty, breathing out slaughter, and thirsting for the blood of Christians; that when Saul was raging, persecuting, bringing letters to Damascus that when he found men and women of this persuasion he should bring them back in chains for punishment; you've heard, haven't you, what the one who, as you confess, is seated in heaven cried out to him? So call to mind what he said, what you've heard, what you've read: *Saul, Saul, why are you persecuting me?* (Acts 9:1-4). Paul, I mean to say, could neither see him nor touch him; and yet he said to him, *Why are you persecuting me?* He didn't say, "Why are you persecuting my family, my servants, my saints"—add another title of honor—"my brothers and sisters." Nothing of that sort. But what did he say? *Why are you persecuting me?* That is, my members, on whose behalf, as they were being trampled upon on earth, the head was crying out from heaven. Because even for your own foot, when it's trodden upon on the ground, your tongue doesn't cry out, "You're treading on my foot," but "You're treading on me."

So why have any doubts about whom you can give to? It's the one who said, *Saul, Saul, why are you persecuting me?* It's the same one who says to you, "Feed me on earth." Saul was raging, and yet it was Christ that he was persecuting. The same applies to you also; pay out on earth, and it is Christ you are feeding. Because this question which bothers you was foreseen by the Lord himself; those who are to be set on his right will also be bothered by it, and when he says, *I was hungry and you gave me to eat,* they will reply, *Lord, when did we see you hungry?* And straightaway they will hear, *When you did it for one of these least of mine, you did it for me* (Mt 25:35-40).

Where your treasure is, there will your heart be also

5. So, if you don't want to give, you have something to accuse yourself of, not something that will excuse you. So it's about these riches that your Lord tells you, "I have given you some very sound and salutary advice. Do you love them? Ship them off; and when you're shipped off yourself, you'll follow them. Follow them, meanwhile, in your heart; *For where your treasure is, there your heart will be also* (Mt 6:21)." If [7] you entrust your treasure to the earth, you are burying your heart too in the earth. But if you are burying your heart in the earth, blush for shame, because you are lying when you give your answer to the words *Lift up your hearts. Lift up your hearts* is said, and straightaway you answer, *We have lifted them up to the Lord.* You're lying to God. Not even for a moment in church do you tell the truth; you lie to God, which you do all the time to other people. You say, *We have lifted them up to the Lord,* and in fact you have buried your heart in the earth; because *where your treasure is, there will your heart be also.*

If you do with your riches what you have heard, if you are the sort of rich man that the apostle describes, not haughty in your ideas, not placing your hopes in the uncertainty of riches, giving things away easily, sharing;[8] so that you store up for yourself a good foundation for the future, in order to lay hold of the true life;[9] now go and question your Lord and God, and say to him, "Look, Lord, I have now shipped off to heaven what I had; or at least, what I still have, I have as though I did not have it.[10] Is the kingdom of heaven worth as much as my patrimony?" It's worth far, far more; in fact it isn't really the sort of thing of which you can say it's worth so much.

This is what your Lord says to you, when you've questioned him about your patrimony: "You are going to live for a time, and afterwards going to die. In my kingdom you are never going to die, but you are going to live forever. You will be a real, true rich man there, where you will never be in want. I mean, the reason you require many animals for transport, lavish banquets for sustenance, expensive garments for clothing, is in order not to be left in want. Is it really the case that you are rich by having many things, and that an angel of mine is poor? He's got nothing; he neither uses a horse, nor rides about in a carriage, nor fills a table with splendid tableware; nor is any garment woven for him, because he is clothed in eternal light. Learn, rich man, to go for the true riches."

You want to have these riches, in order to have the means of tickling your palate and filling your belly,[11] because you fade away, otherwise; the one who will make you really and truly rich, is the one who grants you never to be hungry forever. Because you may have as much as you like, but when dinner time comes,[12] before you come to table you are hungry, and failing, because you are only a miserable wretch after all. Does an angel have to endure all that? Perish the thought! And finally, it is in a spirit of pride that you are so keen on such banquets. They are not the satisfaction of genuine needs, but the dubious adjuncts of office and ambition.[13]

When you are giving thought to increasing your wealth, just see whether you sleep easily. Unless I'm much mistaken, when you've found riches, you have lost repose. While you're awake, you are thinking about the increase of your wealth; when you go to sleep, you dream of brigands. Anxious during the day, fearful during the night, at all times a beggar. The one who promises you the kingdom of heaven wants to make you into a genuine rich man; and you imagine you are going to buy those true riches, that true and blessed life, for as much as you were prepared to redeem these few and laborious days for? Something that is so much more surely ought to be worth much, much more; it is, after all, the kingdom of heaven.

You must hand over not only your property, but also yourself to God.
The example of the martyrs of Thuburbo

6. "And what am I to do?" you say.[14] "Look, holy bishop, I've heard your warnings, I've complied with your advice, I haven't spurned the Lord's command. What I had I gave to the poor, and what I have I share with the needy. What more can I do?"

You've still got something, you've got yourself; you yourself are something more; it's you that are still lacking to the totality of your goods, you that must be added to them. Have you followed your Lord's advice?

"I have," he says.

Why are you lying? You've followed it in one respect, in another you haven't touched it. Listen to what he commands: *Go, sell all that you have, and give to the poor.* He didn't send him away at that point, did he? And in case he should think he would lose what he distributed to the poor, he reassured him by saying, *and you shall have treasure in heaven.*

"Wasn't that enough, then?"

No.

"And what else?"

Come, follow me (Mk 10:21), he says. Do you love him, do you want to follow the one you love? He has run away, he has flown off. Inquire which way he went.

"I don't know which way."

Oh, my dear Christian! You don't know which way your Lord went? Do you want me to tell you which way you must follow? By the way of distress, of abuse, of false charges, of spittle in the face, of slaps and whips and scourges, of a crown of thorns, of a cross, and of death. Why are you holding back? There you are, the way has been shown you.

"But the way is hard," you say; "who could ever follow him along that way?"

Blush for shame, bearded man, blush for shame; you are called a man from manliness.[15] Women have followed him, those whose birthday we are celebrating today. We are celebrating the feast today of the women martyrs of Thuburbo.[16] Your Lord, our Lord, their Lord, the redeemer of our lives, by going first has made of a rough and narrow way a paved road for you, a king's highway,[17] safe and well protected,[18] along which women too were delighted to walk; and are you still holding back? Are you unwilling to shed your blood in return for such blood as that? This is what your Lord is saying to you: "I first suffered for you; give what you have received, give back what you have drunk." Are you, only you, unable to do that? Boys and girls have been able to; delicate, frail men and women have been able to. Rich and outstandingly rich people have been able to; when the trials of suffering suddenly rushed down on them, they weren't restrained by the extent of their wealth, nor captivated by the sweetness of this life; but thinking about that rich man who was finished with riches and discovered torments,[19] they didn't even send on their riches ahead, but rather went ahead of them themselves by martyrdom. With all these examples before you, are you still sluggishly holding back?

And yet you are celebrating the feast of the martyrs.

"It's the birthday of the martyrs today; I shall go along," you say, "and perhaps in my best suit."[20]

Consider with what kind of conscience you come along. Love what you are about, imitate what you are celebrating, do what you admire.

"But I, though, can't do it."

The Lord is near, do not be anxious about anything (Phil 4:6).

"I, though," you say, "cannot do it."

You, my friend, stop being afraid of that fountain. Those women took their fill from it; you too can take your fill from it, if you approach it avidly, if you don't swell yourself up like a hill, but humble yourself like a valley, in order to deserve to receive your fill.

With the world in ruins around us, why be so reluctant to give it up?

7. So, brothers and sisters, these thoughts shouldn't seem hard to us, especially in these times with so much distress all round us.[21] The world was despised by the martyrs when it was flourishing; it was really and truly praiseworthy to despise it while it was flourishing; and now it's loved when it is perishing. They, in their time, despised its blooms, and you, in yours, are embracing its thorns. If you are so reluctant to move, at least allow the ruins of your house to frighten you.

But the pagan is taunting you.[22]

Yes indeed, now is the time for the pagan to taunt you, when the predictions of your Lord are being fulfilled! Surely, though, he would be more correct to taunt you if the things the Lord foretold hadn't been fulfilled. This pagan denies the God whom you worship; it's for you to show, from the things the world is undergoing, that God is truthful, and to rejoice in his promises rather than to let yourself be depressed by his predictions coming true.

He came, you see, at the very time[23] when the world in its declining years, as though it had been made just to be brought to an end, was on the point of overflowing with disasters and calamities, and distresses and troubles. He came for your consolation by coming then; so that you wouldn't fall away under the pressures of a life that is perishing and passing, he promised you another sort of life. Before the world started staggering under all these afflictions and calamities, the prophets were sent; servants were sent to this enormous sick patient, to the human race as to one bed-ridden patient, stretched out and lying there from the east to the west. The capable doctor sent his servants. It came to the point that this patient suffered such a series of critical attacks, that he was clearly going to be in great difficulties. And the doctor said, "This patient is going to be in difficulties, my own presence is necessary."

Now let the stupid patient say to the doctor, "Lord, I've been in great difficulties since you came."

"You fool, you're not in difficulties since, and because, I came; but it's because you were going to be in difficulties that I came."

I'll put it in a nutshell, brothers and sisters; what's the point of my saying so much? *It is a summary word that the Lord has cut short over the earth* (Is 10:23). Let us lead good lives, and for our good life let us not set our hopes on the fleeting good things of this earth. Earthly well-being is a cheap exchange for a good life. That you live well here doesn't count as much as does what you desire here, though by desiring such things you fail even to live well. If you would change your life, change your desires. You are keeping faith with God, and quite simply in order to do well on earth? Is that the sum total of your reason for keeping faith with God? Is that all your faith is worth? Is that the only price tag you give it? Is that all it adds up to for you? If you have something for sale on earth, and are negotiating with a buyer, you set a dearer price, he a cheaper one. "It's worth so much," you say, because you exaggerate the value of what you're selling. And he says, "It's not worth that much, but only so much"; and he gives you[24] a lower price, wishing to buy more cheaply.

Christ the Lord is correcting you. You are saying to Christ your Lord, "Lord, I'm keeping faith with you, and now it's for you to give its value to me on earth."

"You fool, that's not the value of what you are selling; you're mistaken, you don't know what you've got. You're keeping faith, and asking for earth? Your faith is worth more than earth; you don't know how to price it. I, who gave it to you, know how much it's worth. It's worth as much as the whole earth; add the heavens too to the earth, it's worth more than that."

"And what is worth more than earth and heaven?"

"The one who made both earth and heaven."[25]

Turning to the Lord, etc.

NOTES

1. The Maurists have a shorter variant of this sermon as their Sermon 345. The text mainly followed here was published by Dom Frangipane at the beginning of the nineteenth century, and is printed in Migne's supplement to Augustine's works, PL 46, 971-980. But on occasion, and sometimes quite extensively I prefer the Maurist text.

There are different opinions abut the date. It is stated in the sermon itself that it was preached on a Sunday which was also the feast of the martyrs of Thuburbo; and that was celebrated on 30 July. The years in which that day fell on a Sunday during Augustine's ministry were 405, 411, 416, 422, and 428. See O. Perler, *Les Voyages de Saint Augustin*, 296—though he omits to mention 428 as such a year. Kunzelmann follows Frangipane in favoring 428 as the year in which the sermon was preached; but the majority opinion goes to 411; and this means it would have been preached in Carthage. If the minority opinion is correct—and I lean toward it myself—it would have been preached at home in Hippo Regius. See notes 20 and 21 below for arguments in favor of each conclusion.

2. This statement led Kunzelmann to conclude that the sermon was preached on Easter day; but it is by no means a necessary conclusion, since every Sunday, being the Lord's day, commemorates his resurrection.

3. Much more succinct in the Latin, with his favorite *res/spes* jingle: *Si titubas in re, esto fortis in spe*.

4. From here until the end of the little conversation is taken from the Maurist text. We rejoin the Italian edition with "How much, then . . ."

5. I have here transposed two clauses. If I had not done so, the sentence would run, "From your temporal life, which you redeemed at such a vast price, calculate how much you neglect the real worth of the eternal life, which you neglect in order to live a few days more—that's all they are, even if you reach a ripe old age."

6. It is a remark like this that leads Frangipane and Kunzelmann to assign the late date, 428, to the sermon, because it was only in the previous year that the Vandals crossed over into Africa and started their sweep through the provinces, where they were to lay siege to Hippo Regius two years later when Augustine was dying. There is something in the argument, and it certainly appeals to me. But there were, of course, other enemies, other barbarians long resident in the region before the arrival of the Vandals—like the desert tribes over the southern borders, for instance.

7. From here to the end of section 5 I am following the Maurist text, which is for the most part much more coherent than Frangipane, or variations of it in the Italian edition. The differences are sometimes so extensive that I regret I cannot give the alternative text, or texts, in the endnotes.

8. These two phrases are added from the Italian edition.

9. See 1 Tm 6:17-19.

10. See 1 Cor 7:31.

11. Two phrases taken from the Italian edition; the Maurist text reads simply, "to have the means of eating a lot."

12. *Hora quinta*; 11:00 a.m.

13. *Fumus curarum*; literally, the smoke of cares. I wish I could find a translation that is less of a remote paraphrase, but I don't see how I can.

14. Again, I am following the Maurist text, until it comes to an end about halfway through this section.

15. *A virtute vir diceris.*

16. I can find no reference to them in the professional hagiographies, like Butler's *Lives*. But the Maurists inform us, on the authority of Henry Valesius (who sounds to me like Henry of Valois; a royal scholar?), that their names, or the names of some of them, were Maxima, Donatilla, and Secunda.

17. From here on I return to the Italian edition, as the Maurists end here rather abruptly, after a few words more.

18. Omitting *et puram*, and pure—which hardly suits the context; a marginal reflection of a pious reader, I take it to be.

19. See Lk 16:19-24.

20. *Cum meliore tunica.*

21. It is this remark again that led Frangipane to date the sermon later than 427, when the Vandal invasion of Africa began.

22. Now this statement seems to support those who would date the sermon to 411, shortly after the sack of Rome by Alaric, which was the great occasion for pagan taunts against Christianity. But of course these could have been, and no doubt were, repeated with every new calamity at the hands of the barbarians, of which the sack of Rome was only the foretaste and type. So the Frangipane dating still holds good; and I am more and more inclined to support it.

23. The time of the incarnation. This doesn't quite harmonize with what he has just said about the martyrs despising a flourishing world.

24. Correcting the *sibi* of the text—gives himself—to *tibi*.

25. Who is the only true and proper object of your faith.

SERMON 346

ON OUR PILGRIMAGE THROUGH THIS LIFE BY FAITH

Date: uncertain[1]

Only eternal life really deserves the name of life

1. Recollect with me, most dearly beloved brothers,[2] that the apostle said, *As long as we are in the body, we are living abroad, away from the Lord; for we are walking by faith, not by sight* (2 Cor 5:6-7). Our Lord Jesus Christ, you see, who said *I am the way, the truth and the life* (Jn 14:6), wished us to walk both along himself and to himself. How, after all, are we to walk, except along the way? And where are we to walk to, except to the truth and the life, namely eternal life, which alone deserves to be called life? I mean, this mortal life, in which we find ourselves now, is shown up in comparison with that life to be really a death; it is so variable and constantly changing, lacking all steadiness and firmness, terminated after such a brief course. And that's why that rich man who said to the Lord, *Good master, what must I do, in order to obtain eternal life?* received the answer, *If you would attain to life, keep the commandments* (Mt 19:16-17). He already had, of course, some kind of life; the Lord, after all, wasn't talking to a corpse and a non-living man. But because he had asked about obtaining eternal life, the Lord didn't say, "If you wish to attain to eternal life," but *If you wish*, he said, *to attain to life, keep the commandments*; wishing us to understand, surely, that a life that is not eternal doesn't even deserve to be called life, because nothing except eternal life is true life.

Hence the apostle too, when reminding Timothy[3] of the advice to be given to the rich on almsgiving, said, *Let them be rich in good works, let them readily give things away, let them share, let them store up for themselves a good foundation for the future, in order to lay hold of the true life* (1 Tm 6:18-19). Which life did he call the true one, if not eternal life, which alone deserves to be called life, because it alone is a life of bliss? Because of course, those rich people who he said were to be instructed to lay hold of the true life, were enjoying this life in the abundance of their wealth. If the apostle, however, had judged this to be true life, he would not have said, *Let them store up for themselves a good foundation for the future, in order to lay hold of the true life*. All he was doing was warning us that the life of the rich is not true life; a life which is claimed by fools to be not only true life, but indeed a life of bliss.

How, though, can it be blissful if it isn't even true? So only true life is a life of bliss; and only eternal life is true life. We are to understand that the rich do not yet enjoy this through any kind of luxury you like to think of; and that's why they are urged by giving alms to lay a claim to hearing at the end, *Come, you blessed of my Father, receive the kingdom which has been prepared for you from the beginning of the world; for I was hungry, and you gave me to eat* (Mt 25:34-35). That the kingdom is itself eternal life, the Lord went on shortly to show in what follows: *Those will go into eternal burning, but the just into eternal life* (Mt 25:46).

The difference between walking by faith and arriving at sight
is copiously illustrated

2. Until we lay hold of this life, *we are abroad, away from the Lord; since we are walking by faith, not by sight* (2 Cor 5:6-7). He himself said, in fact, *I am the way, the truth and the life* (Jn 14:6). It is in faith that he is the way for us, while it is in sight that he is the truth and the life. *We see now through a mirror in a riddle,* and that is faith; *then, however, it will be face to face* (1 Cor 13:12), and that will be sight. Again he says, *For Christ to dwell in the inner self through faith in your hearts* (Eph 3:16-17); that's the way, on which *we know in part* (1 Cor 13:9). But a little later he says, *to know also the surpassing knowledge of the charity of Christ, that you may be filled up to all the fullness of God* (Eph 3:19); that will be sight, when in this fulness, *once what is perfect has come, what is in part will be taken away* (1 Cor 13:10). Again he says, *For you are dead, and your life is hidden with Christ in God*; that is faith. Then he adds, *When Christ, your life, appears, then you also will appear with him in glory* (Col 3:3-4); that will be sight.

John too says, *Dearly beloved, now we are already children of God, and it has not yet appeared what we shall be*; that's faith. Then he adds, *We know that when he appears, we shall be like him, because we shall see him as he is* (1 Jn 3:2); that will be sight. On this point, when the Lord himself, who said *I am the way, the truth and the life,* was talking to the Jews, among whom were some who had already come to believe, he now directed his words to these in particular, saying, *If you abide in my word, you will truly be my disciples; and you will know the truth, and the truth will set you free* (Jn 8:31-32). These had already believed; I mean, that's how the evangelist puts it: *But Jesus said to those who had come to believe in him, If you abide in my word, you will truly be my disciples; and you will know the truth, and the truth will set you free.* So they had already come to believe, and begun, as it were, to walk in the way, in Christ. And so he is urging them by abiding in it to arrive. To arrive where, if not at what he says: *the truth will set you free*? What is this freedom from, if not from all the the chopping and changing of this present vanity,[4] and from all our perishable mortality? So that is the true life, eternal life, which we have not yet laid hold of, as long as we are abroad and away from the Lord; but we are going to lay hold of it, because we are walking by faith in the same Lord, provided we abide, unshakably steadfast, in his word. You see, insofar as he said, *I am the way,* he also says, *If you abide in my word, you will truly be my disciples.* And insofar as he said *and the truth and the life,* he also says, *and you will know the truth, and the truth will set you free.*

So in this journeying abroad and on this way, that is in faith, what am I to urge upon you, brothers and sisters, but the words of the apostle when he says, *So having these promises, my dearest friends, let us cleanse ourselves from all defilement of flesh and spirit, completing our sanctification in the fear of the Lord* (2 Cor 7:1)? There are people, you see, who aspire to have that light of the most genuine and unchangeable truth handed them on a plate before they believe, when it is impossible for them to behold it except with hearts purified by faith;[5] *Blessed,* you see, *are the purehearted, since it is they who shall see God* (Mt 5:8). They are like blind men, desiring first to see the bodily light of this sun, in order to be cured of blindness; whereas they cannot possibly see it unless they are first cured.

NOTES

1. There is nothing in the sermon, really, to suggest any particular date or place. As for place, though, or rather type of congregation, I wonder if, with the address of *dilectissimi fratres* at the beginning, and the topic, he was not preaching to a community of "servants of God"; most likely, then, his own religious community in Hippo Regius. If that is the case, I ought perhaps, this time, to be excused from translating *fratres* as "brothers and sisters"; there would have been no sisters present.

2. See note 1.

3. I have supplied "Timothy," who is not actually mentioned in the text.

4. See 1:2—and indeed the whole book of Ecclesiastes.

5. See Acts 15:9.

SERMON 346A

ON THE WORD OF GOD AS LEADER OF CHRISTIANS ON THEIR PILGRIMAGE

Date: 399[1]

At a fork in the road on our journey through life stands a man, God made man, directing us to follow the hard rough road to the right, not the broad smooth road to the left

1. Brothers and sisters, we are Christians, and we all want to go on with the journey, and even if we don't want to, the journey is what in fact we have to go on with. Nobody is permitted to stay here; all who come into this life are compelled by the turning wheel of time to pass on. There must be no room for any kind of idleness; keep walking, or you will just be dragged along. As we travel on our journey we have been met at a fork in the road by a certain man; not just a man, in fact, but God who on man's account is man. And he has said to us, "Don't go to the left; that does indeed look an easy and delightful road to pass along, worn smooth by many, and broad; but at the end of that way lies ruin. But there's another way, which involves innumerable labors, difficulties, straitened circumstances, hardships; along which not only are there no delights to be found, but scarcely any humanity is shown either; a road you will have difficulty in walking along; but no sooner do you reach the end, than you come to the very pinnacle of joy, so that you avoid those traps and ambushes, which otherwise nobody can escape."

What the Word of God has foretold has always come true

2. Let us call past times to mind, and the holy scriptures. Isn't that man the Word of God? Didn't that very Word later on *become flesh, and dwell amongst us* (Jn 1:14)? Before he became flesh and dwelt amongst us, didn't that very Word speak through the prophets? God undoubtedly spoke by his Word to Abraham, that his stock was going to be wandering nomads; this though the man who was told so was very old, and Sarah was an old and barren woman; he believed, it happened. That this stock, that is the people born from them according to the flesh, was going to endure slavery in Egypt for four hundred years; it happened. That it was to be delivered from that captivity; delivered it was. That it was going to receive the promised land; it received it.[2] Things both far in the

71

future and soon to occur were foretold, and they came about, and are now still being fulfilled.

The Word of God spoke through the prophets,[3] that that nation would sin, to be delivered into the hands of their enemies because they offended against their God; it all happened. That it would go into captivity in Babylon; this too happened. That Christ the king would come from their stock; Christ came, Christ was born, because the Word himself declared that he would come himself.[4] It was said that the Jews would crucify him;[5] they did so. It was foretold that he would rise again and be glorified;[6] it happened, he rose again, he ascended into heaven. It was foretold that the whole earth was going to believe in his name; foretold that kings would persecute his Church;[7] this happened. It was foretold that kings were going to believe in him; we now have the faithfulness of kings before our eyes—and can we have doubts about the faithfulness of Christ? The lopping off[8] of heresies was foretold; don't we see them too, and groan in the midst of the din they raise all round us? It was foretold that the very idols would be destroyed by means of the Church and the name of Christ;[9] this too we can see being fulfilled. Scandals were foretold in the Church itself, tares too were foretold, chaff was foretold;[10] all this we can also look on with our very own eyes, and we endure it with whatever fortitude we can muster, as granted us by the Lord.

In what respect has this man ever deceived you, the one who has told you, "Go this way"? Say yourself without the slightest hesitation, if you're a believer, with so much experience like that of the one who is speaking to you, "In all these things I find him true, because he has seen fit to be proved true in this way. If he is always telling me the truth, he never deceives me; all this that he says, I hold it all to be true, in no instance has he lied; that's what I know he's like. He is the Word of God; he has spoken through the mouths of his servants, and hasn't deceived me; can what he says from his own mouth be deceitful?" As for the one to whom he is not yet known, who still has his doubts about Christ, let him too say, "I will go this way, in case perhaps he's telling the truth, the one in whom the whole world has now come to believe."

We have to make sure of being in the ark, which is the Church,
if we are to be saved on the last day

3. My brothers and sisters, many who don't believe, or listen to the voice of the holy Fathers,[11] will inevitably find themselves in the same case as that multitude found itself in during the days of Noah; the only ones to escape destruction were those who were in the ark. I mean, if they stopped to think, and changed their ways from their ungodliness and were converted to our Lord, they would make amends for their crimes and misdemeanors, and begging with sighs and groans for his mercy they would most certainly not perish. God, after all, was not unmerciful toward Nineveh, which earned its salvation in three days.[12] What a short period three days is! Yet for all that they didn't despair, with such little time available, of God's mercy, or of inclining him to clemency. So if such

a great city as that had only the space of three days in which to incline God towards mercy, how much more could be done in the space of a hundred years, and two hundred, and three hundred, during which the ark was being constructed![13] From the moment Christ began to fell logs immune to decay[14] from the forests of the nations, that is for constructing the Church,[15] if those people would only change their ways and habits, if they would only appease God by offering him the sacrifice of a contrite heart,[16] they would without the slightest doubt escape unharmed.

So then, people should all be afraid of finding themselves in such a case on that last day. But we too, brothers and sisters, should take steps to change our ways from ungodliness, and to mend our behavior while we have the time, so that that day may find us prepared; because he never lies, the one who says that it is going to come. Beware of doubting it, because it's true. That, after all, is how it was in the days of Noah: *They were eating, drinking, being married, marrying wives, buying, selling, until Noah entered the ark, the flood came and destroyed them all* (Lk 17:21), those who were placing their hopes in this world, and were eager to live in security, but not in the region of security, and none escaped except those who were in the ark.

> *So does this mean, if we wish to enter the kingdom of heaven,*
> *we mustn't marry, or eat and drink, or buy and sell?*

4. But now there are many people saying to themselves, "We are bidden to wait for that day, and not to be found like those who found themselves outside the ark and who perished in that flood. Most certainly, the trumpet call of the gospel terrifies us, the word of God frightens us out of our wits; what are we to do? So does it mean we shouldn't marry wives?" That's what a young man will say, or a growing lad. "So is there to be no eating, no drinking, just fasting all the time?" There are many who will be saying that. And those perhaps who were thinking of buying something will say to themselves, "So is nothing to be bought now, in case we should find ourselves numbered among those who perished in the flood?"

So what are we to do, brothers and sisters? If that's really the case, then it's a matter for lamentation, rather as the apostles felt shock for the human race, when they heard the Lord saying, *If you wish to be perfect, sell all your possessions and give to the poor, and you shall have treasure in heaven; and come, follow me* (Mt 19:21). The man who was told this was shocked, and went away; and while he had called the one, from whom he had sought advice about eternal life, *good master*, he only seemed to be a good master, while the man was able to give correct answers to what he was asked about.[17] The Lord spoke, and the rich man was shattered. But as that man went sadly away, the Lord said, *With what difficulty does the rich man enter the kingdom of heaven!* (Mt 19:23)—as though the kingdom of heaven is shut in the face of the rich. What will happen? It's shut. But he also said, *Knock, and it will be opened to you* (Lk 11:9). And if only as few were to go into the fire as there are rich! But now as it is, many who are numbered among the rich are going to go into the kingdom of heaven, and of those counted among the poor many are going to go into eternal fire, not because they are rich in means, but because they are on fire with greed.

Nor should the rich despair because of what is said
about a camel and the eye of a needle

5. The disciples, though, were shattered. The Lord then said, *"What is difficult for men is easy for God* (Lk 18:27). You were upset by the difficulty, because I mentioned[18] a camel; if it wishes, that enormous beast which is called a camel, can come in here through the eye of a needle." What can this mean? Let's see if it can be shown how. It's not without significance, you see, that John the Baptist too, the forerunner of the Lord himself, had a garment of camel's hair,[19] as though he got his cloak from the judge who was coming after him, to whom he was bearing witness. Let us recognize in the camel mentioned a type of our Lord Jesus Christ; let us mark how great it is, and yet of so humble a neck, that nobody can put a load on it with his own hands, unless it lowers itself to the earth. In the same way Christ too *humbled himself to the death* (Phil 2:8), in order *to destroy the one who had the power of death, that is, the devil* (Heb 2:14). So let's see what the eye of the needle is, through which so great a one came in. Well, in the prick of a needle we can see the sufferings which he spontaneously endured, while in its eye we can see the straits he was reduced to. So now the camel has entered through the eye of a needle; the rich needn't despair; let them enter the kingdom of heaven without a worry in the world.[20]

Poverty as such does not guarantee entry into the kingdom
just as wealth in itself does not result in exclusion

6. But let us realize what sort of rich people. Here comes heaven knows who across our path, wrapped in rags, and he has been jumping for joy and laughing on hearing it said that the rich man can't enter the kingdom of heaven; and he's been saying, "I, though, will enter; that's what these rags will earn me; those who treat us badly and insult us, those who bear down hard upon us won't enter; no, that sort certainly won't enter."

"But just a minute, Mr Poor Man; consider whether you can, in fact, enter. What if you're poor, and also happen to be greedy? What if you're sunk in destitution, and at the same time on fire with avarice? So if that's what you're like, whoever you are that are poor, it's not because you haven't wanted to be rich, but because you haven't been able to. So God doesn't inspect your means, but he observes your will. So if that's what you're like, leading a bad life, of bad morals, a blasphemer, an adulterer, a drunkard, proud, cross yourself off the list of God's poor; you won't be among those of whom it is said, *Blessed are the poor in spirit, since theirs is the kingdom of heaven* (Mt 5:3).

"And here I find a rich man like that—in comparison with whom you've flaunted yourself, and had the nerve to cast your eyes on the kingdom of heaven—I find him poor in spirit; that is, humble, godfearing, innocent, not a blasphemer, following God's will; and if by any chance he has lost in business failures any of this world's goods, he says at once, *The Lord has given, the Lord has taken away; as it pleased the Lord, so has it happened; may the Lord's name be blessed forever* (Jb 1:21). Here you have a rich man who's gentle, humble, doesn't resist,[21] doesn't grumble, follows God's will, and finds his joy in that land of the living;[22] *Blessed*, you see, *are the gentle, because they shall possess the land for their inheritance* (Mt 5:4).

"You, though, are perhaps poor, and proud. I praise the humble rich man; don't I also praise the humble poor man?[23] The poor man has no reason to be conceited, while the rich man has, and he has to struggle against it. This man more than you, this rich man will enter, and against you the kingdom of heaven will be shut, because it will be shut in the face of the godless, of the proud, of the blasphemer, of the adulterer, of the drunkard, it will be shut in the face of the greedy and the grasping. The one who has trusted the promises made has acquired a trustworthy debtor."

But the rich man who is humble, humane, faithful, has this answer to make, and he says, "God is well aware I am not haughty in my ideas; and if I happen to shout sometimes, and say anything harsh, God knows my conscience, that I say these things out of the need to exercise authority; I never, for that reason, consider myself a cut above other people."

"God sees inside the works which follow; those, you see, who are rich in good works give things away easily, they share with the person who has nothing. That, after all, is where humility shows itself, if you are rich and humble. You maintain you are good and godfearing; let what you have be shared between you and the one who hasn't got anything, so that you may store up for yourself a good foundation for the future, in order to obtain the true and blessed life."[24]

If they are like that, they need have no worries; when that last day comes, they find themselves in the ark. They will be part of its fabric,[25] they won't be the prey of the flood. They shouldn't panic, just because they're rich. And if he's a young man, and cannot embrace celibacy, he is certainly allowed to marry a wife.[26] But, because *the time is short, let those who have wives be as though they did not have them, and those who buy as though they did not, and those who weep as though they were not weeping, and those who rejoice as though they were not rejoicing, and those who make use of this world as though they were not doing so; for the form of this world is passing away* (1 Cor 7:29-31).

The judge is certainly going to come, so let us correct ourselves before he does

7. My brothers and sisters, someone will grumble against God and say, "The times are bad, the times are hard, the times are irksome."

And yet the games are being staged,[27] and the times are called hard! How much harder are you, who fail to correct yourself in these hard times! All this crazy parade and ostentation still at full flood, all these superfluous luxuries and pleasures eagerly awaited, and there's no end or limit to greed. How sick our society becomes in the middle of all this! How much licentious self-indulgence has bubbled up everywhere because of the theatres, the organs, the flutes and the dancers! You want to make bad use of what you are aiming at; that's why you won't get it. Listen to the voice of an apostle; *You desire, and you do not have; you kill and you envy and cannot obtain; you quarrel, you ask, and you do not receive, because you ask badly, so that you are eaten up with your desires* (Jas 4:2-3).

Let us come to our senses, brothers and sisters, let us correct ourselves. The judge is going to come, and although he has come[28] in one way, he is still being mocked; he is going to come, and then there will be no room for mockery. My dearest brothers and sisters, let us correct ourselves, because better times are going to come along, but not for those who lead bad lives. This age is already on the wane, and has declined toward old age. Are we going to come back to its youth, and ours? What have we here to hope for? We should already be looking for something else. Don't hope for other times, except for such as we can read of in the gospel. The times are not bad because Christ has come; but because they were bad and hard, one came who would bring us comfort.

Christ has come to heal us; but in this life the treatment is necessarily painful

8. Listen, my brothers and sisters; it was necessary, you see, for the times to be irksome, to be hard. How would we cope, if such a wonderful comforter were not present? The human race was gravely ill, from Adam right up to the end. From the moment we are born here, ever since we were turned out of paradise, life[29] is clearly an illness; but at the end this was going to become more serious, with a possibility of taking a turn toward a recovery of health, and for some toward death. So since the human race was so ill, that great doctor takes over the care of the patient lying in a kind of huge bed, that is in the whole world—but just as any very skilled and experienced doctor observes the periods of an illness,[30] and takes note and looks forward to what turns it is going to take; and first in the milder stages of the patient's illness he sends his assistants; in the same way our doctor too first sent the prophets to examine us. They spoke, they preached; through them he cured a certain number, and restored them to health. They foretold a future critical climax for the malady, and a severe agitation of the patient, for whom the presence of the doctor himself would be needed, and his coming to him in person. And that's what happened.[31]

He came, he was made man, sharing our mortality so that we might be given a share of his immortality. The sick man is still restlessly tossing about; and as he's panting and sweating copiously in his fever, he says to himself, "Ever since this doctor came, I've been suffering worse fevers, been more severely affected, been subject to frightful turmoil. What did he come to me for? I don't think it was for the best that he entered my house." That's what they all say, those who are still sick from the vanity of the world. Why does the vanity of the world make them ill? Because they won't accept from him the curative potion of moderation.

Seeing the poor wretches being tossed about with their anxieties, and preoccupied with the various concerns of this age, which are stifling their souls, God
came as the doctor. And they're not afraid of saying, "Ever since Christ came,
we have been suffering these times; ever since there have been Christians, the
world has been falling entirely to pieces."

You stupid patient! It's not because the doctor has come that your illness has
become graver; the doctor, good, considerate, just, merciful as he is, foresaw
that; obviously, he didn't cause it. He came, after all, to bring you relief, so that
you might really get better. I mean, what is he taking away from you, but what
is simply superfluous? You see, you were panting after things that injure your
health, and becoming addicted to them; the things you were gasping for were
not good for your fever. Is the doctor being rough, when he snatches from the
hands of his patient some fruits that are bad for him? What has he deprived you
of, but a misguided sense of security which you were on the point of grasping?
Rid yourself of your pernicious gut reactions; and then you will see that all this
that you are groaning and grumbling about is part of your cure. Don't suffer
torments against your will by being unwilling to be cured.[32]

It's absolutely necessary that the times should be harsh. Why? To stop us
loving earthly prosperity. It's vital, and it's good medicine, that this life should
be troubled, and the other life loved. Look here; if human idleness can still be
delighted by such earthly things as the race-course and the games, what would
it be like if their activities were never blighted with misfortune? Here they are,
mixed up with so many bitter elements, and still the world is so sweet!

NOTES

1. So Fischer, Kunzelmann, and Lambot, who all date the sermon more precisely to December
of that year. See note 27 below for what is presumably their reason. For myself, I am not entirely
sure that we simply have one sermon here. There are a great many incoherences; sections 7 and 8
seem rather loosely attached to the rest, and are so carelessly put together, that one wonders if we
haven't got here a rough recollection of a sermon, put together by a stenographer who had forgotten
to take his equipment along and was writing the thing up later on from memory. There is no reason
to doubt that the sermon—or sermons—was preached in Hippo Regius; Augustine was rarely away
in the middle of winter.

The full title, given in the supplement to Migne's Patrologia Latina (PLS II, 435), is "On the
Word of God . . .; and that it is necessary for the times to be harsh, lest earthly prosperity should be
loved."

2. See principally Gn 12:1-3; 13:14-17; 15:1-21.

3. We say in the Nicene creed that it was the Holy Spirit who spoke through the prophets. It can
correctly be said, of course, that all the divine persons spoke through the prophets; but it is now
conventional to appropriate this activity to the Holy Spirit. I just wonder if the fact that Augustine
here appropriates it to the Word does not indicate that the additions made to the Nicene creed by
the Council of Constantinople in 381—the last part of the creed, beginning "Lord and giver of life
. . ."—had not penetrated to the Latin-speaking Churches of the West by 399. That Council was

convened as a purely regional council of the East, and only much later on came to be regarded in the tradition as the second ecumenical Council of the whole Church.

4. See Is 7:14, and Mal 3:1, for instance.

5. See Ps 22:12-18; 69:21; and any other texts quoted or alluded to in the passion narratives of the gospels.

6. See Hos 6:2, Jon 2:1, Ps 24:7-10; 47:5, and Dan 7.

7. See Gn 12:3; 18:18; 22:18, Ps 22:27-31, Hos 2:23, and Mt 10:16-23.

8. *Circumcisiones*; an odd word to use. But though the noun, according to Lewis & Short, was only used, and that in ecclesiastical writers, to mean circumcision, the corresponding verb, *circumcidere*, was mostly used in a much wider sense of trimming, clipping, pruning; and it must be in that sense that Augustine is using the noun here. He is no doubt thinking of texts like 1 Cor 11:19, and 1 Jn 2:18-19.

9. See Is 2:18, Ez 30:13, Dan 2:34, Hos 10:8, and Am 7:9. This was happening very much at the time he was preaching, thanks to the stringent new imperial laws against pagan worship, closing the temples; the actual destruction of idols was more the work of fanatical Christian mobs than of imperial officials, especially about the turn of the century. See Sermon 24, note 1.

10. See Mt 18:7, Lk 17:1, and Mt 13:24-30, 37-42; 3:12, etc.

11. From the context, I think he means the prophets and apostles, whose voices he has been summarizing; but he could just possibly mean the Fathers of the Council of Nicaea in 325, who promulgated the Nicene creed—in its shorter form, as we have seen.

12. See Jon 3:3-5.

13. There may have been rabbinic legends current about the construction of the ark taking Noah that long, or at least its taking him a hundred years; he was 500 years old when he begot Shem Ham and Japheth (Gn 5:32), and 600 when the flood came (Gn 7:11). But the ark Augustine really has in mind here, as the next sentence indicates, is the Church, which had been a-building that long— somewhat longer in fact—when he preached this sermon.

14. What the ark was constructed from according to his version; *imputribilis* translating the Hebrew *gopher*, Gn 6:14.

15. *Id est, Ecclesiae*. The most obvious way to construe *Ecclesiae* is as a genitive, in apposition to *gentium*, "of the nations"; but Augustine cannot really be identifying the Church with the nations from among which it is gathered. So I am treating *Ecclesiae* as a dative; literally, "that is, for the Church," which I expand to make it clearer. I think that if that is how he meant it, some rather agile mental acrobatics was being required from his audience.

16. See Ps 51:17.

17. The Latin is much briefer and more obscure. I take Augustine to be referring to the little conversation about keeping the commandments, Mt 19:17-20.

18. Reading *quod nominavi* instead of the text's *quod nominavit*, because he mentioned. But the disciples are being addressed directly, and surely by the Lord himself.

19. See Mk 1:6. Augustine seems to be thinking of John the Baptist getting his cloak from Jesus in much the same way as Elisha received the cloak of his master Elijah, 2 Kgs 2:13.

20. This is surely Augustine at his most ingenious, bizarre and wrongheaded as an interpreter of scriptural images.

21. See Mt 5:39.

22. That is, in the land of the age to come, the kingdom of heaven, as contrasted with this "land of the dying," in which we spend our mortal lives. It is with reference to that land of the living that Augustine always expounds the next beatitude, which he goes on to quote—and in which I have had to translate *terra* by "land" instead of the usual "earth," because of the allusions he is making here.

23. "Yes, but not so much," is the implication of what he goes on to say.

24. See 1 Tm 16:17-19.

25. Because it will be a living ark, the Church constructed out of its members—an image usually applied, of course, to the Church as temple or city; see 1 Pt 2:5, and Rv 21.

26. At last the answer to the questions raised at the beginning of section 4.

27. Particularly during the December holidays, the *Saturnalia*; this is presumably why the scholars agree in dating the sermon to December. But if I am right in suggesting that sections 7 and 8 come from another sermon, that date will only apply to them, and not the rest of the sermon.

28. Substituting *quamquam venit* for the text's *quia venit*, because he has come, or is coming. Another edition reads *quia nondum venit*, because he has not yet come. But this is just another emendation of what is an unsatisfactory reading; and not as good a one, in my opinion of course, as the one I propose myself.

29. Supplying the word *vita*, which is absent from the text. I am supposing it got left out inadvertently somewhere along the line of copyists; but the whole sentence is very peculiar and ill-constructed, ill-thought out, indeed.

30. Reading *aegritudinis* instead of the text's *aegroti*, of the patient. The two words occur together in the next line, *aegritudinis aegroti*; so it would be easy for a copyist here inadvertently to substitute one for the other.

31. I here omit words which break the flow of thought—such as it is; this is a most confused and muddled section—and which have every appearance of being a marginal gloss. They are, after *Ita factum est*, which I translate as "And that's what happened": *quia dixit: Credentem ego reficiam, ego salvabo; ego percutiam, ego sanabo*; because he said, "The one who believes I will refresh, I will save, *I will strike, I will heal* (Dt 32:39)."

32. That is, you suffer them anyway; accept them as part of your cure, and you suffer them willingly. The sentence could, at a pinch, be translated, "You are unwilling to be cured, lest you suffer torments against your will." But that means treating a participle, *nolens*, as a main verb, and in any case does not make such good sense in the context.

SERMON 346B

ON OUR JOURNEY THROUGH THIS LIFE

We are travelers along the way;
our home country is the heavenly Jerusalem

1. That this life of ours, dearest brothers and sisters, is a kind of traveling abroad from the home country of the saints, the heavenly Jerusalem, is what the apostle Paul teaches in the clearest possible way, when he says, *As long as we are in the body, we are traveling abroad from the Lord* (2 Cor 5:6). And because everyone who travels abroad obviously has a home country (nobody, I mean, without a home country can ever be abroad), we ought to know which our home country is, toward which we must ever be hastening, while turning our backs on all the attractions and delights of this life; the country we are on our way to, and where alone we are entitled to take our rest. God, you see, hasn't wished us to find true rest anywhere else but in that home country, because if he also gave us rest here, we would find no pleasure in returning there.

So in saying that Jerusalem is this home country, he didn't mean that earthly city, which *is in slavery with her children*, as the same apostle also warns us. That earthly one, you see, was given as a type and symbol with a special meaning to an earth-bound, material-minded people, who although they worshiped the one God, still desired from him only earthly prosperity. But there is another Jerusalem, which he says is in heaven; yes, there is a Jerusalem above, *which is the mother of us all* (Gal 4:25-26). He calls her a mother, like a metropolis; metropolis, you see, means mother city. So that is the one to which we must be hurrying along, knowing that we are still away abroad, and are on the way.

Nobody arrives except those who are on the way;
but not everyone who is on the way arrives

2. Any people who don't yet believe in and trust Christ are not even on the way; they are going wrong, you see. They too are seeking the home country, but they don't know where or what it is, and they don't know how to get there. What's this I'm saying, that they are seeking the home country? Every soul seeks

rest, and seeks happiness; ask any people whether they wish to be happy, and they will answer without the slightest hesitation that they do. They all cry out that they want to be happy; but how to get to that happiness, and where that happiness is to be found, this they don't know; that's why they go wrong. You don't go wrong, after all, by not going anywhere; it's from going, and not knowing the way you should go, that every kind of going wrong arises.

The Lord calls us back to the right road, to the highway; and when we are made into believers, trusting Christ, we are not yet in the home country, but still we have begun to walk along the highway toward it. So on the one hand we are urging and warning all our dear ones—that is if we remember that we are Christians—those who are straying and going wrong with all sorts of vain superstitions and heresies, to come to the right road and walk along the highway; but on the other, those who are already on the highway ought to be encouraging one another. Nobody, you see, can arrive, except those who are on the right road; but not all who are on the right road necessarily arrive.

So those who don't yet keep to the way are caught in the greater danger; but as for those who are already on the highway, yes they too should not yet consider themselves safe, or they may be held back by the delights of the road itself, and not be drawn on by as much love as they should be to that home country where alone true rest is to be found. The steps, you see, which we take along this highway are the love of God and of our neighbor. If you love, you're running; and the more consistently you love, the faster you run, while the less you love, the more sluggish your progress along the road. But now, if you don't love at all, you're stuck on the road, while if you are longing for the world, you've looked back,[2] your face is not turned toward the home country. What's the use of being on the road if you're not going forward along it, but going backwards? That is, what's the use of being a Catholic Christian—that, you see, is what being on the highway means—and walking along the road, but by loving the world looking back?[3] It means you're going back to where you started from.

If, however, you are drawn away from the Catholic Church through the stratagems of any hostile tempter and bandit you may encounter along this journey, and led either into heresy or into some pagan forms of worship, or any other superstitions and machinations of the devil, you have already lost the way and taken a wrong turn once again.

Let us then run along this way, which is the one Church of God

3. And so, brothers and sisters, because we are Catholic Christians, let us run along this highway, which is the one Church of God[4] as it has been foretold in the holy scriptures. God, after all, did not wish it to be hidden, so that nobody might have any excuse; it was foretold that it would be found throughout the world, and it has been in actual fact presented to the whole world. Nor should we be worried by heresies and innumerable schisms; we should be more anxious if there weren't any, because they too have been foretold.[5] All of us, whether we remain in the Catholic Church or are outside it, bear witness to the truth of

the gospel. What's this I'm saying? We are all proof that everything said in the gospel is true.

How, I mean, was it foretold that the Church of God would be found throughout the nations? As one, set upon the rock, which the gates of hell might not overcome. By the gate of hell is meant the beginning of sin; *the wages of sin is death* (Rom 6:23), and death, of course, belongs to hell. But what is the beginning of sin? Let scripture be questioned: *The beginning*, it says, *of every sin is pride* (Sir 10:13), and if pride is the beginning of sin, pride is the gate of hell. So now, then, consider what it is that has given birth to all heresies; you will find they have no other mother but pride. When people, you see, give themselves a lot of credit, and call themselves holy, and wish to draw the crowds to themselves and tear them away from Christ,[6] it is only out of pride that they have made convenient heresies and convenient schisms. But because the Catholic Church is not overcome by all those heresies and schisms, that is by the daughters of pride, that's why it was foretold, *And the gates of hell shall not overcome it* (Mt 16:18).

How to defeat the stratagems of the devil

4. And so, brothers and sisters, as I had started to say, we are on the highway; let us run along it with love and charity, forgetful of merely temporal things. This highway requires strong, brave travelers, it doesn't welcome the reluctant and the sluggish. There will be many attempts at highway robbery along the way, the devil is lying in wait at every defile, everywhere he is trying to get a foot in the door and take possession; and those he does get possession of, he turns away from the road, or slows them down. When he turns them away, he stops them moving forward at all, or causes them to leave the highway and get entangled in errors and schismatical heresies, and be led away into various kinds of superstition.

Now he tempts us either through fear or through greed; but first of all through greed, by various promises and assurances, or by the seductive attractions of pleasure. When he finds someone who has despised these things, and has, so to say, slammed the door of greed in his face, he begins tempting through the door of fear; which means that if you were now not wishing to acquire anything more in the world, and had thereby shut the door of greed, you haven't yet shut the door of fear, if you are afraid of losing what you have acquired. And so, *be strong in faith* (1 Pt 5:9); don't let anybody lure you into a fraudulent deal by any sort of promise, nobody drive you into a fraudulent deal by any kind of threat. Whatever the world promises you, the kingdom of heaven surpasses it; whatever the world threatens you with, gehenna outdoes it. So if you want to get through all fears safely, fear the eternal pains which God threatens you with. Do you want to trample on all kinds of greed and lust? Desire eternal life, which God promises you. In this way, on the one hand you slam the door in the devil's face, on the other you open it to Christ.

NOTES

1. So Fischer and Kunzelmann. It is probably the tone of the allusions to the Donatists in sections 2 and 3, as also to temptations to revert to paganism, that persuades them of the likelihood of this date. The sack of Rome by Alaric the Goth in 410 was a gift to pagan anti-Christian propaganda (against which Augustine wrote *The City of God*), to which some of the weaker brethren may have easily succumbed; while the great Conference or Colloquy of Donatist and Catholic bishops was being planned and organized, with some faint hopes, perhaps, of ending the schism and drawing the Donatists back into the Catholic fold.

2. See Lk 9:62.

3. I have rearranged the order of words in this sentence, which runs in the text, *et amando saeculum in via ambulat, sed retro respexit*: and by loving the world walking along the road, but looking back. I rearrange it to *et in via ambulat, sed amando saeculum retro respexit*.

4. He will normally, of course, identify the way or road with Christ, in accordance with Jn 14:6. But if tackled on this point here, he would no doubt reply that since the Church is the body of Christ, it shares in his being the way; also—but this is the Church of the saints in heaven—in his being the truth and the life.

5. See Sermon 346A, notes 7 and 8.

6. That is, from the Catholic Church. He has the Donatist heresy and schism, or schismatical heresy, almost exclusively in mind in this passage.

SERMON 346C

ON THE AFFLICTIONS AND DISTRESSES OF THE WORLD

Date: 410[1]

It is foolish to assume that times past were better than present times

1. As often as we suffer any distress or affliction, we must take it as being both a warning to us and a correction. After all, even our own holy books don't make us any promises of peace, security and quiet, while on the other hand the gospel does not keep silent about afflictions, distress and scandals; but *whoever perseveres to the end shall be saved* (Mt 10:22). What good, I mean to say, has this life ever contained from the very first man, from the moment he earned the penalty of death, from the moment he received the curse, the curse from which Christ the Lord has delivered us? So we really mustn't grumble, brothers and sisters, *as some of them grumbled*, so the apostle says, *and perished from the serpents* (1 Cor 10:10.9). What unusual horror, brothers and sisters, is the human race enduring now, that our ancestors didn't have to endure? Or when do we have to endure such things as we know they endured? And you'll find people grumbling about their times, and saying that the times of our parents were good. Suppose, though, they could be whisked back to the times of their parents, they would still grumble even then.

You see, the times in the past you think were good, were only good for the simple reason that they weren't your times. If you have now been delivered from the curse,[2] if you have now come to believe in the Son of God, if you have now been introduced to the sacred books, or become learned in them, I'm astonished that you should reckon that Adam had good times. And your parents carried Adam on their shoulders. Certainly it was that Adam who was told, *In the sweat of your face shall you eat your bread, and you shall work the ground from which you were taken; thorns and thistles shall it produce for you* (Gn 3:18-19). That's what he deserved, that's what he got, that's what he received from the just judgment of God. So why do you think that times past were better than your times? From that Adam right up until today's Adam toil and sweat, thorns and thistles.

Has a flood ever befallen us?[3] Have such harsh times of famine and war ever befallen us, which were written about precisely to stop us grumbling against

God about the present time? Has that time of our ancestors ever befallen us, so very, very remote from our own times, when the head of a dead donkey was sold for such a great amount of gold, when pigeon's droppings were sold for no small amount of silver, when women made agreements about eating their babies; and when one baby was killed and eaten, and another woman was reluctant to kill hers, and a case like that came before the judge, came before the king, so that he found himself to be not so much the judge as the guilty party?[4] And who could possibly remember all the wars or famines of that time? So what dreadful times they must have been! Don't we all shudder with horror when we hear or read about them? So we've more reason to count ourselves fortunate than to grumble about our times.

The only good days are the one eternal day

2. So when were things ever going well for the human race? When was there ever no fear, no grief, when was there ever assured happiness, ever not real unhappiness? If you haven't got something, you're in a sweat to get hold of it. Have you got it? You're shaking with fear of losing it. And what's much worse, both in that sweat and this fear you fondly imagine you are in good health of mind and body. Are you to marry a wife? If she's a bad one, it will be your punishment; if she's a good one, oh dear, oh dear, suppose she were to die! Children not born torment you with disappointment, children born torment you with all sorts of fears. What joy a newborn child brings to people, and immediately they are all fearful they may be mourning it as they carry it out for burial! When or where will life ever be secure? Isn't this whole earth like a great ship carrying its crew and passengers over the tossing waves, in great danger, subject to so many squalls and storms? They are afraid of shipwreck, they are longing to reach port, but at least they already realize they are travelers on a journey.

So which days are good—these uncertain days, days that fly past, days already finished before they come, days that come precisely in order to cease to be? So *who is it that desires life, and is longing to see good days?* (Ps 34:12). Here, though, there is neither life nor good days; good days, you see, mean actual eternity. Days which have no end are what are really called days. *I will dwell*, he says, *forever in his house, for length of days* (Ps 23:6). Again it is said, *Because one day in your house is better than a thousand* (Ps 84:10)—one day without end is better. So let us fix our desires on something like that. It's something like that which is promised us, ordinary, usual words being used for most unusual, extraordinary realities. *Who is the person that desires life?* Every day we talk about life this and life that; but what does it amount to in comparison with that other life? *And is longing to see good days?* Every day too we talk about good days; but examine them a little more closely, and they are not found to be so.

"I spent a good day today."

If you met a friend, you would consider[5] him good, if he was prepared to stop and talk; doesn't one always complain about a friend, if he sees you and just walks past? Well, that's what that good day is like; it sees you, and passes on.

"I've spent a good day"

Where is it? Bring[6] it to me.

"I've spent a good day."

You enjoyed spending it, now lament its passing. So *who is the person that desires life, and is longing to see good days?*

We all reply, "I am."

But after this life, after these days. So if it's being put off, what are we being told to do, in order to reach what's being put off until later? So what am I to do in this so-called life in order to come to real life and good days? What comes next in that psalm: *Curb your tongue from evil, and your lips from speaking deceit; turn away from evil, and do good* (Ps 34:13-14). So do what you're told, and you will receive what you're promised. If you think it is too laborious, and are cast down by the sheer hard labor of the work, let your spirits be raised again by the splendor of the reward.

NOTES

1. So Fischer, Kunzelmann and la Bonnardière. I do not know if they have any external evidence for this. I can see no particular internal evidence for it; I suspect that because this short sermon is talking about trials and tribulations, these learned scholars link it without more ado to the sack of Rome in 410. But of course, there were plenty of other unpleasant public events experienced by Augustine and his contemporaries, that could have prompted this sermon. I would happily date it some years later, say 415-420, and presume that with no evidence to the contrary it was preached in Hippo Regius.

2. Above all the curse of death; but also the one he goes on to quote.

3. See Gn 6—8.

4. See 2 Kgs 6:25-30.

5. The verb so translated is the same as the one just rendered in the previous sentence by "spent"—the verb *duco*; a piece of word play impossible to reproduce in English.

6. The verb *duco* again.

SERMON 347

ON THE FEAR OF GOD

Date: uncertain[1]

How frequently the fear of God is pressed upon us in the scriptures

1. We have been given many commandments, brothers and sisters, about the fear of God, and there are countless divine utterances declaring how useful it is to fear God. I trust you will be happy to listen to me reminding you of a few of them from this abundant store, and discussing them as best I can in the short time at our disposal. Are there any people who are not glad to be wise, or if they are not so yet, don't desire to be so? But what does scripture say? *The fear of the Lord is the beginning of wisdom* (Ps 111:10). Is there anyone who wouldn't love to be a king?[2] But let us listen to the warning given by the Spirit in the psalm: *And now, O kings, understand; be instructed, you who judge the earth; serve the Lord in fear, and exult before him with trembling* (Ps 2:10-11). Which is why the apostle also says, *Work out your own salvation with fear and trembling* (Phil 2:12).

We also read where it's written, *You have desired wisdom; observe justice, and the Lord will grant it to you* (Sir 1:26). We can find many people, you see, who are totally indifferent to justice and as avid as can be for wisdom. These are being taught by divine scripture that they cannot attain to what they have set their hearts on, unless they observe what they are indifferent to. Observe justice, it says, and the Lord will grant you the wisdom you have desired. Who, though, can observe justice, unless they fear God? You see, it says in another place: *The one who is without fear will not succeed in being justified* (Sir 1:22). Accordingly, if the Lord will only grant wisdom to one who observes justice; while the one who is without fear will not succeed in being justified; we have come round again to that principle, *The fear of the Lord is the beginning of wisdom.*

The seven gifts of the Holy Spirit enumerated by Isaiah show us how to climb up from the fear of God to wisdom

2. Then Isaiah the prophet, in presenting us with those seven well-known spiritual gifts, begins with wisdom and ends with the fear of God, as though

87

coming down from the heights to our level; this is to teach us to climb up back again. So he began from where we wish to end; and he arrived at the point where we ought to begin. *There will rest upon him*, he says, *the Spirit of God, the Spirit of wisdom and understanding, the Spirit of counsel and courage, the Spirit of knowledge and piety, the Spirit of the fear of the Lord* (Is 11:2-3). So just as he came down from wisdom to fear, not because he was slipping back but in order to teach; we in the same way must climb from fear to wisdom, not as a matter of pride, but in order to make progress.

The fear of the Lord, after all, *is the beginning of wisdom.* This, you see, is the vale of tears, about which the psalmist says, *He has set steps in his heart in the vale of tears* (Ps 84:5-6). The vale, of course, signifies humility. And who are the humble but the ones who fear God, and with fear crush their hearts in tears of confession and repentance? Because *a crushed and humbled heart God does not spurn* (Ps 51:17). But they should not be afraid they will remain in this vale. You see, in this same crushed and humbled heart, which God does not spurn, he himself has set steps by which we are to rise up to him. That, after all, is what the psalm says: *He has set steps in his heart in the vale of tears, into the place which he has set.* Where are the steps to be climbed? In the heart, he says. But where do we have to climb from? Obviously, from the vale of tears. And where do we have to climb to? *Into the place*, he says, *which he has set.*

What can this place be, but the place of rest and peace? There, you see, is to be found that bright and never fading wisdom. So it was to exercise us in successive steps of doctrine that Isaiah came down from wisdom to fear, from the place, that is, of everlasting peace to the vale of time-bound tears; so that we, by grieving, groaning, weeping in penitent confession, might not remain grieving, groaning, weeping, but might climb up from this vale to the spiritual mountain, on which the holy city Jerusalem, our eternal mother, is built, and might there enjoy undisturbed happiness. So when he had first put wisdom, namely the unfailing light of the mind, he joined understanding on to it; as though to answer those who inquired how they were to reach wisdom, "From understanding."

How to reach understanding?
"From counsel."
How to reach counsel?
"From courage."
How to reach courage?
"From knowledge."
How to reach knowledge?
"From piety."
How to reach piety?
"From fear." So to wisdom from fear, because *The fear of the Lord is the beginning of wisdom.* From the vale of tears to the mountain of peace.

3. *Blessed,* after all, *are the poor in spirit, since theirs is the kingdom of heaven* (Mt 5:3). They are the humble in the vale, they are the ones who sacrifice to God a crushed and humbled heart in fear and trembling. From there they climb up to piety, as not resisting his will, whether in his words, when they don't see the point of what he says,[3] or in his ordering and governing of creation, when so many things happen otherwise than one's personal will desires; here one has to say, *But not what I will, but what you will, Father* (Mk 14:36). *Blessed,* you see, *are the meek, since they shall possess the land as their inheritance* (Mt 5:4); not the land of the dying, but the land of which it is said, *My hope are you, my portion in the land of the living* (Ps 142:5).

Then from this piety they will deserve to reach the step of knowledge, where they will be aware not only of the evil of their past sins, about which they wept at the first step of repentant grief,[4] but also of the evil condition of this mortality and this exile from the Lord they find themselves in now, even when worldly prosperity smiles on them. That's why it's written, *The one who increases knowledge also increases grief* (Eccl 1:18). *Blessed,* you see, *are those who mourn, since they shall be comforted* (Mt 5:5).

From there they rise up to courage, so that the world is crucified to them and they to the world,[5] so that amid all the perversity of this age when iniquity abounds charity does not grow cold;[6] but hunger and thirst for justice is endured until they come to the fullness of it in that immortality of the saints and the company of the angels. *Blessed,* you see, *are those who are hungry and thirsty for justice, since they shall be filled* (Mt 5:6).

However, on account of the disturbing effect of temptations and trials, and of the words *Woe to the world because of scandals* (Mt 18:7), counsel must not be lacking, in case perhaps any failings to which human infirmity is subject should happen to creep in stealthily and little by little. It is impossible, after all, in this mortal life that that step of courage, engaged in continuous conflict with the most cunning of all adversaries, should not sometimes receive a wound, above all through the temptations of the tongue, where, *if anybody says to his brother, "Stupid," he will be liable to the gehenna of fire* (Mt 5:22). So what, then, is the gift of counsel, but what the Lord says, *Forgive, and you will be forgiven* (Lk 6:37)? And that's why, just as in those steps which we learn about from Isaiah the fifth is counsel, so in the gospel, in those praises of blessedness, we find in the fifth place, *Blessed are the merciful, since they shall obtain mercy* (Mt 5:7).

The sixth step with Isaiah is understanding, where hearts are to be cleansed of all the false values of the world and the flesh,[7] so that their purified gaze may be directed toward their true end. That's why the Lord also said in the sixth place, *Blessed are the pure-hearted, since they shall see God* (Mt 5:8).

When, however, the end is finally reached, that's where one now stops, now rests, now enjoys the triumph of total security and peace. And what is the end, but Christ our God? *The end,* you see, *of the law is Christ, for the justification of every believer* (Rom 10:4). And who but Christ is the wisdom of God?[8] And who but Christ is the Son of God? So it is in him that they are wise, and in him that they are sons and daughters of God, whoever become so; and that constitutes full and everlasting peace. That's why, while with Isaiah wisdom is the seventh stage for those climbing upward, the stage from which he himself started to come down by way of teaching us; the Lord too, who is the one that raises us up, put in the seventh place, *Blessed are the peacemakers, since they shall be called sons of God* (Mt 5:9).

Having such promises, therefore, and wending our way toward God by these steps, let us bear with all the hard and rough things of this world, and not let ourselves be broken by its savage fury, because if we overcome it, we shall rejoice in eternal peace. This, you see, is what we are encouraged to do, once the end has been pointed out to us, by the eighth beatitude, *Blessed are those who suffer persecution on account of justice, since theirs is the kingdom of heaven* (Mt 5:10).

NOTES

1. My inclination would be to date this very ingenious sermon fairly late, about 420. It is about much more than the fear of God; about ascending from the gift of the fear of God to the gift of wisdom, according to Isaiah's seven gifts of the Spirit; these being coordinated with the first seven beatitudes, the eighth of which comes in as a kind of coda in the last sentence. I surmise that it was preached to a somewhat select congregation of the better educated and more devout faithful, very possibly in Carthage.

2. Plenty of people, one would imagine!

3. *Ubi non capiunt sensum ejus.* At first it looks as if he is saying "where they don't understand what he says"—in which case it would be difficult either to resist or not resist it. But clearly *sensus* must here mean something more than "meaning" or "sense"; something like "direction," or "aim," like the French *sens*.

4. But the first step was that of fear; he has of course associated the fear of God with weeping in the vale of tears—but he should at least have mentioned fear in this place.

5. See Gal 6:14.

6. See Mt 24:12.

7. *Ab omni falsitate carnalis vanitatis.* As "vanity" is essentially an attribute of "the world," I think I am justified in translating "carnal vanity" into "the world and the flesh." For the cleansing of hearts, see Acts 15:9.

8. See 1 Cor 1:24.

SERMON 348

ON THE FEAR OF GOD

Date: 429-430[1]

Courage and fortitude based on the fear of God;
the kind of charity that casts out fear

1. I have no doubt at all, my dearest brothers and sisters, that there is planted in your hearts that fear of God by which you may attain to a true and solid kind of courage.[2] A man is called brave, you see, who is not afraid of anyone; but his bravery or courage is of a twisted sort if he is not willing first of all to fear God, and so by fearing him to listen to him, by listening to love him, and by loving him not to be afraid. Then he will really and truly be as brave as can be, not with the obduracy of pride, but with the assurance of justice. That's also what's written: *The fear of the Lord is the hope of courage* (Prv 14:26). You see, when you fear the punishment that is threatened, you learn to love the reward that is promised; and thus through fear of punishment you keep on leading a good life, and by leading a good life you acquire a good conscience, so that finally through a good conscience you don't fear any punishment. Therefore, learn how to fear, if you don't want to be afraid.

As John says, I mean, *There is no fear in charity, but perfect charity casts out fear* (1 Jn 4:18). He said it, certainly, and what he said is true. So if you don't want to have any fear, first of all see whether you have the perfect charity which turns fear out of the door. If, however, fear is pushed out before such perfection is achieved, it's a matter of pride puffing up, not of charity building up.[3] Because just as when you are in good health your hunger is driven out by food, not by fussiness; so too when you are in a good state of mind fear is to be driven out not by vanity but by charity.

More about the kind of charity that casts out fear

2. So then, examine your conscience, whoever you are that decline to be afraid. Don't just stroke its surface, get down into yourself, penetrate the inner recesses of your heart. Rummage around there diligently, to see whether there is no poisoned vein sucking in and swallowing the corrosive love of the age,[4]

whether you are not being stirred and caught by the attractions of any carnal pleasure, not being puffed up beyond your proper size by empty boastfulness, not steamed up over futile anxieties; whether you can boldly announce that you have seen every hidden thing you scrutinize in your conscience to be pure and clear of any crooked deeds, words and thoughts; if there's no busy scheming of iniquity tiring you out, no neglect of fairness creeping into your life. If all is well there, then you are right to rejoice; go ahead and rejoice that you are without fear.

What has put it out of the door, though, is the love of God, whom you are loving with your whole heart and with your whole soul and with your whole mind. What has put it out of the door is also your love of your neighbor, whom you are loving as yourself;[5] and that's why you are exerting yourself on his behalf to make sure that along with you he too loves God with his whole heart, his whole soul, his whole mind; because you don't otherwise rightly love even yourself, unless you so love God that you don't love him any the less, when you turn to loving yourself.[6] If, however, you love yourself in yourself, even though you are not vexed within yourself by any kind of greedy desire (and who would ever dare really to make such a boast?), and are therefore very pleased with yourself, the very fact that you are afraid of nothing is something that should give you cause for even more serious alarm. You see, it isn't with any sort of love that fear has to be cast out, but with the upright kind of love with which we love God totally, and our neighbor with the intention that he may love God that way too. But to love oneself in oneself and thus to be very pleased with oneself, is not the justice of charity, but the pride of vanity. And that's why the apostle was quite right to lash out with his rebukes at those who love themselves and are very pleased with themselves.[7]

So then, *it is perfect charity that casts out fear* (1 Jn 4:18). But only that is to be called charity, or dearness, which is not vileness, or cheapness.[8] And what could be cheaper, or more vile than a human being without God? Just look at what he's loving, the person who doesn't love himself in God, but in himself! How right to tell such a one, *Do not think highly of yourself, but fear* (Rom 11:20)! Because he thinks highly of himself, you see, and for that reason does not fear, his never being afraid is of course something dangerously destructive, since it means he is not set on a solid foundation, but being blown about by puffs of pride. Nor can he be gentle and considerate, the man who loves and praises himself in himself; but being haughty and harsh, he doesn't know how to say, *In the Lord shall my soul be praised; let the gentle hear and be delighted* (Ps 34:2).

What good thing, after all, is he loving, the person who is perhaps in love for its own sake with his being afraid of nothing? You see, it could just as well be barbarity as sanity that persuades him of this. Take, for example, some bold, bad bandit, all the more crookedly brave for being so dangerously cruel; because of that very love of himself by which he is in love with his fearing nothing, he plots and plans colossal crimes, in order to exercise what he loves, and to strengthen it by exercising it; the greater the crimes he commits, the greater will be the audacity of one who doesn't know the meaning of fear. So surely it is not to be prized as a great good, this quality that can also be found in the worst sort of man.

The folly of both the Epicureans and the Stoics

3. That's why the philosophers of this world should be laughed out of court; and not only the Epicureans, who hold that even justice itself is up for sale, for the price of the pleasures of the flesh.[9] They say, you see, that the reason the wise man should be just is in order to obtain, or retain, pleasure from the body. Yes, and these too boast of being utterly brave, and say that they are afraid of absolutely nothing. That's because they consider that God doesn't care a snap of the fingers for human affairs, and think that there is no life to come later on, once this one is finished with. And if any adversity overtakes them in this life, they think they are fortified against it in this way, that while they cannot hold onto the pleasures of the body in the body itself, they can, all the same, think about them with the mind, and by gratifying themselves with such thoughts can preserve the bliss of bodily pleasure even against the assaults of bodily pain. Isn't love casting out fear with them too? But it's the love of the most sordid pleasure, or rather the love of the most shameful unsubstantiality; because when the irruption of pain has excluded pleasure itself from the members of the body, it will remain in the mind through the deceptive and unsubstantial image of itself. And this unsubstantiality is loved so intensely, that when the unsubstantial man embraces it with all the energy of his heart, even the sharpest pain is soothed.[10]

So it's not only these people who should be laughed out of court, but also the Stoics as well. Because it was these two schools of the Epicureans and the Stoics, as we can read in the Acts of the Apostles,[11] who had the insolence to throw around their smoke against the light of our Paul. Because the Stoics too present themselves as the bravest of the brave, and it's not because of the body's pleasure but on account of the mind's virtue that they cherish not being afraid for the sake of not being afraid; swollen with conceit, and not healed by wisdom, but hardened by their error. Indeed, they are all the further from health, to the extent that they have supposed their sick minds can be healed by their own efforts.[12] Now this is what they think constitutes health of mind; they say that the wise man should not even feel pity. "You see, if he feels pity," they say, "he suffers pain; but that which suffers pain is not healthy."

What foolish blindness! Suppose it feels less pain to the extent that it is unhealthy? It makes a difference, after all, whether pain is excluded by perfect health, such as the saints will enjoy, both in body and mind, in the resurrection of the dead, which these people don't believe in, because they have such ignorant masters, namely themselves. So it makes all the difference whether a thing is free from pain because of health or because of numbness. I mean, in terms of the health of this mortal condition of ours, healthy flesh feels pain when it is pricked. Which is like the well-disposed mind in this life; when it is pierced with the misery of some sufferer, it shares in the pain out of pity. Flesh, though, that is rendered insensible through some more serious disease, or that is dead through losing the soul, doesn't feel pain even when pricked; which is what the souls of these people are like, who are playing the philosopher, or rather the self-strangler, without God. Just as the body, you see, is alive when animated by the soul, so the soul itself is alive when animated by God. So these people, who feel neither pain nor sorrow nor fear, should consider whether perhaps they are not healthy, but dead.

Two kinds of fear, one to be cast out by love, the other to abide forever

4. Christians, though, should fear, before perfect charity can cast fear out; they should believe, and understand that they are traveling abroad from the Lord,[13] as long as they are living in *the body which is perishing and weighing down the soul* (Wis 9:15). Fear should grow less, the closer we approach to our home country. I mean the fear of those who are traveling abroad should be greater, that of those who are nearing home less, that of those who are arriving none at all. Thus on the one hand fear leads to love, and on the other perfect love casts out fear. Christians, though, should fear, *not those who kill the body, and after that have nothing they can do* (Lk 12:4); *but the one who has the power to kill both body and soul in the gehenna of fire* (Mt 10:28).

There is, however, another *fear of the Lord, which is chaste, abiding forever and ever* (Ps 19:9). So it's not this that perfect love casts out, otherwise it would not abide forever and ever; nor is it without point that after saying *the fear of the Lord*, it adds *which is chaste*, and it's with this addition that it *abides forever and ever*. Why is this, if not because the other fear, which charity casts out, pierces the soul with the dread of losing some creaturely good that is loved, whether it is bodily well-being and quiet, or something of the same sort after death? That, after all, is why we are afraid of both the punishments of the netherworld, and the pains and torments of gehenna.[14] When, however, the soul is on its guard against God's forsaking it, that is the chaste fear that abides forever and ever. About which I would speak more fully, and range more widely, if a sermon already rather too long did not compel me to spare both my old man's feeble powers and also what is possibly your feeling that you have had enough.

NOTES

1. Fischer and Kunzelmann say 425-430; I narrow it down to 429-430 for the reason given in note 2 below. In the last sentence Augustine refers to his *senilibus viribus*, his old man's feeble powers. The sermon was thus almost certainly preached at home in Hippo Regius, because after a journey to Milev, about 100 miles or more to the west, in 426 to preside over the election of a bishop

there, he did no more traveling; this sermon could, I suppose, have been preached during that visit. In fact, on his return from Milev in September, 426, he told his people that he would like to nominate the priest Heraclius as his successor—which was approved—and that from now on, although Heraclius would not be ordained coadjutor bishop as Augustine himself had been, because that was forbidden by the canons of Nicaea, he would be taking over the donkey work of administration, and also of preaching (Letter 213, 5-6). But that almost certainly did not mean that the old man gave up preaching altogether; it would have been wholly out of character, and indeed emotionally impossible, for him to do so. And Possidius in his *Life* says that "he went on preaching the word of God in the Church, with alacrity and power, sound in mind and judgment, until his last illness." See O. Perler, *Les Voyages de Saint Augustin*, 383, note 5.

2. Why the reference to courage or fortitude here? Very possibly because of some approaching crisis. The most likely would have been the Vandal invasion. In that case the sermon would have been preached after May 429; and most likely as the Vandals approached Hippo Regius, which they began to lay siege to in May or June 430; so possibly in April 430.

3. See 1 Cor 8:1.

4. Augustine's knowledge of physiology, let alone cardiology, was crude even, I am sure, by the standards of the limited medical science of those days.

5. See Mk 12:30-31.

6. He has got himself into a rather messy, ill-expressed digression here.

7. See, perhaps, 2 Tm 3:1-5.

8. *Caritas*, the quality of being *carus* or dear, as opposed to *vilitas*, being *vilis* or cheap.

9. A caricature of the genuine teaching of Epicurus—but one which the whole educated establishment of the time, pagan as well as Christian, was unanimously guilty of. See Sermons 150 and 156, in which he also discusses the Epicureans and the Stoics; both sermons were preached in Carthage, possibly to a more sophisticated audience.

10. I don't think Augustine questioned the possibility of this being the case; he is saying that even though it may be true, it is nothing to be proud of, as it indicates a very degraded sense of values.

11. See Acts 17:18.

12. Thus he makes them into the pagan equivalent of the Pelagians, with whom he was so deeply pre-occupied at the end of his life.

13. See 2 Cor 5:6.

14. A curious distinction, but one that was perhaps still half real to Augustine and his contemporaries; the netherworld, *apud inferos*, being simply the place of the dead, the Hebrew *Sheol* and the Greek *Hades*; gehenna being what we now mean by hell.

SERMON 348A

FROM A SERMON TO THE PEOPLE ON THE PELAGIAN HERESY

Date: 415[1]

How the Pelagians try to explain away prayers
for God's help in the keeping of his commandments

1. Those two petitions, *Forgive us our debts, as we too forgive our debtors*, and *Do not bring us into temptation* (Mt 6:12-13), can be raised as objections to the Pelagians, and how do you think they answer them? I was shocked, my brothers and sisters, when I heard. I didn't, indeed, hear it with my own ears, but my holy brother and fellow bishop, our Urbanus who was a priest here, and is now bishop of Sicca,[2] when he got back from Rome, and there crossed swords with someone holding such opinions—or rather mentioned that he had crossed swords with him—when he was being pressed hard by the weight of the Lord's prayer—he was pressing him, you see, and saying, "If it's in our power not to sin, and in our power to overcome all temptations by the sole strength of our will, why do we say to God, *Do not bring us into temptation?*"—what do you think he replied?[3]

"We ask God," he said, "not to bring us into temptation, lest we should suffer some evil over which we have no control—lest I should fall from my horse and break my leg, lest a highwayman should kill me and that sort of thing. These are things, after all, which I do not have," he said, "any control over. Because my temptations to sin I can overcome if I wish to, and it's without God's help that I can do so."

Is that why the Lord himself said
"Watch and pray, lest you should enter into temptation"?

2. You can see, brothers and sisters, what a malignant heresy it is. You can see how shocked you all are. Take care you aren't caught in its coils. I know, you see, the cunning twists and turns of these godless people who have turned away from the truth, and who refuse to be convinced, because they have already fallen so deep into their opinions. Watch out, I beg you. Here you are, you see, he has found something to say: "The reason we say *Do not bring us into*

temptation, is lest something should happen to us which we have no control over, as regards the trials or temptations of our bodies."

So is that why the Lord said, *Watch and pray, lest you should enter into temptation* (Mk 14:38)? Did he say *Watch and pray*, lest you should break a leg, or have a headache, or incur some loss? He didn't say that. But what did he say? What he said to Peter: *I have prayed for you, that your faith may not fail* (Lk 22:32). *I have prayed*, he says, *for you.* God says to a man, the Lord to a servant, the teacher to a disciple, the doctor to a patient: *I have prayed for you*, that your what may not fail? Your what? Your hand, your leg, your eye, your tongue, by any paralysis,[4] that is, any enfeeblement, of your limbs? No; but *that your faith may not fail*. According to these people we have it entirely under our own control that our faith should not fail.

*Instances given of traditional Christian prayers,
and of what Paul says somewhere*

3. Why is God asked on our behalf to grant us what these people say we ought not to ask for from his eternal majesty, but which we have under our own control?[5] Take the blessings, my brothers and sisters, the blessings we call down upon you; they empty them of meaning, make them totally pointless, eliminate them. You have heard me, I believe, my brothers and sisters, when I say, "Turning to the Lord, let us bless his name, may he grant us to persevere in his commandments, to walk in the right way of his instruction, to please him with every good work," and other such.[6] All this, they say, is placed absolutely under our own control. So let me defend both ourselves[7] and you, or else we may find that we are pointlessly giving blessings, and you are equally pointlessly subscribing your *Amen*. Your *Amen*, my brothers and sisters, is your signature, your consent, your agreement.

In case some of them should condemn both us and you, let us defend ourselves with the apostle Paul's help; let us see if he wished for his people the sort of things we pray for over you. Listen to what he said in some place or other. It's a very short thing I have to say. What do you say, Mr New Heretic,[8] whoever you are, listening to me, if you are present here? What do you say? That we have it in our power not to sin, and that we can fulfill this obligation without the assistance of divine grace?

"Yes,"[9] he says.

So we have it in our power not to sin, without any help from God?

"Certainly," he says; "our freedom of choice is quite sufficient for us for this purpose."

So what about what the apostle says, writing to the Corinthians: *We pray to God that you may do nothing evil* (2 Cor 13:7)?

You've all noticed, you've all heard, accepted, and because it's as plain as can be, you have certainly all understood what the apostle prayed for. *We pray*, he said, *to God that you may do nothing evil.* He could have said, "We warn you not to do anything evil, we teach you not to do anything evil, we order you, we command you." And to be sure, if he had said that, he would have said something perfectly in order, because our wills also do contribute something; it's not the case, after all, that our wills do nothing. But they are not sufficient by themselves. However, he preferred to say, *We pray,* in order to emphasize the role of grace, so that those correspondents of his might understand that when they did not do anything evil, they were not shunning evil solely by their own will, but were fulfilling with help from God what had been commanded.

When a command is given, we acknowledge the will's capacity for free choice,
when a prayer is made we acknowledge the need for grace

4. So, brothers and sisters, when a command is given, acknowledge the will's freedom of choice; when prayer is made about what has been commanded, acknowledge the favor of grace. You find each of them in scripture, after all; both the giving of commands and the making of prayers. What is commanded is also prayed for. Notice what I'm saying. We are commanded to understand. How are we commanded to understand? *Do not be like horse and mule, which have no understanding* (Ps 32:9). You have heard it commanded; ask that you may be able to fulfill what has been commanded.

"How," you say, "am I to ask for this?"

Listen to scripture. What are you commanded? *Do not be like horse and mule, which have no understanding.* Because the command has been given, you have acknowledged the role of the will. Listen to where prayer is made, so that you may acknowledge the role of grace: *Give me understanding, that I may learn your commandments* (Ps 119:73).

We are commanded to have wisdom; I can read such a command.

"Where can you read it?" he says.

Listen: *You that are senseless among the people, and foolish, some time be wise* (Ps 94:8). So is wisdom something in our power? I've already said; I've heard the commandment, I've recognized the role of will. Listen to the prayer, so that you may be able to acknowledge the role of grace. We are dealing with the wisdom which has been enjoined upon us. Let us hear what the apostle James has to say: *But if any of you lacks wisdom, let him request it from God, who gives to all lavishly* (Jas 1:5).

Self-control is enjoined upon us.

"Where is it enjoined?"

The apostle writing to Timothy: *Practice self-control* (1 Tm 5:22). It's a command, it's an order, it has to be listened to, has to be carried out. But unless God comes to our help, we get stuck. We try, indeed, to do it by will power, and the will makes some effort; it shouldn't, though, rely on its ability, unless it is assisted in its debility. Yes, certainly, the command is given, *Practice self-control.* But listen to another place of scripture: *And when I perceived that nobody can be self-controlled unless God grants it, and this in itself belonged to wisdom, to know whose gift this is.*

"And what," you say, "did he do?"[10]

I approached the Lord and besought him (Wis 8:21).

Is there any need, my brothers and sisters, to run through many instances? Whatever we are commanded to do, we have to pray that we may be able to fulfill it; but not in such a way that we let ourselves go, and like sick people lie flat on our backs and say, "May God rain down food on our faces," and we ourselves wish to do absolutely nothing about it; and when food has been rained down into our mouths we say, "May God also swallow it for us."[11] We too have got to do something. We've got to be keen, we've got to try hard, and to give thanks insofar as we have been successful, to pray insofar as we have not. When you give thanks, you are taking care not to be condemned as ungrateful; while when you ask for what you do not yet have, you are taking care not to be left empty-handed, because blocked by your own incapacity.

Let us not be deceived by the simplistic Pelagian view;
a reference to Pelagius being exonerated by synods in Palestine

5. So think about these things, my brothers and sisters. Anyone who approaches you and says, "So what are we to do? Have we no control over anything, unless God gives us everything? So it's not us that God will be rewarding, but himself that he'll be crowning"—you can now see that he comes from that vein of thought. It's a vein of thought, but a poisonously vain one.[12] It's been bitten, you see, by the serpent, it isn't a healthy one. That's what Satan, after all, is busy about every day, how to get people thrown out of the Church by the poison of heretics, just as he then got them thrown out of paradise by the poison of the serpent.[13]

As for that man,[14] nobody should say that he was absolved by the bishops. What was absolved was his confession, a kind of correction was absolved, because what he said before the bishops seemed to be Catholic, but the bishops who absolved him were unaware of what he has written in his books. And perhaps he really did correct his errors. We ought not, after all, to despair about the man, who possibly did decide to attach himself to the Catholic faith, and to take refuge in his[15] grace and help. Let's hope this did happen. All the same, it's not the heresy that was absolved, but the man denying the heresy.

NOTES

1. The date is evident enough from the reference in the last section to a council held in Jerusalem, which exonerated Pelagius in July 415. The Maurists call this sermon a fragment; a very considerable one, though it must be conceded that it begins rather abruptly.

2. The full name of the town was Sicca Venerea, presumably because it was dedicated to the goddess Venus, probably in honor of Julius Caesar who claimed descent from her through his fabled ancestor Aeneas the Trojan. Urbanus had only very recently been elected bishop there. He seems to have been employed fairly frequently by the African hierarchy on diplomatic missions, both before and after becoming a bishop himself.

3. The messiness of this sentence faithfully reflects that of the original. Another loose end—the first petition mentioned, *Forgive us our debts* etc., seems to have been forgotten, and in any case hardly has any bearing on the point at issue.

4. The text puts this word in the nominative, like the string of parts of the body just mentioned. I take this to be the inadvertent error of a copyist, and instead of *paralysis* I read *paralysi*, the ablative. He has to explain this Greek word (which we don't really have to do in English), and so adds, *id est, dissolutio*, a very close Latin rendering of the Greek. Does this indicate that he was speaking to a distinctly unsophisticated audience? Does it suggest a provincial congregation in Hippo Regius, rather than a metropolitan, and indeed more cosmopolitan Carthaginian congregation? Possibly so; but then most of the people in almost any congregation would have been scarcely literate.

5. The sentence is treated in the text as an affirmation, not as a question. This strikes me as odd, because it begins with *Quare*, Why. I follow the Maurist text; a later edition gives a peculiar order of words that somewhat wrecks the sense—possibly just a printer's rather than a copyist's error.

6. We have not come across this particular "Turning to the Lord" concluding prayer before. Yet another formula will be found at the end of Sermon 36.

7. All bishops and priests.

8. Pelagius was a contemporary of Augustine's, and had begun criticizing the latter's doctrine of grace, and putting forward his own doctrine of the sufficiency of free will only a few years before this sermon. So it was a new heresy, compared with the Donatism and Manichaeanism that Augustine had been combating in the earlier years of his ministry; and also compared with the Arianism he was to encounter at first hand in the last few years of his life.

9. *Hoc.* Latin had no word for "Yes," but in the Provencal of Languedoc (Tongue of "oc") in southern France, *hoc*, literally "this," was pressed into service as the affirmative particle. Perhaps this was already happening in every day speech in Africa. In Italian and Spanish they turned *sic*, literally "thus," into *si*; while in northern France, the Languedoeuil, it was possibly something like *illic* that was pressed into service to say "Yes."

10. Emending the text's *Et quid, inquit, feci?* "And what, he says, did I do?" to *Et quid, inquis, fecit?*

11. Augustine is ridiculing the simplistic view of the matter which makes grace and free will alternative sources of our activity—we *either* act by free will, *or* are moved by grace. If by free will, we don't need grace; if by grace, we haven't got free will. The view is put forward by the simple Pelagian at the beginning of the next section. Whether Pelagius himself was quite so simplistic may be questioned. What he was originally condemned for—or rather his colleague Coelestius—in a council at Carthage in 411, at which Augustine, apparently, was not present, was the denial of original sin and of the necessity of infant baptism.

12. *Vena est, sed venenum habet.*

13. See Gn 3:4-5.23.

14. Pelagius. He had left Africa very soon after arriving there, even before the Council mentioned in note 11 above. He then went to Palestine, where complaints were made against his teaching by Orosius, a Spanish priest and admirer of Augustine's, and by Jerome, and later on by two refugee bishops from Gaul. But Pelagius denied teaching what he was alleged to teach, his accusers either failed to appear, or to make a good case, and he was absolved, first at a gathering of bishops in Jerusalem, and then by a regional synod at Diospolis, respectively in July and December 415. So this sermon must be dated at least after July 415, and indeed several months after that, considering how long it took for news to travel and letters to reach their destination.

15. He presumably means God, and is just being a little careless in his manner of speaking; grammatically, the antecedent of *ejus*, his, her, or its, is the Catholic faith.

SERMON 349

ON CHARITY

Date: 412[1]

Three sorts of charity: divine, lawful human, unlawful human love or charity

1. A moment or two ago the apostle was talking to us about charity, while his epistle was being read;[2] and he was commending it to us in such a way that we should understand that all other things, great gifts of God though they be, do us no good at all without it. But where charity itself is, it cannot be alone. Let me too, then, give your graces a sermon on the grace of charity.[3] One kind of charity is divine, another human; one human kind is lawful, another unlawful. So about these three kinds of charity or love—what is called *agape* in Greek has these two names with us English speakers[4]—let me say whatever the Lord may grant me.

So my first division, as I said, is into a human and a divine kind of charity; and the human sort I again divided into two, suggesting that there is both a lawful and an unlawful sort. So first of all I will talk about the lawful human kind, with which no fault is to be found; then of the unlawful human kind, which is to be condemned; thirdly of the divine sort, which conducts us through to the kingdom.

On the charity with which wives, children, parents, and so on are loved

2. So, to give a quick instance, the human charity by which one's wife is loved is lawful; by which a prostitute, or someone else's wife is loved, unlawful. Even in the streets and market place[5] the lawful kind of charity is preferred to the prostitute variety; while in the house of God, in the temple of God, in the city of Christ, in the body of Christ, the love of a prostitute leads the lover straight to hell. So have the lawful kind of charity; it's human, but as I said, it's lawful. It's not only lawful, though, in the sense that it's permitted; but also lawful in the sense that if it's lacking, you are very much at fault. It's absolutely right for you to love your wives, to love your children, to love your friends, to love your fellow citizens with human charity. All these names, you see, imply a bond of relationship, and the glue, so to say, of charity.

101

But you will observe that this sort of charity can be found also among the godless, that is, among pagans, Jews, heretics. Which of them, after all, does not naturally love wife, children, brothers, neighbors, relations, friends, etc.? So this kind of charity is human. So if anyone is affected by such hardness of heart that he loses even the human feeling of love, and doesn't love his children, doesn't love his wife, he isn't fit even to be counted among human beings. A man who loves his children is not thereby particularly praiseworthy; but one who does not love his children is certainly blameworthy, I mean, he should observe with whom he ought to have this kind of love in common; even wild beasts love their children; adders love their children; tigers love their children; lions love their children. There is no wild creature, surely, that doesn't gently coo or purr over its young. I mean, while it may terrify human beings, it cherishes its young. The lion roars in the forest, so that nobody dare walk through it; it goes into its den, where it has its young, it lays aside all its rabid ferocity. It puts it down outside, it doesn't step inside with it. So a man who doesn't love his children is worse than a lion. These are human sentiments, but they are lawful.

Unlawful human love

3. Be on your guard against unlawful love. You are the members of Christ, and you are the body of Christ. Listen to the apostle, and shake in your shoes. He couldn't, after all, have said it more seriously, said it more forcefully, couldn't have frightened Christians more sharply off the love of fornication, than when he said, *So taking the members of Christ, shall I make them into the members of a harlot?* Now to prepare the way for this question, he had just said above,[6] *Do you not know that one who cleaves to a harlot is made into one body?* And he quoted the scriptural evidence, where it says, *They shall be two in one flesh* (1 Cor 6:15-16; Gn 2:24). This, you see, was said by God; but about man and wife where it is lawful, where it is allowed, where it is honorable; not where it is disgraceful, not where it is unlawful, not where it is damnable by every reasonable consideration.

Now just as one flesh is effected in the lawful congress of man and wife; so too one flesh is effected in the unlawful congress of harlot and lover. So since one flesh is effected, you should be shaken to the core, you should be horrified by what he added: *So taking the members of Christ*; pay attention, you Christian there, to the members of Christ; don't turn your attention to the members of Christ in someone else, pay attention to the members of Christ in yourself, seeing that you have been bought by the blood of Christ. *So taking the members of Christ, shall I make them into the members of a harlot?* Anyone who isn't horrified at this idea, will find himself horrified by God.[7]

Unlawful human love absolutely incompatible with divine love

4. Again and again I beg you, my brothers[8]—look; let's suppose, what is not the case, that God had promised such people impunity, and had said, "Those

who do such things, well, I will take pity on them, I will not damn them." Let's pretend God has said that. Even with such a promise of impunity, is anyone going to take the members of Christ and make them into the members of a harlot? Nobody will do so, if there is present there the third, divine, kind of love. Remember I listed three kinds of love; I promised I would say about the three of them what God might grant me to say; about the lawful human sort, the unlawful human sort, about that surpassing and divine sort of love.

Let us question divine charity, and let us set before her the two human kinds of charity, and let us say to her, "Here is lawful human charity, with which wives are loved, and daughters, and other secular relations. Here on the other side is the unlawful sort, by which harlots are loved, by which one's maidservants are loved,[9] by which another man's daughter is loved, when she has been neither asked for nor promised in marriage, by which another man's wife is loved. In front of you are two sorts of charity; with which of the two do you wish to stay?"

The man who chooses to stay with that lawful human love doesn't stay with the unlawful variety. You should none of you say to yourselves, "I have them both." If you have them both by admitting into yourself the love of a harlot, you are doing wrong to divine charity, who is living there as the lady of the house. I rather think, you see, that if you are a married man, and are in love with a harlot, you don't bring the harlot into your house, to live with your lady wife. You aren't quite as advanced as all that. You look for the cover of darkness, you look for out-of-the-way corners, you don't parade your shameful behavior. But even those who don't have wives, and are the lovers of harlots slightly less unlawfully, as it were (the reason I said "as it were," is that they too stand condemned, if they are already believers[10]); I rather imagine that even a young man who hasn't yet got a wife will not, if he loves a harlot, bring her to live with his sister, will not bring her to live with his mother, for fear of insulting ordinary human decency, for fear of offending against the honor of his blood.[11] So if you don't bring along the harlot you are in love with to live with your mother, with your sister, for fear, as I said, of offending against the honor of your blood; are you going to bring the love of a harlot along to live in your heart together with the love of God, and offend against the honor of the blood of Christ?

Let us love God, and pray to be given the love of God
as strenuously as the blind man prayed to be given his sight

5. Love God; you can't find anything better to love. You love silver, because it's better than iron or brass; you love gold more, because it's better than silver; you love precious stones more, because they exceed even the value of gold; finally, you love this light of day, which everyone who is afraid of death dreads leaving behind. You love, I repeat, this light of day, just as the man who cried out after Jesus, *Have mercy on me, son of David* (Lk 18:38), longed for it with such a huge love. The blind man was crying out as Jesus was passing by. And how much did he cry out? So much that he wouldn't keep quiet, even when the crowd tried to stop him. He overcame the opposer, caught hold of the savior.

With the whole crowd shouting the man down and trying to prevent him crying out, Jesus stopped, called him and said to him, *What do you wish done for you? Lord, he said, that I may see. Look up, your faith has saved you* (Lk 18:39-42).

Love Christ; long for the light which Christ is. If that man longed for the light of the body, how much more ought you all to long for the light of the heart? Let us cry out to him, not with our voices, but with our behavior. Let us lead good lives, let us scorn the world; for us, let everything that passes away be as nothing. When we live that kind of life, we are going to be taken to task by worldly people who are, so it seems, fond of us; people who love the earth, smack of the dust, think nothing of heaven, breathe in the free air, not with their hearts, but only with their nostrils.[12] They are undoubtedly going to take us to task, and to say, if they see us scorning these human, these earthly things, "What's wrong with you? Why are you so crazy?" They are that crowd, trying to stop the blind man crying out. And a considerable number of them are Christians, who forbid us to live in a Christian way; because that crowd too was walking along with Christ, and yet when that man started yelling loudly to Christ and longing for the light, they were trying to bar him from Christ's favor. There are such Christians; but let us defeat their efforts by leading good lives, and let our lives be our voices crying out to Christ. He will stop for us, because he has already stopped and is standing still.

Christ's passing by and his stopping and standing still

6. Here too, you see, there is a great mystery, with a hidden meaning. He was passing by when that man started crying out; when he cured him, he stopped. Christ's passing by should make us intent on crying out. What is Christ's passing by? Everything he underwent for us in time is his passing by. He was born, he passed by; he isn't still being born, is he? He grew, he passed by; he isn't still growing, is he? He sucked the breast; is he still sucking? He was tired, and slept; is he still sleeping? He ate and drank; he isn't still doing that, is he? Finally, he was arrested, bound, scourged, crowned with thorns, beaten and slapped about, smeared with spittle, hanged on the cross, slain, struck with the lance, buried, rose again; he's still passing by. He ascended into heaven, he is seated at the Father's right hand; he has stopped. Cry out as loudly as you can; now he is restoring your sight.

Because in the very fact that he *was the Word with God,* he was of course standing still, because he wasn't changing in any way. *And the Word was God* (Jn 1:1); *and the Word became flesh.* The flesh by its passing died and suffered many things; the Word stood still. It's by the Word that the heart is enlightened and receives its sight; because it's through the Word that the flesh, which he took on, is treated with honor. Take away the Word, and what is the flesh? Just what yours is. But that the flesh of Christ might be treated with honor, *the Word became flesh and dwelt amongst us* (Jn 1:14). So let us cry out, and lead good lives.

We must of course love our nearest and dearest, but we must love Christ more

7. Love your children, love your wives, even if it's only in worldly matters and a worldly way. Because of course you ought to love them with reference to Christ, and take thought for them with reference to God, and in them love nothing but Christ, and hate it in your nearest and dearest if they don't want to have anything to do with Christ. Such, you see, is that divine sort of charity. What good, after all, would be done them by your fleeting and mortal charity? Still, when you do love them in a human way, love Christ more. I'm not saying you shouldn't love your wife; but love Christ more. I'm not saying you shouldn't love your father, not saying you shouldn't love your children; but love Christ more. Listen to him saying it himself, in case you should suppose these are just my words: *Whoever loves father or mother more than me, is not worthy of me* (Mt 10:37).

When you hear *is not worthy of me*, aren't you afraid? The one about whom Christ says *he is not worthy of me* is not with him; where will the one be, who is not with him? If you don't love being with him, you should be afraid of being without him. Why be afraid of being without him? Because you will be with the devil, if you aren't with Christ. And where will the devil be? Listen to Christ himself: *Go into the eternal fire, which has been prepared for the devil and his angels* (Mt 25:41). If you aren't kindled with the fire of heaven, be afraid of the fire of gehenna. If you don't love the idea of being among the angels of God, be afraid of being found among the angels of the devil. If you don't love the idea of being in the kingdom, be afraid of being in the burning furnace of inextinguishable, everlasting fire. Let fear first win the day in you, and then there will be love. Let fear be the nursemaid;[13] don't let it stay in you, but let it lead you on to charity, as to the schoolmaster.

NOTES

1. So la Bonnardière. She adds that the sermon was preached in the winter, in Hippo Regius. For the season and the year I presume she has some external evidence. As for the place, unless there is evidence to the contrary, I agree with her that the presumption should be that the sermon was preached in Augustine's home base. The full title of the sermon in the Maurist edition is "On charity, and the blind man who received his sight." But that incident is referred to simply in support of what the preacher has to say about charity, and about praying for it.

2. Evidently 1 Cor 13.

3. Literally he says, "give your Charity a sermon on charity." But we have long since settled into the convention of rendering *Caritas vestra* as "your graces."

4. *Apud Latinos,* of course; the two Latin words being *caritas* and *dilectio,* not *amor,* though that will be used here and there in the course of the sermon. We should remind ourselves that *caritas* is the noun from the adjective *carus,* dear. It means "holding dear." So we have to try to import that notion into the English "charity."

5. That is, in secular public life. The Latin begins the sentence *In foro enim,* "For in the market

place," and goes on in the second half to say *in domo Dei . . . etiam meretricis amor* etc.: "in the house of God . . . also/even the love of a prostitute" etc. I find *etiam* totally out of place there, and the *enim* at the beginning not very suitable. So I transfer the *etiam* to the beginning of the sentence: *In foro etiam et plateis*; and either delete *enim* altogether, or place it roughly where *etiam* is in the text: *in domo enim Dei*. Assuming that this represents what Augustine said and the stenographer took down, could the reverse moves have occurred naturally by copyist error in the course of the text's transmission? I think it is possible that it could.

6. In the current text of the New Testament, below, in the next verse; but it is possible that in Augustine's text the verses were in the reverse order. Or, of course, his memory may have been playing him tricks.

7. *Deo horret*; a rather difficult phrase. But here the more material sense of *horreo*, I shudder, is in play. At the judgment the sinners will shudder at the presence of the divine judge. Throughout this passage it seems clear that by the phrase *membra Christi* he is referring not to the Christian as a person, but to his genital organs, which now belong to Christ. That indeed is probably the intention of Paul in the first half of 1 Cor 6:15: *Do you not know that your bodies are the members of Christ?*

8. He is so obviously focusing on the men in the congregation throughout this passage, that it would be a trifle absurd conscientiously to translate *fratres* here as "brothers and sisters."

9. The text—putting all these in the singular—reads *qua diligitur ancilla aliena*, by which someone else's maids are loved. I omit *aliena*, as it is out of place, since the vice he is pointing at is men using their own female slaves in this way. I presume it crept in here through the carelessness of copyists, because of its double occurrence in the rest of the sentence.

10. The implication is that they don't stand condemned by the civil law or by secular custom and *mores*.

11. He is clearly addressing the men of the upper classes, who had a strong sense of family honor, and pride of ancestry—indeed even men of the modest middle classes such as himself; the reason that he never married the concubine of his youth was almost certainly that she did not have enough "class."

12. Reading *non corde sed nare carpentes* instead of the text's *corde, nare carpentes*, breathing it in with heart, with nostrils.

13. *Paedagogus*, the family slave who took the little boys to school.

SERMON 350

ON CHARITY

Date: 427[1]

The whole teaching of the scriptures contained in this one word, charity

1. All the varied plenty and wide-ranging teaching of the divine scriptures is grasped, my brothers and sisters, and kept without any difficulty by the person whose heart is full of charity. It's what the apostle says: *Now the fullness of the law is charity* (Rom 13:10); and in another place, *Now the end of the commandment is charity from a pure heart, and a good conscience, and unfeigned faith* (1 Tm 1:5). But what can the end of the commandment be, but the fulfillment of the commandment? And what is the fulfillment of the commandment but the fullness of the law? So what he said there, *the fullness of the law is charity*, is what he also said here, *the end of the commandment is charity*.

Nor can there be the slightest doubt that the temple of God is the person in whom charity is dwelling. John too, you see, says, *God is charity* (1 Jn 4:8.16). Now when the apostles said these things and urged upon us the absolute primacy of charity, they could only be belching forth what they had themselves eaten. The Lord himself, in fact, feeding them on the word of truth, the word of charity, which he is himself, the living bread which came down from heaven,[2] said, *A new commandment I give you, that you should love one another*. And again, *By this shall everybody know that you are my disciples, if you love one another* (Jn 13:34-35).

He came, you see, to put an end to the corruption of the flesh by the mockery he endured on the cross, and to unfasten the old chain of our death by the newness of his death; and so he made the new man with a new commandment. It was, after all, an old matter, stale news, that man should die. To prevent this prevailing over man forever, a new thing was done, that God should die. But because he died in the flesh, not in his divinity, through the everlasting life of his divinity he did not permit the destruction of the flesh to be everlasting. And so, as the apostle says, *He died on account of our transgressions, he rose again on account of our justification* (Rom 4:25). So because he has brought the newness of life into action against the oldness of death, he himself sets a new commandment against the old sin. Any of you, then, who wish to extinguish the old sin, douse cupidity with the new commandment, and embrace charity. Just as cupidity, you see, is the root of all evil,[3] so in the same way is charity the root of all good things.

2. Charity is in secure possession of the whole length and breadth of the divine utterances, the charity with which we love God and neighbor. After all, the one and only heavenly master teaches us, *You shall love the Lord your God with your whole heart and your whole soul and your whole mind; and you shall love your neighbor as yourself. On these two commandments depend the whole law and the prophets* (Mt 22:37.39-40). So if there's no time or leisure to pore over all the sacred pages, to leaf through all the volumes of the words they contain, to penetrate all the secrets of the scriptures, hold onto charity, on which they all depend. In this way you will hold onto what you have learned there; you will also get hold of what you haven't yet learned. I mean, if you know charity, you know something from which that also depends which perhaps you don't yet know; and in whatever you do understand in the scriptures, charity is revealed; while in the parts you don't understand, charity is concealed. And so it is that those who keep a grip on charity in their behavior, have a grasp both of what is revealed and of what is concealed in the divine writings.

3. Therefore, brothers and sisters, pursue after charity, the sweet and salutary bond of our minds,[4] without which the rich man is poor, and with which the poor man is rich. This it is that endures in adversity, is moderate in prosperity; brave under harsh sufferings, cheerful in good works; utterly reliable in temptation, utterly open-handed in hospitality; as happy as can be among true brothers and sisters, as patient as you can get among the false one's. Acceptable in Abel through his sacrifice, safe in Noah through the flood, absolutely faithful in the wanderings of Abraham, as meek as meek can be in Moses amid insults,[5] so mild and gentle in David's trials and tribulations.[6] In the three young men it innocently awaits the kindly fires; in the Maccabees it bravely endures the ferocious fires.[7] Chaste in Susanna toward her husband, in Anna after her husband, in Mary apart from her husband. Free in Paul for rebuking, humble in Peter for listening and yielding.[8] Human in Christians for confessing, divine in Christ for pardoning.

But what can I say in praise of charity that surpasses in grandeur what the Lord thunders forth through the mouth of his apostle, as he *shows us a more excellent way*, and says, *If I speak with the tongues of men and of angels, but do not have charity, I have become booming bronze, or a clashing cymbal. And if I have prophecy, and know all sacraments, and have all knowledge, and if I have all faith, such that I transfer mountains, but do not have charity, I am nothing. And if I give away all my property, and if I distribute all that is mine to the poor, and if I hand over my body so that I burn, but do not have charity, it profits me nothing. Charity is magnanimous, charity is kind. Charity is not jealous, does not act boastfully, is not conceited, does not behave shamelessly, does not seek its own advantage, is not irritable, does not think evil, does not rejoice over iniquity, but rejoices together with the truth. It tolerates all things, believes all things, hopes all things, endures all things. Charity never falls away* (1 Cor 12:31—13:8).

What a great thing this charity is! The soul of the scriptures, the force of prophecy, the saving power of the sacraments,[9] the fruit of faith, the wealth of the poor, the life of the dying. What could be more magnanimous than to die for the godless,[10] what more kindly than to love one's enemies?[11] It is the one thing that is not cast down by another's good fortune, because it is not jealous. It is the one thing that its own good fortune does not puff up, because it is not conceited. It is the one thing that is not pricked by a bad conscience, because it does not act boastfully. It is steady and unshaken amid reproaches, it is well-disposed in the face of hatred; calm in the face of anger, innocent in the midst of intrigues, groaning in the midst of iniquity, breathing again in the presence of truth. What could be braver than charity, not for paying back insults, but for not caring about them? What could be more faithful, not for vanity, but for eternity?

You see, the reason it endures all things in the present life, is that it believes all things about the future life; and it endures everything that is inflicted on it here, because it hopes for everything that is promised it there. Rightly does it never fall away. So pursue after charity, and by thinking holy thoughts about it bring forth the fruits of justice. And whatever you can find in the praises of charity that is grander than what I have been able to say, let it appear in your behavior. It is right, after all, that an old man's sermon should be not only weighty, but brief.

NOTES

1. Fischer and Kunzelmann say 425-430. The reason becomes apparent when we get to the last sentence of the sermon. Verbraken, however, *Revue des Etudes Augustiniennes*, 1985, has serious doubts about its authenticity. It does, somehow, read like a painstaking imitation of the master.

2. See Jn 6:48-49.

3. See 1 Tm 6:10.

4. See Eph 4:3, Col 3:14. A closer quotation of the latter would have suited the composer's purpose better.

5. See Num 12:3.

6. A somewhat idealized David, one may think; but the allusion is to David's response to the unrelenting hostility of Saul, 1 Sm 21-27.

7. See Dn 3:21-25; 1 Mc 7.

8. See Gal 2:11.

9. "Sacraments" in the quotation of 1 Cor 13:2 rendered the Greek *mysteria*; and of course he understood the word in a much wider sense than we do nowadays. But here, by *salus sacramentorum* he is perhaps thinking of the sacraments as we understand the term—above all of the eucharist.

10. See Rom 5:6-8.

11. See Mt 5:44.

SERMON 350A

ON CHARITY AND ON LOVING GOD ALONE

Date: 399[1]

Every page of scripture tells of charity

1. I am certainly aware that the hearts of your graces are well and truly fed every day on the exhortations of the divine readings and the nourishment of the word of God; all the same, on account of the mutual concern and longing that we have for each other, something should be said to your charity about charity. It's the one topic, you see, for which, if anyone wishes to speak about it, he doesn't have to choose a special reading to provide him with an opportunity for his sermon; every page of the scriptures, after all, wherever you open them, rings of this subject. On this point the Lord himself is a witness, and we are reminded of it from the gospel; because when he was asked which are the greatest commandments of the law, he answered, *You shall love the Lord your God with your whole heart, and with your whole soul, and with your whole mind,* and *you shall love your neighbor as yourself*; and in case you should look for anything else in the sacred pages, he went on to say, *On these two commandments depend the whole law and the prophets* (Mt 22:37.39-40).

If the whole law and the prophets depend on these two commandments, how much more the gospel! It is charity, after all, that renews man; because just as cupidity makes a man old, so charity makes him new. That's why he says, as he grunts and groans in his struggle with cupidity or greed, *I have grown old among all my enemies* (Ps 6:7). But that charity or love belongs to the new man is indicated by the Lord himself in this way: *A new commandment do I give you, that you should love one another* (Jn 13:34). So if the law and the prophets depend on charity, though it is the old covenant that is obviously presented to us in the law and the prophets, how much more must the gospel, which is so plainly called the new covenant, belong only to charity, seeing that the Lord didn't call anything his own commandment, except that you should love one another? He both called this commandment new, and he came here to renew us, and he made us into new men, and he promised us a new, and what's more eternal, inheritance.

110

The charity of the New Testament prefigured in the Old,
and understood plainly even then by certain great lovers of God

2. Because if you are wondering, perhaps, how the law is both called the old testament or covenant, and also depends on charity, though charity renews man, and belongs to the new man, here is the reason. It is an old covenant that is there drawn up, because it makes an earthly promise, and it is an earthly kingdom that the Lord there offers to his worshipers. But even then there were to be found lovers of God who loved him freely for his own sake, and cleansed their hearts by chastely sighing for him. They peeled off the outer shells of the old promises, and came upon the prefiguration of the new covenant that was to come, and they grasped that all the things that are commandments or promises in the old covenant with respect to the old man, are figures or symbols of the new covenant, which the Lord was going to fulfill in the last times, as the apostle says so plainly: *Now these things happened to them as symbols; but they were written for our sake, upon whom the end of the ages has come* (1 Cor 10:11). So the new covenant was being foretold in a hidden way, and being foretold in those figures or symbols.

But when the time for the new covenant came, the new covenant began to be proclaimed openly, and those figures and symbols to be interpreted, and explanations to be given of how the new was to be understood even there, where it was the old that was promised. So the promulgator of the old covenant was Moses; but while he was the one who promulgated the old, he was also one who understood the new.[2] He was promulgating the old to a fleshly, material-minded people, while he himself, being spiritual, was fully aware of the new. The apostles, however, were both promulgators and administrators of the new covenant; but this doesn't mean that what was later made publicly known through the apostles was not there at that earlier time. So charity is there in the old, charity here in the new. But there charity is more hidden away, fear more out in the open; while here charity is more publicly manifest, fear altogether less. To the extent, you see, that charity grows, fear diminishes. As charity grows, that is, the soul's sense of security increases; and where there is complete security there is no fear, with John the apostle saying, *Consummate charity casts out fear* (1 Jn 4:18).

The psalm verse, "Do not be envious of the wicked,"
interpreted as an exhortation to the love of the age to come

3. Thus in talking to your holinesses about this charity, I have also taken this present psalm[3] as a point of departure—because, as I said, whichever of the Lord's pages you read, it admonishes us about nothing else but charity. See for yourselves whether the divine utterances have any other effect but that we should love; see whether they work toward anything else but to set us on fire, to inflame us, to kindle our desire, to get us sighing and groaning until we finally arrive. Human beings having a difficult time here on earth, and finding themselves beset by the greatest trials and temptations, frequently remark with their mortal thoughts and feeble reflections how the wicked usually have the best of

it here for a time, and grow proud in their fleeting prosperity—indeed such thoughts often occur as a temptation to the servants of God,[4] as though they were devoting themselves to God to no purpose at all, if they notice that they lack what they observe the godless to have in abundance. So with humanity in that sort of situation, the Holy Spirit foresaw that we would be tempted like this and wished to change the direction of our love, and prevent us from thinking that we should imitate godless and villainous men the more we see how well they do in the world, simply out of love for the sort of things that their abundant possession of had them strutting about like turkey cocks. And so he said, *Do not be envious of the evil-minded*—it's the beginning of the psalm—*nor jealous of those who work iniquity; since they shall soon wither like grass, and soon fall like the herbs of the meadow* (Ps 37:1-2).

Does the grass never grow and flourish? But it's only for a short time that it flourishes, it will soon dry up; and it's the cold weather that makes it flourish. The coming of the Lord Jesus Christ will be like the hot weather of the year; this present time is like the cold weather of the year. But let us be on our guard against our charity growing cold[5] in the cold weather of the year. Our blossom time has not yet appeared; it is so cold on the outside, but there should be heat in the roots. That's the way, after all, that trees put out leaves in the summer, and are beautiful and fruitful, though they looked so dried up and withered in the winter. Was everything you see on the branches in summer also there throughout the winter? Yes, it was, but it was hiding in the roots. So our time to blossom, which has been promised us, is not yet; may our summer come; it isn't here yet, it's hidden away. We can say more correctly that it isn't apparent, than that it isn't here yet. The apostle, you see, says plainly, *For you are dead.* It's as though he were speaking to trees during the winter. But to show you that while the surface seemed dead, the trees were still alive inside, he immediately went on to say, *and your life is hidden with Christ in God* (Col 3:3). We seem to be living on this earth; just consider where we have taken root. The root of our love is with Christ, it's in God. That's where our blossoming in all its glory is to be found; but it isn't apparent just now.

If the apostle told the rich not to place their hopes in this world, but to hope for the future, how much more ought those to do so, who have vowed to have nothing on this earth!

4. But what did he go on to say? *When Christ appears, your life, then you also will appear with him in glory* (Col 3:4). So now is the time for groaning, then it will be for rejoicing; now for desiring, then for embracing. What we desire now is not present; but let us not falter in desire; let long, continuous desire be our daily exercise, because the one who made the promise doesn't cheat us. I'm not saying, brothers, that nobody should grow cold; nobody should even grow tepid. True, the lovers of the world may well jeer at the servants of God, saying, "Look what we've got, and what we enjoy; where are your good times, your fun?" But you, while you haven't got the things you can see, do have the things you believe in; they for their part don't believe in things that can't be demonstrated. Rejoice then because you have come to believe; you will rejoice

more than ever, when eventually you see. And if you sigh and groan because you cannot point to what you believe, your groans of sorrow will profit you not only for salvation, but also for everlasting glory.

There's nothing they can show us of any great value; their good times are visibly present, ours are in the future. Though it would be truer for us to say that theirs are neither present nor future; I mean, because they love false good times in the present, they won't come to the true ones in the future. If, however, they would turn their backs on the false good times of the present, and find what they can do with what they actually have, and discover what they can acquire with it, they should listen to the advice of the blessed apostle, which he authorizes Timothy to pass on to the rich. He says, you see, *Command the rich of this world not to have proud ideas, nor to place their hopes in the uncertainty of riches, but in the living God, who grants us all things abundantly for our enjoyment. Let them be rich in good works, let them give things away easily, let them share. Let them save up for themselves a good foundation for the future, so that they may lay hold of the true life* (1 Tm 6:17-19).

So then, brothers, if the apostle was determined to turn away the thoughts of those who appeared to be doing very well in the present life from earthly concerns, and to direct them toward heaven; if he didn't want them to rejoice in the present, but to hope for things to come; if the apostle says such things to people who have all this, how much more should that man stretch out his whole heart and soul to what lies ahead in the future, who has decided to have nothing on this earth? To have nothing superfluous, that means, to have nothing which can be a burden, to have nothing which can tie him down, to have nothing which can hinder him. Because even in this time that saying is more truly applicable to the servants of God, *as having nothing, and possessing all things* (2 Cor 6:10). Let there be nothing you call your own, and all things will be yours. If you stick to a part, you lose the whole; after all, what would be sufficient if you were rich, must be sufficient if you are poor.

NOTES

1. This date appears to have been proposed by Dom Morin. The sermon was clearly delivered to a community of "servants of God," of men, that is to say, who had taken what we now call religious vows. Only such a community would, as he says in the first sentence, feed themselves daily on the readings of the holy scriptures. That being the case, it was most probably preached to Augustine's own community of clergy in Hippo Regius. But he could have been invited, of course, to preach to such a community elsewhere. In this context it would be absurd to translate *fratres* as "brothers and sisters"; so here, it will just be "brothers."

2. It was, to our way of thinking, a strange commonplace among all the Fathers, and the scholastics after them, that the great, or spiritual, persons of the Old Testament were fully aware of the new covenant which it prefigured and prepared the way for.

3. Ps 37—than which there are few Old Testament texts more redolent of the old covenant and its earthly, this-worldly promises.

4. Monks, or religious men.

5. See Mt 24:12.

SERMON 350B

ON ALMSGIVING

Date: uncertain

Give from what you have, in order to receive what you do not have

1. *The rich man*, it says, *and the poor man have met each other on the road; but the creator of them both is the Lord* (Prv 22:2). So, brothers and sisters, as it's written, rich and poor have met each other on the road. On what road, if not that of this life? There you are, rich man, you can relieve yourself of your burdens by giving to the poor what you have amassed with such hard work.[1] Give to the person who hasn't got something, because there is something that you too haven't got either. So give from what you have, in order to receive from what you don't have. Let the beggar hammer at your door, while you for your part hammer at the door of your Lord. God treats his beggar as you treat yours. So, *give, and you will be given* (Lk 6:38); but if you're unwilling to, look out for yourself. The poor man, you see, is crying out and saying to you, "I'm asking for bread and you don't give me any; you're asking for life, and you're not getting any. Let's see which of us is laboring under the greater loss; I, who am being cheated of a morsel, or you who are being deprived of eternal life? I, whose belly, or you, whose intelligence,[2] is being chastised? Finally, I, who am being burned up with hunger, or you, who are going to be burned with fire, and handed over as food for the hungry flames?"

I don't know whether the pride of the rich man will be able to find an answer to these words of the poor man. *To everyone who asks you*, says the Lord, *give* (Lk 6:30). If to everyone, how much more to the needy and the wretched, whose gaunt and wan appearance does the begging for them; whose tongues are silent, while their squalor and groans are asking for alms. So listen to me, Mr. Rich Man, and let my advice win your approval. Redeem your sins with almsgiving. Don't sit on your gold like a hen on eggs. Naked you came from your mother's womb, naked you are going to return into the earth.[3] And if you are going to return naked into the earth, for whom are you amassing all these things upon the earth? I imagine, if you could carry anything with you, you would have devoured people alive. Look, you came forth naked, why not be bountiful with your money, whether you've made your pile by fair means or foul? Send ahead

114

what makes you such an admired figure, make balloons of your much admired goods,[4] in order to reach the kingdom of heaven.

After all, if you gave some man ten pounds,[5] for which he later on paid you back three hundred, how delighted you would be, with what high spirits you would kick up your heels for joy! So if a high rate of interest is what you really like, become a money-lender to your God. Give to your Lord from what is in fact his own, because he will pay you back at compound interest. Do you wish to know the precise rate he will pay you back at? For a morsel of bread, for a coin, for an old coat, you will receive eternal life, the kingdom of heaven, endless bliss. Weigh eternal life, everlasting wealth, against that morsel of bread of yours. There's simply no comparison. Give earth, I mean, and you get back the one who made heaven and earth; he himself, you see, is our reward, without whom the rich man is just a beggar, and with whom the poor man is superabundantly rich. I mean, what does the rich man possess, if he doesn't possess God? What doesn't the poor man possess, if he does possess God?

So, brothers and sisters, I'm saying these things to you and admonishing you as a watchman among the people;[6] I'm discharging my duty, and thereby delivering my soul, absolving myself of responsibility. There is one who will inquire about and scrutinize your work. Why, there you are, you all groaned. So that means you are already in the right frame of mind for giving alms. God be thanked for it. The Lord, who has given you understanding, is fully able to bestow on you the fruits of your almsgiving.

NOTES

1. See Sermons 39, 6; 53A, 6; 85; 7; 107A, 5.

2. A contrast we have met before between *ventre* and *mente*. I resist the obvious temptation in this sort of context to translate *mente* by "soul"—because it is a temptation. It is precisely the soul's quality of rational intelligence, the mind, that is doomed to the loss of the beatific vision, if the rich man continues to be hard-hearted.

3. See Jb 1:21.

4. *Fac inflationes rerum permirarum*; literally, make inflations of your much admired goods. But I doubt if they talked about inflation in the monetary sense in those days, though they certainly experienced it. They called it adulterating the coinage. So I am treating *inflationes* as if it means inflated objects, that is, balloons. Did they have balloons in those days? I don't know; perhaps this text is evidence that they did. Anyway, it is a pleasant image: send your wealth up to heaven by balloon.

5. *Solidos*, gold coins of the Roman Empire. It is in fact the word represented by the "s" in "L.s.d."; and so should, pedantically, be translated as "shillings." But it clearly meant much more than shillings did, when we still had shillings; and certainly much more than shillings mean where they do still have them, namely in East Africa.

6. See Ez 33:7.

SERMON 350C

ON ALMSGIVING

Date: uncertain[1]

Give from what you have, in order to receive what you do not have

1. O man, frail of body, changeable in time, breaking up in death, weighed down with honors,[2] worn out with anxieties, listen to my advice: lighten your load by giving to the poor what you have amassed with such labor; give to the person who hasn't got something, because there is something that you too haven't got either—I mean you haven't yet[3] got eternal life. So give from what you have, in order to receive what you do not have. The poor man is hammering at your door; you are hammering at the door of your Lord. God treats his beggar in the way that you treat yours; so *give, and you will be given* (Lk 6:38). If you are not willing to, look out for yourself. The poor man, you see, is crying out and saying to you, "I'm asking for bread and you don't give it to me; you're asking for life, and not getting it. Let's see which of us is laboring under the greater loss: I who am being cheated of a morsel of bread, or you that are being deprived of eternal life? I whose belly, or you whose intelligence is being chastised? Finally, I who am on fire with hunger, or you who are to be burned with fire and handed over to the lively flames?"

I don't know whether the pride of the rich man will be able to find an answer to these words of the poor man. *To everyone who asks you*, says the Lord, *give* (Lk 6:30). If to everyone, how much more to the needy and the wretched, whose gaunt and pallid appearances do the begging for them; whose tongues are silent, while their squalor and their groans are asking for alms?

Weigh up eternal life against your morsel of bread

2. So listen to me, Mr. Rich Man, and let my advice win your approval. Redeem your sins by almsgiving; don't sit on your gold like a hen on eggs. Naked you came forth from your mother's womb, naked you are going to return into the earth;[4] and if you are going to return naked into the earth, for whom are you amassing all these things upon the earth? Send it ahead where you are going to go, organize the transfer of things that are going to perish, so that you may

116

reach the kingdom of heaven. After all, if you gave some man ten pounds, for which he later gave you back a hundred, how delighted you would be, with what a joyful spirit you would kick up your heels!

So if a high rate of interest is what you really like, become a money-lender to your Lord, give your God from what is his own; he will pay you back, you see, at compound interest. Do you want to know the precise rate of interest at which he will pay you back? For a morsel of bread, for a coin, for an old coat, you receive eternal life, the kingdom of heaven, everlasting wealth. There's simply no comparison; I mean, you're giving earth and receiving in return the one who made heaven and earth. He himself, you see, will be our reward, without whom the rich man is a beggar, and with whom the poor man is superabundantly rich. What, after all, does the rich man possess, if he doesn't possess God? What does the poor man not possess, if he does possess God?

NOTES

1. This sermon is clearly just an abbreviated alternative version of the preceding one—possibly descending from a different stenographer.

2. *Onoribus*; but it may possibly be a mistake for *oneribus*, burdens.

3. Reading *nondum* for the text's *nunquam*, never.

4. See Jb 1:21.

SERMON 351

ON THE VALUE OF REPENTANCE

Date: 391[1]

Whoever exalts himself will be humbled,
and whoever humbles himself will be exalted

1. How useful and necessary a medicine repentance is, people will readily understand who remember that they are only human. It's written, you see, *God withstands the proud, but gives grace to the humble* (1 Pt 5:5; Jas 4:6; Jb 22:29; Prv 3:34). And in the gospel the Lord says, *Because whoever exalts himself will be humbled, and whoever humbles himself will be exalted* (Lk 18:14; 14:11); and that tax-collector, who was so anxious to confess his sins, went down from the temple justified more than the Pharisee who was so sure of himself in recounting his merits. Although, yes, he too gave thanks to God, saying, *I thank you, God, that I am not like other men, unjust, adulterers, extortioners; yes, like this tax-collector here too. I fast twice a week, I give tithes of everything whatever I possess*; still, he was preferring himself to the one who *was standing at a distance, and not daring to lift up his eyes to heaven, but was beating his breast, saying, God, be gracious to me, a sinner* (Lk 18:10-14). That Pharisee, after all, wasn't rejoicing so much in his own clean bill of health, as in comparing it with the diseases of others. It would have been more worth his while, since he had come to the doctor, to inform him by confession of the things that were wrong with him, instead of keeping his wounds secret, and having the nerve to crow over the scars of others. So it's not surprising that it was the tax-collector rather who went away cured, since he hadn't been ashamed of showing where he felt pain.

In ordinary visible situations, in order to reach places high up, you stretch yourself up to your full height. God however, though he is the most sublimely high up of all things, is not reached by hoisting oneself up, but by humbling oneself. Which is why the prophet says, *The Lord is near to those who have crushed their hearts* (Ps 34:18); and again: *The Lord is most high, and looks to the humble things, and the high things he knows from afar* (Ps 138:6). He put high things for the proud. So he looks to those other things, to raise them up; these things he knows, to cast them down. After all, when he said that he knows

118

the high things from afar, he showed clearly enough that he attends to the humble things from close by; and yet he had first said that the Lord himself is most high. God alone, you see, cannot be regarded as arrogant, with whatever fanfares he may be pleased to praise himself.

So pride must never think that it can hide itself from God's eyes; God, you see, *knows the high things*. Nor again should it imagine that it is closely united to God by being high; after all, he knows the high things from afar. So any who refuse to humble themselves in repentance, should not think[2] they can draw near to God. It's one thing, after all, to raise oneself up to God; another thing to raise oneself up against God. Those who throw themselves down before him are raised up by him; those who raise themselves up against him are thrown down by him. Solid magnitude, you see, is one thing, the emptiness of a blown up balloon another. Those who are swollen up outwardly are inwardly wasting away. Those on the other hand who choose to be the lowest of the low in the house of God, *rather than to dwell in the tents of sinners*, are themselves chosen by God to dwell in his courts; and as they make no claims for themselves, he claims them for thrones of bliss. Which is why we sing in this psalm so delightfully and truly, *Blessed is the man whose upholding is from you, Lord* (Ps 84:10.5).

You mustn't think that the one who humbles himself remains lying there always; since it is stated that he *will be exalted* (Lk 18:14). And you mustn't suppose that this exaltation of his will occur in the sight of men by means of any terrestrial promotions or elevations. You see, after saying *Blessed is the man whose upholding is from you, Lord*, he went on to tie the thing up and show the spiritual loftiness of his being taken up: *He has arranged*, he said, *ascents in his heart in the vale of weeping, into the place which he has arranged.* So where has he arranged ascents? In the heart, that is in the vale of weeping. That's the equivalent of *Whoever humbles himself shall be exalted.* Just as ascent, after all, signifies exaltation, so the valley indicates humility, and the vale weeping. I mean, just as sorrow is the companion of repentance, so tears are witnesses to sorrow. And how splendidly he goes on to say, *For indeed, the one who has given the law will give his blessing* (Ps 84:5-6).[3]

Why the law was given, you see, was to show up the wounds inflicted by sins, which the blessing of grace would heal. Why the law was given was to make known to the proud their weakness, and to persuade the weak to repent. Why the law was given was so that we might say in the vale of weeping, *I can see another law in my members, fighting against the law of my mind, and taking me captive under the law of sin, which is in my members*; and so that we should cry out in our very weeping, *Unhappy man that I am! Who will deliver me from the body of this death?*; and that when we are heard by the one who raises up the shattered, sets free the fettered, gives light to the blind,[4] we may be succored by *the grace of God through Jesus Christ our Lord* (Rom 7:23-25).

Three kinds of repentance or regret; the first kind: before baptism

2. Now there are three kinds of repentance which, well instructed as you are, you will recognize with me. They are, after all, commonplace in the Church, and known to those who attend regularly.[5] One is the sort that is in labor with the new man, until through saving baptism he is cleansed of all past sins; then, as with the birth of a child, the pains that were bringing it to birth are over and done with, and joy follows on anguish.[6] When any people, you see, who are already of an age to make free decisions of will, approach the sacraments of the faithful,[7] they cannot begin the new life unless they repent of the old. It's only babies that are exempt from this kind of repentance when they are baptized; after all they are not yet capable of making free choices.

However, the faith of those who present them for baptism can avail them for sanctification and the remission of original sin; thus whatever defilement of wrongdoing they may have contracted through others, of whom they have been born, they can be purged of it through the interrogation of these others and the replies they give.[8] The lament in the psalms, indeed, is absolutely true: *Behold in iniquity was I conceived, and in sins did my mother nourish me in her womb* (Ps 51:5). Again, there is what is written, that there is none clean in God's sight, not even an infant whose life has lasted but a day on the earth.[9] So these are the exception; and it is to exceed our limited human measure, to wish to inquire about the rank they may deserve in that *lot of the saints in light* (Col 1:12) which is promised for the future. However, it is piously to be believed, that what is observed so firmly and consistently by ecclesiastical authority throughout the whole world avails for their spiritual salvation. With the exception of these, then, no other human beings can cross over to Christ and begin to be what they were not, unless they have repented of what they were.

This first kind of repentance is enjoined upon the Jews, with the apostle Peter saying, *Repent, and let each one of you be baptized in the name of our Lord Jesus Christ* (Acts 2:38). It was also commanded by the Lord himself, when he said, *Repent, for the kingdom of God has drawn near* (Mt 4:17). John the Baptist too, filled with the Holy Spirit, the Lord's forerunner, who prepared the way for him, had this to say about it: *Brood of vipers, who has shown you to flee from the wrath that is coming? So produce some fruit that is worthy of repentance* (Mt 3:7-8).

The second kind of repentance: regret for this time-bound, perishable, mortal life

3. There is another kind of repentance, though, which we should be practicing with the humility of perpetual supplication[10] throughout the whole of this life, which we are spending in the mortal flesh. First of all, because nobody longs for eternal, imperishable and immortal life without repenting of, or regretting, this time-bound, perishable and mortal life.[11] People are not, after all, born into the new life through the sanctification of baptism in such a way that just as they lay aside there all their past sins, they also immediately shed the very mortality of the flesh and its liability to perish. And even if this were not so, there remains

the truth of what is written, which all of us also experience in ourselves as long as we are in this life, *that the body which is perishing weighs down the soul, and the earthly habitation depresses the mind thinking many thoughts* (Wis 9:15). Because this won't be the case in that state of bliss when *death has been swallowed up in victory* (1 Cor 15:54), who can doubt that whatever kind of temporal well-being we may enjoy, we ought still to be repenting of, or regretting, this life, in order to hasten toward that state of imperishability with all the eagerness we can muster?

That's also the drift, you see, of what the apostle says: *As long as we are in the body, we are traveling abroad from the Lord; for we are walking by faith, not by sight* (2 Cor 5:6-7). So who will be in a hurry and a lather to return to the home country, and to contemplate that sight face to face,[12] unless they regret and are sorry for their exile abroad? It's from the pain of such sorrow or regret that those woeful words burst forth for us all to hear: *Woe is me, since my wanderings have taken me so far.* And in case you should think it is someone not yet a believer who is saying this, notice what follows: *I have dwelt among the tents of Kedar; with those who hate peace I was pacific; when I spoke to them they were exceedingly aggressive* (Ps 120:5-7).

They are the words not only of a good believer, but also of the most strenuous preacher of the gospel and the bravest of martyrs. Because that's also the drift of this passage from the apostle: *For we know that if our earthly house we live in is pulled down, we have a building from God, a house not made with hands, eternal in the heavens. For indeed this is why we are sighing, longing to have our dwelling which is from heaven put on over us; provided, however, that we may be found clothed, and not naked. For indeed we that are in this habitation are sighing, being so weighed down, in that we do not wish to be stripped, but to be given further clothing, so that what is mortal may be swallowed up by life* (2 Cor 5:1-4). So what are we longing for, but to be such as we certainly are not now? And what do our sighs and groans mean, if not that we are sorry for being like this? But when shall we ever not be like this, unless our earthly house is pulled down, so that we may obtain as our lot a heavenly dwelling by the transformation of the whole person in both spirit and body?

That too is why Saint Job did not say that there are trials and temptations in this life, but he said that this very life is itself a trial and temptation, speaking like this: *Is not human life upon earth a trial and temptation?* In the same place he also touched upon the mystery of the fall of man, saying, *Like a slave fleeing his Lord, and reaching shade* (Jb 7:1-2). This life, in fact, should rather be called the shade or shadow of life. Nor is it without significance that Adam the fugitive,[13] after the offense of his sin, hid from the face of the Lord by covering himself with the leaves of trees, which provide dark shady places—*like one fleeing his Lord*, as it says, *and reaching shade.*

All this said, in order to inculcate humility even after baptism

4. All this has been said for one purpose only: to prevent those who have been justified from their previous sins by baptism still daring to be proud, if they

don't commit anything that would cut them off from communion at the altar; as though they can now be completely sure of themselves in their conceit. But instead they should preserve humility, which is practically the only Christian discipline there is. Nor should *dust and ashes be proud* (Sir 10:9), until this whole night has passed, *in which all the beasts of the forest pass by, lion cubs roaring, seeking their food from God* (Ps 104:20-21). Job himself was one who was sought for as such food,[14] which is why he said, *A trial and temptation is human life on earth.* The Lord too said, *This very night Satan has requested to shake you all like wheat in a sieve* (Lk 22:31).

So can there be any in their right mind who wouldn't sigh and groan? Any who wouldn't show by repentance and regret their displeasure at being like this? Any who wouldn't by totally humble supplications present themselves to be heard and helped by God, until all this material for trial and temptation, and this earthly shadow pass away; and until that everlasting day which never fails also shines upon us, and *lights up the hidden places of darkness, and reveals the thoughts of the heart, and then shall everyone have praise from God* (1 Cor 4:5)? Then again, there may be some who can boast that they have so tamed their bodies, that they are crucified to the world as regards every bad work, that they chastise their members and reduce them to slavery, so that sin should no longer reign in their mortal bodies for them to obey their desires;[15] that they worship the one true God, are not devoted to idolatrous rites, not entangled in demonic sacraments, that they do not take the name of the Lord their God in vain, that they await with assurance the everlasting sabbath rest, pay due honor to their parents, are neither stained with the blood of murder, nor defiled with fornication, nor engaged in the dishonesty of theft or the duplicity of lying, nor rendered mean and paltry by coveting another man's goods or his wife.[16] With their own goods they are not wasteful or extravagant, or mean and grasping either; they're not quarrelsome, not abusive, not given to cursing; finally, they may sell all that they have and give to the poor and follow Christ, and plant the roots of their hearts in heavenly treasure;[17] can you think of anything that could be added to such fullness of justice? All the same, I don't want them to boast; they must understand that all this has been granted to them, it doesn't spring from their own selves. What have they got, after all, that they haven't received? And if they have received it, why are they boasting, as though they hadn't?[18]

Certainly, let them lay out the Lord's money; let them take thought for the needs of their neighbors, just as they can perceive that thought has been taken for their own. Indeed, they must not think it is enough to preserve intact what they have received, or they may each hear it said to them, *Wicked and idle servant, you should have invested my money, and I on coming would have collected it with interest,* and have what they have received taken away from them, and be cast out themselves into the outer darkness (Mt 25:26-30). If those who can preserve intact what they have received have to fear such a savage punishment, what hope can there be for those who squander it in an irresponsible and criminal fashion?

So these good people will take part in human affairs, devoting themselves not to material but to spiritual profit; not indeed tied down to secular business, but still, as recruited into God's service, not lazing around either like worthless good-for-nothings in idleness and sloth. So they should give all their alms, if they can, with cheerfulness, either when they are dispensing something to relieve the material necessities of the poor, or when as distributors of the bread from heaven[19] they are building up in the hearts of believers invincible fortifications against the devil. *For God loves a cheerful giver* (2 Cor 9:7). And so they mustn't allow themselves to be broken with weariness at the difficulties which must of necessity arise in order to show us human beings that we are just human. Don't let anger creep in against the one who attacks you spitefully, or the one who, driven by want, asks for help at an awkward time; or who insists on being aided in his business when you are preoccupied with something more important; or the one who in a case of manifest justice opposes what you say out of blind self-interest, or wretched dullness of wits.[20]

Don't give either more or less than is proper; don't speak more than is necessary, or when it isn't even necessary at all. Yes, *beautiful are the feet of those who proclaim the good news of peace, who proclaim good news* (Is 52:7). But all the same, they pick up dust from the dry ground, which is certainly to be shaken off in judgment upon those who with twisted wills reject the offer being made to them.[21] So then, it's not only because of the mortal nature of this life that we ought to practice repentance and regret every day, and because of its ignorance, and because of the evil of the day which would to God it were sufficient, as is said about it, *Sufficient for the day is its evil* (Mt 6:34). This we are instructed to bear with and endure until it passes, and *to wait for the Lord doing manfully* (Ps 31:24), in order to *bring forth fruit with patience* (Lk 8:15). No, it's also because of the dust of this world which sticks to the feet of those who give advice on their journeys of consultation, and because of the losses which they incur in the arduous business of their ministry, which we hope the Lord may compensate them for by greater profits.

The daily sins of the laity and their repentance

5. But if this is the case with the stewards of the word of God and the ministers of his sacraments,[22] the regular soldiers of Christ; how much more with the multitude of other auxiliaries,[23] who form a kind of province of the great king? To avoid offending these with even an unfounded suspicion of avarice, that bravest and most loyal of soldiers, the apostle Paul, served at his own expense; and whenever the necessary funds happened to be lacking, *I plundered other Churches*, he said, *by accepting pay from them in order to minister to you* (2 Cor 7:8). How much more then should provincial Churches, tied down[24] to secular affairs, practice daily repentance! They ought, of course, to be pure and inviolate, innocent of any thefts, robberies, frauds, adultery and fornication and all kinds of self-indulgence, from the cruelty that springs from hatred and the holding of obstinate grudges, finally from all the ugliness of idolatry, the trifling frivolity of the shows, the godless vanity of heresy and schism, and from all

such crimes and misdeeds; still, in the course of managing family affairs, and in the close bond of marriage, they commit so many sins that they seem, not so much to be covered with the dust of this world, as to be smeared with its mud.

This is what the apostle says to them: *Now indeed you are certainly seriously at fault, because you have lawsuits with one another. Why not rather suffer injustice? Why not rather let yourselves be defrauded?* But what he adds on account of some of them is indeed abominable; he says, *You, however, commit injustice, and defraud, and your brothers at that* (1 Cor 6:7-8). Quite apart, though, from injustices and frauds, the mere fact of having lawsuits and litigation between themselves about secular matters is something he says is a fault. This, though, he advises them is something to be tolerated, provided such lawsuits are settled by ecclesiastical judgments.[25]

In the same vein there is also this: *The one who is without a wife thinks about God's affairs, how to please God; but the one who is married thinks about the world's affairs, how to please his wife* (1 Cor 7:32-33); he also makes the same observation about women. Or there's the other thing he says: *And again come together, lest Satan should tempt you on account of your lack of moderation.* To make clear that this is a sin, but conceded to weakness, he immediately added, *But I say this by way of license, not by way of command* (1 Cor 7:5-6). It is only when it is for the sake of begetting children, you see, that the union of the sexes is entirely blameless.[26]

How many other sins there are, whether in talking about other people's affairs and business, which don't concern you; or in futile cackling and laughter, seeing that it is written, *The fool raises his voice in laughter, while the wise man will scarcely laugh even silently* (Sir 21:20). Or there's the greedy and unrestrained appetite for food, which is properly prepared out of the need to keep body and soul together, the proof of excess being the next day's indigestion. Or there are the wrong-headed maneuvers in commerce to buy things cheap and sell them dear. It would be tedious to list all the things that anyone can observe with more certainty and reprehend in himself, if he is not careless about looking into the mirror of the divine scriptures. Although none of them, taken singly, are felt to inflict a mortal wound, like murder [27] and adultery and sins like that; still when they all pile up like a suppurating rash, the more they are, they can kill, or so disfigure our appearance, that they cut us off from the chaste embraces of that bridegroom who is *the fairest in form among the sons of men* (Ps 45:2), unless they are dried up by the medicine of daily repentance.

We beat our breasts every day, saying "Forgive us our debts,
as we too forgive our debtors"

6. But if that's not true, why do we beat our breasts every day? Something we prelates assisting at the altar also do with everybody else.[28] Why too do we say when we pray, as we surely should do all this life long, *Forgive us our debts as we too forgive our debtors* (Mt 6:12)? We are not, you see, praying to have those things forgiven which we believe have already been forgiven in baptism—

if we don't believe that, we are doubting the faith itself. But of course it's about our daily sins that we say this, for which none of us should cease to offer, as best we can, the sacrifices of almsgiving, of fasting, of our very prayers and supplications. So people who take a good look at themselves, and don't deceive themselves with self-flattery, will understand clearly enough in what danger of eternal death, and with what a meager supply of perfect justice we are wandering abroad away from the Lord, although we are already established in Christ, that is on the way,[29] and striving to return along it.

I mean, if we don't have any sins, and still beat our breasts and say, *Forgive us our debts*, by this very fact, and without a shadow of doubt, we sin gravely, since we are telling a lie in the course of the holy mysteries themselves.[30] Thus it is, that insofar as we are linked to our God by faith, hope and charity, and imitate him insofar as we are able, we do not sin, but are children of God; while insofar as through the weakness of the flesh, not yet dissolved in death, not yet transformed in the resurrection, reprehensible and shameless feelings arise, we do sin. And of course it's only proper that we should confess them; otherwise, for our stiff-necked reluctance to do so, we may earn, not the healing of our feeble powers, but the condemnation of our pride. Thus each thing is set down with absolute truth: both, *Whoever is born of God does not sin* (1 Jn 3:9); and what we read in the same letter of John, *If we say that we have no sin, we are deceiving ourselves, and the truth is not in us* (1 Jn 1:8). The former, you see, is said with regard to the beginnings of the new man, the latter with regard to the remnants of the old; in this life, after all, we are playing each part. But the new comes on gradually, and as the old gradually yields ground, it takes its place.

While, however, we are acting each part, we are in the arena; and we aren't only hitting our opponent[31] with good works, but we are also being hit, through our carelessness in avoiding sins. Nor is attention paid right now to which of us wins, but to which of us gets in more blows, which of us battles more bravely, until the one who fell, and envied the man his still standing on his feet, drags some off with him to everlasting death, while others in triumph say at the end, *Where, death, is your striving? Where, death, is your sting?* (1 Cor 15:55). But it is never easier for the enemy to lay us low than when we imitate him by being proud; nor do we throw him more vigorously than when we follow the Lord in humility; nor do we inflict sharper pains on him, than when we heal the wounds of our sins by confession and repentance.

The third kind of repentance: entailing penance for grave sins

7. The third sort of repentance is the one which has to be undergone for those sins which are mentioned in the ten commandments of the law, and about which the apostle says, *Since those who do such things will not possess the kingdom of God* (Gal 5:21). So in this kind of repentance all have to show a greater severity against themselves; in this way, judged by themselves, they will avoid being judged by God, as the same apostle says: *If we judged ourselves, we would*

not be judged by God (1 Cor 11:31). So let those who find themselves in such case take their seats on the bench of their minds against themselves, if they have any dread of the fact that *we must all be presented before the judgment seat of Christ, so that each of us may there receive what we have done through the body, whether good or evil* (2 Cor 5:10). Let them put themselves in the dock before themselves, to avoid this happening to them later on. That, you see, is what God threatens the sinner with, saying *I will accuse you and set you in the dock before yourself* (Ps 50:21). And with the court thus sitting in their hearts, let self-examination appear for the prosecution, conscience be called as a witness, fear be summoned as executioner. Next let a kind of blood of the spirit flow, in the form of a tearful confession.

Finally, the mind itself should pronounce such a sentence, that the persons concerned judge themselves to be unworthy of sharing in the Lord's body and blood; and as they are afraid of being cut off from the kingdom of heaven by the ultimate sentence of the supreme judge, they should for the time being, according to the discipline of the Church, separate themselves from the sacrament of the bread from heaven. Let them hold before their eyes the picture of the judgment to come; so that, while others approach God's altar which they do not approach themselves, they should reflect on how dreadful that punishment is by which, while some receive eternal life, others are cast headlong into eternal death. This altar, after all, which is now set up, exposed to earthly eyes, in the Church on earth for the celebration of the signs and tokens of the divine mysteries, can also be approached by many scoundrelly persons, because God is presenting us in this time with his patience, so that in the time to come he may exercise his severity. They approach, you see, without considering that the patience of God is intending to lead them to repentance. They, however, in line with their stubbornness of heart and their unrepentant hearts are storing up wrath for themselves in the day of wrath and of the revelation of the just judgment of God, who will render to all according to their works.[32]

To that other altar, however, *where Jesus our forerunner has entered on our behalf* (Heb 6:20), where the head of the Church has gone before us, with his other members due to follow in their turn, none of those will be able to have access of whom, as I have already reminded you, the apostle said, *Since those who do such things shall not possess the kingdom of God* (Gal 5:21). Only the high priest, you see, may officiate there, but naturally in his entirety, that is in conjunction with his body, of which[33] he is the head which has already ascended into heaven. It is the body[34] to which the apostle Peter said, *A holy people, a royal priesthood* (1 Pt 2:9). How will those people have either the audacity or the capacity to enter the inner place behind the veil, and that invisible holy of holies,[35] who have ignored the medicine of heavenly discipline, and refused for a short time to cut themselves off from the visible holy place? Those, you see, who have refused to humble themselves in order to be exalted, will be thrown down when they wish to exalt themselves; and any who don't, during this time, provide themselves with a place in the body of the high priest by the merit of obedience and by penitential works of amendment, will be cut off from holy communion with eternity. What a nerve, what impudence they must have, if they then want God to turn his face away from their sins, while now they don't say from the bottom of their hearts, *Since I acknowledge my misdeed, and my sin is always before me* (Ps 51:3)! On what conceivable grounds, I ask you, will God think fit to pardon and remit something, which people do not think fit to acknowledge and admit in themselves?

There is no difference between entering
the kingdom of God and being saved

8. Or what about that other idea, with which those who are so foolishly fond of deceiving themselves like to reassure themselves? While they persist, you see, with their rascally behavior and their self-indulgence, they have the nerve, when they hear the apostle saying *that those who do such things will not possess the kingdom of God* (Gal 5:21), to promise themselves, apart from the kingdom of God, the salvation they desire. And so this is how they talk to each other, while refusing to do penance for their sins and to change their abandoned habits and behavior, some time or other, for the better: "I don't want to reign or rule in the kingdom;[36] it's enough for me to be saved." Well, the first mistake they make is that there won't even be any salvation for those who persevere with their iniquity. There's what the Lord said, after all: *Since iniquity has abounded, the charity of many will grow cold; but it is the one who perseveres to the end that will be saved* (Mt 24:12-13); he was of course promising salvation to those who persevere in charity, not in iniquity. But where there's charity, there can be none of those evil activities which separate one from the kingdom of God. *For the whole law is fulfilled in the one saying, where it is written, You shall love your neighbor as yourself* (Gal 5:14).

Then again, even if there's a difference between those who reign or rule in a kingdom and those who don't, still they all have to be in the one kingdom, or else they will be reckoned among enemies or aliens. All Romans, you see, possess the Roman kingdom, although they aren't all reigning or ruling in it. Anyway, the apostle didn't say, *Those who do such things* will not reign with God, but *will not possess the kingdom of God.* The same thing is also said about flesh and blood: *Flesh and blood will not possess the kingdom of God,* because *this perishable thing will put on imperishability, and this mortal thing will put on immortality* (1 Cor 15:50.53); so that it will no longer be flesh and blood, but from being a mere embodiment of soul, it will be privileged to have the nature and the qualities of an embodiment of spirit.[37]

At the very least they should be terrified by the prospect of that final sentence of our judge, which he wished to be declared to us now, precisely in order that his faithful might be forewarned about it, and forearmed against it; giving *those who fear him a sign, to flee from the face of the bow* (Ps 60:4). Except, you see, for those who will also judge with him, to whom he promised, *You shall sit upon twelve thrones, judging the twelve tribes of Israel* (Mt 19:28)—in this number of judges are to be understood all who have given up everything of their own for the sake of the gospel, and followed the Lord. The number twelve, that is to say, refers to a certain totality. I mean it can't be the case that the apostle Paul won't be included, just because he wasn't one of those twelve. So except for those, whom he also indicated with the name of angels, when he said, *When the Son of man comes to judge with his angels* (Mk 8:38), because angels, of course, are messengers. And we rightly take as messengers all those who bring people the message of heavenly salvation. So the evangelists too can be understood as good messengers; and about John the Baptist it was said, *Behold, I am sending my messenger before my face* (Mk 1:2; Mal 3:1).

So these, as I had started to say, excepted, the rest of the multitude of mankind, as is clear from the words of the Lord himself, will be divided into two parts. He is going to place the sheep, you see, on his right hand, the goats on his left; and the sheep, that is the just, will be told, *Come, blessed of my Father, receive the kingdom which has been prepared for you from the foundation of the world.* It's about this kingdom, of course, that the apostle was speaking when he was making his list of evil actions: *since those who do such things will not possess the kingdom of God* (Gal 5:21). Listen to what those on the left will hear: *Go,* he says, *into the eternal fire, which has been prepared for the devil and his angels* (Mt 25:34.41). So then, who would dare to rely on the name of Christian, instead of listening with complete obedience and fear to the apostle when he says, *For you must be aware of this, knowing that no fornicator, or impure or greedy person, which is the worship of idols, has an inheritance in the kingdom of Christ and of God. Let nobody lead you astray with empty words; for it is because of these things that the wrath of God comes upon the children of unbelief. And so do not let yourselves become their partners* (Eph 5:5-7). And to the Corinthians he has this to say, still more fully: *Do not be mistaken; neither fornicators, nor the worshipers of idols, nor adulterers, nor the effeminate, nor those who lie with men, nor thieves, nor greedy misers, nor drunkards, nor those who curse others, nor the grasping, will possess the kingdom of God.* But notice how he removed fear and despair of salvation from those who committed these things in their old lives: *And these things indeed,* he says, *you were; but you have been washed, but you have been sanctified in the name of our Lord Jesus Christ, and in the Spirit of our God* (1 Cor 6:9-11).

Recourse to the keys of the Church

9. So can any, who find themselves held after baptism in bondage to any of their previous sins, be such enemies to themselves that they still hesitate to change their way of life while there is time, when they are sinning like that, and still remaining alive? It's obvious, you see, that because they are persistently sinning like that, *they are storing up for themselves wrath on the day of wrath and of the revelation of the just judgment of God.* As for the fact, though, that they are still alive, *the patience of God is intent on bringing them to repentance* (Rom 2:5.4). Being therefore entangled in the chains of such death-dealing sins, can they decline to take refuge in the keys of the Church, or put it off, or hesitate

about it, though they can be loosed by them on earth, in order to be loosed in heaven? And can they have the nerve to promise themselves some kind of salvation after this life just because they are called Christians, and fail to tremble at that thunderous truth uttered by the Lord, *Not everyone who says to me, Lord, Lord, will enter into the kingdom of heaven; but the one who does the will of my Father who is in heaven, that is the one who will enter into the kingdom of heaven* (Mt 7:21)?

Why, the apostle, writing to the Galatians, comes to the same conclusion, doesn't he, after listing such sins? *The works of the flesh*, he says, *are manifest, which are fornications, impurities, licentious behavior, the worship of idols, sorcery, enmities, rivalries, jealousies, animosities, dissensions, heresies, envy, drunkenness, rivalries, and things like that; which I warn you, as I have warned you before, that those who do such things will not possess the kingdom of God* (Gal 5:19-21).[38] So let people pass judgment on themselves voluntarily in these matters, while they can, and change their morals for the better; or else, when they no longer can, they will have judgment passed on them, and against their will, by the Lord. And when they have imposed on themselves a sentence of the harshest medicine, but still medicine, let them come to the prelates, by whom the keys in the Church are wielded for their benefit; and now beginning, so to say, to be good children, and observing the rulings of those who play the role of mother in the Church, let them accept from those in charge of the sacraments the manner of making amends required of them. So, in devoutly and suppliantly offering *the sacrifice of a crushed and contrite heart* (Ps 51:17), let them, all the same, do what will not only avail themselves for receiving salvation, but also serve others as an example. This means, that if their sins have not only gravely damaged themselves, but have also been such a scandal to others, and if the prelate considers this will be of value to the Church, they should not refuse to do their penance in the full knowledge of others, even of the whole congregation; they should not jib at this, not add, through shame, the tumor of conceit to an already mortal and death-dealing wound. They must always remember that *God withstands the proud, but gives grace to the humble* (1 Pt 5:5). After all, what could be more unprofitable, more perverse, than not to be ashamed of the wound, which cannot be hidden, and to be ashamed of the dressing on it?

The principles governing excommunication

10. None of you, brothers and sisters, should consider that you should ignore this advice of salutary penance, simply because you may perhaps notice and be aware that many people approach the sacraments of the altar, about whose wrongdoings of this sort you are by no means ignorant. You see, many correct themselves, like Peter; many are tolerated, like Judas; many are unknown until the Lord comes, *who will light up things hidden in the darkness, and manifest the thoughts of the heart* (1 Cor 4:5). I mean there are plenty of people who are unwilling to accuse others, for the simple reason that they are eager themselves to be excused by them. Plenty of good Christians, on the other hand, keep silent,

and tolerate the sins of others which they know about, for the good reason that they lack documentary evidence, and so cannot prove to the ecclesiastical judges what they themselves know. You see, while some things may be true, the judge should not, all the same, be too ready to believe them, unless they can be demonstrated by sure and certain indications.

We, for our part, though, cannot ban any from communion (although such a ban is not a capital sentence, but a remedial one) unless they have either freely confessed, or else been duly charged and convicted by the judgment of some court, whether secular or ecclesiastical. Who, after all, would dare to take each function upon himself and be both accuser and judge of anybody?[39] We can also take the apostle Paul to have briefly suggested a rule of this sort in his letter to the Corinthians, when he listed some such offenses, and gave the form and suchlike for ecclesiastical judgments from some particular instances. He said, you see, *I wrote to you in the letter not to mingle with fornicators; not meaning, of course, the fornicators of this world, or the greedy or the grasping, or the worshipers of idols; otherwise you would have to depart from this world* (1 Cor 5:9-10). People living in this world, after all, cannot help living with others of that sort; nor can they win them for Christ, if they altogether shun their company and conversation. Which is why the Lord used to eat with tax men and sinners, and said, *It is not the healthy who need the doctor, but those who are ill. For I did not come to call the just, but sinners* (Mk 2:17). And that's why the apostle goes on to add, *But now I wrote to you not to mingle, if any brother is named as a fornicator, or a worshiper of idols, or miserly, or given to cursing others, or a drunkard, or rapacious; with persons of that sort not even to take food. For what business is it of mine to judge outsiders? It is for you, is it not, to pass judgment on insiders? On outsiders, though, God will pass judgment. Take away the evil person from among you* (1 Cor 5:11-13).

By these words he shows clearly enough,[40] that it is not rashly, or by any means you like, that evil persons are to be removed from the Church's communion, but by a formal judgment; so that if they cannot be removed by such a judgment, they should rather be tolerated. Otherwise, if anyone is so perversely bent on avoiding the company of evil persons that he withdraws from the Church himself, he will beat in the race to gehenna[41] those he appears to be fleeing from. Here too examples have been set before us in the holy scriptures, as of the harvest, that the chaff is to be borne with until the final winnowing, or of those nets, in which the good fish tolerate the bad until the separation which is going to take place on the shore, that is at the end of the age.[42]

Nor is this place, you see, contradicted by what the apostle says somewhere else: *Who are you to pass judgment on another's servant? It is to his own Lord that he stands or falls* (Rom 14:4). You see he didn't want man to be judged by man on the strength of an arbitrary suspicion, or even by some extraordinary procedure adopted for the occasion, but rather in accordance with Church order, by the law of God; whether on his confessing of his own accord, or his being charged and convicted. Otherwise, why did he say, *If any brother is named as a fornicator, or a worshiper of idols*, etc., unless he meant that naming to be understood by which a person is declared to be such when sentence is passed after due and complete judicial process? Because if mere naming is sufficient, many innocent people are liable to be condemned, since they are often named in the bringing of false charges.[43]

Why choose to imitate the morals of bad clergy, rather than the example of Christ?

11. So those whom we are strongly advising to repent should not go looking for companions in punishment; nor should they be pleased because they can find so many. I mean, they will not burn any the less fiercely, just because they are burning together with many others. You see, this is not a sure counsel of sanity, but the futile consolation of a bad will. Or perhaps they observe that many of their superiors and ministers in high ecclesiastical positions do not lead lives that match the words and sacraments which are administered by them to the people? Oh, miserable creatures, fixing their eyes so intently on these men that they forget Christ! And he having forewarned us so long ago rather to comply with the law of God, than to think we should imitate those who do not do what they say;[44] and having sent the man who was to betray him out to preach the gospel with the others, putting up with him to the very end![45] These people, though, who choose to imitate the bad behavior of their leaders, instead of keeping the commandments of the Lord which they preach, are as absurd and preposterous and wretched as if some traveler were to infer that he has to stand still on the road, when he sees a milestone full of letters giving information about the way, and not walking along it. I mean, why doesn't he rather, if he wants to reach his destination, look out for and follow such companions as will both show him the right way and also walk along it steadily and smartly?

But if people of this sort are lacking, or rather if they are somewhat inconspicuous, because they cannot be lacking—you see, people don't look with such assiduous charity for something to praise and imitate, as they do with malice and suspicion for something to grumble about and deceive themselves with; this partly by not finding any good people, inasmuch as they are themselves bad; partly by being afraid of finding them, inasmuch as they wish to go on being bad always. But still, let us grant that people worthy of imitation are not at all conspicuous nowadays. If any of you think this, fix the gaze of your mind upon the Lord, who became man in order to teach man how to live. If Christ is dwelling in the inner man through faith in your heart,[46] and if you recall that thing that John said, *Whoever says that he abides in Christ, ought himself to walk as he walked* (1 Jn 2:6); in this way you won't lack someone to follow, and when others see you they will stop complaining about the dearth of good people.

I mean, if you don't know what it is to live rightly, get to know the divine commandments. Perhaps, after all, there are many people who do live rightly; but the reason nobody seems to you to live rightly is that you are ignorant of what living rightly means. If however you do know, act on what you know, so that you yourself may have what you are looking for, and may also show others something to imitate. Turn your mind to Christ, turn to the apostles, of whom the last and least[47] is the one who said, *Be imitators of me as I too am of Christ* (1 Cor 4:16). Turn your mind to all those thousands of martyrs. I mean, why do you take such pleasure in celebrating their birthdays with your disgraceful carousals, and take no pleasure in following their lives by decent behavior? There you will see not only men, but also women, finally boys and girls, who were neither taken in through unreadiness, nor perverted through wickedness, nor broken through fear of danger, nor corrupted through love of the world. In this way, finding yourself without any excuses at all, you will be surrounded not only by the unquestionable rightness of the commandments, but also by a countless multitude of good examples.

Why go on ignoring the truth that God's patience is trying to lead you to repentance?

12. But about the salutary value of repentance, let us complete for once what we set out to do. If by now despairing of being healed you are adding sins to sins, as it is written, *The sinner, when he plumbs the depths of evil, is contemptuous* (Prv 18:3); don't be contemptuous, don't despair. Cry out to the Lord even from the depths, and say to him, *Out of the depths have I cried out to you, Lord; Lord, listen to my voice. May your ears be attentive to the voice of my pleading. If you take note of iniquities, Lord, Lord, who will endure? Since with you there is graciousness* (Ps 130:1-4). It was from such depths that the people of Nineveh cried out, and they discovered this graciousness; and the threats of the prophet were more easily discounted, than the humiliation of repentance.[48]

Here perhaps you will say, "But I have already been baptized in Christ, by whom all my past sins were forgiven. I have become vile in the extreme by going back to my old ways; a dog, revolting to the eyes of God, returning to its vomit.[49] *Where shall I go from his Spirit, and where shall I flee from his face?* (Ps 139:7)."

Where indeed, brother, but to the mercy, by repenting, of the one whose authority, by sinning, you have scorned? There is nowhere, you see, anyone can rightly flee to from him, except to him; from his severity to his goodness. What place is there, after all, that will receive you as a refugee, where his presence won't find you? If you climb up to heaven, he is there; if you go down to the underworld, he is present. So take your wings the direct way, and dwell in hope at the end of this age; even there his hand will lead you, and his right hand bring you through.[50] You see, whatever you have done, whatever sins you have committed, you are still in this life, from which God would certainly remove you, if he didn't want to heal you. So why go on refusing to admit that God's patience is trying to induce you to repent?[51] You see, he was unable by crying out to you to persuade you not to turn away from him; but now by sparing you he is crying out to you to come back to him.

Look at David the king; he too, of course, had already received the sacraments of that time, he had already, naturally, been circumcised, which for our fathers took the place of baptism; on this point, you see, the apostle says that Saint Abraham had received it as a seal of the justice of faith.[52] He had also already been anointed with that revered anointing by which the Church's royal priesthood was prefigured. Becoming guilty at a stroke of both adultery and murder,[53] it was not for all that in vain that he cried out, penitent, to the Lord from such a monstrous and dizzy depth of wickedness, saying, *Turn your face away from my sins, and blot out all my iniquities.* On what grounds, in the end, but that he also says, *My iniquity I myself acknowledge, and my sin is always before me?* But what did he offer to the Lord, to appease him? *Since if you had wanted a sacrifice, I would of course have given it; you will not take pleasure in burnt offerings. A sacrifice to God is an afflicted heart; a contrite and humbled heart God does not spurn* (Ps 51:9.3.16-17). So he not only made a devout offering, but also by saying these things he showed us what ought to be offered.

You see, it's not enough to change one's behavior for the better, and to give up bad activities, unless for things you have already done you also make it up to God by the sorrow of repentance, by the groans of humility, by the sacrifice of a contrite heart, with almsgiving thrown in to help you along. *Blessed*, you see, *are the merciful, since God will have mercy on them* (Mt 5:7). It wasn't said, after all, that we should just abstain from committing sins. *But also pray to the Lord*, it says, *about your past sins, that they may be forgiven you* (Sir 21:1). And Peter was also a believer, had already also baptized others in Christ.[54] So take a look at Peter relying on himself, accused and fearful, wounded, weeping and healed.[55] Again, now after the coming of the Holy Spirit from heaven, a certain Simon wanted to buy this selfsame Holy Spirit with money, planning a most infamous and impious transaction, after he had already been baptized in Christ; and yet, when rebuked by Peter, he accepted his advice to repent.[56] There is also what the apostle Paul says, who used to send his letters, of course, to believers: *Lest God should humiliate me when I come to you again, and I should have to mourn many of those who sinned before, and have not repented over the impurity and licentiousness and fornication which they committed* (2 Cor 12:21). So we are surrounded both by instructions on right behavior and by examples of people not only behaving rightly but also repenting, in order to regain the spiritual health that was lost by sinning.

But very well, suppose it is uncertain whether God will pardon you. What do you lose when you beseech God, seeing that you didn't hesitate to lose your spiritual health when you offended God? Who can be certain, after all, that the emperor will grant a pardon either? And yet money is poured out, seas are crossed, the uncertainty of storms braved; and to avoid death, death itself is practically experienced. And yet the keys of the Church are more dependable than *the hearts of kings* (Sir 8:2); we are promised that whatever is loosed by these keys on earth is also loosed in heaven (Mt 16:19; 18:18). And the humility with which one humbles oneself before the Church of God is much more honorable;[57] and a much lighter labor is imposed, and without any risk at all of temporal death, eternal death is avoided.

NOTES

1. This date is suggested by Fischer and Kunzelmann. It would mean that this is one of the first sermons Augustine ever preached, after being ordained priest; and it would also mean that it was preached in Hippo Regius. One strong objection to this date is that he refers once or twice in the course of the sermon to *nos antistites*; and I wonder if any clergy except bishops were called *antistites*. If he had been preaching in the presence of Bishop Valerius, which he may well have been, I suppose he could have included himself as sharing in the bishop's presidency of the congregation; *antistes* meaning in fact one who presides or stands at the head of a group.

But a much stronger objection lies in doubts about the very authenticity of the sermon. It was rejected by no less an authority than Erasmus. True, the Maurists, whose opinion carries enormous weight, disagree with that prince of Renaissance scholars, and consider that both style and content are redolent of Augustine. Here, however, I very definitely cast my vote with Erasmus. The sermon lacks the breath of life that marks Augustine's preaching, even at its least inspired. What we have here, I am convinced, is a preacher of a considerably later date modeling himself on Augustine, pretending indeed to be Augustine. This view will be supported in further notes on the text.

2. Reading *non cogitet* instead of the text's *non cogitat*, are not thinking of drawing near to God.

3. Quite different in modern translations: RSV, "the early rain also covers it with pools."

4. See Ps 146:7-8.

5. *Diligenter attendentibus*; one would normally translate this "those who pay careful attention." But to take it as referring to regular church attendance makes better sense in the context—and is one small pointer to the sermon's not being by Augustine.

6. See Jn 16:21.

7. Not just baptism, but the whole rite of initiation, consisting of baptism, confirmation and first communion.

8. These are the questions put to those about to be baptized on renouncing Satan and so on; also, and more important, the questions put to them about their faith as they are being baptized. Still in Augustine's day, and probably for a century or two later, the baptismal formula was the interrogatory one: "Do you believe in God the Father almighty, maker of heaven and earth?" "I do"—and the neophytes were immersed once; and so on for two more times as they declared their faith in Jesus Christ his only Son, etc., and in the Holy Spirit etc. Now when infants were being baptized it was their parents or godparents who said "I do," while the infant was immersed three times.

9. See Jb 14:4-5, LXX.

10. The Latin says, "with the perpetual humility of supplication." A transfer of the adjective seems called for in English.

11. While this is a perfectly correct use of the verb *paenitet* to mean "to regret" or "to be dissatisfied with," as well as "to repent," it does not seem to me to be characteristic of Augustine. This whole section suggests to me the mind and hand of the admiring imitator, as indeed did the previous one, where the preacher—or composer—was determined to bring in every bit of Augustinian teaching he could muster.

12. See 1 Cor 13:12.

13. Adam is here to some extent taking on an attribute of Cain; see Gn 4:12.

14. By Satan, who with his angels is represented by the lion cubs.

15. See 1 Cor 4:27; Rom 6:12.

16. See the ten commandments, Ex 20:1-17.

17. See Mk 10:21.

18. See 1 Cor 4:7.

19. In this paragraph he is talking of the clergy, and he is referring to them, not just in their administration of the sacraments but in their preaching too, the bread from heaven being the written word of God as well as the Word incarnate. From now until the end of the section he will have the clergy in mind, turning to the laity in the next section. The way this is done is to my mind a definite indication of a hand other than Augustine's.

20. In this last case he is thinking of the bishop hearing and settling disputes as a judge.

21. See Lk 10:10-11. Here we seem to be given a stream of consciousness without any real logical connection between sentences. This, surely, is *not* Augustine.

22. See 1 Cor 4:1.

23. *Stipendiaria multitudo*. In military terms *stipendiarius* just means serving for pay, and so would apply to all the *milites*, the soldiers he has just compared the clergy to. Here, however, it is contrasted with them, and so I translate as "auxiliary"; the irregular forces raised in the provinces to support the regular legions. It is this particular contrast between clergy and laity that I cannot envisage the real Augustine making; and particularly not when the preacher goes on, it seems, to regard the laity as "other Churches." The whole passage reeks of a crude imitation from a later, perhaps considerably later, period.

24. *Obligati*, masculine, qualifying the feminine *Ecclesiae*. This shows how forced is his calling the laity "provincial Churches." He only does so, one presumes, because of his quotation from Paul.

25. He is probably referring to 1 Cor 6:4-5; hardly a text setting up ecclesiastical courts!

26. The almost universal view of the Fathers, for which Augustine alone usually gets the blame. For the contemporary teaching of the Catholic Church on the subject, see the Vatican Council document on "The Church in the Modern World," *Gaudium et Spes*, 49-51.

27. The mortal wound that murder inflicts on the murderer, not the one he inflicts on his victim.

28. The kind of point Augustine makes in other sermons; but there with a suggestion of laughing at the simplicity of the faithful who assumed bishops didn't have to do this. Here, on the contrary, the preacher is saying it very solemnly, rather as if he too was a little surprised at having to do so. The whole tone is very far from that of Augustine himself. "We prelates," *nos antistites*; as remarked in note 1, the use of this word would probably militate against dating the sermon to 391, if by any remote chance it really was preached by Augustine.

29. See Jn 14:6.

30. Saying the Our Father at mass as a preparation for communion.

31. The devil.

32. See Rom 2:4-6.

33. Reading *cui caput est* instead of the text's *qui caput est*, who is the head.

34. Reading *ipsum est cui dixit* instead of the text's *ipse est cui dixit*, he it is to whom. Peter, though, did not address these words to Christ in person, but to his members the Church. The two phrases would sound almost identical to a stenographer, or to a copyist writing to dictation.

35. See Heb 6:19; 9:12.

36. There is an obvious connection in Latin between *regnum* and *regnare*, which is lacking in English between "kingdom" and "reign" or "rule."

37. The difference between what Paul actually calls "a psychic body" and "a pneumatic body." English, of course, has totally changed the meaning both of "psychic" and "pneumatic"; and while we do have the adjective "spiritual" to be a proper translation of *pneumatikos*, we don't have a word "soulish" to be a proper translation of *psychikos*. But it is very important to note how Paul contrasts *psyche*, soul, with *pneuma*, spirit, and in no way treats them as synonyms; and my translation is designed to keep that contrast.

38. He has several times quoted this passage before. Here it is again quoted without the slightest reference to previous use. Does this indicate that with section 9 we have a fragment from another sermon, joined on to the earlier one? Even if that is the case, it is still manifestly, to my mind, the Pseudo-Augustine, or Augustinaster, of a somewhat later epoch.

39. But is this possibility at issue here? It is the slackness of thought throughout that makes it impossible to accept this sermon as Augustine's.

40. Does he?

41. Reading *vincat ad gehennam* with the manuscripts, instead of the *vinciat ad gehennam*, he will bind them to gehenna, of the Maurist and other editors. This emendation makes much less sense than the manuscript reading; and to make the sense of this clear, I have simply added the words "in the race to."

42. See Lk 3:17; Mt 13:47-50.

43. Quite. But how this admirable conclusion can be drawn from the texts quoted, it is very hard indeed to see.

44. See Mt 23:3.

45. See Mt 10:2-5.

46. See Eph 3:16-17.

47. See 1 Cor 15:8-9.

48. See Jb 3.

49. See 2 Pt 2:22.

50. See Ps 139:8-10.

51. See Rom 2:4.

52. See Rom 4:11.

53. See 2 Sam 11.

54. This improbable assumption, that the disciples administered the Christian sacrament of baptism before Christ's final glorification and Pentecost, is presumably based on Jn 4:2.

55. See Mk 14:29.66-68; Lk 22:54-62.

56. See Acts 8:13-24. An emphasis, unusual in traditional comments on the story, on Simon's repentance.

57. Than the humility with which one grovels before kings.

SERMON 352

ON THE VALUE OF REPENTANCE

Date: 398[1]

The occasion for the sermon; the lector reciting Ps 51 without being instructed to do so

1. It is the voice of a penitent that can be recognized in the words with which we responded to the singer of the psalm: *Turn your face away from my sins, and blot out all my iniquities* (Ps 51:9). Since I hadn't prepared a sermon for your graces on this subject, I acknowledge that it is a command from the Lord that I should deal with it. What I intended today, you see, was to leave you all chewing the cud in quiet meditation, knowing how abundantly you have feasted on the word of God.[2] But because you all have such healthy appetites for what is set before you, you are very hungry every day. So may the Lord our God himself grant me sufficient capacity and you some useful listening. I am well aware, of course, that it is your good and sensible will that I am to serve. So let me receive the help, then, both of your prayers and your keen interest; your prayers to God, your interest in the word; so that I may say what the one who is feeding you through me himself considers to be of use to you.

So then, in these words we recognize the voice of a penitent: *Turn your face away from my sins, and blot out all my misdeeds.* Accordingly, I am bidden by God to say something about repentance. You see, it wasn't I who instructed the lector to sing this psalm; but it was that one up there[3] who decided what would be valuable for you to hear, and who instructed this boy[4] inwardly in his heart to give it to you. Let me say something about the value of repentance; especially, too, because the holy anniversary[5] will soon be upon us, which it is right for us to prepare for by humbling our souls and breaking in our bodies.

Repentance as a necessary approach to baptism

2. We find in sacred scripture a threefold consideration of repentance. Nobody, in the first place, can approach Christ's baptism, in which all sins are blotted out, in the right frame of mind without repenting of their old way of life. They aren't really choosing a new life, after all, unless they are sorry for the old one. Now I also have to prove this by the authority of the divine books, whether

those to be baptized have to repent. When the Holy Spirit, previously promised, was sent, and the Lord faithfully kept his promise, the disciples, as you know, on receiving the Holy Spirit, began to speak in all languages, so that everyone among those present recognized his own language. Shaken to the core by this miracle, they begged the apostles for advice about life. Then Peter announced to them that they must worship the one they had crucified, and now in faith drink his blood, which they had shed in their savage rage.

But once our Lord Jesus Christ had been proclaimed to them, and they had acknowledged their guilt, they were pricked to the heart, so as to fulfill in their own persons what the prophet had long ago foretold: *I have been converted into my distress, while the thorn is being stuck in* (Ps 32:4). They were converted, you see, into the distress of sorrow, when the thorn was being stuck in, the thorn of the recollection of sin. After all, they hadn't thought they had done anything bad, as long as the thorn had not been stuck in. But *while Peter was speaking*—so that you may recognize the thorn stuck in, scripture said, *While Peter was speaking, they were pricked to the heart* (Acts 2:37). Accordingly, in the same psalm, after it says, *I have been converted into my distress, while the thorn is being stuck in*, it continues, *I know my sin, and I have not concealed my misdeed. I said, I will declare against myself my offense to the Lord; you, then, have forgiven the impiety of my heart* (Ps 32:5).

So when they were pricked by that thorn of recollection, and said to the apostles, *So what shall we do? Peter said to them, Repent, and be baptized, every one of you, in the name of our Lord Jesus Christ; and your sins shall be forgiven* (Acts 2:37-38). So in the meantime, right now, if there happen to be any present of the group who are preparing to be baptized—I think, you see, they are paying all the keener attention to the word, the closer they are to being pardoned—these are the ones I am first addressing a few words to, so that they may lift up their spirits in hope. Let their love be directed to becoming what they are not, their hatred to what they have been. Let them already in desire conceive the new self that is to be born. Whatever from their past life has been gnawing away at their consciences, whatever has been troubling them, absolutely anything at all, big matter or small, mentionable or unmentionable, they must have no doubt at all that it can be forgiven. Human hesitation must not be allowed to hold against oneself, what God's compassion wishes to forgive.

On Paul's statement, 1 Cor 10:4, that the rock was Christ

3. We should each of us faithfully recall, too, an example offered us in that first people. The apostle says, you see, *All these things were our models* (1 Cor 10:6), when he was talking about such things. I mean, what had he just said? *For I would not have you ignorant, brothers, that all our fathers were under the cloud; and all were baptized in Moses in the cloud and in the sea; and all ate the same spiritual food, and all drank the same spiritual drink. For they drank from the spiritual rock that was following them. Now the rock was Christ* (1 Cor 10:1-4). The one who said that these things were our models, is one whom no

believer has ever contradicted. And while he mentioned many things, he only explained one of them, saying, *Now the rock was Christ.* In explaining a single item, he left us the others to be inquired into; but to save inquirers from going astray by departing from Christ, and to enable them to seek surely, founded on rock,[6] *The rock,* he said, *was Christ.* He said those things were our models, and they are all obscure. Who could unpack these well wrapped models? Who could open them up, who would dare to shake them out? In these densest possible thickets, so to say, and these thick shadows he has lit a light: *The rock,* he says, *was Christ.*

So now that the light has been brought, let us inquire what the other things may mean; what the significance may be of the sea, the cloud, the manna. He didn't explain these things, you see, but he showed us what the rock was. The passing through the sea is baptism. But because baptism, that is to say the water of salvation, has no power to save unless it has been consecrated by the name of Christ, who shed his blood for us, the water is signed with his cross.[7] For that model of baptism to signify this, it was in the Red Sea.[8] The manna from heaven is clearly expounded by the Lord himself. *Your fathers,* he said, *ate manna in the desert, and are dead* (Jn 6:51). How, after all, would they remain alive, seeing that the model could prefigure and foretell life, but could not be life? *They ate manna,* he said, *and are dead*; that is, the manna they ate was unable to set them free from death; not that the manna itself was death, but that it didn't set them free from death. It was the one, you see, who was prefigured by the manna who was going to set us free from death. It was certainly from heaven that the manna came, so notice whom it prefigured: *I am,* he said, *the living bread, who have come down from heaven* (Jn 6:51).

Like keen and careful and attentive students, though, pay close attention to the Lord's words, so that you may make good progress, and know both how to read and to listen to good effect. *They ate,* he said,[9] *the same spiritual food* (1 Cor 10:3). What does *the same* mean, if not the same as we do? I begin to see that what I have undertaken to say is going to cause me some difficulties in expressing and explaining it; but I shall be greatly assisted by your good will, so please let that obtain the necessary facility for me from the Lord. *They ate,* he said, *the same spiritual food.* It should have been enough to say, "They ate spiritual food"; he said *the same.* I can't see how I can understand *the same,* unless it means the same as we too eat.

"What's this, then?" someone will say. "That manna was the same thing as I now receive? So nothing new has come now, if it was already there before. So the scandal of the cross has been canceled out."[10]

So how can it be *the same*? Only because he added *spiritual.* Because those who received that manna in such a way that they simply thought their bodily needs were being satisfied, and their bellies fed, not their minds,[11] didn't eat anything very tremendous—their needs were satisfied. God just fed some of the people, to others he had something to tell. The first sort ate bodily food, not spiritual food.

So whom is he calling *our fathers* (1 Cor 10:1), who he says ate the same spiritual food? Who do we suppose they can be, brothers and sisters, but those who really and truly were our fathers—or rather, not were our fathers, but are so? I mean, they are all among the living.[12] In the same sort of way, you see, the Lord says to some of those who did not believe, *Your fathers ate manna in the desert, and are dead* (Jn 6:49). What, after all, does *your fathers* mean, but those whom you are imitating by your unbelief, whose ways you follow by not believing and by resisting God? It's in this sense that he says to some of them, *You are from your father the devil* (Jn 8:44). Not, of course, that the devil created any human being by his power, or begot any by procreation; and yet he is called the father of the godless, not in virtue of procreation, but of imitation. Just as on the other hand the good are told, *So you are the seed of Abraham* (Gal 3:29), when he is speaking to Gentiles, who did not trace their descent according to the flesh from the stock of Abraham. They were his descendants, you see, not by being born of him but by imitating him. Abraham's fatherhood, on the other hand, is annulled for the unfaithful and they are turned into aliens, when the Lord says to them, *If you were the sons of Abraham, you would do the works of Abraham* (Jn 8:39). And in order to uproot the bad trees who boasted of their descent from Abraham, sons are promised to Abraham out of stones.[13]

So just as the Lord says in this place, *Your fathers ate manna in the desert and are dead*—they didn't, you see, understand what they ate, and so by not understanding, they only ate bodily food—so the apostle too says *our fathers*, not the fathers of the unbelieving, not the fathers of the godless, eating and dying, but our fathers, fathers of the faithful, ate spiritual food, and therefore *the same* food. *Our fathers*, he says, *ate the same spiritual food and drank the same spiritual drink* (1 Cor 10:1.4). There were people there, you see, who could understand what they were eating; there were some there who had a better taste of Christ in their hearts than of the manna in their mouths. Why should I speak of others? First and foremost among them was Moses himself, the servant of God, *faithful in all his house* (Heb 3:2), well aware of what he was dispensing, aware that things had to be provided then which were a closed secret for contemporaries, an open book for the people of the future. So let me put it in a nutshell: whoever understood Christ in the manna, ate the same spiritual food as us; while whoever looked to the manna simply to fill their stomachs, ate as the fathers of unbelievers, and are dead.

In the same way too, the same drink; because *the rock was Christ*.[14] So they drank the same drink as we do, but spiritual drink; those that is, who received it in faith, not those, who merely gulped it down in the body. You heard it was the same drink; *the rock was Christ*. It wasn't, after all, one Christ then, another now. Yes, that was another actual rock, just as it was another actual stone which Jacob put under his head, another lamb killed so that the passover might be eaten;[15] another ram caught by its horns in the thicket ready to be sacrificed, when Abraham was ordered to spare his son, having first been ordered to offer him in sacrifice;[16] one sheep and another sheep, one stone and another stone, still the same Christ, though; therefore the same food, therefore the same drink. Finally, that rock was struck with wood, so that water might flow from it; it was struck, of course, with a rod. Why with something made of wood, not of iron, if not because the cross came into contact with Christ in order to pour out grace for us to drink?[17] So the same food, the same drink—but for those who understood and believed. For those who didn't understand, though, only that manna, only that water; that food for the hungry, that drink for the thirsty; neither that nor this for the believer; for the believer, the same as now. Then, you see, Christ was going to come, now he has come. He was going to come, and he has come; different tenses of the verb, but the same Christ.[18]

The significance of Moses' doubting

4. I also want to say something about the doubts the servant of God, Moses, felt, because the matter has come up. In this too, you see, he was representative of the saints of the Old Testament. Moses had his doubts about the water; when he struck the rock with his rod, so that water flowed out, he doubted. Anyone reading the story, though, could easily fail to notice his doubting, and not understand, because he would be reluctant to inquire too closely.[19] However, that doubting displeased the Lord God, and he noted it, to the extent not only of rebuking, but of punishing it. It was because of this doubting, you see, that Moses is told, *You shall not be the one to bring this people into the promised land* (Nm 20:12). *Climb the mountain and die there* (Dt 32:49-50). God is obviously seen here to be angry. So what about Moses, my brothers and sisters? All that labor of his, all his anxieties for the people, and that charity which prompts him to say, *If you forgive them their sin, forgive it; if not, though, blot me out from your book* (Ex 32:32)—was it all passed over because of a sudden, unpremeditated doubt? And what about the reader's concluding words, when he read the apostle, *Charity never falls away* (1 Cor 13:8)?

Your enthusiasm, when I set some problems before you to be solved, has led me to set you another one, which perhaps you weren't curious about. So let's see, and still make an effort to the best of our ability to penetrate this mystery. God is angry, he says Moses is not going to lead the people into the promised land; he tells him to climb the mountain and die. And yet he gives Moses many instructions about what is to be done, he tells him what to do, how to make arrangements for the people, how he is not to leave them neglected and scattered. He would never, surely, agree to give such instructions to a man he had rejected and condemned. And here's something even more remarkable for you. When Moses was told that he himself would not lead the people into the promised land (that, you see, was what God had decided for the sake of a definite and significant dispensation), another person was chosen in his stead, Jesus Nave; and this man wasn't previously called by that name, he was called Auses.[20] And when Moses entrusted him with the task of bringing the people in, he summoned him, and changed his name, and called him Jesus; so that the people of God would enter the promised land not under Moses but under Jesus, that is to say, not under the law but under grace. But just as that man wasn't the true Jesus, but a model one, so too that promised land wasn't the real one, but a model one. It was a temporary one, you see, for the first people; whereas the one that has been promised to us will be eternal. But eternal realities were being promised and foretold under temporal, time-bound, models and symbols. So just as he wasn't the real Jesus, and neither was that the real promised land, but the model or symbolic one; so too the manna wasn't really heavenly food, but a symbol of it; so too that rock wasn't really Christ, but only symbolically, and so with all the other things.

So then, what kind of consideration does the doubting of Moses demand of us? There too, perhaps, there may be some symbolic or figurative meaning, beckoning persons of understanding, moving them to inquire further, and challenging their intelligence. I observe, you see, after that doubting, and after God's anger, and after the threat of death, and after the removal of Moses from leading the people into the promised land, that God spoke frequently to Moses as to a friend, as he also used to speak previously;[21] to the extent that Moses was set before Jesus Nave himself as an example of obedience, and God admonished him to serve him in the same way as Moses had done; and promised he would be with him just as he had been with Moses.[22] Evidently, my dearest friends, God himself is obliging us not to find fault airily with the doubting of Moses, but to understand it. The rock lying there had a figurative meaning, the rod striking it had a figurative meaning, the water flowing from it had a figurative meaning, Moses' doubting also had a figurative meaning. Moses' doubts began when the wood came into contact with the rock.

Now the quick-witted are flying ahead; let them rather wait patiently for the slow-coaches. Moses doubted when the wood came into contact with the rock; the disciples doubted, when they saw the Lord crucified. Moses figuratively stood for them; he stood for that Peter with his threefold denial. Why did Peter doubt? Because the wood approached the rock. When the Lord himself was foretelling the kind of death he would die, that is his cross, Peter was horrified: *Far be this from you, Lord; this shall not happen* (Mt 16:2). You doubt, because you see the rod hanging over the rock. That's why the disciples then lost the hope they had placed in the Lord; it had somehow been cut off when they saw him crucified, when they mourned him slain. He came upon them after his resurrection talking to one another about this matter, in a sad conversation. He kept their eyes from recognizing him, not to remove himself from believers, but to put them off while they were still doubters, and he joined in their conversation as a third party, and asked them what they were talking about. They were astonished that he should be the only person not to know what had happened—to the very one, in fact, who was inquiring about it. *Are you the only stranger*, they said, *in Jerusalem?* And they went over all that had happened to Jesus. And straightaway they proceed to open up all the depth of their despair, and albeit unwittingly they show the doctor their wounds: *But we*, they say, *were hoping that with him there would be redemption for Israel* (Lk 24:13-21). There you are, doubt arose, because wood had come into contact with the rock. What Moses figuratively stood for was fulfilled.

The meaning of Moses' dying on the mountain

5. Let's take a look at this text too: *Climb the mountain and die* (Dt 32:49-50). The bodily death of Moses stood for the death of his doubting; but on the mountain. What marvelous mysteries! When this has been definitely explained and understood, how much sweeter it is to the taste than manna! Doubting was born at the rock, died on the mountain. When Christ was humbled in his passion, he was like a rock lying on the ground before their eyes. It was natural to have doubts about him; that humility was not holding out hopes for anything very great. His very humiliation naturally made him into a *stone of offense* (Is 8:14; 1 Pt 2:8). But once glorified by his resurrection he was seen to be great, he is now a mountain. So now let that doubt, which was born at the rock, die on the mountain. Let the disciples recognize where their salvation lies, let them summon up their hope again. Notice how that doubting dies, notice how Moses dies on the mountain. Let him not enter the promised land; we don't want any doubting there; let it die.

Let Christ now show us how it dies. Peter trembled, and denied three times.[23] *The rock, you see, was Christ* (1 Cor 10:4). He rose again, he became a mountain; he even gave Peter courage. But doubt must die. How does it die? *Peter, do you love me?* (Jn 21:15-17). It's the inspector of hearts, the knower of hearts, questioning him; and he wants to hear that he is loved, and once isn't enough. He asks this question, he hears the answer to the point of wearying Peter himself. He's surprised, you see, at being questioned by one who knows the answer; but to be asked so many times as well, when once would be enough to answer even someone who didn't know! But it's as though the Lord were saying to you, "I'm waiting; the appointed number must be completed; he must confess three times out of love, because he denied three times out of fear." So the Lord asking that question so many times was the Lord slaying that doubt on the mountain.

The meaning of the cloud, and of various trials
experienced by the Israelites in the desert

6. So what then, my dearest friends, if these things are now crystal-clear? It wasn't to cheat us, but to give us some innocent fun that they were first locked up in obscurity. They wouldn't be grasped, you see, with such pleasure, if they were rendered cheap by being laid out in the open. So now then, let those who will be seeking baptism, whom I had begun to address, look to their business. The Red Sea was baptism, the people were baptized by crossing it. The actual crossing was the baptism, but in a cloud. What was being foretold, you see, was still cloudy and obscure; what was being promised was still being concealed. Now, however, the cloud has gone away, the fine weather of truth made manifest has come; because the veil, too, through which Moses used to speak, has also been removed.[24] This veil was also hanging in the temple, to prevent the secrets of the temple being seen; but the veil was torn in two by the cross of Christ, to open them to public view.[25]

So come to baptism; set out fearlessly on your way through the Red Sea;

don't worry about your past sins following you, like the Egyptians. Your sins were oppressing you with the harsh burden of slavery, but in Egypt, in the love of this world, in exile in a distant country;[26] they were forcing you to engage in earthly pursuits, like making bricks; you were working at muddy activities. Your sins are oppressing you, come to baptism with nothing to fear; the enemy will be able to follow as far as the water, there he will die. Be afraid of something from your past life, believe that something of your sins is going to remain, if a single one of the Egyptians remained alive.[27]

But I hear the voice of the sluggards:[28] "I," he says, "am not afraid of past sins; I don't doubt they are all forgiven me in the holy water, and also through the charity of the Church; but it's future sins I'm afraid of."[29]

So do you prefer to stay behind in Egypt? Right now escape from your present enemy, who has already been oppressing you, and already enslaved you. Why think up enemies for yourself in the future? What you have already done will remain done, even if you don't want it to; what you think you are going to do won't be done if you want it not to be.

"But the way is dangerous; I mean, even when I've crossed the Red Sea, I won't yet be in the promised land. That people was led a long journey through the desert."

Right now, get yourself liberated from Egypt. So what's the trouble then? Do you think the one who rescued you from the old captivity won't still be there to help you along the way? Can't the one who delivered you from your old enemies put down your new foes? Just cross over fearlessly, go on walking fearlessly, be obedient. Don't be a bitter disappointment to this Moses, whose obedience was typified by that one.[30]

I admit, there's no lack of enemies. Just as there was no lack of them to pursue them as they escaped, so there was no lack of them to obstruct them as they went on their way. Yes, dearly beloved, they did indeed represent us. Meanwhile, don't let there be anything in you which can sadden Moses; don't be the bitter water, which that people couldn't drink after the Red Sea. There too, you see, they underwent temptation and trial. And yet when this sort of thing happens, when the people become bitter, we show them Christ, what he endured for their sake, how he shed his blood for them; and they quieted down, as though we were putting wood into the water.[31]

You will certainly have Amalek as an enemy barring your progress.[32] That was when Moses prayed, when he stretched out his arms; and when he dropped his arms, Amalek grew stronger; when he stretched out his arms, Amalek fell back. Let your arms too be stretched out, let the Amalek fall back who is tempting you and barring your progress on this journey; be watchful and sober in prayer, in good works;[33] not, though, apart from Christ, because that stretching out of the arms was the cross of Christ. The apostle is being stretched out on it, when he says, *The world has been crucified to me, and I to the world* (Gal 6:14). So let Amalek fall back, be defeated, and not bar the passage of God's people. If you drop your arms from doing good works, from the cross of Christ, Amalek will prevail.

All the same, you mustn't think that you are in every respect or immediately going to be strong, or on the other hand going to fail utterly by despairing. After all, that alternation of failure and of strength in the arms of God's servant Moses was, perhaps, your alternation. Sometimes, you see, you fail in your trials and temptations, but don't totally succumb to them. He let his arms droop a little, but didn't collapse altogether. *If I were to say, My foot has slipped; behold, your mercy, Lord, would come to my help* (Ps 94:18). So don't be afraid; the one is present on the journey to help you along, who was not absent in Egypt to set you free. Don't be afraid, step out along the road, be confident and throw care to the winds. Sometimes he lowered his arms, sometimes he lifted them up; anyway, Amalek was defeated. They were able to wage war, they were not able to win.

A second kind of repentance, to be practiced by everyone every day

7. And so we are reminded to talk now about a second kind of repentance. I suggested, you remember, that it is considered in scripture under three headings. There is the first kind for the *competentes* and those thirsting to come to baptism;[34] this I have illustrated from the holy scriptures. Well, there's another sort of repentance for every day. And where can I show you this daily repentance? I have no better place to show it in than in the daily prayer, in which the Lord taught us to pray, showed us what we should say to the Father, and put the matter in these words: *Forgive us our debts, just as we too forgive our debtors* (Mt 6:12). What debts, brothers and sisters? Since debts here can only be understood as sins, are we praying for the debts that he canceled in baptism to be canceled over again? Undoubtedly every single Egyptian who was pursuing us is dead. If there's nothing left over from the enemies who were pursuing us, what are we praying to have forgiven, if not the drooping of our arms against Amalek? *Forgive us, just as we forgive.* He provided a medicine, he sealed a bargain. First he dictates a prayer, next he replies to you praying. He knows what rules govern the way things are done in heaven, and how you can obtain the things you desire. "Do you want to be forgiven? Forgive," he says.

What, I mean to say, have you got that you can grant God, by whom you want something to be granted to you? Is Christ the savior still walking about on earth? Is Zacchaeus still now joyfully receiving him in his house? Is Martha still entertaining him, and preparing dinner for him?[35] He doesn't need any of these things, he is seated at the right hand of the Father. But, *when you did it for one of the least of mine, you did it for me* (Mt 25:40). That's the stretching out of arms, under which Amalek fell back. And so you spend money on the poor; perhaps, when you give something to the hungry, you will have less of what you have given—but in your house, not in heaven. But here also on earth, the one at whose orders you have been generous, himself makes up for what you have given. When the apostle was talking about this matter, he said, *The one who supplies seed for the sower, will also furnish bread for food* (2 Cor 9:10). You're God's workman, you see, when you give to the needy; you're sowing in winter something to reap in summer. So why are you dreading, O you of little faith, that in this great household such a great master won't feed his workman? It will all be there too—but what is enough for you. God will give everything to your need, nothing to your greed. So work away fearlessly, stretch out your arms, let Amalek fall back.

But in this respect, as I said, when you've given something from your household store, you see less there in any case than what you could see before; you don't see it there, when you've given it, until God gives it back to you again. Tell me, though, when you pardon someone from your heart, what are you losing? When you pardon the person who sins against you, what will you have less of in your heart? It's from there, you see, that you are forgiving, but you're not giving anything away.[36] On the contrary, indeed, a kind of wave of charity was sweeping over your heart, and so to say welling up from an inner spring; you nurse hatred against your brother, you have blocked up the source. So not only do you lose nothing when you pardon, but you are watered more abundantly than ever. Charity is not limited at all; you place a stone of offense there, and you're limiting yourself. "I'll get my own back, I'll get my revenge, I'll show him, I'll do it." You're all steamed up, you're wearing yourself out, when by granting him pardon you could be without a care in the world, live without a care in the world, pray without a care in the world.

Because look here, what are you going to do? You're going to pray. Why should I say when? You're going to pray today. Or aren't you going to pray? Full of anger and hatred, you're threatening vengeance; you're not forgiving from the heart. Here you are, you're saying your prayers; here you are, the time for prayer has come, you begin either to hear or to say those words.[37] When the first ones have been said and heard, you are going to come to this verse. Or if you're not going to come to it, where are you going to go? In order not to pardon your enemy, will you deviate from Christ? Certainly, if you deviate, make a detour, in the prayer, being unwilling to say *Forgive us our debts*, because you can't say *just as we forgive our debtors*, in case you should get the swift reply, "I forgive in the same way as you in your turn forgive"—so because you can't say this, and don't want to forgive, you will bypass this verse, make a detour round it, and say what comes next: *Do not suffer us to be led into temptation* (Mt 6:13); there too your creditor will catch you, the one whom you were trying, as it were, to avoid meeting face to face.

It's like when you run into someone in the street to whom you owe some money; if there is a side entry to hand, you leave off where you were going, and go down this other passage, to avoid seeing your creditor face to face. That's what you consider you have done with this verse; you've avoided saying "Forgive, just as I forgive," in case he should forgive in the same way, that is, not forgive, because you aren't forgiving; and you refused to say it, to avoid meeting your creditor face to face. Whom are you avoiding? Who are you anyway, doing the avoiding? To what place will you go, where you can be, and he can't? You'll find yourself saying, *Where shall I go away from your spirit? And where shall I flee from your face? If I climb up to heaven, you are there; if I go down to hell, you are present.* How much further can a debtor flee from Christ, than to go down to hell? Even there this creditor is present. What are you going to do, but what comes next? *I will take*[38] my wings directly, and fly to the uttermost parts of the sea (Ps 139:7-9); that is, I will meditate in my hope on the end of the age,I will live in your commandments, I will lift myself up on the two wings of charity. So fulfill the two wings of charity; *Love your neighbor as yourself* (Mk 12:31), and don't cling to the hatred, which makes you flee from your creditor.

The third kind of repentance for deadly sins

8. There remains the third kind of repentance, about which let me say something briefly, so that with the Lord's help I may keep my promise and complete what I have proposed. It involves a heavier and more sorrowful kind of penance, for those who are properly called penitents in the Church, who are barred from sharing in the sacrament of the altar, in case by receiving it un-worthily they should eat and drink judgment upon themselves.[39] There is a serious wound involved; perhaps adultery has been committed, perhaps murder, perhaps some sacrilege, a grave matter, a grave wound, lethal, deadly; but the doctor is almighty. Already, after the suggestion of the deed, and the liking of the idea and consent to it, and finally the perpetration of it, let the sinner be like one four days dead, and stinking. But not even this one has the Lord forsaken, but he has cried out, *Lazarus, come forth outside* (Jn 11:39-43). The weight of the grave has yielded to mercy, death has yielded to life, the underworld has yielded to the world on high.

Lazarus was raised up, he came forth from the burial mound; and he was bound, as people are who do penance when they confess their sins. They have already come forth from death; because they wouldn't confess unless they were coming forth. The very act of confessing is a coming forth from a hidden and dark place. But what does the Lord say to his Church? *Whatever you loose*, he says, *on earth, shall be loosed in heaven* (Mt 18:18). Accordingly, after Lazarus has come forth, because the Lord has exercised his prerogative of mercy by bringing to confession one who was dead, hidden away and stinking; now the ministers of the Church carry out the rest: *Loose him, and let him go free* (Jn 11:44).

But, my dearest friends, none of you should propose this kind of penance to yourselves, none of you prepare yourself for this kind; still, if it does happen to come to it, none of you should despair. It wasn't so much the crime that Judas the traitor committed, as his despair of pardon that brought him to total destruc-tion. He wasn't worthy of mercy, that's why no light shone in his heart to prompt him to have recourse to the gentle kindness of the one he had betrayed, like those who had crucified him.[40] But he killed himself in despair, and hanged himself with a noose, suffocated himself.[41] What he did to his body is what happened to his soul. Even the breeze of this air, you see, is called spirit. So just as those who pull something tight round their throats kill themselves by stopping the spirit of this air entering their lungs; so too those who despair of God's merciful kindness, suffocate themselves inwardly by their very despair, making it impossible for the Holy Spirit to look in on them.

9. At this point, pagans are in the habit of making fun of Christians about the penitential discipline which has been established in the Church; and against some heresies the Catholic Church has held firmly to this truth about doing penance. There have been people, you see, who said that for some sins no penance should be allowed; and they have been excluded from the Church, and declared heretics.[42] Over whatever sins you like to think of our loving mother the Church never loses her tenderness of heart. So the pagans too are in the habit of poking fun at us on the point, though they don't really know what they are talking about, because they haven't yet encountered the word of God, which *makes eloquent the tongues of babes* (Wis 10:21). "You folks," they say, "make people sin, when you promise them pardon if they do penance. This is to destroy morality, not to defend and encourage it."

To support this opinion they pile up words, as much as each of them can; whether shouting or just stammering, they never keep quiet. Yet even when we talk to them, even if they are beaten in argument, they don't admit it. All the same, would your graces please note how they can be beaten, because the Lord's mercy has established everything in the best possible way in his Church. They say we are licensing sins, because we promise a haven to repentance. If access to repentance were to be closed off, wouldn't that sinner all the more readily add sins to sins, the more he despaired of being forgiven them? I mean, he would say to himself, "Here I am, I've sinned, here I am, I've committed a crime, now I've no chance of pardon. Repentance is fruitless, I am to be damned; why shouldn't I now live as I like? Because I can't find any charity there, at least let me feed my cupidity here. After all, why should I hold myself back? There, every door is closed to me; here, whatever I refrain from doing, I lose, because I won't be given the life that comes after this one. So why not serve my lusts, to satisfy them to the full, and do whatever I am disposed to, though not allowed to?"

Perhaps he would be told, "But, you poor wretch, you will be caught, you will be charged, tortured, punished." Bad men know people say these things, and in human society carry them out. They also notice that many live bad and criminal lives and their sins go unpunished. They can conceal them, or buy their way out of what they can't conceal; right up to old age they can buy impunity for an abandoned life of lechery, blasphemy, sacrilege. They count it all up, and say to themselves, "What? Didn't that man who did all those dreadful things die in old age?" What you don't pay attention to, is that the reason that sinner, that criminal died as an old man is that God was demonstrating his patience in him, waiting for him to repent. Which is why the apostle says, *Are you unaware that God's patience is leading you to repentance?* That man, however, accord-

ing to the hardness of his heart and his unrepentant heart, has stored up for himself wrath on the day of wrath and of the revelation of the just judgment of God, who will pay back to each one according to his works (Rom 2:4-6).

So there's a need for fear to take hold of people's minds here, a need for those who don't want to sin to reflect that God is present with them, not only in public, but also privately at home; not only in the house, but even in the bedroom, at night, on their beds, in their hearts. So if you take away the haven of penance and repentance, you increase sins out of desperation. So there you are; they're not saying anything at all, those people who imagine that the reason sins increase is that the Christian faith does offer a haven of repentance.

So what, then? Ought not God to have made provision for preventing sins from again increasing because of there being this hope of indulgence? Just as he has made provision, you see, against their being added to because of despair,[43] so he ought to have provided against their being added to because of hope. I mean, just as those who have despaired really do add to their sins, so too those who have pinned their hopes on pardon can also add to their sins; you might say to yourself, "I will do whatever I want. God is good; when I turn back to him, he will pardon me."

Yes, sure, say to yourself, "When I turn back to him, he will pardon me"—if you can be sure of tomorrow. Doesn't scripture warn you about this, when it says, *Do not delay turning back to the Lord, nor put it off from day to day; for suddenly his wrath will come, and in the time of vengeance he will destroy you* (Sir 5:7). There you are; in either case God's providence has been wide awake on our behalf. To stop us adding to sins out of despair, the haven of repentance and penance is opened to us; again, to stop us adding to them through misplaced hope, we are given total uncertainty about the day of our death.

NOTES

1. Fischer, Kunzelmann, and van Bavel all suggest 396-400. From the last sentence of section 1, the sermon was evidently preached not long before Easter; on the Saturday before the second Sunday in Lent, in all probability; see next note.

This is not the only sermon Augustine preached entirely off the cuff, because of a mistake made by the reader. See for example his *Expositions of the Psalms* 138 (139), which begins, "I had prepared a short psalm for us, which I had given directions to be sung by the lector. But when the moment came, it seems, he was flustered and read another one instead. So I have preferred to follow God's will in the lector's mistake, rather than my own in my original purpose." This is the authentic sermon, of which Sermon 351, in my view, is a rather sorry imitation.

2. It being Lent, most probably the Saturday before the second Sunday, which used to be among one of the four Ember times of the year, there had evidently been several long readings.

3. Just *ille* in the Latin; but no doubt with a gesture pointing up to heaven.

4. The lectors, or readers—it was one of what used to be called the minor orders—were usually boys who would be receiving some sort of education from the adult clergy; the ancient, informal equivalent of contemporary minor and major seminaries.

5. Of Good Friday and Easter.

6. See Mt 7:24.

7. An allusion, presumably, to the baptismal liturgy of Holy Saturday.

8. Red with the blood of Christ.

9. Saint Paul; but Augustine is almost treating the text here as if it was Christ who said it—which, of course, in Augustine's view he did, through Paul. But here he is practically conflating the texts from Jn 6 and 1 Cor 10.

10. The eucharist as the memorial of Christ's passion contains and perpetuates the scandal of the cross.

11. The favorite contrast between *ventrem* and *mentem*; not quite such a perfect rhyme as *spes* and *res*, but still easy to remember.

12. See Mk 12:27.

13. See Lk 3:8.

14. And the water they drank came from the rock, struck by Moses with his rod.

15. See Ex 17:6; Gn 28:11; Ex 12.

16. See Gn 22:13. All these different things mean Christ. In this last instance he is signified both by the ram caught by the horns (Christ stretched out on the cross), and by Isaac carrying the wood for the sacrifice (Christ carrying his cross).

17. But if Moses had struck the rock with a rod of iron, this would not have bothered Augustine; it would have represented the lance with which Christ's side was pierced.

18. It was the common teaching of the Fathers and the scholastic theologians after them, that "our fathers" in the Old Testament believed in Christ quite as explicitly as we do; they, however, in the Christ who was going to come, we in the Christ who has come.

19. It is indeed an obscure story; not easy to see in what Moses' sin of doubting God consisted. Num 20:10-11 are perhaps the crucial verses. The Lord had told Moses to *speak* to the rock (v.8), and it would produce water. In v.10 Moses asks the people if they really expect him to produce water from the rock, and he strikes it twice, in a gesture, one supposes, of extreme irritation with the rebellious people. This, it would appear, showed that he did not really believe what God had said to him.

20. See Nm 13:16. I have to keep the names as Augustine had them in his version, straight from the Greek Septuagint, because of the significance of the name Jesus. In our modern versions they are respectively Joshua son of Nun and Hoshea. Joshua is in fact only another form of Hoshea, both meaning something like "May Yahweh save"; and Jesus is just the Greek form of Joshua, which in the Aramaic of our Lord's time may have become Jeshua.

21. See Ex 33:11.

22. See Jos 1:1-9.

23. See Mk 14:66-72.

24. See 1 Cor 3:12-18; Ex 34:34-35.

25. See Mk 15:38.

26. See Lk 15:13-20.

27. See Ex 14:28.

28. See *Alice in Wonderland*, by Lewis Carroll, chapter IX, "The Lobster Quadrille."

29. An almost universal reason in those days for deferring baptism, even till one was on the point of death. What would they do, ordinary, not very heroic and saintly people wondered, about the sins they were sure to commit after baptism—especially sexual sins—since there would be no second baptism to wash them away? A text like Heb 10:26-31 would serve to confirm them in their hesitation.

30. Moses, now a type of Christ by his obedience.

31. See Ex 15:23-25.

32. See Ex 17:8-13.

33. See 1 Thes 5:6; 1 Pt 4:7.

34. See Is 55:1. The *competentes* were those who had already enrolled themselves in the group

preparing to be baptized at the Easter vigil. It was a technical term, meaning "the seekers," or "the askers," for which there is not now any proper equivalent in liturgical English; so I keep the Latin word.

35. See Lk 19:6; 10:40.

36. *Inde enim dimittis, sed nihil amittis*; you are forgiving from there, but not losing anything.

37. To hear them, because at mass they were said by the celebrant alone. At other times of prayer, at home, of course, they were said by the faithful themselves.

38. The text follows the psalm in beginning the sentence with "If." But it is clear from the context that Augustine deliberately omitted it.

39. See 1 Cor 11:29.

40. See Acts 2:37.

41. See Mt 27:3-5.

42. Like the Montanists, for example, in the late second century. Augustine's compatriot of that time, Tertullian, was also this kind of rigorist, and joined this sect about the year 200.

43. By providing the Church with the sacrament of penance, or reconciliation.

SERMON 353

Date: 394[1]

Moral exhortations, developing 1 Pt 2:1-3

1. I would indeed like my sermon, being that of a concerned and solicitous pastor, to strike home to the ears and minds of all of you who are entrusted to my care; all the same, it is most particularly addressed now to those of you whose spiritual infancy is indicated by the cradle of the sacraments from which you have so recently emerged. It is to you above all, you see, that God is speaking so coaxingly through the apostle Peter: *So laying aside*, he says, *all malice, and all guile and flattery, and envy and fault-finding, like new-born infants desire the reasonable and innocent milk; so that you may grow up by means of it into salvation, if you have tasted that the Lord is sweet* (1 Pt 2:1-3). Well, that you have so tasted, I can bear witness; I myself administered this sweetness to you in my role of wet-nurse.

So then, act as you have been admonished to on the model of holy infancy; lay aside malice, guile, flattery, and envy and detraction. You must hold on to this harmless innocence in such a way that you don't lose it as you grow up. What is malice, but a love of doing harm? What is guile but doing one thing and pretending to do another? What is flattery, but leading astray with deceitful praise? What is envy, but hatred of another's good fortune? What is fault-finding, but criticism that is more waspish than truthful? Malice takes delight in another person's ills; envy is tormented even by another person's well-being. Guile is two-faced;[2] flattery two-tongued; fault-finding inflicts wounds on people's reputations. The innocence, on the other hand, of this holy infancy of yours, being the daughter of charity, *does not rejoice at iniquity, but rejoices together with the truth* (1 Cor 13:6). It is *simple as a dove*, and thus *cunning as a serpent* (Mt 10:16); clever, not at doing harm, but at avoiding those who do.

It is to keep this kind of innocence that I am urging you. *For of such is the kingdom of heaven* (Mk 10:14), namely of the humble, that is to say those who are little ones in spirit. Don't despise it, don't shrink from it. This littleness is proper to great souls. Pride, on the other hand, is the misleading greatness of the weak; when it takes possession of the mind, it casts it down by raising it up, empties it out by puffing it up, dissipates it by stretching it out. A humble person cannot harm anyone, a proud person cannot be harmless or innocent. I'm talking about the kind of humility which doesn't wish to excel in things that are going to pass away, but fixes its thoughts on something eternal, which it cannot reach by its own powers, but only assisted by grace. This humility is incapable of wishing people ill, which contributes nothing to their true good. When we come to pride, however, it is constantly giving birth to envy. But can you be truly envious without wishing the person ill, whose good fortune is tormenting you? So envy, then, goes on to give birth to malice; from which proceed both guile and flattery and fault-finding, and every sort of bad action which you don't want to experience at the hands of others. So it is that if you preserve a kindly humility, which is qualified in the holy scriptures as a holy infancy, you can be quite sure of the immortality of the blessed. *For of such is the kingdom of heaven.*

If you are not to treat human beings proudly,
how much less should you oppose yourself obstinately to God

2. Furthermore, if you are not to treat human beings proudly, you should above all take care not to oppose yourself obstinately to God. After all, if you shouldn't do to anybody else what you don't want to suffer at anyone else's hands, and we none of us wish to endure disobedience from those who are subject to our authority; how much more care should we take that none of us should behave toward God in a manner that we don't like other human beings to behave toward us?

Accordingly, those people are cheating their own souls, who reckon that it's enough if they don't do to anybody else what they don't want done to themselves, and then proceed to corrupt themselves with such a life of dissipation, that they are in fact doing their level best to do to God what they don't want done to them by other people. I mean to say, they don't want their houses turned upside down by anyone, and yet they are turning God's house in themselves upside down by their wretched blindness, their deafness to the cry of the apostle: *Are you all unaware that you are God's temple, and that the Spirit of God dwells in you? But if anyone demolishes God's temple, God will demolish him. For the temple of God, which is what you are, is holy* (1 Cor 3:16-17). Don't deceive yourselves, any of you. So how can they imagine they are preserving their innocence in their relations with other people, when they are doing themselves such harm, that they do themselves out of God as a guest, and are punished by him as an avenger?

Hence it also happens that those who slither away and spread themselves in harmful pleasures not only cease to be temples of God, but also become ruins in which evil demons lurk,[3] whom they proceed to beg favors of and to worship; and *their last state*, as it says, *becomes worse than the first* (Lk 11:26). And so, just as the apostle Peter earlier on addressed you that have been born again of immortal seed[4] on the subject of malicious longings to do harm, to treat people in a way they hate; so later on the same apostle turns to the filthy and unlawful pleasures of the flesh, and abominable sacrileges, which don't indeed seem to involve doing harm to others by treating them in a way they don't like; but do involve disobeying God to whom all things are subject, and treating the Lord of lords in a way people don't like being treated by their own household slaves; and he addresses you with the words, *Since Christ, therefore, suffered in the flesh, arm yourselves too with the same thought. Because whoever has suffered in the flesh has ceased to sin, so as to live for the rest of the time in the flesh no longer by human desires, but by the will of God. For the time that is past is enough for having carried out the will of the nations, in lusts and pleasures and revels, drinking bouts and the abominable worship of idols* (1 Pt 4:1-3).

The time past, you see, is quite enough for having, so to say, been slaves under the domination of the Egyptians, in the muddy works of sin. Already the Red Sea, namely the baptism of Christ consecrated by his blood, has overthrown the real Pharaoh,[5] destroyed the Egyptians; you need be in no dread of your past sins, as of enemies pursuing you from the rear. For the rest, give your thoughts to making your way through the desert of this life, and to reaching the promised land, the heavenly Jerusalem, the land of the living.[6] Don't let your hearts, like inner taste buds, lose their sense of taste out of contempt for the word of God, like loathing for the manna; don't ever grumble about the nourishment coming from heaven out of a longing for Egyptian foods.[7] Never commit fornication, as some of them did, and never tempt Christ as some of them tempted him.[8]

If in your thirst for the faith of the nations[9] you should encounter some bitterness from those who oppose you, like that of the waters which Israel was unable to drink, imitate the patience of the Lord, so that those waters may turn sweet by your throwing in, as it were, the wood of the cross.[10] If you should be bitten by some temptation creeping up on you like a serpent, apply the same cure of the cross, by gazing on that serpent lifted up, like death conquered and led in triumph in the flesh of the Lord.[11] If the Amalekite adversary should attempt to block and hinder your journey, let him be defeated by your doggedly persevering in stretching out your arms in yet another indication of the cross.[12] Be true and complete Christians; don't imitate those who are Christians in name, empty vessels in good works. I say it again, and it has to be said so often: *The time that is past is enough for having carried out the will of the nations* (1 Pt 4:3).

Loathe and detest the dogs which return to their vomit;[13] loathe and detest the cleaned and empty house, into which seven other spirits, more wicked still, are brought, so that *the last state of the man is worse than the first* (Lk 11:25-26). What you must do is keep hold of the one who has cleaned you up as permanent resident in your house. For *we command and beg you not to receive the grace of God in vain* (2 Cor 6:1). For the time that is past is enough for having carried out the will of the nations. Listen also to the apostle Paul:[14] *For just as you have presented your members to be slaves of uncleanness and iniquity making for unrighteousness, so now present your members to be slaves of righteousness, making for sanctification* (Rom 6:19).

NOTES

1. Fischer and Kunzelmann actually suggest 391-396; in any case, a sermon preached before Augustine was ordained bishop. I have abbreviated the title, which in its fullness—it is only the idea of some copyist of a manuscript—runs, "On the octave of the *infantes*, whom he exhorts, in the words of the apostle Peter: *Therefore, laying aside all malice,*" etc.

2. The Latin says "two-hearted"; *duplicat cor.*

3. See Rv 18:2.

4. See 1 Pt 1:23.

5. The devil; see Ex 14:26-28.

6. See Rv 21:10; Gal 4:26; Ps 27:13.

7. See Nm 11:4-6; 21:5.

8. See 1 Cor 10:8.

9. *Si vobis fidem gentilium sitientibus.* "Thirsting for the faith of the nations" is a rather odd expression, as the word *Gentiles* normally stands for those who do not believe—as it has been doing already in this sermon. I was tempted to make a simple change in word order, and read, *Si vobis fidem sitientibus gentilium amaritudo aliqua resistentium . . . occurrerit*, which would give the sense, "If in your thirst for the faith you should encounter some bitterness from the Gentiles who oppose it." But the reading of the text is tolerable, and there appears to be no manuscript support for changing it.

10. See Ex 15:23-25.

11. See Jn 3:14; Nm 21:8.

12. See Ex 17:8-13.

13. See 2 Pt 2:22.

14. He appears to think that the whole of the previous quotation came from 1 Pt 4:3.

SERMON 354

Date: 403[1]

The reason the world hates us is that we,
the body of Christ, preach Christ, our head

1. The Lord reminded us, when the gospel was read, that whoever believes in him, believes in the one who sent him.[2] Our faith most truly holds that he was sent to us as our savior; since Christ is being preached by Christ himself, that is by the body of Christ spread throughout the whole world. He was in heaven, you see, and he said to the savage persecutor on earth, *Why are you persecuting me?* (Acts 9:4). In this way the Lord affirmed that he is also here in us. In this way the whole Christ grows; because just as he is here in us, so we too are there in him.[3] This is brought about by the cement of charity. The one who is our head is the savior of his body.

So Christ is preaching Christ, the body preaching its head, and the head looking after its body. And that's why the world hates us, as we have heard from the Lord himself.[4] It wasn't, you see, just to a few apostles that he said this, that the world would hate them; and that they ought to rejoice when people belittled them and uttered every kind of evil against them, because this would make their reward greater in heaven.[5] The Lord wasn't speaking to them alone, when he said these things; but he was speaking to his whole body, speaking to all his members. Any who wish to be in his body and be his members, mustn't be surprised that the world hates them.

Our enemies are not only those outside;
the worse ones are the worldly people inside

2. Now many people receive the sacrament of his body; but not all who receive the sacrament are also going to have the place in his company promised to his members. Nearly all people indeed say the sacrament is his body, because all are feeding together in his pastures; but he is going to come and separate them, and place some on the right, some on the left. And each section is going to say, *Lord, Lord, when did we see you and minister to you?* or else *Lord, when*

did we see you and not minister to you? Each section is going to say that; to one, all the same, he will say, *Come, you blessed of my Father, take possession of the kingdom;* to the other, *Go into eternal fire, which has been prepared for the devil and his angels* (Mt 25:31-41).

So we ought not to think that our only enemies, dearly beloved, those of us who are members of Christ with a good conscience; we ought not to think that our only enemies are those who are openly so outside. Much worse are those who seem to be inside, and are really outside. They love the world, you see; and that's why they are bad. And indeed they think about us in terms of what they themselves love, and they envy us whatever worldly fortune we may have, which we ourselves deplore.[6] About our inner prosperity, however, they know nothing, because they haven't had a taste of it; but they don't realize that the world smiling on us in temporal matters is more of a danger to us than a distinction; because they don't know at all how to tell the difference between these different kinds of enjoyment.

If we didn't have enemies, we couldn't carry out the Lord's command to love our enemies, and pray for those who hate us

3. It's on this sort of thing that I wish to reassure your graces, seeing particularly that you have come together here in considerable numbers, you that have a higher goal set before you than others; that is to say, you have a more honorable place in the body of Christ, through his gift, not through your own merits, because you are practicing the continence which has been granted you by God. This too, I mean, becomes a matter for suspicion for bad people who are jealous of us. The reason it is snapped at, though, is to test its real quality. You see, if by professing absolute chastity we are seeking human admiration, we cave in under the weight of human criticism.

While you are a chaste servant of God, there's the world, suspecting you perhaps of shameless and lewd behavior, and gladly lingering over the business of slandering you. The worst suspicions, of course, seem to taste sweet to the malevolent soul. If you, though, chose to practice continence in order to win human admiration, you have caved in under human disapproval, and lost everything that you set before yourself as your goal.

On the other hand, if you know how to say with the apostle, *Our boast is this, the testimony of our conscience* (2 Cor 1:12), not only does the world not diminish your reward by its criticisms, but it actually makes it ampler yet. You, however, must pray for the world, that your reward shouldn't mean its death. Because here too, you see, we are being tested, dearly beloved; because if we didn't have any enemies, there wouldn't be anybody for us to pray for as the Lord commanded us, when he said, *Love your enemies, pray for those who hate you* (Mt 5:44). How can we test ourselves, how can we question our hearts, whether we are capable of doing this, if we have no experience of enemies, of any malicious critic, anyone pulling us to pieces, anyone speaking evil of us? So you can see that bad people too are needed by the good. We are in a kind of goldsmith's furnace, that is to say, in this world. If you are not gold, you are burnt up together; if you are gold, your straw is the bad person; if you too are straw, you will both be smoke together.

4. However, the first thing for you to realize, dearly beloved, is that in the body of Christ, the more excellent members are not the only ones. After all, married life too is something to be admired, and has its place in the body of Christ; just as in our own bodies too there is a place for other parts as well as those that are located in a nobler position, like the senses in the face, occupying a superior place in the body; but unless the feet were supporting it, whatever is most exalted in the body would be lying flat on the ground. That's why the apostle says, *And our less honorable parts are the more necessary. God has arranged the body, so that there should be no rifts in the body* (1 Cor 12:23-25).

Now we know that there are members of Christ who lead the married life—if they are members of Christ, that is if they are believers, if they are either hoping or waiting for the age to come, if they know why they bear the sign of Christ; just as we know that they pay honor to you, that they reckon you to be better than they are themselves. But just as they honor you, so ought you to show equal honor and respect to them. I mean, if there is a special holiness in you, be afraid of losing it. How? Through pride. The holiness of the chaste perishes one way if they commit adultery; it perishes another way if they become proud. And I make bold to say that those who lead the married life are better, if they hold onto humility, than those who are chaste and proud. Your graces should consider what I am saying very carefully. Take the devil; was he ever charged at God's judgment seat with adultery or fornication? He doesn't do anything of that sort, as he doesn't have flesh. The one thing that casts him into eternal fire is pride and envy.

5. When pride has crept into a servant of God, straightaway envy is to be found there too. The proud person cannot help being envious. Envy is the daughter of pride; but this mother is unable to be barren; wherever she is, she immediately gives birth. Now to avoid this being the case with you, just think about this point, that in the time of persecution it wasn't only Agnes the virgin who was crowned, but also Crispina the married woman.[7] And perhaps, which can scarcely be doubted, there were at that time some religious who fell away, and many married people who fought and won.

And so it's not for nothing that the apostle says to all the members of Christ, *Each thinking the other superior to themselves, and outdoing one another in mutual respect* (Phil 2:3; Rom 12:10). Indeed, if your thoughts run on these lines, you won't be great in your own eyes. After all, what you should rather be thinking about is what you lack, instead of what advantages you have. As for what you have, be careful you don't lose it; as for what you haven't got yet, pray hard that you may get it. It's on all the ways in which you fall behind others that your thoughts should dwell, not on all the ways in which you excel them. I mean, if you're thinking how much better you have done than the other person, beware of getting a swollen head. But if you're thinking how much you're still falling short, you start groaning; and when you groan, you are worrying about yourself, you will be humble, you will walk more securely, you won't tumble over a cliff, you won't be puffed up like a balloon.

When charity builds up, it does not allow knowledge to be puffed up

6. And if only we could all just let our thoughts dwell on the one thing, charity![8] It's the only thing, you see, which both surpasses all things, and without which all things are worth nothing, and which draws all things to itself,[9] wherever it may be. This is the thing that *is not jealous*. You want to know why not? Notice what follows: *is not puffed up* (1 Cor 13:4). First among the vices, as I started to say earlier, is pride, next envy. It's not envy, you see, that has given birth to pride, but pride that has given birth to envy. It's only a love of excelling, after all, that is envious. A love of excelling is what we call pride. So since pride is first in order, while envy comes next, the apostle did not want to put first in his praise of charity that it is not puffed up, and next that it is not jealous; but first he said *is not jealous*, and next *is not puffed up*. Why so? Because after he had said *is not jealous*, as though you were going to ask the reason why it isn't jealous, he added, *is not puffed up*. So if the reason it isn't jealous is that it isn't puffed up, if it were puffed up it would be jealous.

Only let this attitude take root in you, and the soul is set firm and solid, because it is not being puffed up. *Knowledge*, says the apostle, *puffs up*. So what, then? Must you run away from knowledge, and are you going to choose to know nothing, rather than be puffed up? What on earth am I talking to you for, if ignorance is better than knowledge? Why am I arguing the point with you? Why am I making these distinctions? Why am I reminding you of what you know, introducing you to what you don't know, if knowledge is to be avoided, in case it should puff one up? So then, love knowledge, but put charity first. If knowledge is there by itself, it puffs up. But because *charity builds up* (1 Cor 8:1), it doesn't allow knowledge to be puffed up. So knowledge only puffs up, where charity is not building up; but where it is building up, knowledge is set firm and solid. There is no puffing up where the rock is the foundation.

God's way of saving us from conceit by not always answering our prayers

7. What a temptation, though, being puffed up, that is, being conceited, really is! It was because of this vice that even such a great man as that apostle of ours said that he had a sting applied to him in the flesh, an angel of Satan, to be buffeted by. Being buffeted means being boxed about the head, to stop you

lifting it up; because it's particularly in the head that knowledge puffing you up, that is making you conceited, is to be feared. He said, you see, *Lest the greatness of my revelations should make me conceited.* So that's where he had to fear conceit, where there was a revelation of great matters. *Lest the greatness of my revelations should make me conceited, there was given me a sting in my flesh, an angel of Satan to buffet me. About this I besought the Lord three times to take it from me. And he said to me, My grace is sufficient for you; for power is perfected in weakness* (2 Cor 12:7-9).

The sick man is asking that the plaster, which the doctor is applying to him for his health, should be removed when the sick man wishes. The doctor says, "It doesn't sting, then it doesn't heal." You say, "Take it away, because it stings." The doctor says, "I won't take it away, because it's healing you." Why did you, though, go to the doctor in the first place? To be healed, or not to suffer any inconvenience? So the Lord didn't listen to Paul to do what he wanted, because he listened to him to preserve his health. In fact, there's nothing very special about God listening to you to do what you want; nothing very special about that. Don't imagine that's something tremendous, if someone's heard when he prays for something he regards as important. Inquire what he's praying for, inquire in what respect he is heard. I mean, you mustn't regard it as a great thing to be heard with respect to what you want; regard it as a great thing to be heard with respect to your true advantage.

Even the demons were heard and given what they wanted, and allowed to go into the pigs they had asked for.[10] Even their chief, the devil, was listened to, and given what he wanted; his request to test and tempt Job wasn't refused; this, though, was so that Job might pass the test, the devil be put to confusion.[11] The Israelites, too, were listened to; and while the food was still in their mouths, you know what they got for it.[12] So don't regard it as a great thing to be heard and given what you want. Sometimes God gives you what you ask for because he is angry, and refuses you what you ask for because he is gracious. When, however, you ask God for the things that he himself commends, he himself commands, he himself promises for the future, then you need have no qualms about asking; press on with your prayers as much as you can, in order to obtain these things. They are granted, you see, by God in his graciousness; they are bestowed not by his anger, but by his mercy. But when you ask for temporal things, ask for them with moderation, ask for them with fear. Leave it to him to give them if they are for your good, not to give them if he knows they will be bad for you. What's bad, what's good for you, though, is something the doctor knows, not the patient.

There are humble religious, there are proud religious

8. So there are humble religious, there are proud religious. The proud ones shouldn't promise themselves the kingdom of God. The place which dedicated chastity leads to is certainly higher; but *the one who exalts himself will be humbled* (Lk 14:11). Why seek the higher place with an appetite for the heights,

when you can make it simply by holding on to lowliness? If you exalt yourself, God casts you down; if it's you yourself that cast yourself down, God lifts you up. It's the Lord's own pronouncement which nothing can be either added to or subtracted from.[13] People though who have dedicated themselves to chastity are sometimes so outrageously proud, that they are even ungrateful to their own parents, by considering themselves superior not only to other people in general, but also to their parents. Why? Because these practiced procreation, while they themselves declined to get married. How could those who declined to get married have even been ungrateful, if their parents hadn't produced them?

"But a son is better than his married father, because he himself hasn't taken a wife; and a daughter is better than her married mother, because she herself hasn't looked for a husband."

If prouder, in no way better; if better, then without a doubt because humbler. If you want to discover whether you are really better, question your soul, ask whether you can see any conceit there. Where there's swollen conceit, there's emptiness; where the devil finds an empty space, he busily sets about building himself a nest.

It is good for proud religious to fall, so that they may
be humbled on the very point on which they pride themselves

9. Finally, my brothers and sisters, I make bold to say that it is a good thing for proud religious to fall, so that they may be humbled on the very point on which they pride themselves. What good, after all, does chastity do anyone who is dominated by pride? Such a person scorns that by which human beings are born, and yearns for that by which the devil fell. You have declined marriage, you have done well; you have chosen the better course—but don't grow proud. It's from marriage that human beings are born; it's from pride that angels fell. If I were to consider your good points one by one, you are better than your father, because you have declined marriage; and you there are better than your mother, because you have declined marriage. Yes indeed, the holiness of virginity is better than wedded chastity. If these two are just compared with each other, this is better than that; who doubts it? But now add another pair, pride and humility. If I question you about these two, and tell you to answer me about them, "Which is better, pride or humility?" you answer, "Humility." Join it to the holiness of virginity. Pride, on the other hand, should not only be absent from your virginity, but shouldn't either be present in your mother. If you, after all, cling to pride, and your mother to humility, the mother will be better than the daughter. I will now compare you again. A moment ago, when I took the points singly, I found you to be the better; now when I take them in pairs, I don't hesitate to prefer the humble married woman to the proud virgin.

And to prefer her on what grounds? Notice how I make the preference in my first comparison. Married chastity is good, virginal integrity is better. I was comparing two good things, not a bad thing and a good thing; I was distinguishing the good and the better. Going on, though, to those other two which I set before you, pride and humility, can we possibly say, "Pride is good, but humility is better"? No, but what do we say? Pride is bad, humility is good; and pride is a great evil, humility a great good. So then, if one of these two is bad and the other good; the bad one is joined to your greater good, and the whole becomes bad. The good one is joined to your mother's lesser good, and makes it into a great good. The mother will have a lower place in the kingdom of heaven, since she is married, than the daughter, since she is a virgin. The virgin daughter, you see, will have a higher place, the married mother a lower place, but still both will be there; just as one star is bright, another star dim, but still both are in the sky.

But if your mother is humble, and you proud, she will have some sort of place there; you on the other hand will have no place. And if you have no place there, where will you find another place, but with the one who fell from there, and then threw down the one who was still standing? The devil fell from there, and from there threw down the man who was still standing. He threw down the one who was standing; but Christ came down and raised up the one who was lying flat on the ground. Notice, though, what your Lord raised you up by; he raised you up by humility. *Becoming obedient unto death, he humbled himself* (Phil 2:8). Your chief is humble, and are you going to be proud? The head is humble, and is the member proud? Perish the thought. Any who love pride don't really wish to belong to the body of a humble head. But if they are not there, let them see where they will be. I myself don't want to say, in case I should appear to be frightening you too much. Or rather, if only I really did frighten you, and really did achieve something! If only any man or any woman among you who was like that should not be so any further! If only I were pouring these words into you, and not just pouring them out on the ground! Everything, though, is to be hoped for from the mercy of God; because the one who instills fear instills sadness; the one who instills sadness, brings comfort; while if any are comforted, it means they have been corrected.

NOTES

1. Fischer and Kunzelmann simply say before 410—I cannot say on what grounds; I take the mean between 396, when Augustine was ordained bishop, and 410. The full title runs, "Preached to religious (*continentes*), in which he first gives them courage in the face of their detractors and the envious, and then tells them to beware of pride."

The *continentes*, or those dedicated to celibate chastity, are clearly a mixed congregation of men and women; gathered to hear him on some special occasion, no doubt, in the main church of the town. This, I rather think, was not Hippo Regius, but some other town he had perhaps been asked to visit by its bishop, in order to address the men and women religious there. It is a curiously unsatisfactory sermon in some ways, frequently rather ill-expressed. I get the impression that Augustine was somewhat ill at ease himself. Perhaps the last two sections give us the clue; the monks and nuns there—or rather some of them—had been getting above themselves, and this in a way that was causing some gossip, if not scandal.

2. See Jn 12:44.

3. The line of reasoning is not exactly either clear or compelling.

4. See Jn 15:18-21.

5. See Mt 5:11-12.

6. He is presumably referring to gifts and endowments, usually of land and rents, made to religious communities by the devout.

7. Saint Agnes, the very popular girl martyr of Rome, martyred some time in the middle of the third century, whose feast is celebrated on 21 January; and Saint Crispina, a married woman with several children, martyred at Theveste in Africa on 5 December 304. See Sermon 286, 2, note 6; also *Expositions on the Psalms*, 120 (121), 13 and 137 (138), 14.

8. An allusion here, I think, to Lk 10:32, the one thing necessary.

9. And here an allusion to Jn 12:32; *And I, if I am lifted up from the earth, will draw all things to myself.*

10. See Mt 5:8-13.

11. See Jb 1—2.

12. See Nm 11:4.19-20.31-33. What they got for it was "a very great plague" after they had gorged themselves on the quails.

13. See Rv 22:18-19.

SERMON 354A

FRAGMENT FROM A SERMON ON THE GOODNESS OF MARRIAGE

Date: unknown[1]

A means of obtaining pardon for what is not lawful

1. *Let whoever can receive this, receive it* (Mt 19:12).[2] "But I can't," he says. You can't?

"No, I can't." To your aid there comes a particular authority from the apostle, to feed you on milk, to the effect that *if they cannot practice continence, let them marry*. Let something be done, in order to obtain indulgence. The function of indulgence is to save you from landing in eternal punishment. Let what is lawful be done, in order to be pardoned for what is not lawful. He indicates this by what comes next: *I prefer them to marry, rather than to burn* (1 Cor 7:9). He made a concession, I'm saying, to incontinence, because he feared something worse; he feared eternal pains, he feared what's awaiting, what's in store for adulterers. Even the fact that married couples, overcome by desire, make use of their conjugal rights more than is necessary for having children, I place among the things for which we say every day, *Forgive us our debts, as we too forgive our debtors* (Mt 6:12).

NOTES

1. It is impossible to date, or place, such a short fragment as this, which is preserved in the florilegia of Bede and Florus. From the style and tone, though, I would be inclined to date it early.
2. The reference is to making oneself a eunuch for the sake of the kingdom of heaven.

164

SERMON 355

Date: 425[1]

An important distinction between one's conscience and one's reputation

1. What I'm going to talk about is the matter for which I wanted your graces to come here today in greater numbers than usual, as I asked you to yesterday. We[2] live here with you, and we live here for you; and my intention and wish is that we may live with you in Christ's presence forever. I think our way of life is plain for you to see; so that I too may perhaps make bold to say what the apostle said, though I can't of course be compared with him: *Be imitators of me, as I too am of Christ* (1 Cor 4:16). And that's why I don't want any of you[3] to find an excuse for living badly. *For we aim at what is good*, says the same apostle, *not only in the sight of God, but also in the sight of men* (2 Cor 8:21).

As far as we are concerned, our consciences are all that matters; as far as you are concerned, our reputation among you ought not to be tarnished, but influential for good.[4] Mark what I've said, and make the distinction. There are two things, conscience and reputation; conscience for yourself, reputation for your neighbor. Those who, being clear in their consciences, neglect their reputations, are being cruel; especially if they find themselves in this position, a position about which the apostle says, when he writes to his disciple, *Showing yourself to all around you as an example of good works* (Ti 2:7).

How Augustine established a monastery in the bishop's house

2. So then, in order not to detain you long, especially because I am sitting down as I talk, while you will soon get tired as you're standing: you all know, or almost all of you, that we live in the house which is called the bishop's house in such a way as to imitate, to the best of our ability, those holy people about whom the book of the Acts of the Apostles says, *Nobody called anything their own, but they had all things in common* (Acts 4:32).[5] But some of you, perhaps, are not such keen examiners of the way we live that you know this in the way I would like you to know it; so let me spell out in more detail what I have just said in a few words.

I, whom by God's grace you see before you as your bishop, came to this city as a young man;[6] many of you know that. I was looking for a place to establish a monastery, and live there with my brothers. I had in fact left behind all worldly hopes, and I did not wish to be what I could have been;[7] nor, however, was I seeking to be what I am now. *I have chosen to be a nobody in the house of my God, rather than to dwell in the tents of sinners* (Ps 84:10). I separated myself from those who love the world; but I did not put myself on an equal footing with those who preside over Churches.[8] Nor did I choose a higher place at the banquet of my Lord, but a lower, insignificant one; and he was pleased to say to me, *Go up higher* (Lk 14:10). So much, though, did I dread the episcopate, that since I had already begun to acquire a reputation of some weight among the servants of God, I wouldn't go near a place where I knew there was no bishop.[9] I avoided this job, and I did everything I could to assure my salvation in a lowly position, and not to incur the grave risks of a high one. But, as I said, a servant ought not to oppose his Lord. I came to this city to see a friend, whom I thought I could gain for God, to join us in the monastery. It seemed safe enough, because the place had a bishop.[10] I was caught, I was made a priest,[11] and by this grade I eventually came to the episcopate.

I brought nothing with me; I came to this Church with only the clothes I was wearing at the time. And because what I was planning was to be in a monastery with the brothers, Father[12] Valerius of blessed memory, having learned of my purpose and desire, gave me that plot where the monastery now is. I began to gather together brothers of good will, my companions in poverty, having nothing just like me, and imitating me. Just as I had sold my slender poor man's property[13] and distributed the proceeds to the poor, those who wished to stay with me did the same, so that we might live on what we had in common. But what would be our really great and profitable common estate was God himself.

I arrived at the episcopate. I saw that the bishop is under the necessity of showing hospitable kindness to all visitors and travelers; indeed, if a bishop didn't do that he would be said to be lacking in humanity. But if this custom were transferred to the monastery it would not be fitting.[14] And that's why I wanted to have a monastery of clergy in this bishops' residence. This then is how we live; nobody in our company is allowed to have any private property. But perhaps some do have some; nobody's allowed to; if any do have it, they are doing what is not allowed. But I have a good opinion of my brothers, and believing the best of them, I have always refrained from making any inquiries, because to make such inquiries would, so it seemed to me, indicate I had a low opinion of them. I knew, you see, and I still know, that all who were living with me knew about our purpose, knew about the law governing our life together.

The case of Januarius

3. We were also joined by the priest Januarius. He seemed to get rid of all he had by honestly distributing it, but he didn't get rid of it all. Some assets, that is, some money, remained with him, which he said was his daughter's.[15] His

daughter, by God's grace, is in a monastery of women, and we have good hopes for her. May the Lord direct her course, so that she may fulfill our hopes for her, by his mercy, not by her own merits. And because she was under age, and could do nothing with her own assets—while we could appreciate the splendid sincerity of her profession, we had some fears about the slipperiness of youth—it was arranged that that money should be kept, as if it were the girl's, so that when she came of age, she could do with it what befitted one of Christ's virgins, when she could do it finally to best advantage.

Before this time came, he himself drew near to death; and swearing consistently that it was his own, not his daughter's, he made a will about it. A priest, a companion of ours, staying together with us, living on the Church, professing the common life, made, I'm telling you, a will. He made a will, he said who would be his heirs. Oh, what a sad blow for that company of ours! What fruit, not produced by the tree which the Lord had planted! He made the Church his heir.[16] I don't want these gifts, I don't like the taste of such bitter fruit. I myself had recruited him for God, he had made profession in our company: this is what he would keep to, this is what he would observe. He would have nothing?[17] He shouldn't make a will. He had something? He shouldn't pretend to be our companion as one of God's poor.

This has been a great grief to me, brothers and sisters. I'm telling your graces, on account of this grief I have decided not to accept this inheritance for the Church. Let what he left belong to his children, let them do with it what they like. It seems to me, you see, that if I were to accept it, by that very fact I would be his partner in an action that displeases me and causes me real pain. This is what I did not wish to conceal from your graces. His daughter is in a monastery of women, his son in a monastery of men. He disinherited both of them; her, with words of praise, him with a clause in the will severely censuring him. Now I have recommended the Church not to accept such legacies, which really belong to disinherited children, except when they have come of age. The Church keeps such property for them.

Then again, he has left his children an occasion for a quarrel which troubles me greatly. The girl says, "It's mine, you know that my father always said that." The boy says, "My father should be believed, because he couldn't possibly lie when he was dying."[18] And what a really bad thing this wrangling is! But if these children are both servants of God, we can quickly put an end to this dispute between them. I will listen to them as a father, and perhaps better than their own father. I will see what the rights of the matter are, as God wills, together with a few of the faithful and respected brethren taken, by God's favor, from among your number, that is from this congregation. I will hear the case between them, and as the Lord grants us, I will settle it.

Augustine's policy about legacies left to the Church, and his answer to some critics

4. All the same, please, don't let any of you blame me because I don't want the Church to receive this legacy; first, because I detest his action; secondly,

because it's my policy. Many of you will praise what I am going to say, but some too will criticize it. It's very hard to satisfy both parties. You heard just now when the gospel was read, *We have sung to you, and you did not dance; we have wailed for you, and you did not mourn. John came, neither eating nor drinking, and they say, He has a devil. The Son of man came, eating and drinking, and they say, Look, a greedy man, a toper of wine, a friend of taxmen* (Lk 7:31-34). So what am I to do in the face of those who are ready to find fault with me and bring their teeth to bear on me, if I accept legacies from those who are disinheriting their children in anger? Again, what am I going to do with those to whom I sing, and they refuse to dance? Those who say, "Look why nobody gives anything to the Church of Hippo; look why those who are dying don't make it their heir. It's because bishop Augustine in his goodness"—you see, they are biting me by their very praise, caressing with their lips, and digging their teeth in—"waives everything, accepts nothing."

I certainly do accept things, I assure you I accept good offerings, holy offerings. But if anyone is angry with his son, and disinherits him on his deathbed, if he lived, wouldn't I try to placate him? Wouldn't I have the duty to reconcile him with his son? So how can I wish him to be at peace with his son, when I have my eyes on his inheritance? But certainly, if he does what I have often urged people to do—he has one child, let him think of Christ as the second; he has two, let him think of Christ as the third; he has ten, let him make Christ the eleventh, and I will accept it. So because I have done this in a number of cases, they now wish to turn my goodness, or their estimate of my reputation, in another direction, to find fault with me in another way, that I refuse to accept the offerings of the devout. They should consider how many I have accepted. What's the point of listing them all? Here you are, I'll just mention one; I accepted the inheritance of Julian's son.[19] Why? Because he died without children.

The case of Boniface's legacy

5. I refused to accept the legacy of Boniface,[20] not out of softheartedness, but out of fear. I didn't want the Church of Christ to be a shipping company. There are indeed many people who make a fortune from ships. Yet should there be just one mishap, should a ship go aground and be wrecked, were we going to hand people over to the torture, at the customary marine inquest into the loss of a vessel, and have those who had been saved from the waves tortured by the judge?[21] But we would not hand them over;[22] no way, I mean, would it be proper for the Church to do that. So would it pay the resultant fine and damages? But what would it pay them from? It's not right for us to keep a reserve fund; it's not the bishop's business to save up gold, and repulse the beggar's outstretched hand. There are so many asking every day, so many groaning, so many needy people pleading, that we have to leave several of them unhappy, because we haven't got enough to give all of them something; and should we set up a fund to insure against shipwreck? So it was to avoid this that I did it, not out of generosity. Nobody need praise me for it, but nobody should blame me either.

Certainly, when I have granted a son what his father, dying in anger, took away from him, I have done well. Let those who wish praise me, those who don't want to praise me, at least spare me. What more, my brothers and sisters? Anyone who wants to make the Church his heir after disinheriting his son, should look for someone else to accept the legacy, not Augustine; or rather, by God's grace, may he not find anyone to take it. How that admirable action of the holy and venerable bishop Aurelius of Carthage filled the mouths of all who knew about it with the praises of God! Someone who had no children, and apparently no hope of any, gave all his property to the Church, keeping only the use of it to himself during his life. Children were in fact born to him, and the bishop gave back the endowment he had made, without his in the least expecting it. The bishop had the right not to give it back— but according to the civil law, not according to the law of heaven.

Augustine's change of policy about depriving of their clerical
status those who do not keep his rules

6. Certainly your graces should also know this, that I have told my brothers, who stay with me that anyone who possesses anything should either sell it and distribute the proceeds, or donate it to the common fund; let the Church have it, through which God provides for us. And I have given them until Epiphany, for the sake of those who either haven't divided their property with their families, and have left what they have with their brothers, or who have not yet done anything about what is theirs, because they were waiting till they came of age. Let them do whatever they like with it, provided they are prepared to be poor together with me, and we all look together for support purely and simply to the mercy of God. But if they don't want to do this, as perhaps some don't—well certainly I'm the one, as you know, who determined to ordain no one a cleric unless he were willing to stay with me; on such terms that if he chose to turn away from his purpose, I would have the right to deprive him of his clerical status, because he was throwing over his membership in a sacred association, which he had promised and begun.

Well here and now, in the presence of God and of yourselves, I am changing my policy: those who wish to keep some private property, for whom God and the Church are not enough, may stay where they like and where they can; I will not deprive them of their clerical status. I don't want to have any hypocrites. It's bad—who would deny it?—it's bad to fall away from one's commitment; but it's worse to pretend to have such a commitment.[23] Look, this is what I am saying, listen: someone who deserts the fellowship of the common life which he has taken on, which is praised in the Acts of the Apostles, is falling away from his vow, falling away from his holy profession. He should watch out for a judge—but God, not me. I myself am not depriving him of his clerical status. I have set before his eyes what great danger he is in; let him do what he likes. You see, I know that if I decide to degrade someone who does this, he won't lack patrons, he won't lack supporters, both here and among bishops, to say,

"What has he done wrong? He's unable to take this kind of life with you; he wants to stay outside the bishop's residence, he wants to live on his own income; should he forfeit his clerical status for that?"

I for my part know what an evil it is to make a holy commitment and not carry it through. *Make your vows*, it says, *and pay them to the Lord your God* (Ps 76:11); and, *It is better not to make a vow than to make one and not perform it* (Eccl 5:4). Take a virgin, for example; if she was never in a monastery, and is a dedicated virgin, it is not lawful for her to marry. She isn't compelled to be in a monastery; if however she has started off living in a monastery, and left it, and yet remains a virgin, half her life has collapsed. In the same way a cleric too has made a commitment to two things: both holiness of life and the clerical state. The holiness, meanwhile—as for the clerical state, God has placed it on his shoulders through the people;[24] it's more of a burden than an honor, but *who is wise and understands these things?* (Ps 107:43)—so he has made a commitment to holiness; he has committed himself to live together in a community, he has professed *how good and pleasant it is, brothers dwelling in unity* (Ps 133:1). If he falls away from this commitment, and remains outside as a cleric, he too has fallen away from half his life. What's it got to do with me? I'm not judging him.

If he preserves sanctity of life outside, he has fallen away from half his life; if he stays inside and is just pretending, he has ruined the whole of it. I don't want him to have any need to pretend. I know how men love the clerical state; I won't deprive anyone of it who doesn't want to live in community with me. Those who wish to live with me have God. If they are prepared to be provided for by God through his Church, not to have any private property, but either to distribute it to the poor or put it in the common fund, let them stay with me. Those who don't want this may consider themselves free; but they should also consider whether they can have eternal felicity.[25]

A further report on the situation promised after Epiphany

7. That must be enough for your graces for the time being. What I do with my brethren—I have good hopes, you see, that they will all obey me willingly, and that I am not going to find any of them possessing anything, except by necessity of religion,[26] not out of sheer possessiveness—so what I do, I will inform your graces after Epiphany as God wills; and I won't conceal from you how I settle the dispute between the brother and sister, the two children of the priest Januarius. I have talked at length; please excuse the talkativeness of old age, that is also the timidity of ill-health.[27] I, as you can see, have now grown old in years; ill-health made me an old man long ago. Still, if God is pleased with what I have said now, he will give me strength, I won't let you down. Pray for me, that as long as there is a soul in this body, and any kind of strength supplied to it, I may serve you in preaching the word of God.

NOTES

1. The sermon was preached after Christmas, either at the end of December or the beginning of January; at any rate, shortly before Epiphany, 426. The best account of the whole situation which gave rise to the occasion for this and the next sermon is to be found in F. van der Meer's *Augustine the Bishop*, chapter 8, "The clergy and the ascetics," section 1, "The *Episcopium* as monastic community."

2. He and his clergy.

3. The Maurist text reads "any of us," meaning any of us clergy, I presume.

4. *Non pollui, sed pollere*, wordplay impossible to reproduce in translation.

5. A text he recalls right at the beginning of his *Rule*.

6. Back in 391, when he was 37.

7. A very successful orator, and eventually, in all likelihood, a distinguished political career, either at the imperial court or as governor of some province of the empire.

8. Literally, he says "over peoples," each local Church constituting a *populus*, a people.

9. In case he was promptly elected bishop there. Bishops in those days were not appointed by the Holy See, or any "higher authority," but elected by the clergy and people of the city or town in question. These electors, though, would often ask the primate of Africa, the bishop of Carthage, to provide them with a bishop from among his numerous clergy; and as several of Augustine's fellow "servants of God" in his monastery became bishops, he himself after becoming a bishop may well have been asked to supply a vacant see, now and then, with an occupant.

10. Valerius, who was however, in spite of his Latin name, a Greek, and wanted a good Latin speaking priest to assist him in his pastoral duties.

11. *Presbyter*, not *sacerdos*, the word usually behind the English "priest," signifying one who offers sacrifice or presides over sacred ceremonies. *Presbyter*, a word simply meaning an elder (which is why the Presbyterian Churches have elders), signifies the second grade in the Church hierarchy only. So, of course, does "priest" in the context of this and the next sermon; so I have decided to keep it, with some slight misgivings, having earlier thought I should just transliterate "presbyter."

12. *Senex* Valerius, literally, "the old man Valerius"; but *senex* was a formal, almost official title of respect for a senior bishop, in particular for *the* senior bishop of a province; Valerius may well have been the senior bishop or primate of Numidia by seniority. "The old man" in English, on the other hand, is a distinctly informal, though often affectionate way of referring to the man in charge. So I opt for "Father."

13. Back in his home town of Thagaste, presumably, where he had first established his monastery, to which he was hoping to bring back the friend he had come to visit in Hippo Regius. Now he is setting up a new monastery, with new companions on the site given him by Valerius.

14. The manuscripts read, "if this custom in the monastery *missa esset*," which I have more or less translated. The Maurists emend it to read *permissa esset*, if it were permitted in the monastery. But they have a footnote which shows that they do not really believe in their emendation. They wonder if *missa esset* was not really put for *omissa esset*, if this custom were omitted in the monastery. Or else whether, keeping *missa esset* in the sense of transferred to the monastery, Augustine means that it would be unfitting, not for the monastery, but for the bishop to leave all hospitality to the monks. The point is, Augustine cannot be saying that it was unfitting for monks to show hospitality to wayfarers and the poor; this was universally regarded as one of their chief social responsibilities—and still is. Augustine was not thinking, one concludes, about preserving the cloistered seclusion of the monks, but of the duty of the bishop to share the burden of hospitality with them. Which is why he begins the next sentence—in the Maurist text—"And that's why . . ."

15. Januarius was almost certainly a widower when he joined the community, as no mention is made in the subsequent story of provision for his wife. But he could well have been ordained a priest before his wife's death.

16. The Church of Hippo Regius. Januarius had already died, and it was on his death that his will came to light.

17. So the Maurists: *Nihil haberet?* Another text reads *Nihil habebat?* "He had nothing?"

18. As the father had censured his son in his will, it is hard to see what point the son was making in opposition to his sister.

19. *Filii Juliani hereditatem.* The most natural translation is the one I have given; but then he goes on to say that he, presumably Julian, died without children. He is, I think, indulging in a deliberate oxymoron, or contradiction; Augustine accepted what would have gone to Julian's son, if he had had one, because he didn't have one. But if readers think that is too difficult to swallow, they can take *filii* as being in apposition to *Juliani*, and translate "the inheritance of son Julian."

20. So the Maurists; another text reads *Bonifati, id est Fati, Fatus* being the man's well-known nickname. As it would sound so odd in English to say "of Boniface, that is, Face," I keep with the Maurists, though the longer is probably the more authentic reading.

21. The extraordinary, and indefensibly brutal, Roman legal procedure of examining witnesses under torture.

22. So the Maurists; the other text has *nos* for *non*, and the sense, making the sentence into a question, "But would we hand them over?"

23. And if the threat of being degraded from the clergy remained, the inference presumably is, as in fact he says in the last section, that several would continue to keep their private property secretly, while remaining in the community, for fear of losing their status.

24. *Per populum.* The Maurists read *propter populum*, for the sake of the people. But that looks like an emendation made at a time when the people no longer had any say at all in choosing, or designating, their clergy. I think in Augustine's time they did still have a residual say—they certainly had in the choice of bishops, and it was by popular acclamation and force that Augustine himself had been made a priest.

And here he points to a most important distinction between a vocation to the priesthood and a vocation to the religious life; a distinction which has been almost entirely lost sight of in the last few centuries since the Council of Trent. A vocation to the priesthood, properly speaking, is not an inner prompting from the Holy Spirit that one would like to be, or ought to be, a priest. It is, properly speaking, a call, a summons from the Christian community that they want you to be a priest. It should be exactly the same kind of vocation, differing only in degree, as the vocation to be a bishop or a pope. This comes from the Church, and one is normally obliged to accept it, even though one doesn't want it—and even if one does, it is considered decent to show reluctance. Whoever heard of anyone saying, "I think I have a vocation to be a bishop"; or of vocations campaigns urging men to consider whether or not they have vocations to be bishops? The same should apply, in principle, to the vocation to the priesthood.

A vocation to the religious life, on the other hand, cannot possibly be imposed on anyone by the Church or the community. It must be a spontaneous response to some inner call from God.

25. The old man is certainly being excessively harsh here.

26. Presumably property held in trust for religious purposes; like Eraclius, for example, Augustine's future successor, having a fund with which he built the shrine for Saint Stephen; or held in trust for members of the family, like Januarius holding money, as Augustine and everyone else thought, in trust for his daughter.

27. Anything less timid than the preacher of this sermon it is hard to conceive.

SERMON 356

SAINT AUGUSTINE'S SECOND SERMON ON THE WAY OF LIFE OF THE CLERGY
WHO WERE LIVING WITH HIM

Date:426[1]

Recapitulation of what was said in the previous sermon

1. Your graces are owed a sermon today about us clergy ourselves. As the apostle says, you see, *We have become a spectacle to the world, both to angels and to men* (1 Cor 4:9); those who love us look for something to admire in us, while those who hate us tear us to pieces. We, however, set in the middle between both parties, have the duty, with the help of the Lord our God, so to protect both our way of life and our reputation, that our admirers are not put to shame by our detractors. Now many of you know from holy scripture how we wish to live, and how by God's grace, we already do live; to remind you of it, though, the actual reading from the book of the Acts of the Apostles shall be chanted to you, so that you may see where the pattern is described which we desire to follow. So while it's being chanted, I want you to pay very careful attention, so that after its recital I may, with God's help, say to attentive ears what I have decided on.

And the deacon Lazarus read: *When they had prayed, the place where they were gathered was shaken, and they were all filled with the Holy Spirit, and began to speak the word of God with confidence to everyone who wished to believe. Now the multitude of believers had one soul and heart, and they none of them said that what they possessed was their own, but they had all things in common. And the apostles were testifying with great power to the resurrection of the Lord Jesus; and great grace was upon them all. Nor was there anyone in need among them. For as many of them as owned estates or houses sold them, and brought the proceeds from them and laid them at the feet of the apostles; while distribution was made to each as each had need* (Acts 4:31-35).

When the deacon Lazarus had chanted the passage, he handed the volume to the bishop, and Augustine the bishop said:

I too want to read. It gives me more pleasure, you see, to be reading these words than to be arguing my case with my own words. *When they had prayed, the place where they were gathered was shaken, and they were all filled with*

173

the Holy Spirit, and began to speak the word of God with confidence to everyone who wished to believe. Now the multitude of believers had one soul and heart, and they none of them said that what they possessed was their own, but they had all things in common. And the apostles were testifying with great power to the resurrection of the Lord Jesus; and great grace was upon them all. Nor was there anyone in need among them. For as many of them as owned estates or houses sold them, and brought the proceeds from them and laid them at the feet of the apostles; while distribution was made to each as each had need.

A brief recall of the case of the priest Januarius

2. When the bishop finished reading, he said: You have heard what our wishes are; pray that we may be able to live up to them. It has, however, become imperative that I should deal with the matter more thoroughly, because, as you already know, a priest who was a member of our community, the sort of community to which the reading you heard just now when we were reciting it bears witness, made a will as he was dying, because he had property to make a will about. There was something he called his own, while living in a community where nobody was allowed to call anything his own, but they had everything in common. If any friend and admirer of ours were to sing the praises of this community in the presence of one of our detractors, and say, "All bishop Augustine's companions live with him exactly as it is written in the Acts of the Apostles," that detractor would immediately shake his head, and bare his teeth, and say, "Do they really live in the way you say they do? Why are you lying? Why honor with false praise men who don't deserve it? Wasn't there recently a priest with a position in their community who made a will, and disposed of what he possessed as he wished, and left it as a legacy? Do they really have everything in common there? Does nobody really call anything his own?"

What could my admirer do under the hammer blows of these words? Wouldn't that detractor be, so to say, stopping up his mouth with lead? Wouldn't he bitterly regret having praised me? Wouldn't he be covered with shame and put completely out of countenance by the other's words, and curse either me or that man who made the will? This is why it was imperative that we should give the matter this thorough airing.

The happy result of Augustine's investigations
into the affairs of his community members

3. So then, I've news for you to rejoice at. I have found all my brothers and my fellow clergy who live with me, priests, deacons, subdeacons, and my nephew Patrick,[2] to be such as I desired. But there are two who haven't yet done what they had decided to about their poor little properties; the subdeacon Valens, and the nephew of mine I have just mentioned. The subdeacon was prevented from doing so, both by his mother still being alive, because she was being supported by it, and by his waiting too till he came of age, so that the action he

took might be fully confirmed and ratified.[3] But he hasn't yet taken it,[4] because he owns those small fields in common with his brother, as an undivided property. He is eager, though, to bestow it on the Church on such terms that those of his household who are in mind for a life of holiness may be supported from it as long as they are in this present life. It's written, you see, and this is something the apostle says, *Anyone who does not provide for his own, and especially for his domestics, is denying the faith, and is worse than an unbeliever* (1 Tm 5:8). But there are still some slaves likewise owned jointly with his brother, not yet shared out. He is planning to emancipate them, and cannot do so until they are shared out, because he still doesn't know which will belong to him. Making the division, certainly, belongs to him as the elder, and then having the first choice belongs to his brother. His brother too is serving God; he is a subdeacon to my holy brother and fellow bishop, Severus, in the Church of Milev. The business is under way, due to be completed without delay, of sharing out and emancipating those slaves, so that he can give the property to the Church and provide for their support from it.[5]

As for my nephew, from the time of his conversion[6] and his coming to live with me, he too has been prevented from doing anything about his few small fields by the unwillingness of his mother who had the use of them, and who only died this year. There are some issues outstanding between him and his sisters, to be settled soon with the help of Christ; so that he too may do what befits a servant of God, what his very profession, and this reading, requires.

The deacon Faustinus

4. The deacon Faustinus, as almost all of you know, was converted to the monastery here from a military career in the world.[7] He was baptized here, and then ordained deacon. But because what he possessed, *de jure*, not *de facto* as the lawyers say,[8] was little enough, he just left it behind and it was held by his brothers. He has never given it a thought since his conversion, nor has he asked for anything from his brothers, nor has anything been asked of him. Now that it has come to this point of time, on my advice he has divided the property, and given half to his brothers, half to the poor Church that is established in the same place.

The deacon Severus

5. You know to what sort of trial and affliction the deacon Severus has been subjected by God; but he hasn't lost the light of reason.[9] He had bought one house here for his mother and sister, whom he was eager to bring here from his native place. He didn't buy it, though, with his own money, because he didn't have any, but with a collection taken up by religious laymen, whose names he gave me when I asked for them. I cannot say what he has done with the house, or what he's planning, except that he has placed the whole thing at my disposal, so that what I myself wish may be done about it. He still has some problems

with his mother, of which he has made me the judge, so that when these are settled, I may do what I wish with the house. What can I wish, though, under God's direction, but what justice commands and filial piety requires? He also has some fields in his native place; he is arranging to dispose of them in such a way that there too a benefaction may be made to the poor Church established in that place.

The deacon of Hippo

6. The deacon of Hippo[10] is a poor man; he has nothing to bestow on anyone. And yet from the fruit of his labors before he joined the clergy he had bought a few slaves. Today in your presence he is going to emancipate them through the episcopal register.[11]

The deacon Heraclius

7. The deacon Heraclius is constantly before your eyes, his works are brilliantly evident to the eyes of all of us.[12] It is thanks to his work and the money he has spent that we have the memorial chapel of the holy martyr.[13] On my advice he has also bought a property with his money, because he wanted that money to be distributed by my hands, in whatever way I pleased. If I were greedy for money, or in this case were to care more for meeting the obligations I have toward the poor, I would have accepted the money.[14]

"Why didn't you?" someone will ask.

Because that property which was bought by him and given to the Church, is still not bringing anything in to the Church. You see, he didn't have enough for the price demanded; what he had to borrow to pay for it is still being paid back from its rents.

I'm an old man; how much income from that property can be expected to accrue to me? Can I promise myself I am going to live so many years, until it has finished paying off its own price?

So while it's scarcely paying back over a long period of time more than part of the price paid, I could have had the whole sum very soon, if I had wished to accept it. I didn't do it, I had different ideas. I confess to you and to him, I still had my doubts about his youth, and I was afraid, seeing that they are only human, that perhaps his mother would not be pleased, and would say the lad had been unduly influenced by me, so that I could swallow up his paternal inheritance, and leave him destitute. That's why I wanted his money to be invested in that property, so that if things should later have turned out otherwise than we wish—which God forbid!—the estate could be returned to him, and the bishop's reputation suffer no damage. I know, you see, how much my reputation means to you; as for me, my conscience is enough.

He also bought that plot behind the church which you all know, and built a house on it with his money. This too you know; that a few days before the talk I had with you about this affair,[15] he donated it to the Church. He had been waiting to finish it, you see, so that he could donate it all complete. However there was no need for him to build the house, except that he was thinking his mother was going to come here. If she had come earlier, she would have been living on her son's property; if she comes now, she will be living in the work of her son's hands.[16]

I bear him witness, he has remained poor; but he has remained in possession of charity. He had been left a few slaves, who are in fact already living in the monastery, whom however he is going to emancipate today through the Church register. So let nobody say "He's rich"; nobody think it, nobody speak ill about him, nobody in this way tear himself and his own soul to pieces with his teeth. He hasn't got any money, money saved up; I just hope he can pay back what he owes!

The rest of the deacons

8. The others, that is the other deacons,[17] are poor. By God's grace they are depending on God's mercy. They have nothing about which they need to do anything. Having no means, they have finished with the greedy desires of the world. They are living with us in a common fellowship. No distinction is made by anyone between them and those who have brought something to the community. The unity effected by charity is always to be put before the advantage of an earthly inheritance.

The priests

9. There remain the priests; I have wanted, you see, to come to them like this step by step. Let me say at once, they are God's poor. They have brought nothing to our community house except the charity than which nothing is more precious. However, since I know that rumors have been going around about their wealth, they don't have to be obliged by me to do anything, but their name does have to be cleared to you by my words.

The case of Leporius

10. I'm telling those of you who are unaware of it, because a great many of you in fact know it very well; that while the priest Leporius came of a distinguished family in the world, and was born within that family to the most honorable position,[18] he gave up everything he possessed, so that I received him here quite penniless; not because he never had anything, but because he had already done what this reading encourages people to do. He didn't do it here, but I know where he did do it. The Church is one, it is the unity of Christ; wherever a good work is done, it also belongs to us, if we rejoice together over it. There is a garden in a place you know; there he has established a monastery for his people, because they too are given to the service of God. This garden doesn't belong to the Church, but nor does it to Leporius himself.

"So to whom does it belong?" someone will say.

It belongs to the monastery situated there. But what is true is that up until the present moment he was looking after them in such a way that he kept in his own hands the rents needed to support them, and paid them out, so it seemed, himself. But to avoid this giving a toehold to people who like chewing over their suspicions and never having their fill of them, he and I agreed that the members of that monastery should now cope with their own affairs as if he himself had already departed this life. When he does die, after all, he isn't going to go on providing for them, is he? It's better that he should see them leading a good life under God's guidance, living in such a way under Christ's discipline that he simply rejoices on their account, and doesn't have to occupy himself with their needs.

As for the building of the hostel which you can now see completed, I myself laid this task on him, I myself gave the orders for it. He was most willing to comply with my wishes, and as you can see, he has done the work. It was also on my instructions that he has put up the basilica for the Eight Martyrs,[19] with the resources God has provided through your generosity. He began it, you see, with the money which had been given to the Church for the hostel, and when he had started building, devout people who desire to have their works recorded in heaven gave their help to the extent each wished, and up the building went. We have the work in front of our very eyes; just look, everyone of you, at what has been done.[20]

As for the money involved, let the critics believe me that he doesn't possess it; let them stop their backbiting, or they may break their teeth. With the hostel money he had bought a house in Carraria,[21] which he thought he would find useful for its stones; but it turned out that the stones of this house weren't needed for the building, because stones were provided from elsewhere. So the house remains as it was, and brings in some rent, but to the Church, not to the priest. So nobody should say anymore, "In the priest's house, at the priest's house, in front of the priest's house." Look, that's where the priest's house is; where my home is, that's where his home is. He hasn't got a home anywhere else—apart from wherever he has God.[22]

Settlement of dispute between Januarius' children

11. What else are you expecting? Except that I remember I also promised that I would report to you what I had settled between the two children of the priest Januarius, brother and sister, that is; because a difference had arisen between them about some money—but still a difference as between siblings, with no damage done, by God's grace, to charity. So I had promised I would hear the case between them, and whatever it was, would settle it with a formal judgment. I was prepared to be the judge; but before I could act as such, they themselves settled the matter I was to have passed judgment on. I found nothing to make a judgment on, only something to rejoice over. They fell in wholeheartedly with my wishes and my advice, that they should share equally between them the money their father had left, the Church forgoing any claim to it.

Augustine ready to answer any further criticisms
that may be leveled against him and his clergy

12. After this sermon of mine people are going to talk; but whatever people may say, some of it will reach my ears, in whatever direction the wind is coming from. And if it's such that we need yet again to clear ourselves, I will answer the slanderers, I will answer the adverse critics, I will answer the skeptics, those who don't trust us, their leaders; I will answer them as best I can, and as the Lord enables me to. Meanwhile, there's no need to do so now, because perhaps they aren't going to say anything. Those who love us will be free to rejoice, those who hate us will cover their disappointment in silence.

Still, if they do sharpen their tongues, what they, together with you, will hear from me, by God's grace, will be my answers, not my counter-charges. I am not going to name any names, you see, and say, "So-and-so said this, So-and-so spread this slander," because it's possible, as can indeed happen, that false reports will be brought back to me. All the same, whatever is brought back to me, I will speak about it to your graces, if it seems advisable. I want our life to be lived openly before your eyes. I know that those who are looking for an excuse for leading bad lives look assiduously for examples of people leading bad lives, and defame many people so that they may appear to have found themselves companions in ill-doing. That's why we have done what it was our job to do; there is nothing more we can do. We are always before your eyes. We desire nothing of anyone, other than your good works.

Gifts should be offered to the community,
not to its individual members

13. And I beg you, my brothers and sisters, if you wish to give anything to the clergy, you must realize that you oughtn't to do it in such a way as to encourage their vices, so to say, against me. Whatever you wish to offer freely, offer to all of us together. What is common to us all will be distributed to each as each may need. Stick to the collection box, and we shall all have it. It pleases me immensely to think of that as our manger, so that we can be God's beasts, and you God's field. Nobody should give a cloak, or a linen tunic, except to the common store. Then whoever gets one, will get it from the common store.

As for myself, since you know[23] that I wish to have in common whatever I do have, I don't want your graces to offer me such things as I alone could, as it were, with propriety make use of. I'm offered, for example, a very expensive cloak; perhaps it would be suitable for a bishop to wear it, although it isn't suitable for Augustine to do so, that is to say a poor man, born of poor parents.[24] Now people are going to say that I wear expensive clothes, which I couldn't have had either in my father's house or in my old secular profession. That's not right; I should have the sort of clothes that I can give to my brother, if he hasn't got some. Clothes such as a priest can wear, such as a deacon and subdeacon can suitably wear, those are the ones I am willing to accept, because I am accepting them for the common store. If anyone gives me anything better, I sell it. Yes, that's what I am in the habit of doing, so that when a garment cannot be for common use, the price of the garment can be. I sell it, and I distribute the proceeds to the poor.[25]

If a donor likes the thought of me myself having something, he—or she—should give me the sort of thing I am not ashamed of. You see, I confess to you that I am ashamed of expensive clothes, because they are not suitable for this religious profession of mine, not suitable for what I'm now reminding you of, not suitable for this body, not suitable for these grey hairs. I also want to say this: if anyone in our house, in our community should happen to be ill, or just recovering from illness, so that he has to take some food even before the time for dinner; I won't forbid religious lay men or women to send in whatever they consider they should send in. Nobody, though, shall take his dinner or supper outside.

Those clergy who stay in the monastery, and are found to be hypocrites, by in fact continuing to possess property, will be struck off the roll of the clergy

14. Look, I am telling you, you have heard what I say, they, the clergy, can hear me too. Any of them who wishes to have his own property, and live off his own income, and act against these instructions of ours—it's not enough for me to say that he won't remain with me, he won't even continue to be a clergyman. I had said, you see, and I know I said, that should they be unwilling to undertake community life with me, I wouldn't deprive them of their clerical status, they could stay somewhere else, live somewhere else, live as best they could for God. And yet I placed before their eyes what a bad thing it is to fall away from one's commitment. I preferred, you see, to have even crippled colleagues than to mourn over dead ones. Because anyone who is a hypocrite is dead.

So just as if any of them wishes to stay outside and live off his own income, I won't deprive him of his clerical status; so now, because the others have chosen, by God's grace, this community life, any of them who lives it hypocritically, who is discovered to have his own property still, I won't permit him to make a will about it, but I will strike him off the roll of the clergy. Let him appeal against me to a thousand councils, let him sail overseas against me[26] wherever he likes, certainly wherever he can; so help me God, wherever I am bishop, that man cannot be a clergyman. You have heard me, they have heard me. But I hope in our God and in his mercy, that just as they have accepted my arrangements in a cheerful spirit, so they may observe them with simplicity and fidelity.

The case of the priest Barnabas

15. I have said that the priests living with me as my companions have nothing of their own, and among them is also the priest Barnabas. But I have heard rumors tossed around about him, above all that he has bought a villa from my dear and honored son, Eleusinus.[27] It's not true; Eleusinus donated it to the monastery,[28] he didn't sell it. I myself am a witness to this. What more you want,

I don't know. I myself am a witness; he donated it, he didn't sell it. But while people don't believe he could have donated it, they believe he sold it. Happy man who did such a good work that nobody would believe it! Anyway, believe it now, at least, and stop listening so gladly to malicious gossip. I've now told you—I myself am a witness.

It's also said about Barnabas that in the year he was in charge he deliberately ran up debts, so that I, wanting the debts to be paid, would give in to his request to be granted the farm at Victoriana;[29] as though he had said to me, "To enable me to pay my debts, give me the farm at Victoriana for ten years." This too is simply not true. But there was something which gave rise to the rumor. He did contract debts that had to be paid. I paid off some of them, insofar as I could. There remained something which was also owing to that monastery which God had established through him.[30] So since this debt remained outstanding, we started looking around for means of paying it off. Nobody offered to rent that farm, other than a man who was offering a rent of forty *solidi*.[31] But we saw that the farm could yield much more than that, to pay off the debt more quickly. So I entrusted it to him, so that the brothers should not look for a profit from letting the farm, but should put down whatever the farm yielded to the reduction of the debt. It's a matter of trust.

The priest is quite ready for me to put somebody else in charge, who would pay the brothers from the farm's profits. I would like it to be one of you that I commit it to, preferably one of those who regaled me with such stories. You see, there are also religious people among you who were upset at his being blamed on the strength of a false rumor, and who yet believed he had done it. So let one of them come along to me, undertake the administration of the farm, sell its produce at the proper price, so that the money still owed can be the more readily paid, and the priest's responsibility for it can cease as from today.

The site on which the monastery has been established was also donated by my honored son Eleusinus, already mentioned, to the priest Barnabas before he was ordained a priest; it was on that site that he established the monastery.[32] But still, because the site had been donated in his name, he changed the title deeds, so that possession of it might be in the name of the monastery. As regards the farm at Victoriana I myself am begging, I myself urging, I myself beseeching some religious person to hold it in trust, and do the Church this service, to get the debt paid off as soon as possible. But if no lay person is found willing, I myself will put someone else in charge; this man will not go back there.

Nobody should tear the servants of God to pieces, because it doesn't do the tearers any good. The reward, indeed, of God's servants increases with false calumnies, but the punishment coming to their detractors increases too. It is not, I mean, just for nothing that it was said, *Rejoice and exult, when they speak ill of you, uttering falsehoods, because your reward is great in heaven* (Mt 5:11-12). We don't want, though, to have a great reward at your expense. Let us have a smaller reward there, and still reign there together with you in the kingdom.

NOTES

1. Preached in January, shortly after the Epiphany. See Sermon 355, note 1.

2. His sister's son, named after his grandfather, Augustine's father Patricius. In translations of the *Confessions* (IX, 9, 13), and in all books about Augustine, he is always called Patricius; but the English form of this name is Patrick, so Patrick let Augustine's nephew be. He was probably a subdeacon; and the Maurist text, in a rather confused reading, explicitly makes him one.

3. I think the *legitima aetas* when one came of age under Roman law must have been 25, and not 21.

4. The suggestion is that his mother has now died.

5. Yet another tiny monastery, to be established on a small plot of land, for Valens' ex-slaves. One suspects that most of these small religious communities, mushrooming everywhere, had a rather ephemeral existence.

6. To the religious life, not to the Christian religion.

7. *De militia saeculi.* It could be a metaphorical expression, suggesting that Faustinus had led a very worldly existence, or simply that he had been in government employment as a civil servant. Or was he, perhaps, the Faustinus whose somewhat spectacular and very public conversion is mentioned in Sermon 279, where see note 6? But that had occurred 24 or 25 years, earlier, and in Carthage. However, I take it he had been a soldier, discharged in the normal way after 25 years' service, and so was a man of distinctly mature years; possibly indicated by his being mentioned first among the deacons.

8. What they said then was *jure non corpore*; which I am assuming was the equivalent of the later legal expression.

9. So his affliction, Van der Meer reasonably suggests (*Augustine the Bishop*, 204), was blindness.

10. Odd that he is given a title rather than a name. Would he have been the equivalent of the archdeacon of a later period? Van der Meer, op. cit., wisely offers no explanation. It looks as if before joining the clergy the deacon of Hippo had been some sort of small craftsman in town, like a cobbler or cabinet maker, and had bought the slaves to help him in his business.

11. *Episcopalibus gestis.* Such legal proceedings, presided over by bishops, were recognized as valid in civil law.

12. He was clearly Augustine's favorite among the clergy—to be nominated as his successor a few months later. See Letter 213.

13. Saint Stephen, whose relics had reached Hippo Regius only a year or so earlier. See Sermon 318, note 1.

14. Instead, presumably, of advising Heraclius to invest it in the property. But then the reason he apparently gives for not accepting the money is that the rent from the property is all being used up in paying back the extra money borrowed to buy it. The whole case is certainly rather baffling. However, the solution to the puzzle is probably as follows: the first "because" after the question is not in fact his answer to the question—how characteristic of his tortuous mind! This first "because" is simply explaining how he himself is gaining nothing from the whole transaction. His answer to the question comes in the next paragraph: he didn't want Heraclius' mother to say that he had persuaded Heraclius, still very young, to give his family inheritance away to the Church. By having it invested in an estate, he was avoiding its simply being spent; it was always there, available to be given back, should Heraclius decide, as we would say nowadays, that he didn't have a vocation. The business of paying back money borrowed to buy the villa is all an irrelevant complication, only serving to show how Augustine is getting nothing out of the deal.

15. Presumably before Sermon 355.

16. Which is now the property of the Church.

17. The Maurists read "subdeacons." But he had already dealt with subdeacons earlier on in section 3. He began with them, Valens and his own nephew, Patrick. And as he will say in the next section, he is working his way up the hierarchical ladder. These other deacons presumably include

the reader Lazarus. They were all probably too young to be able to dispose of their property, even if they had any.

18. As the eldest son, possibly, of the senior branch.

19. See Sermon 313G, 3.

20. The sermon was perhaps being preached in this basilica.

21. A suburb of Hippo Regius, no doubt.

22. Following the Maurists, *sed ubicumque habet Deum*. Another text reads *sed ubique habet Deum*, but he has God everywhere.

23. Emending the *sciam* of all texts, "since I know," to *sciatis*. *Sciam* could make better sense in the Maurist text, which runs the previous sentence into this one, altering it to read, "It's from the common store that I too receive things for myself, since I know I wish to have in common whatever I do have. I don't want your graces to offer . . ."

24. On the social and economic class to which Augustine belonged see, for example, G. Bonner's *St Augustine of Hippo: Life and Controversies*, chapter 2, "Augustine's Life, I." The author quotes with approval I. Marrou as saying that Augustine's father belonged "to the petty bourgeoisie on the way to proletarianization." Revised edition, 1986, 37.

25. The poor brethren, I suppose, as well as the poor of the parish.

26. To the imperial court at Ravenna. This severity is directed only against those who have elected to stay in the monastery as from this moment, and are then caught cheating. Any who wished to pull out now could do so, and could remain in the diocese as what we would now call diocesan or secular clergy. But hitherto Augustine had refused to have such clergy, only ordaining those who were willing to stay in the monastery, leading the regular monastic life.

But the whole matter is a little problematic. There were clearly other monasteries in the diocese, like the one established by the priest Barnabas which will be mentioned in section 15. And the diocese of such a comparatively large city as Hippo Regius, with quite an extensive rural hinterland, cannot have been served just by clergy, in particular priests, from the bishop's residence. So he had probably relaxed his original rule a few years earlier, and had sometimes been willing to ordain priests who were not proposing to live in a monastery.

27. A layman of prominent family.

28. A monastery which Barnabas had established himself, not the one in the bishop's residence.

29. A place about 30 miles from Hippo Regius, mentioned in *The City of God*, XXII, 8, as a place where a miracle was performed in a memorial chapel dedicated to Saints Gervase and Protase; a young man delivered from diabolical possession.

30. Money owed, it seems, by Barnabas to his monastery.

31. The word signified by the s in L.s.d; but clearly worth much more than a shilling. It was a gold coin, though much debased from its original value. The man was perhaps offering a rent of something like £40 a year.

32. It seems quite clear to me that the founder of the monastery was Barnabas, not Eleusinus, who was simply the generous lay benefactor. But van der Meer and the Italian translation both take it that it was Eleusinus who established the monastery. The text can be read either way.

SERMON 357

IN PRAISE OF PEACE

Date: 411[1]

How the lovers of peace should deal with those who hate it

1. This is the time to encourage your graces, with all the strength God grants me, to love peace, and to pray to the Lord for peace. So let peace be our beloved and our mistress, our hearts be the chaste couch we share with her, enjoying together a quiet mutual trust, and not an association of bitter wrangling, in the loving relationship of inseparable friends. It's harder to praise peace than to possess her. If we wish to praise her, you see, we have to rally our powers, put our ideas together, weigh our words; but if we wish to possess her, we can do so without the slightest effort.[2]

Those who love peace are of course to be praised; but as for those who hate her, rather than provoking and challenging them by harsh words, it's better for the time being to pacify them by just giving them factual information[3] and even just keeping quiet. The true lover of peace also loves his enemies. Just as if you love this daylight, after all, you don't get angry with the blind, but feel sorry for them, because you know what a good thing it is that you enjoy the use of; and therefore, observing what a good thing they are deprived of, you realize they deserve your pity. And if you had the means, the skill, the medicines, you would be in a greater hurry to cure than to condemn them. In the same way, if you are a lover of peace, whoever you may be, have pity on the person who doesn't love what you love, doesn't have what you have.

The thing you love, in fact, is such that it doesn't make you jealous of anyone who possesses it with you. He has peace together with you, and he doesn't thereby restrict your possession of it. Anything material that you love, it's difficult for you not to be jealous of someone who has it. Again, if you have a mind to share with your friend the material you possess, so that your benevolence may be admired, so that even in these temporal things charity may be displayed; so if you're willing to share your earthly possession with your friend, like an estate, a house, or anything of that sort, you share it with one, and admit him to your company, and enjoy it together with him. You think, perhaps, of admitting a third, and a fourth partner; you are already considering how many

184

it has room for, how many it can stand, whether it is a house for lodging them or a field for supporting them. And you say, "It won't now take a fifth partner, it's impossible for a sixth to live with us, when will such a small property ever support a seventh?" So others are excluded, not by you, but by limited space. Love peace, have peace, be in possession of peace, take to yourself as many others as you can to be in possession of peace with you. The more people it is possessed by the more extensive it will be. An earthly house hasn't got room for many; the property which is peace grows ever bigger the more inhabitants it has.

To love peace is to have it

2. What a good thing it is to love it! This, you see, is the same as having it. Is there anyone who doesn't wish what he loves to increase? If it's only a few people that you want to be at peace with you, then your peace will be small. If you want this possession to increase, add another possessor. Because this thing I've just said, brothers and sisters, "It's a good thing to love peace, and loving it is having it," just think how much it's worth! What voice would suffice to praise this saying, what heart to reflect on it: "To love it is to have it"? Consider all the other things which set people on fire with greed. Observe someone else loving farms, silver, gold, a large family, stately well-furnished houses, pleasant and valuable estates. Does he love this? He does. The one who loves it doesn't straightaway have it, does he? It can happen, after all, that the lover of all these things remains empty-handed. When he hasn't got them he loves them, he's on fire with greed to get them; when he starts getting them, though, he's tormented with the fear of losing them. He loves honors, perhaps, loves authority. How many men yearn for the positions of authority they have been denied the chance of occupying! And it usually happens that their last day overtakes them before they attain to what they love.

So just how much must it be worth, when you have something the moment you love it? You don't go looking for what you love with its price in your pocket; you don't go cap in hand to a patron with whose help to attain to it. Look, just stay where you are, love peace, and what you love is right there with you. It's a thing of the heart. Nor do you share peace with your friends in the same way as you share bread. If you want to share bread, of course, the more people you break it to, the less there is left where that came from. Peace, though, is like that bread which increased in the hands of the Lord's disciples as they broke and distributed it.[4]

Heretics hate peace, as the bleary-eyed hate light;
each to be treated gently

3. Be at peace therefore, brothers and sisters, with each other. If you want to draw others to peace, you must first have it yourselves, first hold on to it yourselves. Let what you have glow in you, so as to kindle others. Heretics hate

peace, and the bleary-eyed hate the light. Does it follow therefore that light is bad, because the bleary-eyed cannot endure it? The blear-eyed hate light; and yet it is on account of light that the eye was created. So those who love peace and want what they love to be possessed by others with them, take pains to increase the possession by adding other possessors. So they should take pains to cure the eyes of the bleary-eyed, by any means available, any effort called for. They are cured reluctantly, they don't like it while they are being cured; but as soon as they can really see the light, they will be delighted. Suppose they do get angry; don't get tired of persevering. Be yourself the first to observe, lover of peace, and to take delight in the beauty of your beloved, and be on fire to draw others to her. Let them see what you see, love what you love, hold fast what you hold fast.

Your beloved, whom you love, is addressing you; she says to you, "Love me, and immediately you have me. Bring along with you as many as you can to love me; I will remain chaste and undefiled. Bring along as many as you can; let them discover me, hold me, enjoy me. If many people seeing this light don't spoil it, can many lovers spoil me? But they don't want to come, because they lack the means with which to see me; they don't want to come, because the splendor of peace dazzles the bleary eyes of dissension." Notice the pitiful voice of the bleary-eyed. They are told, "It has been decided that Christians should have peace."[5]

When they received that sort of message, they said to one another, "Woe betide us!"

Why?

"Because unity is coming."

What's this? What words are these, "Woe betide us, because unity is coming"? With how much more justice could you say, "Woe betide us, because dissension is coming"? God forbid, though, that dissension should come; that is darkness for those who are able to see. Because unity is coming, we should all rejoice, brothers.[6] Why are you terror-stricken? Was the word, "A wild beast is coming, fire is coming"? Unity is coming, light is coming.

If they wish to answer you truthfully, they will say, "We aren't terror-stricken because a wild beast is coming; we aren't cowards, after all. What terrifies us is that light is coming, because we are bleary-eyed."

So we must take pains to cure them, somehow. We have to share with them something that does not become restricted by sharing, we have to share with them as best we can, to the best of our ability, as God may grant us.

The congregation exhorted to show the Donatists
a Christian and Catholic meekness

4. Accordingly, dearly beloved, I implore your graces to show them a Christian and Catholic meekness. Right now all our concern is to cure them. The eyes of the injured[7] are inflamed and itching, curing them calls for great care, they have to be treated very, very gently. None of you, please, should engage in a

dispute with them, none of you wish even to defend your faith by hot argument, in case a spark should be struck by a dispute, in case an excuse should be given to those who are simply looking for an excuse.[8] Sure, you get some abuse; put up with it, pretend you didn't hear, ignore it. Remember the man needs to be cured. Notice how mild doctors are toward those whom they are healing even with painful, stinging treatment. They hear themselves abused, they apply the treatment, they don't return abuse for abuse. Let it be just a word in exchange for a word, as there is one person to be healed, another doing the healing, not two having a quarrel. Put up with it, I beg you, my brothers and sisters.

"But I won't put up with it," he says, "because he's speaking ill of the Church."

This is what the Church is asking of you, to put up with his speaking ill of the Church.

"He's slandering," he says, "my bishop. He's making gross accusations against my bishop, and am I to keep quiet?"

Let him make his accusations, and yes, keep quiet; not by way of consent, but of forbearance. This is a favor you are doing to your bishop, if for the time being you don't let yourself get mixed up in a slanging match. Understand that this is a critical time; be advised. How many people there are who speak ill of your God! You hear them, and do you imagine he doesn't? You know about it, and does he not know? And for all that, *he makes the sun rise upon the good and the bad, and sends rain upon the just and the unjust* (Mt 5:45). He is showing his patience, putting off the exercise of his power.[9] In the same way you too must appreciate the occasion, don't provoke those with swollen eyes to make them worse by rubbing them.

Are you a lover of peace? Be still, there in your heart with your beloved.

"And what am I to do?"

There's plenty you can do. Put a stop to wrangling, turn to prayer. Don't repel with abuse someone showering you with abuse, but pray for him. You want to speak against him; instead, speak to God for him. I'm not telling you to keep quiet, but rather to choose carefully where you speak, in whose presence you speak while keeping quiet, your lips tight shut, your heart crying out loudly. Where that man can't see you, that's where you must be a good friend on his behalf.

But you can give this kind of peaceable answer to one who doesn't love peace, and wants to pick a quarrel: "Whatever you may wish to say, however much you hate me, detest me as you please, you are still my brother. What can you do in order not to be my brother? Whether you're good or bad, whether you like it or not, inescapably you are my brother."

And he says, "How am I your brother, O my foe, my enemy?"

"By the very fact of your saying this, you are my brother."

It seems very strange; he hates, he detests me, and he's my brother?

Well, would you rather I believed him, though he doesn't know what he's talking about? The one whose health I'm seeking, so that he may see the light and acknowledge that he is our brother? So would you prefer me to believe him that I'm not his brother, because he hates me, and not rather believe the light itself? Let us hear what the light itself has to say. Read the prophet: *Listen, you that are fearful, to the word of the Lord.* The Holy Spirit is speaking through Isaiah the prophet: *Listen, you that are fearful, to the word of the Lord. Say, You are our brothers, to those that hate you and that detest you* (Is 66:5, LXX). What's this? The light has flashed out, revealed where brotherhood really is, and still the bleary-eyed says, "Close the shutters."

No; you, rather, turn your eyes to the light; you, trapped in the dark, recognize your brother who isn't trapped in the dark; and say, say without a qualm, say in God's words, not mine: *Say,* says God, *You are our brothers.* To whom? *To those that hate you.*[10] After all, what's so wonderful about your saying it to those who love you? *To these that hate you and that detest you.* Why all this? Listen, and observe the gain such behavior brings. As though you questioned the Lord your God, and said, "Lord, how am I to say, You are my brother, to someone who hates, who detests me? Tell me why." *That the name of the Lord may be held in honor. May it appear at least in joyfulness; let them, however, blush for shame* (Is 66:5). Observe, I beg you, what is gained by patience, by such persistent meekness. *Say, You are our brothers.* Why? *That the name of the Lord may be held in honor.*

But why doesn't he acknowledge you as his brother? Because he has held in honor the name of a man.[11] So then, say, " My brother; though you hate, though you detest me, you are my brother. Acknowledge in yourself the sign of my Father. It's the word of our Father. Bad brother, quarrelsome brother, still my brother is what you are. You, after all, say, just as I do too, *Our Father, who art in heaven* (Mt 6:9). We say one and the same thing; why aren't we in one and the same body? I beg you, brother, acknowledge what you say together with me, and condemn what you do against me. Pay attention to the words coming out of your mouth. Listen, not to me but to yourself. Notice to whom we say, *Our Father, who art in heaven.* It isn't just a friend, just a neighbor, but the very one to whom we say this, that is commanding us to reach agreement. Together in the presence of the Father we have one voice; why don't we together have one peace?"

The fervor of charity, as against the inflamed swelling of dissension, to be exercised above all in prayer during the solemn fast after Pentecost

5. Say that kind of thing ardently, but say it gently. Say it aglow with the fervor of charity, not with the inflamed swelling of dissension; and pray hard to the Lord with us bishops during these solemn fast days.[12] The due we are now paying to God, let us also pay for this cause. We are already, you see, solemnly fasting after Pentecost; and of course we would be fasting, even if we didn't have this cause. So what do we owe to our brothers, whose cure and restoration to health is our present concern in the name of the Lord our God, our physician, as we make our offering to him on their behalf, not presuming to have ourselves the physician's skilful hands? But what are we to do? Let us pray to the physician

himself, fasting in humility of heart, in pious confession, in fraternal respect. Let us show piety toward God, charity toward these brothers of ours.

Let your almsgiving also be more frequent, to ensure that your prayers are heard the more readily.[13] Be hospitable, keep open house. It's the time for it; the servants of God are coming.[14] Now's the time, now's the chance, why let it slip by? Pay attention to what you have in the cellar and pantry[15] of your house. Also pay attention to what you are depositing up above, what you are saving for yourself, the one and only treasure you can rely on without a qualm. Deposit it above, entrust it not to your slave but to your Lord. You can't fear, can you, any thief creeping in there, any burglar breaking in, any turbulent enemy grabbing it there? Make sure you have something that can be paid back to you. Nor will you be paid back merely what you have deposited. The Lord wants you to be a money-lender at an exorbitant rate of interest—but to him, not to your neighbor.

NOTES

1. The sermon was preached in Carthage, on the first of the Pentecost Ember days, Wednesday 17 May. See O. Perler, *Les Voyages de Saint Augustin*, 288, note 1. This was just before the great Conference, or Colloquy, between Catholic and Donatist bishops, and aimed at setting the tone for that occasion.

2. He will only explain how in section 2. First, though, he characteristically changes tack.

3. Just *docendo*, "by teaching," in the Latin; hardly a procedure, one would have thought, to appease bitter enemies.

4. See Mk 6:41-44.

5. Decided at the imperial court, that peace in Africa between Catholics and Donatists should be seriously negotiated at the Conference, due in a few days' time, to be presided over by the tribune Marcellinus.

6. Here, I think, he is rhetorically addressing the Donatist leaders.

7. Reading *sauciorum*, as the Maurists suggest, instead of the *sanctorum* of their text, "the eyes of the saints." But the Donatists could only be called saints by Augustine in a tone of biting sarcasm, and such an attitude would hardly fit with what he is urging upon his congregation here.

8. An excuse, an *occasio*, what for? He doesn't say, but presumably to break off the negotiations, or to refuse to attend the Conference.

9. Much neater in the Latin: *Ostendit patientiam, differt potentiam.*

10. Here he has got into a conversation with the bleary-eyed Donatist. But his conversation continues, I think, with the Catholic whom he is instructing to tell the Donatists that they are his brothers.

11. Donatus. I have omitted from the text a word, *homines*, that is entirely redundant and impossible to construe, as far as I can see; it is fairly evidently the product of dittography. The text runs, *quia nomen hominis homines honorificavit.*

12. The Ember days after Pentecost. This sermon was preached on the Wednesday, the next on the Friday, 19 May.

13. Following one manuscript. The rest read, "For our almsgiving must increase, to ensure that our prayers. . . ."

14. All the African bishops, assembling for the Conference.

15. He actually says "dining room," *cenaculo*; but I am presuming that this term could be transferred to the cellar and pantry that supplied the dining room.

SERMON 358

Date: 411[1]

To be defeated by truth is to be victorious; the victory of truth is charity

1. May your holinesses' prayers come to the aid of us bishops in the responsibility we carry for you, and for our enemies and yours,[2] for the salvation of all, for public order,[3] for the common peace, for the unity which the Lord has commanded, which the Lord loves. Help us at one and the same time to speak about this to you, and to rejoice over it together with you. Of course, if we love peace and charity, we ought to talk about them always. Much more so therefore at this time, when peace is being loved in such a way, that those people are in real danger of loving it and holding onto it themselves, those to whom we do not render evil for evil,[4] and with whom, as it is written, *though they hate peace, we are at peace* (Ps 120:7), and because we speak peace to them, they wish to overwhelm us. So those people, being of that nature, are caught in a deadly trap between love of peace and the shame of humiliation, and since they refuse to acknowledge defeat, they are taking no steps to be undefeated. Those, you see, who refuse to be defeated by truth, are defeated by error.

Oh, if only charity rather than animosity could overcome them! We for our part love, cling to and defend the Catholic Church, not on the strength of human arguments, but of divine testimonies; and we are inviting its enemies to be reconciled with it and enter its peace. What am I to do with someone who pleads for a part and brings an action against the whole?[5] Isn't it good for him to lose the case, because if he loses he will hold onto the whole, while if he wins, he will be left with the part—or rather if he appears to win, because it's only truth that ever wins. The victory of truth is charity.

The evidence of scripture on the universality of the Church

2. So why, brothers and sisters, should I use many words, and mine at that, to commend to you the Catholic Church which is bearing fruit and growing throughout the whole world? We have the words of the Lord on its behalf, and on ours. *The Lord*, he says, *said to me: My son are you, I today have begotten*

190

you. Ask of me, and I will give you the nations as your inheritance, and as your possession the very limits of the earth (Ps 2:7-8). So why, brothers,[6] are we wrangling about possession of the property, and not rather reciting the sacred title deeds? Let us imagine[7] we have come before a judge. The argument is about possession, and this is not an argument in a lawsuit, but an argument about love. Well anyway, a litigant over possession of some earthly property goes to law precisely in order to exclude his adversary; we are doing so in order to bring our adversary in. When the litigant over an earthly property hears his adversary saying, "I wish to take possession," he replies, "I won't allow it." I, on the other hand, am saying to my brother, "I want you to possess it with me." It's he, making an issue of it, who replies, "I refuse."

And so I'm not afraid that the Lord will condemn me, and rebuke me like those brothers, or rather that brother who appealed to him among the people, and said, *Lord, tell my brother to divide the inheritance with me.* At once the Lord uttered a rebuke, because he hated division; *Tell me, man,* he said, *who set me up as a judge, or a divider of the inheritance between you? I, though, say to you, beware of all greed* (Lk 12:13-15). I don't fear that rebuke. I'm appealing, you see, to my Lord; I admit, I'm appealing. I'm not, however, saying, *Lord, tell my brother to divide the inheritance with me,* but I'm saying, "Lord, tell my brother to share in unity with me." Look, I'm reciting the title deeds of this property, not with the intention of possessing it alone, but of convincing my reluctant brother to possess it with me. Look, here are the title deeds, brother: *Ask of me,* it says, *and I will give you the nations for your inheritance, and for your possession the very limits of the earth.* It was said to Christ; so it was said to us, because we are the members of Christ. Why run off with just a part, or remain in just a part? Look, get your hands on the whole property, as in the title deeds. You are inquiring about the limits within which you may take possession, as inquiries are usually made, with consultation of documents, between owners who have common limits. The one who has given you all limits, hasn't left you confined within any limits.

Some more evidence from scripture

3. Listen to some more evidence from the holy title deeds. It is said of the Lord Christ under the figure of Solomon. *He shall lord it from sea to sea, and from the River as far as the bounds of the earth. Before him shall bow down the Ethiopians, and his enemies shall lick the dust. The kings of Tarshish and the islands shall offer presents; the kings of the Arabs and Seba shall bring gifts. And all the kings of the earth shall worship him, all nations shall serve him* (Ps 72:8-11). When these words were first spoken they were believed; now that they are being fulfilled, they are denied. So then, take possession of the inheritance with me *from sea to sea, and from the River,* namely the Jordan,[8] where Christ's teaching started from, *as far as the bounds of the earth.* Why won't you? Why are you so hostile to this promise and this inheritance, to your own wealth?

Why won't you? Is it because of Donatus? Because of Cecilian? Who was

Donatus? Who was Cecilian?[9] Men, of course. If they were good men, it was
with their own goodness, not mine; so too if bad men, with their own badness,
not mine. As for you, accept Christ, and pay attention to Christ's apostle, so
jealous for him: *Was it Paul who was crucified for you? Or was it in the name
of Paul that you were baptized?*. But to prompt him to say this, notice what it
was that shocked him: *Each one of you is saying, I indeed am Paul's man, I
though am Apollo's, I however am Cephas', but I am Christ's. Has Christ been
divided up? Was it Paul who was crucified for you? Or was it in the name of
Paul that you were baptized?* (1 Cor 1:12-13). If not in the name of Paul, much
less in the name of Cecilian, and much, much less in the name of Donatus.[10]

And yet still, after these words of the apostle, after the manifestation of the
Church and its spread throughout the world, I will be told, "I'm not quitting
Donatus, I'm not quitting heaven knows which Tom, Dick or Harry,[11] or Parmenianus. A thousand names, a thousand schisms. Will you deprive yourself,
by following a man, of such a great inheritance as you heard about just now—
from sea to sea, and from the River as far as the bounds of the earth? Why not
keep hold of it? Because you love a man? What's a man, but a rational animal,
made of the dust of the earth?[12] So that's why you are an enemy, because you
are *licking dust* (Ps 72:9). You should despise it, rather. Don't lick the dust of
the earth, but instead place your hopes in the one who made heaven and earth.
This is our hope, this testimony here: *The God of gods, the Lord, has spoken
and summoned the earth, from the rising of the sun to its setting* (Ps 50:1). Don't
remain with the earth, but go instead to where the earth has been summoned.

Charity should be bringing Catholics and Donatists together

4. And who could recite all the testimonies to be found in the holy title deeds
of this property? So why aren't they converted to the Church, if not because this
is the voice of the Church itself: *Let those who fear you and know your testimonies be converted to me* (Ps 119:79)?[13] The Church has seen what it said in the
psalm. You heard it a moment ago, the words are fresh in your ears and your
hearts: *I have seen the end of every consummation.* "Consummation," meaning
completion, not consumption;[14] and "end," also meaning completion, not abo-
lition. *I have seen the end of every consummation; your commandment is
exceedingly broad* (Ps 119:96). *I have seen the end of every consummation.*
What is this end? *Your commandment is exceedingly broad.* For *the end of the
commandment is*—now you say it with me. [The people all shouted] *charity
from a pure heart* (1 Tm 1:5).

You have all said, what you have always heard to good effect: *The end of the
commandment is charity from a pure heart*—the end by which we are completed, not the one by which we are consumed. This end is broad, because it is
a commandment of God about which it says "your commandment is exceedingly broad": *A new commandment I am giving you, that you should love one
another* (Jn 13:34). Notice how broad this commandment is. Where is it broad?
Not in the flesh, surely? In the heart, rather. Because if it were also broad in the

flesh, you, my eager listeners, would not be as cramped as you are for space. It's broad in the heart. See where it's broad, if you've got the wherewithal to see it,[15] and then hear from the apostle how broad this commandment of charity is: *The charity of God has been poured out in our hearts* (Rom 5:5). He didn't say "shut in," but "poured out"; the phrase "shut in," you see, rings a note of cramped space, whereas "poured out" suggests expansive breadth.

So then, *your commandment is exceedingly broad.* Lord our God, please certify that it's because of this breadth that we are inviting our brothers to share in the possession of peace. Is it that you wish to be bishops? Be so with us.[16] The people don't want two bishops in every Church? Be brothers with us in the inheritance. Let us not put obstacles in the way of Christ's peace for the sake of our honors. What honor are we going to receive in the peace of heaven, if we now defend our honor by wrangling on earth? Let the dividing wall of error be removed, and we can be together. Acknowledge me as your brother; I am acknowledging you as my brother—but apart from schism, apart from error, apart from dissension. Let these things be put right, and you are mine. Or don't you want to be mine? I, if you put yourself right, want to be yours. So then, with error removed from between us, like a *wall of partition* (Eph 2:14), consisting of contradiction and division, be my brother, and let me be your brother, so that we may both be the brothers of the one who is both my Lord and yours.

Let the matter be negotiated

5. We say this out of a love of peace, not out of lack of confidence in the truth. This, you see, is what we wrote back, this is the proposal you have read;[17] because we aren't running away from discussing and negotiating the matter. On the contrary, we are pressing for it to be discussed and negotiated, so that when I have demonstrated to you where possession lies, I may in this way share the inheritance with him. Let him come fearlessly, let him come without a qualm, let him come well instructed; I don't wish to prejudge the case by authority.[18] Let us open our eyes to the one who cannot be mistaken; let him teach us what the Church is. You have heard the testimonies about it. It cannot be contaminated by human delinquency, since it has not been redeemed by human justice.

And yet, while the issue about the Church is one thing, the issue about persons another,[19] and they are quite distinct from each other, we aren't afraid of facing the issue of persons either, whom they have accused, and been unable to convict. We know they were cleared, we have read the documentation of their being cleared. Even if they hadn't been cleared, I would never set up a Church because of them, and build one on sand, and pull down one built on rock;[20] because *on this rock*, he said, *I will build my Church, and the gates of the underworld shall not overcome it* (Mt 16:18). *Now the rock was Christ* (1 Cor 10:4). *Was it Paul that was crucified for you?* (1 Cor 1:13). Hold on to these texts, love these texts, repeat then in a fraternal and peaceful manner.

An appeal to avoid any disorders, and to leave the business of arguing
the case to the bishops, and to help them by prayer and fasting

6. Please don't any of you, my brothers and sisters, burst in on the place where the conference is being held. In fact, if it's at all possible, avoid passing through that area at all, in case perhaps an opening should be found for quarrelling and wrangling, or some excuse given, and those who are looking for excuses should grasp that excuse; especially since those who have little fear of God, and don't give a fig for this admonition of ours, ought at least to have a healthy respect for the severity of the secular authorities. You have read the edict of his honor,[21] publicly posted up. Not indeed that it was posted up on account of you who fear God and don't ignore the admonitions of your bishops; but in case there should be any who don't care about these things and who do ignore them. So such people should look to it, in case perhaps what the apostle said should apply to them: *For the one who resists authority is resisting what God has ordained. For rulers are not to be feared for good works, but for bad* (Rom 13:2-3).

Let us avoid all disorder, all occasions for disorder. Perhaps you will say, "We are keen to know what we are to do." And what task am I to lay upon you?[22] What are perhaps the more effective works of piety. We bishops are arguing and debating on your behalf; you can be praying on ours. You can also assist your prayers, as I have already urged upon you, with fasting and almsgiving. Add these wings to your prayers, on which they can fly to God. Engaged in this business, you may well be of more use to us than we are to you. We are none of us, you see, in this grave debate, relying on ourselves; all our hope is in God. Nor, after all, are we better than the apostle, who says "Pray for us." *Pray for me*, he says, *that the word may be given me* (Eph 6:19). So you are pleading for us to the one in whom we have placed our hopes, so that you may have reason to rejoice over the result of our debate.

Hold fast to these things, brothers and sisters, I beg you, by the name of the Lord himself, by the author of peace, the sower of peace, the lover of peace;[23] I beseech you to beseech him peaceably, to plead with him peaceably. And remember to be the sons and daughters of the one about whom it is said, *Blessed are the peacemakers, for they shall be called sons of God* (Mt 5:9).

NOTES

1. Preached in Carthage two days after Sermon 357 on Friday, 19 May. O. Perler, however, in *Les Voyages de Saint Augustin*, 290, thinks this sermon was preached several days later, between 26 and 31 May, because it refers to the two letters the Catholic bishops wrote to Marcellinus (Letters, 128 and 129), the second of which, he says, cannot have been written before 25 May. However, all Augustine says here, at the beginning of section 5, is *Hoc rescripsimus*, "This is what we wrote back"; and in fact Letter 128 by itself covers all the points made in this sermon. Finally, the reference to fasting in section 6 suggests to my mind that we are still in the Pentecost Ember days.

2. The Donatists. I translate the opening words as referring to "us bishops," rather than to "me," because here I am sure he is soliciting the congregation's prayers primarily for the impending Conference, and not for himself as the preacher of this sermon. But it is true he does go on to refer to his own task as the preacher.

3. *Pro quiete.* The leadership of the bishops was very necessary to ensure there were no sectarian riots at a critical moment like this.

4. See 1 Pt 3:9. In saying they were in danger of loving peace, he is of course being ironical in what is meant to be a benign way.

5. The Donatists were constantly referred to as the *pars Donati,* the party, or part, of Donatus, whereas the Catholic Church was precisely catholic, or universal; not restricted to a *part* of the world, North Africa, or to an ecclesiastical *party.*

6. Here the Donatists.

7. So the Maurist text. Another, published by Lambot, has "Let them imagine."

8. He is wrong here; the River, without qualification, in the Old Testament is the Euphrates.

9. The figures at the origin of the Donatist schism, Cecilian the bishop of Carthage, to whose election and ordination in 310 vigorous objection was taken by what came to be the Donatist party, on the grounds that he and the bishops who ordained him, or at least one of them, had been *traditores,* traitors, by handing over, *traditio,* the sacred books to the persecuting authorities; and Donatus, the man who was elected by that party, not immediately to replace Cecilian, but after one short-lived predecessor.

10. Some manuscripts leave out Cecilian, and simply read, "If not in the name of Paul, much less in the name of Donatus." The omission looks rather like the correction of a scribe, who didn't think Augustine could really be bracketing the Catholic Cecilian with the schismatic Donatus.

11. *Nescio quem Gaium, Lucium.* These two were the Latin equivalent of Tom, Dick, and Harry. They are introduced to disparage Parmenianus, who was real enough, and Augustine wrote a work against him in several books. He was a Donatist controversialist of an earlier generation. But he was not one of the Donatist leaders who started schisms within the schism.

12. See Gn 2:7.

13. How can this be a reason for their not being converted to the Church? He is implying, presumably, that the Donatists neither fear God nor know his testimonies. And I think he is going on to imply that they also lack charity—but he is going to do it by exhorting them to reflect on the meaning of charity.

14. *Consummatio* never does mean consumption; but perhaps the less educated often mixed it up with *consumptio.*

15. Meaning eyes in the heart, purified by faith—and by charity too.

16. See Letter 128.

17. The answer of the Catholic bishops to the tribune Marcellinus' convocation of the Conference.

18. I think he must mean here the imperial authority; because of course he goes on immediately to appeal to the authority of Christ.

19. About Cecilian and the bishops who had ordained him. See note 9 above.

20. See Mt 7:24-27.

21. *Viri illustris,* an official rank; he means the imperial tribune, Marcellinus.

22. Following the Maurists; the alternative text reads, "There is something I would lay upon you."

23. So the Maurists; the alternative text reads, ". . .by the author of peace, the establisher of peace, the sower of peace."

SERMON 358A

DISCOURSE OF SAINT AUGUSTINE ON THE VALUE OF BEING MERCIFUL

Date: uncertain[1]

Being merciful, or kindhearted,
makes us share in other people's sorrows

1. I very much wish to address your holinesses on the subject of being merciful or kindhearted, and its real value. Although I have often experienced how forward you are in every kind of good work, still it's necessary that we should have a word or two on the subject, carefully condensed in summary form.[2] We are to discuss, then, what being merciful or kindhearted essentially is. It is nothing other than feeling a soreness of heart caught from others. It gets its Latin name, *misericordia*, from the sorrow of someone who is miserable; it is made up of two words, *miser*, miserable, and *cor*, heart. It means being heartsore. So when someone else's misery or sorrow touches and pierces your heart, it's called *misericordia*, or soreness of heart.

And so observe, my brothers,[3] how all the good works which we perform in our lives are really an expression of being merciful or heartsore. For example, you offer some bread to a hungry man; offer sympathetic kindness from the heart; don't do it contemptuously, or you'll be treating a fellow human being like a dog. So when you perform a work of mercy, if you're offering bread, feel sorry for the hungry; if you're offering drink, feel sorry for the thirsty; if you're handing out clothes, feel sorry for the naked; if you're offering hospitality, feel sorry for the stranger and traveler; if you're visiting the sick, feel sorry for the people who are ill; if you're burying the dead, feel sorry for the deceased; if you're patching up a quarrel, feel sorry for the quarrelers.

We do none of these things, if we love God and our neighbor, without some sorrow of heart. They are good works which confirm that we are Christians. You see, the holy apostle says, *While we have the opportunity, let us do good to all* (Gal 6:10). And again, what does he say himself in the same place[4] about such good work? *This I say, however; that the one who sows sparingly will also reap sparingly* (2 Cor 9:6). He has introduced sowing time, promised a harvest.

No need for works of mercy in heaven

2. But when you are sowing, because you are doing a work of kindhearted mercy, you are *sowing in tears* (Ps 126:5), since you are feeling sorry for the person you are helping. One day, all the same, after we've reached the end, there will be no need for sowing these seeds of kindheartedness; because in that kingdom, those who have here been sorely tried for God's sake will not be miserable or wretched. No, but in very truth, in that final balancing of accounts, to whom will you offer bread, where nobody's hungry? What naked person will you find to give clothes to, where all are robed in immortality? To whom will you show hospitality, where all will be living in their true home country? What sick people will you visit, where there is universal and eternal health? What dead will you bury, where all live forever? What quarrels will you patch up, where that full and perfect peace reigns of which we have here received the promise?

So there will be no works there, no soreness of heart. Why not? Because you are already *bringing in the sheaves* (Ps 126:6), not casting the seed. So let us not falter; we are sowing in tears, that is to say, in hardship, pain and sorrow. And so you shouldn't falter in the works of mercy; you will, after all, receive the reward of your sowing.[5] Winter sows in hardship; but has the harshness of winter ever deterred the countryman from casting in the soil the fruit of such painstaking labor? He goes along and casts in the soil what he had gathered from the soil, what had been sifted from the soil. Out he goes, and casts it in the soil, shivering with cold, tireless and undeterred. What makes him tireless in the cold? It's faith and hope that shake off any temptation to sluggishness. Can he see the harvest? But he believes it will spring up. Is he already gathering the crop? But he hopes he is going to gather it in. And it is with this faith, this hope that he encourages himself to cast seed in the soil notwithstanding the hardship of the freezing weather, so that he may be sure, with God's generous help, of being able to obtain a crop whose abundance accords with the hard work he has put into it.

NOTES

1. Such a short sermon is impossible to date. Quite why it has been inserted in the series in this place, in the middle of sermons relating to the Donatists and the Conference of 411, it is not easy to understand.

2. Why was it necessary? I think he must have been addressing a somewhat specialized group of people; hence, most likely, a small religious community. I don't think in those days they had any such lay associations as the Church can boast of nowadays, like the Saint Vincent de Paul Society, or the Catholic Women's League.

3. On the assumption that he is addressing a small religious community of men, I don't include sisters in his *fratres*.

4. He talks in the same section about sowing and reaping, but about sowing and reaping in the flesh and the spirit. The text Augustine actually quotes comes from a different place altogether.

5. See Gal 6:9.

SERMON 359

ON THE DISPUTE AND ON CONCORD WITH THE DONATISTS

Date:411[1]

On what makes concord between brothers so difficult

1. The first reading from the divine scriptures, from the book called Ecclesiasticus, commended three excellent things to us that are most worthy of consideration: *concord between brothers, and the love of neighbors, and a husband and wife in agreement with each other* (Sir 25:1). These things are certainly good, delightful and admirable in purely human affairs. But in divine matters they are much more significant. Is there anyone, after all, who doesn't rejoice over brothers in concord with each other? And what is indeed deplorable is that such a great thing is so rare in human affairs; the thing is admired by all, actually practiced by so few. Happy indeed are those who embrace in themselves what they cannot help admiring in others. There are no brothers who don't admire brothers living in concord with each other. And what makes it so difficult for brothers to live in concord with each other? The fact that they are at odds about earth, that they want to be earth. Right at the beginning, you see, the man who was a sinner heard, *Earth you are, and to earth you shall go* (Gn 3:19). From this we should be able to work out and examine the words which the man who is just ought to hear in the opposite sense. If the sinner was rightly told, *Earth you are, and to earth you shall go*, the just man is rightly told, "Heaven you are and to heaven you shall go."

Or aren't the just the heavens, seeing that it is most plainly said about the evangelists, *The heavens tell of the glory of God*? And indeed that this is being said about them is made sufficiently clear by what follows: *And the firmament proclaims the works of his hands*. The ones he called heavens he also called the firmament. *Day bellows the word to day, and night to night points out knowledge. There are no languages nor dialects in which their voices may not be heard*. You ask whose, and the only answer you can get is, the heavens'. So it was said about the apostles, said about those who proclaimed the truth. Thus it continues, *Into all the earth their sound went forth, and to the ends of the wide world their words* (Ps 19:1-4).

There are no languages nor dialects in which their voices may not be heard.

198

When the Holy Spirit came upon them, and God began to dwell in the heaven which he had made out of earth, they spoke, with the Holy Spirit generously filling them, in the tongues of all nations.[2] That's why it says, *there are no languages nor dialects in which their voices are not heard*. And because they were sent from there to preach the gospel throughout all nations, *into all the earth their sound went forth, and to the ends of the wide world their words*. Whose? Those of the heavens, who are rightly told "Heaven you are, and to heaven you shall go," just as the sinner was rightly told, *Earth you are, and to earth you shall go*.

So if brothers wish to live in concord with each other,
they should not love earth

2. So if brothers wish to live in concord with each other, they should not love earth. But if it is their wish not to love earth, they must not be earth. Let them seek possession of a property which cannot be divided, and they will always live in concord. What does discord between brothers spring from, the upsetting of natural family feeling? How is it there is one womb between them, and not one spirit, if not because their souls are bent double,[3] and each of them only has eyes for his own portion, and spends all his efforts on improving and adding to his own portion, and wishes to have unity in the possession of his own piece, while possessing division with his brother?[4]

"This is a fine property; whose is it?"

"It's ours."

"A large property." That's the sort of thing that is usually said. "Is it all yours, brother?"

"No; I have a partner here; but if God wills, he will sell me his share."

The flatterer replies, "May God see to it." May God see to what? That the squeeze may be put on the neighbor, and he may sell his share to his neighbor?

"May God see to it. You have the right idea, may God bring it about for you."

Since the sinner is praised in the desires of his soul, and the one who practices iniquity is blessed (Ps 10:3).

What could be more iniquitous than to wish to get rich through the other person's poverty? And yet there's so much of this going on; *the one who practices iniquity is blessed*. And perhaps he has succeeded, perhaps he has put the pressure and the squeeze on, turned the screw, twisted the arm, not of any old partner, but maybe of his own brother: "It's better that I should buy it, rather than a stranger." And the other one, squeezed out so easily, has some consolation, if he's a just man. He should listen to the scripture, which he heard just now. He is weighed down with want, his brother is full of fatness—but he's full of earth, empty of justice. Notice, earth, what that poor man hears: *Do not be afraid when a man becomes rich, nor when the glory of his house is multiplied; since when he dies, he will not take it all with him* (Ps 49:16-17).

As for you, poor man, hold on to what you won't leave behind when you die, and what you will possess while living forever. Hold on to justice, don't regret it. Does it depress you, that you are poor on earth? The one who created the earth was poor here too. The Lord your God is consoling you, your creator is consoling you, your redeemer is consoling you. Your brother, who is not grasping, is consoling you. That Lord of ours, you see, was prepared to be our brother; the only brother completely to be trusted without a shadow of doubt, with whom concord is to be possessed. I said he isn't grasping, and possibly I find he is. Yes, he's grasping; but it's us he wants to grab, us he wants to get possession of. It was for us that he paid such a huge price, himself; a price to which nothing can be added. He gave himself up as our price, and became our redeemer. He didn't give himself up as the price, after all, in such a way that the enemy would let us go, and keep possession of him.[5] He gave himself to death in order to slay death. Yes, by his death he slew death, he wasn't slain by death; and with death slain, he delivered us from death. Death, you see, was alive and kicking while we were dying; it will die when we are living, when it will be told, *Where, death, is your striving?* (1 Cor 15:55).

The right way of giving to everyone who asks something of you

3. So that was the sort of brother who was appealed to by one brother against his brother, brothers between whom, on account of earth, there was no concord; and he said to him, "*Lord, tell my brother to divide the inheritance with me* (Lk 12:13). He took the lot, he doesn't want to give me my share, he ignores me; he may at least listen to you." What concern was it of the Lord's? The way we think, though, low people thinking low thoughts, crawling on the earth, fixed in this life, and not wishing to hurt anybody, and frequently thereby hurting them all the more gravely, what would we have said? "Come, brother, give your brother back his share." That's not what the Lord said. And where could better justice be found than with him? Who could hope to find such a judge, to appeal to against the avarice of his brother? Wasn't that man delighted at finally discovering such a great relief to his wrong? Undoubtedly he was hoping for really effective assistance, when he said to such a judge, *Lord, tell my brother to divide the inheritance with me.* Yet what did the judge say? *O man, who appointed me a divider of the inheritance between you?* (Lk 12:14). The Lord repulsed him, he didn't give him what he was being asked for, he didn't grant him a gratuitous favor.

What was the problem? What was he to lose by it? What in any case was so difficult about doing such a favor? He didn't give him what he wanted. And what about, *To everyone who asks you, give* (Lk 6:30)? He didn't do this, the one who has given us an example of how we should live. How are we, then, going to do it? Or how shall we give what costs us something, if we don't grant a favor that costs us nothing, by which we spend nothing, lose nothing? The Lord didn't give this particular thing; nevertheless, he didn't give nothing. He refused a lesser favor, but bestowed something more than he was asked for. He said, he said quite plainly, *To everyone who asks you, give.* What if someone asks of you, I'm not saying something that it's unprofitable to give, but that it's disgraceful to give? What if some woman asks for what a woman asked of Joseph? What if some man asks for what the false elders asked of Susanna?[6] Does that apparently general rule have to be followed even here? Perish the thought! So shall we in such a case act against the instructions of the Lord?

On the contrary, let us act according to the Lord's instructions, and not give bad things to those who ask for them, and even so we shall not be acting against this maxim. What was said, after all, is, *To everyone who asks you, give*; what was not said, is, "Give everything to one who asks you." *To everyone who asks you, give.* Most certainly, give; give him something. He's asking for something bad, it's for you to give him good things. That's what Joseph did. He didn't give the shameless woman what she was asking for; and yet he did give her what it was right she should hear, so that she wouldn't have his example to justify her shamelessness; he both avoided falling into the pit of lust, and also gave her sound advice about chastity. This, you see, was his answer: *Far be it from me to do this thing to my master, that I should defile his bed, though he has entrusted to me all that is in his house* (Gn 39:8-9). If a slave bought for cash kept such faith with his master, what sort of faith should a wife keep with her husband? This was to admonish her: "I, a slave, will not do this to my master; ought you, his wife, to be doing this to your husband?"

Susanna too gave something, and didn't send them away empty-handed, if they had been willing to take her advice about chastity. Not only, you see, did she not consent to them, but she did not, either, keep quiet about why she didn't consent. *If I consent to you*, she said, *I am lost to God; if I do not consent, I cannot escape your hands; it is better, though, to fall into your hands, than to be lost to God* (Dan 13:22-23).[7] But what's the meaning of, *it is better to fall into your hands than to be lost to God*? You are already lost to God, simply by seeking such things.

So hold on to this rule: give whenever you are asked, even if not precisely what you are asked for. That's what the Lord did. That man was asking for— what? The division of the inheritance. The Lord gave him—what? The death-knell of greed. What did he ask for? *Tell my brother to divide the inheritance with me.* What did he receive? *Tell me, man, who appointed me a divider of the inheritance between you? I, though, have this to say to you both.* What? *Beware of every kind of greed* (Lk 12:13-15). And I'll tell you why. Perhaps, you see, you are asking for half the inheritance precisely in order to get rich. Listen:

A certain rich man's territory was successful, that is, it showed great profits, and was blessed with many crops. *And he thought to himself, saying, What am I to do, where am I to store my crops?* And thinking hard, *I have realized*, he said, *what I must do; I shall pull down the old barns, I shall put up new ones, I shall fill them. You see, I shall make them bigger than the old ones were. And I shall say to my soul, You have many goods; take your fill, enjoy yourself. God said to him, Fool*, you think you're so very shrewd. You know indeed how to pull down old structures and build new ones; you, though, have remained in the old, worn-out ruins of yourself, where you should have been pulling down the old structures in yourself, so that you would no longer savor the things of earth.

Fool, what have you said, who have you said it to? You have said to your soul, *Enjoy yourself, you have many goods. This very night your soul will be required of you, to which you have made such promises. Whose shall they be, the things you have promised?* (Lk 12:16-20). So then, *do not be afraid when a man becomes rich, because he will not, when he dies, take it all with him* (Ps 49:16-17).

About concord among Christians

4. There you have the kind of advice on how to achieve concord, which the Lord gave brothers who were at loggerheads; they should lay aside greed, and would straightaway have their fill of truth. So let us acquire an inheritance like that. How long shall we go on talking about concord between brothers over earthly matters, which is rare enough, unreliable enough, difficult enough? Let's talk about that brotherly concord which ought to be, and can be, very real. Let all Christians be brothers, let all the faithful be brothers, let those be brothers who have been born of God and of the womb of mother Church by the Holy Spirit; let them be brothers, let them too have an inheritance to be possessed,[8] and not divided. Their inheritance is God himself. The one whose inheritance they are, is himself in turn their inheritance. How are they his inheritance? *Ask of me, and I will give you the nations as your inheritance* (Ps 2:8). How is he their inheritance? *The Lord is the portion of my inheritance and my cup* (Ps 16:5). In this inheritance concord is preserved; for this inheritance there is no litigation. Any other inheritance may be acquired by litigation; this one is lost by litigation. Those who don't wish to lose this inheritance avoid the wrangling of litigation.

And when perhaps they seem to be wrangling over it, they are not in fact doing so. But perhaps they appear to be wrangling, or are assumed to be wrangling, when what they are wishing to do is to consult the interests of their brothers. Notice in what a concordant spirit they wrangle or litigate, with what peaceable intentions, what good will, what justice, what fidelity. We too, after all, seem to be wrangling or litigating with the Donatists; but in fact we are not. A man is litigating, you see, when he wishes his opponent ill; he's litigating when he wishes his opponent's loss to be his own gain; for something to be snatched from the other and to accrue to himself. That's not what we are like. You people[9] know this too, you that are litigating outside the unity; you too know this, you that have been acquired as a result of division; you know that this lawsuit is not an action of that sort, because it is not prompted by ill-will, because it is not aiming at the opponent's loss, but rather at his gain.

What we were hoping for, you see, was that those with whom we appeared to be litigating, or even still appear to be doing so, should acquire the inheritance together with us; not that they should lose it in order that we might acquire it for ourselves. In a word, our tone is quite different from that brother's, who appealed to Christ as he was walking this earth. Because we too are appealing to him in this case, as he is seated in heaven; and we are not saying, *Lord, tell my brother to divide the inheritance with me* (Lk 12:13); but, "Tell my brother to possess the inheritance with me."

About the Conference recently held with the Donatists at Carthage

5. That such are our wishes is also borne out by the published *Acts* of the Conference.[10] That such were our wishes is indicated not only by our speeches, but by our letters which were given to them.[11] Do you value the episcopate? Keep it together with us. In you there is nothing that we hate, nothing we detest, nothing we abominate, nothing we condemn, except human error. It's human error, we said, that we detest, not divine truth. But what you have that is God's, we acknowledge; what you have as your own deviation, we wish to correct. The sign of my Lord, the sign of my emperor, the mark[12] of my king I acknowledge in the deserter; I go looking for the deserter, I find him, approach him, accost him, take him by the hand, bring him along, correct him; I do no violence to his regimental mark or badge. To anyone really paying attention and being observant, this is not a matter of litigating, but of loving.

We said that it is possible in one Church, for the sake of peace, for brothers[13] to be in concord with each other; concord between brothers is, surely, a beautiful thing. Is it not possible, after all,[14] we said, for there to be two bishops, so that they both take their seats in one single basilica, one on the bishop's throne, the other as a visitor; one on the bishop's throne, the other seated next to him as a colleague?[15] Or again that one should preside over his brother's[16] congregation, the other in turn over his?

We said that *repentance for the forgiveness of sins had been preached through all nations by the apostles, beginning from Jerusalem* (Lk 24:47). We said: "Let us suppose that Cecilian had an entirely bad case; is one man having a bad case, are two, five, ten men going to prejudice the salvation of so many thousands of the faithful, spread in the most variegated abundance throughout the whole world?" We said all that.[17] Abraham believed, and he was promised all nations;[18] Cecilian sinned, and are all nations lost, so that the wrong he did should outweigh what Truth had promised? These things were said; they are there to be read. Against the divine examples, the testimonies which assert that the Church is to be spread throughout the whole wide world, the Church whose unity we hold fast to in the name of the Lord, they themselves were able to answer precisely nothing.

The case of Cecilian

6. So then, saving the case of the Church, confirmed and unchangeably fixed and established, as on a foundation of rock so that the gates of the netherworld may not defeat it;[19] so saving this then, we also came to the case of Cecilian, not in the least worried now about whatever he might be found to have done wrong. After all, could we possibly be going to argue that if as a man he were found to be in any way to blame, judgment would be given that we were all to be either

condemned or rebaptized because of one man's fault? And we said, "Saving the case of the Church, which is not prejudiced at all by the sin of Cecilian—the Church is neither given the prize for Cecilian's virtue, nor declared the loser for Cecilian's fault—let us also see what sort of case there is against him."

We agreed to look into it, but as the case of a brother, not of a father or mother. Our father is God, our mother the Church; Cecilian was our brother, or is our brother; if good, a good brother, if bad, a bad brother, still a brother. If we find him to be innocent, where will you now be, who have also fallen into the vice of human calumny? But if he's found to have done wrong, if he's found guilty, not even in that event have we been defeated, because what we take our stand on is the unity of the Church, which is undefeated. Let him be found guilty through and through, I condemn the man, I don't desert Christ's Church. That, we said, is what we have guaranteed; from then on we will not recite his name at the altar among the bishops whom we believe to have been faithful and innocent. That is all we have guaranteed; are you going to rebaptize the whole world just because of Cecilian?

So with this assurance firmly settled, the case of Cecilian was opened for investigation. He was found to be innocent, he was found to have been attacked by false accusers. He was condemned once in his absence, three times absolved when he was present; condemned by a faction, absolved by true judgment of the Church. All this was read out, all of it duly attested as genuine. They were asked whether they had anything to say in rebuttal. When they had used up all the twists and turns of their false accusations, or when they were able to offer nothing against the plain evidence of the documents, or against the innocence of Cecilian himself, judgment was given against them. And still they go on saying, "We won." I hope they do win, but over themselves, so that Christ may obtain possession of them; may he win the case against them, the one who has redeemed them.

Many Donatists, though, did really win, by acknowledging defeat

7. And yet there are many of them over whom we can rejoice. Many of them were profitably defeated, because in fact they were not defeated. Human error was defeated, the human being was saved. The doctor, after all, is not striving against the patient; even if the patient is doing so against the doctor, it's the fever that is defeated, while the patient is cured. The doctor's intention, surely, is to win; and that is also the fever's intention, to win. The patient is kind of placed in the middle; if the doctor wins, the patient is saved; if the fever wins, the patient will die.

So in our struggle, the doctor was striving for a cure and health, the patient was on the side of the fever. Those who took some notice of the doctor's advice won the day, they overcame the fever. We have them with us in the Church, in good health and glad of it. They used to speak ill of us before, because they didn't acknowledge us as their brothers; the fever, you see, had disturbed their wits. We, though, love them even while they abominate us and rave against us, and we were putting ourselves at the service of the raving patients. We were standing up to them, struggling with them, and in a kind way wrangling and litigating; and yet we were doing it out of love. All who serve invalids of that sort, after all, make nuisances of themselves; but it is for their welfare and salvation that they do so.

Some of them are sluggish and lethargic, others frenzied in their violence. The case of a priest whose tongue they cut out

8. We have found some, though, who are sluggish and reluctant to move, and who say, "It's true, my lord, it's true; there's nothing more to say."

So what are you waiting for? Come over, act.

"My dead father is there, my mother is buried there."

You've mentioned someone dead and buried. You're alive, there's still someone here to talk to. Your parents were Christians of the party of Donatus; perhaps their parents too were Christians; their grandparents or great-grandparents were certainly pagans. So those who first became Christians, did they freeze up against the truth when they carried out their pagan parents for burial? Did they bow to the authority of their dead parents, and not rather prefer the living Christ to their dead parents? So if it's here that true unity is to be found, outside of which you are bound to die forever, why do you wish to follow your dead parents, dead to you and to God? What have you got to say? Answer!

"What you say is true. there's nothing more to be said. What do you want me to do?"

Goodness knows what kind of habit is holding such people in its grip. They are lethargic, suffering from the opposite kind of disease; they are going to die of sleep. Others are frenzied, they are very troublesome. Because even if the lethargic ones are going to die, at least they don't make trouble for those who are trying to serve them. The frenzied ones make a great deal of trouble, and being quite out of their minds, they roam about, insane and raving and armed, looking for people they can kill, people they can blind. Yes, we have just received the news, they cut out the tongue of one of our priests.[20] These people are in a frenzy. It's a test of charity, they too must be loved. Many of them, seeing the light, have wept bitterly; many have seen the light. We know this, a number of these frenzied people have come to us. Every day they weep over their past deeds, nor can they have enough of tears when they observe the fury of those who are still raving, still drunk on their futile nonsense. So what do we do? Charity obliges us to be at the service of such people. And although we are a troublesome nuisance to both sorts, both by shaking the lethargic and by restraining the frenzied, still we love them both all the same.

Fraternal concord in Christ

9. A good thing indeed it is, *concord between brothers*; but notice where: in Christ. *And the love of neighbors* (Sir 25:1). What if even now he's not a brother

in Christ? Because he's human, he's a neighbor; you should love him too, in order to gain him too. So there you are, in concord with your brother Christian, and loving your neighbor, even though you are not yet in concord with him, because he's not yet your brother in Christ, not yet born again in Christ, doesn't yet know about the sacraments of Christ; he's a pagan, he's a Jew; still he's a neighbor, because he's a human being. So if you love him, you have also attained another strand of love, by another gift, and in this way there are two things in you: *concord between brothers, and the love of neighbors*. And it is of all those who maintain concord between brothers and who love their neighbors that the Church consists, wedded to Christ and submissive to her husband, so that we get the third strand, *a husband and wife in agreement with each other* (Sir 25:1).

Which is why I am admonishing your graces, and urging you in the Lord to think lightly, my brothers and sisters, of things present, which you can't carry with you when you die. Be on your guard against sin, on your guard against injustice of all sorts, on your guard against worldly appetites and greed. It is only then, you see, that our profit from you[21] is undiminished, and our reward full of joy in the Lord. I mean, even if we say what has to be said, even if we preach what has to be preached, and absolve ourselves of our debt to the Lord in the Lord's sight, because we haven't kept quiet about what we fear, haven't kept quiet about what we love, so that the sword of the Lord's vengeance, whoever it may fall upon, will not find anything to charge the look-out with;[22] still, we don't want our reward to be assured with all of you being lost, but with all of you being found. I mean, the apostle Paul too was sure of his reward, and yet what did he say to the people? *Now we live, if you stand fast in the Lord* (1 Thes 3:8).

I am talking to all of you, and to your graces, fathers and brothers,[23] by the Lord's command. I am also speaking on behalf of my brother, your bishop, whose joy you ought to be,[24] by obeying the Lord our God. Certainly this church has been constructed for you, in the Lord's name, by his labors, thanks to the generous contributions and the sympathetic and devout assistance of faithful brothers and sisters. This church has been put up for you; but it is you, rather, who are the Church. What has been built for you is a place for your bodies to enter; but it's your minds that ought to be the place for God to enter. You have honored your bishop by wishing to call this basilica the Florence.[25] But it's really you that are his Florence or flowering. Because that's what the apostle says: *My joy and my crown is what you are in the Lord* (Phil 4:1).[26]

Whatever there is in the world, it fades away, it passes. As for this life, what is it but what the psalmist said: *In the morning it will pass like the grass, in the morning it will flower and pass away; in the evening it will fall, it grows hard and withers* (Ps 90:5-6). That's what *all flesh is* (Is 40:6). That's why Christ, that's why the new life, that's why eternal hope, that's why the consolation of immortality has been promised us, and in the flesh of the Lord has already been given us. It was from us, after all, that that flesh was taken which is now immortal, and which has shown us what he accomplished in himself. It was on our account, you see, that he had flesh. I mean, on his own account *in the*

beginning was the Word, and the Word was with God, and the Word was God
(Jn 1:1). Look for flesh and blood; where is it to be found in the Word? Because
he wished really and truly to suffer with us and to redeem us, he clothed himself
in *the form of a servant* (Phil 2:7), and came down here though he was here, in
order to be plainly visible though he had never been absent; and he that had
made man wished to be made man; to be created of a mother, though he had
created his mother. He mounted the cross, he died, and showed us what we
already knew about, being born and dying. In his humility he went through with
these hoary old experiences of ours, so familiar, so well known.

We knew all about being born and dying; what we didn't know about was
rising again and living forever. So in his humility he took to himself our two old
things; in his sublimity he accomplished two other great and new things. He
raised up flesh, he lifted flesh up to heaven, he is seated as flesh[27] at the right
hand of the Father. He wished to be our head; the head has pleaded for the
members; because even when he was here, he said, *Father, it is my wish that
where I am, there these also may be with me* (Jn 17:24). Let us hope firmly for
all this with respect to our flesh too, resurrection, transformation, inperishability,
immortality, an eternal abode; and let us so conduct ourselves that we achieve
it. That will be Florence, the real flowering Florence.

NOTES

1. The sermon was preached at Bizerta, Hippo Diarrhytus, a few months after the great Conference at Carthage. O. Perler suggests late September as the month (*Les Voyages de Saint Augustin*,
298). The fuller title given by the Maurists is: "On the text of Sir 25:2 on concord among brethren
and love of neighbors, etc.; on the dispute . . ."

2. See Acts 2:1-4.

3. See Lk 13:11, the woman who had been bent double by Satan for eighteen years. Being so
affected meant she could only look down at earth, and not up at heaven. Such are the souls he has
in mind here.

4. An odd manner of talking, which will gradually explain itself, especially as he goes on to
apply the theme to the Donatists.

5. Which would be the case with an ordinary ransom payment, or the handing over of a hostage.

6. See Gn 39; Dn 13.

7. Augustine's text, or paraphrase, is very far from either of the Greek texts the Latin could have
been translated from, that of the Septuagint or that of Theodotion.

8. The text reads *dandam*, to be given. Some manuscripts have *tenendam*, to be held. I am
guessing that *dandam* was carelessly written by a stenographer, falling behind a little, for *possiden-
dam*.

9. Turning to the Donatists—first to their bishops who are actively engaged in the litigation,
then to their lay followers.

10. Held at Carthage at the beginning of June, just a few months previously.

11. Letters in fact addressed to the tribune Marcellinus, who presided over the Conference;
Augustine's Letters 128 and 129, in particular 128. Letter 129 is a response to a memorandum sent

to Marcellinus by the Donatists, and deals with a number of particular points of procedure. But it too testifies to the concern of the Catholic bishops for peace.

12. Here we have the language of sacramental character, with the worldly analogue from which it is taken clearly evident. Roman soldiers were branded, or otherwise indelibly stamped, with the emperor's mark or "character," as a sign of the service they owed him. The sacramental mark or character Augustine has primarily in mind is that of baptism; but secondarily also that of order. The Catholics acknowledged the validity of Donatist orders, and that is what raised the issue he is about to discuss.

13. He means particularly brother bishops.

14. In the text this is a statement. But as such it contradicts what is said in *Letter* 128; whereas, taken as a question, it repeats the suggestions made in that letter. The situation envisaged after the hoped for reunion of Donatists and Catholics was, that in each town where both parties had basilicas and bishops this would continue to be the case; but that the two prelates would take it in turn to preside, each in his own basilica, while the other joined him like any other visiting bishop; or else that they should preside fraternally, each in turn in the other's basilica.

Only after these suggestions does *Letter* 128 go on to say that if the Christian congregation cannot stomach such a dual episcopate, then both should resign, and one single successor to them both be elected and installed.

15. The text actually reads, "one on the Christian throne, the other seated next to him on a heretical one as a colleague." I cannot believe, however, that Augustine would have introduced this harshly discordant note into an otherwise irenic discourse on concord. So I am assuming that the words *Christiana* and *in haeretica* were added, perhaps by the ultra-Catholic stenographer when he made his fair copy.

16. So one manuscript. The others omit the word "fraternal."

17. See Letter 129, 3 and 5. About Cecilian's case, see Sermon 128, note 9.

18. See Gn 12:3.

19. See Mt 16:18.

20. See *Letter* 185,30, written to Count Boniface about ten years later; there he says the unfortunate victim was a bishop. For a general account of such Donatist atrocities see also *Letter* 133, where he mentions a similar attack on one of his own diocesan priests in Hippo Regius.

21. Reading *fructus noster in vobis* instead of the text's . . . *in nobis*, that our profit is undiminished in ourselves. But this hardly makes sense. I think the "our" includes all the bishops and clergy present.

22. See Ez 33:1-6.

23. Here, I think, he turned to the bishops and clergy seated in the apse behind him. It is only they who would have been addressed not only as "brothers," but also as "fathers." The Maurists, however, do suggest emending *secundum jussionem Domini, patres et fratres*—which I have translated—to *secundum jussionem domni patris et fratris*, which would mean translating the sentence, "I am talking to all of you and to your graces by command of my lord, my father and brother," that is the local bishop. It is an ingenious suggestion, but still leaves us with the awkwardness of that opening, *Loquor vobis et caritati vestrae*. Two distinct groups do seem to be envisaged here.

24. See Phil 4:1.

25. The bishop's name was Florentius. See Sermon 15A for the commencement of the building of the new basilica the previous year.

26. The connection of this text with their being their bishop's *florentia* lies in the *corona* or crown of those days being always in fact a wreath of flowers, or of bay or laurel leaves in the case of the prize awarded to athletes.

27. The text simply reads *sedet ad dexteram Patris*. But as he has been emphasizing that Christ raised up *carnem*, and lifted *carnem* up to heaven, I cannot help feeling that Augustine insisted too that it was *caro* that took its seat at the Father's right hand; and that he said, *sedet ad dexteram Patris caro*—or even *carnem*, boldly making the verb *sedet* transitive. But a copyist, familiar with the credal formula being alluded to, *sedet ad dexteram Patris*, would either have just overlooked the final *caro/carnem*, or deleted it as not belonging to the creed.

SERMON 359A

SERMON PREACHED AT TUNEBA ON PATIENCE AND ON THE GOSPEL READING
ABOUT THE STEWARD

Date: uncertain[1]

On Christian hope

1. As long as we are in this world, if we take care to have our hearts lifted up above, the fact that we are walking here below won't be to our disadvantage. We are walking here below, after all, in this flesh. So by fixing our hope up above, we have set it like an anchor on firm ground,[2] able to hold against any of the stormy waves of this world, not by our own strength but by that of the one in whom this anchor of our hope has been fixed. Having caused us to hope, after all, he will not disappoint us, but will in due course give us the reality in exchange for the hope.[3] *For hope*, as the apostle says, *which is seen is not hope; for why should anyone hope for what he can see? But if*, he goes on, *we hope for what we cannot see, we wait for it with patience* (Rom 8:24-25).

On the necessity of patience

2. It's about this patience that I wish to speak to your graces whatever the Lord grants me to say. The Lord Jesus Christ too, you see, says somewhere in the gospel, *By your patience shall you gain possession of your souls* (Lk 21:19). It also says in another place, *Woe to those who have lost patience!* (Sir 2:14). Whether it's called patience, or endurance, or tolerance, the same thing is signified by several names. We, though, should fix in our hearts not the variety of sounds, but the unity of the thing itself, and have inside us what we outwardly give names to. Those who realize they are living the life of strangers in this world, in whatever country they may find themselves as regards the body; who know they have an eternal home country in heaven; who are confident that that is the region of the blissful life which one is at liberty to long for here below, not at liberty to possess here; who are burnt up with such a holy, such a chaste desire—they know how to live here patiently.

Patience doesn't seem to be needed when things are going well, but when they are going badly. Nobody patiently tolerates what is enjoyable. But anything we tolerate, anything we bear with patiently, is harsh and bitter; and thus patience is not needed when you're happy, but when you're unhappy. However, as I started to say, any who are on fire with a yearning for eternal life, in whatever country they may be happily living, must of necessity live patiently, because they have reluctantly to tolerate the fact of their being strangers and exiles, until they reach the desired home country after loving it so long. Love expressed in desire is one thing, love satisfied by sight another. I mean, you love both when you desire and when you see. Your love, when you desire, is aimed at arriving; your love, when you see, at staying. Now if the desire of the saints burns so hot when fueled by faith, what will it be like when fed by sight? If we love like this while we believe what we cannot yet see, how shall we love when we actually do see?

Faith and hope

3. That's why the apostle mentions these three things, which he urges us above all to assemble and construct[4] in the inner self: faith, hope, charity. And when he was praising these three, he said at the end, *but the greatest of these is charity. Aim at charity* (1 Cor 13:13—14:1). So what is faith, what is hope, what is charity, and why is charity the greatest? *Faith*, as it's defined somewhere in scripture, *is the ground of things hoped for, the conviction of things which cannot be seen* (Heb 11:1). When you hope, you don't yet have what you are hoping for, but by believing it you resemble someone who does possess it. *For faith*, he says, *is the ground of things hoped for*, it isn't yet the thing itself which we will eventually take hold of, but our very faith stands for the thing itself. I mean you haven't got your hands on nothing when you have them on faith, nor are they empty if they are full of faith. The reason faith is greatly rewarded is that it doesn't see, and yet believes. I mean, if it could see, what reward would there be?[5]

That's why the Lord, when he had risen from the dead and shown himself to the disciples not only to be seen by their eyes but also to be handled and felt by their hands[6]—but that's why after convincing their human senses that he, the one who had risen, was the same as the one who a short while before was hanging on the cross, and after spending as many days with them as he considered sufficient for confirming the gospel and supporting faith in the resurrection, why he ascended into heaven, so that he would not be seen anymore himself, but would be held onto by believing. I mean if he were here all the time, and were plainly visible to these eyes, there would be no reason for praising faith.

Now, however, people are told, "Believe," and they want to see. The answer they're given is, "In order to see eventually, for the time being believe. Faith does the earning; sight is the reward. If you want to see before you believe, you're demanding to be paid before doing the job. What you want has its price. You want to see God; the price of such a tremendous good as that is faith. Do you want to arrive, and not want to walk? Sight is possession, faith is the way to it. If you shirk the hard work of the journey, how can you expect the joy of possession?"

4. But faith doesn't falter, because it is supported by hope.[7] Take away hope, and faith falters. How after all, when you're walking somewhere, will you even move your feet, if you have no hope of ever getting there? If, though, from each of them, that is from faith and hope, you withdraw love, what's the point of believing, what's the point of hoping, if you don't love? Indeed, though, you can't even hope for anything you don't love. Love, you see, kindles hope, hope shines through love. But when we attain to the things which we have been hoping for while believing in and not seeing them, what faith will there be then to be praised? Considering that *faith is the conviction of things which cannot be seen* (Heb 11:1), when we do see, it won't still be called faith. After all, you will be seeing, not believing.

Again, it's the same with hope. When you have the real thing, you're not hoping for it anymore. *For why should anyone hope for what he can see?* (Rom 8:24). There you are, when we finally arrive, we are finished with faith, finished with hope. What about charity? Faith turns into sight, hope turns into the real thing; now there will be sight and the real thing, not faith and hope. What about charity? Can we really be finished with that too? After all, if it was already burning hot for something that couldn't be seen, obviously when it can see it, it will be burning more hotly than ever. So it was very well said, *but the greatest of these is charity* (1 Cor 13:13), since faith is succeeded by sight and hope succeeded by the thing hoped for, charity succeeded by nothing at all; it is its very self that grows, its very self that increases, its very self that is perfected by that contemplation.

The mere fact of being in lonely exile here is an evil
from which we all pray to be delivered

5. Hence, as we long for the face of God, and sigh for the true home of everlasting happiness, it makes no difference, however much worldly happiness we may be flooded with, however full to overflowing we may be with abundance of this world's goods; obsessed with that desire, shall we not regard our earthly exile as something wretched in itself, and in that very sense of wretchedness[8] do we not plead with God, saying, *Lord, deliver me* (Ps 7:1)? A poor man says *Deliver me*, and you assume he's asking to be delivered from poverty. A rich man says *Deliver me*; perhaps he's ill. On the contrary, he's in good health, and he's rich, and he cries out *Deliver me*. What from, if not from what the prayer itself says: *Deliver us from evil* (Mt 6:13)?

However good their circumstances may be, Christians must of necessity cry out continually, *Deliver us from evil*. If they are crying out, *Deliver us from evil*, there clearly is some for them to be delivered from; if there is some for them to be delivered from, they are in evil straits; if they are in evil straits, however many good things they may have which they can delight in, they also have something they must tolerate until they can enjoy God. So tolerance is absolutely necessary in this life for the poor, the rich, the healthy, the sick, for captives, for free persons, for exiles and foreigners, for those settled in their own country; tolerance is necessary, because all alike are exiles and foreigners in the world. And until they are delivered from this exile, and are united to that truth, to that unchanging reality for which they have been sighing in their exile, they are beset with trials and temptations, and cry to God with complete sincerity of heart, *Deliver us from evil.*

The example of Job

6. But people who are down on their luck see others who in this world are called fortunate and said to be blessed, and they want to be like that themselves, and they imagine that when they are like that themselves, they won't any longer be in evil straits. This is a twisted frame of mind, and not a Christian one, marked by greed, not by faith; they think there is nothing for them after this life. I don't say, "Happy in this life are those who have plenty of everything." Far be it from me to say so; but if they think there is nothing after this life, they are never happy. Reason, after all, assures us, truth assures us that nobody can be happy here—I mean happy as wisdom judges the matter, not as avarice judges it. And there you are, as soon as I have posed the question, everyone has decided that a person can be happy.[9] And I start looking for such people, to see whether any are to be found on this earth. Am I saying, "Happiness is being healthy, being rich, being loaded with honors, living safe and sound with all one's family?" No; what I'm saying is, "Happiness is not lacking anything."

And straightaway comes the answer, "So the rich are happy, because they don't lack anything."

If they lack nothing, they don't covet; if they do covet, they lack something. What you notice is their means, what I question is their greed. How can they lack nothing if they are not satisfied with what they have, and long to have more? You can see that when they've made their pile, it's nothing but firewood to feed the flames, not to satisfy them. So if their greed burns more fiercely the more they have, I'm not just saying they are needy; but that they are needier than those beggars there. The beggar's greed, after all, is satisfied with a few coins, while the whole world is not enough for the greed of the wealthy hoarder.

Here you may well reply, "What if they aren't looking around for anything more than what they have?"

I'll praise them if I find them, warmly congratulate them. They have set limits to something naturally boundless, they have been able to say to covetousness *Thus far* (Jb 38:11). It shows great strength of character, great mental control, to be able to fix a limit, to break in the greedy appetite, to restrain covetousness, to set bounds to the fires of lust. That's real virtue, I admit, real virtue.

All the same, according to the definition I gave, I won't yet call them happy. I mean, what did I say? What is happiness? Not lacking anything.

"Well there you are; these people don't lack anything. They have plenty of everything, and are looking for nothing more."

I've still got a question to ask: Don't they want to have more?

Answer: "They don't."

Aren't they afraid of losing what they have?

Answer: "They are."

So how can you say they lack nothing? Even if they are not lacking in means, they are lacking in security. And is there anyone who can provide them with such security in this world, that what they possess cannot be lost? From whom can they receive any assurance about things that of their nature totter and stagger so unsteadily, slither and slide about in such uncertainty? Many people have gone to sleep rich and woken up poor. So nobody can give them this assurance. And they themselves know this, and that's why they are afraid. So it's vital for them to screw up their courage, for it to receive more strength, greater, more solid firmness, so that just as they set bounds to greed, in the same way they may not be worried about losing what they have, and may have the strength of mind to be able to say, when they have in fact lost everything, *Naked I came from my mother's womb, naked shall I return to the earth. The Lord has given, the Lord has taken away; as it pleased the Lord, so has it happened; may the Lord's name be blessed* (Jb 1:21). A great athlete of God indeed this man was, because he was also wrestling with a great opponent!

So let's suppose some people of such mettle, such greatness of soul, that their heads don't swell over the things they have, and their spirits aren't broken when these things are lost and destroyed; but they have things as though they did not have them, and use this world as though they were not using it.[10] And so they have vast means at their disposal, namely the will of their Lord, like that man we have just mentioned: *As it pleased the Lord*, he said, *so has it happened; may the Lord's name be blessed*. "I'm rich—it's the will of my God; I'm poor—it's the will of my God." See how they have carried out what all of us sing but few of us act upon: *I will bless the Lord at all times, his praise always on my lips* (Ps 34:1). What's *at all times*? Both when things are going well and when they're going badly; that's *at all times*, that's *always*. Those people are truly rich who are rich inwardly, not within the walls of their houses, but within the thoughts of their hearts; in their consciences, not in their bank balances. They can't lose such riches even if they are shipwrecked. I mean they can emerge from the waves stripped of everything, and yet with their coffers full.

Am I to think we have found some people who are happy? If happiness is not lacking anything, why should such people, whoever on earth they may be, not be considered happy? I rather think that we have found even such people as that to be lacking something; if they still lack anything, they are not yet happy.

"Look, they don't covet anything, look, they aren't worried about any losses, prosperity doesn't go to their heads, adversity doesn't unnerve them. In what way are they not yet happy?"

If I find they lack anything, I dare not pronounce them happy.

"And in what respect," someone will say, "are you going to find these people lacking anything?"

I certainly find them so. If they believe in God, they still lack something, they are still God's beggars. Yes, it may happen that such people don't say in the prayer, *Deliver us from evil* (Mt 6:13); but they do say, "We are in need."

"What are they in need of?"

Of eternal life. This they do not yet have. Their lives are spent in the midst of trials and temptations.

Look at Job himself, challenged to love God freely, for nothing—because this was the challenge the devil threw down to him, when all his possessions were destroyed, when he had lost the comfort of his children, and was left only with his wife, to tempt him, not to comfort him; when he was also smitten with terrible sores from head to foot,[11] so that he was deprived even of the poor man's patrimony. The poor man's patrimony, you see, is health, which if the rich man doesn't have, whatever he does have is gall and wormwood to him. Perhaps you can find a poor man who doesn't need the rich man's patrimony; you certainly won't find a rich man who isn't also in need of the poor man's patrimony. It was the poor man's patrimony, that is to say, health, which Job lost when he was smitten with terrible sores from head to foot. He wasn't for all that induced to ascribe folly to God, and in his troubles to be displeased with God; he was always pleased with God. At the promptings of the serpent with whom he was invisibly wrestling, the new Eve suggested he should blaspheme: *Say something against God,* she said, *and die. And he said, You have spoken like the silly woman you are. If we have received good things from the hand of the Lord, can we not endure bad things?* (Jb 2:9-10).

She was Eve, but he wasn't Adam. Adam was defeated in paradise, Job was victorious on his dunghill. But still, among all the things he had to suffer, he said somewhere, *Is not human life on earth a trial and a temptation?* (Jb 7:1). So, being saddled with this human life, he was certainly saddled with a trial and a temptation. He wished to be delivered from this trial and temptation. He too was still lacking that life where there is no trial or temptation. If he lacked it, he wasn't yet happy. And thus, whatever sort of person you may set up here, you will be describing, depicting, aiming at something you won't find; nobody can be happy on this earth.

Back to where he started

7. What had I proposed? To talk about patience. If it hasn't slipped your graces' memory, that's what I proposed. And so let us see how patience is such a great good, that thanks to it we can endure even earthly happiness.[12] Anyone who hasn't got it, falls by the wayside. Anyone who falls by the wayside on the journey, won't arrive at the longed for home country. You can see, then, how true it is that it's by our patience that we gain possession of our souls.[13]

A consideration of death

8. So as long as we are living here, however fortunate our circumstances, let us live patiently. Now all of us, or almost all of us, are afraid of dying. Sickness may befall us, or it may not. The loss of our dear ones is something we fear; it's possible we may lose them, it's possible we won't. Whatever bad thing you may

fear on this earth, it may possibly happen, it may possibly not. Death cannot possibly not happen. It can be delayed, it can't be eliminated. And yet everybody works so hard to put off the evil day; everyone keeps watch, or digs in, or bolts the doors, or sails the seas, or plows the fields. On land, in the house, wherever they may be toiling away, the reason people toil away is not in order not to die, but just in order to die a little later.

Just reflect, my dearest friends, how much work just about everyone puts into dying a little later. If we spend all that labor on merely dying a bit later, how much should be spent on never dying at all? This too is to be counted among the things to be put up with, and among the things to be tolerated and endured patiently: the fear of death, with which every soul has to wrestle. Notice, in fact, what the apostle says: *We groan, being weighed down*, on this earth under this load of perishable flesh, *in that we do not wish*, he says, *to be stripped, but to be clothed over, so that what is mortal may be swallowed up by life* (2 Cor 5:4). We are indeed, he says, being weighed down by the load of the perishable body, and we are groaning under the weight of this body, and we don't want to be stripped. What does that mean, we don't want to be stripped? We don't want to lay aside this corpse we are groaning under. No, we don't want to put it down. What an unluckily sweet burden it is! *We groan*, he says, *being weighed down*.

"So put it down willingly, if you're groaning under the load."

In that we do not wish, he says, *to be stripped.*

"Well, what do you want?"

But to be clothed over.

"So that you have two loads to carry?"

No, he says.

"But why, then?"

So that what is mortal may be swallowed up by life.

Our wish, you see, is to attain to eternal life. We wish to reach the place where nobody dies, but if possible we don't want to get there *via* death. We would like to be whisked away there while we are still alive, and see our bodies changed, while we are alive, into that spiritual form into which they are to be changed when we rise again. Who wouldn't like that? Isn't it what everybody wants? But while that's what you want, you are told, *Quit*. Remember what you have sung in the psalm: *A lodger am I on earth* (Ps 119:19). If you're a lodger, you're staying in someone else's house; if you're staying in someone else's house, you quit when the landlord bids you. And the landlord is bound to tell you to quit sooner or later, and he hasn't guaranteed you a long stay.[14] After all, he didn't sign a contract with you. Seeing that you are lodging with him for nothing, you quit when he tells you to. And this too has to be put up with, and for this too patience is very necessary.

The unjust steward

9. That servant saw that his master was going to order him to vacate his job, and he took thought for the future, and said to himself, *My master is going to*

throw me out of the job. What am I to do? I am unable to dig, I am ashamed to beg. Hard work rules out one solution, shame the other. But as he racked his brains over the problem, he wasn't left without a solution. *I have hit upon what I must do, he said. He summoned his master's debtors, brought out their files. Tell me, you, how much do you owe? And he said, A hundred barrels of oil. Sit down, quickly make it fifty; take your bill. And to another, You there, how much do you owe? A hundred bushels of wheat. Sit down, quickly make it eighty. Take your file* (Lk 16:3-7). What he reckoned was this: "When my master throws me out of the job, these people will take me in, and I will not be forced by want either to dig or to beg."

Why Jesus told this parable

10. Why did the Lord Jesus Christ present us with this parable? He didn't approve, surely, of that cheat of a servant; he cheated his master, he stole from him, and didn't make it up from his own pocket. On top of that he also did some extra pilfering; he caused his master further loss, in order to prepare a little nest of quiet and security for himself after he lost his job. Why did the Lord set this before us? Not because that servant cheated, but because he exercised foresight for the future, to make Christians blush, who make no such provision, when even a cheat is praised for his ingenuity. I mean, this is what he added: *Behold, the children of this age are more prudent than the children of light.* They perpetrate frauds in order to secure their future. In what life, after all, did that steward insure himself like that? What one was he going to quit when he bowed to his master's decision? He was insuring himself for a life that was going to end; won't you insure yourself for one that is eternal? So don't go in for cheating, but, he said, *make friends for yourselves, with the mammon of iniquity make yourselves friends* (Lk 16:8-9).

This means giving alms

11. Mammon is the Hebrew word for riches, just as in Punic the word for profit is *mamon*. So what are we to do? What did the Lord command? *Make yourselves friends with the mammon of iniquity, so that they too, when you begin to fail, may receive you into eternal shelters* (Lk 16:9). It's easy, of course, to understand that we must give alms, that a helping hand must be given to the needy, because it is Christ who receives it in them. It's what he said himself: *When you did it for one of the least of mine, you did it for me* (Mt 25:40). Again, he said somewhere else, *Whoever gives one of my disciples just a cup of cold water in the name of a disciple, amen I tell you, he shall not lose his reward* (Mt 10:42). We can understand that we have to give alms, and that we mustn't really pick and choose about whom we give them to, because we are unable to sift through people's hearts. When you give alms to all and sundry, then you will reach a few who deserve them. You are hospitable, you keep your house ready for strangers; let in the unworthy, in case the worthy should be excluded. You cannot, after all, be a judge and sifter of hearts.

Although, even if you could: "He's a bad fellow, he isn't a good man"; I myself will add, "There's still your enemy. *If your enemy is hungry, feed him* (Rom 12:20; Prv 25:21). If you are obliged to do good even to your enemy, how much more to someone unknown to you, because even if he's a bad man, still he isn't an enemy." We can understand very well that people who do this sort of thing are acquiring friends for themselves, who will receive them into eternal shelters, when they have been turned out of this job or agency. After all, we are all stewards, and we have to do something with whatever has been entrusted to us in this life, so that we can account for it to the great householder. And from the one to whom more has been entrusted, a stricter account will be required.[15] The first reading that was chanted terrified everybody, and above all it terrified those who are set over whole communities, whether they are the rich, or kings, or princes, or judges, whether they are bishops, or those in charge of churches.[16] We are all, every single one of us, going to give an account of our own particular job or agency to the householder. The agency itself is only for a time, the agent's reward is forever.

But if we conduct this agency in such a way that we can give a good account of it, we can be sure of having greater things entrusted to us after the lesser ones. *Be in charge*, he said, *of five properties* (Lk 19:19); that was the master speaking to his servant who gave a good account of the money which he had received in order to invest it. He is calling us to greater things if we do well. But because it's difficult in a large agency, not to be at fault in many ways, that's why we shouldn't stop giving alms, so that when we come to present our accounts, we may find not so much the stern, incorruptible judge as the kindhearted father. If he begins to examine everything, after all, he will certainly find plenty to condemn. We ought to come to the aid of the wretched on this earth, so that we may be treated according to what's written: *Blessed are the merciful, since God will show mercy to them* (Mt 5:7); while in another place, *Judgment without mercy upon those who have not shown mercy* (Jas 2:13).

What the kingdom of heaven can be bought for;
all the wealth of Zacchaeus, and a cup of cold water

12. So then, *make yourselves friends* (Lk 16:9). Everyone of us has the means to do so. Nobody should say, "I'm poor." Nobody should say, "Let the rich do it." Those who have more should do more for more people. Does that mean the poor too don't have the means to do anything? Zacchaeus was rich, Peter poor. The one paid half his wealth to buy the kingdom of heaven, the other bought as much with one fishing net and one little boat.[17] Just because the former bought it, you see, it doesn't mean there was nothing left for the latter to buy. That's not the way the kingdom of God is up for sale, so that when one purchaser has bought it, another finds nothing he can buy. Look, the patriarchs bought it, and kept it as something for us to buy in our turn. Did they buy one thing, we another? No, it's exactly the same thing. It's always being bought and always being put up for sale right up to the end of the world. You needn't be afraid of being

excluded from the auction; you've no grounds for saying, "He's going to buy it; after all, what he can bid puts it beyond my reach." The one who has put it up for sale answers you, "Bring what you have; it's all there for you to buy too."

I said that Peter bought it all on the strength of the one little fishing boat he had. The whole of it was there for that widow to buy, who put two farthings in the treasury.[18] She put in two coins, and bought the whole kingdom. That's because by leaving herself nothing, she put in very much. And as I said a little while ago,[19] what could be cheaper than *a cup of cold water* (Mt 10:42)? The kingdom of heaven is also worth as much as that. Anyone who hasn't got a boat and nets, who hasn't got the wealth of Zacchaeus, who hasn't even got the two coins that widow had, at least has a cup of cold water. I suppose the reason he added *cold*, was in case you would be worried by the thought of firewood. But then perhaps at the proper moment, you can't even lay your hands on a cup of cold water to offer a thirsty man. You can't lay your hands on one, and you feel for the thirsty person. God sees what you have inside you; he doesn't have eyes for the capacity of your hand, what he does have eyes for is the will of your heart. You too have bought the property; be reassured on that score. This property is called peace: *Peace on earth to people of good will* (Lk 2:14).

Why it is called the mammmon of iniquity

13. But let's get back, brothers and sisters, to a point we had overlooked. What's the meaning of *the mammon of iniquity* (Lk 16:9)? What did the Lord wish to warn us about? Are we meant to commit fraud in order to have something to give alms with? Many people do do that, but what they do is not good. They grab a lot of money by such means, and give some of it in alms, and think they are getting their sins forgiven as by a corrupt judge. The one you give something to rejoices, but the one you grab it from laments. God has his ears between them in the middle; *With him there is no respect of persons* (Rom 2:4). He listens more to the one who is groaning against you than to the one who is giving thanks for you. So you should none of you persuade yourselves that because the Lord mentioned *the mammon of iniquity*, one may resort to fraud, robbery, extortion, and anything else that is displeasing to him, for the sake of giving alms.

So why did he say, *Make yourselves friends with the mammon of iniquity*? What I understand, brothers and sisters, is simply that mammon means gold, that is riches. I mean, let's speak in English[20] which you can understand. There are true riches, there are false riches. False riches are what iniquity calls riches, because the true riches are to be found with God. True riches are what the angels have, seeing they lack nothing. As for the riches which we seem to have, we seek them as a kind of remedy for our infirmity. If we were really healthy, we wouldn't go looking for these riches. These are the riches which iniquity calls riches. That's why he said, *Make yourselves friends with the riches of iniquity*, not meaning the riches which you acquire by iniquity, but the riches which iniquity calls riches, though they aren't the true riches.

A comparison in a psalm between the true riches and the false

14. Listen to how these which are not the true riches are called riches by iniquity. A psalm says somewhere—a man is groaning in it, and wishing to be delivered from some alien sons, and he says to the Lord, *Deliver me from the hands of alien sons, whose mouths have spoken vanity, and whose right hands are right hands of iniquity.* They talk about nothing but fraudulent deals and prepare themselves for such frauds, these people about whom he says their *right hands are right hands of iniquity.* He isn't going to accuse or name any fradulent cheat.[21] But what is he going to say? *Whose sons are like well set saplings, their daughters smart and adorned in the likeness of the temple. Their cellars are full, bursting out from this one to that. Their oxen are fat, their sheep fertile, multiplying in their lambing. There are no ruined walls, no crying in their streets.* What marvelous temporal happiness he has described! So where's the iniquity, where's the vanity? Listen to what follows: *Blessed they called the people which has these things* (Ps 144:11-15).

There you have the iniquity, because they called the people blessed which has these things in abundance. They had no eyes for the other blessedness, they didn't seek the other kind, which is the true one. They used up all their desire on earthly well-being and happiness. They refused to lift up their hearts up above. But the man who's groaning and wishing to be delivered from such a crew, what does he say? *Blessed the people whose God is the Lord* (Ps 144:15). There you have the true riches; the other sort, though, are the riches of iniquity. Let any who possess those riches of iniquity use them to make friends with, before they depart from this agency. If they make friends with them, you see, they are using them well. Aren't they real riches in their hands? After all, they do have other true riches; they count God as their riches. They are using earth to trample on earth.

Finally, you love these riches. The Lord said to some rich man or other who was very attached to his possessions, "Do you love what you possess? Transfer it where I tell you to; don't lose it."

But how?

Make for yourselves treasure in heaven, where no thief can approach it, nor moth spoil it (Lk 12:33).[22] By loving your riches, you are going to lose them. Transfer them where you can't lose them; deposit them in the place you are going to come to.

Another way of taking the mammon of iniquity

15. So, he says; *make yourselves friends with the mammon of iniquity, so that they too may receive you into eternal shelters* (Lk 16:9). This saying can also be interpreted like this: suppose the mammon of iniquity does mean money made dishonestly. Your father made his pile by usury. He made you rich. You don't approve of your father's usury. Don't be the heir to his iniquity, just be the heir to the money from iniquity. Don't you imitate your father by being a money lender at extortionate rates. But now there's all that pile of money in

your house. Use it to make friends with the mammon of iniquity; it's not a question of your being dishonest and giving the proceeds in alms, but of using a pile already made dishonestly. If your father had learned how to rob, you must learn how to pay out.

Why the difference in the amounts of the debts
the unjust steward rescheduled?

16. But why make fifty from a hundred, why eighty from a hundred?[23] By fifty from a hundred he wished to signify a half. That, you see, is what Zacchaeus did: *Half my goods I give to the poor* (Lk 19:8). By making eighty from a hundred he wished to signify two tenths. After all, to give twenty out of a hundred, so that eighty remain, is to give two tenths. In this matter they used to give one tenth.[24] But the Lord said in the gospel, *Unless your justice abounds more than that of the Pharisees and scribes, you shall not enter into the kingdom of heaven* (Mt 5:20). So if the justice of the Pharisees and scribes was to give a tenth, how will your justice abound unless you give at least two tenths? To give more is the same as to abound.

Concluding words on the subject of patience

17. So you are making friends, you are reaching out in hope, you are exercising the muscles of your desire, you are patiently tolerating the present, whether it's going well or badly with you, since for someone who is seeking well-being and happiness up above, even happiness and well-being here below are things to be tolerated. They are tolerated, you see, because as long as we are wandering in exile, anything that holds us back from our God is regarded as an evil. And the heart that is fighting against being corrupted by prosperity is engaged in a severer struggle than the one that is fighting against being broken by adversity. So it's through this sort of patience that we can be sure, once this world comes to an end, or once our lives come to the end which is hastening to meet each one of us in the not so very distant future, that we can be sure of those eternal shelters, because we have made ourselves friends with the mammon of iniquity.

NOTES

1. There is nothing at all to indicate the date of this sermon. About the place Dom Lambot, who has edited the text, suggests that Tuneba in the title is the same as a place called Thunuba by the second century geographer and astronomer, Ptolemy, who locates it in the province of Proconsular Africa, about halfway along the road between Carthage and Augustine's home town of Thagaste. See O. Perler, *Les Voyages de Saint Augustin*, 411.

2. See Heb 6:19.

3. The *res* in exchange for the *spes*.

4. It is one of his favorite metaphors to envisage all the scriptures as a gigantic *machina*, a derrick or scaffolding for constructing the edifice of faith, hope and charity.

5. Since seeing is itself the reward faith earns by believing.

6. See Lk 24:39.

7. The quotation from Heb 11:1 at the beginning of the previous section implies that hope is supported by faith. But this need not be seen as a contradiction or inconsistency; they support, or ground, each other.

8. *Miseratione ipsa*; a most unusual use of this word, which properly means pity or compassion. But he must be employing it here as an extension of *miseria*, wretchedness.

9. Emending the text's *judicavit omnis homo eum esse posse felicem*, every man has judged that he (someone else) can be happy, to *judicavit omnis homo hominem esse posse felicem*. My guess is that a copyist left out the "hom" of *hominem* by simple haplography, and that the surviving "inem" was then corrected to *eum*.

10. See 1 Cor 7:31.

11. See Jb 1:12—2:9.

12. There is a gap in the Latin text in the middle of this sentence; so one cannot be sure of the translation. I take him to be making a little joke.

13. See Lk 21:19.

14. *Nec diem mansionis constituit*; literally, "and he has not established the day of stay." I wonder if *diem mansionis* ought not to be emended to *diu mansionis*, with *diu* being used idiomatically as a noun; thus meaning "length of stay."

15. See Lk 12:48.

16. These last, if they are being distinguished from bishops, must, I suppose, be parish priests, insofar as such beings existed in the Church as organized in those days. The first reading, presumably not from the gospels, may have been Wis 6.

17. See Lk 19:1-10; 5:1-11.

18. See Mk 12:41-44.

19. In section 11 above.

20. Latin, of course, is what he said.

21. Printed as a question in the text. I think it makes better sense to treat it as a statement.

22. Augustine is associating this text with the story of the rich man who asked Jesus what he must do to inherit eternal life; see Lk 18:22.

23. He is referring to the amounts the steward told the debtors to substitute for their real debt; Lk 16:6-7.

24. See Mt 23:23—the tithes (tenth part), which the Pharisees used to pay; also Lk 18:12—the boast of the Pharisee praying in the temple.

SERMON 360

ON THE VIGIL OF MAXIMIAN, ABOUT A DONATIST WHO HAS RETURNED
TO THE CHURCH

Date: 411[1]

The convert's address

1. God be thanked, brothers and sisters; rejoice with your brother, who *was dead and has come to life, was lost and is found* (Lk 15:32). Thanks for the patience and mercy of the Lord our God; for his patience, because he still waited while I was dragging my feet; for his mercy, because he was willing to receive me as I returned. This is the vineyard where I was not working, as I had used up all my strength in that of a stranger. O vineyard beloved of my Lord,[2] not only were my labors of no use to you, but I was even serving your enemy against you. I was dripping with sweat, when I was not gathering for you.[3]

Thanks to the one who planted you, who does not keep back the wages even of the workers who have been called at the last hour. I come late, but I do not despair of my tenner.[4] *I was previously a blasphemer and a persecutor, and I spoke insultingly of you. But I obtained mercy, because I acted in ignorance* (1 Tim 1:13). I held by the teaching of my parents, you see; not of the patriarchs, not of the prophets, not of the apostles, but of the parents of my flesh. I gave my acquiescence to flesh and blood;[5] but then, being defeated, I acquiesced in the truth, and having returned, I found rest in the unity.

Was I not reading the same scriptures as I read even now? But even that teacher of the nations, that chosen vessel,[6] Saul turned into Paul, the proud man became the least,[7] the raider turned shepherd, the wolf turned ram, was *a Hebrew of the Hebrews, as regards the law a Pharisee* (Phil 3:5-6), instructed in the law *at the feet of the teacher Gamaliel* (Acts 22:3); and yet he did not know that Christ, whom he had read of in the prophets, was seated in heaven, and did not permit him to be worshiped on earth. He unwittingly sang of faith in his passion and his resurrection,[8] and erroneously devastated it in his rage. According to the prophets, in whom he had been born and brought up, Christ had already risen from the dead and was seated in heaven; and he himself was still blinded by the lie of his relatives, that his disciples had stolen him from the tomb.[9]

In the same way I too was having the truth about the Catholic Church, as it is spread throughout the whole world, dinned into me from every side by the words of the divine scriptures; and the false accusations about the betrayers leveled against it by my relatives made me deaf. I'm not comparing myself with Paul's merits, but with his sins. Even if I haven't been found worthy to be as good as he was; still, before receiving the remedy of correction, I was not as bad. He failed to recognize the bridegroom in the books he read, and I failed to recognize the bride. The one who revealed to him what's written about Christ's glorification: *Be exalted over the heavens, God*; also revealed to me what follows about the spread of the Church: *over the whole earth your glory* (Ps 57:5.11). The evidence of both texts is plain to those who can see, but hidden from the blind. It was the baptism of Christ that opened his eyes,[10] the peace of Christ that opened mine. He was made new by the washing of the holy water;[11] whereas it was charity that covered the multitude of my sins.[12]

NOTES

1. Kunzelmann and Fischer suggest the date, linking this odd little sermon with the Conference of 411. If, as they also suggest, it was preached back in Hippo Regius, then it would have been preached a few weeks after Sermon 359; so the vigil of Maximian must have been celebrated in the last three months of the year. This Maximian was most probably a convert Donatist who resigned as bishop of Bagai, in Numidia, and was then very severely beaten up and practically left for dead on a dunghill by Donatists who regarded him as a traitor. But he survived, went with his complaint about such treatment to the imperial court in Ravenna, and was instrumental in getting the laws against the Donatists made much more severe. All this happened between 402 and 404. See O. Perler, *Les Voyages de Saint Augustin*, 243, note 5, and 254. Perhaps he had died since then, and was venerated as a quasi-martyr. His feast, according to Holweck's *Dictionary of the Saints*, was kept on 3 October. That could well have been when this sermon was preached, on Augustine's way back to Hippo Regius.

The sermon is not in fact *about* a converted Donatist, but *by* a converted Donatist—possibly composed for him by Augustine. But that means it was certainly a Donatist clergyman, probably a bishop, as I don't think any layman would have been asked to preach, or have agreed to do so. So, as I have suggested, it may have been preached in some other small town between Bizerta and Hippo Regius. I think, in fact, that this is more likely. There would surely be other references to the event in Augustine's writings, especially his letters, if the preacher here had been the ex-Donatist bishop of Hippo Regius, or even one of his priests.

2. See Is 5:1.

3. See Lk 11:23.

4. My *denarius*; Mt 20:9.

5. See Gal 1:16. The text actually reads *Non acquievi carni et sanguini*, which is indeed what Paul says in the verse being alluded to. But the speaker here had just said, in other words, that that is what he did do—he had followed the teaching of his parents. Here he is contrasting himself with the converted Paul, whereas just now he had compared himself with the unconverted Saul. The *Non*, I am sure, was introduced by a copyist, reproducing the scriptural text literally.

6. See 1 Tm 2:7; Acts 9:15.

7. See 1 Cor 15:9.

8. When he sang the psalms.

9. See Mt 28:13-15.

10. See Acts 9:18. In fact the scales fell from Saul's eyes before he was baptized.

11. See Eph 5:26.

12. See 1 Pt 4:8. But here he means, not his own charity, but that of the Church, expressed in its peace.

SERMON 361

ON THE RESURRECTION OF THE DEAD

Date:411[1]

Comment on the text, Let us eat and drink, for tomorrow we die

1. I noticed, when the apostle's letter was read, a praiseworthy reaction of your faith and your charity, how you shuddered at the people who say, *Let us eat and drink; for tomorrow we die* (1 Cor 15:32), because they think that this life, which we have in common with cattle, is the only one, while after death everything a human being consists of comes to an end, and there is no hope of another, better life; and they like to tickle the itching of undisciplined ears in this way. So let's make this the starting point of our discussion, and let this be, as it were, the hinge of my sermon, to which anything else the Lord may be pleased to suggest to me may be referred.[2]

Two questions to be considered: the truth of the doctrine of the resurrection of the dead, and the kind of life to which the dead rise

2. The resurrection of the dead, you see, is our hope; the resurrection of the dead is our faith. It is also our charity, which blazes up at the proclamation of things that cannot yet be seen, and grows hot with a desire so huge that it gives our hearts the capacity to receive the bliss which is promised us for the future, enlarging them as long they believe what they cannot yet see. So this charity also of ours ought not to be preoccupied with these temporal and visible things, in such a way that we hope we are going to have something of the sort in the resurrection; such things as that, if we despise them now, we live better lives and are better people, such things, that is to say, as the pleasures and delights of the flesh.

And so take away faith in the resurrection of the dead, and the whole of Christian doctrine collapses. Having established faith, though, in the resurrection of the dead, we haven't thereby straightaway reassured the Christian spirit, until we have distinguished that life which is going to be in the future, from this one which passes away. And so the matter is to be put like this: if the dead do not rise again, there is no hope of a future life for us; but if the dead do rise again,

225

there will indeed be a future life, but the second question is, what sort of life it will be. And so the first thing to be discussed is whether there is going to be a resurrection of the dead; while the second thing to be discussed is what sort of life the saints will have in the resurrection.

It is those who are not Christians who deny the resurrection of the dead;
Christians only argue about what sort of life it will be in the resurrection

3. So those who say the dead do not rise again are not Christians; while those who think that when the dead rise again they are going to live a carnal kind of life are a carnal kind of Christians. So whatever argument there may be against the opinion of those who deny the resurrection of the dead, it is against outsiders, of whom I don't imagine there are any present here.[3] So my argument could seem superfluous, if I linger on it in attempting to teach that the dead do rise again. Christians, after all, who already believe Christ, who in no way think the apostle can be lying, are to be governed by the weight of authority. So it's enough for them to hear, *If the dead do not rise, our preaching is vain, vain too is your faith. If the dead do not rise*, he says, *neither has Christ risen* (1 Cor 15:14.13). But if Christ has risen again, in whom Christians find salvation, then it is not, clearly, impossible for the dead to rise again; since the one who raised his Son, and the one who raised his own flesh,[4] have given a demonstration in the head which would be a model for the rest of the body, which is the Church.

So a discussion of the resurrection of the dead could be superfluous, so that we should now proceed to the one which Christians usually have among themselves, about what we shall be like when we have risen again, how we shall live, what our business will be, whether there will be any business or none at all; if there won't be any, are we going to live idly with nothing to do; or if we do do anything, what shall we do; finally, are we going to eat and drink, are there going to be conjugal relations between male and female, or will there be a simple and incorrupt common life;[5] and if that's how it is, what sort of life it will be, with what sort of motions, what sort of shape the bodies themselves will have. These are questions for Christians, saving the faith in the resurrection.

Concern for the carnal minded and almost pagan Christians obliges
him to discuss the question of the resurrection itself

4. So I would promptly pass on to this kind of discussion, insofar as it can be engaged in and brought to any conclusions by human beings for human beings, such as either I am or you are, if it were not that a certain anxiety for our brothers and sisters who are excessively materialistic, and almost pagan, obliges me to linger a little over that first question that is asked, whether the dead do in fact rise again at all. Because I take it that there are no pagans present here at the moment, but that you are all Christians. Pagans, though, and scoffers at the idea of resurrection never stop muttering in the ears of Christians every day, *Let us eat and drink; for tomorrow we die*. And there's what the apostle said, introduc-

ing his concern and adding his own words to this quotation,[6] *Bad conversations corrupt good habits* (1 Cor 15:32-33). So as I am apprehensive about such dangers, and bear a heavy responsibility for the weak, out of a loving concern for them which is that of a mother as well as a father I will say something about this, something sufficient, maybe, for Christians, because it is a greater devotion to the scriptures that has brought along all those who are gathered here today.

It isn't, after all, the solemn celebration of any feast day that has brought even the theater crowds along to the church of God. Some people, you see, are in the habit of assembling, not out of piety, but out of the excitement of a feast day. It's this consideration[7] that has led me to say something first about the resurrection of the dead; and then, if the Lord gives me the ability, about what sort of life the just will enjoy after it.

If people take care to make wills for the sake of those they will leave behind them, how much more should they give some thought to their own souls!

5. *I am afraid*, says the apostle, *that just as the serpent led Eve astray by his cunning, in the same way your minds too may be corrupted from the chastity which is in Christ* (2 Cor 11:3). Now the minds of these people are corrupted by that sort of conversation, *Let us eat and drink; for tomorrow we die* (1 Cor 15:33.32). Those who love these things, who pursue these things, who assume this is the only life there is, who hope for nothing further, who either don't pray to God, or pray to him for this life alone, who find any talk of diligence very tedious, will be very downcast when they hear me saying all this.[8] They want to eat and drink; for tomorrow they die. If only they would give genuine thought to the fact that they are going to die tomorrow! Can there be any, after all, so mindless, so perverse, so hostile to their own souls, that they don't reflect, when they are about to die the next day, on how everything they have worked for has come to an end? That, you see, is what is written: *On that day shall all his schemes come to nothing* (Ps 146:4).

And if people take care, as the day of their death approaches, to make wills for the sake of those they are leaving behind, how much more should they give some thought to their own souls! Will you give thought to those you are leaving behind, and give none to yourself, who are leaving all these things behind? Look, man; your children will have what you leave them, you yourself won't have anything; and you're giving all your thought to what is being used up on the road they are passing along behind you as travelers, none to where they may arrive at the end of their travels. So if only people really did give some thought to death!

But when the dead are carried out to burial, people's thoughts do turn to death, and you hear them saying, "Poor soul! That's how it was; he was walking about only yesterday," or, "I saw him only a week ago, we had a conversation about this and that; yes, man is nothing at all."

Yes, they mutter things like that. But perhaps while the dead person is being mourned, while the funeral is being arranged, and preparations being made for it, when the cortège sets off, while the coffin is being laid in the grave, this kind of talk is to be heard. But once the dead have been buried, even this kind of thought is buried too. All those death-dealing preoccupations return, people forget whom they have buried, those who are going to follow them to the grave start thinking about the succession. Back they go to their frauds, their extortions, their perjuries, their drunkenness, to the endless pleasures of the body which are, I don't say going to vanish when they've been exhausted, but already vanishing while they are being sampled. And what is much more pernicious, from the burying of the dead an argument is drawn for the burial of the heart, and they say, *Let us eat and drink; for tomorrow we die.*

Against the argument that nobody has ever returned from the dead

6. They also mock the faith of those of us who assert that the dead are going to rise again, and they say to each other, "Look, this man has just been laid in the grave; let his voice be heard. But his can't be; then let me hear the voice of my father, my grandfather, my great-grandfather. Who has ever risen again from there? Who has ever indicated what goes on among those in the netherworld? Let us do ourselves proud while we are alive; but when we're dead, even if our parents, or dear ones, or relatives bring things along to our graves, they will bring them for themselves, the living, not for us, the dead."[9]

Scripture too, in fact, has mocked such practices, when it says about people who are insensible to good things that are presented to them, *As if you were to lay a banquet,* it says, *around a dead person* (Sir 30:18). And it's obvious that this doesn't benefit the dead, and that it's a custom of the pagans, and that it doesn't flow from the channel of justice derived from our fathers the patriarchs; we read about their funerals being celebrated; we don't read of funeral sacrifices being offered for them. This can also be observed in the customs of the Jews;[10] for while they have not inherited from their ancestors the fruit of virtue, still they have retained the ancient customs in a number of their celebrations and ceremonies.

And as for the objection some people bring from the scriptures: *Break your bread and pour out your wine on the tombs of the just, but do not hand it over to the unjust* (Tb 4:17), this is not the occasion, indeed, to expatiate on it; but still I will say that the faithful can understand what is being said.[11] It is well known, after all, to the faithful how the faithful do these things out of a religious respect for their dear departed; and that such rites are not to be granted to the unjust, that is to unbelievers, because *the just man lives by faith* (Rom 1:17), this too is known to the faithful. So nobody should try to turn a remedy into a hurt, and attempt to twist a rope from the scriptures, and with it lob a deadly noose over his own soul. It's as plain as a pikestaff how that text should be understood, and this celebration of Christians is open and above board and entirely salutary.

Wake up the faith sleeping in your heart, like Christ asleep in the boat,
to answer these jibes of unbelievers

7. So then, as I had started to say, let us take a look at this question, because of the people who murmur in the ears of the weak, *Let us eat and drink; for tomorrow we die* (1 Cor 15:32); because they say, "Nobody has risen again from there; I haven't heard anyone's voice, from the time my grandfather was laid to rest there, or my forefather, or my father." Answer them, Christians, if you are Christians—unless,[12] maybe, while you wish to get drunk with the mob, you are loath to answer those who are trying to corrupt you. You have a perfectly good answer you can make; but you are all being tossed about by the lust for pleasure, and you actually desire to be sucked down and buried alive. A craving to get drunk swells up and hurtles like a kind of breaker over the soul, driven on by gusts of evil persuasion.

So you are enduring a great storm; you don't want to answer the one who is trying to corrupt you, because you want to be nice to him, since he's offering you a drink; but the tidal wave of that craving is rearing up its crest, and threatening to engulf your heart like a boat. Christian, Christ is asleep in your boat; wake him up, he will command the storm, and everything will be calm.[13] At that time, you see, when the disciples were being tossed about in the boat and Christ was asleep, they represented Christians being tossed about while their Christian faith is asleep. You can see, after all, what the apostle says: *For Christ to dwell*, he says, *by faith in your hearts* (Eph 3:17). As regards, you see, his presence in beauty and divinity, he is always with the Father; as regards his bodily presence, he is now above the heavens at the right hand of the Father; but as regards the presence of faith, he is in all Christians. And the reason, therefore, that you are being tossed about hither and thither is that Christ is asleep; that is, the reason you don't overcome those cravings that are stirred up by the gusts of evil persuasion, is that faith is asleep.

What does that mean, faith is asleep? It has been drugged. What does that mean, it has been drugged? You have forgotten it. So what does it mean, to wake up Christ? Waking up your faith, remembering what you have believed. So then, recall your faith, wake up Christ; your very faith will command the waves you are being troubled by, and the winds of persuasive perversity. They will fade away immediately, immediately everything will grow calm; because even if the evil persuader doesn't stop speaking, he no longer rocks the boat, no longer whips up the waves, no longer swamps the vessel in which you are sailing.

The fact of Christ's resurrection is the answer to all objections

8. So what are you doing when you wake Christ up? What had that evil chatterer said to you? What had that corrupter said, corrupting good habits with his evil conversation?[14] Certainly, what he said was this: "Nobody has ever come back from there, I have never heard from my father, nor my grandfather. Let someone come back from there, let him tell us what goes on there."

You now, with Christ woken up in your boat, recalling your faith, should answer him like this, and say: "Fool, if your father rose again, you would believe; the Lord of all things has risen again, and you don't believe? Why, after all, did he wish to die and rise again, if not so that we might all believe and trust one man, and not be deceived by many? And what would your father do, if he rose again and spoke, only to die once more? Observe with what power and authority that one rose again, who *dies now no more, and death will no longer lord it over him* (Rom 6:9). He showed himself to his disciples and faithful believers; they felt and handled the solidity of his body, since it wasn't enough for some of them to see what they had remembered, unless they could also touch what they saw.[15] Faith was confirmed, not only in the hearts but also in the eyes of men. He ascended, after giving these demonstrations, into heaven, he sent the Holy Spirit to his disciples, the gospel was preached.

"If you think we are lying about this, question the whole wide world. Many things that were promised have come about; many things that were hoped for have been fulfilled; the whole world is flourishing in the Christian faith. They don't dare to belittle the resurrection of Christ—not even those who haven't yet believed Christ. There's evidence for it in heaven, evidence on earth; evidence from the angels, evidence from the shades of the dead.[16] Is there anything left that does not cry out? And you go on saying, *Let us eat and drink; for tomorrow we die* (1 Cor 15:32)!

Examples from nature to illustrate the resurrection

9. "But you are filled with sorrow over the burial of your dear one, because you haven't immediately heard his voice. He was alive, he's dead. He used to eat, he eats no more. He used to feel things, he has no more feelings. He takes no part in the joys and pastimes of the living.

"Would you mourn for the seed, when you went plowing? So if there was anyone so unversed in practical matters, that when the seed is taken out to the fields, and put in the ground, and buried when the clods are broken; so if there was anyone so ignorant even of what was going to happen soon, that he mourned for the wheat, because he remembered the summer, and thought to himself and said, 'Oh, this grain which has now been buried! With what toil it was reaped, carried, threshed, cleaned, stored in the barn! We saw how lovely it was, and congratulated ourselves over it. Now it has been taken away from our sight. I see the earth plowed up; but the grain I can perceive neither in the barn nor here.' He would be mourning and lamenting the grain as though it were dead and buried, he would be shedding many tears, observing the clods and the earth, but not being able to see the harvest. How he would be laughed at by any unlearned Tom Dick or Harry—but not unlearned in that matter; uninstructed indeed in other matters, but well enough instructed in the business over which he was lamenting, being so absurdly uninstructed!

"And what would those who knew say to him, if by any chance the reason he was mourning was that he didn't know any of this? 'Don't be downhearted. What we've buried is certainly no longer in the barn, it's not in our hands; we shall come to this field, and you will be delighted to see the beauty of the crop, where now you are grieving over the bareness of the plowland'. Anyone who knew what was going to spring from the grain would also rejoice over the plowland; while the one who was skeptical, or rather plain stupid, and to speak more accurately, totally lacking in experience, would doubtless perhaps grieve at first, but if he trusted those who had experience would go away comforted, and with those who had experienced it would hope for the harvest."

If the grain stays like this, and is not made to die, it will stay alone

10. But harvests are regularly seen every year; while of the human race, on the other hand, one final harvest will grow ripe at the end of the world. It cannot now be shown to our eyes; but we have been given experience of it in the one principal grain. The Lord himself says, *If the grain stays like this, and is not done to death, it will stay alone* (Jn 12:24), speaking of his own being done to death, because there is to be an abundant and multiple resurrection of those who believe in him. An example was given with one grain, but such an example as all those who wish to be grains could trust absolutely. Though as a matter of fact, the whole of creation too speaks of resurrection, if we aren't too deaf to hear; so that we ought to be able to work out what God is going to do all at once with the human race at the end, when we can see so many similar things happening every day.

The resurrection of Christians will happen just once; the sleeping and waking of animals is a daily occurrence. Sleeping is like death; waking up is like resurrection. From what happens every day, believe what is only going to happen once. The moon, through all the months, is born, waxes, comes to the full, wanes, is consumed, is renewed. What happens with the moon every month, happens with the resurrection just once in the whole of time; just as what happens with sleepers every day, happens with the moon every month. Where do they come from, where do they return to, the leaves on the trees? Into what secret places do they depart, from what secret places do they arrive? It's winter;[17] certainly, though, the trees, which now look dead, will grow green again when the spring comes. Is now the first time this has happened, or was it also like this last year? Of course it was also like this last year. Everything is cut off from autumn into winter, it comes back again through spring into summer.[18] So the year comes back to life in due season, and shall human beings, made to the image of God, perish totally when they die?

More down to earth examples

11. But someone who observes the changes and renewal of things somewhat superficially may say to me, "Those leaves have rotted, new ones have been born." But if he considers the matter more carefully, he will see that even the leaves which rot yield themselves to the forces of the earth. Where, after all, does the earth get its richness from, if not from the rotting of earthy things?

Those who cultivate the countryside are well aware of this; and those who don't, because they always live in town, should certainly know, from the gardens near the town, with what diligent care the worthless off-scourings of the city are kept, by whom they are even bought for a price, where they are carried to. Certainly all this could be thought by people with no experience to be worthless rubbish, void of any further use. And is anyone ready to spare a glance for a lump of dung? What people shrink from glancing at, they take great care to save.

So what seemed to have been already used up and thrown away goes back into the richness of the earth, the richness into sap, the sap into the root. And what passes from the earth into the root wanders up by invisible channels into the trunk, is distributed through the branches, passes from the branches into the seeds, from seed into fruit and leaves. There you are—what you shuddered at in the putrefaction of dung, you admire in the fruit and the greenery of the tree.

The objection that the bodies of the dead turn to dust

12. I don't want you now to raise me the objection you usually raise: "The body of a dead person, once buried, doesn't remain entire; because if it did so remain, I would believe it would rise again." So the Egyptians are the only ones, are they, who can believe in the resurrection, because they diligently cure the corpses of the dead? They have the custom, you see, of drying bodies, and rendering them almost the color of bronze.[19] So according to these people, who are ignorant of the hidden recesses of nature, where all things are kept safe for the creator, even when they are withdrawn from human perception, only the Egyptians are justified in believing in the resurrection of their dead, while the hope of other Christians is entirely in doubt.[20]

Often enough, I mean, when tombs have been opened and laid bare, either because they are so old,[21] or out of some need that is not sacrilegious, the bodies have been found to have rotted away, and people have sighed and groaned, accustomed as they are to delight in the appearance of the human body, and have said to themselves, "Can it really be the case that these ashes will have that beautiful appearance, will be brought back to life, brought back to the light of day? When will this happen? When may I hope for something alive from these ashes?" As you say this, at least you can see ashes in the tomb. Think back over your own age, if you are, for example, thirty, or fifty years old or more. In the tomb there are at least the dead person's ashes; as for you, what were you fifty years ago? Where were you? The bodies of all of us here, who are now talking or listening, will be ashes in a few years' time; a few years ago they weren't even ashes. So will the one who was able to prepare for existence what was not, be unable to repair for renewed existence what already was?

Blessed are those who do not see, and yet believe

13. So let there be an end to the mutterings of these people who speak evil things, and corrupt good habits with their evil conversations.[22] Set your feet

firmly on the way, set them there, so that you don't leave the way, not so that you stick on the way, but as it is written, *So run, that you may attain* (1 Cor 9:24). Let Christ flourish always in your hearts, the Christ who wished to show in the head what the other members should hope for. We indeed are toiling away on earth; our head in heaven now neither dies, nor fails in any way, nor suffers anything at all. He did, all the same, suffer for us, because *he was handed over on account of our sins, and rose again on account of our justification* (Rom 4:25). We know this by faith, while those he showed himself to learned it by their eyes.

That doesn't mean, though, that we are rejected, because he rose again and we haven't been able to see him with our bodily eyes. We have the Lord's own testimony on our behalf—what he said to the doubting disciple, who sought to believe by touching. I mean, when he cried out, convinced by feeling the scars, and said, *My Lord and my God,* the Lord countered, *Because you have seen me,* he said, *you have also believed; blessed are those who do not see, and yet believe* (Jn 20:24-29). So wake up, all of you, to what is your real blessedness, don't let any evil persuader shake out of your hearts what Christ has fixed in them.

About the idea that only Christ was in a position to rise again

14. And I don't want to be told that other thing, either.[23] It's something, you see, said by all who have bowed, even unwillingly, to the authority of Christ. I mean, almost none of the pagans, even those who refuse to attach themselves to Christ in devotion, or put off doing so, dare to object to him personally;[24] while they dare to object to Christians rising again, they don't dare do so to Christ. They bow to the head, and continue to revile the body. But when the body hears the abuse of those who already acknowledge the head, it shouldn't suppose it has been cut off from the head, but rather that it is supported by it. Of course, if we had been cut off, we ought to fear the voices of our abusers. But that we haven't been cut off, he himself testifies, by saying to Paul, while he was still Saul, persecuting the Church, *Saul, Saul, why are you persecuting me?* (Acts 9:4).

He had already passed through the impious hands of the Jews, already penetrated the infernal regions, already risen again from the tomb, already ascended into heaven, already enriched and strengthened the hearts of believers with the gift of the Holy Spirit, seated at the right hand of the Father and interceding for us. He wasn't going to hand himself over to death yet again, but to deliver us from death; so what could he still endure from the rage of Saul? How could that hand touch him, even though he was the one, as it is written, who was *breathing out slaughter* (Acts 9:1)? He could launch an attack on Christians, toiling away on the ground; on Christ, though, when and how could he do so? All the same, he cries out on behalf of his members, and he doesn't say, "Why are you persecuting my people?" After all, if he said, "Why are you persecuting my people?" we would think he meant his servants. But servants are not joined as closely to their master as Christians are to Christ. This is altogether another kind of conjunction, another arrangement of members, another union of charity. The head is speaking on behalf of the members, and he doesn't even say this: "Why are you persecuting my members?" but he says, *Why are you persecuting me?* He wasn't touching the head, but he was touching what was joined to the head.

I have often said this already,[25] but as it is an apt comparison and puts the matter very neatly, it bears repetition. Somebody treads on you in a crowd, squashes your foot, while doing nothing to your tongue. So what's the meaning of your tongue yelling, "You're treading on me"? The pressure's on the foot, there's no harm done to the tongue, but it is all one compact body. *And if one member suffers, all the members suffer with it; and if one member is honored, all the members rejoice with it* (1 Cor 12:26). So if your tongue can speak on behalf of your foot, can't Christ in heaven speak on behalf of Christians? So your tongue doesn't speak for your foot by saying like this, "You're treading on my foot," but "You're treading on me," though it hasn't been touched itself. Recognize him as your head, when he speaks for you from heaven, and says, *Saul, Saul, why are you persecuting me?*

So, brothers and sisters, why have I been saying all this? In case perhaps those people may creep in among you, about whom the apostle says, *Evil conversations corrupt good habits*, because they say, *Let us eat and drink; for tomorrow we die* (1 Cor 15:33.32); and in fact they say to you—they dare not object to Christ, you see, they tremble before the sovereign authority established throughout the whole world; but as it is written, *The sinner will see and be angry, he will grind his teeth and waste away* (Ps 112:10); he can grind his teeth, he can waste away, but he dare not speak ill of Christ—so it's in case they should speak to you like this and say, "Only Christ was in a position to do so." Sometimes, you see, they even say it from the heart, while sometimes they say it out of fear. As for you, though, pay attention both to what they dare to say, and what they don't dare to say.

How to answer their exaggerated praise of Christ and their
disparaging of Christians

15. So they are going to say, "You tell me that Christ has risen again, and from that you hope for the resurrection of the dead; but Christ was in a position to rise again from the dead." And now he begins to praise Christ, not in order to do him honor, but to make you despair. It's the deadly cunning of the serpent, to turn you away from Christ by praising Christ, to extol deceitfully the one he doesn't dare to disparage. He exaggerates the sovereign majesty of Christ in order to make him out quite unique, to stop you hoping for anything like what was demonstrated in his rising again. And he seems, apparently, to be all the more religiously respectful of Christ, when he says, "Look at the person who dares to compare himself with Christ, so that just because Christ rose again, he can imagine he's going to rise again too!"

Don't let this perverse praise of your emperor disturb you. The insidious tricks of the enemy may disturb you, but the humility and humanity of Christ should console you. This man emphasizes how high above you Christ is lifted up; Christ, though, says how low he came down to you. So answer this man, wake up that faith. It's a storm, there are huge waves, the boat is at risk, Christ is asleep.[26] Wake up that faith, don't forget what you have believed. You will give him an answer straightaway, once the gospel faith has come awake in you. You won't be without resources in replying; after all, it won't be you speaking. Christ abiding in you will snatch up your tongue as his instrument, like his sword, using your heart and your voice like the owner living in you, and he will stand up to your opponent and make you secure. All you have to do is to wake him up when he's asleep; that is, to recall the faith you had forgotten.

Christ, to be the mediator, took on our mortality,
to enable us to share in his immortality

16. Well, what am I going to say now, to help you reply to such people? I won't say anything new, but simply what you have already believed. So wake up that faith, and answer the person who says, "Only Christ was able to do it, the rest of us cannot." Answer and say, "The reason Christ was able to, was because he is God; yes, he certainly could, because he's God. If because he's God, then because he's almighty; if because he's almighty, why should I despair of his being able to do in me to what he demonstrated in himself on my account?"

Then I ask what Christ rose again from.

He will answer, "From the dead."

I ask how he came to be dead. I mean to say, can God die? That divinity too, the Word equal to the Father, the skill of the almighty craftsman, *through whom all things were made* (Jn 1:3), unchangeable wisdom, *who abiding in herself renews all things* (Wis 7:27), *reaching mightily from end to end and disposing all things pleasantly* (Wis 8:1)—can that die?

"No," he says.

And yet Christ died. How did he come to die? Plainly, because *he did not consider it robbery to be equal to God, but he emptied himself, taking the form of a servant.*

But what did he say before that? *Who, since he was in the form of God* (Phil 2:6-7). Had he taken the form of God, or was he in it by nature? The apostle distinguishes; when he mentioned the form of God, he said *was*; when he referred to the form of a servant, he said *taking*. So Christ was something; he took something, in order to be one thing with that which he had taken. In the form of God he was equal to God, as the evangelist, that fisherman, states it: *The Word was in the beginning, and the Word was with God,, and the Word was God* (Jn 1:1); that's the same as, *Since he was in the form of God, he did not consider it robbery to be equal to God.* Anything, you see, that does not belong by nature, but is unlawfully usurped, is robbery. An angel usurped equality with God, and fell, and became the devil; a man usurped equality with God, and fell, and became mortal. This one, though, was born equal, because he was not born in time, but was always born to the everlasting Father as the everlasting Son, through whom all things were made; and so he *was* in the form of God.

But in order to be the mediator between God and humanity, between the just one and the unjust, between the immortal one and mortals, he took on something from the unjust and the mortals, retaining something with the just one and the immortal one. With the just and immortal one, you see, he retained justice, from the unjust and the mortals he took on mortality, and thus became the reconciler in the middle, throwing down the wall of our sins; which is why his people sing to him, *And in my God I will leap over the wall* (Ps 18:29). In this way he gave back to God what sins had alienated from him, he bought back with his blood what the devil had got possession of. He died for us, and he rose again for us. He carried our sins, not as something inherent to him, but as something he just wore, as Jacob wore the skins of goats, in order to seem hairy to his father as he blessed him.[27] Esau, the bad man, had his own proper hairiness, while Jacob, the good man, wore an alien hairiness. Sins, that means, are inherent to mortal human beings. But they weren't inherent to the one who said, *I have the authority to lay down my life, and I have the authority to take it up again* (Jn 10:18).

So death in our Lord was a sign of alien sins, not a penalty for his own. In all other human beings, though, mortality is the penalty for sin; it is derived, you see, from the very origin of sin, from which we all come; from the fall of that man, not from the coming down of this one. It's one thing, I mean, to fall, another to come down. The one fell out of wickedness, the other came down out of kindness. *For just as in Adam all die, so in Christ shall all be made alive* (Rom 8:3). So as one carrying the sins of others, *for what I did not seize*, he said, *I then discharged the debt* (Ps 69:4); that is, I died, though I had no sin. *Behold, he says, the prince of this world will come, and in me he will find nothing.* What's *he will find nothing in me?* He won't find in me anything that deserves death. What deserves death, you see, is sin.

So why will you die?

He continues, and says, *But that all may know that I do the will of my Father, arise, let us go hence* (Jn 14:30-31). And he gets up and proceeds to his passion. Why? Because he was doing the will of his Father, not because he, in whom there was no sin, owed anything to the prince of sinners.

So our Lord Jesus Christ brought divinity with him, but took on mortality from us. He took this in the womb of the virgin Mary, joining himself, the Word of God, to human nature, like a bridegroom to his bride in the virginal bridal chamber, so that *he like a bridegroom might come forth from his chamber* (Ps 19:5).

*Christ rose again in what he took from us,
not in what was proper to himself*

17. So come back to what I was saying. Mortality came to all human beings from sin; in the Lord, however, it was the result of kindness and mercy, and yet

it was genuine all the same, because such perfect flesh was real and genuine, and genuinely mortal, having *the likeness of the flesh of sin* (Rom 8:3); not the likeness of flesh, but the likeness of the flesh of sin; real flesh, you see, but not the flesh of sin. After all, as I said, he hadn't taken that mortality as the deserts of sin, seeing that *he had emptied himself, taking the form of a servant, and becoming obedient to the death* (Phil 2:7.8). So what was he, and what did he have? He was divinity, which had mortality. Now that in which he died was also that in which he rose again.

Now take a look at those who say, "It was possible for Christ alone to rise again, not though for you." But you must answer and say, "Christ rose again in what he had taken from us. Take away the form of a servant, there would be nothing in which to rise again, because there would be nothing in which to die. So why, by praising my Lord, do you wish to pull me down the faith, which my Lord built up in me? It's as a result, you see, of his taking the form of a servant that he died. But he rose again in the same respect as he died. So I certainly need not despair in the least about the resurrection of a servant, since it was in the form of a servant that the Lord rose again."

Or suppose they attribute Christ's rising again from the dead to his power as a man; because they are also in the habit of saying this, that he was such a just man that he was even able to rise again from the dead—if I may for the moment speak as they do, and not say anything about our Lord's divinity. He was so just that he deserved to rise again from the dead. Well in that case he could in no way have been deceiving us, when he promised resurrection to us as well.

A summary of what has been said

18. So everything that has been said, brothers and sisters, is directed to providing you with material against those who say that the dead do not rise again. Something was said, if you remember, as far as God was pleased to suggest what was needed, some evidence was given from nature and some everyday examples; and also evidence of the omnipotence of God, for whom nothing is difficult, so that if he was able to make something that was not, much more is he able to repair what had been; and also about the Lord and Savior Jesus Christ himself, about whom it is common ground that he rose again, and that his resurrection only occurred in the form of a servant, because death too, from which he would have to rise, could only occur in the form of a servant. Therefore, since we are servants, we ought to hope in our form for what he was pleased to demonstrate to us first in the form of a servant. Let the tongues then fall silent of those who say, *Let us eat and drink; for tomorrow we die* (1 Cor 15:32). Right away come back with the answer, yes all of you too, and say, "Let us fast and pray; for tomorrow we shall die."

A brief reflection on the last day; the example of Noah's times

19. It remains for us to say what the life of the just will be like in the resurrection. But as you can see, the time allotted for today has been used up.

So chew the cud over what I have given you, and as for what I still owe you, pray that I may pay it back some time or other. Above all bear in mind why we have been speaking; it's particularly because of these festive days, my brothers and sisters, being celebrated by the pagans.[28] Look to yourselves; this world is passing. Recall the gospel in which the Lord foretells that the last day is going to be just as it was in the days of Noah: *They were eating and drinking, buying and selling, marrying wives and husbands, until Noah entered the ark; the flood came, and destroyed them all* (Lk 17:27). You have the Lord giving you the clearest advance warning, and saying elsewhere, *Do not let your hearts be weighed down with drugs*[29] and drunkenness (Lk 21:34). *Let your loins be girded, and lamps burning; and be like houseboys waiting for their master, when he comes from the wedding* (Lk 12:35-36). Let us be waiting expectantly for his coming, don't let him find us sunk in a torpor.

It's disgraceful for a married woman not to desire her husband; how much more disgraceful for the Church not to desire Christ! A husband comes to the embraces of the flesh, and is received by his chaste wife with intense longing. The Church's bridegroom is going to come to give us an eternal embrace, to make us his everlasting co-heirs; and we live in such a way, that not only do we not desire his coming, we even dread it! How true it is that that day is going to come as in the days of Noah! How many it is going to find like that, even those who are called Christians! That's why the ark is taking so many years in the building,[30] so that those who do not yet believe may wake up. That ark took a hundred years to build,[31] and they didn't wake up to say, "It can't be without reason that the man of God is building an ark; it must mean the imminent destruction of the human race"; and then to placate the wrath of God, and be converted to a way of life that pleases God, as the Ninevites did. They, you see, produced the fruit of repentance,[32] and appeased the wrath of God.

The example of Nineveh

20. Jonah proclaimed, not the mercy, but the wrath to come. He didn't say, you see, "Three days, and Nineveh shall be overthrown; but if you repent within these three days, God will spare you." He didn't say that. He only threatened the city's overthrow, and foretold that alone. And yet they didn't despair of God's mercy, they turned to repenting, and God did spare them.[33] But what are we to say? That the prophet lied? If you understand it merely literally, he does seem to have said something untrue; if you understand it in a spiritual way, what the prophet said did happen. Yes, Nineveh was overthrown. Consider what Nineveh was, and see how it was overthrown.

What was Nineveh? They were eating and drinking, buying, selling, planting, building, spending time on perjuring themselves, lying, getting drunk, committing crimes, being corrupt. That's what Nineveh was. Look at Nineveh now: they are mourning, grieving, afflicting themselves in sackcloth and ashes, fasting and prayer. Where is that other Nineveh? It has been overthrown of course, because it is no longer constituted by those previous activities.

How to enter the ark which Christ is building

21. So then, brothers and sisters, even now the ark is being built, and those hundred years are these times; this whole stretch of time is signified by that number of years. So if those people deserved to perish, who took no notice of Noah building the ark, what do those deserve who take no notice of the salvation offered while Christ is building the Church? There is as much difference between Noah and Christ as between slave and master; or rather, as much as between God and man; because slave and master can also be called two human beings. And yet, because human beings didn't believe while a human being was building the ark, they were given as an example to posterity to be on its guard against. Christ, God, man for our sakes, is building the Church. He has placed himself as the foundation for this ark; every day timbers immune to decay,[34] faithful men and women who renounce this world, are entering into the structure of the ark; and still it's being said, *Let us eat and drink; for tomorrow we die* (1 Cor 15:32)!

So you, brothers and sisters, as I have said, must say against them, "Let us fast and pray; for tomorrow we die." They, after all, say *Let us eat and drink; for tomorrow we die*, because they have no hope of resurrection; we, though, who already believe and proclaim the resurrection, with the prophets speaking of it and Christ and the apostles foretelling it, we who hope we are going to go on living after this death, we must not fall away, nor weigh down our hearts with drugs and drunkenness. Rather, as we wait, expectant and alert, loins girded and lamps burning, for the coming of our Lord, let us fast and pray, not for the reason that tomorrow we shall die, but in order that we may die secure and without a care in the world.

As for what remains, then, brothers and sisters, require it of me in the name of the Lord some other time. Turning to the Lord, etc.

NOTES

1. The Italian edition suggests the winter of 410-411. What their grounds are for the year, I do not know; Augustine tells us that it is winter in section 10. He also refers to a festival being celebrated by the pagans at the time. While the *Saturnalia*, at the turn of the year, was the greatest of these, there were also special celebrations for the dead, called the Parentalia, toward the end of February; and I think it more likely that this sermon was preached coincidentally with them. So I would assign it, accepting the Italian edition's suggestion, more precisely to February, 411. There is no reason to suppose it was not preached at home in Hippo Regius, but perhaps to a somewhat special group (see note 3 below) and thus not in any of the city's main basilicas.

2. Augustine had clearly chosen the reading of 1 Cor 15; probably verses 1-28, because he intended to preach on the resurrection. But gratified by the audience reaction to this particular verse, he chose it as his dominant text.

3. This may perhaps indicate that this was a sermon preached to a special group, not to an ordinary Sunday congregation, when there would usually have been a number of non-Christians present.

4. That is, both the Father and the Son.

5. I think he means a common life in which all sexual distinction has been abolished, where there will be no more male or female, as in Gal 3:28; hence the next question.

6. From Is 22:13. The words Paul goes on to add are also a quotation, this time from a play, *Thais* by the poet Menander.

7. What sort of consideration? He is being very obscure, or perhaps deliberately vague. Were any of the "theater crowds" present after all? I think they must have been; not, evidently, because it was a big feast of the Church, but perhaps because it was the time of the *Parentalia*.

8. Reading *audiunt nos . . .*, instead of the text's *audiant nos . . .*, should be very downcast.

9. An allusion to the sacrificial offerings made at the graves of the dead; a pagan custom which lay behind the banquets that African Christians celebrated with great gusto at the tombs of the martyrs, and which Augustine inveighed against from the moment of his ordination.

10. That is, that such sacrifices and sacrificial meals for the dead are not celebrated by them.

11. That is, that it refers—of course by a spiritual interpretation—to the offering of mass for the dead. It is only the faithful who understand this, because non-Christians and catechumens were ostensibly barred from knowing about the eucharist by the threadbare "discipline of the secret."

12. Reading *nisi* instead of the text's *ne*, lest perhaps.

13. See Mk 4:37-39.

14. See 1 Cor 15:33.

15. See Lk 24:36-40; Jn 20:25.

16. See Mt 27:52-53.

17. So we can date the sermon to the winter.

18. Reading *in hiemem . . . in aestatem*, instead of the text's *in hieme . . . in aestate*, in winter. . . in summer.

19. Here the Latin text adds, "They call them *gabbaras*." But the Maurists inform us that the sentence is absent from the manuscripts, so one wonders how it got into the edited text. As well as the manuscripts, the Maurists also made use of an earlier edition published in Louvain. So I suspect this is the comment of a learned 16th century scholar from that city of scholars.

20. Printed as a question in the text. It seems fairly obvious to me that it is a statement.

21. Like prehistoric graves, I suppose, accidentally dug up. I doubt if there was any deliberate archaeological or palaeontological excavation of such sites undertaken in those days.

22. See 1 Cor 15:33.

23. That is, that Christ was the only one who could rise from the dead. But he doesn't actually say what this other thing is until the end of this long section and the beginning of section 15.

24. While they refuse to *apprehendere* Christ, they dare not *reprehendere* him.

25. This means he was preaching to a congregation who heard him regularly; this supports my inference that it was one in his own diocese of Hippo Regius, since he certainly wasn't in Carthage in the winter of 410-411.

26. See Mk 4:37-39.

27. See Gn 27:16.21.

28. I suggest in note 1 that they are the February *Parentalia* on behalf of the dead.

29. *Crapula*. But as this word means exactly the same as the next, *ebrietate*, one can scarcely translate "drink and drunkenness," and "booze and drunkenness" would hardly do. So I offer a modern equivalent.

30. He means here the ark which is the Church.

31. The figure is arrived at by putting together Gn 5:32—Noah 500 years old when he begot Shem, Ham and Japheth; and Gn 6:11—the flood starting in the 600th year of his life.

32. See Lk 3:8.

33. See Jon 3.

34. In Gn 6:14, the ark is to be constructed of *gopher* wood, which in the Septuagint, and hence in Augustine's Latin version, becomes "squared timbers." And sometimes Augustine sticks to that, as in his sermons on Saint Quadratus, whose name, "Squared," rather asks for it; see Sermons 306B, 3, note 8, and 306C, 2, note 8. But again, as here, he sometimes mixes up Noah's ark with the ark of the covenant, which in Ex 25:10 is to be made of *shittim* wood; and this becomes in the Septuagint "aseptic," in Augustine's Latin *imputribilis*.

SERMON 362

ON THE RESURRECTION OF THE DEAD

Date: 411[1]

Carrying on from the previous sermon; on the nature of the life
of the just after the resuurection

1. Remembering the promise I made, I have had suitable readings chanted from the gospel and the apostle.[2] Any of you who were present at the previous sermon, you see, will remember that we divided the question proposed to us on the resurrection into a twofold discussion; first we would discuss, for the sake of those who doubt it, or even those who deny it, whether there is going to be a resurrection of the dead; while after that we would inquire, as best we could, according to the scriptures, what kind of life the just are going to have in the resurrection. So we lingered so long on the first part, where we dealt with the dead rising again, as you no doubt remember, that there was no time to deal with the second question, and thus we were forced to put it off until today. So this is the debt your eagerness is demanding of me, and I acknowledge that this is the time for me to pay it.

So let us all beg the Lord together, with earnest devotion from the heart, both that I may suitably pay the debt, and that you may profitably receive it. This, after all, is the bigger question, it must be admitted; but mightier than any difficult question is charity, whose slaves all of us ought to be, so that God who ordered this undertaking may turn all our difficulties into ease and joy.

A reminder of what was said in the previous sermon

2. You remember that we gave an answer on that day to some people who say, as the apostle taxes them with it, *Let us eat and drink; for tomorrow we die*; to which he added, *evil conversations corrupt good habits*, and then concluded like this, *Be sober, you just, and do not sin; for some people have no knowledge of God; I say it to your shame* (1 Cor 15:32-34). I hope we have all heard these words of the apostle, and taken them to heart, and whoever have so heard them and taken them to heart, may they show it by their actions. Those who hear, you see, are like a field receiving the seed from the sower; those who take to heart

241

are like the one who breaks up the clods and covers what has been sown; while those who act according to what they have heard and taken to heart, they are the ones who spring up harvest, and *bring forth fruit with patience* (Lk 8:15), *some thirtyfold, some sixtyfold, some a hundredfold* (Mk 4:20). For these it is not the fire that is being prepared, as for the chaff, but the granary, as for the grain.[3] So it's in these hidden granaries that that perpetual bliss is itself set apart for the just in the resurrection of the dead; and that's where scripture assures us they are to be received.

The hidden, or withdrawn nature of the place of the just indicated by the parable of the seine, and also other comparisons

3. It also mentioned them in another place under the name of vessels, when the Lord Jesus Christ said that the kingdom of heaven is like a seine, that is to say, nets; you see some nets, are called a seine. So, *the kingdom of heaven*, he said, *is like a seine thrown into the sea, and collecting things of every kind; pulling it out when it was full, and sitting on the shore, they selected the good ones into vessels, while the bad ones they threw away* (Mt 13:47-48). Our Lord wished to indicate that the word of God is now being thrown over the peoples and over the nations, in the way a seine is cast into the sea. It is now collecting with the Christian sacraments both good people and bad; but not all whom the seine hauls in are also stored in the jars. The jars, you see, are the dwellings of the saints, and the quiet retreats of the life of bliss, where it isn't anyone that's called Christian who can come, but only those who are called so in such a way that they really are so.

Certainly, though, both good and bad are swimming about within the seine, and the good are putting up with the bad, until they are separated at the end. It also says somewhere, *You will hide them in the hidden place of your countenance* (Ps 31:20). He was talking about the saints, you see. *You will hide them*, he says, *in the hidden place of your countenance*, that is, where the eyes of men can't follow them, nor the thoughts of mortals; to signify certain places set apart, so hidden, so concealed, he said it was in the hidden place of God's countenance. Are we to think materialistically and literally of God having a kind of huge face, and of there being in his face some material receptacle, where the saints are to be hidden away? You can see, brothers and sisters, how materialistic such an idea is, and how totally it is to be spat out from the hearts of all the faithful. So what must we understand by the hidden place of God's countenance, but something that is known only to God's countenance?

So when granaries are talked of, to signify places set apart, and elsewhere they are called jars; they aren't, of course, the granaries we know, nor the jars. I mean, if it was one such thing, it wouldn't be called the other. But because things unknown to us are intimated, insofar as they can be, by similarities familiar to people, take each thing named in this sense, that you should understand a place set apart by the names of both granary and jars. But if you ask what sort of withdrawn place, how set apart, listen to the prophet saying, *You will hide them in the hidden place of your countenance.*

We are still sighing in this life for our true home country

4. Be that as it may, brothers and sisters, in this life we are still wandering exiles, still sighing in faith for I know not what kind of home country. And why "I know not what kind," seeing that we are its citizens, unless it is because by wandering away *into a far country* (Lk 15:13) we have forgotten our true native land, and so can say about it, "I know not what kind of place it is"? This amnesia is driven from our hearts by the Lord Christ, king of that country, as he comes to join us in our exile; and by his taking of flesh, his divinity becomes a way for us,[4] so that we may proceed along it through Christ as man, and abide in Christ as God.

So what now, brothers and sisters? That secret place, which *eye has not seen, nor ear heard, nor has it come up into the heart of man* (1 Cor 2:9)—what eloquence can be adequate for me to unfold it to you, or what eyes will enable us to see it? Sometimes we can know something which for all that we are unable to express; but what we don't know, we are not capable of ever expressing at all. So while it could be that, if I knew those things, I would still be unable to express them to you, how much more difficult must my expression of them be, seeing that I too, brothers and sisters, am walking together with you by faith, not yet by sight?

But is this true just of me, or also of the apostle himself? You see, he comforts us for our ignorance, and builds up our faith, when he says, *Brothers, I do not consider myself to have apprehended. One thing, however, forgetting what lies behind, stretching out to what lies ahead, according to intention I follow toward the palm of the calling from above* (Phil 3:13-14); which is how he demonstrates that he is still on the way. And in another place, *As long*, he says, *as we are in the body, we are in exile abroad from the Lord; for we are walking by faith, not by sight* (2 Cor 5:6-7). And again, *For it is by hope*, he says, *that we have been saved. But hope which can be seen is not hope; for why should anyone hope for what he can see? But if we are hoping for what we cannot see, we wait for it with patience* (Rom 8:24-25).

So he will only try to explain what he believes, not what he knows

5. This being so, then, brothers and sisters, be ready to hear the same voice from me as is to be heard in the psalms, a dutiful voice, humble, gentle, not conceited, not rowdy, not headstrong, not rash. A psalm says somewhere, you see, *I have believed, for which reason I have spoken* (Ps 116:10). And the apostle introduced this text, and then added, *We too believe, for which reason we also speak* (2 Cor 4:13). So do you want me to tell you things I know? I won't mislead you; listen to what I have believed. Don't let it seem cheap stuff in your eyes, just because you are hearing what I have believed; you are hearing, after all, a genuine confession of faith. If I were to say, though, "Listen to what I know," you would be hearing some very rash presumption. So then all of us, brothers and sisters, and all too, if we are to trust the writings of the saints, who have lived in the flesh before us, and through whom the Spirit of God has spoken, in

order to impart to the human race just as much as needs to be signified to exiles, we all speak what we believe; the Lord himself, however, speaks what he knows.

So what does it matter, if the Lord was the only one who could actually know the things he said about the life that is going to be forever; while others who follow the Lord only speak because they have believed? We find our Lord Jesus Christ himself, who knew what he could speak about, declining for all that to say it. He said somewhere, you see, to his disciples, *I still have many things to say to you; but you are unable to take them now* (Jn 16:12). It was on account of their weakness that he put off saying what he knew, not on account of any difficulty he would have himself. We, on the other hand, on account of the common weakness of us all, make no attempt to give fitting expression to something we know; but instead we explain as best we can things that it is fitting for us to believe; and you, for your part, must grasp it as best you can. And if any of you, perhaps, can grasp more than I can express, don't waste your time on this thin little trickle, but hurry off to the abundant fountain, since with him *is the fountain of life, in whose light we shall see light* (Ps 36:10).

Our faith in the resurrection has already been discussed

6. So that there is, indeed, a resurrection, we have already discussed; that's what we believe, what we ought to believe; that's what we speak, because that is what we have believed,[5] if we are Christians. We have observed the mighty arm of the Lord laying low the pride of the nations on all sides, and building up the faith far and wide throughout the world, as was promised long before it happened; and observing all this, we are being built up to believe things which we cannot yet see, so that we may eventually receive the sight of them as the reward of faith. So since it is perfectly plain to our faith that there is going to be a resurrection of the dead; so plain, indeed, that any who doubted it would have to be utterly shameless to call themselves Christians; the question is now raised what sort of bodies the saints will have, and what their future life is going to be like. Many people have supposed, you see, that the resurrection will indeed happen, but only with respect to souls.[6]

Questions about the resurrection are raised

7. There's no need, however, after the last sermon, to argue at length that bodies also rise again. But that raises this sort of question; if there are going to be bodies, what sort of bodies are they going to be? Such as they are now, or of quite another fashion? If of another fashion, what is that fashion? If such as now, will it therefore be for the same activities?

That it won't be for the same activities is laid down by the Lord; that they won't be such[7] as they are now is what the apostle teaches. I mean, it won't be for the same life, nor for the same mortal and perishable and passing deeds, nor for the joys of the flesh nor for the consolations of the flesh. So if not for the same things, it follows they won't be such as they are now. So how, if bodies won't be such as they are now, will the flesh rise again? Now we have the resurrection of the flesh stated in the rule of faith, and it is in confessing it that we are baptized.[8] And everything we confess there, we confess from the truth and in the truth, in which *we live and move and are* (Acts 17:28).

You see, it is by certain time-bound and passing and fleeting events and deeds that we are prepared for eternal life. All the things that have taken place so that we might hear something salutary, that miracles might occur, that our Lord might be born, be hungry and thirsty, be arrested, be treated with abuse, be beaten, be crucified, die, be buried, rise again, ascend into heaven—they are all over and done with, and when they are preached about, they are proclaimed as the time-bound and transitory objects of our faith. Does it mean that because the events themselves are passing, what is being built up by them is also passing?

Would your holinesses please concentrate, in order to grasp the point through a comparison? An architect uses scaffolding and machinery that is going to be removed, in order to build a house that is going to remain. I mean in this building so vast and spacious, which we can see, while it was being put up there were all sorts of scaffolding and machinery here which are not here now; because what was being built with them now stands here completed. So in the same way, brothers and sisters, something was being built in Christian faith, and certain temporary mechanical devices have done their work and been finished with.[9] The fact, you see, that Christ rose again is over and done with; he isn't, after all, still rising again. And his ascending into heaven is over and done with; he isn't still ascending, after all. But his being now in that kind of life where *he dies no more, and death no longer lords it over him* (Rom 6:9); the fact that in him is also living forever that very nature of humanity which he took, and in which he was willing to be born, willing too to die in and be buried—all this is what has been built, all this remains forever. The machinery, though, by which it was built is over and done with. Christ isn't always, after all, being conceived in a virginal womb, or always being born of the virgin Mary, or always being arrested, or always being condemned, scourged, crucified, buried. All these events are classed as so much machinery, for building up by their means what remains and lasts forever. This resurrection, though, of our Lord Jesus Christ has been deposited in heaven.[10]

How Christ is the foundation of the heavenly Jerusalem

8. Would your graces please observe a wonderful building? These earthly buildings, of course, press down on the ground with their weight, and all the weight in this immense structure is bearing down on the ground by the force of gravity—and unless it is held up, it will sink to lower and lower depths, where its weight is dragging it. So because it is being built on earth, a foundation is first laid in the ground so that on this foundation the builder may put up his edifice without any further worries. That's why he places the most stable and solid mass right at the bottom, something that will be suitable to support what is placed on top of it; and the more massive the building, the more massive the

foundation prepared for it. But it is in the ground, in the earth, as I said, because what is being built on top of it is also, of course, being located on the ground, on earth.

That Jerusalem of ours, though, still in exile, is being built in heaven. That's why Christ, its foundation, preceded it into heaven. That, you see, is where our foundation is, and the head of the Church, because a foundation too is also called a head;[11] and indeed that is what it is. Because the head of a building too is its foundation; its head isn't where it is finished, but where it starts growing upward from. The tops of earthly buildings are raised up high; yet they set their head firmly in the solid ground. In the same sort of way the head of the Church has gone ahead into heaven, and is seated at the right hand of the Father. Just as men go about their work, when for laying foundations they bring along suitable material to make a solid base, to ensure the security of the mass that is going to be placed on top of it in the construction of the edifice to be; so in the same sort of way, by all those things that took place in Christ, being born, growing up, being arrested, enduring abuse, being scourged, crucified, killed, dying, being buried, it was like material being brought along for the heavenly foundations.

Let us take care to build on Christ, the one foundation

9. So now that our foundation has been laid in the heights, let us get ourselves built on it. Listen to the apostle: *No other foundation*, he says, *can anyone lay, besides the one which has been laid, which is Christ Jesus* (1 Cor 3:11).

But what comes next? *But let each of you see what you build on top of the foundation, gold, silver, precious stones, wood, grass, stubble* (1 Cor 3:10.12). Christ is indeed in heaven, but also in the hearts of believers. If Christ has the first place there, the foundation is rightly laid. So if you are building on it, you may build without a qualm, if you build, to match the worth of the foundation, gold, silver, precious stones. If however, by building wood, grass, stubble, you fail to match the worth of the foundation, at least stick to the foundation, and because of the dry and fragile things you have constructed on it, prepare yourself for the fire. But if the foundation is there, that is if Christ has obtained the first place in your heart, while the things of this world are loved in such a way that they are not put before Christ, but the Lord Christ is put before them, so that he is the foundation, that is holding the first place in your heart, then *you will suffer loss*, he says; *but you yourself shall be saved, in such a way, though, as if by fire* (1 Cor 13:15).

This is not the time to urge you to build gold, silver, precious stones, rather than wood, grass, stubble on such a grand and sturdy foundation. But at least take what I say now very briefly with the same seriousness as if it were said at length and in many words. After all, brothers and sisters, I know very well that if any of you, on account of the things you now love, were threatened by some judge with being thrown into prison, where you would have to endure only smoke, you would much rather lose all those things than suffer in that place. I don't know how it is, though, that when mention is made of the fire that is going to be there on judgment day, people all shrug it aside, and while they are really afraid of the flames in the hearth, they don't give a snap of the fingers for the flames of gehenna. What's the explanation of this insensitivity, of such perversity of feeling? If people would only at least fear what the apostle says, *by fire*, as you fear being burned alive, which only happens to you for a few moments until you lose consciousness and thus render all those flames superflous. You fear it, all the same, and avoid doing anything forbidden by the law, in case you should suffer that torment of a single moment.

We should be hoping for the same sort of resurrection
as has occurred already in the case of the Lord

10. But as I said, brothers and sisters, there is no time now to discuss that point. What I do say is that what we ought to hope for in the resurrection of the dead is what has already been portrayed in our head, what has been portrayed in the body of our Lord Jesus Christ. Any people who are hoping for something else are not now building on that foundation, not only not building gold, silver, precious stones, but not even stubble. They are putting it all outside, you see, because they are not putting it in Christ. So our Lord rose again in the very same body in which he had been buried. Resurrection is what Christians have been promised. So we should be hoping for the same sort of resurrection as in the case of our Lord has preceded the faith of us all. The reason he went ahead first, you see, was so that our faith might be built up on that foundation.

Well then, what does this mean? How shall we not be such as we are now? The flesh of our Lord Jesus Christ, after all, rose again, but it has ascended into heaven. On earth[12] it maintained human functions, but this was to convince them that it was what had been buried that had also risen again. There isn't such food, though, as that in heaven, is there? I mean, we read that angels too performed human functions on earth. They came to Abraham, and ate; and the angel went with Tobias, and ate.[13] What are we too say—that that eating was a phantom show, and not real?[14] Isn't it as clear as day that Abraham killed a calf, baked bread, and placed it all on the table; that he served the angels and they ate? All these things happened as plainly as could be and were described as plainly as could be.

Human beings eat from necessity; angels simply to show that they can

11. So what does the angel say in the book of Tobit? *You saw me eating, but you were seeing with your vision* (Tb 12:19). Was that because he wasn't actually eating, but only seemed to be eating? On the contrary, he really did eat. So what's the meaning of *you were seeing with your vision*? Would your holinesses please concentrate on what I am saying—concentrate on prayer more than on me, so that you may understand what I say, and I may say it in such a way as will be right for you to hear and to understand what you hear. Our bodies, as long as they are perishable and due to die sooner or later, suffer from the need

for constant renewal and refreshment, a need that also gives rise to starvation. That's why we get hungry and thirsty; and if we extend our hunger and thirst for a longer period than our bodies can bear, they become unhealthily wasted and thin, diseased and shrunken, because their energy is being drained away without being replenished; and if this goes on too long, even death will follow. Because something is always leaving our bodies in a kind of continual flow or current; but we don't thereby feel our strength deserting us, because we take in more to replace it by eating and drinking. What is supplied in bulk, you see, leaves us little by little; which is why we spend only a short time over our meals, while our strength and energy takes much longer to desert us, having been recharged when we were at table.

It's like oil in a lamp, which in a moment is poured in, but is used up over a longer period little by little. But when it has almost all been used up, the feebleness of the flame is now like the lamp's starvation, and straightaway we come to its help to restore that brightness, and keep the lamp alight, refreshed by its food when we add the oil. It's the same with our strength and energy, which we obtain by feeding ourselves; it drains away and deserts us in a steady flow, but little by little. I mean, it's precisely what's going on in us right now, and in all our actions and movements; and what has been received never stops leaking away, even in our moments of rest; and if it's all entirely used up, a person dies in the same sort of way as a lamp goes out. But in order not to die, that is not to go out—not that one dies in the spirit, but so that this bodily life of ours may not go out, and the body may, so to speak, wake up—we hurry to replace what has been used up, and are said to restore ourselves. When you talk of restoring, what are you restoring, if nothing has decayed?

So it's through this kind of need and decay that we are all also going to die, because this body is such that death is being kept in store for it as its due. This mortality, you see, is signified by the skins with which Adam and Eve were clothed, and then expelled from paradise.[15] Skins, after all, suggest death, because they are usually flayed from dead cattle. So while we are carrying around this weakness subject to decay, which even if it never lacks food but is restoring its strength thereby, still cannot ensure that death isn't going to come— after all, the whole condition of the body brings it eventually through successive stages, even if it goes on living here a long time, to the terminus of old age, beyond which it will find nowhere further to go except death; I mean that lamp too, even if you keep on putting oil in it, is still unable to go on burning forever, because even if it isn't extinguished by other accidents, the wick itself eventually fails, and is used up by a kind of old age. So while we carry around such bodies as this, their tendency to decay makes us needy, our need makes us hungry, our hunger sets us eating.

Angels, on the other hand, don't eat out of need. It's one thing, after all, to do something because you can, another to do it because you have to. Human beings eat in order not to die; angels eat in order to adapt themselves to mortals. If angels, you see, don't have to fear death, they don't need to restore what is decaying; if they don't need to restore what is decaying, they don't eat because of need. But those who saw the angel eating, assumed it was because he was hungry. That's what he was referring to when he said, *You were seeing with your vision.* He didn't say, after all, "You used to see me eating, but I didn't eat"; *you used to see me eating,* he said, *but you were seeing with your vision;* that is, "I was eating in order to adapt myself to you, not because I was suffering from any hunger or need, under whose compulsion you have been in the habit of eating; and that's why, when you see anyone eating, you guess it's being done out of need, because you assess what you see by your own habits." That's the meaning of *you were seeing with your vision.*

We too, after the resurrection, will be under no necessity of eating or drinking

12. So what follows, my brothers and sisters? *We know,* as the apostle says, *that Christ rising again from the dead dies now no more, and death no longer lords it over him. For in that he died to sin, he died once; while in that he lives, he lives to God* (Rom 6:9-10). So if he dies no more, and death no longer lords it over him, we should be hoping that we too are going to rise again like that, to be forever in the state into which we shall be changed by rising again. As for eating and drinking, even though we have the power, we will not be under the necessity of it. At that time, though,[16] there was a reason why the Lord should do this, because those to whom he wished to adapt himself were still in the flesh, to whom he also showed his scars. The one, after all, who made eyes for the blind man which he hadn't received in his mother's womb, was not incapable of rising again without his scars. Indeed, if he had wished before his death so to alter the needs of his mortal flesh, that it was under no necessities at all, and lacked nothing, he could naturally have done so. After all, he had it in his grasp, because he was God in the flesh, and the Son is almighty just as the Father is almighty. I mean, he did in fact change his own flesh before his death into whatever he wished; thus on the mountain, when he was with his disciples, his countenance shone like the sun.[17]

This, of course, he did by his divine power, wishing to show that he could change even his very flesh from being under any need, so that he wouldn't die if he did not wish to. *I have the power,* he said, *to lay down my life, and I have the power to take it up again. Nobody can take it from me* (Jn 10:18). Great indeed the power by which he was able even not to die; but greater still the loving kindness by which he was willing to die. The reason, you see, he did by loving kindness what he was also able by power not to do, was to lay the foundation for us of resurrection; so that the mortal element which he carried around for our sakes would both die, because we are going to die; and would rise again to immortality, so that we might hope for immortality. And that's why it's not only written that before his death he ate and drank, but also that he was hungry and thirsty; while after the resurrection only that he ate and drank, not though that he was hungry and thirsty; because in a body that was not going to die anymore there was none of the need imposed by decay, requiring the necessity of restoring tissues, but there was the power of eating. This was done for the sake of adapting himself to others, not to supply the needs of his flesh, but to persuade the disciples of the true reality of his body.

What about the apostle's remark that flesh and blood
shall not gain possession of the kingdom of God?

13. Against all this weight of evidence, some people raise a problem for us from the apostle himself; just see what they object, in fact, to this argument. The flesh, they say, will not rise again; because if it does, it will gain possession of the kingdom of God; but the apostle says openly, *Flesh and blood shall not gain possession of the kingdom of God* (1 Cor 15:50). You heard it, when the apostle was being read. We say the flesh rises again, and the apostle exclaims, *Flesh and blood shall not gain possession of the kingdom of God.* So are we proclaiming something against the apostle, or did he proclaim something against the gospel? The gospel bears witness with a divine voice: *The Word became flesh, and dwelt amongst us* (Jn 1:14). If it became flesh, it became true flesh—I mean, if it wasn't true flesh, then it wasn't flesh. Just as Mary's was true flesh, so Christ's, which was taken from her, was true flesh. It was this true flesh that was arrested, scourged, slapped about, hung up on the cross; this true flesh that died, this true flesh that was buried, this true flesh that also rose again from death. The scars are evidence for this; the eyes of the disciples see them, and they still hesitate for the wonder of it; their hands touch and feel, to rescue their minds from doubt. Against all that evidence, brothers and sisters, which our Lord Jesus Christ wished to convince the disciples of in this manner, as they were going to proclaim it throughout the wide world; against this evidence does the apostle really seem to be fighting when he says, *Flesh and blood shall not gain possession of the kingdom of God?*

One simple solution of the problem

14. We could solve this problem just like this, and stand up to the quibbling fault-finders—all the same, while we shall offer such a solution, by which a quick answer can be given, we shall also consider more carefully why the apostle said what he did. So let me say how we can most easily answer the objection. What have we got in the gospel? That Christ rose again in the same body as was buried; that he was seen, that he was touched and handled, that to the disciples who thought he was a spirit he said, *Feel and see, that a spirit does not have flesh and bones, as you can see that I have* (Lk 24:39). What does the apostle oppose to this? *Flesh and blood,* he says, *shall not gain possession of the kingdom of God* (1 Cor 15:50). I wholeheartedly embrace each statement, and I don't say they clash with each other, or else I myself may be clashing with the goad. So how can I embrace them both? I could quickly, as I said, answer like this: The apostle said, *Flesh and blood cannot gain possession of the kingdom of God by inheritance.* He was speaking correctly; you see, it's not the place of

flesh to possess, but to be possessed. After all, it isn't your body that possesses anything, but your soul that possesses things through the body, just as it also possesses the body itself. So if the flesh rises again in such a way as to be owned, not to own, to be possessed, not to possess, what's so surprising about flesh and blood not possessing the kingdom of God, because it will of course be possessed itself?

The flesh, you see, gains possession of those who are not the kingdom of God, but the devil's kingdom; and that's why they are enslaved to the pleasures of the flesh. Thus too, that paralytic was being supported by his pallet; but when the Lord healed him, he said to him, *Take up your pallet and go to your home* (Mk 2:11). So in this way, cured of his paralysis he owns his flesh and takes it wherever he likes; he isn't being carted by the flesh where he doesn't want to go, and he now carries his body instead of being carried by it.[18] Now it's quite clear that in that resurrection the flesh will not have the allure, the power of attraction to lead the soul, by tickling its fancy with various blandishments, where the soul doesn't really wish to go—and often enough it's overcome, and says, *I can see another law in my members fighting back against the law of my mind, and taking me prisoner under the law of sin, which is in my members.* The paralytic is still being carried on his pallet, is not yet carrying it. So let him cry out, *Unhappy man that I am, who will deliver me from the body of this death?*; and let him answer himself, *The grace of God through our Lord Jesus Christ* (Rom 7:23-25).

So when we have risen again, the flesh will not be carrying us, but we shall be carrying it; if it's we who are carrying it, it's we who shall possess it; if it's we who possess it, it's we who shall not be possessed by it, because now that we have been delivered from the devil's grip, we are the kingdom of God; and thus *flesh and blood shall not gain possession of the kingdom of God.* So let those fault-finders just shut their mouths, because they really are flesh and blood, and cannot think anything but thoughts of flesh. Because about them, as they persist in the same *prudence of the flesh* (Rom 8:6)—which is why they can deservedly be called flesh and blood—it can rightly and truly be said that *flesh and blood shall not gain possession of the kingdom of God.*

The problem may also be solved in this way: that such people as are called flesh and blood (it's about such, you see, that the apostle also says, *our wrestling is not against flesh and blood* (Eph 6:12), must change to a spiritual way of life and *by the spirit put to death the deeds of the flesh* (Rom 8:13), or they will not be able to gain possession of the kingdom of God.

What the apostle really meant by the sentence

15. "But all the same," someone will say, "what did the apostle really mean? After all, the truest sense of his words will be the one that is opened up by the context of the passage."

And so let us for preference listen to him, and see from the whole surrounding context of scripture what he wished us to understand in this place. This then is what he said: *The first man was from the earth, earthly; the second man is from heaven. As the earthly one is, such too are those who are earthly; and as the heavenly one is, such too are those who are heavenly. Just as we have borne the image of the earthly man, let us also bear the image of the one who is from heaven. But this I must say, brothers, that flesh and blood shall not gain possession of the kingdom of God, nor what is perishable of imperishability* (1 Cor 15:47-50).

So let's see the whole thing, bit by bit. *The first man*, he says, *was from the earth, earthly; the second man is from heaven. As the earthly one is, such too are those who are earthly,* all, that is, who are going to die; *and as the heavenly one is, such too are those who are heavenly,* all, that is, who are going to rise again. The heavenly man, after all, has already risen again and ascended into heaven; we are now being incorporated into him by faith, so that he is our head, while the members are to follow their head in due order, and so that what has been demonstrated in advance in the head is to be repeated at the proper time in the members; while for the time being we are to go on bearing the image of this[19] by faith so that in due course we may come to the full reality and direct sight. That, after all, is what he says somewhere else: *But if you have risen again with Christ, seek the things that are above where Christ is, seated at the right hand of God; savor the things that are above, not the things that are on earth* (Col 3:1-2). So while indeed we have not yet risen again in ourselves, as Christ has in the body, still we too are said to have risen again with Christ through faith; so in the same way he bids us meanwhile bear the image of the heavenly man, of the one, that is, who is already in heaven, by faith.

Why the second man is said to be from heaven, and not in heaven

16. But if you ask why he said the second man was not in heaven but from heaven, whereas the Lord himself took his body from earth, because of course Mary was descended from Adam and Eve; you should understand that the earthly man was called so with reference to earthly desire. Now that passion, by which human beings are born through the union of male and female, is a very earthly one, and by it they also contract original sin from their parents. The body of the Lord, on the other hand, was created from a virginal womb without any such passion, although Christ did take flesh from the earth, which we understand the Holy Spirit to be telling us, when he says, *Truth has sprung from the earth* (Ps 85:11). All the same he is not an earthly, but a heavenly man, and is said to be from heaven. After all, if he has granted this to his faithful by grace, so that the apostle can rightly say, *For our domicile is in heaven* (Phil 3:20), how much more is he himself a heavenly man, and justly said to be from heaven, seeing that no sin was ever to be found in him? It was because of sin, after all, that the man was told, *Earth you are, and into earth you shall go* (Gn 3:19).

So that heavenly man is most rightly said to be from heaven, since his domicile never moved from heaven, although the Son of God also became Son of man by taking a body from earth, taking, that is, *the form of a servant* (Phil

2:7). For it was only the one that had descended who also ascended.[20] Because even if others ascend, whoever he may grant this to, or rather if they are lifted up to heaven by his grace, even so it is he that ascends, because they become his body, and in this way it is just one who ascends. This is a great sacrament in Christ and the Church, as the apostle explains, where it is written, *And they shall be two in one flesh* (Eph 5:31; Gn 2:24). That's why it's also said, *Therefore they are not now two, but one flesh* (Mk 10:8). That's how it is that *Nobody has ascended into heaven except the one who descended from heaven, the Son of man who is in heaven* (Jn 3:13). The reason he added *who is in heaven*, you see, was in case anyone should reckon that his domicile had been moved from heaven, when he appeared on earth to human eyes in an earthly body.

So then, *just as we have borne the image of the earthly man, let us also bear the image of the one who is from heaven* (1 Cor 15:49), for the time being by faith, by which we have also already risen again with him; so that we may have our hearts lifted up above, *where Christ is, seated at the right hand of God* (Col 3:1); and in this way let us seek the things that are above, and savor them, not the things that are on earth.

A difference in meaning between "body" and "flesh"

17. But he was dealing with the resurrection of the body; this, you see, is how he had begun the passage:[21] *But someone will say, How do the dead rise? With what sort of body are they coming?* (1 Cor 15:35). And the reason he had said *The first man was from the earth, earthly, the second man from heaven; as the earthly man is, such too are those who are earthly; and as the heavenly man is, such too are those who are heavenly*, was so that we might hope that what had come about first in Christ's body would also come about in ours; and that although we don't yet experience this in actual reality, we should in the meantime hold on to it by faith. That's why he added, *Just as we have borne the image of the earthly man, let us also bear the image of the one who is from heaven.* But in case we should assume we were going to rise again for the same sort of activities, involving processes of decay, as we used to engage in according to the first man, he immediately added, *But this I must say, brothers, that flesh and blood cannot gain possession of the kingdom of God* (1 Cor 15:47-50).

And he wants to indicate what he meant by flesh and blood, that he doesn't mean the very fact of being a body, but is signifying liability to decay by the expression "flesh and blood," a liability that will not then be experienced. The body, you see, that is not subject to decay is not properly called flesh and blood, but simply body. If it's flesh, I mean, it's subject to decay and mortal; but if it now dies no more,[22] it is now no more subject to decay; and therefore, while retaining its own specific nature without being subject to decay, it is not now called flesh, but body; and if it does happen to be called flesh, it is not now properly so called, but on account of a certain specific similarity. Just so we can, possibly, talk about the flesh of angels because of this kind of similarity, when they have appeared as men to human beings, while in fact, there were bodies there, not flesh, because there was no inner liability to decay.

So because we can, in virtue of this similarity, call a body flesh which is not any longer subject to decay, the apostle was anxious to explain what he meant by "flesh and blood," that he meant liability to decay, not the specific nature; and so he immediately went on to add, *Nor shall what is perishable gain possession by inheritance of imperishability* (1 Cor 15:50); as though to say, "What I meant by *flesh and blood shall not gain possession of the kingdom of God*, is the same as what I said now, that *what is perishable shall not gain possession of imperishability*.

How the Lord answered the Sadducees, when they called
in question the resurrection of the dead

18. And in case anybody should say, "So if imperishability cannot be possessed by what is perishable, how will our bodies manage to be there?" listen to what follows.[23] It's as though, you see, the apostle were asked, "So what is it you're saying? Have we professed our faith in *the resurrection of the flesh*[24] all for nothing? If flesh and blood shall not gain possession of the kingdom of God, then it's all for nothing that we have believed that our Lord rose again from the dead in the body in which he was born and crucified, and that in it he ascended into heaven before the very eyes of his disciples, the heaven from where he cried out to you, *Saul, Saul, why are you persecuting me?* (Acts 9:4)." This really did happen to Paul, the holy and blessed apostle, who was giving birth in tender maternal love to his children, begotten in Christ through the gospel,[25] with whom he was *still in labor until Christ should be formed in them again* (Gal 4:19); that is, until they should bear in faith the image of the man who is from heaven. I mean, he didn't want them to remain with the ruinous assumption that they were going to do the same kind of things in the kingdom of God, in that eternal life, as they used to do in this life, occupied with the pleasures of eating and drinking, of marrying husbands and wives, and producing children[26] according to the flesh. You see, it's the flesh's liability to decay that requires these activities, not the specific nature of flesh.

So, as I remarked some time ago,[27] the Lord had already established, in the gospel which was chanted just now, that we are not going to rise again for such activities. The Jews,[28] you see, certainly believed in the resurrection of the flesh; but they thought it was going to be such that they would have the same kind of life in the resurrection as they led in this world. And so, with such fleshly, gross ideas about it they were unable to answer the Sadducees, when they put their problem about the resurrection; whose wife a woman would be whom seven brothers had had in turn, each of them wishing to raise up seed for his dead brother from his wife.[29] The Sadducees, I mean, were a particular sect of the Jews which didn't believe in the resurrection. So when the Sadducees put this problem, the Jews were uncertain and hesitant, and couldn't really answer it, because they assumed that the kingdom of God could be possessed by flesh and blood, imperishability, that is, by what is perishable. Along comes Truth, he is questioned by the misguided and misguiding Sadducees, that problem is put to the Lord. And the Lord, who knew what he was saying, and who wished us to believe what we didn't know, gives an answer by his divine authority which we are to hold by faith. The apostle, for his part, explained it to the extent that it was granted him to; which we, as best we can, must try to understand.

So what did the Lord say to the Sadducees? *You are mistaken,* he said, *not knowing the scriptures, nor the power of God. For in the resurrection they marry neither husbands nor wives; for neither do they start dying again, but they will be equal to the angels of God* (Mt 22:29-30; Lk 20:36). Great is the power of God. Why do they not marry husbands or wives? Because they won't start dying again. It's where one generation departs, you see, that another is required to succeed it.[30] So there will be no such liability to decay in that place. And the Lord himself passed through the usual stages of growth, from infancy to adult manhood, because he was bearing the substance of flesh that was still mortal; but after he has risen again at the age at which he was buried, are we to imagine that he is growing old in heaven? So, *they will be,* he says, *equal to the angels of God.* He eliminated the assumption of the Jews, refuted the objection of the Sadducees; because the Jews did indeed believe the dead would rise again, but they had gross, fleshly ideas about what activities they would rise again for. *They will be equal,* he said, *to the angels of God.* You have heard about the power of God; now hear about the scriptures as well: *About the resurrection,* he said, *have you not read how the Lord spoke to Moses from the bush, saying, I am the God of Abraham, the God of Isaac, and the God of Jacob? He is not the God of the dead, but of the living* (Mk 12:26-27).

Paul's account of life after the resurrection

19. So then, that we are to rise again has already been said; and that we rise again to the life of the angels, we have heard from the Lord; but in what specific form we are to rise again, he has shown us himself in his own resurrection. It's because that specific form, however, will have no tendency to decay that the apostle says, *But this I must say, brothers, that flesh and blood shall not gain possession by inheritance of the kingdom of God; nor shall what is perishable gain possession by inheritance of imperishability* (1 Cor 15:50); to show that by the expression "flesh and blood" he wished us to understand the tendency to decay of a mortal and merely soul-animated body.[31] Then he goes on himself to solve the problem, which his anxious hearers might raise with him, being more careful himself about what the children would understand than children usually are about the words of their parents. So he adds something, and says, *Behold, I tell you a mystery.* Hush your thoughts, man, whoever you may be; you had started, I know, to conclude from the apostle's words that human flesh is not to rise again, when you heard, *Flesh and blood shall not gain possesion of the kingdom of God;* but lend your ears to the words that follow, and correct the hasty assumption of your thoughts. *Behold,* he says, *I tell you a mystery; we shall all indeed rise again, but we shall not all be changed* (1 Cor 15:51).[32]

So what does this mean? Change, of course, is either for the worse or for the better. So if a change has been posited, about which we cannot yet see what sort it will be, whether into something better or into something worse; so let him go on himself to explain which; what business is it of ours to guess? And perhaps the apostle's authority will not allow you to slip into error through human guesswork, putting two and two together and making five; and perhaps he will explain clearly what sort of change he wishes us to understand here. So what's the situation? When he says *We shall all rise again, but we shall not all be changed,* I observe that all are going to rise again, both good and bad alike; but let us see who will be changed; and from this let us understand whether that change is going to be for better or for worse. If this change, you see, concerns the bad, it will be for the worse, if the good, it will be for the better. *In an atom,*[33] he says, *in the twinkling of an eye, at the last trumpet. For the trumpet will sound, and the dead will rise again imperishable, and we shall be changed* (1 Cor 15:52). So now this change will be for the better, since he says, *and we shall be changed.* But he hasn't yet expressed as fully as it needs to be, to what extent our bodies will be changed for the better. What this "better" is hasn't yet been said. After all, when they change from infancy through to adolescence, they can be said to be changed for the better, where even though they grow less feeble, they still are feeble, all the same, and mortal.

Explaining the atom of time, and the twinkling of an eye
in which the dead are all going to rise again

20. So let's go over each point a little more carefully. *In an atom,* he says. It appears to people a difficult thing for the dead to rise again; it's wonderful how the apostle removes all the doubts and difficulties from the hearts of the faithful. You say, "The dead can't rise again."

I say, that not only do the dead rise again, but they do so with a speed such as you certainly weren't conceived and born at. I mean, what a long time it takes for a human being to be formed in the womb, to be completed, to be born; then to reach full stature by growing through the stages of life! Is that how you are going to rise again? No; but *in an atom,* he says.

Many people don't know what "atom" means. It comes from the Greek *tomē,* which means cutting; so *atomos* in Greek means what cannot be cut. But you can talk about an atom in material bodies, and about an atom in time. In material bodies, if anything can be found which is generally held to be impossible to divide, it means some particle so minute that it leaves no room to cut it. But an atom in time is a brief moment, which leaves no room to divide it. For example, so that the slower minds may grasp what I am saying: there's a stone; divide it into parts, and those parts into pebbles, the pebbles into grains like those of sand, and again divide the grains of sand into the finest dust, until you come, if possible, to something so tiny it can't be divided any further; that is an atom in the case of material bodies. In time, on the other hand it can be understood like this: a year, for example, is divided into months, months are divided into days, days can be divided still further into hours, hours still further into somewhat extended portions of hours which admit of further divisions,[34] until you come to such a small point of time, a kind of drop of a moment, that it can't be held and lingered on in any way whatever, and therefore can't be divided; this is an atom of time.

So you were saying that the dead don't rise again; not only do they rise again, they do so with such speed that the resurrection of all the dead is going to happen instantaneously, in an atom of time. And to impress upon you the speed of such an atom, after saying *in an atom*, he straightaway went on to show how much action and movement can occur in an atom of time, by saying *in the twinkling of an eye* (1 Cor 15:52). He realized, you see, that saying *in an atom* was rather obscure, and he wanted to say it more plainly so that it could be the more easily understood. What is the twinkling of an eye? Not the moment when we close or open the eyes with the eyelids—when we blink; no, by the twinkling of the eye he meant the emission of rays in order to observe something.[35] As soon as you turn your gaze there, you see, the ray emitted reaches the sky, where we look upon the sun and moon and stars and constellations, separated from the earth by such an immense distance.

As for the last trumpet, he means the last, final signal. *For the trumpet*, he says, *will sound, and the dead will rise again imperishable, and we shall be changed* (1 Cor 15:52). By "we," of course, he meant the faithful, and those who rise again first to eternal life. So that change, because it will affect the devout and the holy, will be for the better, not for the worse.

The nature of the change

21. But what is this change? What's this he said, *We shall be changed*? Does it mean the loss of the specific form which now exists, or only of the perishability and liability to decay, which led him to say, *Flesh and blood cannot gain possession of the kingdom of God; nor shall what is perishable gain possession by inheritance of imperishability*? And to prevent this moving his hearers to despair about the resurrection of the flesh, he added, *Behold, I tell you a mystery; we shall all rise again, but we shall not all be changed* (1 Cor 15:50-51). And in case we should suppose the change will be for the worse, *and we*, he says, *shall be changed*. So it remains for him to say what sort of change it is going to be. *For it is necessary*, he says, *for this perishable thing to put on imperishability, and for this mortal thing to put on immortality* (1 Cor 15:52-53). If this perishable thing puts on imperishability and this mortal thing puts on immortality, there will no longer be any perishable flesh. So if there's no more perishable flesh, all mention of perishing and decay in flesh and blood will fall away; even proper mention of flesh and blood will fall away, because these are words that imply mortality. And if that's the case, it's true both that the flesh will rise again, and that because it is changed and becomes imperishable, *flesh and blood shall not gain possession of the kingdom of God*.

If, however, anyone wishes to understand that change as taking place in those whom that day will then find still alive; so that those who are already dead rise again, while those who are still alive are changed; so that it is in their name we are to suppose the apostle was speaking, when he said *and we shall be changed*; even so the same conclusion will follow, that that imperishability will certainly apply to all, *when this perishable thing puts on imperishability, and this mortal thing puts on immortality. Then shall the word that has been written come true: Death has been swallowed up in victory. Where, death, is your striving? Where, death, is your sting?* (1 Cor 15:54-55).

The body, though, which is no longer mortal, cannot properly be called flesh and blood, which are earthly bodies; but it is called body, because it can now be called a heavenly one. Just as when the same apostle was speaking of different kinds of flesh, *Not every flesh*, he said, *is the same flesh. There is one kind in human beings, another in cattle, another in fish, another in birds, another in snakes. And there are heavenly bodies*, he said, *and earthly bodies* (1 Cor 15:39-40). In no way, however, could he talk of heavenly flesh, though bodies could be called flesh, but only earthly ones. Every kind of flesh, after all, is a body, but not every kind of body is flesh; not only because heavenly bodies aren't called flesh, but also some earthly ones, like wood and stones, anything of that sort. So even in this respect flesh and blood are unable to gain possession of the kingdom of God, because when the flesh rises again it will be changed into the kind of body in which there will no longer be any mortal tendency to decay, and which therefore will no longer be properly called flesh and blood.

Against those who say there is only a spiritual resurrection

22. But pay close attention now, brothers and sisters, I beg you; it's not something to make light of, it's a question of our faith, which we have to guard not only against the pagans, but also against some perverse people who want to be called and to be seen as Christians. There was no lack of people, you see, even during the time of the apostles, to say that the resurrection has already taken place, and thereby to turn the faith of some upside down. It's about these that the apostle says, *who have strayed into error about the truth, saying that the resurrection has already taken place; and they have overturned the faith of some* (2 Tm 2:18). Now it is not insignificant that he didn't say they have gone astray from the truth, but *about the truth*. All the same they didn't hold on to the truth.[36]

So then death is eliminated, and will simply not exist at all. As the apostle says, *what is mortal will be swallowed up by life* (2 Cor 5:4). The same thing is said, you see, about the Lord, that he has swallowed death.[37] It's not, after all, as though death somehow withdraws, having some kind of independent existence or substance of its own; but it will simply cease to be in the body where it was, so that you can still see the specific form, hold onto the specific form, but when you look for perishability and mortality you can't find it. So has perishability gone away somewhere? No, but right there it has been abolished, right there swallowed up. That's why, after saying *It is necessary for this perishable thing to put on imperishability, and for this mortal thing to put on immortality*, he goes on to say, *then shall the word which has been written come true: Death has been swallowed up in victory. Where, death, is your striving? Where, death, is your sting?* (1 Cor 15:53-55). And he didn't say, "Death has departed in victory," but *Death has been swallowed up in victory.* So how did they go astray about the truth? By asserting truly one resurrection, but denying the other.

The difference between the resurrection of the wicked and of the good

23. You see, there is indeed a resurrection according to faith, whereby everyone who believes rises again in spirit. In fact it is those who have first risen again in the spirit that will have a good second resurrection in the body. Because those who haven't previously risen again in spirit through faith, will not rise again to that change in the body, whereby all liability to decay and to perishing will be taken away[38] and swallowed up, but to that other penal kind of wholeness or completeness. Because the bodies of the wicked too will be whole and complete, nothing in them will appear diminished; but this wholeness of body will be for their punishment, and there will be a certain, if I may say so, a certain strength of body, a kind of decaying strength. Because where there can be pain, you cannot say there is no decay; although that strength[39] isn't worn out with the pain, lest the pain itself should die. It is not, I think, too far-fetched to suppose that this decay is prophetically signified by the name of worm, and the pain by the name of fire. But because the strength of body will be such that it doesn't succumb to death as a result of its pains, nor get changed into imperishability and immunity to decay, in which there is no pain, that's why the text runs like this: *Their worm will not die, and their fire will not be put out* (Mk 9:48; Is 66:24).

The change, on the other hand which means freedom from perishable decay will be that of the saints. So it will apply to those who have now experienced resurrection of the spirit through faith; the resurrection about which the apostle says, *But if you have risen again with Christ, seek the things that are above where Christ is, seated at the right hand of God; savor the things that are above, not the things that are on earth. For you have died, and your life is hidden with Christ in God* (Col 3:1-3). Depending on how we die according to the spirit and rise again according to the spirit, so later on we die according to the flesh and rise again according to the flesh. Death according to the spirit is no longer believing the futilities you used to believe, no longer doing the bad things you used to do. Resurrection, according to the spirit is believing the salutary things you used not to believe, and doing the good things which you used not to do. You used to regard earthly idols and images as gods, you have come to know the one God and to believe in him; you have died to idolatry, risen again in the Christian faith. You used to be a drunkard, you are now a sober person; you have died to drunkenness, risen again in sobriety. In the same way, when one gives up any kind of bad activity there is a kind of death in the soul, and in one's good deeds it rises again. *Put to death*, says the apostle, *your members which are on the earth, uncleanness, disorderly behavior, evil lusts, and avarice*, he says, *which is the worship of idols* (Col 3:5). So when we have put these members to death, we rise again in the good works that are their opposites, in holiness, in tranquillity, in charity, in almsgiving. Now just as the death according to the spirit precedes the resurrection according to the spirit, so in the same way the death according to the flesh is going to precede the resurrection according to the flesh.

Evidence for the double resurrection from the apostle

24. So we should be aware of each kind of resurrection, both the spiritual and the bodily kind. The spiritual kind is referred to by the text, *Arise, you that are asleep, and rise up from the dead* (Eph 5:14); and by that other one, *Upon those who were sitting in the shadow of death light has risen* (Is 9:2); and by the one I mentioned a short while ago, *If you have risen together with Christ, seek the things that are above* (Col 3:1). It is to the bodily resurrection, on the other hand, that what the apostle is now saying refers, where he had put this sort of question to himself: *But someone says, How do the dead rise again? With what kind of body will they come?* (1 Cor 15:35). So it was a matter of the resurrection of the body, in which the Lord had gone ahead of his Church. So it's about this that he says, *It is necessary for this perishable thing to put on imperishability, and for this mortal thing to put on immortality* (1 Cor 15:53); all this on account of what he had said, *Flesh and blood shall not gain possession of the kingdom of God* (1 Cor 15:50).

Now in another place we have the same apostle Paul's clearest testimony about the resurrection according to the spirit and about the resurrection according to the flesh. The mortal body, you see, which is, or was, animated by the soul, is being called flesh. So this is how the apostle speaks: *But if Christ is in you, the body is indeed dead because of sin, but the spirit is life because of justice.* There you are, the resurrection according to the spirit is already being understood as achieved through justice; just see whether the resurrection of the body is also to be hoped for. After all, he didn't want to call the body mortal, but dead; and yet he made it plain in what follows that this is what he meant. And so he goes on to say, *So if the Spirit of the one who raised Jesus from the dead is dwelling in you, the one who raised our Lord Jesus will also give life to your mortal bodies through his Spirit dwelling in you* (Rom 8:10-11).

That's how those people *went astray about the truth*,[40] those who denied one resurrection. If they had denied every kind, you see, they would have gone astray from the truth, not just *about the truth*. But because *they went astray about the truth*, they confessed one, the one according to the spirit, while they denied the other, which we are hoping for in the resurrection of the flesh, *saying that the resurrection has already taken place*; if they hadn't said this, in such a way as to prevent people believing in and hoping for the one which is going to occur in the body, he wouldn't go on to say about them, *they overturn the faith of some* (2 Tm 2:18).

25. But listen now to the clearest possible testimony from the Lord himself in the gospel according to John. In one place he declares both resurrections, both the one which occurs now according to the spirit, and the one which is going to happen later on according to the flesh, in such a way that none who in any way call themselves Christians and submit to the authority of the gospel can be left in any doubt at all; in such a way too that there is no entry left for the twisters who wish to unsettle Christians by means of what is apparently the Christian faith, by injecting it with their poison so as to kill the souls of the weak. But listen to it from the volume of the gospel itself. The reason, you see, that I am performing the office of reader as well as of expositor is so that this sermon of mine may be supported by the authority of the holy scriptures, and not built upon the sand of human guesswork, if something happens to slip one's memory.

So listen to the gospel according to John; the Lord is speaking. *Amen, amen I tell you, that whoever hears my word and believes the one who sent me has eternal life, and does not come to judgment, but has made the passage from death to life. Amen, amen I tell you, that the hour is coming, and now is, when the dead will hear the voice of the Son of God; and those who hear shall live. For just as the Father has life in himself, so too he has given the Son also to have life in himself; and he has given him authority also to execute judgment, because he is the Son of man. Do not be surprised at this, that the hour is coming in which all who are in the grave will hear his voice; and those who have done good will come forth to the resurrection of life; but those who have done evil to the resurrection of judgment* (Jn 5:24-29). I imagine that many of you understand that the Lord himself distinctly and openly indicated each kind of resurrection in this passage, both the one according to the spirit through faith, and the one according to the flesh through that trumpet we all know about so well.[41]

All the same, let us go over these words very carefully, so that it may be clear to all the listeners. *Amen, amen I tell you, that whoever hears my word and believes the one who sent me has eternal life, and does not come to judgment, but has made the passage from death to life.* This is the resurrection according to the spirit, which occurs now through faith. But it might seem to be stated in such a way that it is still a long way off in the future; because although he didn't say "is going to pass from death to life," but *has made the passage from death to life,* still the use of the past tense might seem to be figurative, as with *they have dug my hands and my feet* (Ps 22:16), which was being foretold as still to come in the future. So to avoid this misunderstanding he goes on to explain it more simply: *Amen, amen I tell you,* he says, *that the hour is coming and now is when the dead will hear the voice of the Son of God; and those who hear shall live.* What he said above, *has passed from death to life,* is the same as what he now says, *shall live.* But in case his saying *The hour is coming* should result in this only being hoped for at the end of the world, when the resurrection of bodies also is going to take place, he added *and now is.* Those who hear this voice shall live, with the life, that is to say, which he indicated earlier, saying *has passed from death to life.* So here he indicated those who are not doomed to the penalty of judgment, because they forestall the judgment by their faith, and make the passage from death to life.

Exposition of the passage continued; the future resurrection of the body

26. So it remains for him to show the future judgment between the good and the bad; because so far he has only mentioned the good as profiting from the present resurrection, which is according to the spirit. And so he goes on to say, *And he has given him authority to execute judgment, because he is the Son of man.* He introduced the grounds on which he received authority to judge: *because he is,* he said, *the Son of man.* I mean, insofar as he is the Son of God, he has an everlasting authority together with the Father. Now he goes on to explain how the future judgment is going to take place. *Do not be surprised,* he says, *at this, that the hour is coming in which all the dead who are in the grave will hear his voice and come forth; those who have done good, to the resurrection of life; but those who have done evil, to the resurrection of judgment.* Earlier on, when he said *The hour is coming,* he added, *and now is,* in case we should think he was foretelling the hour in which at the end of the world the resurrection of bodies is going to occur. So here, because that is precisely what he wished us to understand, he didn't add *and now is* when he said *the hour is coming.*

Again, he talked earlier on of the dead hearing the voice of the Son of God, but he made no mention of graves. So we were to distinguish the dead through spiritual error, who rise again now through faith, from those dead whose corpses in their graves are going to rise again at the end of the world. So here, precisely so that we may hope for that resurrection of bodies at the end, *All,* he says, *who are in their graves will hear his voice, and will come forth.* Again, he said above, *will hear the voice of the Son of God; and those who hear shall live.* What need was there to add *those who hear,* when it could have been said like this: "will hear the voice of the Son of God and shall live," unless he was speaking of those who are dead in terms of spiritual error, many of whom hear and don't hear, that is don't comply, don't believe? Those, however, who hear in the way he wished to be heard, when he said *Whoever has ears to hear, let him hear* (Mk 4:9), they are the ones who shall live. So then, many will hear, but *those who hear shall live,* that is, those who believe. Because those who hear in such a way that they don't believe, shall not live. From this it is apparent about which death and about which life he was talking at that point; about the death, namely, which only affects the bad, precisely insofar as they are bad; and about the life which only touches the good insofar as they become good.

Here, though, where he is referring to those who are going to rise again in the body, he doesn't say, "They will hear his voice, and those who hear will come forth." After all, they will all hear the last trumpet, and come forth, because we shall all rise again. But because *we shall not all be changed* (1 Cor 15:51), he goes on to say, *those who have done good, to the resurrection of life; but those who have done evil, to the resurrection of judgment.* And so above, where it's a matter of coming to life again through faith according to the spirit, they all come to life again to the same life of the same sort; their life isn't divided into the two kinds of blessed and wretched, but they all belong on the same good side. And that's why, after saying *those who hear shall live* he didn't add, "those who have done good, for eternal life, but those who have done evil, for eternal punishment." You see, he wished this simple expression *shall live* to be taken in a good sense only, in the same way as he had said earlier on, *has made the passage from death to life*; and he didn't say to what life, because to come to life again from death through faith cannot be to a bad life.

Here, however, for the first time, it isn't "They shall hear his voice, and shall live"—this expression *shall live*, you see, he wishes to be taken throughout this reading in a good sense. But what he said was, *shall hear and come forth*, by which term he indicated the bodily movement of bodies from the places they had been buried in. But because coming forth from their graves won't be to the good for all of them, *those who have done good*, he said, *to the resurrection of life*—even here he wished life to be understood in a good sense only; *but those who have done evil, to the resurrection of judgment*—putting judgment, evidently, for punishment.

Your flesh will rise in the same form as that in which the Lord
appeared, and your life will be the life of the angels

27. So then, brothers and sisters, none of you should now be asking with misguided shrewdness what sort of shape bodies will have in the resurrection of the dead, what sort of movements, what sort of gait. It's enough for you to know that your flesh will rise in the same form as that in which the Lord appeared, in the form, of course, of a human being. But don't, because of this specific form, worry about any tendency to perish; if you're not worried about that, you see, you won't be worried either by that statement, *Flesh and blood shall not gain possession of the kingdom of God* (1 Cor 15:50); nor will you be caught by the snare of the Sadducees, which you couldn't avoid if you imagined that people rise again in order to marry wives, and beget children, and engage in the activities of this mortal life.

If you ask what sort of life it will be, what human being could possibly explain? It will be the life of angels. Anyone who can show you the life of the angels, will show you the life they will have; because they will be equal to the angels.[42] But if the life of the angels is a secret, none should inquire further; else they may go astray and not reach what they are inquiring about, but what they have made up for themselves, because in that case their inquiries are being made hastily, and they are in too much of a hurry. You, though, keep walking on the way; you will get to the home country if you don't leave the way. So hold on to Christ, brothers and sisters, hold on to the faith, hold to the way; it will lead you right through to what you cannot see now. In that head of ours, after all, there has appeared what is to be hoped for in the members; in that foundation there has been demonstrated what is to be built up in our faith, so that it may later on be completed in what we see. Otherwise, when you assume you can see, something may appear to you, by a false imagination, to be real which is not so, and you may leave the way and deviate into error, and not reach the home country to which the way is leading, not attain to the sight, that is, to which faith is leading.

*It is easier to say what there will not be in that life,
than what there will be*

28. You will say, "How do the angels live?" It's enough for you to know this, that they don't live a life subject to decay. You can be told more easily, you see, what there will not be in that life, than what will be there. After all, even I, my brothers and sisters, can briefly run through some of the things with you that will not be found there; and the reason I can do this is that we have experienced these things, and know the things that will not be found there, while what there is to be found there we have not yet experienced. *For we are walking by faith, not yet by sight; as long as we are in the body, we are wandering abroad in exile from the Lord* (2 Cor 5:6-7). So what kind of thing will not be found there? Marrying wives in order to have children; because there will be no death there. There won't be any growing up there, because there won't be any getting old; there won't be taking of nourishment, because there won't be any diminishment; there won't be any business, because there won't be any neediness. There won't even be any of those praiseworthy works of innocent people, which the poverty and the necessities of this life oblige them to engage in. You see, I'm not only saying there won't be any of the activities there of robbers and usurers, but that there won't either be any of the things which innocent people engage in because of the need to relieve human necessities.

It will be a perpetual sabbath, which is celebrated by the Jews in a temporal sense, but is understood by us to be eternal. There will be inexpressible peace and quiet, quite impossible to describe; but as I have said, to describe it at all we are reduced to saying what won't be found there. It is to that peace and quiet that we are wending our way, for that which we are spiritually born again. Just as we are born, you see, in the flesh for toil and hardship, so we are spiritually born again for peace and quiet; as he cries out to us indeed: *Come to me, all you that labor and are overburdened, and I will give you rest* (Mt 11:28). Here he feeds us, there he perfects us; here he makes promises, there he keeps them; here he communicates in code, there he makes it all clear and manifest.

But when in that state of bliss we have been saved and brought to perfection both in spirit and in body, there will be none of these activities; not even any of those which are to be praised here below in the good works of Christians. What Christian, I mean, is not praised for offering bread to the hungry and drink to the thirsty, for clothing the naked, taking in the stranger, calming the quarrelsome, visiting the sick, burying the dead, consoling the grief-stricken? Great works, full of kindness and compassion, full of praise and grace. But not even these will be found there, because the works of mercy are called forth by the needs of misery. Who will you feed, where nobody's hungry? Who will you give a drink to, where nobody's thirsty? Or are you still going to clothe the naked, where all are clothed in immortality? You heard a short while ago about the apparel of the saints, when the apostle said, *It is necessary for this perishable thing to put on imperishability* (1 Cor 15:53). Where he talks about putting on, he indicates a garment. This is the garment that Adam lost, so that he had to be given a coat of skins.[43]

Or are you going to take in the stranger and foreigner, where all are living in their home country? Will you visit the sick, where all enjoy the best of imperishable health? Bury the dead, where they live forever? Reconcile the quarreling, where all is peace? Console the sad, where all are rejoicing forever? So because all miseries will have been brought to a simultaneous end, these works of mercy will also come to an end.

All our activity will consist of Amen and Alleluia

29. So what will be going on there? Haven't I already said that it's easier for me to say what won't be than what will be happening there? This I do know, brothers and sisters, that we are not going to slumber and do nothing, because sleep too is something that has been given to the soul as a support for its defects. Indeed, the frail body will not tolerate unremitting attention activating its mortal senses, unless the senses are dowsed and this frailty is repaired to enable it to endure this very activation. And just as there is going to be a renewal of the body from death in the future, so now waking up is a similar renewal from sleep. So there won't be any sleep there. After all, where there's no death, there won't either be the image of death.

Not, however, that you should allow the fear of boredom to creep up on you, when you are told that you will be awake all the time, and won't be doing anything. I can say—and how indeed it's going to be I cannot say, because I can't even see it yet; still, there's something I can say without impudence, because I'm saying from the scriptures what our activity will consist of there. Our whole activity will consist of Amen and Alleluia. What do you say, brothers and sisters? I can see that you hear and are delighted. But don't let yourselves again be depressed by the flesh-bound thought that if any of you were to stand and say Amen and Alleluia all day long, you would droop with fatigue and boredom; and you will drop off to sleep in the middle of your words, and long to keep quiet; and for that reason you might suppose it is a life you can well do without, not at all desirable, and might say to yourselves, "Amen and Alleluia, we're going to say that forever and ever? Who will be able to endure it?"

So I will tell you if I can, as best I can. It isn't in fleeting sounds that we shall be saying Amen and Alleluia, but with the affection of the mind and heart. After all, what does Amen mean, and what's Alleluia? Amen, "It's true"; Alleluia, "Praise God." So now, God is unchangeable truth, without defect, without advancement, without loss, without gain, without the slightest tendency[44] to falsehood, perpetual and stable, and always remaining imperishable; on the other hand, the things we are involved in here in this created world and this life are no more than the symbols of things signified by material bodies, things in which *we walk by faith* (2 Cor 5:7). But when we see *face to face* what we now see *through a mirror in a riddle* (1 Cor 13:12), we shall then say with quite a different, an inexpressibly different feeling of love, "It's true"; and when we say this, we shall of course be saying Amen, but with a kind of never satisfied satisfaction. Because there will be nothing lacking, you see, that's why complete satisfaction; but because what is not lacking will always be giving delight, that's why, if one can so put it, it will be an unsatisfied satisfaction. So just as you will be insatiably satisfied with the truth, so you will be saying with insatiable truth, Amen.

But now who can possibly say what it is like, *what eye has not seen, nor ear heard, nor has it come up into the heart of man* (1 Cor 2:9)? And so because we shall see the truth without any distaste and with perpetual delight, and gaze upon it with the most evident certainty, we shall be fired with love of this truth and cling to it with a sweet and chaste embrace—a non-bodily one, of course; and so we shall also praise him with the same kind of voice, and say, Alleluia. All the citizens of that city, you see, will be urging[45] each other to equal heights of praise with the most ardent charity toward one another and toward God, and so they will be saying, Alleluia, because they will be saying, Amen.

The banquet of the blessed in the contemplation of the truth

30. This life of the saints, therefore, will also fill their bodies, now changed to a heavenly and angelic state, and so animate and quicken them with immortality, that none of the processes of decay that are necessary here[46] will distract them or turn them away from that utterly blissful contemplation and praise of the truth. Thus the truth itself will be their food; while their resting in it will be like reclining.[47] When it says, you see, that they will recline and feast, as the Lord says, *that many will come from the east and the west, and will recline with Abraham and Isaac and Jacob in the kingdom of my Father* (Mt 8:11); what is signified is that they will feed on the food of truth as they enjoy a wonderful rest. Such food, you see, nourishes, and is not diminished; it fills, and remains entire; you are brought by it to perfection and completion, while it suffers no depletion. Such is that food; not like the food here, which is diminished while it nourishes, and is itself finished in order that those who receive it may not finish their lives. So too, that reclining in the kingdom will be eternal rest; the fare at that banquet will be unchangeable divine truth; that feasting on it will be eternal life, that is the actual knowledge of the truth. Because *this*, he said, *is eternal life, that they may know you, the one true God, and the one you have sent, Jesus Christ* (Jn 17:3).

Be at leisure, and see that I am God

31. That that life will continue forever in the contemplation of the truth, not only inexpressibly but also delightfully, is something that is borne witness to by

many passages of scripture; it is impossible to mention them all. Among them is this one: *Whoever loves me keeps my commandments; and I will love him and will show myself to him* (Jn 14:21). As though he were being asked for the profit and the reward, because his commandments are being kept, *I will show myself,* he says, *to him,* thus placing perfect bliss in his being known as he is. In the same sense we also have this other text: *Beloved, we are children of God, and it has not yet appeared what we shall be. We know that when he appears, we shall be like him, because we shall see him as he is* (1 Jn 3:2). That's why the apostle Paul also says, *Then it will be face to face* (1 Cor 13:12); because he also said somewhere else, *We are being transformed into the same image from glory to glory, as by the Spirit of the Lord* (2 Cor 3:18).

And in the psalms it says, *Be at leisure, and see that I am God* (Ps 46:10). It is then that he will be seen most perfectly, when we are supremely at leisure. But when will we be supremely at leisure, if not when all the times of toil have passed away, all the times of the necessities we are now tied down by, as long as the earth goes on producing thorns and thistles for sinful man, so that he has to eat his bread in the sweat of his brow?[48] So when the times of the earthly man have been transacted in every respect, and the day of the heavenly man perfected in every respect, we shall see in a supreme manner, because we shall be supremely at leisure. When all decay and need, after all, is at an end in the resurrection of the faithful, there will be nothing anymore for which we will have to toil and labor. It says *Be at leisure and see,* in the same way as if it said, "Recline and eat."

So we shall be at leisure and we shall see God as he is; and on seeing God we shall praise him. And this will be the life of the saints, this the activity of those at rest, that we shall praise him without ceasing. We won't just praise him for one day; but just as that day has no end in time, so our praise will have no end at which it stops; and that's why we shall praise him forever and ever. Listen to scripture saying this too to God, saying what we all desire: *Blessed are those who dwell in your house; they will praise you forever and ever* (Ps 84:4).

Turning to the Lord, let us beseech him for ourselves, and for all the people standing with us in the courts of his house; may he be pleased to guard and protect them, through Jesus Christ his Son our Lord, who lives and reigns with him forever and ever. Amen.

NOTES

1. This inordinately, not to say monstrously long sermon was preached a few days, perhaps a week, after Sermon 361 in February, or possibly early March, 411. See Sermon 361, note 1.

2. From the gospel, probably Mt 22:23-33, or possibly the parallel passage, either from Lk 20:27-28, or Mk 12:18-27; or indeed from a Latin translation of Tatian's *Diatessaron*; and from the apostle, 1 Cor 15:35-58.

3. See Mt 3:12.

4. See Jn 14:6. Surely he really ought to say, "makes a way for us," since as he goes on at once to remark, it is Christ the man who is the way.

5. See 2 Cor 2:13.

6. A view very widely prevalent among Christians today.

7. Reading *quia non talia*, instead of the text's *quia non ad talia*, that it won't be for such as now.

8. Baptized in confessing the Apostles' creed, according to the interrogatory formula of baptism then still employed: "Do you believe in God the Father Almighty . . .?" "I do"—and you are dipped a first time; "And in Jesus Christ his only Son our Lord . . . to judge the living and the dead?" "I do"—and you are dipped a second time; "And in the Holy Spirit . . . and life everlasting?"—and you are dipped a third time.

9. *Perfecta sunt*. But he is getting just a little bit muddled, it seems, with his comparison. There he said the building *perfectum stat*, while the scaffolding etc. is no more; now here he says that the equivalent of the scaffolding, which he indeed calls *quaedam machinamenta temporalia*, has been completed—like the building? Well, yes and no; because while they were temporal, temporary events, as he goes on to point out, he cannot bring himself to say—quite rightly so—that they have just been dismantled, or moved off the site, like scaffolding and cranes.

10. That is, Christ in his risen glory is the finished building—in one sense or perspective; but it is a finished building to which the rest of his body, the Church, is constantly being added.

11. No more usually, I suspect, in Latin than in English. But we do talk about the head waters of a river, a kind of equivalent to a building's foundations, that from which a thing starts.

12. He means after Christ's resurrection, but before his ascension. See Lk 24:42-43.

13. See Gn 18:1-9; Tb 12:19.

14. That is certainly what the author of Tobit suggests—but not, apparently, in the version Augustine knew.

15. See Gn 3:21-24.

16. Again, after his resurrection, Lk 24:42-43.

17. See Mt 17:2.

18. Flesh and body, of course, being represented by the pallet, and the man himself representing the soul.

19. The Latin just says, "bearing this," *hoc*, without indicating what "this" refers to. But I think mine is the only feasible interpretation, as will become clear in the next few sentences.

20. See Jn 3:13.

21. Reading *praeposuerat* instead of the text's *proposuerat*.

22. See Rom 6:9.

23. But you will have to wait until sections 19—21 to hear what that is, and how it is expounded.

24. In the Apostles' Creed, the creed professed at baptism.

25. See 1 Cor 4:5.

26. Following a suggestion of the Maurists. The text reads simply *eos*, producing them.

27. Not in this sermon, nor in Sermon 361, preached a few days earlier.

28. He is following the dubious practice of the fourth gospel in employing the term "Jews" to mean the Pharisees; because of course the Sadducees, with whom he is about to contrast these "Jews," were also Jews.

29. See Mt 12:18-27. It is worth noting—something Augustine would easily fail to do—that in verse 28 one of the scribes (that is, one of the "Jews") observed that Jesus had answered well. So presumably at least this man's ideas about the resurrection were not all that fleshly or gross.

30. How much more succinct in the Latin: *ibi enim successor ubi decessor*!

31. He talks of the *animalis corporis*. But by *animalis* he doesn't mean "like an animal." Neither Paul nor Augustine is thinking here of our bodily, generic similarity to other animals; they mean precisely a body that is "ensouled," not yet, as the resurrection body will be, "enspirited."

32. The Latin versions all differ here diametrically from the Greek. What Paul actually wrote was, "We shall not all fall asleep (that is, die), but we shall all be changed."

33. *in atomo.* I have to keep the word "atom," because he will be explaining it at length in the next section. One would normally translate by "instant," an indivisible unit of time, a split second, perhaps—only by definition it cannot be split. When the atom is split, it is thereby shown not in fact to be an atom.

34. Evidently there was as yet no official division of hours into minutes and seconds; a refinement which perhaps only came in with the invention of clocks by medieval monks.

35. Augustine's theory of sight; the eye and sense of sight is not a passive receptor of light, it is an active transmitter of rays which require light as a medium to function in. So he identifies the twinkling of an eye with what we would now call the speed of light, though he thought it was even swifter than we now know it is; he thought it was instantaneous.

36. What the significance of this distinction is, he will suggest at the end of the section.

37. See 1 Pt 3:22, where the Vulgate and all old Latin versions add, after "at the right hand of God," *swallowing down death, so that we may be made heirs of eternal life.*

38. Reading *absumetur* instead of the text's *assumetur*, will be taken.

39. Reading *firmitas* instead of the text's *infirmitas*, that weakness. But he is surely carrying on with his paradox.

40. Last mentioned in section 22 above.

41. Mentioned in 1 Cor 15:52; section 20 above.

42. See Lk 20:36.

43. See Gn 3:21. The garment he lost was the garment of innocence and grace.

44. So the text, *sine alicujus falsitatis inclinatione.* The Maurists, folllowing an earlier scholar, Morel, suggest . . . *falsitatis inquinatione*, without the defilement of any falsehood. I see no need for this emendation.

45. Reading, as the Maurists suggest, *Exhortantes* instead of the text's *Exultantes*, will be exulting. This indeed leaves the sentence hard to construe, with no transitive verb to govern the reflexive pronoun *se.*

46. Shorter, but definitely opaque, in the Latin: *nulla corruptio necessitatis.* He is probably referring to the body's excretory functions.

47. He is referring to the custom of reclining on couches to eat at a banquet.

48. See Gn 3:17-19.

SERMON 363

ON THE CANTICLE OF EXODUS, 15:1-21

Date: 414[1]

We must follow the example of Saint Paul in reflecting
on and interpreting the scriptures

1. Our thoughts, my dearest brothers and sisters, in reflecting on and discussing the holy scriptures must be guided by the indisputable authority of the same scriptures, so that we may deal faithfully both with what is said clearly for the purpose of giving us spiritual nourishment, and what is said obscurely in order to give us spiritual exercise. Who, after all, would dare to expound the divine mysteries[2] otherwise than as has been practiced and prescribed by the mind and mouth of an apostle? Now the apostle Paul says, *I do not wish you to be unaware, brothers, that our fathers were all under the cloud, and all passed through the sea, and were all baptized in Moses, and in the cloud, and in the sea; and they all ate the same spiritual food, and all drank the same spiritual drink. Now they drank from the spiritual rock that was following them; but the rock was Christ. With most of them, though, God was not well pleased. For they were laid low in the desert. But these things have become our models, so that we should not be longing for bad things, as they longed for them.* And a little later, *All these things*, he says, *happened to them by way of a model; but they were written for our correction, upon whom the end of the ages has come* (1 Cor 10:1-6.11).

How the crossing of the Red Sea was a model or type of our baptism

2. And so from this text, dearly beloved, none of the faithful will have the least doubt that the passage of that people through the Red Sea was a model or type of our baptism. Thus under the leadership of our Lord Jesus Christ, who was at that time signified by Moses, we have been delivered through baptism from the devil and his angels, who like Pharaoh and the Egyptians were wearing us down in our subjection to the mud of the flesh as with the work of making bricks. Therefore, *let us sing to the Lord; for he has been gloriously magnified; horse and horseman he has hurled into the sea* (Ex 15:1). As far as we are concerned, you see, they are dead, because they cannot lord it over us anymore;

270

because our very misdeeds, which made us into their subjects, have been, so to say, sunk and obliterated in the sea, when we were set free by the bath of holy grace.

Let us sing, then, to the Lord; for he has been gloriously magnified; horse and horseman he has hurled into the sea; pride and the proud he has obliterated in baptism. Now indeed the humble who are subject to God can sing this song; because for the proud who are seeking their own glory[3] and magnifying themselves, God has not been gloriously magnified. But the ungodly who have been justified by believing in *the one who justifies the ungodly*, so that *their faith may be reckoned as justice* (Rom 4:5), so that *the just may live by faith* (Rom 1:17), lest by *being unaware of God's justice and wishing to establish their own, they should not be subject to the justice of God* (Rom 10:3); these can with the most genuine sincerity sing of the Lord as their helper and protector for salvation, their God whom they honor.[4] They are not, you see, of that conceited number who, *while knowing God, have not honored him as God* (Rom 1:21). And so they say, *God of my father* (Ex 15:2). He is the God, you see, of father Abraham, who *believed God, and it was reckoned to him as justice* (Rom 4:3; Gen 15:6).

And that's why, as little ones, not relying on our own justice but on his grace, we magnify the Lord, since he it is that *crushes wars* (Jdt 16:3), seeing that *he is our peace* (Eph 2:14). And that's why *the Lord is his name* (Ex 15:3), to whom we say with Isaiah, *Take possession of us* (Is 16:13, LXX). *The Lord is his name.* We were not, and he made us; we were lost, and he found us; we had sold ourselves, and he bought us back. *The Lord is his name. Pharaoh's chariots and his army he hurled into the sea* (Ex 15:4). And the worldly pride and arrogance, and the troops of innumerable sins which were fighting for the devil in us, he obliterated in baptism. The devil had placed *teams of three* (Ex 15:4, LXX) in each chariot, who were to terrorize us by haunting us with the fear of pain, the fear of humiliation, the fear of death. All these things were sunk in the Red Sea, because *together with him*, together with the one who for our sakes was scourged, dishonored and slain, *we were buried through baptism into death* (Rom 6:4). Thus he overwhelmed all our enemies in the Red Sea, having consecrated the waters of baptism with the bloody death which was utterly to consume our sins.

But if our enemies *went down into the depths like a stone* (Ex 15:5), the only ones the devil remains in possession of, and the only ones who have the hardness of the devil, are those about whom it is written, *When the sinner has come into the depths of evil, he behaves disdainfully* (Prv 18:3). They don't believe, you see, that they can be forgiven for what they have done; and in that mood of despair they plummet to greater depths than ever. But, *Your right hand, O Lord, was glorified in might; your right hand, Lord, shattered your enemies; and in the greatness of your majesty you crushed your adversaries. Indeed, you sent out your wrath, and it consumed them like stubble* (Ex 15:6-7). We, that is, feared your wrath, and believed in you, and all our sins were consumed. I mean, why was it *by the spirit of the Lord's wrath that the water was divided, and the waters froze like a wall, the waves froze in the midst of the sea* (Ex 15:8), when it was by this division of the water, this freezing of the waves, that a way lay open for the people he had delivered? So why was it not rather by the spirit of the mercy of the Lord that the water was divided? It can only be because dread of the wrath of God, which that sinner disdains who comes into the depths of evil, is precisely what drives us to baptism, so that we may be set free by passing through the water as a way and not be drowned in it.

The enemy said, I will pursue and catch them; I will divide the spoils, and will satisfy my soul; I will slay with the sword, my hand shall prevail (Ex 15:9). And the enemy[5] does not understand the power of the Lord's sacrament, which is available in saving baptism for those who believe and hope in him; and he still thinks that sins can prevail even over the baptized, because they are being tempted by the frailty of the flesh. He doesn't know where, and when, and how the complete renewal of the whole person is to be perfected, which is begun and prefigured in baptism, and is already grasped by the most assured hope. It will be, after all, when *this mortal thing puts on immortality* (1 Cor 15:53), and when, once *every principality and power has been totally set aside, God will be all in all* (1 Cor 15:24.28). For the time being, though, as long as *the perishable body is weighing down the soul* (Wis 9:15), the enemy says, *I will pursue and catch them. But you sent forth your Spirit, and the sea covered them* (Ex 15:9.10).

Now it's not called the spirit of God's wrath, when the sea covered his enemies; and a little earlier on it said, *By the spirit of your wrath the water was divided*, when it was in fact by this means that God's people passed through and were delivered. But of course God does not seem to be angry with those whose sins go unpunished, and who thereby grow heavier than ever. That's why they are compared to lead[6] and sink down to the depths; all the more so, the more they see that those who have been justified by faith, and are tolerating present evils in the hope of the future life, are living in toil and trouble, which the Spirit of God is strengthening them to endure. So God sent forth his Spirit both to comfort and to exercise the just in their difficulties; and the sea covered the ungodly, who were not only thinking that there was no difference between themselves and the others, but in fact reckoning that God was angry with the just, who were being afflicted with such trials, and being favorable to themselves, who were enjoying such prosperity.

Thus *they went down like lead into the mighty water. Who is like you among the gods, O Lord? Who is like you, glorious among the holy ones*, who do not glory in themselves, *marvelous in majesty, performing prodigies?* These things that happened then, you see, were foretelling something that was going to be, since they were models for us.[7] *You stretched out your right hand, the earth devoured them* (Ex 15:10-12). Certainly at that time no yawning chasm of the earth swallowed up any of the Egyptians; they were covered by water, they perished in the sea. So what's the meaning of *You stretched out your right hand, the earth devoured them*? Or are we correct in understanding God's right hand to be the one of whom Isaiah says, *And the arm of the Lord, to whom has it been it revealed?* (Is 53:1)? That, you see, is the only Son, whom the Father did not spare, *but handed him over for us all* (Rom 8:32). And thus he stretched out his right hand on the cross, and the earth devoured the godless, when they thought of themselves as victorious, and of him as despicable in defeat. *The earth*, you see, *was handed over into the hands of the godless, and he covered the face of its judges*[8] (Jb 9:24), that is his divinity. Thus the Lord steered his people, as though they were being carried on that wood, where the earth, that is the flesh of the Lord stretched out on the cross, devoured the godless. I mean, the people weren't even crossing the sea in a ship, where *you steered* would be the appropriate word. But all the same it says, *You steered your people with your justice*, as they were not relying on their own justice, but living by faith under your grace; *this people of yours which you set free* (Ex 15:13). *The Lord*, you see, *knows who are his own* (2 Tm 2:19).

The journey through the desert stands for the journey through life,
after baptism, to our true home country

3. *You encouraged in your strength*, that is, in your Christ, *because the weakness of God is stronger than men* (1 Cor 1:25). Even if he was crucified out of weakness, still *he lives by the power of God* (2 Cor 13:5). *You encouraged in your strength, and in your holy restoration* (Ex 15:13). Insofar, that is, as the mortality of the flesh has been restored in him by his resurrection, and in him *this perishable thing has already put on imperishability* (1 Cor 15:54), we have been encouraged in our hopes for the future, and in our endurance of all these present ills. There remains, you see, after baptism the crossing of the desert, by a life that is lived in hope, until we come to the promised land, to the land of the living where God is our portion,[9] to the eternal Jerusalem; until we get there, the whole of this life is the desert for us, the whole of it a trial and a temptation.[10] But in the one who has overcome the world[11] the people of God has overcome all things. Just as in baptism, after all, our past sins, like enemies pursuing us from the rear, are obliterated, in the same way after baptism, in the journey of this life, when we eat the spiritual food and drink the spiritual drink,[12] we overcome everything that bars our way.

The name of our emperor, in fact, has terrified the enemies barring our way. Previously, you see, the wrath of the nations was roused to destroy the name of Christian; but when their wrath was of no avail, it turned into grief, and more and more, as faith spread and occupied every corner, grief turned into fear, until even the proud ones of this world, like the birds of the sky, would come seeking refuge and protection under the shade of that plant which had grown so much from the tiniest mustard seed.[13] In the same way, in this canticle too, where those things are recorded that happened to them as models, the order is kept of the wrath, the grief and the fear of the nations. *The nations heard*, it says, *and were angry; grief seized hold of the Philistines dwelling there. Then the chiefs of Edom made haste*, that is they were deeply troubled, *and also the princes of the Moabites; trembling gripped them, all the inhabitants of Canaan wasted away. May trembling oppress them, and fear of the greatness of your arm. May they turn to stone until your people passes by, Lord, until this people of yours passes by, which you have won* (Ex 15:14-16).

That's how it happened, that's how it still happens. The enemies of the Church, aghast with amazement, turn to stone until we pass by to our home country. But as for those who have tried to stand in our way, just as Amalek at that time was overcome by the outstretched hands of Moses,[14] so now are these by the sign of the Lord's cross. And thus we are brought in and planted on the mountain of the Lord's inheritance, which has grown from the small stone which Daniel saw[15] and has filled the whole earth. This[16] has been prepared as a dwelling for the Lord. *For the temple of God is holy*, and the sanctification of his house which comes from him.[17] *For the temple of God is holy*, says the apostle, *the temple which you are* (1 Cor 3:17).

And in case anybody's thoughts should turn to the earthly Jerusalem, where that temple bore for a time, as was necessary and fitting, a symbolic significance, Moses made it clear that he was talking of the eternal kingdom, which is the eternal inheritance of God, the eternal Jerusalem. He went on, you see, to say, *Which your hands have prepared, Lord, who reign always, and unto everlasting and still more* (Ex 15:17-18). Is there anything that goes beyond "unto everlasting"? Who could say such a thing? So why did he add *and still more*? Perhaps because we are used to understanding "everlasting" as meaning an excessively long time,[18] and so here *and still more* was added to signify the true "everlasting," which is without end. Or else because God reigns *always* in the heavenly places, which he established forever and ever, *set a commandment and it shall not pass away* (Ps 148:6); and reigns *unto everlasting* in those who after transgressing the commandment have later on been converted and had their sins forgiven; and reigns *still more* over those whom he set as a most just punishemnt under the feet of his people. No one at all, I mean, escapes from his sovereign authority, seeing that all creatures are constrained by his eternal law, which governs most justly the distribution of all gifts and payments, of all rewards and punishments according as they are deserved. *For God withstands the proud, but gives grace to the humble* (1 Pt 5:5).

How we too should join Moses and the sons of Israel, Mary the prophetess and the daughters of Israel, in singing this song

4. *Because the cavalry of Pharaoh with their chariots and charioteers entered the sea; and the Lord brought back on them the waters of the sea. But the children of Israel walked on dry ground through the middle of the sea* (Ex 15:19). This is what Moses sang and the sons of Israel, what Mary the prophetess sang and the daughters of Israel with her; what we too now should sing, whether it means men and women, or means our spirit and our flesh. *Those who belong to Christ Jesus*, you see, as the apostle says, *have crucified their flesh with its passions and desires* (Gal 5:24). This can be suitably understood in the drum which Mary took, to accompany this song; flesh,[19] you see, is stretched over wood to make a drum. So they[20] learn from the cross how to accompany in confession the sweet strains of grace. So then, we have been made humble through baptism by God's loving kindness and grace, and there too has been

quenched our pride, through which the proud enemy used to lord it over us, so that now *whoever boasts should boast in the Lord* (1 Cor 1:31). Therefore, *let us sing to the Lord, for he has been gloriously magnified; horse and horseman he has hurled into the sea* (Ex 15:21).

NOTES

1. Fischer and Kunzelmann propose 412-416, and say the sermon was preached in Hippo Regius. It was possibly preached at Easter time, but hardly at the Easter vigil, when this canticle would have been sung. My guess is that it was a kind of conference given later on to a particular group, not a sermon preached to an ordinary congregation; the most likely group would have been a religious community of monks, or perhaps, in view of the reference to both men and women in the last section, a mixed group of monks and nuns meeting together to have this canticle expounded to them.

2. *Sacramenta.* He clearly means the mystical or allegorical meanings of scripture.

3. See Jn 7:18.

4. See Ex 15:2.

5. Augustine means the devil.

6. See Ex 15:10.

7. See 1 Cor 10:6.

8. Reading *judicum* instead of the text's *judicium*, judgment, which is very difficult to construe; if it means anything, it would make the sentence run, "and his judgment covers the face." But the Septuagint has "of his judges" here; and while Augustine's Latin text may have departed from that, I think it is unlikely in this case, and that we have a simple instance of scribal error. His treatment of his texts here, however, is so utterly bizarre, that one cannot say with any certainty what the reading of any one text is.

9. See Ps 142:5.

10. See Jb 7:1.

11. See Jn 16:33.

12. See 1 Cor 10:3-4.

13. See Mk 4:31-32.

14. See Ex 17:8-13.

15. See Dan 2:34-35.

16. That is, in Augustine's view, though not in the original context of the canticle, the whole earth. He is now commenting on Ex 15:17 without actually quoting it.

17. This last redundant and almost meaningless phrase must, I think, be reproducing his Latin version of the last phrase of Ex 15:17.

18. As when we grumble about the everlasting rain, or drought, or recession.

19. That is, skin. See Ex 15:20.

20. That is, those who belong to Christ Jesus.

SERMON 364

SERMON OF SAINT AUGUSTINE THE BISHOP ON SAMSON[1]

Appeal to the congregation

1. In this reading which has been chanted to us, dearest brothers,[2] there are contained many divine mysteries, and exceedingly obscure ones. It is because they cannot be explained in a short time, and for that reason alone, that I have decided to have the psalms of morning prayer finished earlier, so that you wouldn't be wearied by a longer sermon than usual. And because you are due to leave the church at the customary time, please listen attentively with your customary silence and stillness to what has to be said.

Samson's strength a matter of grace, not nature;
his dubious morals excusable as being prophetic

2. As for Samson, though, dearest brothers, the sort of strength he had came from grace, not nature; because if he had been naturally strong, he would not have been deprived of his strength when his hair was cut off.[3] And where did the secret of that tremendous strength lie, if not in the fact that *the Spirit of the Lord was accompanying him* (Jgs 13:25)? So that strength belonged to the Spirit of the Lord. In Samson we have a vessel, in the Spirit we have what fills it. A vessel can be filled and emptied; and every vessel gets its contents from elsewhere. That's why it was grace that was being emphasized in the case of Paul, when he was called *a chosen vessel* (Acts 9:15).

So let us see what kind of riddle Samson put to the Foreigners.[4] *From the eater*, he said, *there issued food, and from the strong there came forth sweetness* (Jgs 14:14). The riddle was betrayed, reported to the friends, solved; Samson was beaten. Whether he is a just man is wholly uncertain; the justice of this man is profoundly obscure. What was read, I mean, both that he was overcome by a woman's coaxing and that he went in to a harlot, all seems, to those who have a limited understanding of the hidden ways of the truth, to call his merits in question. Well, a prophet too was ordered by the Lord's command to take a harlot to wife.[5] Perhaps we will be able to say that these things were not criminal or reprehensible in the Old Testament, seeing that what he either said or did was all prophetic.

So let us inquire what it meant that he was beaten, what it meant that he won, what it meant that he gave in to a woman's blandishments, what it meant that

276

he told her the secret of the riddle, what it meant that he went in to a harlot, what it meant that he caught some foxes and set fire to his enemies' crops by means of the foxes' tails, to which he tied firebrands. He could, of course, have set fire to the crops by a much simpler method, if he hadn't been thinking of some hidden meaning in the foxes. Wouldn't fields of dry stalks burn, unless fire was dragged through them by foxes? So we should realize that great things are lurking here beneath the surface.

Samson represented Christ in his fullness

3. What was Samson, then? If I say, "He was representing Christ," it seems to me I am saying something true. But straightaway people thinking it over begin to wonder, "And is Christ overcome by a woman's blandishments? And how can Christ be understood to have gone in to a harlot? Then again, when does Christ have his head shaved, his locks of hair shorn, when is he stripped of his strength, bound, blinded, made sport of?" Wake up, faith, notice what Christ is, not only what he did, but also what he suffered. What did he do? He performed the feats of a strong man, he suffered as a weak man. In his one person I can perceive each thing; I can see the strength of the Son of God, I can see the weakness of the Son of man. There's yet another point, because the whole Christ, as scripture presents him to us, is both head and body; just as Christ is the head of the Church, so the Church is the body of Christ.[6] And it isn't such indeed by itself; it's together with its head that it constitutes the whole Christ. So the Church has within it strong members, it has weak ones; it has those who are being fed on solid bread, it has those who still need to be reared on milk.[7] I will add something else, which has to be admitted; in the very companionship of the sacraments, in the fellowship of baptism, in the sharing at the altar, the Church has just members, has unjust ones. Now, after all, the body of Christ which you know about is the threshing floor; later on it will be the granary.[8] Still, as long as it is the threshing floor, it does not refuse to put up with straw; when the time comes for storing, it will separate the wheat from the straw.[9]

So Samson did some things in the role of the head, some in the role of the body, everything, however, in the role of Christ. Insofar, you see, as Samson performed feats of strength and wonders, he represented Christ the head of the Church; while insofar as he acted wisely, he bore the likeness of those in the Church who live just lives; where he happened to be taken unawares, and to have acted foolishly, he represented those who are sinners in the Church. The harlot whom Samson took to wife[10] is the Church, who before she came to acknowledge the one God committed fornication with idols, whom later on Christ joined to himself. After she was enlightened, though, and received the faith from him, she also won the right to know through him the sacraments of salvation, and to have revealed to her by him the hidden things of heavenly mysteries.

That very riddle, after all, which runs, *From the eater there issued food, and from the strong there came forth sweetness* (Jgs 14:14), what else does it signify but Christ rising from the dead? From the eater, of course, that is from death which devours and consumes all things, there issued that food which said, *I am the living bread, who have come down from heaven* (Jn 6:41). The one whom human iniquity had made sour, and to whom it had given the bitterness of vinegar and gall to drink, is the one from whom the people of the Gentiles, on being converted, received the sweetness of life; and thus from the mouth of the dead lion, that is from the death of Christ who *lay down and slept like a lion* (Gn 49:9), there came forth a swarm of bees, that is of Christians. As for what he says, *You would not have found out my riddle unless you had plowed with my heifer* (Jgs 14:18), the heifer is also this Church which had revealed to her by her husband the secrets of the faith, the mysteries of the Trinity, of the resurrection, of the judgment too and the kingdom, and published them as far as the ends of the earth through the teaching and preaching of the apostles and the saints, and promised to all who understood and acknowledged them the rewards of eternal life.

Samson's companion stands for the heretics

4. It continues, *Samson was angry, because his companion had married his wife* (Jgs 14:19-20). This companion stands for all heretics. This is a key notion, my brothers. You see, the heretics, who have divided the Church, have wished to elope with and marry the Lord's wife. I mean, they went out from the Church[11] and away from the gospels, having attempted by a kind of impious adultery to snatch the Church, that is the body of Christ, into their own party. That's why that faithful servant and friend of the Lord's bride speaks to her and says, *For I have betrothed you to one man, to present you as a chaste virgin to Christ;* and with the zeal of his faith and a stinging rebuke he touches on the person of the corrupt companion of Christ; *and I am afraid,* he says, *lest as the serpent seduced Eve, so too your good sense may be corrupted from the truth which is in Christ Jesus* (2 Cor 11:2-3). Who, though, are the companions, that is the heretical deserters, who have wished to snatch the bride of the Lord, if not Donatus, Arius, Mani, and other vessels of error and ruin? It's about such that the apostle says, *I hear that among you,* he declares, *there are divisions. For one says, I indeed am Paul's man; another, though, I am Apollo's; while another says, I am Cephas' man* (1 Cor 1:11-12).

Accordingly, let us see what this mystical Samson[12] did, when he was offended by a foreigner over his wife. You see, he caught foxes, that is the adulterous companions, of whom it says in the Song of Songs, *Catch for us the little foxes that are spoiling the vineyards* (Sg 2:15). What does "catch" mean? That's come to grips with them, convince, refute them, so that the vineyards of the Church may not be spoiled. What else is catching foxes, but overcoming heretics with the authority of the divine law, and so to say binding and tying them up with the cords provided by the testimonies of the holy scriptures? He catches foxes, ties their tails together and attaches firebrands. What's the meaning of the foxes' tails tied together? What can the foxes' tails be, but the backsides of the heretics, whose fronts are smooth and deceptive, their backsides bound, that is condemned, and dragging fire behind them, to consume the crops and works of those who yield to their seductions?

One says now to people, "Don't listen to the heretics, don't agree with the heretics, don't be led astray by the heretics." They answer, "Why not? Didn't So-and-so and Such-and-such listen to heretics? And didn't some other Christian commit so many evils, so many adulteries, go in for so many extortions? And did anything bad happen to him?"

That's the front of the foxes, which those seduced by them observe; and at their back end there's fire. "Nothing has happened to him now," he says. Just because he's going on his way, does it mean he's dragging nothing behind him? He's going to come to the fire at the back end. Do you suppose, though, that because the heretics are dragging fire behind them, to burn up the crops of the enemies, they won't also be burnt up themselves? Without a doubt, after all, when the foxes set fire to the harvest, they were of course burnt up themselves. So judgment is going to come upon the heretics from behind; they have behind them what they don't see now. They wheedle and flatter, they put on a front of being free; in God's judgment their tails have been tied together, that is, they are drawing fire behind them, because their impudence goes ahead of their punishment.

The deeds of Samson and Christ compared

5. That he went in, though, to a harlot, if he did it without a reason, whoever it is that has done it, he's impure. But if he did it as a prophet, it's a sacred sign. If he did not go in to lie with her, he went in, perhaps, by reason of some mystery. But we don't read that he lay with her. It continues, *But his enemies were waiting for him at the gates of the city, in order to seize him when he had come away from the harlot to whom he had gone in; he, though, was sleeping.* Observe how it is not written that he had intercourse with the harlot, but it's written that he was sleeping. *When he rose,* it says, *he went out in the middle of the night, and took away the gates of the city itself, with their bars, and carried these same gates to the top of a mountain* (Jgs 16:2-3), and the Foreigners were unable to seize him.

He took away the gates of the city, through which he had gone in to the harlot, and carried them up a mountain. What does this mean? Hell and the love of a woman, scripture joins the two together;[13] the harlot's house was a representation of hell. It is rightly put for hell, because it turns nobody away, draws to itself everyone who enters. In this place we can recognize the works of our redeemer; after the synagogue, to which he had come, was separated from him by the devil, after it had shaved his head,[14] that is had crucified him in the place called Calvary, or baldness, he descended into hell; and the enemies were guarding the place where he was sleeping, that is the tomb. and they wanted to seize one they had not been able to see. *He though was sleeping.* The reason it said this there, is that it wasn't a true death.[15] Its saying *he rose in the middle of the night,* signified that he rose secretly. He suffered openly, you see, but when he had risen he only showed himself to his disciples and a select few.[16] So then, that he went in, they all saw; that he rose again only a few knew about, held him and fondled him.[17] All the same, he removes the gates of the city, that is, he takes away the gates of hell. What's taking away the gates of hell, if not depriving death of its dominion? It used to receive the dead, you see, and never release them. But what did the Lord Jesus Christ do after taking away the gates of death? He went up to the top of a mountain; we know, after all, that he both rose again and ascended into heaven.

The mystery of Samson revealed and fulfilled by Christ

6. What, though, is the meaning of his strength lying in his hair? Pay close attention to this too, brothers; he didn't have his strength in his hand, nor in his foot, nor in his breast, nor even in his head, but in his hair, in his locks. What is hair, what are locks? We can see for ourselves, and if we ask the apostle he will answer us: *Hair is a veil* (1 Cor 11:1); and Christ had his strength in a veil, when the shadows of the old law were covering him. So Samson's hair was a veil; because in Christ one thing was seen, and another perceived by the mind.[18] What's the meaning, though, of Samson's secret being betrayed, and his head being shaved? The law was ignored, and Christ suffered; they wouldn't, after all, have slain Christ, if they hadn't ignored the law; I mean, they themselves knew very well that it was not lawful for them to kill Christ. They said to the judge, *It is not lawful for us to kill anyone* (Jn 18:31). Samson's head was shaved, the thickets were laid bare,[19] the veil was removed, and Christ, who had been hidden, appeared openly.

But the hair grew again and once more clothed the head, because the Jews were unwilling to acknowledge Christ even when he rose again. He was in fact in the treadmill, he was blinded, he was in the prison house; the prison house, or the treadmill, is the toil and trouble of this world. The blinding of Samson, however, points to those who have been blinded by unbelief, and so have not known Christ either performing miracles or ascending into the heavenly sphere. So the blindness which they inflicted on him, signified the blindness of the Jews. Christ was both arrested and killed by the Jews; but he, rather, slew those who killed him. *So his enemies brought him in to make fun of him* (Jgs 16:25). Here now you should observe the image of the cross; he stretched out his hands, you see, to the two columns as to the two beams of the cross; but while being destroyed himself, he overwhelmed his adversaries, and his own death meant the slaughter of his persecutors. And that's why scripture concludes like this: *He killed more when he was dead than he had killed when he was alive* (Jgs 16:30). This mystery was very clearly fulfilled by our Lord Jesus Christ; because our redemption was accomplished by him in his death in a way that it had certainly not been celebrated by the life of him who lives and reigns forever and ever.[20] Amen.

NOTES

1. This is the first of thirty-three sermons classified by the Maurists as dubious—some more so than others. They in fact regard this one as probably authentic; I myself would say, possibly authentic in parts, like the curate's egg. In fact, though, it is a sermon of our old friend Caesarius of Arles, making some use of one by Augustine. Possidius mentions "a discourse on Samson and a verse of Ps 57(58)" in his Index to Augustine's works. Bits of it, no doubt, are to be found in what is really a singularly bad sermon.

2. Not "and sisters" here, because it rather looks, from the reference to the psalms of the morning office in the next sentence, that the speaker was addressing a monastic, or at least a clerical community. He was almost certainly not Augustine, but Caesarius. This first section is absent from all the manuscripts available to the Maurists, though they knew of it from earlier printed editions. The psalms of the morning office would have been got through more quickly than usual, one presumes, by being simply monotoned instead of being sung to more elaborate chants with antiphons. It all smacks of a later and quite different ecclesiastical setting from that of Hippo Regius in Augustine's time.

3. See Jg 16:19.

4. The *Allophili*. This is the word, *allophylos* in the Greek, with which the Septuagint regularly translates "Philistines." They, I suppose, were the foreigners, the Gentiles, *par excellence*, and there was also a certain similarity in sound. The background for this whole sermon is really Jgs 14-16. Indeed, it must have been a very long reading.

5. See Hos 1 and 2.

6. See Eph 4:15; Col 1:18.

7. See 1 Cor 3:2.

8. So the latest edition (presumably among the works of Caesarius) in the CCL. The Maurists have "is on the threshing floor . . . will be in the granary"; a fairly evident scribal "correction."

9. See Lk 3:17.

10. The preacher, possibly Augustine in this section, is confusing Samson with Hosea. The Philistine woman Samson married was not a harlot, but later on he did visit a harlot.

11. See 1 Jn 2:19.

12. Mystical, because he represented the mystery of Christ.

13. See Prv 9:11-18.

14. Correcting the text's *decalcavit*, which either means had whitewashed him or had trampled on him, to *decalvavit*, literally had made him bald. With the reference to Calvary following immediately, this must be what the preacher said. He is referring, of course, to Delilah having Samson's locks shaved off, Jgs 16:19, and is conflating this episode with Samson's visit to the harlot of Gaza, 16:1-3. I am pretty certain we have Caesarius here, not Augustine. I do not recall Augustine ever referring to the Jews simply as "the synagogue," though the contrast between Church and Synagogue soon became a commonplace of patristic and medieval polemics.

15. Augustine could not possibly have said this! What, perhaps, the preacher meant was that Christ's descent into hell was not a definitive and final entry into the realm of the dead. The text followed by the Maurists, fairly evidently corrected by a rightly scandalized scribe, runs, "He though was sleeping there. The reason I said this is that it was a true death."

16. See Acts 10:41.

17. See Mt 28:9.

18. He means, I take it, Christ's humanity and divinity respectively.

19. See Ps 29:9.

20. And our redemption means our old selves being killed. One presumes that is what the preacher meant.

SERMON 365

ON PSALM 16:7, *I WILL BLESS THE LORD, WHO GRANTS ME UNDERSTANDING*[1]

God to be praised from the heart, as well as with the mouth

1. We have been singing, and saying, *I will bless the Lord* (Ps 16:7); I hope from the heart, and not only with the mouth. Because if it's with the mouth and not from the heart, *the praise of the Lord is ugly in the mouth of a sinner* (Sir 15:9); nor does the outward confession of praise avail one in the mouth, if there is no inner profession of charity in the heart. Consider, brothers and sisters: charity is not a virtue of the mouth; where it fixes its abode is where the beauty of the bridegroom's darling is to be found. And where is this beauty to be found? *All the glory of the king's daughter is within* (Ps 45:13). That glory is nothing else but beauty, that beauty is nothing else but charity, charity is nothing else but life. So then, in order to be alive, love; if you love, you are beautiful. Love is a good thing, love is a beautiful thing; if that beautiful thing is lacking, you are not alive. You have indeed the appearance of being so, but not the reality within. Just let that tomb supported on its many pillars be opened up, let that marble slab be smashed, and what else will confront us but a grisly corpse, stinking bones, ashes, worms? And so yes, there is a fine appearance, but it conceals a dead man, the sight of whom fills you with such horror that you scream.

Do you imagine, though, that a dead man can say, *I will bless the Lord?* On the contrary, as scripture testifies, *The dead will not praise you, Lord, nor any of those who go down to the netherworld* (Ps 115:17). Open the gospel, you will hear the Lord rebuking the devil, and saying to him, *Hold your tongue* (Mk 1:25). Why? Because *the dead will not praise you, Lord, nor any of those who go down to the netherworld*. Nobody praises someone they don't love; or if an enemy does praise him, he loves the virtue which he is praising in his enemy. Anyone who sins is waging war on God, and so can neither praise God nor praise God's virtue,[2] because praise is something good, which doesn't go with sin. Anyone who praises somebody insincerely is really disparaging him, or making fun of him rather than praising him. Take away charity from the heart, all that's left is a lie. Would you like a lie to praise the truth, and God to receive tributes from the very source that blasphemes him? Wise men don't value being praised by the insane and the wicked; shall God be praised by an impure and utterly impudent heart, and by a blasphemous and utterly mindless mind?

So then, say, *I will bless the Lord, who grants me understanding* (Ps 16:7).

You are not insane, your sanity has been restored, you have some understanding. Praise your God who grants you understanding, who endows you with an eye; understanding to grasp things, an eye to observe them; to grasp what is *the breadth and length* (Eph 3:18) of God's love, to observe *the author and finisher of faith* (Heb 12:2); to grasp charity, to observe Christ—charity in order to love him, Christ in order to bless him, and in loving and blessing him to know him as the Lord who grants you understanding; and in knowing him to live, because *This is eternal life, that they may know you the only God, and Jesus Christ whom you have sent* (Jn 17:3).

Such understanding a gift of grace, not a natural endowment

2. But where, I ask you, do you get this understanding from? Here comes someone putting a shot across our bows, and saying, "The one who gave us our nature gave us understanding. Our nature is good, our understanding good. Let me acquire this good, that's enough for me. It won't, after all, be a debased understanding; and I will bless the Lord from the source he has granted me understanding from, that is to say, from nature."

So, Mr. Heretic, you've acquired a nature that is good, have you? The apostle had better shut up and feel ashamed of himself. *It is not the good I wish to*, he says, *that I do* (Rom 7:19). And yet he has acquired a nature that is good, and in this nature that is good he cannot do the good he wishes to. He wishes, he longs, he strives; wishes weakly, longs pointlessly, strives in vain; and against what he wishes, what he longs and strives for, he doesn't achieve this good. Indeed, how good is this nature, whose will is so feeble, whose longings so ineffective, whose strivings so futile!

Let the philosophers play their part, and show themselves most grateful to you for quite gratuitously conferring upon them a nature that is good. What follows? They know all about the heavens, they know all about the earth, they know all about the sea, they pry into the deeps, they investigate the mysteries of nature, they know the distinctive features, the differences, the essences of things; about all these things they give a rational account. What next? Carry on, say some more. After so many and such great achievements they fall away, and they have not glorified him as God, and have become futile in their thoughts, and have grown foolish, all the while thinking themselves to be wise, and *have changed the likeness of God into the likeness of a calf that eats grass* (Ps 106:20), and have spent themselves in the error of the Baalim, and *the god of this world has blinded them* (2 Cor 4:4), and they have been handed over to shameful passions, and have become like the things they worshiped.[3] And yet they enjoyed a nature, and through nature an understanding, that were both good! You crazy fool, can you see this nature granting them an understanding with which to bless God, and not rather granting them an understanding with which to curse God and rise up against their creator?

You, on the other hand, brothers and sisters, say rather, "*I will bless the Lord who has granted me understanding* (Ps 16:7); unless he had granted it, I would not have understood; unless I had understood, I would not have blessed him. He has granted me understanding, he has given me an eye." Nature is blind; it doesn't bestow what it lacks itself. Make your own understanding, and you will make your own blindness; *the light that is in you is darkness* (Mt 6:23). Say, therefore, *Enlighten my darkness, lest I fall asleep in death* (Ps 13:3). What does falling asleep in death mean? Hoping for something from nature, *making flesh your arm* (Jer 17:5), fashioning an understanding for yourself. If you do this you are not only in death, but you are falling asleep in death, you are more than four days dead, more than stinking.[4] If you were only in death, you could be brought back to life. But in this very death you are sleeping a more than iron sleep; you are taking your ease in it; it's all over with you.

"I knew that I could not otherwise be self-controlled, unless God were to give it"

3. But do you wish to know what action a man took who really did acquire a nature that is good? Did he say, like you, "In virtue of a nature that is good I have a good understanding, and the one who granted the first hasn't denied me the second"? Let us stamp on the scorpion, crush it, let the mouth of iniquity be stopped up.[5] Read: *I have acquired a good soul.* Carry on, let us hear what sort of treasure you have gotten, which may perhaps turn into coals—and if only into coals which heaped upon your head may burn up your superfluities![6] *And since I was exceptionally good, I entered into an undefiled body; and as I knew that I could not otherwise be self-controlled, unless God were to give it—and this was itself a matter of wisdom, to know whose gift it was—I approached the Lord and prayed* (Wis 8:20-21). That you have really and truly acquired a nature that is good, who would deny? I mean, even the devil's nature is good, and everything that God has made is good; but in virtue of this nature that is good will you, do you think, have a wise understanding, by which you can abstain from the lusts and *desires which war against the soul* (1 Pt 2:11), if God does not give it to you? Learn, Mr. Heretic, learn at last: *And I knew that I could not otherwise be self-controlled unless God were to give it.* And this is the chief part of wisdom, which is entirely a matter of understanding, to know by what means you can control yourself, and that you cannot otherwise control yourself than with God's help alone. Oh, outstanding nature, which cannot abstain from anything, and cannot do otherwise than collapse, if God does not give the understanding by which not to collapse!

So then, let us sing, brothers and sisters, let us sing, *I will bless the Lord, who has granted me understanding* (Ps 16:7). He has given us our nature, given us understanding; he has healed nature, healed understanding. In each case the kindly Samaritan has shown compassion; he has come down, has bandaged the wounds, sponged them with the wine which we know about,[7] taken care of the sufferer, brought him along to the inn which is the Church, entrusted him to the inn-keeper.[8] To which inn-keeper? To the Holy Spirit, who lives in the holy Church. He accepted the money, money which the one who pays for the wretched of the earth had poured out from the purse that was ripped open,[9] and healed with his oil, his anointing,[10] the wounds of nature lying there at its last gasp; and with the same oil, which he lit, he enlightened my darkness, and made my understanding lucid. If you do not believe this, he will not be a Samaritan for you, and you will die of your wounds, having rebuffed the hand of the healer.

Understanding is a gift of the Holy Spirit, which Christ bought for us by his passion

4. Let the apostles be questioned, and let them tell us who it was that on that fiftieth day from the Lord's resurrection granted them understanding. Or maybe it was they themselves who raised that terrifying racket, by which the place was shaken in which they were awaiting the promise of the Father?[11] Maybe it was they who kindled that fire from above which had them all burning brightly? Maybe they themselves created those fiery tongues? It was they, perhaps, who procured for themselves those divine gifts, of which understanding is one, and poured them out upon themselves to their heart's content? Any who say this have no part in this sacred number fifty;[12] nor do any receive understanding who imagine that understanding is given according to nature.

So when was understanding given, if not when the Spirit was also given? Let us deal with this together; you are already disconcerted, already losing countenance; and if only you may be so disconcerted as to be built up in the truth, so put out of countenance as to receive honor and glory! What, then, is the Holy Spirit but the promised endowment of the Father, but the gift of the Son? If he is promised, you have someone he is promised by, because things that are promised are outside our control; and a thing would be promised in vain which was either under our control when it was promised, or which could be taken possession of when we liked. What I promise you is what you do not have, and it is with me when I promise it, so that what I promise may come down to you. The Holy Spirit is also a gift, and one surpassing every gift, and a gift which is owed to nobody, and a gift that is granted gratis, for nothing.

Christ was born, and laid in a manger to become the food of pious beasts of burden.[13] Yet he suffered thirst and weariness, he was sold by his own friends, handed over and accused by the Jews, scourged by the Gentiles, crowned with thorns, crucified, finally shut in by a stone; to what end all this? To buy you a gift, which he would later on present you with when you believed—or rather, would present you with so that you might believe; because if he had not given it first, you would never have believed, either before or after.[14] It follows that if you have this gift from nature, you are rendering vain and meaningless the death of Christ, his passion, his cross. He dies to no purpose, to obtain for you what you already have with you, to bestow on you what you already possess. Give back to the Lord the lowliness of the manger, give him back the curse of the cross, give back the generous shedding of his blood; it is all fruitless. You are entirely self-sufficient, all this is pointless. You are rich, and among the goods of your rich nature you count understanding, which nature gave you, not grace, and which you do not owe to the creator, except insofar as he bestowed on you the nature which has provided you with understanding.

5. You realize, I imagine, the mistake. And if only your loins would correct you![15] Then you might realize it better, and by realizing seek, and by seeking obtain the spirit of understanding and counsel and fear,[16] which would ensure your ending up wiser, ensure your becoming more careful, and more submissive to the Lord. Even if I, brothers and sisters, were not dealing with these matters, there would still be something else to instruct you; and you would deal with them within yourselves. If, you see—which God forbid—you had slipped into such a gross and stupid error, as to imagine that it was nature that had endowed you with the understanding which you have gotten solely from the grace and mercy of God, your loins would correct you and cry out, *Why are such thoughts coming up into your hearts* (Lk 24:38)? Question yourselves, each one of you, take your pulses, examine yourselves, and don't go looking outside yourselves; interrogate your loins, and they will tell you, "There has been *a law in my members opposed to the law of my mind* (Rom 7:23); I am prone to every kind of misconduct, the waves of lust so overwhelm me that I am sunk every day, and collapse into the depths of sin. Envy rears its head, pride rears its head, lechery rears its head, they close ranks to attack wretched me. If I steer away from Charybdis, I run upon Scylla.[17] If I repel lust, I succumb to anger; if avarice doesn't subdue me, drunkenness lashes me; if I abstain from robbery, I close my hands and my heart to the poor; if I close my ears to malicious gossip, death comes in through the windows—that is to say, through my eyes I drink in incitements to lust and self-indulgence. In a word, if I caulk one seam, a hundred others open up, through which I take on board the hostile storm, and finally founder."

These are the points your loins insist upon with you, and being conscious of their own infirmity they instruct you, rebuke you, correct you, and *right into the night* (Ps 16:7). What sort of night? That of your fog-bound conscience, whose darkness you like to wrap yourself in and hold in front of you like a shield against the light of truth, placing all your hopes in your own strength. But let your loins correct you. It says somewhere in scripture, *In the loins and haunches there is power* (Jb 40:16).[18] But seeing that your haunches are so lacking in staunchness,[19] and your loins are so flabby, they are instructing you and saying, "If there is so much weakness, such feebleness in the loins which are the seat of strength, what will be the case with the rest?" So when our loins instruct us, and teach us how *vain is the help of men* (Ps 108:12), what remains for us to do but to gird up our loins, so that they don't falter and flag?

When our floorboards at home start gaping, either because they are so old, or because of the excessive heat, or as the result of the weather, or from any other cause at all, we immediately fasten them together with nails and cords. This is what should be done with your loins, that is your strength; they are getting loose, they are in disarray, they are cracking up, the whole structure is falling apart. You have nails in the Crucified; hammer them in hard, and all the better the deeper they go. But don't apply them to a tottering edifice; this will only shore up a structure that has fallen into ruin. The nails of the cross have the power to raise up the fallen, to revive the feeble, to hold up those who are slipping. Drive them in, hammer them into the marrow of your bones, into your very soul. By such correction you will be healed, and once healed you will say to the Lord, *For you I will guard my strength* (Ps 59:9); my strength comes from you, my strength is for you.

Turning to the Lord, etc.

NOTES

1. The Maurists, whose text is followed here, are extremely doubtful of this sermon's authenticity. They could not lay their hands on any manuscripts of it—and evidently none has been found since, or at least none has been edited. So they get their text from one earlier printed edition. They consider the style to be very different from Augustine's. It is a very self-conscious, mannered style. While Augustine in his early years could also be very self-consciously mannered, he was characteristically more expansive, more exuberant than the preacher of this sermon. In any case the sermon is aimed at the Pelagians, who only confronted Augustine after 411, long after he had stopped bothering about carefully polished rhetoric. So in my humble opinion the doubts of the Maurists can safely be transformed into a certainty that this sermon is not authentic. No date can therefore be meaningfully assigned to it—no date, that is, within Augustine's lifetime.

2. So the little qualification our preacher has made does not apply; why then did he make it?

3. See Rom 1:21-28; Ps 115:8.

4. See Jn 11:39.

5. See Ps 63:11.

6. See Prv 25:22; Rom 12:20. The preacher's little elaboration of this text develops, and not very successfully, an Augustinian conceit about one's hair representing one's superfluities; that is to say, for him, one's wealth over and above what supplies one's basic needs.

7. A reference to the eucharist.

8. See Lk 10:33-35.

9. See Jn 19:34.

10. See 1 Jn 2:20.

11. See Acts 1:4. The Pentecostal event of Acts 2:1-4 did not include a shaking of the place; this has been imported from Acts 4:31.

12. Representing both the unity of the Church and the life of the world to come, according to the Augustinian symbolism of the number fifty. See Sermons 276, 6; 252, 8-10.

13. Meaning devout Christians, represented by the ox and the donkey.

14. After what? This last phrase seems wholly redundant, not to say meaningless.

15. See Ps 16:7.

16. See Is 11:2.

17. Charybdis is a whirlpool, Scylla a reef opposite this on the other side of the straits of Messina, between Sicily and the Italian mainland; both personified in Greek legend into two voracious female monsters.

18. But in the context of Job it is not a general remark; it is part of the description of Behemoth, who is usually identified with the hippopotamus.

19. The Latin talks of your *lumbi* being so *elumbes*.

SERMON 366

ON PSALM 23, *THE LORD IS MY GUIDE, AND I SHALL LACK NOTHING*

Date: uncertain[1]

*The sermon is addressed particularly to those
who are shortly to be baptized*

1. To you, dearly beloved, who are hastening toward the baptism of Christ,
we are handing over this psalm in the name of the Lord, to be learned by heart;
so we must explain its inner meaning, with divine grace to enlighten us. It's a
psalm, you see, which in a special way contains the remedy for the fall of the
human race, and simultaneously the discipline and the sacraments of holy
Church. Let the ears of your hearts, therefore, be open in silence to listen, so
that the seed of the word may find the furrows of your total attention prepared
for it, and that what the thirsty ground now receives it may, on being made drunk
in due course on the blood of Christ,[2] turn into tall standing stalks and a plentiful
crop of wheat.

*An affirmation of confidence in God's protection
and of the infinite wealth he bestows on us*

2. *The Lord is my guide, and I shall lack nothing* (Ps 23:1). A great way, my
dearest friends, to begin singing God's praises. He has affirmed and fortified,
you see, his confidence in God's protection, he has strongly asserted the infinite
extent of his riches. *The Lord is my guide*, that has fortified his confidence in
God's protection; *and I shall lack nothing*, that has asserted the infinite extent
of his riches. But let us inquire who is doing the praising, how important and
what sort of person it is. It's that man, dearly beloved, yes it's that man who was
going down from Jerusalem to Jericho and fell among thieves.[3] Stripped of the
dignity of his original creation, and laid low by the poisoned dart of death, man
was lying on the ground powerless and naked. When the trumpet of the law and
the prophets peals forth, he attempts to get up by his own power; but pulled back
by the pain of his wounds, he falls back more heavily than ever into the dire
state he was lying in. Because *the law*, as the apostle says, *never brought
anything to perfection* (Heb 7:19).

288

That Samaritan of ours, namely Christ, whom the Jews called a Samaritan,[4] which means Guardian,[5] took pity on him when he was passing the same way, that is when he had come in the flesh as the Just One[6] to die for us sinners. He lifted him up from the ground, and placed him on his own mount; and carrying him like a straying sheep on his own shoulders into paradise, from which he had fallen, he called him back into the hundred, that is into the perfect number.[7] *For he it is*, as the prophet says, *that has borne our sins and has grieved for us* (Is 53:4). Now say, Man, seated on the mount of the Lord's mercy, on the shoulders of the Lord's love, say as, being known yourself, you recognize[8] your creator and Lord, say, *The Lord is my guide*. Which of course you couldn't say, lying there, unless you had been picked up by the Lord. So it's the one who is carrying you that is your guide. After all, when you say, *The Lord is my guide*, no proper grounds are left for you to trust in yourself.

And so you must beware of ever becoming conceited about your own merits. You didn't have any, after all, when the Lord came to pick you up. In fact he found you naked, without any clothes; he found you beaten up, not in good health; he found you lying on the ground, not standing on your own feet; he discovered you straying, not returning on your own. Beware of boastfulness, beware of it; because the one who took pity on you and raised you from the ground when you were half dead, carries you if you are humble, throws you off if you start thinking too much of yourself. You see, when you say in a spirit of fear, as you walk in innocence, *the Lord is my guide*, you will confidently be able to add, *and I will lack nothing*; since *nothing is lacking for those who fear him* (Ps 34:9), and *the Lord will not deprive of good things those who walk in innocence* (Ps 84:11).

On the pastures of Christians and the shepherd who feeds them there

3. I mean, to convince yourself that you will lack nothing, add what comes next: *In a place of pasture, there he has settled me; he has reared me on the water of refreshment* (Ps 23:2). Acknowledge, Man, what you have been, where you have been, under whom you have been. You were a straying sheep, in a trackless and waterless desert, feeding on thorns and thistles. Placed under a hireling, you had no security when the wolf came. Now, however, the true shepherd has come looking for you, you have been lovingly hoisted onto his shoulders and brought back to the sheepfold, that is to the house of God, which is the Church, where Christ is your shepherd, and the sheep stay together in one flock. This shepherd is not like the hireling, under whom you had a wretched and difficult time, under whom you were in constant fear of the wolf.[9] But do you want to know how deeply this shepherd cares for you? He laid down his life for you. He says himself in the gospel, after all, *The good shepherd lays down his life for his sheep* (Jn 10:11). That is what he did. I mean, to the wolf who was lurking on the lookout for you he presented himself to be killed in your stead. Nor do you need anyone else to shut and open the door of your pen, because Christ is for you both shepherd and door; he himself is both pasture and

provider. *I*, he says, *am the gate of the sheep. Whoever enters through me will be saved, and will walk out and walk in and will find the pastures* (Jn 10:9).

The pastures, then, which this good shepherd has prepared for you, in which he has settled you for you to take your fill, are not various kinds of grasses and green things, among which some are sweet to the taste, some extremely bitter, which as the seasons succeed one another are sometimes there and sometimes not. Your pastures are the words of God and his commandments, and they have all been sown as sweet grasses. These pastures had been tasted by that man who said to God, *How sweet are your words to my palate, more so than honey and the honeycomb in my mouth!* (Ps 119:103). It is the same person[10] who also cries out to the Lord's sheep about these pastures, and says, *Taste and see how sweet is the Lord* (Ps 34:8). Read the decalogue, then, in the Old Testament: *You shall not kill, you shall not steal, you shall not utter false witness* (Ex 20:13.15-16), and the rest. Read the New Testament's praise of the commandments: *Blessed are the poor in spirit, since theirs is the kingdom of heaven; blessed are the gentle, since they shall take possession of the earth by inheritance* (Mt 5:3.5), and the rest that follows, or similar things; and much more, scattered throughout the prophets and apostles.[11]

It's about these pastures, surely, that the shepherd cries out to the sheep, *Work for the food that does not perish* (Jn 6:27). The reason, though, it does not perish is that *the word of the Lord abides forever* (Is 40:8). The word of the Lord is your food, and not only food, but also your drink. Listen to him saying through the prophet, *Those who eat me will be hungry still; those who drink me will be thirsty still* (Sir 24:21). Again, to him saying himself, *My flesh really is food and my blood really is drink* (Jn 6:55). These pastures, though, are not far from the water of refreshment; the one place for both of these is the Catholic Church of God, where the commandments of life are your pastures, and where is to be found the *fountain of water leaping up to eternal life* (Jn 4:14), with whose streams you will be refreshed when you are baptized in order to be restored in Christ. Unless your pastures, then, are irrigated by this water, it will be impossible for you to be reared, because the commandment of God can neither germinate without the baptism of Christ, nor be eaten so as to satisfy the soul.

The paths along which we are instructed to walk

4. So when by means of the water of Christ's refreshment you have begun to be fit to be fattened on the taste of the sweet pastures, then you will understand, and you will cry out with joy and say, *He has turned back my soul, he has led me by paths of justice for the sake of his name* (Ps 23:3). The devil through sin overturned your soul, and turned it away from God; God the Father through Christ turned it back to himself, not for your merits, but for the sake of his name. So then, once you are already enlightened, already converted and turned back to him, already a believer,[12] already fattened on the divine pastures through the water of refreshment, you will say, *He has converted my soul.* This is a confession rightly to boast about, if there is no shift in your conscience. You will make

it truly, you see, and with an unalterable conscience, if you say it, not on account of your merits, but for the sake of his name.

But what are the paths of justice, by which he has led you? Listen to your leader: *How wide,* he says, *and spacious is the road that leads to destruction; but tight and narrow is the road that leads to life* (Mt 7:13-14). Every path, after all, is a kind of short-cut. So it is not by the delights of the world, by the opulence of gold and silver, conspicuous also with your precious stones and expensive clothes, endowed with every kind of honor and title of nobility, your head swollen with all the wisdom of the philosophers, that God has arranged for you to go to the kingdom of heaven. Because all these things, and others like them, which are given[13] to be used well, become for those who use them badly a wide and spacious road, one traveled, that is, in hope that can be seen only;[14] and it leads them, when they are deprived of this present life, not to the hope[15] in which they did not place their hopes, but to destruction. *For they have slept their sleep, and all the men of wealth have found nothing in their hands* (Ps 76:5).

It is by the paths of justice that he has arranged for you to go; that is by mercy and truth. *For all the ways of the Lord are mercy and truth* (Ps 25:10). He wants you to ignore the wide and spacious road, and advance along narrow paths and short-cuts, that is by way of hunger and thirst, of nakedness and fasting, by way of obscurity, of poverty, of patience, of contempt for all things of the present, while clinging to the promised hope.[16] Would you like, though, to hear a plain statement of the short-cut, by which the paths you are told to walk along bring you? *You shall love the Lord your God with your whole heart and with your whole soul; and your neighbor as yourself. For on these two commandments depends the whole law, and the prophets* (Mt 22:37-40). So in order to get there quickly, if you are in a hurry to reach the kingdom of heaven, proceed along these two paths, which are the sum of them all and make one road; so that when you finally arrive, you may rejoice that you have traveled them all diligently and without fatigue.

The Lord your God is with you on the road

5. So keep to these paths, confine your steps to them, picking your way between the ambushes the devil lays for you in his rage, so that you may sing confidently to the Lord and say, *For even if I walk in the midst of the shadow of death, I will fear no evils; since you are with me* (Ps 23:4). The shadow of death is the road of sin, on which that good-for-nothing bandit the devil spreads the nets of deception to catch those who are walking straight. It's a shadow, because light has nothing in common with darkness. The apostle teaches us to repudiate the works of this shadow when he says, *Let us cast aside the works of darkness, and put on the armor of light; let us walk honorably as in the day, not in orgies and drunkenness, not in debauchery and shamelessness, not in quarreling and jealousy* (Rom 13:12-13). So then, as long as you remain in this present life, you are walking in the midst of vices, of worldly pressures, which are the shadow of death. Let Christ shine in your heart, who lights the lamp of

our minds with the love of God and neighbor; and you will not fear any evils, since he is with you. *I will not desert you*, he says through the prophet, *nor abandon you* (Jos 1:5). Again in the gospel, *Behold, I myself will be with you every day until the close of the age* (Mt 28:20). Your guardian[17] is reliable; the Lord your God is with you. Beware of deserting this companion of yours by being boastful, and of remaining deserted yourself in the shadow of death.

The rod of discipline, the staff of mercy, the table of delight

6. And so, since you realize that you are being assailed in the shadow by the stratagems of the enemy intending to discourage you, take up the rod of discipline, and lean confidently on the staff of mercy, so that when Christ, *the sun of justice* (Mal 4:2), has shone upon you to help you, you may truthfully say, *Your rod and your staff have given me comfort* (Ps 23:4). It's a rod, you see, that herds[18] the proud, according to what is said about Christ in the second psalm: *You will herd them with an iron rod, and shatter them like a potter's vessel* (Ps 2:9). A staff, however, supports the feeble and the weary. So remember the rod of correction and discipline, and don't get conceited and proud when you have been filled with the good things of God's gifts, and start grumbling against him; because in his anger he will shatter you with it like a potter's vessel.

Remember too the staff of assistance, and don't trust in your own virtue, or ever say, "I am holy, I can't stumble." Our weakness makes us liable to many slips and falls, nor is its dominant feature the holiness of its works while it is still set in earth that *produces thorns and thistles*, nor can it boast of any kind of purity. So as long as it is due to *return to the earth from which it was taken* (Gn 3:18.19), it is unable, unless it is controlled by the staff of divine grace, to stand on its own feet. And so whether you are prospering in God, or whether you are being tossed about by storms of trials and temptations, throw yourself entirely upon the staff of God's mercy, so that when you recline upon it to be feasted upon spiritual gifts, you may suitably say, delighted at the taste of his sweetness, *You have prepared a table in my sight against those who oppress me. You have made my head fat with oil, and your beaker of heady wine, how noble it is!* (Ps 23:5).

This is what the universal Church sings throughout the whole wide world, supported by the staff of grace. This is what she preaches against heretics, Jews and Gentiles who distress her with their mockery, as she glories not in herself but in the Lord.[19] The table of delight, you see, is the passion of Christ, who offered himself for us as a sacrifice to God the Father on the table of the cross, thus bestowing on his Catholic Church the banquet of life, that is to say giving us his body to satisfy our hunger, and his blood to make us drunk. Fed and vitalized at this table, the Church exults against those who distress her, having the hope of eternal life through her life, the Lord Christ, who has anointed her lavishly with *the oil of gladness* (Ps 45:7) through the Holy Spirit. It was on account of this table that the apostle rebuked the Corinthians who were in the habit of sitting down to meals in idol-houses, saying, *You cannot share in the*

table of the Lord and the table of demons; you cannot drink the cup of the Lord
and the cup of demons (1 Cor 10:20-21).

7. So when the divine grace to which you are hastening[20] has conducted you
to it, you will recognize the table of the spiritual banquet, and then each one of
you, having acknowledged the truth, can exult and give thanks to God, and can
properly and confidently say, *And your mercy shall follow me all the days of my*
life (Ps 23:6). You have the great comfort of God's glory accompanying you.[21]
That is to say, on account of your miserably weak condition, the mercy of God
follows behind you. But first, in order to show you the route to eternal life, it
anticipates you, that is to say it goes ahead of you, according to what it says in
another psalm, *My God, his mercy will anticipate me* (Ps 59:10). His mercy
anticipates you, that is it leads you to the road which you are still ignorant of, it
calls you to God when you have been dumped far away from God. It attracts
you while you are still a slave of sin, in order to set you free, so that by walking
along the road all the days of your life you may avoid going astray.

It also follows you, as your rearguard, in case the serpent lying in wait for
your heel,[22] the devil with whom you are at war, should trip you up. Robbers,
you see, either kill you by attacking from the front or by leaping out behind you.
That's why the mercy of God both goes ahead of you and follows behind you,
so that you may walk along in the center, safe and sound and without a qualm,
all the days of your life. So you have the hope and the glory, not in yourself but
in the mercy of God going ahead of you and following you. It was as a sinner
that you were anticipated by it, so that you could be saved; it was not as a just
person that you were found, so that you could boast that you pleased God on
your own.

8. Notice, though, where he is leading you, if you don't spurn his lead. It's
not into a field of worldly wretchedness, to gain your bread among thorns and
thistles with toil and sweat.[23] It is not into the perils of the sea, to pursue, *on a*
frail piece of wood (Wis 10:4), uncertain profits in the course of trade. It is to
the house of God that he is leading you, not as a guest for a time, to move on
from there in due course, but as a permanent inhabitant in it. It continues, you
see, *And that I may dwell in the house of the Lord for length of days* (Ps 23:6).
The house of the Lord is paradise; length of days is eternal life. You won't be
hungry there, or thirsty, nor will you toil away in the heat of the sun and the
moon, and you won't feel the cold and the storms of winter. There is no sadness
or grief there. Yours will be the everlasting blessedness of the company of the
saints. You will rejoice with them, and exult, as you live and praise God forever
and ever. It says in another psalm, you see, *Blessed are those who dwell in your*
house; they will praise you forever and ever (Ps 84:4).

This, dearly beloved, is the hope of your faith. You have approached the Lord to declare your faith;[24] make haste, and take pains by good behavior to grasp what you have declared your faith in. It is not, after all, for the sake of this present life that you are becoming Christians, but for the sake of the life to come, which the Lord Christ himself lavishes on you when you believe and persevere in him: who lives and reigns with the Father in the unity of the Holy Spirit forever and ever. Amen.

NOTES

1. This sermon has better manuscript support for its authenticity than the previous one. But for all that the Maurists are fairly certain on grounds of style that it is not one of Augustine's. Mlle. la Bonnardière, on the other hand, thinks it is. My own hesitant inclination is to side with the Maurists.

It was addressed to those who were "hastening to baptism"; so whatever year it was preached in, and by whatever preacher, it was presumably preached in Lent—and from the final paragraph we can conclude that it was preached on the occasion of the *redditio symboli*, the "giving back" of the creed; that is to say, if I am not mistaken, on the fourth Saturday or Sunday of Lent. If Augustine was the preacher, its strong whiff of anti-Pelagianism (all the manuscripts insert it among the anti-Pelagian treatises) would suggest a date after 411; and the place would certainly be Hippo Regius. If the preacher was a devoted disciple of Augustine's, someone like his successor Heraclius, for example, the place would be the same, the date twenty to thirty years later.

2. When, on being baptized, his audience are admitted to the Eucharist.

3. See Lk 10:30-35. The man is interpreted as representing Adam, and thus the entire human race.

4. See Jn 8:48.

5. Roughly correct; Samaria, *Shomron* in Hebrew, comes from the root *shamar*, meaning to guard or watch.

6. See Acts 3:14.

7. See Lk 11:3-7.

8. See Gal 4:9.

9. Perhaps it would not be fair to ask him whom he has in mind as the hireling. I suppose one could answer, anyone setting up as a *guru*, a guide to life, who is not Christ nor a follower of Christ's.

10. David, as Augustine and all his contemporaries assumed; and through David, Christ himself.

11. He has so far only quoted the law and the gospel.

12. Only after baptism would the catechumens rank formally as "believers," as among the faithful, the *fideles*.

13. Reading *dantur* instead of the text's *datur*. As it stands, the text is very defective, several relative pronouns seeming to have more than one antecedent. The Maurists suggest reading *non datur*, which would give the whole passage the rather different sense, ". . . become for those who use them badly, to whom it is not given to use them well, a wide and spacious road . . ."

14. See Rom 8:24. Such hope, the preacher implies, is not really hope at all.

15. I am tempted to emend this *spem* to *rem*, giving the sense, "not to the real thing, in which they have not placed their hopes." If *spem* here is not a mistake of a stenographer or copyist for the *rem* actually spoken, and if the preacher did say *spem* here, then to my mind this would be a strong indication against Augustinian authorship, since Augustine could hardly let an occasion pass by for contrasting *res* and *spes*.

16. A passage roughly modelled on 2 Cor 6:4-10.

17. The good Samaritan.

18. It is the same word, *regit*, as I have translated in the first verse of this Ps 23, "is my guide."

19. See 1 Cor 1:31.

20. The grace of baptism.

21. An allusion here to the shining cloud of God's glory that escorted the Israelites through the Red Sea and accompanied them in their journey through the desert. As this pillar of cloud sometimes went ahead of them and sometimes followed behind, it provided a very vivid symbol for the doctrine of prevenient and subsequent grace; that is to say, the grace that is given to us before we take any step toward faith and conversion, and the grace that follows on them. See Saint Thomas, *Summa Theologiae*, Ia IIae, q.111, a.3 (English translation, volume 30; ed. Thomas Gilbey, O.P., Blackfriars and McGraw-Hill, London and New York, 1972). There he quotes Augustine's work on *Nature and Grace*, 31: "Grace anticipates us, *praevenit*, so that we may be healed; it follows us, *subsequitur*, so that once healed we may grow strong; it anticipates us so that we may be called, follows us so that we may be glorified."

22. See Gn 3:15.

23. See Gn 3:18-19.

24. This is the clue to the sermon's being preached on the occasion of the *redditio symboli*. See note 1 above. The Latin, admittedly, simply says, "You have approached the Lord to believe, *credere*"; but this word does seem here to be used in a pregnant, technical sense.

SERMON 367

ON LUKE'S GOSPEL, 16:19-31, ABOUT THE RICH MAN AND LAZARUS[1]

The gospel narrative of the rich man, and Lazarus must
be a warning to the rich, who are reluctant to give alms

1. Your holinesses will have noticed, my dearest brothers and sisters, and together with me, I rather think, will have taken a very close look at the opulence of the rich man and the extreme need of the beggar; one of them positively stewing in food, and the other fainting with hunger. Both, of course, human beings, both creatures of flesh, both mortal; but not both equal. A common nature, but not a common kind of life. Neither of them immune from the liability to death; and yet one of them is feasting in fine style, and the other is getting dirtier and dirtier in his rags and wretchedness. The one was enjoying choice foods and the inventiveness of the cooks; the other was waiting to see if any scraps would fall from his table.

Let the rich listen now, those who are reluctant to give alms; let them note that we are all born according to one law, all live by one and the same light of day, all breathe the same air, are all also finally snuffed out by one and the same death; though even if this didn't intervene as a rule, that poor man wouldn't have lasted long.[2] This Lazarus, lying there naked and covered with sores, is carried up in the hands of angels to Abraham's bosom. And lo and behold, the rich man, well fed in his finery, is locked up in the prison of Tartarus.[3] Where now is that garment of fine linen? Where is that varied life of affluence and inexhaustible plenty? Don't all these things pass, with death, like a shadow?

We brought nothing into this world, says the apostle, *and what is more we cannot take anything out of it* (1 Tm 6:7). We neither take nor snatch anything away with us. What if we could take something—wouldn't we be devouring people alive? What is this monstrously avid appetite, when even huge beasts know their limits? The time they pounce on something, you see, is when they are hungry; but when they feel satisfied, they spare their prey. It is only the avarice and greed of the rich that is forever insatiable. It's always snatching, never satisfied; it neither fears God nor respects man;[4] neither spares father nor acknowledges mother; neither goes along with brother, nor keeps faith with friend. It oppresses the widow, moves in on the orphan's property; it hails freedmen back into slavery, presenting false documents. The property of the dead is seized, as though those who do this sort of thing were not also going to die themselves. So what is this insanity of souls, prompting them to forgo life

296

and have an appetite for death, to acquire gold and lose heaven? But it's because nobody gives a thought to God, that's why judgment waits for them in death.

The rich man is refused mercy in his torment, because he had neglected mercy during his life

2. How right it was for the rich man to be told, *Because you received good things during your life, and Lazarus likewise bad things; now on the contrary he is being comforted, you though are being tormented* (Lk 16:25). Let the rich pay heed to these words, those who are unwilling to give alms. Let them take note that punishment is meted out to those who are unwilling to dole out assistance. Let them note the poor man enjoying cool refreshment, let them note the rich man stewing in the juice of heavier pains. *Father Abraham*, he says, *send Lazarus, to dip the tip of his finger in water and cool my tongue; because I am being tormented in these flames* (Lk 16:24). He, though, replies, *Remember, son, that you received good things in your life, and Lazarus likewise bad things.* Pains are apportioned in return for riches, refreshment in return for poverty, flames in return for purple, entertainment in return for nakedness, so that the equal balance of the scales may be maintained, and that standard of measurement may not be proved false which says, *With the measure you mete out, shall it be meted out to you* (Mt 7:2). The reason the rich man is refused mercy in his pain is that while he lived he neglected to show mercy. The reason the rich man's pleas in his torment are ignored is that he ignored the poor man's pleas on earth.

Rich and poor need each other

3. Rich and poor are two things opposed to each other; but again they are two things needed by each other. Neither would be in want if they supported each other; and none would be in difficulties if they both helped one another. The rich were made for the poor, and the poor were made for the rich. It is the task of the poor to pray, and of the rich to provide; God's business is to apportion great things in return for small. From the small amount of the rich man's alms there springs a great crop. The field of the poor is fertile, it soon yields a profit to its owners. The poor are the way to heaven, by which one comes to the Father. So begin to provide for them, if you don't want to lose the way.

Start in this life to unshackle the fetters with which your inheritance has you chained up. In order to be sure of free access to heaven, throw away from yourself the burden of wealth, throw away your voluntary chains, throw away all the irksome business and the anxieties that have been been leaving you no peace all these years. Give to anyone who asks you, so that you yourself may receive; be generous to the poor, if you don't want to be food for the flames. Give something on earth to Christ for him to pay back to you in heaven. Forget what you are, and think about what you are going to be. The present life is fragile, and always on the verge of death. Nobody can stay here, but we are all obliged to pass along. We come without wishing to, we go against our will, because we

are bad. If, however, we send something along in advance, we won't come to a
chilly reception and poor hospitality. What we give to the poor, you see, we are
sending on ahead of us; but whatever we snatch and grab, we leave it all behind
here.

NOTES

1. While all the manuscripts available to the Maurists attribute this sermon to Augustine, they
themselves, together with earlier editors, are very doubtful, again on grounds of style. I share their
doubts, more on grounds of the way the subject is treated. But readers should judge for themselves;
compare Sermons 113A and 113B which are on this passage, and also several others which refer to
it, sometimes at length: Sermons 14, 3-5; 15A, 2-5; 20A, 9; 33, 4; 41, 4-5; 102, 3.

2. A more or less unintelligible and totally pointless aside: *quae*—death—*si non intercederet,
nec ipse pauper duraret.*

3. A suitably mythical name for the netherworld. See 2 Pt 2:4.

4. See Lk 18:2.

SERMON 368

SERMON OF AUGUSTINE THE BISHOP PREACHED ON THE TEXT
"WHOEVER LOVES HIS SOUL WILL LOSE IT"

Date: uncertain[1]

If nobody ever hated his own flesh, much less did anyone ever hate his own soul

1. Just now, brothers and sisters, while the divine reading was being read, we heard the Lord saying, *Whoever loves his soul*[2] *will lose it* (Jn 12:25). This statement seems to be contradicted by what the apostle says: *Nobody ever hated his own flesh* (Eph 5:29). So if there's nobody who ever hated his own flesh, how much less anybody who ever hated his own soul? The soul, clearly, is much more important than the flesh, because it is the inhabitant, the flesh merely the dwelling; and the soul is the master, the flesh the servant; the soul the superior, the flesh the subject. So if nobody ever hated his own flesh, who can there ever have been to hate his own soul?

That being the case, the present reading from the gospel has landed us with no small problem; because in it we heard *Whoever loves his soul will lose it.* It's dangerous to love the soul, or it may perish. But if the reason it is dangerous for you to love your soul is that it may thereby perish, the reason why you ought not to love it is that you don't want it to perish. But if you don't want it to perish, that means you love it.

"But because I'm afraid of losing it, that's why I don't love it—and of course, what I'm afraid of losing, I love . . ."

And the Lord says somewhere else, *What does it profit a man, if he gains the whole world, but suffers the loss of his own soul?* (Mt 16:26). There you have it, that the soul is to be so loved as to be preferred to gaining the whole world; and yet the one who loves his soul is to observe that if he loves it he will lose it. You don't want to lose it? Don't love it. But if you don't want to lose it, you cannot not love it.

The wrong kind of love of the soul which springs from hatred,
and the right kind of hatred of the soul which springs from love

2. So there are people who love their souls in the wrong way; and this is what the word of God means to correct—not that they should hate their souls, but that

299

they should love them in the right way. It's by loving them badly, you see, that they lose them, and you're left with an enormous kind of back to front contradiction; still the fact remains, that if you love it in the wrong way you will lose it, if you hate it in the right way you will keep it safe. So there is a certain wrong way of loving the soul, and a certain right way of hating it; but the wrong way of loving springs from hatred, and the right way of hating springs from love.

What's the wrong way of loving the soul? When you love your soul in all kinds of iniquity. Listen to how this wrong kind of love springs from hatred: *But whoever loves iniquity, hates his own soul* (Ps 11:5). Observe on the other hand how the right kind of hatred springs from love: in the same place the Lord went on to say, *But whoever hates his soul in this age will find it for eternal life* (Jn 12:25). Obviously, you love very much what you wish to find for eternal life. What use, after all, is what you love for a time? Either you are removed from it, or it is removed from you; when it's you that are eliminated, what ceases to be is the actual lover; when that thing is eliminated, what vanishes is what you loved. So where either the lover ceases to be or the thing loved, it's not worth loving. But what is worth loving? What can be with us forever? If you want to have your soul safe forever, hate it for a time. So the right way of hating springs from love; the wrong way of loving springs from hatred.

The right kind of love must drive out the wrong kind

3. What, then, is the right way of loving the soul? Do you imagine the martyrs didn't love their souls? You can certainly see nowadays, if anyone is in peril of his life,[3] life of this present age, how his friends rush around to save it; how they rush off to the church, how the bishop is begged to intervene; if there is anything he can do, to be quick about it, to hurry up. Why all this? For the sake of a soul. And everyone is agitated, each one decides to drop every other business and get a move on; all haste is applauded, all delay complained of. Why? For the sake of a soul. What does that mean, for the sake of a soul? So that a man should not die. Didn't the martyrs know how to love their souls? And yet all this is for the sake of a soul, so that a man should not die.

A person's real death is iniquity. If you run a hundred miles for the sake of this life, how many miles should you run for the sake of eternal life? If you are in such a hurry to gain a few days, and those so uncertain—I mean, the man delivered from death today doesn't know whether he'll die tomorrow—still if there's all this rushing around to gain a few days, because even up to old age our days are few, how much rushing around should there be for the sake of eternal life? And yet people are so sluggish and slow about taking any steps toward it. You will have difficulty in finding even someone who has suffered making slow, hesitant moves for the sake of eternal life. So there's plenty of the wrong sort of love around; while very few people have the right sort of love. I mean, just as there's nobody who doesn't love his own soul, so too there's nobody who doesn't love his own flesh. So it can happen that both what the apostle said is true: *Nobody ever hated his own flesh* (Eph 5:29), and that the soul is not truly loved.

So let us learn then, brothers and sisters, how to love our own souls. Every pleasure provided by the world is going to pass away. There is a love that is useful and a love that does harm. Let love be hampered by love; let the love that does harm retire, and the love that is of use take its place. But it's because people don't want to retire from that sort, that this other sort can't gain entry to them. They are full up, so they can't hold anything else. They must pour something out, and then they can hold some more. They are full, you see, of the love of sensual pleasures, full of the love of this present life, full of the love of gold and silver, of the possessions of this world. So those who are full in this way are like jars. Do you want honey to gain entry into a jar from which you haven't yet emptied the vinegar? Empty out what you have, in order to take and hold what you don't yet have. That's why the first step is to renounce this world, and then the next is to turn back to God.[4] When you renounce, you are emptying out; when you turn back to God, you are being filled—but only if it's done, not merely with the body, but also with the heart.

The right order of love, and progress in it

4. The question arises, brothers and sisters, how this love grows. You see, it has its beginnings, it has its increase, it has its perfection. And we clergy need to know who are just beginning, so that we may encourage them to increase; who haven't even begun, so that we may advise them where to begin; who have both begun and grown, so that we may urge them on toward perfection. The first thing for your graces to note is this: what people always love and value before anything else is themselves, and from there they go on to value other things. If you value gold, you first value yourself, and from there gold; because if you were to die, there wouldn't be anyone to possess the gold. So with each and every one of us love begins with oneself, and cannot but begin with oneself. And nobody needs to be advised to love himself; this is innate, after all, not only in human beings but also in animals. After all, you can see, brothers and sisters, how not only huge wild beasts and large animals, like oxen and camels and elephants, but also flies, but also the tiniest little worms, how they don't want to die, and how they love themselves. All animals shrink from death. So they love themselves, they want to take care of themselves; some do it by speed, others by hiding, others by resisting and fighting back. All animals, nevertheless fight for their lives, they don't want to die, they want to take care of themselves. So they love themselves.

Something else also starts being loved. But what is this something else? Whatever it is you have loved, it is either the same as yourself, or it is inferior to you, or it is superior to you. If what you love is inferior to you, love it to console yourself with, love it as something to work at, love it as something to use, not as something to tie yourself to. For example, you love gold; don't tie yourself to gold. How much better are you than gold? Gold, after all, is shining earth; you though were made to the image of God in order to be illuminated by God. Since gold is one of God's creatures, yet it wasn't gold that God made to his image, but you; it follows that he placed gold under you. So this sort of love is to be treated lightly. Such things as these are to be acquired for use; one mustn't let oneself be stuck to them, as with glue, by the bonds of love. You shouldn't make extra limbs for yourself, which will cause you great pain and torment when they start being lopped of. So what, then? Rise up from this love by which you love things lower than you are; start loving things that are your equals, that, are the same as you are. But what need is there of many examples? If you want, you can do it very shortly.

A quick way to reach the perfection of love

5. In fact the Lord himself has told us in the gospel, and made it abundantly clear, what the proper order is for our obtaining true love and true charity. This is how he put it: *You shall love the Lord your God with your whole heart, and with your whole soul, and with all your strength; and your neighbor as yourself* (Mk 12:30-31). So first of all, love God, then yourself; after that love your neighbor as yourself. First learn, though, how to love yourself, and in this way love your neighbor as yourself; because if you don't know how to love yourself, how will you be able to love your neighbor in truth? Some people, you see, assume that they are appropriately and legitimately loving themselves, when they snatch other people's property, when they get drunk, when they make themselves the slaves of lust, when by a variety of false slurs they make unjust profits. Such people as these should listen to scripture saying, *Whoever loves iniquity, hates his own soul* (Ps 11:5). So if by loving iniquity you not only don't love yourself, but in fact hate yourself, how will you be able to love either God or your neighbor?

So if you want to keep the order of true charity, act justly, love mercy, shun self-indulgence; begin, according to the Lord's instruction to love not only friends but also enemies.[5] And when you strive to maintain these standards faithfully with your whole heart, you will be able to climb up by these virtues, as by a flight of steps, to being worthy to love God with your whole mind and your whole strength. And when you reach this happy state of perfection, you will reckon all the desires of this world as nothing but dung,[6] and with the prophet you will be able to say, *But for me to cling to God is good* (Ps 73:28).

NOTES

1. All the authorities are agreed that this is a genuine sermon of Augustine's, one noted by Possidius in his *Index*, 8 (PL 46, 17) as "On the apostle: *nobody ever hated his own flesh*; and from the gospel: *Whoever loves his life will lose it.*" But it comes to us through the filter of Caesarius of Arles, being included among his works in the CCL edition of the Latin Fathers, volume 4, 705-708. That being so, it is hard to attempt any assignment of date to Augustine's original sermon; but not

impossible, and my inclination would be to regard it as a sermon of his old age, between 424 and 430. There is a certain softening of his harshness toward the love of things below us; we are now allowed to love them *ad consolandum*, to console ourselves with them (section 4). But that could, I suppose, be Caesarius and not Augustine.

2. Normally one would translate *animam* here by "life." But now I have to keep "soul" for reasons that will soon become evident.

3. He means from the law—under sentence of death.

4. An allusion to the ceremony of admittance to the catechumenate, in which the candidate first stood on a goatskin and facing to the west (the region of darkness) renounced Satan and all his pomps; and then turning round toward the east (the region of light), confessed his faith in Christ.

5. See Mt 5:44; Lk 6:27.

6. See Phil 3:8.

SERMON 369

SERMON PREACHED IN THE RESTORED BASILICA ON CHRISTMAS DAY

Date: 412[1]

The eternal is born in time

1. Our savior, born of the Father apart from any day, and through whom every single day has been made, wished to have as his birthday on earth this particular day we are now celebrating. Any of you that are filled with wonder by this day, should rather be marveling at the eternal day[2] abiding before all days, creating all days, born on this day, delivering us from *the evil of the day* (Mt 6:34). Go on being filled with wonder; the one who bore him is both mother and virgin; the one she bore is both speechless infant and Word. Rightly did the heavens speak, angels celebrate, shepherds rejoice; rightly were astrologers[3] changed, kings troubled, little children crowned.

Give suck, mother, to our food; give suck to *the bread that came down from heaven* (Jn 6:58), and was placed in a manger, like fodder for pious beasts.[4] There, you see, *the ox has acknowledged its owner, and the donkey the manger of its Lord* (Is 1:3), that is to say the circumcised and the uncircumcised,[5] by adhering to *the cornerstone* (Eph 2:20); their firstfruits being respectively the shepherds and the Magi. Give your breast to the one who made you such that he might be made in you, who both gave you the gift of fertility when he was conceived, and did not deprive you of the honor of virginity when he was born; who before he was born chose for himself both the womb from which he would be born and the day on which he would be born.

And he made what he chose, so that he might come forth from there *like a bridegroom from his chamber* (Ps 19:6), to make it possible for him to be seen by mortal eyes, and to indicate, by the lengthening of the light of the year,[6] that he had come as the light for our minds. The prophets sang that the maker of heaven and earth would be found on earth with men;[7] the angel announced that the creator of flesh and spirit would come in the flesh.[8] John from the womb saluted the savior in the womb; the old man Simeon acknowledged God in the infant; the widow Anna acknowledged the virgin mother. These, Lord Jesus, are the testimonies to your birth, before the waves were subjected to the tread of your feet, or bowed to your commands; before the winds were hushed at your bidding, the dead came back to life at your call, the sun faded at your death, the earth quaked at your resurrection, the heavens opened at your ascension; before you had done any of these and other marvels in the prime of life. You were still being carried in your mother's arms, and were already acknowledged as Lord of the world. You were yourself a tiny boy of the seed of Israel, and yourself *God with us, Emmanuel* (Mt 1:23).

The eternal begetting of the Word

2. What must that other coming to birth of our savior be, the one in which he is coeternal with the Father who begets him, when this one from the virgin has stupefied the world, been acknowledged and accepted by devout faith, but mocked by unbelief, while it has been feared by the pride it has overcome?[9] What indeed can that coming to birth be, by which *in the beginning was the Word, and the Word was with God, and the Word was God* (Jn 1:1)? What is this Word, the utterance of which did not mean silence either before or after it was uttered? What is this Word without time, through which were made all times; which neither opened anyone's lips when it started, nor closed them when it ended; a Word which has no beginning in the mouths of speakers, and *opens the mouths of the dumb*; a Word which is not the product of the eloquence of any nation, and which *has given eloquence to the tongues of babes* (Wis 10:21)? What indeed, I say, is that generation to which no father has given way by dying, because none has preceded it by living?

Let us lift up our souls to him, as best we can with his help, leaving behind all intervals of space and time, all sense of extension which governs our usual perception of days and bodies; to see if we are capable somehow or other of grasping one born who is not preceded by the one who begets, and one begetting who is not followed by the one who is begotten; Father and Son; and not both equally fathers, nor both equally sons, but both equally eternal; not each begetting nor each being born, but neither living without the other. Let us reflect that the Father has eternally been begetting and the Son has eternally been born, if we can; if we cannot, let us believe it. There isn't anything we are capable of saying here;[10] but all the same, it *is not placed very far from any one of us; for in him we live, and move, and are* (Acts 17:27-28).

Let us pass beyond our fleshly condition, in which parents live before their children, because they have had to grow up in order to be able to beget children, and as their children grow up, they themselves are already getting old. Parents were alive when the children were not yet born, because again when the parents are dead, the children are still going to be alive. Let us also pass beyond the condition of our souls; they too give birth to something by thinking, which they have within them by knowing. But they can lose it by forgetting, just as they didn't have it at all before they knew it. Let us pass beyond all bodily, time-bound, changeable things, in order to see, far above all things, the one through whom all things were made.[11] Our ascent takes place in the heart, because the one to whom[12] we are ascending is near. We, though, are far away from him, insofar as we are unlike him. So it is his likeness that ascends to him, which he fashioned in us and then refashioned. But as long as this is not yet perfect, our weak eyes can only blink, and are not able to gaze directly at the inexpressible *brilliance of eternal light* (Wis 7:26). So if the fine point of the mind cannot yet grasp his splendor, *who shall declare his coming to birth* (Is 53:8)? But all the same, *the Word became flesh and dwelt amongst us* (Jn 1:14).

Let us worship the one who was born today,
to become Emmanuel, God with us

3. So as regards this coming to birth, whose anniversary we are celebrating today, this birth by which he saw fit to come through Israel and become Emmanuel, God with us in the weakness of the flesh, not with us in the iniquity of the heart; drawing near to us in what he took to himself from what was ours, and delivering us through what he remained in what was his—that is to say, the Lord visited his servants,[13] sharing our weakness and subjection to death, in order to set us free by his unchangeable truth;[14] so as regards this coming to birth, which human frailty is to some extent at least capable of grasping; not that one which remains above all things without time, without mother; but this one which happened in time, without father, in the midst of all things; let us praise, love and worship this son of the virgin and husband of virgins, born of an uncorrupted mother, and making fruitful with incorruptible truth, so that by his mercy we may confound the devil's cunning and lead him captive in triumph. The devil crept in to deceive us by corrupting a woman's mind; Christ came forth to liberate us, born of a woman's uncorrupted flesh.[15]

NOTES

1. This is the suggestion of Lambot and Perler, *Les Voyages de Saint Augustin*, 316. If the sermon is authentic, it can really only have been preached on Christmas Day, 412, because that seems to have been one of only two winters that Augustine spent in Carthage after he was ordained bishop. Other sermons preached that winter in January, 413, were the series on successive days from 19 to 20 January, Sermons 111, 23, 53, 277; possibly also Sermon 25A. The other winter that saw Augustine in Carthage was that of late 419; but in that year he returned to Hippo Regius before Christmas. See Perler, 356-360; 470.

However, many scholars from the Maurists onward question the authenticity of the sermon, and as I proceeded with the translation I was more and more inclined to agree with them. Its rhetoric is very high-flown, and not quite in the manner of Augustine even at his most rhetorical. The Maurists seem to suggest that it was composed by a certain bishop Vigilius, trying to pass it off as one of Augustine's, in order to support his own, entirely orthodox, anti-Arian polemic. There are any number of little characteristic Augustinianisms in it, embedded like currants in a suet pudding.

2. Another of his names for the Son, who can be called Day from Day as well as Light from Light. See, for example, Sermon 226.

3. He says *magi*, and is of course referring to the Magi. But for us that is simply the name for

the three wise men, whereas in Latin for the people of Augustine's time it very definitely meant magicians, wizards, or as I translate, astrologers, whose activities were seriously frowned on by the Church.

4. That is, for the devout faithful; see Sermon 365, 4, note 13.

5. The ox, a sacrificial animal, representing the Jews; the donkey standing for the Gentiles.

6. With the days beginning to grow longer from the winter solstice, which used to be, or was assumed to be, 25 December.

7. See Bar 3:35-37.

8. See Lk 1:30-33.

9. The allusion of the last phrase, I imagine, is primarily to Herod's fears when he heard the Magi's news.

10. So the Maurists. Dom Morin's edition has "There is nothing here we wish to say"—which makes very poor sense indeed.

11. See Jn 1:3.

12. So the Maurists. The text published by Dom Morin reads "the thing to which . . ." But on either side of this sentence the pronouns in question are all personal and masculine.

13. See Lk 1:68.

14. See Jn 8:32.

15. The Maurists add, "who with the Father and the Holy Spirit is blessed forever. Amen."

SERMON 370

ON THE LORD'S NATIVITY

Date: uncertain[1]

Four ways in which human beings have come into existence

1. Today is a day that has conferred upon the human race the great joy of now having the hope of eternal life. The first man, you see, in whose fall we all fell, whose downfall meant our subjection to death, was not born, but made, with no father, no mother, by the work of God's hands. This was the first fashioning of a human being, of Adam *from the earth* (Gn 2:7). The second fashioning of a human being is the one by which the woman is created from the side of the man.[2] The third fashioning of a human being is the one by which human beings are born of man and woman. The fourth fashioning is that of God and man, by which Christ was born of a woman without a man.

Of these four ways of fashioning human beings, we are familiar with only one; the other three are present not to the eyes in our bodies, but to the faith in our hearts. Of the man made from the earth without father, without mother, we have no direct knowledge; of the woman made from the side of the man we have no direct knowledge; we have believed what we have read and heard. The third way we are familiar with, by which human beings are born every day from the embrace of male and female. So now there was one fashioning without man and woman, now another from man without woman, now the third from both man and woman; there remained the fourth, from woman without man. But this fourth has liberated the other three. The first and the second, you see, had a great fall, the third they produced from their downfall, in the fourth they found salvation.

All ages and qualities of life should rejoice in the birth of the savior

2. So let virgins, then, exult for joy; it was a virgin that gave birth to Christ. They must not imagine that anything she had vowed was disfigured in her; she remained a virgin after giving birth. Let widows exult for joy; the widow Anna recognized the infant Christ. Let married women exult for joy; the married Elizabeth prophesied that the Lord Jesus Christ would soon be born; no grade

308

was overlooked, there was none from which the salvation of all would fail to receive a testimonial. Is it only virgins, after all, that reach the kingdom of heaven? Widows too arrive there. Of great merit was that holy widow, Anna. She had lived with her husband for seven years from her virginity; after his death she had attained to a very advanced age,[3] and in her holy old age she was waiting for the savior's infancy; a woman full of years waiting to see a little one, an old grannie waiting to acknowledge a little one, waiting to see the savior coming into the world as she was on the point of leaving it.

And in the male sex the same three grades are set before us. Christ himself was born as a boy; let boys exult and be glad, as they vow continence to a boy. He did indeed consecrate perfect chastity, seeing that he conferred fertility on his mother, without depriving her of virginity. That old man Simeon had lived a long time, his age being comparable to Anna's,[4] and he had received the reply *that he would not see death before he had seen the Christ of the Lord* (Lk 2:26).

How eagerly the birth of Christ had been awaited by the prophets of old

3. You must appreciate, brothers and sisters, what a tremendous desire possessed the saints of old to see the Christ. They knew he was going to come, and all those who were living devout and blameless lives would say, "Oh, if only that birth may find me still here! Oh, if only I may see with my own eyes what I believe from God's scriptures!" And to prove to you how great was the desire of the saints who knew from the holy scriptures that a virgin was going to give birth, as you heard when Isaiah was read: *Behold a virgin shall conceive in the womb, and shall bear a son, and his name shall be called Emmanuel* (Is 7:14). What Emmanuel means the gospel declares to us, saying, *which is interpreted, God with us* (Mt 1:23). So don't let it surprise you, unbelieving soul, whoever you are, don't let it strike you as impossible that a virgin should give birth, and in giving birth remain a virgin. Realize that it was God who was born, and you won't be surprised at a virgin giving birth. So then, to prove to you how the saints and just men and women of old longed to see what was granted to this old man Simeon, our Lord Jesus Christ said, when speaking to his disciples, *Many just men and prophets have wished to see what you see, and have not seen it; and to hear what you hear, and have not heard it* (Mt 13:17).

This old man was much too late to hear, but in good time to see. He wasn't expecting to hear Christ speaking, since he recognized him while he was a speechless baby. And this was granted to him when he was already decrepit, as though he were longing and sighing and saying in his prayers every day, "When will he come? When will he be born? When shall I see him? Do you think I'll make it? Do you think he'll find me here? Do you think these eyes of mine will see the one by whom the eyes of my heart will be opened?" These are the sort of things he used to say in his prayers, and for his pains he received the reply that *he would not taste death unless he had first seen the Christ of the Lord* (Lk 2:26). Mary his mother was carrying him as a baby; Simeon saw him, and recognized him. By what means did he know the one he recognized? Was the one who was born outwardly also revealed inwardly? He saw him, and he recognized him. Simeon recognized the infant that said nothing, and the Jews killed the young man that performed miracles.

So when he recognized him he took him in the crook of his elbows, that is in his arms, and embraced him. He was carrying the one by whom he was being carried. Christ after all is *the wisdom of God* (1 Cor 1:24), who *reaches from end to end mightily, and disposes all things sweetly* (Wis 8:1). How great[5] he was there, and how little he had made himself! Made little, he was seeking the little ones. What do I mean, he was seeking the little ones? Those who are not proud, not too full of themselves; instead he was gathering together the humble and the meek. He was ready to be placed in a manger, in order to be the fodder of pious beasts of burden.[6] So Simeon took him in his arms, and said, *Now, Lord, you are letting your servant go in peace.* You are letting me go in peace, because I now see peace. So why are you letting me go in peace? *Because my eyes have seen your salvation* (Lk 2:28-30). The salvation of God is the Lord Jesus Christ; *Declare from day to day his salvation* (Ps 96:2).

All grades in the community can bear witness to the newborn Christ

4. So then, young boys, you have the boy Jesus; holy old men, you have the old man Simeon. While if you are looking for some married man to give his testimonial to the Lord, consider Zechariah. So nobody should look for anything else, my brothers and sisters, Christian believers, whether virgin or widow or married woman, or boy or celibate, or married man; whatever more you may want to be than that, you won't find any way in which it belongs to Christ. We don't find that adulterers offered their testimonial to Christ, or fornicators, or the impure. And that he should receive testimonials from such as you are is something that he has bestowed on you, that he has given you. We are none of us, after all, holy by our own powers.

So let us exult for joy, dearly beloved. From today on the days start growing. Believe in Christ, and the day grows in you. Have you come to believe? The day has started. Have you been baptized? Christ is born in your heart. But did Christ, when he was born, remain as he was? He grew up, he reached young manhood, but he never took the downturn into old age. So let your faith also grow up, let it discover the solid strength of maturity, let it never get worn out with age. In this way you will belong to Christ the Son of God, the Word in the beginning with God, the Word who was God; but the Word which became flesh to dwell among us.[7] Majesty was hidden there, and weakness was apparent. Simeon took the weakness in his arms, but inwardly he recognized the majesty. Let none of you make light of the one who was born, if you wish to be reborn. His part was to be born for our sakes; let it be our part to be reborn in him, who lives and reigns forever and ever. Amen.

NOTES

1. The Maurists are very doubtful about the authenticity of this sermon, but contemporary scholars mostly accept it—all of it, that is, except the first section, which all agree is not from the master. As I proceeded with the translation, I became more and more convinced that we have here an eager "Augustinaster" doing his best to imitate his hero. There are, to my mind, too many lapses of intelligence for this ever to have been preached by Augustine. I would not be surprised if it turned out to have come to us through the filter of Caesarius of Arles.

2. See Gn 2:22.

3. To the age of 105, by my calculations, the same age as that reached by the great heroine Judith (Jdt 16:23). In Lk 2:37 she is said to have been a widow for 84 years—not to have been 84 years old as all modern translations tamely say. Married at 14 (that is the presumption), living with her husband for seven years till his death, a widow for 84, brings her to 105. See Sermon 196, 2, note 6.

4. He is being presented, presumably, as a widower. Married men will have to wait until section 4 and Zechariah before their legitimate existence in this connection is acknowledged.

5. The Latin says *Quantus ibi erat, et quam magnus*, which is only translatable, if one is to be literal, as "how great he was there, and how great."

6. The faithful. See Sermons 365, 4, note 13 and 369, 1, note 4.

7. See Jn 1:1.14.

SERMON 371

Date unknown[1]

The two nativities of Christ

1. The savior was born for us today; and that's why the true sun has risen today for the whole world.[2] God became man, so that man might become God; and in order that the slave might be turned into a lord,[3] the Lord *took the form of a slave* (Phil 2:7). The one who dwells in heaven came to dwell on earth, so that the human inhabitants of earth might become inhabitants of heaven. So the savior has been born for us;[4] born though of the Father always, of his mother just once. We have accepted in faith two nativities of our Lord Jesus Christ, first a divine, then a human one; but each, of course, wonderful, that one being accomplished without a mother's, this without a father's contribution; one of them eternal, for the creation of temporal beings;[5] the other temporal, to render them eternal. So he is equal to the Father in the form of God, subject to the Father in the form of a slave.[6] He, the creator of time, was born in time. And he was made so small that he could be brought forth by a woman; but he remained, of course, so great, that he was never separated from the Father.

So these two nativities of the Lord are even attested by the way two of the evangelists begin their gospels. One, you see, has this to say about the divine nativity: *In the beginning was the Word, and the Word was with God, and the Word was God. This was in the beginning with God. All things were made through him, and without him was made nothing* (Jn 1:1-3). But about the human nativity, this is what the other states: *The book of the genesis of Jesus Christ, son of David* (Mt 1:1). So this is the Lord's birthday, this is the day of his second nativity; *let us exult and rejoice on it* (Ps 118:24). Nor is it without significance that, with the days lengthening from now on, the light begins to increase today; so that this day rightly extends the course of the sun, along which it has brought to us this other one, by whom we are to be released from the darkness of death.[7]

So in announcing that he was going to come, the prophets went like lamps ahead of the day of his rising, and proclaimed with the clearest, the most brilliant fanfares the miracles he was going to perform in the flesh. It was right, after all, that his coming should be foretold, in case it should be doubted when he came.

And so this God of ours lived a human life among human beings; he appeared, you see, as a man to those who saw him, as God to those who could understand; offering his humanity to the public gaze, keeping his divinity for those who believed. So while the sight of his weakness saved the weak, the contemplation of his divinity calls for the strong.

God became man to present us all with one like us whom we could follow

2. I beg you, dearest friends, notice what a great mystery of truth this is. For the salvation of mankind he had given the law, sent the prophets; and once[8] these remedies for curing our infirmities had been tried out first, God was eager to offer himself to the human race for its salvation. Obviously, human beings couldn't see God himself in his proper substance; while at the same time there could be no question of their placing their hopes in a mere human being. So what was to be done in this case? They had no business to follow a man, a man who could be seen was not to be followed; God was to be followed—but he couldn't be seen. So in order to present human beings both with one who could be seen by human beings and with one whom human beings might properly follow, God became a human being. And then while he was already living among men, and standing together with the three apostles whom he had led apart into a secret place, he suddenly shone out before them, resplendent in the divine style of glory,[9] which the apostles who were present could scarcely gaze upon, for the weakness of their human senses.

He wished to be born in the human way, so that we might be born in him, and in order to ratify the sacraments of rebirth for his future worshipers. In this way we, who were trapped by that first birth and held liable to its consequences, might by accompanying our savior's steps obtain the sure protection of the second birth;[10] and born again by it in God and from God, might snap the chains of the ancient death, when we received the pledge of salvation, which is the Holy Spirit.

So when God wished to appear visibly to people, and desired also to teach them in person what he had first laid down in the law, he tempered the force, the power of the divine, by taking on the human, and *made the darkness his cover round about him* (Ps 18:11), when he concealed himself in the tent of the flesh. So it is in such a wonderful and inexpressible mystery that Christ our Lord[11] is held to be both man and God; man through his mother, God through the Father. And in this way it comes about that each of those things that he said is true: *The Father is greater than me* (Jn 14:28); and *I and the Father are one* (Jn 10:30); because in his divinity he is equal to the Father; by his incarnation he is subject to the Father.

How God and man can be mixed together

3. Some people, however, are in the habit of asking how man and God could be mixed together. They look for an explanation of this mystery, which hap-

pened once; while they are themselves totally unable to give an explanation of one that happens all the time; that is, how the soul is mixed with the body, to make a human being. So just as a bodily thing and an unbodily one are joined together to make a human being; in the same sort of way a human being was joined to God, and it made Christ. And yet, for Christ to be made, those two unbodily things, namely the soul and God, could be joined and mixed together more easily than one unbodily and another bodily thing can be, that is, soul and body, to bring a human person into existence.

But if God, the creator of heaven and earth, while being God became man, and *humbled himself to the death, even death on the cross* (Phil 2:8), how much more ought dust and ashes never to be proud? Notice, brothers and sisters, just how much God humbled himself for the sake of humanity. How much ought slaves to abase themselves, when even the Lord descended to such total humility? It's this humility, my dearest friends, that if people possess it to the full, will also develop into charity. Because while one reckons himself superior to another, love creates equality.[12] For that reason we human beings should not have a low opinion of ourselves, seeing that it was on our account that God was prepared to undergo all these things.

You are called Christ's brothers and sisters, Christ's heirs

4. And I certainly, brothers and sisters, for whom I long to spend myself and be spent over and over again, have always held you in great esteem. All the same this matter raises you even higher in my estimation, when I consider how great is my God's respect for humanity. You, of course, are the price of the Lord's incarnation, the price of his blood; you are the members of Christ, Christ is your head. For your sakes he didn't put off being born, didn't put off suffering everything for your sakes; he even endured the cross itself for this purpose—to fit you out as a family for himself. You are called Christ's brothers and sisters, you are called his heirs.

Accordingly, dearly beloved, you should each and every one of you regard yourselves as persons in whose presence it would be disgraceful for you to sin; as persons in whose presence, should you even think of doing something wrong, you should be ashamed. *For you were bought for a great price; glorify and carry God in your body* (1 Cor 6:20). This is the one who was born for you, this the one who offered himself for you; this the one who, if you conduct yourselves worthily, dwells in you. Let us so conduct ourselves then, *meditating on the law of the Lord day and night* (Ps 1:2), that we may deserve to comprehend him, to see him. Let us so conduct ourselves that because God was pleased to come down for the sake of us human beings, we human beings may be able to ascend to him.

NOTES

1. Again the Maurists are very doubtful about this sermon's authenticity; and again, as I proceeded with the translation, I came wholeheartedly to share their doubts. There are, to be sure, a number of genuine echoes of Augustine here, and of his ideas; but again it all smacks of the work of a devoted, but not very skillful imitator, an "Augustinaster," who again may possibly have been Caesarius of Arles.

2. This suggests that the sermon was being preached at the Mass at dawn of Christmas.

3. This is one of a number of expressions which the Maurists regard as utterly un-Augustinian.

4. Here I omit a sentence that baffles me completely. I find it impossible to construe, and any sense it may make appears to have nothing to do with the subject immediately in hand. I suspect it started as a shorthand comment in the margin, which came to be copied very unintelligently into the text. It runs: *passus est diem partus repudiatae Legis conceptus*. My guess is that it is alluding to the tradition that Christ suffered on 25 March, the same day as he was conceived—the feast of the Annunciation; and that this was thought to have something (I cannot think what) to do with the replacement of the Mosaic law by the gospel.

5. An allusion to the creation of all things through the eternally begotten Word, Jn 1:3.

6. See Phil 2:6-7.

7. This is another conceit which the Maurists consider quite alien to the genuine Augustine. Whether the sun is being thought of as bringing us Christ (in the mythical chariot of the sun) as "this other day" or as "this other sun," is not specified. It could be either or both.

8. Reading *quando* for the text's *quia*, because.

9. *In illa divini cultus claritate*; a rather odd use of the word *cultus*. It will be picked up in the next sentence with reference to future worshipers, *cultoribus*. This is another passage which the Maurists cannot accept as coming form the lips of Augustine. See Mk 9:2-3.

10. Here, of course, the preacher is not talking about Christ's two births, the divine and the human ones, but about our two, our birth in the flesh and our rebirth in baptism.

11. Emending the text's *Deus noster* to *Dominus noster*, for obvious reasons, and with plain enough justification.

12. Augustine could never, I am sure, have expressed himself as carelessly, as ineffectively as this. And the next sentence is a fairly glaring *non sequitur*.

SERMON 372

ON THE LORD'S NATIVITY

Date: 400[1]

The two nativities of Christ

1. Your faith, dearly beloved, which has gathered you all here in this big and representative crowd, is well aware that *a savior was born for us today* (Lk 2:11). He was born of the Father always, of his mother once; of the Father without reference to sex, of his mother without the use of it.[2] With the Father, of course, there was no womb to conceive him in, with his mother there was no male embrace to beget him. By the first nativity from the Father nature was preserved; by the second nativity from his mother the seeds of grace were sown.[3] In the former he retained the majesty of the divine substance; in the latter he took on fellowship with us in our human mortality. And the reason he was prepared to come through this latter birth was so that he might *become obedient to the death* (Phil 2:8), and by dying might conquer death.

Each of these births is inexpressible, each of them marvelous. What human mind, after all, would be capable of grasping, what tongue of explaining, how Christ is always born of the Father, or in these last times of his mother? Who could really understand the Father being coeternal with the Son, who fittingly speak of the virgin mother; understand him begetting without beginning, without end, speak of her conceiving without lust, giving birth without damage to her virginity? Each birth is marvelous, because it is divine. So whether the human mind considers that one or this one, it most properly says, *His coming to birth who shall explain?* (Is 53:8). And as for me, what am I to do, brothers and sisters? Far be it from me, far be it from the tongue of the servant to keep silent, when it is the birthday of the Lord. So let me say what I can, what I have read.

Christ both bridegroom and giant

2. The blessed David, speaking of Christ, says in the psalms, *He pitched his tent in the sun, and he, like a bridegroom coming forth from his chamber, exulted as a giant* (Ps 19:4-5). Today, you see, he came forth from his sacred chamber,

that is from the hidden and undefiled retreat of the blessed virgin's womb. From there he came forth as the son of a virgin, as the bridegroom of a virgin—the son, that is to say, of Mary, the bridegroom of the Church. The apostle, after all, was speaking to the universal Church when he said, *I joined you to one man, to present you as a chaste virgin to Christ* (2 Cor 11:2).

To such a wedding feast for Christ as this the Father first invited the people of the Jews. But what does the gospel say? *Those who were invited were not worthy* (Mt 22:8). Next the multitude of all the nations was invited; they filled the Church, they received from the Lord's table, not cheap dishes or low grade wine, but a foretaste of the flesh and blood of the shepherd himself, of the slain Christ himself. The innocent lamb was himself slain at his wedding feast, he was slain at the wedding; and all those he invited he fed on his own flesh. Being slain, he prepared the banquet; rising again, he celebrated the wedding. When he was slain he willingly endured his sufferings; when he rose again he married the wife who had been arranged for him. In the virgin's womb he received human flesh as a kind of pledge; on the cross he shed his blood as a priceless dowry; in his resurrection and ascension he confirmed the contract of this eternal marriage. *For he ascended on high, he led captivity captive, he gave gifts to men* (Eph 4:8). What gifts? The Holy Spirit, through whom charity has been poured out upon human minds,[4] and the Church has been attached inseparably to Christ as her husband.

So he came forth today like a bridegroom from his sacred chamber, and as the psalm continues, *he exulted as a giant to run the course* (Ps 19:5). He came forth as a bridegroom, he exulted as a giant. Beautiful and strong; beautiful as a bridegroom, strong as a giant. Beautiful so as to be loved, strong so as to be feared; beautiful to give pleasure, strong to win victories. Where in the sacred scriptures is the beauty of this bridegroom to be found? *Handsome in form above the sons of men; grace is poured out on your lips* (Ps 45:2). Where is the giant's strength to be found? *The Lord strong and mighty, the Lord mighty in battle* (Ps 24:8). Each quality, though, that is both beauty and strength, had been seen and understood by Isaiah, when he said, *Who is this who is arriving from Edom, the crimson of his garments from Bozrah, so handsome in the robe of his garment with strength?* (Is 63:1). So this prophet, who called him both handsome and strong, knew him as bridegroom and giant.

Human life is a torrent, in which Christ comes as a life-saver

3. So, dearly beloved, *he exulted as a giant to run the course* (Ps 19:5). Which course, if not the course of our mortality, which he was willing to share with us? This course is the way along which the human race passes. They all pass along it, you see, starting on it when they are born, finishing it when they die. And this stream of the human race from beginning to end is constantly issuing from the hidden sources of nature. It was from this rapid and turbulent stream that Christ was willing to drink. You heard just now in the psalm, *From the torrent he drank in the way* (Ps 110:7). This torrent has brought us to birth, has

carried us on to death. As though from the hidden source of a spring, Christ has taken to himself the very depths of the sea.[5] Each for our sake—he was both born and died.

Now human beings, caught in the middle of this river, more often than not take pleasure in the allurements and attractions of the world, which dredge up the mud of this torrent, and which plunge into the depths of hell those who greedily gulp the waves as they pass through them, and in this way effectively get killed. They are eager to stand in this rushing torrent, and to fix their steps firmly in an essentially slippery substance.[6] And that is why *from the torrent the Lord drank in the way*. What does it mean, *drank in the way*? Drank while passing along. He drank, you see, and passed along, he didn't stay; nor did he *stand in the way of sinners* (Ps 1:1).

Again, human beings dread death; because all are bound to be swept away by the tremendous force of this torrent. Christ, though, could not be afraid of the death he had spontaneously taken on. That's why it said, *He exulted as a giant to run the course*. He came down, you see, and ran; he ascended, and took his seat. You know that, because you are in the habit of confessing it in the creed: "After he had risen, he ascended into heaven, he is seated at the right hand of the Father." This course run by our giant was succinctly and beautifully turned into song by the blessed Ambrose, in the hymn you sang a few moments ago:

From the Father he came forth,
To the Father he returned;
His outward course to the realms of death,
His homeward course to the throne of God.[7]

If we ask, dearly beloved, why all this was done, we shall discover it was all done for our sakes. He came down, you see, so that we might ascend; he died, so that we might live; he rose again, so that we might rise again; he ascended into heaven, so that we might learn to think lightly of earthly things, and to raise up our hearts to the things that are above. Finally, to lift up our hope after him, he first lifted up his own flesh; and to give us hope that this was going to follow in our case, that which he had received from us went on ahead.

NOTES

1. The Maurists are again extremely doubtful about the authenticity of this sermon; but this time I do not altogether share their doubts, while not being absolutely sure of its genuineness. The style, for the most part, does strike me as vintage Augustine—a fairly early vintage. The reference at the end to the congregation's having just sung one of Ambrose's hymns is in my view a point in favor of authenticity, rather than telling against it as the Maurists argue. So impressed had Augustine been by the hymns he heard the people singing in Milan at the time of his conversion, that I am sure he would have lost no time in introducing them into the Church of Hippo Regius when he became bishop.

2. This rather feeble antithesis—and there will be other similar weaknesses—is one of the things

cited by the Maurists as evidence of inauthenticity; they consider it "insufficiently accurate," *haud satis accurate pronuntiatum*, for Augustine. But we have from time to time found him capable of much less "accurate pronouncements" than that.

3. This is, I must admit, a very peculiar contrast between nature and grace to find Augustine making, if he is the one who made it. His usual contrast is between created, especially human, nature and grace, whereas here "nature" must be referring to the divine nature. And again, to the best of my knowledge Augustine rarely uses the word "nature" of God, preferring to talk of the "divine substance." But if this is, as I suggest, a fairly early pre-Pelagian sermon, such looseness of theological language would not argue strongly against Augustinian authorship.

4. See Rom 5:5.

5. At first sight a very confused image; but in fact true to the biblical picture of the world, according to which the deep of Gn 1:2, the abyss, as well as being usually identified with the sea, was also thought of as underlying the whole world; the dry land resting on top of it, supported on pillars (Ps 74:3), rather like a contemporary oil-drilling rig. And it was from the abyss, the deep, that rivers drew their supply of water.

6. *In re labili*, the emendation suggested by the Maurists of the text's *in republica*. As text, this makes no sense; but it could have been a monastic reader's skeptical comment in the margin, to the effect that politics, public affairs, *res publica* are the *res labilis* in which it is absurd to try to stand firm, as people "in the world"—and a good many medieval monks—so often tried to do. Then, as so often happened, the marginal comment passed into the text, and in this case, cuckoo-like, pushed aside the genuine reading.

7. This is the fifth verse of the hymn for the second vespers of Christmas in the old Dominican breviary—I believe in the Roman breviary it had, like all the old hymns, been rewritten to suit the "classical" taste of the Renaissance, after the Council of Trent. It runs:

> *Egressus ejus a Patre,*
> *Regressus ejus ad Patrem;*
> *Excursus usque ad inferos,*
> *Recursus ad sedem Dei.*

SERMON 373

Date: 413[1]

Christ manifested to the Magi as to the firstfruits of the nations,
having been announced first to the shepherds as representatives of the Jews

1. The solemnity we are celebrating today has been given the Greek name of Epiphany, because it's about the manifestation of the Lord. Today, that is, he is being presented to us as manifested to the Magi, who had come as the firstfruits of the nations to worship one who had been born, we are told, only a few days before. He is that cornerstone who coupled together, as it were, in his own unity the two walls, coming from different angles, of the circumcision and the uncircumcision, of the Jews that is to say and the Gentiles, and who thus *became our peace, who made both into one* (Eph 2:14). Therefore, that he might be announced to the Jewish shepherds, angels came from heaven;[2] and that he might be worshiped by the Gentile Magi, a star shone brilliantly from the sky.[3]

So whether by means of angels or of a star, *the heavens declared the glory of God*; so that by the grace of the one who was born the apostles too might declare it, carrying news of the Lord like the heavens, and that *their sound might go forth to all the earth, and their words to the ends of the wide world* (Ps 19:1.4). And since this news has also come as far as us, *we believe, therefore we also speak* (2 Cor 4:13).

The wonderful paradoxes involved in the story

2. So then there are many things to be considered, brothers and sisters, in this reading from the gospel which we have heard. Magi come from the east, they are seeking the king of the Jews, though there had previously been so many kings of the Jews, whom they had not sought. They are seeking, though, not a grown man, or one of great age, conspicuous to human eyes on a lofty throne, with a mighty army, spreading terror by force of arms, splendid in purple, with a diadem of dazzling jewels;[4] but a newborn baby, lying in a cradle, eager for the breast, not notable for any adornment of the body, any strength of limb, any wealthy parents, or for his age, or for the power of his family.

And they are seeking the king of the Jews from the king of the Jews; from Herod they are seeking Christ;[5] they are asking a grown man about an infant, someone famous about someone unknown, someone wealthy about someone needy, someone strong about someone weak; and yet[6] someone contemptuous about someone to be worshiped, one in whom no royal state could be seen, but in whom true majesty was to be worshiped.

The fate and destiny of the holy innocents

3. Finally, Herod is afraid, the Magi are eager; they are longing to find the king, he is in dread of an end to his kingdom. Both, to conclude, are seeking: they, one through whom they can find life; he, one he was determined to kill; he, one against whom to commit a great sin; they, one who would forgive them all their sins.[7] Herod accordingly kills many little children, in his determination to bring about the death of just one. And while he carried out this most celebrated[8] and cruel slaughter of so many innocents, he was himself the first one he slew by such an utterly wicked deed.

Meanwhile the Magi were kneeling in adoration before our king, before the speechless, infant, Word, and little children were dying for him. Whether lying in the manger or sucking the breast, having as yet not spoken at all, he was already finding believers; and not yet having suffered himself, he was already making martyrs. O blessed babes, only just born, never tempted, never engaged in the struggle, already crowned as victors! Let those have doubts about your reward in your suffering for Christ, who also don't think that the baptism of Christ is of any use for babies.[9] You were not indeed of an age to believe in Christ who was going to suffer; but you already had the flesh in which to endure suffering for the sake of Christ who was going to suffer. In no way would the grace of the infant savior abandon these infants, seeing that he had come *to seek what was lost* (Mt 18:11), not only by being born in the flesh, but also by hanging on the cross.[10]

I mean, if he was able, as soon as he was born, to have angels proclaiming him, the heavens declaring him,[11] the Magi adoring him, he was also able to prevent these children dying for him here, if he knew that by such a death they would be lost, and not rather be living in much greater bliss. Perish, indeed perish the thought that Christ who came to set mankind free, should have done nothing about rewarding those who were slain on his behalf, seeing that while he was hanging on the cross he prayed for those by whom he was himself being slain.[12]

The Jews compared to milestones, which give directions
along the way without moving along it themselves

4. What am I to say about the miserable state of the Jews, who answered the inquiries of the Magi about the Christ by producing a prophecy that indicated the place, by designating Bethlehem? They were like the builders of Noah's ark, providing others with the means of escape, and themselves perishing in the

flood.[13] Like milestones, they showed the way, and were incapable of walking along it.[14] They were asked where the Christ was to be born. They answered, *In Bethlehem of Judah. For thus it was written by the prophet*—they were repeating from memory, you see, what had been written about this:[15] *And you, Bethlehem, land of Judah, are not the least among the leaders of Judah; for from you shall come forth the king who is going to be the shepherd of my people Israel* (Mt 2:5-6; Mic 5:2).

The inquirers heard and went on their way; their informants spoke and stayed where they were. Divided from each by contrary sentiments, the former became worshipers, the latter persecutors. Nowadays also the Jews continue to provide us with something similar. There are quite a few pagans, you see, to whom we present the clear testimonies of scripture to show them that Christ had been prophesied beforehand, and they suspect that they may have possibly been made up by Christians; so they prefer to trust the texts of the Jews. And just as the Magi did at that time, they leave these fruitlessly reciting, while they themselves go off faithfully to worship.

Today's feast offers us a spiritual spectacular

5. And so let us exult in the Lord as we celebrate the Lord's feast day; not only the day on which he was born of the Jews, but also the one on which he was manifested to the nations. It is pleasant to contemplate all the details, and bringing them all together in one purview, to let our minds gaze upon a spiritual spectacular. The Christ is born; a virgin conceives, gives birth as a virgin, suckles as a virgin, granted fertility without loss of integrity. Angels proclaim him, shepherds glorify him, the heavens declare him, the Magi desire him, kings are in dread of him, the Jews point the way to him, Gentiles worship him. Raging foes are frustrated, infants receive crowns of victory, believers are lost in wonder.

What is this sublimity of one so lowly, this strength of one so weak, this greatness of one so small? Assuredly that Word made all these things come about, through which *all things were made* (Jn 1:3). The Word, which was far away from us, *became flesh, to dwell amongst us* (Jn 1:14). And so let us acknowledge in time the one through whom all times were made; and in celebrating his temporal feast, let us long for our eternal reward.

NOTES

1. The date is a pure guess on my part. The reference in section 3 to those who deny the point of infant baptism, indicates that it was preached after the Pelagian controversy arose, but not very long after. This points to two possible years, 412 or 413. If it was preached at Epiphany 412, it was preached at home in Hippo Regius, while if it was the following year, January 413, it was preached

in Carthage. The rather self-conscious elegance of the style inclines me to favor the latter. At this time in his ministry, Augustine only seems to have taken more than usual pains over his style when preaching to the more sophisticated audiences he would find in the great metropolis.

The text has been embellished in several places by later copyists and editors. The Maurists, following one of their oldest manuscripts, have judiciously pruned these pious excrescences by putting them in brackets. I ignore the minor ones, and put the rest in the endnotes.

2. See Lk 2:8-14.

3. See Mt 2:1-2. Here the Maurists' oldest manuscript actually adds a clause they are probably wise to omit: "and that the Magi as the sample of the nations might be saved, they were admonished by a new light among the stars."

4. Here some manuscripts add what surely started as a pious reflection in the margin: "or exulting in his cross, by which he redeemed all the martyrs who confessed him; or rising again from hell, or ascending into heaven."

5. Here there is another such addition: "... God and man, from an earthly king and man, the king of heaven who had made man."

6. And here another: "Herod the persecutor about Christ the ruler of themselves and others."

7. Some wordplay here: a contrast between *in quem grande peccatum committat*, and *qui omnia sibi peccata dimittat.*

8. So that one ancient manuscript. The rest emend *celebratissimam* to what they clearly consider a more suitable *saevientissimam*, most savage. There is again in this sentence a piece of wordplay, contrasting *perfecit*, carried out, with *interfecit*, slew, at the end of the sentence.

9. The Pelagians. See note 1.

10. Here another addition: "by descending into hell, and ascending into heaven, and sitting at the right hand of the Father."

11. See Ps 19:1.

12. See Lk 23:34.

13. Gn 6 says nothing about others helping Noah build the ark. Is this just an assumption of the preacher's, that Noah must have employed a considerable work-force in his dockyard? Or was there some rabbinic *midrash* to that effect?

14. See Sermon 199, 2, which was also preached on the Epiphany, for this comparison.

15. This aside is contained in that one ancient manuscript favored by the Maurists, and omitted by all the rest—as also by the Maurists themselves, rather cravenly in my opinion. It does not strike me as the sort of comment a copyist or reader would put in the margin, while it is the sort of comment Augustine himself would make. He is emphasizing that the scribes knew the passage by heart, and did not have to "search the scriptures" in order to find it, when the Magi came along with their question.

SERMON 374

ON THE LORD'S EPIPHANY

Date: 402[1]

> *The Magi must have had the meaning of the star*
> *they had seen revealed to them by angels*

1. The annual celebration of this day exacts an annual sermon from me, a debt owed to your ears and minds. Today our savior led the Magi to himself from such a faraway nation. They came to worship an infant, the Word of God. Why did they come? Because they had seen an unusual star. And how did they know it was Christ's star? I mean, they could see a star; could it speak to them and say, "I am the star of the Christ"? There can be no doubt that they were shown this by some other means, by some revelation. Still, a king had been born in unusual circumstances, one who was to be worshiped by foreigners. Hadn't kings been born before in Judea, or throughout the whole earth in different nations? Why was this one to be worshiped, and worshiped by foreigners, with no army to cow them, but in the poverty of the flesh, concealing the majesty of his power?

When he was born, he was worshiped by Israelite shepherds, to whom angels had proclaimed him;[2] but the Magi were not of the nation of Israel. They worshiped the gods of the nations, that is to say demons, whose deceptive powers were constantly leading them astray. So they saw some unusual star, they were astonished; they undoubtedly asked themselves whose sign it might be, this new and unprecedented thing they had seen. And they certainly heard the answer, evidently from angels, from some revealing suggestion. You will ask, perhaps, "From good angels, or bad ones?" Bad angels too, indeed, that is to say demons, confessed that Christ was the Son of God.[3] But why shouldn't they have also heard it from good angels, seeing that it was their salvation that was already being sought by worshiping Christ, and not iniquity that was controlling them? So it could have been angels saying to them, "The star you saw is the Christ's; go and worship him where he has been born, and at the same time indicate precisely who and what it is that has been born." When they heard this, they came and worshiped him. They offered gold, frankincense and myrrh, according to their custom.[4] Such were the gifts, after all, that they were accustomed to offer their gods.

324

Christ pointed out to the Gentiles by the Jews themselves

2. Before they did this, of course, before they found him in the city where he had been born, they came with their inquiry, *Where has the king of the Jews been born?* (Mt 2:2). Couldn't they have also come to know this by revelation, just as they had come to know that that star was the star of the king of the Jews? Couldn't the same star have led them to that city, just as later on it led them to the place where the infant Christ was to be found with his mother?[5] Of course it could have, but still that didn't happen, so they have to make this inquiry from the Jews. Why did God want to have this inquiry made of the Jews? So that while they point out the way to the one in whom they don't believe, they might be condemned by their own action in doing so. Notice how at this point the Magi become the firstfruits of the nations,[6] giving all the greater glory to their deliverer, the more impious the religious practices they have been delivered from. They inquire, *Where is the one who has been born king of the Jews?* When Herod hears the name "king," he trembles as at the threat of a rival.[7] He summons the learned lawyers, he asks them to indicate according to the scriptures where the Christ would be born. They answer, *In Bethlehem of Judah* (Mt 2:3-5). The Magi went on and worshiped him; the Jews stayed behind, though they had shown where he was.

What a significant dispensation! Still today we are using the volumes of the Jews to convince people; their volumes are making Christian believers. Thus we show pagans something they are unwilling to believe; because sometimes pagans put this sort of question to us, when they see that what has been written in the scriptures has been fulfilled in such a way that they can't possibly deny it; things happening through the name of Christ among all nations that have been foretold in the holy books—kings coming to believe, idols overthrown, a revolution in human affairs. And sometimes they have the nerve to say, "You saw all these things happening, and you wrote them up as though they had all been foretold." This is what one of their own poets did; those who have read it will catch the reference. He told the story of someone going down to the underworld, and coming to the region of the blessed, where he was shown the rulers of the Romans that were going to be born, who as the writer knew had been born.[8] He was, you see, telling the story of past events; but he wrote of them as though they were future events being foretold. "In the same way you people too," the pagans say to us, "have seen all these things happening, and you have written volumes for yourselves in which these things can be read about as predicted."

Oh, the glory of our king! How appropriate that the Jews were conquered by the Romans, and yet not absorbed! All the other nations subjugated by the Romans took over the laws and customs of the Romans; this nation was both conquered and still remained with their own law; as far as the worship of God is concerned, they preserved their ancestral customs and rites. Even though their temple has been demolished and their ancient priesthood extinguished, as foretold by the prophets,[9] they still keep circumcision and a certain way of life which distinguishes them from other nations. For what purpose but for bearing witness to the truth? The Jews have been dispersed everywhere, carrying the books in which Christ is proclaimed and presented just as he was foretold, so that it can now be pointed out to the pagans. I bring out a volume, I read a prophet, I point out how the prophecy has been fulfilled; the pagan has his doubts, he wonders whether I had fabricated it all myself. My enemy has the same volume, handed down to him from of old by his ancestors. From this I convince them both; the Jew, because I know that it was prophesied and has been fulfilled; the pagan, because I certainly didn't fabricate it.

The one true sacrifice offered to the one true God

3. So don't let the demons, with their specious divination, lead astray the careless and those who are idly curious about temporal affairs; nor deceive the godless with their proud disdain, and exact from them the honor of being offered sacrifices. Truly divine things have been foretold by the disciples of one divine man.[10] True sacrifice is owed to the one true God. Before the era of grace, this sacrifice was foreshadowed and prefigured by various sacrificial victims. What was going to be accomplished in one way was foretold in many ways by divine providence, to show how great this true sacrifice would be. He is the medico, and he is also the medicine; the medico because he's the Word, the medicine, because *the Word became flesh* (Jn 1:14). He is the priest, he the sacrifice. He it is that changed the way of the Magi;[11] he that also now changes the lives of the wicked.

It is his manifestation in the flesh, which in Greek is called Epiphany, that the nations who have been justified in spirit[12] are all celebrating together in today's solemnity. Let us hope that the solemn celebration may refresh our memories, piety may be invigorated by our devotion, charity may be more fervent in our congregation, truth may shine upon the ill-disposed.[13]

NOTES

1. Again, this date is pure guesswork on my part, based on the sermon's style. The opening sentence indicates that Hippo Regius was the place. All this, of course, if it is a genuine sermon of Augustine's. The Maurists doubt it, largely because of two points in its content this time: the preacher's argument that the Magi must have been told by angels that the star they had seen heralded the birth of the king of the Jews; and the explanation of their gifts as being what they customarily offered to their gods, which differs from that given in Sermon 202, 2. Neither point seems to me inconsistent with Augustinian authorship. But I must confess that the last section does give me pause; see note 13 below.

2. See Lk 2:9-13.

3. See Mk 5:7.

4. See Mt 2:11.

5. See Mt 2:9-11.

6. See 1 Cor 16:15.

7. Reading *tanquam aemulum contremiscit*, instead of the text's *tanquam aemulus* . . ., like a rival.

8. Virgil, writing about Aeneas being guided through the realms of the dead by his late father Anchises, *Aeneid*, 6, lines 752-887.

9. See Heb 7:12.

10. The Maurists confess that the text here is confused. As it stands, the disciples of the one divine man (Christ) are in this context the prophets.

11. Possibly an allusion to Mt 2:12, where the Magi are warned in a dream to return home by another way. But even so, the deeper meaning of the preacher would have been that Christ changed the idolatrous star-gazing ways of the Magi who, we must never forget, were thought of as *magicians*, wizards, practitioners of the black arts, which the demons were always trying to involve people in.

12. See 1 Tm 3:16; 1 Cor 6:11.

13. The sermon ends with a very forced piece of rhetoric, a series of phrases ending respectively with the words *solemnitas, pietas, caritas*, and *veritas*. This whole final section does rather smack of a labored imitation of Augustine rather than of the genuine article.

SERMON 375

ON THE LORD'S EPIPHANY

Date unknown[1]

Christ the cornerstone, manifested first to the Jews, then to the Gentiles

1. Epiphany, in English,[2] is manifestation. Christ was manifested to the Jews a few days earlier, when he was born; while today he is declared to the Gentiles by means of a star. *The ox acknowledged its owner, and the donkey its master's manger* (Is 1:3). The ox from the Jews, the donkey from the Gentiles; both came to the one manger, and found the fodder of the Word. The Magi who came to worship Christ, and who represent the firstfruits of the nations,[3] had not received the law, had not heard the prophets; a star was the language of heaven for them. As though they were told, "What advantage have I looked for from you? *It is the heavens that declare the glory of God* (Ps 19:1)."

And yet Herod was troubled, and inquired of the Jews where the Christ was to be born. And they answered, *In Bethlehem of Judah* (Mt 2:5); and they quoted the evidence from the prophet; and when the Magi went off to worship, they themselves remained unmoved and motionless. They are milestones on the causeway; they point the way, and don't walk along it themselves. Still, the Magi went off to Bethlehem; but when they had found the town, how could they find the house? Lo and behold, the star which shone in the sky, and led them along on the earth, *stood over the place where the child was* (Mt 2:9).

What service from the elements, and what wickedness from the Jews! Herod was troubled, as if Christ had come to seek and find an earthly kingdom. The lion of heaven[4] was born, and the little fox of the earth was troubled. The Lord said of Herod, *Go, tell that fox* (Lk 13:32). Because it was troubled, what did it do? It slaughtered infants. What did it do? It slaughtered infants in place of the infant Word.[5] They were made martyrs by the shedding of their blood, before they could confess the Lord with their mouths. And these are the firstfruits that Christ sent to the Father. An infant came, and infants went; an infant came to us, infants went to God. *From the mouths of infants and sucklings you have perfected praise* (Ps 8:2).

Let us rejoice, *the day has dawned for us.*[6] The Magi, as firstfruits of the nations, represented us. The Jews acknowledged him when he was born, the

Gentiles acknowledged him today.[7] Divergent walls have come to the corner-stone, the Jews from there, the Gentiles from here. You have seen and you know that the further walls are from the corner, the further they are from each other; as they approach the corner, so they approach each other; when they reach the corner, they join each other. This is what Christ did. Jews and Gentiles were far away from each other, the circumcision and the uncircumcision, people of the law, and those without the law, the worshipers of the one true God, and of many false ones. How far away! But he *is our peace, who has made both one* (Eph 2:14).

But those who came from the Jews are to be counted as being in a good wall; because those who came did not remain in the ruin. We have become one, they and we; but in the one, not in ourselves. Of what stock was Christ born? Of the Jews. That's what you find written: *Salvation is from the Jews* (Jn 4:22); but not only for the Jews. He didn't say, after all, "Salvation is for the Jews," but *Salvation is from the Jews*. They seized him, and they lost him; they bound him, and he put them to flight;[8] they saw him, and killed him. We haven't seized him, and we hold onto him; we haven't seen him, and we believe in him; we came later, and we are going on ahead. Those who went in front of us have lost the way; we though have both found the way and by walking along it we shall reach the home country.

NOTES

1. The Maurists have doubts about the authenticity of this sermon, which I certainly share. The preacher confuses the Herod of this story, Herod the Great, with the Herod Antipas, his son, whom Jesus called a fox. Augustine on the other hand, in his work *The Harmony of the Gospels* 7, and elsewhere, clearly distinguishes them. Apart from that slip, we do seem to have in this short sermon several Augustines mixed together rather crudely; observe, for example the preacher's treatment of the Jews at the end, both as one of the two walls joined together in Christ the cornerstone, and as the people who rejected Christ. Both attitudes, of course, authentically Augustinian, but here, I feel, slapped together as though there were no tension between them at all.

2. *Latine* of course, in the Latin text.

3. See 1 Cor 16:15.

4. See Rv 5:5.

5. In the Latin the connotation in the word *infans* of incapacity for speech is unmistakable.

6. *Nobis illuxit dies*. My memory tells me this is a line from one of Ambrose's hymns, but fails to tell me which one. See Ps 118:27.

7. The text says "yesterday," but the Maurists sensibly suggest reading "today." Perhaps some copyist was copying the sermon the day after Epiphany.

8. This seems to be an allusion to one of the Samson stories; see Jgs 16:7f.

SERMON 375A

ON THE SACRAMENTS

Date: 397[1]

Christ both lamb and lion

1. As the truth has it, that resounded through the apostles, and *their sound went forth into all the earth, and their words to the ends of the wide world* (Ps 19:3-4), *Christ our passover has been sacrificed* (1 Cor 5:7). This had previously been foretold by the prophet: *Like a sheep he was led to be slaughtered, and like a lamb in the presence of his shearer he was without voice, thus he did not open his mouth.* Who is this? Obviously the one about whom he goes on to say, *In humility his judgment was taken away. His generation, who shall relate?* (Is 53:7-8). I can see this model of such humility in a king of such power and authority. Because this one, who is like a lamb not opening its mouth in the presence of the shearer, is himself *the lion from the tribe of Judah* (Rev 5:5). Who is this, both lamb and lion? He endured death as a lamb, he devoured it as a lion. Who is this, both lamb and lion? Gentle and strong, lovable and terrifying, innocent and mighty, silent when he was being judged,[2] roaring when he comes to judge.

Or perhaps both in his passion lamb and lion, and also in his resurrection lamb and lion. Let us see him as a lamb in his passion. It was stated a moment ago: *Like a lamb in the presence of his shearer he was without voice, thus he did not open his mouth.* Let us see him as a lion in his passion: Jacob said, *You have gone up, lying down you have slept like a lion* (Gn 49:9). Let us see him as a lamb in his resurrection: the book of Revelation, when it was talking about the eternal glory of virgins, *They follow the lamb*, it said, *wherever he goes* (Rv 14:4). The same book of Revelation says, what I mentioned just now, *The lion from the tribe of Judah has conquered, to open the book.* Why a lamb in his passion? Because he underwent death without being guilty of any iniquity. Why a lion in his passion? Because in being slain he slew death. Why a lamb in his resurrection? Because his innocence is everlasting. Why a lion in his resurrection? Because everlasting also is his might.

330

2. Who is this lamb and lion? How can you ask who he is, if this is what he was before: *In the beginning was the Word*; if this is where he was before: *and the Word was with God*; if this is what sort of Word he was: *and the Word was God*; if this is the kind of power he had: *all things were made through him*; if this is what he became: *and the Word was made flesh* (Jn 1:1.3.14)? If you want to know how he was either from the Father without a mother, or from his mother without a father, *his coming to birth who shall declare?* (Is 53:8).

Begotten from all eternity, co-eternal with his begetter; remaining the Word, becoming flesh; creator of all times, created at the appropriate time; the prey of death, the predator of death; *deformed in posture beyond the sons of men* (Is 53:2-3), *handsome in figure beyond the sons of men* (Ps 45:2); *knowing how to bear infirmity* (Is 53:3), and how to bear it away; so sublime that he could do lowly things; so lowly that he could do sublime things; the God of man, and a man who is God; both firstborn and creator of the firstborn;[3] only Son, and also brother of many;[4] born of the Father's substance, and made a partner with the adopted children;[5] both Lord of all, and slave of the many.

This is the lamb, *who takes away the sins of the world* (Jn 1:29); this is the lion, who has conquered the kingdoms of the world. We were asking who this one is; let us ask who those are for whom this one died. Was it perhaps for the just and the holy? That's not what the apostle says, but rather that *Christ died for the ungodly* (Rom 5:6); not of course so that they might remain ungodly, but so that the ungodly might be justified by the death of the just, and that by the shedding of sinless blood, the liability of sin might be cancelled.[6]

NOTES

1. The most recent editor of the text suggests 396 or 397. In that text the heading of the sermon runs, "Here begins another sermon on the sacraments, preached on the same day." The same day as which? Hardly as Denis 3 (this sermon being Denis 4), which has already appeared in this series as Sermon 228B. The editor of this sermon in the appendix to Augustine's works in Migne's *Patrologia Latina* (PL 46, 828-829)—Dom Frangipane at the beginning of the nineteenth century?— seems to suggest that it may have been Sermon 229. But seeing that both Denis 3 and Denis 5 have almost exactly the same heading, we must conclude that the scribe or copyist of Folio 5, from which these sermons have been edited, did not mean on the same numerical day, but simply on Easter Day. Nobody questions the authenticity of the sermon.

2. See Mk 15:5.

3. See Heb 12:23.

4. See Heb 2:11-12.

5. See Gal 4:5-6.

6. See Col 2:14. One manuscript here concludes with the words, "End of sermon on the sacraments on Easter Day." It is abundantly clear that the sermon is not about the sacraments at all.

SERMON 375B

SERMON OF AURELIUS AUGUSTINE ON THE FIRST HOLY DAY OF EASTER

Date: 391[1]

We all have to die; blessed are the martyrs who repaid Christ's
dying for them by themselves dying for him

1. We heard the gospel; the resurrection of our Lord Jesus Christ was read.[2] Christ rose again, so that means Christ had died. Resurrection is proof of death, while the death of Christ is the extinction of fear. Let us not be afraid to die; Christ died for us. Let us die in the hope of eternal life; Christ rose again so that we might rise again. In his death and resurrection we have a task prescribed for us and a reward promised us; the task prescribed is suffering, the reward promised is resurrection. The martyrs carried out the task completely; let us carry it out by godliness,[3] if we cannot do it by martyrdom. It doesn't, you see, fall to everyone's lot to suffer for Christ and to die for Christ; yet simply to die does fall to everyone's lot. Fortunate are those to whom what has to happen did happen for Christ's sake. There was no escaping, I mean, the necessity of death; but there was no necessity of its being death for the sake of Christ. Death is going to come to all, but not for all will it be death for Christ.

Those to whose lot it fell to die for Christ paid back, after a certain fashion, what had been spent for them. Christ had spent for them his dying for them; they paid it back to him by dying for him. But how could needy wretches pay anything back, if the Lord with his fortune hadn't given them the means? And so it was precisely what Christ had spent on the martyrs that gave them the means of paying it back to Christ. This, you see, is the voice of the martyrs: *Unless the Lord had been in us, they would perhaps have swallowed us alive* (Ps 124:1-2); our persecutors, he is saying, would no doubt have swallowed us alive. What's the meaning of "alive"? Knowing that we would be doing something evil if we denied Christ, and yet we would have done such a great evil alive, that is knowingly; and in this way they would have swallowed us alive, not dead. What does "alive" mean? Knowingly, not in ignorance. And by what strength did they not do what the persecutors were trying to force them to do? Let us question them, let them tell us themselves. Here you have their reply: *Unless the Lord had been in us.* So he gave them what would be paid back to him. Thanks indeed be to him; he is rich, and what's written about him is true: *He became poor, to make us rich* (2 Cor 8:9). We have been enriched by his poverty, healed by his wounds,[4] raised up high by his humility, justified by his death.

The Jews cannot boast that they defeated Christ

2. *What shall I repay the Lord for all that he has paid to me?* is what some martyr was saying. Listen to what follows. He was considering, you see, and wondering what he could repay the Lord; and what did he say? "*I will take the cup of salvation* (Ps 116:12-13); this is what I will repay the Lord, the cup of salvation, the cup of martyrdom, the cup of suffering, the cup of Christ." That's what the cup of salvation is, because our salvation is Christ. "So I will take," he says, "his cup and I will repay him." It's about this cup that he himself also said to the Father before he suffered, *Father, if it can be so, let this cup pass from me* (Mt 26:39). He had come to suffer, he had come to die, he had death entirely in his power. Or, if you think I'm lying, listen to Christ himself: *I have the power*, he says, *to lay down my life, and I have the power to take it up again. Nobody can take it from me, but I lay it down of myself, and I take it up again* (Jn 10:18.17).

You heard the power he has? Nobody can take his life. The Jews have no reason for boasting. The part they play in Christ's death is sin, not power. Christ died, because it was his will; he himself says in a psalm, *I myself went to sleep, and I slumbered* (Ps 3:5). They clamored, *Crucify him, crucify him* (Lk 23:21). They held him, they hanged him. Thus they are pleased to think that they had the power to do it. *I myself went to sleep.* And what next? *And I slumbered.* Indeed, a three days' slumber. So what next? *And I rose again, since the Lord upheld me* (Ps 3:5). He is speaking in the form of a servant[5] when he says *the Lord upheld me*, just as he is in another place: *Will not the one who goes to sleep take steps to rise again?* (Ps 41:8).[6] They, to kill him, hanged him on the cross; but *I myself went to sleep*, because when I so willed I laid down my life, and when I so willed I rose again.

Christ speaking in two voices, human and divine

3. So the very cup he wanted to pass from him is the one he had come to drink. So what's the meaning, Lord, of what you said, *Father, if it can be so, let this cup pass from me* (Mt 26:39)? You said to your disciples, as you were going to your passion and death, *My soul is sorrowful to the point of death* (Mt 26:38). So what I'm looking for in these words is those other words of yours, *I have the power to lay down my life, and I have the power to take it up again* (Jn 10:18). From where do I hear, *My soul is sorrowful to the point of death*? Nobody can take your life away; why are you filled with sorrow? You have the power to lay down your life; why are you saying, *Father, if it can be so, let this cup pass from me*?

He answers your question, and says to you, "Man, in my flesh I took you to myself; so then, if I took you to myself in my flesh, didn't I also take you to myself in my voice? When I say, *I have the power to lay down my life, and I have the power to take it up again,* I am speaking as myself as maker; when I say, *My soul is sorrowful to the point of death,* I am speaking as you, as the thing made. Rejoice over me as myself in me;[7] recognize yourself in me. When I say, *I have the power to lay down my life,* I am your helper; when I say, *My soul is sorrowful to the point of death,* I am your mirror."

4. Haven't you read that he died? We don't deny it, do we?[8] If we deny his death, we also deny his resurrection. He died in virtue of his readiness to be a human being; and he rose again in virtue of his readiness to be a human being, because we too are human beings, and we are going to die, and we are going to rise again. Did the Word in him die? Could that suffer anything, which *in the beginning was the Word, and the Word was with God, and the Word was God* (Jn 1:1)? What can such a Word as that suffer? And yet it was necessary that he should die for us; he was unable to die, and it was necessary that he should die. *In the beginning was the Word, and the Word was with God, and the Word was God.*

Where's the blood? Where's the death? There's no death in the Word, is there, no blood in the Word? If there's neither death in the Word nor blood in the Word, where is our price? Or isn't his blood our price? So what would he pay this price with, if he just remained the Word, if the Word did not take flesh? Flesh, though, made alive and animated by a human soul, so that since the Word could not be killed, only the flesh would be killed, which was animated by its own soul. The soul, after all, couldn't be killed either. By adhering to the divinity this soul was one spirit with the Word, as a result, that is to say, of the Lord clothing himself with it; not as a result of its believing in him, as it says about us, *Whoever joins himself to the Lord is one spirit* (1 Cor 6:17). We, after all, when we were unbelievers, were unworthy and alienated from God; but it was by believing that we adhered to God. But that soul was created worthy of adhering to God, when it was taken up, all fresh and new, into the unity of the divine person. When this single unity of two unequal spirits departed from it, the flesh died. It had been made alive by this unity of two spirits in a new way and with a new kind of life, that is to say it had a marvelous kind of twin life; by this it was abandoned for just a short time. God, I mean, as spirit, and his image the human spirit, are both immortal.

5. So this is roughly how the Lord our God, our savior, addresses us, saying, "Men, I made man upright, and he has made himself crooked.[9] You have withdrawn from me, you have got lost on your own; but I am going to seek what had got lost.[10] You have withdrawn from me," he says, "and you have forfeited

life; *and the life was the light of men* (Jn 1:4). There you have what you abandoned, when in Adam you all perished. *The life was the light of men.* What life? *In the beginning was the Word, and the Word was with God, and the Word was God. In him was life*;[11] you were all laid out in your death. As Word, I had no means of dying; you, as human beings, had no means of living."

Because the Lord Christ is so amenable, I have made his words my own; if he has made mine his own,[12] how much more may I adopt his! As though speaking in silence, through the events themselves, our Lord Christ says, "I had no means of dying; you, man, had no means of living. I took from you the means by which to die for you; now you take from me the means by which to live with me. Let's strike a bargain; I give to you, give something to me. From you I receive death; from me receive life. Bestir yourself; notice what I am giving, what I am receiving. Though sublime in heaven, I received from you lowliness on earth. Though I am your Lord, I received from you *the form of a servant* (Phil 2:7). While I am your health, what I received from you were wounds; while I am your life, what I received from you was death. While I am the Word, I became flesh, in order to be able to die. I had no flesh with the Father; it was from your lump[13] that I received what I would spend for you"—the virgin Mary was part of our lump; that's where Christ took flesh from us, that is from the human race. "I took flesh from you, in which to die for you; receive the life-giving spirit[14] from me, with which to live with me. In a word, I died from what is yours; see to it that you live from what is mine."

The whole Christ is Word and soul and flesh

6. So, brothers and sisters, when you hear "He was born of the Spirit from the virgin Mary, he suffered, was flogged, was slapped in the face";[15] when you hear, "Christ suffered these things," do not imagine that that Word, who was in the beginning with God, could suffer any such thing in his own nature and his own proper substance. But then on the other hand, can we say that the Word of God, *God the only-begotten* (Jn 1:18), did not suffer for us? He did suffer, but in his soul and flesh which were capable of suffering. He took, after all, *the form of a servant* (Phil 2:7), in order to suffer as a human being. He had, you see, both soul and flesh, because he had come to set free the whole person, not by losing life, but by granting life.

But let us provide a comparison, from which you may grasp more quickly what I am saying; for example, when the martyr Stephen, or Phocas[16] or any other suffered and was killed and buried, it was their flesh alone that was killed and buried, while their souls could be neither killed nor buried; and yet we are quite right in saying, "Stephen or Phocas or anybody else died for the name of Christ." In the same way, when the only-begotten Son of God suffered and was killed and buried, it was of course only his flesh that was killed and buried; but his soul, and much more his divinity, could not be killed. And that's why[17] we say without a qualm that the only Son of God, that is God the only-begotten Son of God, died for us and was buried.

Thus it was of course true and no lie, what Christ the Lord himself said, he being the Truth[18] without any falsehood: *For God so loved the world that he gave his only-begotten Son, so that everyone who believes in him might not perish, but might have eternal life* (Jn 3:16). And the apostle says something similar about God the Father: *Who did not spare his own Son, but delivered him up for us all* (Rom 8:32). But do you wish to know what Christ is? Don't only think of the flesh which lay in the tomb; don't only think of the soul, of which he said, *My soul is sorrowful to the point of death* (Mt 26:38); don't only think of the Word, because *the Word was God* (Jn 1:1); but remember that the whole Christ is Word and soul and flesh.

The errors of the Apollinarists and the Arians about the soul of Christ

7. Take care, however, not to subtract anything from the soul of Christ. The Apollinarist heretics, you see, said that he didn't have a mind; that is to say, his soul didn't have intelligence, but the Word did duty for its mind and intelligence. That's what Apollinaris said. The Arians, though, say, "He didn't have any kind of soul at all."[19] So you, then, must faithfully hold that the whole Christ is most certainly Word and soul and flesh. And when you hear, *My soul is sorrowful* (Mt 26:38), you must understand it of a human soul, not a brute soul; a soul without intellect, after all, is the soul of a beast, not a human one. So Christ is one, Word and soul and flesh. What is a human being? Soul and flesh. What is Christ? Word and human being, and thus Word and soul and flesh, one Christ.

When you hit a man with your fists, what part of him are you striking, soul or flesh? You admit that it's the flesh. And yet the soul cries out, "Why are you striking me? Why are you hitting me?" If you said to the soul, "Who touched you? I'm whacking the flesh, not you," wouldn't whoever heard you saying this laugh at you, and put you down as either stupid or plain crazy? So in the same way, those who scourged the flesh of the Word who is God,[20] or slapped his face, cannot say, "We scourged, or slapped the face of the flesh, not the Word or the soul of Christ"; in fact, they scourged the whole Christ, or slapped him in the face, that is they scourged or slapped the Word and the soul and the flesh; it wasn't, after all, his dead body that they scourged or slapped in the face. And while, of course, they were unable to kill on the cross either his soul or his very divinity, which is the true life, still they were delighted in their hearts and their ill-will to be slaying the whole Christ.

Anyone, after all, who's going after somebody to kill him, wants the whole of him extinguished, just as the whole light of a lamp is extinguished when it is dashed to the ground, so that it gives no light at all, when some malefactor sees that it is obstructing his activities. This cannot, of course, happen in any way at all with human beings, that is that the whole person should be extinguished, because of course while they have one element that is mortal, they have another that is immortal; the only thing that's mortal in them, after all, is the flesh. Much less, though, could Christ the only-begotten Son of God be totally extinguished, though the Jews thought they were eliminating him; of his three elements, that is, one eternal and divine, and two temporal, that is human ones, he only had one that was mortal, that is his flesh; while the soul he had and supremely the divinity were without a shadow of doubt immortal. And that is why he alone by his suffering death for a very short time was able to redeem us from our eternal death, because he was not only flesh and human soul, but being God and soul and flesh he was the one only-begotten Son of God. *For it was the one who descended to the lowest parts of the earth that also ascended above all the heavens* (Eph 4:9-10). This was something a mere man could not do.

Christ's triumph over death

8. So without a worry in the world, *let us exult and rejoice* (Ps 118:24), dearest brothers and sisters, because we have been redeemed by the death of the one, who even when slain triumphed over his enemies. For when he was slain he slew death, and delivered us forever from its hands,[21] *and ascending on high took captivity captive*, and by sending the Holy Spirit *gave his gifts to men* (Eph 4:8); and even while lying in the tomb, he was able to bring the faithful thief into paradise.[22]

NOTES

1. This date is purely my personal guess; none of the scholars suggests any particular date. My reasons for dating it so early, in fact the first Easter after Augustine's ordination to the priesthood, are first, that such a long sermon on Easter day indicates the still inexperienced pastor; secondly, in a reference to the Arians in section 7 he doesn't mention their main error, but only a comparatively secondary conclusion from it. Had he been preaching later on, after he had started his work on the Trinity in about 400, let alone after the arrival of the Arians in North Africa with Gothic mercenaries about 420, he would certainly have mentioned their refusal to accept the Word as consubstantial with the Father. The sermon, like all the Easter sermons, was preached in Hippo Regius, given its genuine authenticity, which nobody seems to question.

2. Almost certainly according to Matthew; Mt 28:1-15, or even, very likely, the whole chapter.

3. See 2 Tm 3:12: *All who wish to live in a godly way in Christ will suffer persecution.* So godliness necessarily involves suffering, even if not martyrdom in the full sense.

4. See Is 53:5.

5. See Phil 2:7.

6. In the Hebrew it is the psalmist's enemies saying exactly the opposite. Augustine's text represents a reinterpretation of the verse by the Septuagint Greek translators.

7. Reading *Gaude de me in me* with Denis and Frangipane; a later edition of the text reads . . . *de me in te*, over me in you.

8. The only people who would have denied the reality of Christ's death would have been the Docetists some centuries earlier, and also the Manichees of Augustine's time. What they really denied was the reality of the incarnation.

9. See Eccl 7:29.

10. See Lk 10:19.

11. Reading *In ipso vita erat*. The text simply reads *Vita erat*, He was life. A copyist could have

inadvertently left out *In ipso*, because he had just started another sentence, a line or two above, with *Vita erat*; The life was the light of men.

12. When he said, *If it can be so, let this cup pass from me.*

13. Mankind compared to a lump of dough—one of Augustine's favorite figures for the fallen human race, which he will regularly call a *massa damnata*, a batch or lump that has been condemned in the bakery, as unfit for human consumption. His only New Testament source for the figure is Rom 11:16, where Paul uses it in an altogether more positive sense. Paul also uses the word for the lump of clay from which the potter can make vessels for honorable and dishonorable use, Rom 9:21.

14. See 1 Cor 15:45.

15. In the recitation of the creed, no doubt. But I think it unlikely that the credal formula in Hippo Regius contained such details of Christ's passion as that he was flogged and slapped in the face. These I take to be the preacher's elaboration of the phrase "he suffered."

16. Why Phocas—and which Phocas anyway? The cult of Stephen, of course, was very popular in the African Church, but there is no evidence, apart from this allusion here, to any Saint Phocas being honored there. The editor of the text in PL 46—Frangipane?—suggests that of the three Saints Phocas, of whom one was from Antioch, and two from Sinope on the Black Sea coast of Asia Minor, one a bishop of the town, the other a market gardener, it was the last named who is being referred to, as he was very popular with sailors for doing miracles at sea, and ships from Sinope would no doubt have been seen from time to time in the harbor of Hippo Regius. In any case such a devotion would have spread widely among seafarers, wherever they sailed from.

17. Not because his soul and divinity could not be killed; but because in the analogy we say Stephen or Phocas died, not just that their flesh died; the passion or action is referred to the one whole person. In fact, implicit in his argument is the unity of person of the Word incarnate, which he will go on shortly to state quite explicitly.

18. See Jn 14:6.

19. Apollinaris was a staunch supporter of Athanasius in his fight against the Arians; he was also a member of the Alexandrian school of theology, which insisted above all, in its christology, on the unity of person of the Word incarnate; and it was to accentuate this unity that Apollinaris said that in Christ the Word took the place of a human mind. The strongest reaction against this error came from the school of Antioch, represented by Diodore of Tarsus, and later by Theodore of Mopsuestia, who insisted on the full and complete humanity of the Word made man.

The Arians' denial that Christ has a human soul at all was a little known by-product of their principal thesis that the Word, the Son, is a creature, the first of all creatures, but still a creature of almighty God. So being on the created side of the creator/creature dividing line, he could act as the soul, the vivifying principle, of the flesh he took.

20. Or "of the Word of God." The Latin, *Verbi Dei*, is ambiguous.

21. See Ps 49:15.

22. See Lk 23:43.

SERMON 375C

PREACHED ON THE THURSDAY OF EASTER WEEK

Why Thomas was allowed to touch the risen Christ,
while Mary had been told not to

1. Today's reading of the holy gospel[2] has again revealed the Lord to the servants, Christ to the apostles, and it convicts, while convincing,[3] the unbelieving disciple. One of the twelve disciples, you see, the apostle Thomas, refused to trust, not only the women, but also the men who told him of the resurrection of the Lord Christ. And this, certainly, was an apostle who was to be sent out preaching the gospel. So when he began to preach Christ later on, how did he expect to be believed himself about what he had not himself believed? I rather think he used to feel ashamed of himself, when unbelievers started heckling him.

His fellow disciples say to him, his fellow apostles indeed, *We have seen the Lord.* And his answer to that was, *Unless I put my hands in his side, and touch the places of the nails, I will not believe* (Jn 20:25). He wanted his faith to be backed by touching. Well, if the Lord had come in order to be touched, how can he say to Mary in that part of the reading that was read first, *Do not go on touching me, for I have not yet ascended to the Father* (Jn 20:17)? To a woman who believes he says *Do not go on touching me*; to a man who does not believe he says, "Touch me." Mary, you see, had already run to the tomb, and had at first thought that the Lord standing there was the gardener, and had said, *Sir, if it is you that have taken him away, tell me where you have put him, and I will take him away.* But the Lord answered her with her name, *Mary.* She immediately recognized the Lord in the way he said her name; he called her by it, and she knew him. By calling her name he gave her the happiness of knowing him. So as soon as she heard her name spoken with that authority and tone he was accustomed to use, she herself answers in the way she is accustomed to: *Rabboni* (Jn 20:15-16). So Mary had now believed, and the Lord says to her, *Do not go on touching me, for I have not yet ascended to the Father.*

339

For Thomas to touch Christ was the cure for his unbelief

2. But now in that part of the reading which sounded most recently in your ears, what did you hear Thomas saying? "I won't believe, unless I touch." And the Lord says to this Thomas, "Come, touch, *put your hands into my side, and do not be incredulous, but believing* (Jn 20:27). I," he is saying, "if you don't think it's enough for me to offer myself to your eyes, am also offering myself to your hands. Perhaps, you see, you are one of those who sing in the psalm, *In the day of my trouble I sought the Lord with my hands in the night in his presence* (Ps 77:2)." Why was he seeking with his hands? Because he was seeking in the night. What does that mean, was seeking in the night? He was carrying the darkness of unbelief in his heart.

This happened, though, not only on his account, but also on account of those who were going to deny that the Lord had real flesh. It would have been possible, after all, for Christ so to heal the wounds in his flesh that no trace of scars remained; it would have been possible for him not to carry the traces of the nails in his hands and feet, not to carry the trace of the wound in his side; but he permitted those scars to remain in his flesh in order to remove from people's hearts the wound of unbelief, and to take care of their real wounds with the signs and traces of his own wounds. This one, you see, who permitted the signs of the nails and the lance to remain in his body, knew that some time or other there were going to be godless heretics with such twisted minds, that they would say our Lord Jesus Christ both lied about his flesh, and told lies in so many words to his disciples and our evangelists, when he said, "Touch and see." There you have Thomas with his doubts. What sort of doubts? *Unless I can touch him, I can't believe.* He gratuitously[4] makes faith depend upon touch. *Unless I touch him,* he says, *I will not believe* (Jn 20:25). What, do you suppose, will a Manichee say? "Thomas saw, and Thomas touched, and Thomas felt the places of the nails, and it wasn't real flesh." So if he had been present then, he wouldn't have believed even by touching.

3. So would your graces please note what a horrifying pestilence this is, what a detestable deceit, what an unbelievable impiety. Notice what a difference there is between Saint Mary Magdalene, who as soon as she heard *Mary,* at that one word from Christ believed he had risen—so between her faith and that of the two men who, as soon as they saw Christ in the breaking of bread, immediately believed,[5] what do we suppose is the difference? What can it be? She saw him, it would seem, in the half light of dawn,[6] they saw him in broad daylight; yet both they and she believed on seeing. Later he appeared to all the disciples, and *they thought they were seeing a spirit* (Lk 24:37). He relieved them of this vain idea, and implanted in them the surest truth.

They thought they were seeing a spirit. That's what the Manichees also think, that Christ was a spirit, that he wasn't flesh. Very well, remain in such a faith yourself, if Christ wished his disciples to remain in it. You think Christ was a spirit, and appeared as a phantom, that is, as though there wasn't real flesh in Christ; that's what the disciples thought too. You have been wounded with the disciples, let yourself be healed with them. When the disciples thought this, that

Christ was a spirit, and that what they were seeing was more of an apparition than a reality, what did the Lord do? *"Why, he said, are thoughts coming up in your hearts?* No enemy has come at you from outside, and inside you thoughts are murdering your souls, your own thoughts about me. *Why are thoughts coming up in your hearts?"* What sort of thoughts? *Because they thought they were seeing a spirit.*

The Lord fears such thoughts, afraid they may kill the faith of the disciples. So be afraid yourselves of having such thoughts. No patient is unconcerned about what the doctor fears. *Why are thoughts coming up in your hearts? See my hands and my feet; feel and see, that a spirit does not have bones and flesh, as you can see that I have* (Lk 24:38-39). They saw, and they touched, and they believed, they proclaimed the good news. And the Manichees still contradict about Thomas. "I won't believe, unless I touch"; so then, *Do not be incredulous* (Jn 20:25.27). The Lord's scars were false, were they, and the words of the Manichee are true? Perish the thought! On the contrary, the Lord's words are true, the bones the Lord showed them were true and real, the scars were real. They were real limbs and body which he carried up to heaven; but decay and liability to decay he did not carry up to heaven. It was flesh that said, "Death is dead."

What was meant by Mary being told not to touch Jesus

4. Let's get back to that question about Saint Mary. Here we have him being touched by the disciples: *Feel and see that a spirit does not have bones and flesh, as you can see that I have* (Lk 24:39). He's touched by doubting Thomas, who exclaims, *My Lord and my God.* And to him the Lord says, *It is because you have seen that you have believed. Blessed are those who do not see, and believe* (Jn 20:28-29). "Those to whom you proclaim me outdo your faith. You proclaim what you have seen, proclaim what you have touched, proclaim what you scarcely believed even by seeing and touching; and yet those who have neither seen nor touched are going to believe you. You see me, and you don't believe me; you touch me, and you scarcely believe me; others hear you, and believe in me."

But you are asking, "Why is it that Thomas is allowed to touch, and Mary is told, *Do not go on touching me?"* He gave the reason in that very place: *For I have not yet,* he said, *ascended to the Father* (Jn 20:17).

"What is all this? Here you are on earth, and you don't allow yourself to be touched; when you've ascended, who can touch you? While you are still on earth, you repulse the hand right there beside you."

In this place we can make a very neat guess, and say, "The Lord did well to reserve touching him to the incredulous; he forbids this woman to touch him, because she had already believed in him. What need, after all, was there for her to touch and seek one whom she had recognized on hearing him?

But all the same he didn't keep quiet, but went on to give the reason. *Do not go on touching me.* Why not? *For I have not yet ascended to my Father;* touch me as I ascend to the Father.

What's "Touch me as I ascend to the Father"?
Touch me as equal to the Father.
What's "Touch me as equal to the Father"?
Touch me as God, that is, believe in me as God.

It's easy to believe what you can see. It's the form of a servant,[7] taken on for your sake, it's a garment God is wearing; it isn't a great thing to see flesh. The Jews also saw, who killed me; the nations did not see, and believed.

So, he is saying, in the way you can see me, limbs in the flesh, the likeness you know, in the way you can see me *do not go on touching me*; that is, don't stick there, don't just look that far, don't let this be the final goal of your faith. I want you, indeed, to believe that I am a man, but don't stick there; stretch out the hand of faith further, don't stick there.

The error of Photinus to be avoided, that Christ was only a man

5. Don't touch in the way that the heretic Photinus touched;[8] he said Christ was a man, nothing more; so he didn't grasp the truth, he didn't understand, he didn't really touch that *The Word was made flesh, and dwelt amongst us* (Jn 1:14). So to stop her thinking of Christ as only a man—"*Do not go on touching me* (Jn 20:17). In front of you is simply my garment; keep in mind its having been made in heaven.[9] Stretch out the hand of your heart, and then you are touching me when I ascend to the Father." That's how all those have touched who have confessed, *He ascended into heaven, he is seated at the right hand of the Father.*[10]

There you are, that's how the Church touches, which was being represented by Mary. Let us touch Christ, let us touch him. Believing is touching. Don't just stretch your hand out as far as the man; say what Peter said, *You are the Christ, the Son of the living God* (Mt 16:16). So don't see Christ as only a man; because if you touch him in the way the heretic said, you will be like Photinus. But again, don't shun Christ the man, just don't stop there. I'm not telling you to turn away from there; what am I telling you? Don't stop there. The person who wants to stop and stay somewhere on the way doesn't reach his lodging. Get up, start walking; Christ as man is your way, Christ as God is your home country. Our home country, *the truth and the life* (Jn 14:6); our way, *the Word was made flesh, and dwelt amongst us* (Jn 1:14). We were being lazy about walking; the road, the way, came to us. Because the road has come to us, let's start walking. Christ the man is our road. Don't let's abandon the road, and then we shall attain to him as the only-begotten Son of God, equal to the Father, surpassing the whole of creation, coeternal with the Father, day without day, the craftsman of faith. Let that be the reason for our walking, let us touch that.

Christ is touched by faith, as in the case of the woman
suffering from the flow of blood

6. That, finally, is how the woman touched him who was suffering from a flow of blood. What faith there must have been in her, for the Lord to say to her, "Now betray yourself and show yourself openly to the crowd; receive praise from the same source as you received your health!" *Go, daughter, your faith has healed you, go in peace* (Mk 5:34). If you're asking what faith, listen: *She said to herself, If I can touch the hem of his garment, I shall be healed* (Mk 5:28). She touched in order to obtain what she had believed; she didn't touch in order to have the fact that she had believed publicly approved of.[11] Then the Lord starts asking, and saying *Who touched me?* (Lk 8:45).

So don't you know, Lord, who touched you? You can see thoughts, and you ask questions about actions? What's the meaning of *Who touched me?*

I will show you who touched me; faith touched me; it's faith that by its touch made power go out from me. Where I have never been, where I have never walked, where I wasn't born, that's where they have believed in me. *A people whom I did not know became my servants* (Ps 18:43).

What a splendid touch, what belief, what insistence! And this is what a woman did, worn out with loss of blood, like the Church afflicted and wounded in its martyrs by the shedding of their blood, but full of the strength of faith. She had previously spent her fortune on doctors, that is on the gods of the nations, who had never been able to cure her;[12] to this Church the Lord has presented not his bodily but his spiritual presence. So now this woman who's touching and the Lord who's being touched know each other. But in order that those who needed to know how to obtain salvation might be taught how to touch, he said, *Who touched me? And the disciples answered, The crowds are jostling you, and you can say, Who touched me?* As though you were in some lofty place where nobody can touch you, is that how you ask who touched you, while you are being jostled continuously by the crowds? The Lord said, *Someone touched me* (Lk 8:45-46). I felt one woman touching me more than the whole crowd jostling me. The crowd knows well enough how to jostle; if only it could learn how to touch!

Jesus Christ, true God and true man

7. Let the conclusion of our talk, brothers and sisters, be this: that we should believe our Lord Jesus Christ to be before Abraham,[13] before Adam, before heaven and earth, before angels and archangels and thrones and dominations and principalities and powers,[14] before all things that have been established and made, whether things that can be seen or things that cannot; coeternal with the Father without any space of time, any number of years, equal to the Father, the Father's true only-begotten Son, the power and wisdom of the Father;[15] equally everlasting, equally immortal; and truly immortal, because altogether unchangeable; equally invisible, because incorporeal; equally mighty, and indeed almighty. Such let us believe the only-begotten Son of God to be.

But remember, when we say, *and in Jesus Christ his only Son our Lord*, remember what follows: *who was born of the Holy Spirit and Mary the virgin.*[16] He was born of his mother without a father here below on earth, having already been born of the Father up above without a mother before time was, the one who was going to make time. Now, near the end of all times, he was begotten in true flesh of true flesh. But his flesh, while having *the likeness of the flesh of sin* (Rom 8:3), was not the flesh of sin. And why did it have the likeness? Because it was mortal. And why was it not the flesh of sin? Because it had come through the faith of the virgin. Now it was this very flesh of Christ that grew, this very flesh that came to the age of manhood. It was in this flesh that Christ was hungry, was thirsty, ate, drank, felt tired, rested, slept; in this flesh all those things, sin nowhere in it at all. In it he suffered, in it he was revealed openly as man, concealed as God, seeking man in a man, seeking the one that was lost through the one that was taken on.

So it was in this flesh that he suffered unworthy things from men for the sake of man himself. It was true flesh that was held by the Jews; it was true flesh that ate the passover with the disciples. It was true flesh that the Jews knocked about, true flesh that the Jews crowned with thorns, true flesh that unbelieving they hanged upon the tree; true flesh that when the soul had departed miserable unbelievers pierced with the lance; true flesh that disciples took down from the tree, and placed in a tomb; true flesh that Truth brought back to life; true flesh that Truth showed to the disciples after the resurrection; the scars of true flesh that Truth presented to the hands of those who would touch him. Let Falsehood then be ashamed, because Truth has conquered.

NOTES

1. The date 402-404 is proposed, I believe, by Dom Morin. The sermon was, of course, preached in Hippo Regius.

2. The whole of Jn 20.

3. This is a double translation of the single Latin word *convincit*, which can mean both "convict" and "convince"—and does, I think, mean both here.

4. Emending the text's *ultra*, besides, into *ultro*. One editor reads *vel*, He even makes . . .

5. See Lk 24:30-31.

6. *Quasi in subobscuro*; I presume this is the rather pointless point he is making. Why he should bring in the two disciples on the road to Emmaus at all, it is hard to see.

7. See Phil 2:7.

8. Photinus was bishop of Sirmium in Hungary in the middle of the 4th century.

9. *Serva factum in caelo.* The word *factum* need not necessarily refer to the *vestimentum*, the garment of the first phrase, which is how I have translated it. But if it doesn't, it would mean "Keep in mind what has been done in heaven." Now would Augustine ever refer to the eternal begetting of the Son—which is in general what he is thinking of here—to the divinity of Christ, as *factum*? I really doubt it. So here, by suggesting that Christ's humanity was made in heaven, as I interpret him, he is pointing through it to what it was made for: to clothe the divine Word; and hence to Christ's equality with the Father.

10. In the Apostles' Creed.

11. Reading, *ut quod crediderat probaretur,* instead of the text's *ut quod non crediderat probaretur,* in order to have what she had not believed put to the test. What that might mean I cannot conceive. I think a copyist inadvertently slipped in another *non,* having just written *non tetigit,* she didn't touch; or else a copyist, being stupidly clever, thought that the first sentence, *Tetigit ut quod crediderat . . .,* had to be balanced here by *non tetigit ut quod non crediderat . . .*

12. See Lk 8:43.

13. See Jn 8:58.

14. See Col 1:16.

15. See 1 Cor 1:24.

16. From the Apostles' Creed, in the form used by the African Church as its baptismal creed.

SERMON 376

ON THE SUNDAY AFTER EASTER

Date: 411[1]

How could the risen Christ enter a room through closed doors?

1. Your graces heard, when the holy gospel was read, how our Lord and savior Jesus Christ, after his resurrection, came in to his disciples when the doors were closed.[2] A marvelous miracle; but you stop marveling, if you reflect that it's God. I mean, it would be marvelous if a mere man had done this. Ascribe it to omnipotence, not to a phantom.[3]

"But he came in while the doors were closed."

My answer to you, so that you may know it was real flesh, is that he showed them his scars to be touched.[4]

"But[5] it isn't in the nature of a solid body to enter through a closed door."

In the same way it isn't in the nature of a solid body to walk on the waves of the sea.

"But he entered through closed doors," you answer me;[6] "give me the solidity of flesh there."

He walked on the waters of the sea; you too, give me the weight of flesh there.

Do you want to be convinced that this is the work of omnipotence? He also gave the power to do it to Peter.[7] What he wished, he gave to others, what was proper to himself, he reserved to himself. The one, after all, who entered alive through closed doors, was the one who at his birth did no damage to his mother's virginity. So then, brothers and sisters, let us marvel and believe, let us believe and obey, let us obey and hope to receive what we have been promised, if we do what we have been told; because to do what we have been told, we have the help of the one from whom we hope to receive what we have been promised.

NOTES

1. So Poque, adding that the sermon was preached in Hippo Regius in the Basilica of Peace. The Maurists, whose text is followed in this edition, said that they had no manuscripts to work on, and that they were simply reproducing earlier printed editions, which give this sermon as only the first section of a longer one, the rest of which will be found on the next page here as Sermon 376A. The Maurists agree that this section has no obvious connection with the rest; hence the sensible decision to treat the whole as two distinct sermons.

2. See Jn 20:19.26.

3. See Lk 24:37.

4. See Lk 24:39-40.

5. Omitting *sicut* of the text: But just as it isn't . . . The text makes this one sentence with the next—the scribe not realizing, in my opinion, that we have here a characteristic Augustinian conversation.

6. Reading *respondes mihi* instead of the text's *responde mihi*: answer me.

7. See Mt 14:25-29.

SERMON 376A

ON THE SUNDAY AFTER EASTER

Date: 425[1]

The unveiling of the heads today of the recently baptized is a sign of freedom

1. Today is called the octave of the "infants"; they are to unveil their heads, as a sign of freedom.[2] This spiritual birth, you see, means freedom, while birth in the flesh properly speaking means slavery. A person, of course, has two births, being born and being born again. We are born to toil, we are born again to rest; we are born to misery, we are born again to eternal felicity. Take these children, infants, babies, sucklings, clinging to their mothers' breasts—and how much grace has been conferred on them without their knowing it, as you yourselves can see; because they are called infants,[3] they too have their octave today. And these old people, young people, teenagers, they're all infants.

They have one infancy, in fact, that goes with being old, another that goes with being young and new. I mean those whom you see born very recently are born old, and there is in them when they are born, if one may so put it, a young old age.[4] Our old self is called Adam, from whom we are born; our new self is Christ, through whom we are born again. So these here are also new and young, and have been born again to another life.

The newly baptized exhorted not to imitate bad Christians

2. Here, then, are our infants, being mixed in today with the faithful, and as it were flying from the nest. So I have an obligation, as having given birth to them, to address them in particular. As you will recall, I mean, brothers and sisters, when the fledglings of swallows and house sparrows begin to fly from the nest, their mothers fly round them with a lot of noise, and with their anxious loving voices warn their children of the dangers.

So we know that many of those who are called the faithful live bad lives, and that their behavior doesn't correspond with the grace they have received; they praise God with their tongues, blaspheme him with their lives. But we know of others among these many, as in an abundant heap of chaff, groaning like grains of wheat at the threshing, but consoling themselves with the hope of the granary

348

that awaits them. We know that there are these two kinds of people in the Church. We know the Church is the Lord's threshing floor; we are hoping for the winnowing on the day of judgment, we are looking forward to the heap of corn in the resurrection, we are longing to claim the granary in eternal life.[5] There won't be any chaff there, just as in hell there won't be any grain.

So now, my brothers and sisters, while we know there are these two sorts of people in the Church, the godly and the ungodly, the good and the bad, those who fear and those who ignore God, what we don't know is to which sort these here will attach themselves. What we wish, however, they know very well themselves, but whether our wishes will be realized in them—well, human ignorance tires us out with anxiety, and sometimes torments us with false suspicions. That's the kind of lesson we learn on this earth, where one cannot live without trials and temptations.

So let me warn you, holy seedlings, let me warn you, fresh plants in the field of the Lord, not to have it said of you what was said of the vineyard of the house of Israel: *I expected it to produce grapes, but it produced thorns* (Is 5:2). Let him find good bunches of grapes on you, seeing that he was himself a bunch of grapes trodden in the winepress for you. Produce grapes, live good lives. *For the fruit of the Spirit*, as the apostle says, *is charity, joy, peace, tolerance, kindness, goodness, gentleness, faith, self-control, chastity* (Gal 5:22). When our farmer comes to us, whose laborers we are, while he produces growth from within—I mean, we know how to plant and water outwardly, but as the apostle says, *Neither the one who plants is anything, nor the one who waters; but God who produces growth* (1 Cor 3:7), who now sees how you listen, who now observes how you fear him, or are now beginning to fear him—so when that farmer comes, may he find in you what the apostle said: *My joy and my crown, all of you that are standing firm in the Lord* (Phil 4:1).

Imitate the good, beware of the bad

3. Brothers and sisters, my sweetest children, dearest children, imitate the good, beware of the bad. You see, I know that bad people are going to come to you, and are going to try and persuade you to indulge in drunkenness, and they are going to say to you, "Why not? Aren't we too very staunch believers?" Yes, I know they will, that's what saddens me, that's what I'm afraid of. If you, now, say firmly, "Brother, I don't even want *you* to do what you are doing; but if I can't lead you over to my good example, at least don't drag me over to your bad one"; these people, as commonly happens, will start getting headaches.[6] Your neighbor, or his wife, is going to say to you, "There's a good witch-doctor here, a good healer here, somewhere or other there's an astrologer." What you say is, "I'm a Christian, that sort of thing is forbidden me." And if he says to you, "Why not? Am I not a Christian too?" you are going to say, "But I am one of the faithful."[7] And he will answer you, "And I too have been baptized."

Members of Christ become the devil's angels. Because he's possessed by the enemy, he tries to catch another one too for him. May the one who has prepared these traps for you[8] find you prepared. That's why I'm speaking, that's why I'm calling you to witness, that's why I'm not keeping quiet, that's why I'm shaking my garments, that's why I'm claiming to be excused at the judgment seat of my God. I will say to my God, "Lord, I didn't keep quiet; Lord, I didn't hide the talent you gave me, but invested it." What he might say to me is, *Wicked servant, you should have given, I would have collected* (Mt 25:26-27). "Look, Lord, I did give, it's for you now to collect."

And if, perhaps, your fancy's ever tickled by old bad habits, you have someone you can appeal to for help. Your helper is greater than your attacker. That's why you groan, that's why you pray, that's why you say, *Lead us not into temptation.* Notice too, my brothers and sisters, what you say just before: *Forgive us our debts,* in order to carry out what follows: *as we also forgive our debtors* (Mt 6:13.12). You give alms, you receive alms; you pardon, you are pardoned; you are generous, you are treated generously. Listen to God, saying, *Forgive, and you will be forgiven; give and things will be given to you* (Lk 6:37-38).

Keep the poor in mind. I say this to all of you;[9] give alms, my brothers and sisters, and you won't lose what you give. Trust God. I'm not only telling you you won't lose what you do for the poor; but I'm telling you plainly, this is all that you won't lose; you will lose the rest. Come now, let's see if you can cheer the poor up today. You be their granaries, so that God may give to you what you can give to them, and so that he may forgive whatever sins you have committed. *Shut an alms up in the hearts of the poor, and it will pray for you to the Lord* (Sir 29:12, Vulg), to whom be all honor and glory forever and ever. Amen.

NOTES

1. This is simply my own guess, based on style and tone. Like all his Easter sermons, this one was clearly preached in Hippo Regius; or if not in the city, at least in the diocese.

2. That the newly baptized at Easter were given white garments to wear throughout Easter week, to be discarded when they were "mixed with the faithful" on the following Sunday, is common knowledge. That they were also given special veils or headgear to wear is something not mentioned in liturgical histories and commentaries. Veiling the head, presumably with a fold of the toga, while offering a sacrifice, was an element in the traditional pagan Roman religion.

3. It is a confused, unconstruable sentence. But he is evidently saying that the babies among the newly baptized were infants in two senses: as actual babies, and as born again Christians, like the others he goes on to list.

4. I have transferred this second part of the sentence, beginning "and there is in them," to this place from the end of the section, where it seems out of place.

5. A strange way of stating a simple enough thought: *horreum in vita aeterna sumere cupimus.* It would surely have been more natural to say, *in horreum vitae aeternae sumi cupimus,* we long to be taken into the granary of eternal life.

6. He surely means *you* will get a headache sometimes, and then they will try to lead you astray with what follows.

7. As distinct from a catechumen, who would also rank as a Christian, but not as a *fidelis.*

8. The devil.

9. That is, I imagine, not only to the *infantes,* whom he has been addressing in particular up till now.

SERMON 377

ON THE LORD'S ASCENSION

Date: 425[1]

Christ, the king of glory

1. Who, I ask you, dearly beloved brothers and sisters, could worthily utter a time-bound word about the eternal Word? How may the lowest kind of things suffice to express the great ones? The heavens praise him, angelic hosts praise him, celestial powers praise him, the lights of heaven praise him, the constellations praise him, as best it can even the earth praises him; not so as to praise him worthily, but so as not to convict itself of ingratitude. Who will ever explain, who describe, who even form an idea of the one who *reaches mightily from end to end, and disposes all things sweetly* (Wis 8:1), and how he exulted to run his course, so that his going out might be from the height of heaven, and his return as far as the height of heaven?[2] If he reaches everywhere, where does he come out from? If he reaches everywhere, where does he go to? He is not extended through places, nor does he vary with time, nor does he come and go; while abiding in himself, he encompasses everything in his entirety. What spaces are there that do not have within them the almighty, that do not hold the infinite and the immeasurable, that do not welcome him when he comes?

If you are thinking of the Word, I've said nothing. But in order to teach the humble how to say something about himself, *he humbled himself, taking the form of a servant* (Phil 2:8.7). In this form he came down,[3] in this form he made progress in the study of wisdom,[4] in this form he practiced exemplary patience, in this form he fought bravely, in this form he died, in this form he conquered death and rose again, in this form he returned to heaven, having never departed from heaven. Blessed, therefore, is he in the firmament of heaven,[5] *who became a curse for us*, in the apostle's words, *in order that the blessing of Abraham might be found among the nations* (Gal 3:13.14).

He exulted like a giant (Ps 19:5). What sort of giant? One who conquered death by dying. What sort of giant? He smashed the gates of hell; he came out and ascended. *Who is this king of glory*, on whose account some princes are told, *Take away your gates, princes; and lift yourselves up, everlasting gates*? Lift yourselves up, he's tall, you're low, you can't take him; lift yourselves up. Why this? *That the king of glory may come in.* They are terrified; *Who is this king of glory?* (Ps 24:7-8). He isn't recognized. He isn't only God, but also man; he isn't only man, but also God. He suffers; is he definitely God? He rises again; is he definitely man? Or is he both God and man? After all, he really suffers, and he really rises again.

Now this is said twice in one and the same psalm: *Take away your gates, princes, and lift yourselves up, everlasting gates, and the king of glory will come in.* And this is repeated after the same words, in a way that might be thought superfluous and unnecessary. But in the repetition of the same words pay attention to how they end, and notice why it's said twice. It's as if, you see, to the one who rises again once and ascends once, gates are opened twice, both those of hell[6] and those of heaven. It's a new thing, after all, God present in hell; it's a new thing, a man taken up into heaven. At each moment, at each point, princes are terrified: *Who is this king of glory?*

How can we tell this? Listen to the reply given to each. The first questioners are told, *The Lord, the valiant and mighty, the Lord mighty in war* (Ps 24:8). What sort of war? Undergoing death for mortals, suffering alone for all, the almighty not resisting, and yet conquering death in dying. Great indeed, then, is the king of glory, even in the netherworld. This is also repeated to the heavenly powers: *Take away your gates, princes, and lift yourselves up, everlasting gates.* Or are those not everlasting gates, whose keys were entrusted to Peter?[7] But because he lifts up a man also with him to heaven, it's as if he isn't recognized there either, and they ask, *Who is this king of glory?* But there, because he is no longer a contender but the winner, because he isn't fighting, but celebrating his triumph, the reply here isn't *The Lord mighty in war,* but *The Lord of hosts, he is the king of glory* (Ps 24:9-10).

NOTES

1. In older editions than that of the Maurists this sermon was headed "On the Lord's nativity." The Maurists corrected this to "On the Lord's ascension" from the manuscripts; but the only kind of manuscripts they had were lectionaries, which are not very sure guarantees of authenticity; so they are hesitant about this, while conceding that the sermon has something of Augustine's style about it. On the assumption that it is authentic, I would tentatively date it rather late, about 425.

2. See Ps 19:5-6.

3. See Jn 3:13.

4. See Lk 2:52.

5. See Dn 3:56, Vulgate; Song of the Three Young Men, 34, Revised Standard Version Apocrypha.

6. Hell, *inferi,* is being thought of more as the realm of death than of eternal punishment.

7. See Mt 16:19.

SERMON 378

ON THE DAY OF PENTECOST

Date: 420[1]

The gift of the Holy Spirit is an earnest of eternal life

1. God takes pleasure in a solemn festivity which is an expression of active piety and of fervent charity. That is, after all, the effect of the presence of the Holy Spirit, as the apostle teaches us when he says, *The charity of God has been poured out in our hearts through the Holy Spirit which has been given to us* (Rom 5:5). So the coming of the Holy Spirit filled a hundred and twenty men and women gathered together in one place.[2] When the Acts of the Apostles were read, we heard that there were gathered together in one place one hundred and twenty persons, holding on to the promise Christ had made. He had said, you see, that they should stay in the city until they were vested with power from on high. *For I*, he said, *will send what I have promised upon you* (Acts 1:4; Lk 24:49). Faithful in his promises, generous in keeping them. After ascending into heaven, he sent what he had promised while on earth.

We now have a pledge of eternal life to come and of the kingdom of heaven. He didn't cheat us of what he had so recently promised, and is he going to cheat us of what we are looking forward to in the future? When people enter into a business contract, and wish to have their minds set at rest by financial guarantees, they all, for the most part, receive or give an earnest. And the earnest given creates confidence that the property of which an earnest has already been handed over will in due course follow. The earnest Christ has given us is the Holy Spirit. And the one who could not possibly cheat us has all the same given us security, when he gave us this earnest; even if he hadn't given it, he would most certainly grant us what he has promised. What has he promised us? Eternal life, as the earnest of which he has given us the Holy Spirit. Eternal life is the possession of those who have reached home; the earnest is the reassurance of those who are still on the way there.

You see, it is better to call it an earnest than a pledge.[3] I mean, while these two things seem to be much the same as each other, there is still a difference between them that is not to be ignored. Both when a pledge is given and when an earnest is given, the reason it's done is to ensure the fulfillment of a promise;

353

but when a pledge is given, you give back what you have received, once the matter has been settled for which you received the pledge; when an earnest is given, though, it isn't taken back, but is added to for the matter to be settled.

So we have an earnest; let us thirst for the very fountain from which the earnest comes. As an earnest we have a kind of dew-fall in our hearts of the Holy Spirit; if any are aware of this sprinkling, they should long for the fountain. Why, after all, do we have an earnest, if not to save us from fainting from hunger and thirst on this journey? We are hungry and thirsty, you see, provided, that is, we acknowledge ourselves to be travelers. Those who are traveling, and know they are traveling, long to reach home; and because they are longing for home, they find the traveling irksome. But if they love traveling, they forget home, and don't want to go back. Our true home is not such that we should put anything else before it.

Sometimes, you see, while people are traveling, they get rich. They were needy at home, they travel and become rich, and don't want to go back. As for us, we were all born traveling a long way away from our Lord, from the moment when he breathed the breath of life into the first man.[4] Our home country is in heaven, its citizens the angels. Letters were sent to us from our home country, urging us to return, and they are read out every day in our congregations. May the world grow cheap in our eyes, may we learn to love and prefer the one by whom the world was made.

NOTES

1. About this sermon, for which they have better manuscript sources, the Maurists are just a little less hesitant than about the last one. They say it is either one of Augustine's or of someone very familiar with his sermons. Sharing their confidence, I would ascribe it to his later years, about 420.

2. The number 120 comes from Acts 1:15. Augustine is quite right, in my view, in regarding this group of 120 people as the recipients of the Holy Spirit in Acts 2; Acts 2:1 states "They were *all* there together in the same place." The tradition which seems to have taken root in the Catholic mind, that the Holy Spirit came only upon "our Lady and the apostles," is a bad one, and not in accord with the text.

3. For the distinction between a pledge and an earnest (between *pignus* and *arrha*), see Sermons 23, 8, and 156, 16. The New Testament reference is to 2 Cor 1:22.

4. See Gn 2:7.

SERMON 379

SERMON OF SAINT AUGUSTINE ON SAINT JOHN THE BAPTIST

Date: uncertain[1]

The mystery of John the Baptist

1. The blessed John,[2] whose birthday is being celebrated today, stood out as so great a man among men, that the Lord Christ[3] bore this kind of witness to him, saying, *Among those born of women none has arisen greater than John the Baptist* (Mt 11:11). We heard, when the holy gospel was read, how wonderfully he was conceived when there was no hope of such a thing, with what a testimonial from the Holy Spirit he was begotten; his father, because he did not believe, was struck dumb; so when John was announced by the angel and not believed, he deprived his father of speech, and when he was born he loosened his father's tongue.[4] So then, receive now from me the inner significance and meaning in this great and mysterious affair.[5]

John bears witness to Christ

2. John was sent before the Lord Christ.[6] Prophets had also been sent beforehand through previous ages; there was no lack of them to proclaim Christ. In fact, from the very origins of the human race Christ did not cease to prophesy himself and foretell his own coming.[7] Last of all was born John, a human being, but one than whom none greater had ever existed. However, the Lord Jesus was going to come, not only a human being but also God; both God and human, of course; God always, human at a point in time; God before all times, human in time; God before the ages, human at the end of the age. God, who made man, thought fit for the sake of man to become what he had made. So when the Lord Jesus Christ was about to come, who is more than man, in case he should be thought to be only a man, it was right and necessary that a great man should bear him testimony.

Let us listen to both Jesus and John in their testimony about each other

3. I have put it very briefly. The brighter minds have no doubt grasped it all, but those who are slower on the uptake must not just be left behind. What I have

just said must be unfolded more openly again, with the Lord's help.[8] Christ the Lord, I am saying, is not only God, not only man, but both God and man; God who made us, man who remade us. John, however, was only a man. But how great a man? Listen to what God and man has to say about him. O Lord Jesus Christ, who is John? How great is John? *Among those born of women*, he says, *none has arisen greater than John the Baptist* (Mt 11:11).

O John, great man, than whom none greater has arisen among those born of women, now you tell me: Who is this? Tell me, great man; who is this who is thought to be only a man?

Hear who he is: *One whose sandals*, he says, *I am not fit to carry* (Mt 3:11).[9]

Hear who he is: I'm telling you John's words about the Lord Christ: *The one who has the bride*, he says, *is the bridegroom; but the bridegroom's friend—* mentioning himself—*stands and listens to him, and rejoices on account of the bridegroom's voice* (Jn 3:29). Again, here's another testimony of John's: *We*, he says, *have all received from his fullness* (Jn 1:16).

The mystery of the Word

4. Try and understand, my brothers and sisters, recall the saving mystery, have a hunger for the Word of God, grasp what I am proclaiming, and let us together find joy in the truth. Christ the Lord—inquire of John the evangelist who it was, and how great, that on our account became so little. Let him say about the Lord Christ, *In the beginning was the Word* (Jn 1:1). What does Moses say? *In the beginning God made heaven and earth* (Gn 1:1). What does John say? *In the beginning*, not "God made the Word," but *was the Word*. The Word was, before heaven and earth were made in the beginning; the Word was, so that this might be made—but God's Word, in case through familiarity with human words you should think lightly of the Word through which it was made. Listen to John: *The Word was with God, and the Word was God.* What sort of God, how great a God? *All things were made through him, and without him was made nothing. What was made in him was life, and the life was the light of men. And the light shines in the darkness, and the darkness did not grasp it* (Jn 1:3-5).

The difference between the light and the lamp

5. So why does it say, *The darkness did not grasp it*? You must be light in order to grasp it. May faith make you light, so that you may have your fill of sight.[10] *For as long as we are in the body, we are traveling abroad from the Lord* (2 Cor 5:6); if we are traveling abroad from the Lord, we are travelling abroad from the light. So what then? Shall we remain in darkness? Perish the thought. *Approach him and be enlightened* (Ps 34:5). Again, after John the evangelist has said, *The light shines in the darkness, and the darkness does not grasp it*, what does he add, in order for them not to remain darkness? *There was a man sent by God, whose name was John.* God could not be seen; a lamp was lit. *There was a man sent from God, whose name was John.* So intense was the

light in Christ, that blear-eyed hearts couldn't take it; they were provided with the solace of a lamp, so that the lamp might bear witness to the daylight. You see, *there was a man sent by God whose name was John. This man came for witness, to bear witness to the light.* Why? Because *the light shines in the darkness, and the darkness did not grasp it.*

So John comes, a man adjusted to the darkness by his human mortality and weakness. May he come and say about Christ what human weakness does not grasp. That's why he came, to bear witness to the light. And it goes on, *He himself was not the light.* Who wasn't? John. *He himself was not the light, but to bear witness to the light.* To what light? It goes on, *That was the true light.* The true one. What sort of true light? *which enlightens every man coming into the world* (Jn 1:5-9), therefore John too. If it enlightens every man, it therefore also enlightens John, than whom none greater has arisen among those born of women. If it enlightens every man, John spoke the truth when he said, *We have all received from his fullness* (Jn 1:16).

In what way John was, and was not, light

6. So was John not light? What can we say against the gospel? The other John, who was also truthful, testifies and says, *He himself was not the light* (Jn 1:8). The apostles were called light, and was that one not light, than whom none greater has arisen among those born of women? But how do we prove that the apostles were called light? Listen to the Lord Christ speaking to the apostles: *You are the light of the world* (Mt 5:14).[11] John too was light. I dare not deny John what was given to the apostles; nor would I deny what the Lord Jesus said himself, who was pleased to bear John such witness as that *none greater than John the Baptist has arisen among those born of women* (Mt 11:11).

So let the one who promised enlightenment solve this problem, let him solve it clearly. Listen. *He was not the light* was said, just so that you would not suppose you were enlightened by him. For enlightening you, he was not the light. Finally, to teach you how he was not the light, he immediately went on to mention the one in comparison with whom he was not the light; *That was the true light.* He added *true.*

What's this you're saying, *true*?

Which enlightens every man (Jn 1:8-9); because the light which is lit, or enlightened, is not a light by its own power, but by participating in the light. The true light, which enlightens, cannot be extinguished; the lamp can both be lit and be extinguished. In what way were the apostles called light? In the way of a lamp. How is this to be demonstrated? To save me from seeming disrespectful, listen to the Lord a few moments later: *You are the light of the world*, and he continues, *Nobody lights a lamp and puts it under a bushel* (Mt 5:15); so you are light in the way a lamp is.

What about John? Let the Lord himself be heard again; he said about John in so many words, *He was a burning and a shining lamp* (Jn 5:35). The apostles a lamp, John a lamp. Rightly did the lamp recognize himself, and submit himself to the daylight; *I am not worthy*, he said, *to undo the strap of his sandal* (Jn 1:27). He did well not to give himself a high place, or else he might have been blown out by the wind of pride.

John, like Paul the friend of the bridegroom, directs us to Christ

7. There you are, we have learned[12] through John, and through a man, that we are to believe in Christ, and not to place our hopes in any man, but in Christ. There you have the great man, than whom none greater has arisen, and see where he directs you to. John, the friend of the bridegroom, is jealous not for himself but for the bridegroom,[13] like the blessed apostle Paul. He too was a friend of the bridegroom, and how did he show he didn't want hopes to be placed in himself? Fleshly-minded people were making divisions among themselves at that time, and some were saying, *I am Paul's man, others, I am Apollo's, others, I am Cephas' man, others, I am Christ's* (1 Cor 1:12). Three voices of the chaff here: *I am Cephas' man*, that is Peter's, is still a voice of chaff.[14] *I am Christ's*; that is now wheat grain, that is the heap which will be revealed at the end when the threshing floor has been winnowed, and which will fill the granary of eternal life.

So at that juncture Paul the apostle, being jealous for the bridegroom and not for himself, rebuked them and thrust them away from himself. He deals with his own case;[15] what's in it, after all, for himself? He says, *Has Christ been divided up? Paul was not crucified for you, was he? Or were you baptized in the name of Paul?* (1 Cor 1:13). Sure, you've done me an honor, sure, you have wished to be mine. Stop wishing to be mine in case we perish together, but let us all rather be his, so that we may remain, and not be blown away, at the winnowing. *Paul was not crucified for you, was he?* I am the friend, he is saying, of the bridegroom; I am jealous for the bridegroom, not for myself.

Reflect, my brothers and sisters, and notice what I'm saying. If someone goes abroad and entrusts his bride to a friend, and while he's abroad this loose woman casts a wanton eye on his friend, her protector, wouldn't this man be horrified at the other's lust, afraid of losing his own good faith? In the same way, notice where John too directed his admirers:[16] *I indeed*, he said, *am baptizing you in water. But the one who is coming after me is greater than I am, the strap of whose sandal I am not worthy to undo. He will baptize you with the Holy Spirit* (Jn 1:26-27.33). Come through me, but don't remain in me. Pass on to him, since he created both you and me,[17] because he is the one who gives us life. *We have all*, he says, *received from his fullness* (Jn 1:16).

Where we[18] have received from is where you have received from. Let us drink from it together, in order not to die of pride. So John passed people on to Christ. However just people may be, however pre-eminent in grace, however luminous their wisdom, however great the merits that set them on a pinnacle, they are only mountains. Pay attention to the psalm:[19] *I lifted up my eyes to the mountains, from where my help shall come* (Ps 121:1); because *there was a man sent by God, whose name was John; this man came to bear witness to the light*

(Jn 1:6-7). So you've lifted up your eyes to the mountain John, from where your help may come, because he is bearing witness to the light. Continue with the psalm, don't stop on the mountain: *My help is from the Lord, who made heaven and earth* (Ps 121:2). That is Christ; *All things were made through him* (Jn 1:3). He is the constructor of the world; he is, you see, the Word of the Father; the Father made all things through the Word.

Don't despise the humble garment.[20] Or has he grown cheap in your eyes, because he has been hidden? After all, could you endure him, if he was openly revealed? We must be grateful to him for clothing himself in a human being, and thereby adjusting himself to our weakness, in order to make us partakers of his divinity. Sing the faith, in order to arrive at sight.[21] Walk along the road that will bring you to the home country. He stays there where we are going, he came as the way by which we are to return there. But he came in such a way as not to depart from there; he ascended into heaven in such a way as not to abandon us here.[22]

NOTES

1. The sermon exists in two forms, the one published by the Maurists in the seventeenth century, and the other published by Dom Lambot in 1949, which is considerably longer. My choice will, as usual, be eclectic, though in general showing a preference for the shorter text, since in those leisurely days of manuscript copying sermons were more likely to be added to than abbreviated.

2. So the Maurists; Lambot has "Saint John the Baptist."

3. So Lambot; the Maurists have "Our Lord Jesus Christ"

4. See Lk 1:5-25.57-61. It is more than likely, however, that apart from the prologue the whole of Lk 1 was read: 1:5-80. The testimonial John received from the Holy Spirit was his father's being struck dumb and later recovering his speech, to chant the *Benedictus*.

5. So the Maurists: *Accipite ergo in hujus rei mysterio magnum sacramentum.* Lambot has a longer passage altogether: "It is difficult not only to explain but even to think worthily about the great and profound mystery of such a great man as this. However, to the best of my ability, as far as God grants, on account of the solemnity of the day accept from me, I say, the inner significance and meaning of this matter, because this is above all what you ought, and what you are expecting, to hear."

6. So Lambot; the Maurists, "the Lord Jesus Christ."

7. So the Maurists. Lambot, at the end of the previous sentence, added, "and to foretell his coming"; and in this sentence reads, "... did not cease to be prophesied about and have his coming foretold." His text continues, "We cannot, of course, run through all the prophecies. But those who are keen students of the divine scriptures both know what I have passed over in silence, and recognize what I say."

As regards such prophecies from the origin of the human race, the text the preacher most likely had in mind was Gn 5:15.

In the rest of this section Lambot's text has a whole number of slight additions to the Maurist one, which I am following. They are not sufficiently significant to note individually.

8. These three sentences from Lambot's text are absent from that of the Maurists.

9. From here until the end of section 6 is lacking in the Maurist text.

10. See 2 Cor 5:7; 1 Cor 13:12.

11. As a matter of fact, Jesus was not speaking just to the apostles, but to "the disciples," all of them: Mt 5:1.

12. So the Maurists, who rejoin us here. Lambot has, "So we say, through John."

13. Here the Maurists abandon us until further notice.

14. That the preacher should even consider the possibility that this was less a voice of chaff than "I am Paul's man, I Apollo's," to my mind argues strongly against at least these longer additions to the Maurist text coming from Augustine. The words indicate an ambience of a strong papalist piety, always tempted to put Peter (and thus the Pope) on a par with Christ; and there was certainly none of this in Augustine's African Church. Of course this could be a copyist's comment.

15. *Facit secum.* The text makes this into a question, which I don't quite know how I would translate; perhaps, "Does he back himself?" But then comes along the next rather opaque little question, *Quid enim sibi?*

16. Here the Maurists rejoin us, with a different phrase introducing what John said, to chime in with where we left them at note 13: "He says, you see, to those who come to him . . ."

17. Here the Maurist text ends.

18. I think this is the preacher referring to himself and his fellow clergy.

19. Possibly the psalm sung as a responsory.

20. The flesh which the Word became.

21. See 2 Cor 5:7.

22. A very disjointed, incoherent ending; yet another indication, perhaps, of the inauthenticity at least of these added portions. One manuscript adds at the end, as the subject of the sentence, "Jesus Christ, the Son of God, who was willing to become flesh and suffer for us, forever and ever. Amen."

SERMON 380

ON THE BIRTHDAY OF JOHN THE BAPTIST

Date: uncertain[1]

Today we are celebrating John the Baptist's birth
not his death, as some people suppose

1. For people who are keeping still, even a weak voice from the speaker is enough.[2] But if you want to listen in real stillness, brothers and sisters, don't have your minds in your ears, but ears in your minds. The Church believes and hands down to us that this day has dawned for celebrating the feast of John the Baptist. We must, of course, believe about this day what the whole world acknowledges without exception. But because nobody doubts that it is John's day, not the John who wrote the gospel, but John the Baptist, the Lord's forerunner, the man who was revealed to be all the greater, the more lowly he presented himself as being; thus when he was thought to be the Christ, he said that he was not worthy to undo the sandal strap of the one whom he acknowledged as his Lord, in order to earn the right to be his friend.[3]

Some people, however, think that what is being celebrated today is his death. The first thing your holinesses should understand is that today is the day of his birth, not his death. The gospel reading, indeed, discloses that his birth preceded the birth of the Lord by six months. And since there is general agreement in the Church on the tradition that the Lord's birthday falls on 25 December,[4] it remains that today, 24 June, is to be taken as the birthday of John.

The two births of Christ, one eternal, the other in time

2. So John preceded the Lord, not as a master goes before a pupil, but as a runner goes before a judge; not to impose his authority on him, but to do him a service. Now John's own testimony on the subject runs like this: *The one who is coming after me was made before me,*[5] because he was before me (Jn 1:15). The Lord came after John when he was born of the virgin Mary, not when he was born of the Father's substance. You see, we have been taught about two births of the Lord, one divine, the other human, both of them, however, marvelous; the former without mother, the latter without father; that one eternal, in

361

order for him to create the one in time; this one in time, in order for him to bestow on us the eternal one.[6] The one, you see, about whom it is said by John, not the Baptist but the evangelist, that *In the beginning was the Word, and the Word was with God, and the Word was God*, and that *all things were made through him, and without him was made nothing* (Jn 1:1.3); the one who was so great in the form of God that he was equal to God,[7] the one who timelessly constructs all times, the one who is from no age, before all ages, and judge of the age; this one was made so small that he could be born of a woman; but he remained so great, that he did not leave the Father.

All the prophets bore him witness and did him homage, like lamps doing the same for the coming daylight; they foretold him, coming before him by birth, following behind him as his adherents by belief. It was necessary, you see, that his coming should be foretold, and the miracles he would perform. These miracles, to those who understood them rightly, would indicate that he was God; while in his human aspect he would appear as a man to those who saw him, little for the little ones, but humble for the proud; by his littleness teaching us human beings to recognize our littleness, and not to imagine ourselves big, by swelling up, as distinct from growing up. Pride, you see, is a swelling tumor, not genuine bigness. So to heal the human race of this tumor, he the physician, he the medicine, not only provided a remedy, but made himself into the remedy, and appeared as a human being among human beings, offering himself as a man to those who saw him, keeping himself as God for those who believe in him. The sight of his humanity, you see, healed the sick and weak; the contemplation of his divinity looks for the healthy and the strong.

No human beings yet were capable of seeing God in a human being, nor could they see anything except the human being. And for all that they must not place their hopes in a human being. So what should be done? Human beings can see a human being, human beings mustn't follow a human being. God was to be followed, but he couldn't be seen; a man was not to be followed, but he could be seen. So in order to present humanity both with one who could be seen by human beings and with one whom human beings might follow, God became man. O man, on whose account God became man, you ought to consider yourself to be something great; but first come down low in order to go up high; because God too came down low when he became man. Stick close to your cure, imitate your master, acknowledge your Lord, embrace your brother, understand your God. That's what he is, this one so great and so small, *a worm and no man* (Ps 22:6), and yet through him man was made. So that's what he is. What is John, but what the Lord says about him, but what the truthful one says about him, but what Truth says about him? After all, if we have to believe John about the truth, surely we must believe Truth about John.

Showing against the Arians that the Word was not created

3. First of all let the sharer in truth give his witness to Truth; and then let the maker of man give his witness to the man. First let us hear what John has to say

about Christ, and then what Christ has to say about John. Let us listen to the first one, but understand the later one; let the one who was born first speak first, but let him be confirmed by the one by whom he was made. *He is coming after me, he says, and he was made before me* (Jn 1:15). Here now, those who believe that the one through whom all things were made was himself made before the rest,[8] misrepresent these words, or use them to misrepresent us, and say, "There you are, he was made; John says, *He is coming after me, and he was made before me.* Explain to me the meaning of *he was made before me.*" I'm quoting their words, and presenting them for discussion. "You are in the habit of maintaining," they say, "when anything is said about Christ to show him as less than the Father, that such a statement is to be referred to him as man; so that his being in the form of God means he is equal to the Father, while his *having emptied himself and taken the form of a servant, being made in the likeness of men, and found in habit as a man* (Phil 2:6-7), means that the Father is greater. So what will you say to this statement of John's, *he was made before me?*"

Listen to what we do say; but first of all note this point, that when the apostle was distinguishing each nature, and yet commending one and the same person in each,[9] he did not say, "taking the form of God." What, though, did he say about the form of God? *While he was in the form of God,* is what he said, looking back to that other apostle who had been called before him, in whose gospel it is stated, *In the beginning was the Word* (Jn 1:1); or rather looking back to that light by the grace of which that other apostle said this. John did not say, after all, "In the beginning God made the Word"; he could have said it like that, in the way Moses said, because he was talking about the creation made by the Lord God, *In the beginning God made heaven and earth* (Gn 1:1). So while he could have said, had he shared the opinion of the Arians, "In the beginning God made the Word," he didn't say this, but he said, *In the beginning was the Word.* What was in the beginning was not made.[10] Everything, after all, that God made, he made with the Word: *He spoke, and they were made; he commanded, and they were created* (Ps 148:5). Between the one speaking that it should be made and what is made by the speaker, there is a vast difference; but if there is a speaker, he has a Word; if he has a Word, he made things through the Word; if he made things through the Word, he did not make the Word.

Another objection of the Arians

4. "Why does that follow"? they say. "Or haven't you also heard about the earth: *The earth was invisible and unordered* (Gn 1:2)? If the reason," they argue, "that you say the Word was not made is that it says *the Word was,* then the earth wasn't made either, because it says *The earth was.*"

What blind and heretical nonsense! Pay attention, if you have anything to pay attention with; listen, if you have anything to listen with; don't let sounds beat in vain upon ears whose heart is not[11] being enlightened by the truth. I am going to repeat the words of the same passage of scripture, which you found there when you read it, and which you left out when you were making difficulties. So now, you think the same sort of thing was said about the Word of God, when it says *In the beginning was the Word* (Jn 1:1), as was said about the earth, because it says *The earth was invisible and unordered*. I, however, will now recite to you the earlier words in this book of Genesis, which the servant of God, the writer,[12] spoke before he said *The earth was*, to make it quite clear that it was made; he first said, *In the beginning God made heaven and earth* (Gn 1:1). There you are; I have first declared to you the earth as made, and made of course by God, with the scripture thundering out and dinning it into your resistant ears, *In the beginning God made heaven and earth*.

These things had been made; but they hadn't yet been embellished, hadn't been brought to light as yet. The earth was not yet distinct, but all the same it was already made. But in case you should immediately think that the earth had been made in such a way that there was nothing in it to be embellished, he went on to say—it had indeed been made, because in the beginning God made heaven and earth—*now the earth*, which God made, *was invisible and unordered*. He was showing you what it was like, the earth that had been made; not that an earth was, which had not been made. So John could have said, "In the beginning God made the Word; now the Word was," in the same manner as *In the beginning God made heaven and earth; now the earth was*; so that this would have been the order of the words: "In the beginning God made the Word, and the Word was with God," giving us to understand that the Word which was with God was the Word which God had made. As it is, though, what you hear is *In the beginning was the Word*.

Why do you put yourself so far beyond the pale[13] as to look for things before the beginning? Yes indeed, you have put yourself beyond the pale in your error; you are talking from the lowest depths and fixing your gaze on the lowest depths. If you must speak from the lowest depths, I would rather you stretched your heart out upwards, and cried to the Lord from the depths;[14] then he would scatter the clouds befogging your flesh, the light which came in humility would open your eyes to humility; you would see, *In the beginning was the Word, and the Word was with God, and the Word was God; this was in the beginning with God* (Jn 1:1-2). Let Paul too say, *Who while he was in the form of God*. What does John say about his human birth? *And the Word became flesh* (Jn 1:14). Let Paul too say, *He emptied himself, taking the form of a servant* (Phil 2:6-7).

What the meaning was of John saying "He was made before me"

5. So[15] what were you saying about the words of John the Baptist? Repeat them to me now, say them again now. What did John the Baptist say? *He is coming after me*. I recognize their births, one from a barren woman, the other from a virgin. Barrenness was turned into fruitfulness; virginity remained after fruitfulness.

"But if John," he says, "had meant that he was made in this sense, in that he was born of the virgin, he would not have said *He was made before me* (Jn 1:15), because he had been made of the virgin after him. So what can *he was made before me* mean, but that in the beginning the Word had been made? That, after all, is how he was before John; because born of the virgin he came after John."

Stand by for the answer, and if you are not hell-bent on quarreling, take good note of it. What you wish to understand, after all, is really rather obscure, and quarreling will only raise you more smoke than ever, which would hinder you from understanding. First of all consider that scripture text which teaches you to be docile: *Be meek in listening to the word, so that you may understand* (Sir 5:11 Vulg). So bear with me for a little while; perhaps we shall discover in what sense it was said, *He was made before me*; provided we don't take it to mean that the Word was made, through whom all things were made.

"How?" he says.

If I can, I'll tell you. If I can't tell you, that still doesn't mean that there isn't anything to be said by someone who can tell you. However I hope and believe that the majesty of that only-begotten Son, who though he was the Word became a speechless infant, will dispel the infant speechlessness of my tongue, and bring to birth in my mouth, what he has caused to be conceived in my heart. So here you are; let me say it as best I can; understand it as best you can; and don't find fault with what you can't understand, as though you were already grown up. Instead, wait patiently, so that you may deserve to grow up.

Certainly this is what puzzles you, how it could say, *The one who is coming after me has been made before me* (Jn 1:15). By all means, let it puzzle you as a seeker, not as a quarreler. Certainly, I too am seeking with you. Together we shall find, if together we seek; we shall both receive if we both ask; to each of us it shall be opened, if we both knock.[16] *He is coming after me*, he says; recognize his birth from the virgin Mary. *He has been made before me*. What's the meaning of *he has been made before me*? Understand it in the sense of "he has been placed before me." The one who is coming behind me has got ahead of me. It's as if two people are walking on a journey, and one's slower, the other faster, and the slower one goes on ahead a bit; but after a while the faster one follows, and the slower one who's ahead looks back at the faster one following, and says, "He's coming after me." And lo and behold, he accelerates, and draws nearer, and comes up beside him, and passes him, and he sees in front of him the one he had looked back at behind him. Certainly, if he were somewhat taken aback by his speed and surprised at it, couldn't these be his very words, "Here's a man who was after me, and has been made before me"?[17] What does that mean, "The one who was after me has been made before me"? "The one who was walking behind me has been made by his speed to get in front of me."

I mean, if whenever you read "has been made," you are only going to understand that one who was not has been formed; then you are going to say that the Lord God was made, about whom it says, *The Lord has been made into a refuge for me* (Ps 94:22); *The Lord has been made my helper* (Ps 30:10); and *He has been made into salvation for me* (Ps 118:14). Made how often? And it was he that made all things! So understand the words rightly with me. After all, this same John didn't keep quiet either about what the Word was.[18] So you shouldn't think that the Word was indicated when he said *He has been made before me*; so you should realize that what *he has been made before me* refers to, is that he has taken precedence over me, that he has been glorified more than me, that when people look at me, the forerunner, they acknowledge as the Lord the one whom I preceded in birth, whom I proclaimed in the course of my duty to him; that the Lord has become their hope and their rallying point. He has been glorified as the Son of God, made first before me, according to what the apostle says, *Therefore God has exalted him, and bestowed upon him a name which is above every name, that at the name of Jesus every knee should bow, of heavenly beings, earthly beings and infernal beings* (Phil 2:9-10). So his glory did not begin to be, but it began to be known. He was made before John, in the sense that he took precedence over John in honor.

Further testimonies to the pre-eminence of Christ

6. But let us see if it was right that he should. Question John himself: "This one who came after you, why was he put before you? The one who was following you, why was he preferred to you?"

He continues, *Because he was before me* (Jn 1:15). That's the same as, *In the beginning was the Word* (Jn 1:1). So it was quite right that he should be made before me, *because he was before me.* Before John, before Abraham, before Adam, before heaven and earth, before angels, thrones, dominions, principalities and powers.[19] Why before them? Because *all things were made through him* (Jn 1:3). Let the servant acknowledge his lowly status, let the Lord declare his majesty. Let this same John say, *I am not worthy to undo the strap of his sandal* (Jn 1:27). He would have been humbling himself very much if he had said, "I am worthy." After all, what if he had said he was worthy to do that? Would it be to sit in judgment at the right hand of the Father? Would it be to come to judge the living and the dead? What if he had said he was worthy to undo the strap of his sandal? Notable humility, if this is what the friend of the bridegroom is worthy of. He was going to say, you see, that he was the friend of the bridegroom; and in case anyone should possibly be so thoughtless as to think that that friendship meant equality, he says he is his friend out of love, he throws himself at his feet out of awe and fear. And it isn't enough for him to cast himself at his feet; he says he isn't even worthy to undo the strap of his sandal. Humble indeed, if he said he was worthy to undo it; but because he says he is not even worthy to do that, he is worthy to be raised up on high from this lowly position.

Let him say even more openly, say even more distinctly, what the meaning is of *He is coming after me, he has been made before me.* He also gave the reason, you see: *because he was before me.* Because, *In the beginning was the Word*; and *Since he was in the form of God, he did not think it robbery to be equal to God* (Phil 2:6). *It is necessary*, he says, *for him to grow, but for me to diminish* (Jn 3:30). It was necessary for the one who came later to grow, and for the one who came first to diminish. If the one who came later grew, he was made before the other by growing. *It is necessary*, he said, *for him to grow, but for me to diminish.* That's the meaning of *he was made before me.*

And how did Christ grow, and John diminish? In age and in human birth John came before the Lord. They both grew with the years, in the stature of the flesh, and reached a particular size, as adult human beings. But John was a man, Christ was God and man. If we suppose that Christ grew in his divinity, we are being absurd, and going altogether astray. Something grows, after all, to make progress. God has nothing in which to grow; I mean if he does have something in which to grow, he was smaller before he grew. So let's get back to the form of the flesh in Christ. That grew along with John, it didn't grow while he diminished. So let us perhaps refer it to their glory, and understand *It is necessary for him to grow, but for me to diminish* in the same way as *he is coming after me, and he was made before me.* John, you see, was playing the part of mankind, and speaking in the role of the human race, which Christ had come to save. Now we have said, brothers and sisters, that God was humble enough to come to the proud man.[20] Let man recognize himself as man, let God be shown to man for what he is.

Even if the reason Christ came had been for man to be humbled, and for man to grow from lowliness and humility, it would still have been necessary for man's glory now to give way, and for God's glory to be commended; so that man's hope might be in God and not in himself, as the apostle says: *Whoever glories, let him glory in the Lord* (1 Cor 1:31). So he is quite right to say to man, *What do you have that you have not received? But if you have received it, why do you glory as though you had not received it?* (1 Cor 4:7). John was manifesting this type of human humility, because the more Christ's fame and reputation spread abroad—not the stature of Christ, not the divine majesty of Christ, not the divine wisdom, not the Word of God, but that fame which started from practically nothing, and now fills the whole wide world; the glory of Christ, not the glory of man, so that man might acknowledge his lowliness, and God might communicate and share his divinity.[21]

Indeed, brothers and sisters, God's glory is our glory. The more we delight in glorifying God, the more does it profit us. God, after all, will not be exalted any higher just because we are giving him honor; let us only humble ourselves, and we are exalting him. It is written, you see, *I will exalt you, Lord* (Ps 30:1). What's the meaning of *I will exalt you*? He was on earth, was he, and you placed him in heaven? And is a man exalting God? What's the meaning of *I will exalt you*? I will confess that you are highly exalted. So let human beings confess that they are just human; let them first decrease, in order to grow. Let John say, decreasing to a lowly level, that he is not worthy to undo the strap of his sandal, and let him know he has been enlightened by sharing in his light.

John a lamp, not the true light

7. This, you see, is what John the evangelist said about him: *He was not the light* (Jn 1:8). Was he perhaps slighting John by saying *He was not the light*, when the apostles were told by the Lord, *You are the light of the world* (Mt 5:14)? Did the apostles put themselves before John? They don't do that, or they

would be condemning the Lord as a liar, for saying, *Among those born of women none has arisen greater than John the Baptist* (Mt 11:11). Not of course in bodily stature, but in the grace of wisdom, in the grace of salvation he was given a share of. So what can it mean, *He was not the light, but in order to bear witness to the light*? Why did he say this?

I know, says he, what I'm saying, to bear witness to the light. You see, there was a true light, quite distinct from John.

So it's not that John was not a light in any sense at all, But it's in comparison with this light that you must understand *He was not the light*; in relation to what he went on to say that there was a true light. How do you distinguish this true light?

Which enlightens, he says, *every man coming into this world* (Jn 1:9).

So if every man, then John too. But to save us from giving the impression that we are getting from these words what was not actually said, though it is to be understood from what follows, let John himself say, *From his fullness we have all received* (Jn 1:16).

So there was a true light. John, the light enlightened and lit, Christ the light enlightening and lighting. I mean, to show you that John was a light, let the Lord bear witness to him as well. He bore witness to his Lord, witness to the truth about his Lord, which he received from the Lord. He had, after all, received from his Lord what he should say about his Lord. The other, though, had not received from his servant what he should say about his servant. Christ in himself bears witness to John, and Christ in John bears witness to himself. So let Truth itself bear witness, and let us hear that John is a light. It was said to the Jews about John, *He was a lamp, burning and shining* (Jn 5:35). And a lamp, of course, is a light; not like the daylight, but still it is a light. So a lamp is lit to shine, and John was enlightened to speak. So if John was enlightened to speak, the lamp should recognize itself for what it is, in order not to be blown out by the wind of pride.

But perhaps the disciples were light, and John a lamp? What the Lord said about John, after all, was *He was a lamp, burning and shining*, while about the disciples he said, *You are the light of the world*. Was he putting his disciples before John? Are the faithful too, whom Paul addresses, to be preferred to John, the ones to whom he says, *You were once darkness, but now light in the Lord* (Eph 5:8)? So the apostles are light, and the faithful are light, justified sinners, unbelievers turned believers. Still, were the disciples not also called a lamp? Pay attention, perhaps they were, and not in another place, but right there, to show in what sense he had called them light; because they are not the true light which enlightens every man coming into this world. Follow the words of the gospel: *You are the light of the world. A city set on a mountain cannot be hidden*.

But he was talking about a city, not about light.

Go on following: *Nor do they light a lamp and place it under a bushel tub* (Mt 5:14-15). The sort of light you are is the sort John is; a lamp lit and enlightened. Like the person or persons whose words had anticipated this: *You will light my lamp, Lord; my God, light up my darkness* (Ps 18:28). Darkness in the apostles? We too were once, etc. . . .[22]

. . . as of that reprobate and blasphemer: *I was previously a blasphemer, and persecutor and overweening*. There you have the darkness; let the lamp be lit: *but I obtained mercy* (1 Tm 1:13). And to show you that he was speaking about them when he said, *Nor do they light a lamp and place it under a bushel tub, but on a lampstand, to shine on all who are in the house*, he immediately goes on, *So let your light shine before men, that they may glorify your Father, who is in heaven* (Mt 5:15-16). The Father is glorified, the Son is glorified, because the Father glorifies the Son and the Son glorifies the Father.[23]

So let man acknowledge his lowly state, and acknowledge that the exalted God humbled himself on his account, so that man, having humbled himself by the confession of sin, might be exalted by the attainment of justice. There are these two things: the Lord and John, humility and glory; God, humble in glory, man humble in infirmity; God humble on man's account, man humble on man's account. God, you see, is humble in order to be a help to man; man is humble in order not to be a hindrance to himself.

Further ways in which Christ grew, John diminished

8. So let us recognize these two things in the very differences of their deaths. We read that John suffered martyrdom for the truth; was it for Christ? It wasn't for Christ if Christ isn't truth. It certainly wasn't for his name, and yet it was for Truth itself. I mean the reason John was beheaded, after all, was not that he had confessed Christ. But he was urging self-control, he was urging justice; he was saying *It is not lawful for you to have your brother's wife* (Mk 6:18). The law, you see, which had commanded this, had also commanded about those who died without children, that brothers should take the wives of their brothers, and raise up seed for their brothers.[24] Where this reason was lacking, the only motive was lust. It was this lust that John was rebuking, a chaste man rebuking an incestuous one; because this too is what he represented: *It is necessary for him to grow, but for me to diminish* (Jn 3:30).[25]

The commandment had already been given that if anyone died without seed, his closest relation should take his wife and raise up seed for his brother. After all, why had God commanded this if not to signify in this way that the brother's seed was to be raised up to the brother's name? The commandment, you see, was that the child to be born would have the name of the deceased. Christ was deceased, the apostles took his wife, the Church. Those whom they begot of her they did not name Paulians or Petrians, but Christians.

So let both their deaths also speak of these two things: *It is necessary for him to grow, but for me to diminish*. The one grew on the cross, the other was diminished by the sword. Their deaths have spoken of this mystery, let the days do so too. Christ is born, and the days start increasing; John is born, and the days start diminishing. So let man's honor diminish, God's honor increase, so that the honor of man may be found in the honor of God.

NOTES

1. The Maurists are inclined to accept the authenticity of this sermon; but they say the text has been interpolated and tampered with in rather odd ways; and they have tried to straighten it out. For my part, the more I proceeded with the translation, the more convinced I became that this is in no way at all a sermon of Augustine's, but a pastiche of Augustinian sentiments and expressions cobbled together by a very inexpert imitator and no doubt sincere admirer—possibly a century or so later in Visigothic Spain, where the composer was engaged in somewhat puerile verbal combat with the Arian conquerors.

2. This looks like a genuine Augustinian touch; he often mentions the weakness of his voice. But the rest of this introduction immediately raises doubts in my mind. It is the merest flannel. No, the admiring Augustinaster quite cleverly picked on that opening touch to lend his work verisimilitude.

3. See Jn 1:27; 3:29. He has forgotten how he began the sentence, and so fails to end it.

4. Literally, "the eighth day before the Kalends of January."

5. *ante me factus est*. This, in Latin, is a perfectly correct translation of the Greek, and should be translated in English as "has been placed before me." But, as will be evident in section 3, the Latin *factus est* is ambiguous; as well as representing the perfect, which it really does here, it can also be taken as an aorist, which is how the preacher's Arian opponents, if not the preacher himself, evidently did take it; and how therefore it has to be translated here into English.

6. The substance of this section is also to be found in Sermon 371,1; and there these two phrases run, "that one eternal, in order for him to create beings in time; this one in time, in order for him to make them eternal." And that is what the manuscripts say here too. But the Maurists emended two plural adjectives *temporales* and *aeternos*, into the singular, and changed the gender from masculine to feminine: *temporalem . . . aeternam*.

7. See Phil 2:6.

8. The Arians.

9. The Latin does not use the words "nature" and "person"; but the doctrine being expounded is clearly that of the Council of Chalcedon in 451. This does not mean that Augustine, who died in 430, could not have uttered these words; his statements on the person of Christ frequently anticipate the definition of Chalcedon. But I have the feeling here that the preacher is echoing that Council, while still speaking in the *persona* of Augustine.

10. Here I omit a sentence that I can make very little sense of: *Neque enim praecessit aliquid de facto Verbo*. Its most obvious meaning (if it has any at all!) is "Nor did anything of the made Word precede." But as the preacher is at pains to insist that the Word was not made, he cannot really have intended to say that. It can also be construed as meaning—and this I presume is what it did mean to whoever scribbled it in the margin: "Nor did anything of what had been made precede the Word." It is indeed, I suggest, a hastily scribbled marginal comment, a rather pointless one, that was subsequently copied into the text.

11. Reading *cujus cor veritas non illustrat* instead of the text's *cujus cor veritas illustrat*. Negatives are the easiest particles in the world to omit when copying, or otherwise writing.

12. He means Moses, whose most common title was "the servant of God."

13. This translates *factus extremior*. *Extremior* is a very odd word, being the comparative of what is already a superlative. I somehow cannot hear Augustine using such a form of debased Latin; it is to my mind an indication of the inauthenticity of the sermon—as indeed is this whole childish argument. I doubt if any of the Arians Augustine encountered would have initiated it.

14. See Ps 130:1.

15. The text begins section 5 a few sentences lower down, at "But if John." This seems to me the more natural place to begin it.

16. See Lk 11:9.

17. He wouldn't say that in English, of course. The trouble is that *factus est*, was made, has been made—we have already noted that little ambiguity in note 5 above—does duty for the past and

perfect tenses of *fio*, I become. And that, of course, is what John's words mean. The whole problem is really a non-problem, raised by a deficiency in the Latin language.

18. He said the Word was God, Jn 1:1. The preacher does seem to be equivocating a little between the evangelist and the Baptist.

19. See Col 1:16; Eph 1:21.

20. Not, I am sure, in this sermon; but it is an Augustinian commonplace. This is a piece of clumsy imitation on the part of this Augustinaster.

21. Another unfinished sentence.

22. Here, according to the Maurists, there is a gap in the text (a fairly slight one, it would seem), which was filled in some of the manuscripts by the first part of Sermon 126. Something is needed to link up with the next paragraph.

23. See Jn 17:1. This is either a marginal comment which has crept into the text, or yet another indication that the whole sermon is nothing but a pastiche of characteristic Augustinian concepts and expressions.

24. See Dt 25:5-6; for the commandment broken by Herod see Lv 18:16; 20:21.

25. The reasoning here is almost totally opaque! But the preacher is trying to bring a comparison between the two laws about marrying and not marrying brothers' wives, into the comparison between Christ and John. John, insisting on the law forbidding a man to marry his brother's wife, is insisting on a "diminishing" law. Christ and the apostles, on the other hand, as he goes on to say, represent the law commanding brothers to marry a deceased brother's wife, and thus exemplify a law of growth. I cannot conceive that the genuine Augustine would ever have been quite so silly!

SERMON 381

ON THE BIRTHDAY OF THE APOSTLES PETER AND PAUL

Date: uncertain[1]

*In Peter the weak things of the world were chosen to confound the
strong; in Paul sin abounded that grace might abound the more*

1. As the belief of the Romans assures us, today is the day of the apostles
Peter and Paul, on which, having roundly defeated the devil, they earned the
victor's crown. Since a solemn feast is held in their honor, let our respects also
be paid to them with a formal sermon. May they hear our praises, may they pour
out prayers on our behalf. The common memory, basing itself on the tradition
of the fathers, knows that they did not actually suffer in the course of the same
day between sunrise and sunset. So Paul suffered on Peter's birthday, not the
day he emerged from his mother's womb to join the ranks of mankind, but the
one on which he was released from the bonds of the flesh and born into the light
of the angels. And so it is that, while each was given his own day of martyrdom,
they are now both celebrated on the same day.[2]

To me this looks like a splendid sign of harmony; the last of the apostles
comes to meet his fellow apostle, the first of them, called on the same day,
crowned on the same day;[3] the one chosen before the Lord's passion, the other
after his ascension; different in the order of time, equal in the bliss of eternity;
the one from being a fisherman, the other from being a persecutor.[4] In Peter the
weak things of the world were chosen, to confound the strong;[5] in Paul sin
abounded so that grace might abound the more.[6] In each of them what shone
forth was the great grace and glory of God, who made them deserving, did not
find them so.

What else, after all, was he good enough to demonstrate in first choosing to
call fishermen to the kingdom and only later on emperors, but that *whoever
boasts, let him boast in the Lord* (1 Cor 1:31)? Because of course he wasn't
being indifferent to the salvation of the well-born, the learned, the powerful,
when he put before them the low-born, the unlettered and the weak. But unless
the weak had been chosen first in all their unimportance, the proud would not
have been cured of their self-conceit. If the rich had been the first to be called
by Christ, they would have thought, and have said, that all they were chosen for

372

was their wealth, their fluency in talking, the fine style of their teaching,[7] the brilliance of their knowledge, their nobility, their breeding, their tranquil mode of life, their royal authority.

Thus, their heads swollen with temporal and secular[8] well-being, as though they were doing Christ a favor by being what they were, they would assume that he was paying them their due, not bestowing a favor on them; and they would neither understand nor grasp[9] what they were going to be by God's grace. So how much better for him now, how much more suitable for him first *to lift up the needy from the ground, and exalt the poor from the dunghill, in order to set them with the magnates of his people* (Ps 113:7-8); so that the endowment of intelligence and learning might not only be from God, but be quite evidently from God? With what joy then, and with what glory to God do we behold the wealth of emperors being set at nought by the soul of a fisherman, the prayers of emperors being poured out at the tomb of a fisherman, with the result that the latter is not spurned on account of what he did not possess, and the former do not grow haughty on account of what they do!

As regards Christ's making Paul into a preacher of his out of a persecutor, I would rather the apostle himself explained how important it was for our salvation that even those with great crimes and wickedness on their consciences ought never to despair of God's mercy. *It is a human word*, he says, *and worthy of complete acceptance, that Christ Jesus came into this world to save sinners, of whom I am the first. But it was for this reason that I obtained mercy, so that Christ Jesus might demonstrate all forbearance in me first of all, for the sake of those who were going to trust him to bring them to eternal life* (1 Tm 1:15-16). Would anyone, I mean, in the hands of the almighty physician, despair of being restored to health when informed of such a wonderful example, when contemplating him spreading the good news of the faith which he once used to lay waste, and noting that he not only escaped the punishment due to a persecutor, but also earned the crown due to a teacher, and that by believing himself he shed his own blood for the name of the one whose blood he had been thirsting ferociously to shed in his members?

So then Rome, the head of the nations, has these two lights of the nations lit by the one who *enlightens every man coming into this world* (Jn 1:9); one light in which God has exalted the most abject lowliness, the other in which he cured the wickedness that deserved to be condemned. With the former let us learn not to be proud, with the latter not to despair. How simply these great examples have been set before us, and how salutary they are! Let us always commemorate them, and in praising them glorify that *true light* (Jn 1:9). So none of us should get a swollen head about having a high position in the world; Peter was a fisherman. None of us, reflecting on our own iniquity, should run away from God's mercy; Paul was a persecutor. The former says, *The Lord has become the refuge of the poor* (Ps 9:9); the latter says, *Let me teach the wicked your ways, and the godless will be converted to you* (Ps 51:13).

NOTES

1. The Maurists somewhat grudgingly acknowledge the authenticity of this sermon. It carries Augustine's name, they say, in the ancient lectionaries, and the style is not altogether alien to his. On this point I am inclined to differ from them, and to cast my vote against authenticity; the style from time to time strikes me as that of the earnest but not very competent imitator. As it survives only in lectionaries, one may well wonder if it is complete.

2. In other words, Paul was martyred on the anniversary of Peter's martyrdom. My doubts about the style being Augustine's are already beginning to arise.

3. He appears to be saying that Paul's conversion on the road to Damascus occurred on the anniversary of Peter's call by the shores of Lake Galilee—with what warrant in the legendary lore of the early Church I cannot say. Otherwise one could interpret him as tautologically saying martyred on the same day—called to martyrdom, crowned as a martyr, on the same day. As we shall see, he is rather inclined to the vice of tautology.

4. A better contrast in Latin: *ille ex piscatore, iste ex persecutore.*

5. See 1 Cor 1:27.

6. See Rom 5:20.

7. *eloquentiae doctrinam*, literally, the teaching of eloquence. I am treating it as another of those curious inverted genitives. This whole list of things the rich would boast about is a very uneven, ill-assorted one; one of several instances of flawed style which make me question the sermon's authenticity.

8. A quite superfluous tautology, the two words meaning almost exactly the same thing.

9. Another feeble tautology; this is such a common fault in the essays of my seminary students—filling in space by saying the same thing in two ways, as in a sentence of this kind: "He declared or asserted that he was unwilling or reluctant to join in the party or celebration"—that it convinces me we have here the hand of an amateur student of Augustine, not of the master himself.

SERMON 382

Date: uncertain[1]

The preacher asks the congregation for their prayers,
and introduces the subject: "Love your enemies"

1. Jesus the son of Nave[2] was fighting in the desert, and Moses was praying. They weren't both fighting and both praying, but one was fighting, the other praying. It was what you would expect, that the one who was fighting did not grow faint, because the other was winning the battle by his prayers. In the same way I too appear to be speaking; but I am speaking while others are praying, in order that by their prayers I may benefit from what the Lord said: *Open your mouth wide, and I will fill it* (Ps 81:10). If Joshua was helped by just one person praying, and was not defeated, how much more shall I be helped, for whom not just one but many are beseeching my God? Now my heart will not be afraid of speaking, because *my mouth will speak the praise of the Lord* (Ps 145:21).

Our Lord and savior Jesus Christ commands us to do something and promises us something. What he commands us to do is to be done here; what he promises us is to be obtained elsewhere. What he commands us to do has a limit, because it is to be done in the course of time; what he promises us has no limit, because it is eternal. What he commands is work, what he promises us is wages. Here your holinesses should take note of how great is his mercy toward us, in that he set us work to do here which has a limit, gives us wages in heaven that have no limit. And that's why we ought first to do the hard work here, and after that to receive the reward in heaven, rather than wanting to receive the reward here and after that to do the work. There were some people, you see, about whom the Lord said, *Amen I tell you, they have received their reward* (Mt 6:2). But you, perhaps, are all agog for the reward, and lazy about the hard work;[3] how can you have the nerve to ask God for what he has promised you, and not do what God has commanded you? First carry out the command, and in this way go on to demand fulfillment of the promise. First, I repeat, listen to his command, and only then require him to keep his promise.

What he commands us to do, you see, is to love our enemies. *Love your enemies*, he says, *do good to those who hate you and pray for those who speak*

375

ill of you. You have heard what the work is, wait for the wages:[4] *so that you may be*, he said, *children of your Father who is in heaven, who makes his sun rise upon the good and the bad, and sends rain upon the just and the unjust* (Mt 5:44-45).

2. Look at the Lord himself, who did precisely what he commanded. After so many things the godless Jews committed against him, repaying him evil for good, didn't he say, as he hung on the cross, *Father, forgive them, because they do not know what they are doing* (Lk 23:34)? He prayed as man, as God with the Father he heard the prayer. Even now, you see, he prays in us, prays for us, is prayed to by us. He prays in us as our high priest, prays for us as our head, is prayed to by us as our God. So when he was praying as he hung on the cross, he could see, and he could foresee; he could see all his enemies, he could foresee that many of them would become his friends. That's why he was interceding for them all. They were raging, he was praying. They were saying to Pilate *Crucify!* (Lk 23:22); he was crying out, *Father, forgive.* He was hanging from the cruel nails, but he didn't lose his gentleness. He was asking for pardon for those from whom he was receiving such hideous treatment.[5]

They were raging, barking furiously all round him, shaking their heads at him—their far from sane heads—and as one man, like so many raving lunatics, raging on all sides against the supreme physician set there in their midst. He was hanging there and healing them.[6] He was suspended there, and yet dispensing goodness.[7] He wouldn't come down from the cross, because out of his blood he was preparing a medicine for their frenzy. Finally, after his resurrection he cured those whose utter insanity he had tolerated as he hung on the cross. There you have why Christ came; not to destroy what he had found, but *to seek and save what had been lost* (Lk 19:10), so that by loving his raging enemies, he might make them into believers and his friends.

3. But in case you should say it's too much to expect of you, to imitate your Lord, though *he suffered for you, leaving you an example, so that you might follow in his footsteps* (1 Pt 2:21), take a look at Stephen, your fellow servant. He was a human being like you, he was born of the same sinful lump as you, he was redeemed with the same price as you were too, he was a deacon, he used to read the gospel, which you also read or hear. There he found it written, *Love your enemies* (Mt 5:44). He learned the lesson he read there, he carried it out in practice.[8] When he was being murdered by the Jews under a hail of rocks, not only did he not utter any threats against them, but over and above that he prayed for pardon for those who were stoning him. Kneeling down, you see, he began praying, and said, *Lord, do not hold this sin against them* (Acts 7:60). They were stoning him, he was praying for them; they were pursuing him with rage, he was

peaceably following Christ. They were blinded by their malice; for him the heavens were opened, he saw the Son of God, and he was enlightened by wisdom.[9] They were hurling stones, he was shooting prayers ahead, as though he were saying, "Lord, if you kill these enemies now, whom will you later on make into friends?"[10]

How Stephen's prayer won the conversion of Saul

4. I mean, to show your holinesses how much weight the holy martyr's prayer carried, come back with me to that young man called Saul, who while Stephen was being stoned was keeping the coats of those who were doing the stoning, as though to be seen as himself throwing the stones with the hands of them all. Later on, as you know—because I know whom I'm talking to, I'm talking to my brothers and sisters, I'm talking to my Father's children, I'm talking as a disciple to my fellow disciples[11]—later on, *he received letters from the chief priests, so that whomever he might find to be followers of the Christian way, men and women, he should bring in chains to Jerusalem*, to be tortured and punished. *As he was going on his way, suddenly there shone around him a light from heaven. He fell down and heard a voice saying to him, Saul, Saul, why are you persecuting me? And he said, Who are you, Lord? And the Lord answered, I am Jesus the Nazarene*, he said, *whom you are persecuting. It is hard for you to kick against the goad* (Acts 9:1-5; 26:14), because you won't hurt the goad, but your feet which you are kicking with. What have you got against me? *Why are you persecuting me?* Why are you rearing up against me to your own harm, and not rather humbling yourself for your own good? But against all the evils you are committing against me, for which indeed I ought to have destroyed you long ago, my servant Stephen has prayed for you.[12]

He was struck down a persecutor, he was raised up a preacher. Let me say it plainly, let me say it more explicitly; he was struck down *a son of perdition* (Jn 17:12), raised up *a vessel of election* (Acts 9:15); he was struck down as Saul, raised up as Paul.[13] Because if Stephen hadn't prayed like that, the Church would never have had Paul. But the reason Paul was raised up from the ground is that Saint Stephen was heard when he bowed down to the ground.

We are inclined to ask God to punish our enemies; he teaches us to imitate Christ on the cross and pray for them

5. But against these great and splendid examples, this is how you go about it, whoever you are who don't love: Kneel down, beat your forehead on the ground, cry out and say, "O God, kill the bad man." You as well, praying like that for a man to die, are a bad man praying against a bad man, and that now makes two bad men. You are crying out and saying, "O God, kill the bad man." He will answer you, "Which one of you?" Would your holinesses please reflect, I'm saying things you all know. A human judge doesn't himself kill the man he finds guilty, but he gives the order and the executioner kills him. The judge says "Put him to death," and the torturer does so.[14]

And so you, when you say, "Lord, kill my enemy," are making yourself the judge and expecting God to be the torturer. God will answer you, "Most certainly not; I will not be the torturer of the sinner, but rather his liberator, because *I do not desire the death of the sinner, but rather that he may be converted and live* (Ez 33:11). Because if I had the same kind of will as you have, I would have killed you first, before you came to me uninvited.[15] Haven't you blasphemed me? Haven't you provoked me with your evil deeds? Haven't you wished to blot out my name from the earth? Haven't you ignored me in my commandments or in my servants? If I had killed you then as my enemy, whom would I now be making into my friend? So why are you now, with your bad prayer, trying to teach me to do what I never did in your case?[16] So rather let me," God says to you, "let me teach you to imitate me. Hanging on the cross I said, *Father, forgive them, because they do not know what they are doing.* I have taught this to my soldiers, taught it to my martyrs. You too first be my martyr witness, my recruit against the devil. Otherwise you will in no way fight and win, unless you pray for your enemies."[17]

NOTES

1. The sermon exists in two versions, one that of the Maurists, the other published in the *Revue Bénédictine* in 1970. The Maurists fairly firmly deny its authenticity, saying that it has all the appearance of being a pastiche of texts, and quoting an earlier editor who dismisses it as "the patchwork of an unskilled hand." I think they must be right in the main; some things just don't hang together very naturally. But there is a lot of genuine Augustine in it. It is not really a sermon celebrating Stephen's feast day anyhow, in spite of its title; but a sermon on our obligation to love our enemies, Stephen only being brought in toward the end to reinforce this lesson. Insofar as the body of it, apart from the patches stuck onto it, is authentic, I would date it fairly early, even before 396, and I would infer from a number of points that it was not preached in Hippo Regius but in a Church, perhaps Carthage, perhaps a smaller place, which Augustine was visitng or passing through.

2. Joshua the son of Nun for us; see Ex 17:8-13. This whole introduction, up to "because my mouth will be speaking the praise of the Lord," is omitted by RB.

3. So the Maurists. RB has, "But you perhaps are slow about receiving the reward for the work," which hardly fits into the argument.

4. So the Maurists. Instead of this sentence RB has: "A hard commandment, but a great reward. *Love your enemies*—this is the work—*do good to those who hate you, and pray for those who speak ill of you.* And in case you should stand aghast at the hard work, he immediately added the wages:"— which is rather repetitious.

5. So the Maurists. This sentence is omitted by RB.

6. Here the Maurists add, "*Father*, he said, *forgive them.* Take note, brothers and sisters; what great loving kindness!"

7. *Pendebat, et tamen impendebat.*

8. So the Maurists, from "he used to read the gospel" to this point. RB has instead: "as you also know."

9. So the Maurists, from "Kneeling down." RB has instead: "*Lord*, he said, *do not hold this sin against them*; as though to say, 'Let me die in the flesh; don't let these people perish in mind.'"

10. So the Maurists, from "as though he were saying." RB omits.

11. This parenthesis, from RB, is omitted by the Maurists.

12. So the Maurists, from "*And he said, Who are you, Lord?* RB has much the same content, but arranges it quite differently.

13. So the Maurists; RB omits this last phrase about Saul and Paul.

14. So the Maurists; RB omits this sentence.

15. *antequam invitatus venires.* To translate *invitatus* as "uninvited" instead of as "invited" may seem rather bold; but as "invited," it doesn't seem to make sense. Perhaps I could suggest that a *non* has slipped out of the text; but I am inclined to think that the syllable *in* is doing double duty, both as negative prefix and as part of the word "invited." This could be under the influence of the very similar word *invitus*, unwilling. I am again following the Maurist text here. RB leaves out the first part of this sentence, and construes "before you came . . ." with the question that follows.

16. RB omits this last question.

17. RB phrases the last three sentences rather differently. The Maurists add at the end: "May he be good enough to grant us this, etc."

SERMON 383

ON THE ANNIVERSARY OF HIS ORDINATION AS BISHOP

Date: uncertain[1]

The two kinds of reflection which this anniversary
provokes in the bishop

1. Every day, indeed, and every minute of the day, and with altogether unceasing concern, dearly beloved, should a bishop be pondering on what a burden of pastoral responsibility he bears, and what sort of account he will have to render for it to his Lord. However, every time the anniversary of my ordination comes round, I then find myself supremely conscious of the burden of my office, as though it were at that moment first being placed upon my shoulders. There is this difference, though, that on the day when I first received it I thought only of how I was to carry it out; whereas subsequently, and especially on the day when it is celebrated as a feast day, I have not only been taking thought with careful foresight, how matters should be conducted from now on for the future; but I have also been anxiously recalling how they have been conducted up till now in the past, so that I may continue to imitate myself in what I have done well, and take care, where anything blameworthy transpires, not to repeat it, and pray for it to be pardoned. In this way I hope to clear myself of the devil's accusations, where I can, by sedulously trying to act rightly; and where I cannot do this, to defeat him by devout and sincere confession.

Just as future sins, you see, are committed through indifference to justice, so past ones are confirmed by the defense of injustice. So then, just as charity looks to the future to stop sins being committed, in the same way humility erases the ones that have been committed. They cannot, of course, be now uncommitted, so to say, by doing right; but they can at least be forgiven by not being proud. We have, to be sure, learned to say to our Father who is in heaven, *Forgive us our debts, as we too forgive our debtors* (Mt 6:12). For us to be able to say this honestly, we have of course also to love our enemies; though we ought not to have any, except where justice obliges us to. I mean, if people are our enemies because we indeed deserve ill of them, we don't have to trouble about forgiving them their debts, but rather to be afraid of having to pay our own. Because if they hate us on account of our wrongdoing, it is not they who are our debtors, but we who are theirs.

380

He pardons his debtors, but urges them to change their ways

2. So on this anniversary of my becoming bishop let me first address a few words to my debtors, who quite unwittingly plead my cause with God by incurring the debts which I can forgive, in order to earn in advance the forgiveness of my own debts. And so it's to you that I'm talking, whether you are present or absent, you whose enemy I become by preaching the truth, to whom the good advice I give seems burdensome, whose wills I am compelled to cross by seeking your welfare. What I have to say to you is, *Be not like horse and mule, which have no understanding* (Ps 32:9). These animals, you see, are supremely in the habit of attacking with teeth and hoof those who handle them to cure their wounds. You don't spare me, I don't spare you; you oppose me, I oppose you; you resist me, I resist you. The struggle puts us on a par with each other, but the cause we are fighting for sets us apart. You are the enemy of the doctor, I of the disease; you of my care and kindness, I of your serious illness.

They were paying me back evil, he says, *for good; I, however, was praying* (Ps 35:12). What was I praying, if not, *Father, forgive them, because they do not know what they are doing* (Lk 23:34)? *When they speak ill of you*, he says, *and utter every kind of evil against you because of justice, rejoice and exult, since your reward is great in heaven* (Mt 5:11-12). You people, though, must correct your perversity, and acknowledge my charity. Pay me back love for love; I don't want your perdition to earn me a greater reward. These few words must now suffice for my debtors, whom I forgive, so that I may be forgiven.

He asks those whom he has offended or injured in any way to forgive
him such debts, and assures them of his love for them

3. From now on I must also address myself for a short while to those of you in whose debt I stand. Because, as the apostle says, *I am a debtor to Greeks and barbarians, to the wise and the foolish* (Rom 1:14). Because I too, within my limited powers and within the small area entrusted to my pastoral stewardship, am a debtor not just to some people, but to all. Now, however, I am talking about those debts which I long to have forgiven me, not the ones whose payment should be required of me.[2] I am not, after all, quite so conceited and vain as to have the effrontery to say, that from the moment I shouldered the load of this office nobody has ever been wrongfully hurt by me. For that to be the case is, I won't say impossible, but certainly difficult for any person occupied and distracted by so many and such irksome calls upon his time; how much more so for me, familiar as I am with my infirmity, which night and day I offer up to the Lord our God to be cured, together with my prayers and yours on my behalf!

So then if, when I've been flustered by the rush and difficulty of such a variety of cares, I haven't perhaps listened to someone in the way expected of me; if I've looked at anybody more severely than was needed; if I've spoken to anyone more harshly than was required; if I've upset anyone with a troubled heart or in need of help by an unsuitable answer; if some poor man has perhaps been pestering me while I was concentrating on something else, and I have waved him aside or put him off, or even hurt his feelings with a curt shake of the head; if anyone has entertained some false suspicion about me, as one person so easily can about another, and I have shown greater indignation than was warranted; if there is anyone who has not had on his conscience what I have in all too human a way suspected him of; to you I confess that I am in your debt for these and suchlike offenses; and at the same time I ask you to believe that I really love you. A mother hen, after all, often treads in some narrow space on the chicks she is fostering, though not with her whole weight, and she doesn't thereby cease to be a mother.

Forgive, so that you may be forgiven. Forgive one who loves you the debts he has incurred in his difficulties, since not even against your enemies should you hold the debts incurred by their cruelties. In a word, I beg you all, commend to the Lord, yes you, commend to him the care and responsibility I have for you—in return, you see, I can justly call upon your care and responsibility for me—so that he may graciously pardon whatever I have done to offend in the past, and not severely hold me to account for it. As for the time that lies ahead of me under this burden, may he guide my steps along the road, and make me pleasing to his eyes and useful to you, so that when you appear in his presence, you may be found to be, not my horror and punishment, but *my joy and my crown* (Phil 4:1).

NOTES

1. The Maurists turn this sermon down on the point of style; they think it lacks Augustine's flair, *ingenium*. But they inform us that Bossuet regarded it as genuine. As a bishop himself, he perhaps found that the sermon spoke to him more shrewdly; but as a scholar, he was not quite in the same class as the monks of Saint Maur. If it is genuine, I would date it to not much more than ten years after Augustine's ordination as bishop; to between 405 and 410. And if it is genuine, it must certainly have been preached in Hippo Regius.

2. That is to say, the sermons and the pastoral care he owes them.

SERMON 384

What God is

1. It is salutary indeed, brothers and sisters, for the holy and divine scriptures to be chanted to us regularly, every day in fact, for the nourishment of our souls. In the age to come, though, may they take their fill at the eternal banquet, according to the prophet's words, *I shall take my fill when your glory is revealed* (Ps 17:15). What this future glory will be like, however, how richly it will flourish, with what splendor it will blaze out, while we can sing its praises, we cannot possibly explain. Why not? Because we read, *Eye has not seen, nor ear heard, nor has it come up into the heart of man, what things God has prepared for those who love him* (1 Cor 2:9). So if that's what has to be said about the eternal good things of heaven, which the almighty Lord has prepared for his holy, Catholic and faithful peoples, what must God himself be, who has prepared such great and wonderful things?

What, I repeat, must almighty God be like? What but unfathomable, inexpressible, incomprehensible, surpassing all things, beyond all things, apart from all things? He excels, after all, every one of his creatures, he goes far beyond everything he has made, he surpasses the whole universe. I mean, if you are looking for greatness, he is greater; if for beauty, he is more beautiful still; if for delightfulness, he is still more delightful; if for splendor, he is more brilliant; if for justice, he is more just; if for strength, he is stronger; if for fatherly care, he is kinder. Reason, after all, in no way allows us to equate the thing made with its maker, or the work with its craftsman. As we may read in the prophet, *The one who made mighty things is mightier himself; and the one who made beautiful things is more beautiful than they are* (Wis 13:4.3).

The divine Trinity is one, and the divine unity is three

2. That is how we proclaim the outstanding sublimity of this one and only godhead, provided though we do it like Christians, not like Jews. Let us together confess the mystery of the divine Trinity. For just as the Father is almighty and inexpressible, so too is the Son almighty and inexpressible; so also the Holy Spirit, indivisibly tied in with the Father and the Son, is inexpressible and boundless. For Father and Son and Holy Spirit, one almighty God, one in trinity,

383

one in power, unity, trinity, everlasting majesty, wielding one authority throughout the universe, exists as trinity in unity and unity in trinity; but neither divided as trinity, nor separated as unity.

Armed and equipped, therefore, with this Catholic faith, dearly beloved, let us briefly interrogate the dastardly Arian heretics, who are so impiously pushing themselves forward these days, and leading astray many of our Christians with their deceitful corruptions. Let us ask them how they pray to the Lord, seeing that that they hold opinions against the Lord. They answer us, and say, "We pray to the Lord, of course, as a trinity; but as we read the scriptures: to the Father as greater, to the Son as less, to the Holy Spirit as the lowest in rank; because Christ himself says, *The Father is greater than I* (Jn 14:28).

To all this we reply, "Is that, I ask you, how you pray and worship God?"

"Certainly; that's how we read the scriptures, that's how we worship, that's how we pray."

To them we say, "So if that's how you worship God and pray to him, that is not worshiping and praying to the one great God, but making three gods; and what has become of what we read in the divine law, *Hear, O Israel; the Lord your God is one God* (Dt 6:4)? And again it says somewhere else, *You shall adore the Lord your God, and him alone shall you serve* (Dt 6:13). I mean, if the Father is one thing, the Son another, and the Holy Spirit another, there is now not one trinity, but a division of power; but how can discordant power stand, when according to what we read in the gospel, *A house divided against itself, or a kingdom, cannot stand* (Mk 3:24-25)?

But how can divinity be split off from itself when brightness may in no way be separated from light, or heat from the sun? So there you are, as we can see, there are three things in the sun, and they are absolutely inseparable. But let's see what these three things are; the sun's course, its brightness, its heat. We see the sun, after all, running its course in the sky, shining on us, giving heat. So divide the sun if you can, Mr Arian, and then by all means divide the Trinity.

But perhaps it's difficult for reason to make these distinctions in the sun, because it's in the sky, and positioned a long way away from us. Here you are, let us put forward another element which is less than the sun, and here on earth with us; I mean fire, which we have to hand, and yet it is not to be divided. Fire too, you see, has three things, and they cannot be split up; that is, its motion, its light, and its heat. If therefore, impious, detestable heretic, you cannot split up the created sun and fire, how can you split up God, the creator of all things?

Scriptural texts supporting the doctrine of the Trinity

3. Now listen and learn how this great and single Trinity has been indicated from the very origins of the human race. Hear about it in the law and the prophets, in the psalms and in the gospel, hear it plainly stated without a shadow of doubt in the apostle. Hear about it, I say, in Genesis: *God made man to the image of God²* (Gn 1:27). To show at the same time how the Trinity is inseparable, he says in the same book, *And the Spirit of God was being wafted over*

the waters (Gn 1:2). Listen to the prophet, saying in the person of Christ, *The Spirit of the Lord is upon me, which is why he has anointed me, has sent me to proclaim good news to the poor* (Is 61:1). Listen to it in the psalms: *By the word of the Lord were the heavens fixed firm, and by the breath of his mouth all their might* (Ps 33:6); and again, *Give me back the joy of your salvation, and confirm me with the sovereign spirit* (Ps 51:12). Listen to the same thing confirmed in the gospel: The Lord Christ says to the apostles, *All authority has been given to me in heaven and on earth; go and baptize all nations in the name of the Father and of the Son and of the Holy Spirit* (Mt 28:18-19). Listen to the apostle: *Oh, the depths of the riches of the wisdom and knowledge of God! How inscrutable are his judgments, and unsearchable his ways!. For who has ever known the mind of the Lord, or who has ever been his counselor? Or who ever first gave to him, and was repaid? Since from him and through him and in him are all things; to him be glory forever and ever* (Rom 11:33-36).

Thus it has been sufficiently and clearly proved from the scriptures of the Old and New Testaments that the divine unity is an inseparable trinity; let us therefore utterly reject the heretics, following what the apostle says; *Shun a heretic after one correction* (Ti 3:10), and let us now confirm our faithful congregations in this Catholic faith. There are indeed no greater riches or treasures or honors, no greater wealth of this world than the Catholic faith, which saves sinners, gives light to the blind, heals the sick, baptizes catechumens, justifies the faithful, restores the penitent, helps the just to grow in justice, crowns the martyrs, preserves virgins, widows and married couples in a chaste way of life, ordains clergy, consecrates bishops, prepares us all for the kingdom of heaven, has a share with the holy angels in the eternal inheritance. As indeed the Lord himself assures us with his promise, *In the resurrection they marry neither wives nor husbands, but they will be equal to the angels of God* (Mt 22:30); through Christ our Lord.[3]

NOTES

1. All authorities from the Maurists onward, as well as their predecessors, regard this sermon as spurious; it is not hard to see why. It probably comes from within the century or so after Augustine's death, when the Arian barbarian Goths and Vandals, Burgundians and Franks and other Germanic tribes, occupied all the western provinces of the Roman Empire. It clearly presupposes Augustine's doctrine from time to time; even presupposes the Athanasian creed, the *Quicunque vult*, which is usually dated to about 500. So a date about 530, a hundred years after Augustine's death, and from the uncompromising tone of the sermon a place like Spain, would be quite likely. See Sermon 380, note 1.

2. How this text is intended to reveal the Trinity defies comprehension. All that I can think of is that the author—did he really preach the sermon, or is it a written composition in the form of a sermon?—had in mind Augustine's working out of a trinitarian image in the human mind of the divine Trinity, in the last seven books of his *On the Trinity*.

3. An inappropriate ending, where there has been no concluding prayer.

SERMON 385

ON OUR LOVE FOR ONE ANOTHER[1]

Human love can be bad as well as good

1. We are advised, dearest brothers and sisters, in the Old as well as in the New Testament, in what way we should maintain perfect charity. This, you see, is what the Lord himself said in the gospel: *You shall love your neighbor as yourself* (Mk 12;31).[2] So let us deal for a little while with the love of human beings for each other; because there are warped kinds of human love. You love someone else in a warped manner, if you love yourself in a warped manner; but if you love yourself in the right way, you also love the other person in the right way. For example, there are shameful, detestable kinds of love; the loves of adulterers, the loves of corrupt persons, unclean loves. Evil loves are reprobated by all human laws and divine laws. So put away these unlawful kinds of love; let us investigate the lawful ones.

Various grades of lawful love

2. Lawful love starts from marriage; but that is still a fleshly form of it. You can see that it is shared with the animals; and those sparrows, which are chirping away there, have marriages and build nests, and together sit on the eggs, together feed the fledglings. It is, to be sure, a lawful kind of love among human beings, but as you see, it's fleshly. The second grade is love of your children, but this too is still fleshly. It is not, after all, particularly praiseworthy for people to love their children, but it is abominable when they don't. I mean, am I going to praise as something remarkable in a human being what I can see in a tigress? Snakes love their children, lions and wolves love their children. So don't imagine that it is anything very remarkable that you love your children; with this kind of love you are still on a par with snakes; if you don't love your children, you are letting snakes beat you. I am now speaking about respectable kinds of love; you see, I have excluded those shameful kinds.

Another grade of love, that of our kindred, already seems to be proper to human beings, if it isn't just a matter of habit.[3] I mean, the love which extends beyond our relations is greater than the love which is confined within the circle of kinship. When you love your relations, you are still loving your own blood. Try loving others who are not related to you, give a welcome to strangers. This love has now expanded very widely. It only grows, though, by extending itself

386

from married partners to children, from children to kinsfolk, from kinsfolk to strangers, and from strangers to enemies. But to reach that final point it has to go up many steps, many grades.

From friendship based on habit to friendship based on reason

3. So consider what I am going to say about friendship. There are friends—excepting always that friendship, which shouldn't even be called friendship, being the product of a bad conscience; there are people, you see, who do bad things together, and that's why they seem to be inseparable, because they are bound together by a bad conscience. So apart from that nefarious sort of friendship, there is a kind of friendship which is still merely fleshly, that arises from the habit of living together, chatting together, going around together, so that people feel sad when they are left or thrown over by friends with whom they were in the habit of chatting and getting together. Two people meet, they go around together for three days, and now they don't want to separate. And this pleasant kind of friendship is honest and decent enough, of course; but let us continue to examine it, because we are inquiring about the grades of this love; and let us see how we may arrive at such a love or friendship as I have mentioned.[4]

So there is this friendship arising from habit, not from reason; animals too go in for it. Let two horses but eat together, and they desire each other's company. If one of them goes ahead the next day, the other one hurries after, desiring, so it seems, its friend; it can hardly be controlled by its rider, and goes on challenging him with its impetuosity, until it catches up. When it reaches the one that has gone ahead, it calms down. It was carrying the rider's weight, but it was being urged on by the weight of love; it has come at last, as it were, to its proper place, and has rested there.[5] This sort of friendship arising from habit is still to be found in animals; let us continue to rise up from this sort too. There is another, higher kind of friendship, arising not from habit but from reason, by which we love a person because of mutual trust and benevolence in this mortal life. Any love or friendship we find which is superior to this is divine. Let people start loving God, and the only thing they will love in other human beings is God.

The love involved in friendship must be gratuitous

4. The first thing, you see, that your graces should observe, is how the love involved in friendship ought to be gratuitous. I mean, the reason you have a friend, or love one, ought not to be so that he can do something for you; if that's why you love him, so that he can get you some money, or some temporal advantage, then you aren't really loving him, but the thing he gets for you. A friend is to be loved freely, for his own sake, not for the sake of something else. If the rule of friendship urges you to love human beings freely for their own sakes, how much more freely is God to be loved, who bids you love other people! There can be nothing more delightful than God. I mean, in people there are

always things that cause offense; still, through friendship you force yourself to put up with things that offend you in a person, for the sake of friendship. So if you ought not to break the ties of friendship with a human being just because of some things in him you have to put up with, what things should ever force you to break the ties of friendship with God? You can find nothing more delightful than God. God is not something that can ever offend you, if you don't offend him; there is nothing more beautiful, nothing more full of light[6] than he is.

But you are going to say to me, "I can't see him; how can I love someone I can't see?" Here's how you can learn to love someone you can't see; I am now going to show you how you should strive to see what you cannot see with these eyes. Here you are, you love a friend; what do you love in him? You are loving him freely, gratuitously. But perhaps this friend of yours, to pass over other things, is an old man; it can happen after all, that you have an old man as a friend.[7] What do you love in the old man? His bent and twisted body, his white hairs, the wrinkles in his face, his sunken cheeks?[8] If it's just the body you can see, there is nothing more unsightly than old age; and yet you love something, and you don't love the body which you can see, which is unsightly. How can you see what you love? After all, if I ask you, "Why do you love him?" you're going to answer me, "He is a faithful man." So you love faith in him. If you love faith, the eyes with which faith can be seen are the very eyes with which God can be seen. So start loving God, and you will love other people on account of God.

God is not to be loved for the sake of any reward

5. Listen to a splendid instance. The devil is certainly the accuser of the saints; and because he cannot drag us before the sort of judge he can deceive, he is unable to bring false charges against us; he knows in whose presence he is speaking. So because he can't bring false charges against us, he looks for true ones to bring. That's why he tempts us, in order to have true accusations to make. So this adversary of ours, who envies us the kingdom of heaven, who doesn't want us to be in the place he was cast out of: *Does Job*, he says, *worship God for nothing?* (Jb 1:9). So here we are, being challenged by the adversary to worship God for nothing, when in his search for something to object against Job, he thought he had found something serious, because he said, *Does Job worship God for nothing?* This was not because he had seen into his heart, but because he had seen how rich he was.

We ought to be on our guard against loving God for any reward. What's the point, after all, of loving God for a reward? What sort of reward is it that God is going to give you? Whatever else he gives you, it's less than he is. You are worshiping him not freely, not gratuitously, in order to receive something from him. Worship him freely, and you will receive God himself; God, you see, is keeping himself for you to enjoy him. And if you love the things he made, what must he that made them be like? If the world is beautiful, what must the architect of the world be like? So tear your heart away from the love of creatures, in order to cling to the creator, and to be able to say what is written in the psalm, *But for me it is good to cling to God* (Ps 73:28).

Loving what God has made instead of God is a kind of adultery

6. But if you forsake the one who made you and love the things he made, by forsaking the one who made you, you become an adulterer. That's what the letter of James says loud and clear, calling them adulterers. *Adulterers!* And why adulterers? You ask why? *Do you not know*, he says, *that friendship with this world is enmity with God? So whoever wants to be a friend of this age is thereby constituted an enemy of God's* (Jas 4:4-5). He was expressing what he meant by saying *Adulterers!* The soul which forsakes the creator for love of the creature is an adulteress. There is nothing more chaste than love of him, nothing more delightful; once you forsake him, my soul, and embrace the other, you become unclean. In order to be worthy of his embrace, my soul, let go of these other things, and cling to him freely, for nothing. It was in that connection that the psalm said, *But for me to cling to God is good.* In the previous verse it had said this: *You have destroyed all who play the whore away from you* (Ps 73:28.27). And as though to show you what playing the whore means, he added, *But for me to cling to God is good*; I don't want anything else but him; to cling to him, that is my good, that is my free, gratuitous good; and that's why it's also called grace, because it is to be had free, gratis and for nothing.

So when you start loving God freely and for nothing, you can throw care to the winds, because you are both loving your friend for nothing, and also loving him to this end, that he may love God together with you.[9] Take a look, after all, at that common friendship we started from, in the course of which we climbed steps or grades; take a look at that. A husband loves his wife, and a wife her husband; without a shadow of doubt he wants her and she wants him to be safe and well. She wants to have him safe and sound, she wants to have him doing well. She loves him to this end, that she herself wishes to be safe and sound and to do well; what she wishes for herself, she also wishes for him. She loves her children; who would ever wish their children to be anything but safe and well? She loves her friend; who would ever wish their friends to be anything but safe and sound? To this extent indeed, that should anything happen to your friend, you tremble, you're upset, you start worrying, you rush off to prevent it happening; when it does happen you wring your hands. So what does this show that you want? To have your friend safe and well. So if all who love anyone or anything wish to have the object of their love safe and well, let them understand where true safety or well-being is to be found, and they will start loving that in itself, and be obliged to love this true well-being or safety in and for their friends as well.

Well-being in this world is to be used, eternal well-being
or salvation is to be loved

7. If you are looking for God with the eyes in your head, consider the three youths delivered in the fire.[10] If you are looking for God with faith, consider the Maccabees crowned in the fire.[11] That other kind of well-being or salvation is to be loved, this kind is to be used; it is, you see, necessary to use it, because it is transitory and doesn't last long. I mean, what the doctors call health or well-being, brothers and sisters, is not the real, true kind; it is just a sort of alleviation for us, because life in this fragile flesh is a continuous sickness. You imagine, do you, that people are sick when they have a fever, and in good health when they are hungry? "He's well," they say. Do you want to see how bad it is to be hungry? Leave him without medicine for a week, he's dead; but because you set before him the appropriate medicine every day, he stays alive.

The medicine for hunger, of course, is food; the medicine for thirst, drink; the medicine for weariness, sleep. The medicine for sitting down is walking about; the medicine for walking about is sitting down; the medicine for fatigue is slumber; the medicine for slumber is being awake. And notice how feeble the human body is; the very aids I mentioned, if you take them and persist in them, your health suffers. When you were hungry, you looked for the aid of food; here's the aid of food; you eat it, you satisfy your hunger. If you do more than satisfy your hunger, your health suffers. You look for a drink to aid you in your thirst; if you drink too much, you choke, where just now you were being driven by thirst. You've got tired through walking, you want to sit down; sit down perpetually, and see if you don't get tired of that. So whatever remedy you take to eliminate some inconvenience, if you persist in it, your health suffers.

True health or well-being is eternal life

8. So what is this well-being really, this health, brothers and sisters, so soon to pass, so fragile, so perishable, so vain? Indeed, indeed, it's as it says: *For what is your life? It is a mist that appears for a moment* (Jas 4:14). So *whoever in this life loves his soul will lose it. But whoever in this age hates his soul, will keep it safe for eternal life* (Jn 12:25). What is eternal life? True well-being, real health. And if you now consider your friend, whom you love in this world, wishing him to be safe and well; because you yourself are now eager for that well-being and health which is eternal, you now love him to that same end; and everything you want to do for your friend, you want to do it to this end, that he may enjoy that health and well-being with you. You love justice, you see; you want him to be just. You love being under God; you want him too to be under God. You love eternal life; you want him to reign with you there forever.

Then there's that enemy of yours who, as you are all too well aware, is hounding you; it is, in fact, wickedness that is hounding you. With him you ought to be angry in a compassionate way; he is suffering from a fever in the soul. So just as a worldly friend loves his own soul by the standards of this world, and wishes to rid his friend of a fever, since he loves him as himself with respect to present health and well-being; in the same way you, whoever they are that you love, should love them with respect to eternal life. When you find them suffering from anger, indignation, hatred, iniquity, do your best to rid them of such diseases of the spirit, in the same way as the worldly friend deals with diseases of the body. Love in fact to this end, that you may make them what you also are, and perfect charity will be found in you.

If you turn out to be like this, then love your wife or husband to this end, love your children to this end, to this end love your relative, your neighbor, the unknown stranger, your enemy, and perfect charity will be found in you. If it is, then you are overcoming the world,[12] and the prince of this world is being driven out outside. I mean, you have heard what the Lord said: *The prince of this world has been thrown outside* (Jn 12:31), because he himself was going to suffer, and by his passion was going to reproduce his love in us all. *Greater love has nobody than this, that a person should lay down his life for his friends* (Jn 15:13). So in order to be loved, he first loved; in order that nobody should be afraid of dying for his name, he first died for all. So in order to build up charity in all our hearts, he threw the devil outside. Outside where? From the hearts of human beings. Greed and cupidity bring him in, love and charity put him out.

As the Lord has rescued us from the devil, let us take pains
to fill ourselves with good things

9. We, however, brothers and sisters, should reflect very carefully upon the aforementioned[13] steps or grades of charity, in order to avoid repaying the Lord evil for good. And because he came and tied up the strong man, that is the devil, and removed us all, who were his gear, from his power,[14] we must by his grace empty ourselves of all evil, and take great pains to fill ourselves with an abundance of good things. We should be afraid of that thing the Lord himself said: *When the unclean spirit goes out of a person, it walks about through dry places, seeking rest, and it cannot find any; after this it goes back, and finding the house it had gone out of unoccupied, it brings along with it seven other spirits more wicked than itself; and the last state of that person has become worse than the first* (Lk 11:24-26). So in order that nothing like that should happen to us too, let us endeavor as best we can to bring in virtues in the place of vices, so that we may attain eventually to the mercy of God.

NOTES

1. This is roughly the title given the sermon by the Maurists. The sermon is also published, among those of Saint Caesarius of Arles, in the contemporary *Corpus Christianorum* volumes, where it is given the following cumbersome title: "This admonition of Saint Augustine shows that there are several grades in perfect charity and love, which are useful and very necessary." The

beginning and the ending, according to the Maurists, are the work of Caesarius; we may have some Augustine in the middle, but more likely some anonymous patchwork artist of an "Augustinaster."

2. The preacher, or composer, forgets to point out, what he has just hinted at, that Jesus is quoting Lv 19:18.

3. *Si non sit consuetudinis*. I cannot see the point of this qualification.

4. Does he mean love of enemies? Could that be called, exactly, the love of friendship? Evidence here, perhaps, of the careless patchwork technique of this Augustinaster.

5. This is elaborating on Augustine's famous dictum, *Amor meus pondus meum*, my love is my weight. Weight, in his natural philosophy, is the force, not quite gravity, which pulls things to their "proper place"; heavy things like earth downward to the lowest place, light things like fire upwards to the top place. Augustine will associate this theme of my love being my weight with one of his favorite texts, Wis 11:20, *You have arranged all things in measure, number and weight*. See, for example, *The Trinity*, XI, 18; also *The Literal Meaning of Genesis*, IV, 3, 7-12.

6. Reading *lucidius* with some manuscripts, instead of the *dulcius*, nothing sweeter, of the text.

7. This wry remark has a genuine Augustinian flavor to it—Augustine preaching as an old man. The theme, however, is one he does touch on from time to time. So our patchwork artist could well have taken this little passage from a genuine sermon.

8. No dentures in the ancient world!

9. This hardly seems a conclusion from what has just been said. Rather, it takes up the line of thought as it was left at the end of section 4.

10. Shadrach, Meshach and Abednego, in the fiery furnace, Dan 3. Consider them if you want to see God in this way, because—I presume—there appeared a fourth figure in the furnace, like a son of God, Dan 3:25. But bringing these three and the Maccabee brothers into this context is very peculiar. There seem to be several lines of thought tangled up together in the composer's/preacher's mind. If he couldn't sort them out, I don't think I will bother to attempt the job.

11. See 2 Macc 7.

12. See Jn 16:33.

13. He says *suprascriptos*, the above written. Does this give the show away, and prove that this is not a real sermon, but a somewhat laborious composition?

14. See Lk 11:22.

SERMON 386

How we should love our enemies

1. Turn your minds, please, my brothers and sisters, to that charity which the divine scriptures praise so much, that nothing else can equal it. When God warns us that we must love one another, is he only warning you to love the person who loves you? That is mutual love, and it is not enough for God. You see, he wanted you to get as far as loving your enemies, when he said, *Love your enemies, do good to those who hate you, pray for those who persecute you; so that you may be the children of your Father who is in heaven, who makes his sun rise upon the good and the bad, who sends rain upon the just and the unjust* (Mt 5:44-45). What do you say to that? Do you love your enemy? Perhaps you will reply, "I can't do it, I'm too weak." But take steps to make progress, to ensure that you can do it; above all because you are going to pray to a judge whom nobody can deceive, who is going to try your case.

So appeal to this judge, where there is no clerk of the court to scare you, no beadle to remove you, no advocate to be bought to plead your case or utter words which you haven't learned. But the only Son of God himself, equal to the Father, seated at the Father's right hand as his assessor, your judge, has taught you just a few words, which any illiterate person can get by heart and repeat, and in these words he has made your case for you. He has taught you the heavenly law, as to how you should plead. But perhaps you will reply, "By whom am I to make my petition? By myself in person, or through someone else?" The one who has taught you to pray,[2] he is the one who presents your plea for you, because you were guilty. Rejoice, because the one who is now your counsel will then be your judge.

So because you are going to pray, you are going to plead your case in a few words, and you are going to come precisely to these words: *Forgive us our debts, as we too forgive our debtors* (Mt 6:12). You see, God is saying to you, "What are you giving me, so that I should forgive you your debts? What gift are you offering, what sacrifice of your conscience are you laying upon my altars?" Straightaway he taught you what you should ask for and what you should offer. You ask, *Forgive us our debts*; and you offer—what? *As we too forgive our debtors.* You are in debt to the one who cannot be deceived; you also have your own debtor. God is saying to you, "You are my debtor, that man is yours; I treat you, my debtor, in the same way as you treat yours. Offer me a gift from what

393

you have spared your debtor. You are asking me for mercy; don't be sluggish in showing mercy yourself. Pay attention to what scripture says, *I desire mercy more than sacrifice* (Hos 6:6; Mt 12:7)." Never offer a sacrifice without mercy; because your sins will not be forgiven unless you offer it together with mercy.

But I suppose you may say, "I haven't got any sins." However careful you may be, brother or sister, still while you are living in the flesh in this age, you are acting under pressure and in tight spots, and you find yourself in the midst of innumerable temptations; you simply cannot be without sin. Sure, God is saying to you, "Don't worry at all about sin, don't forgive your debtors, if you haven't got anything for me to forgive you; instead, demand payment from your debtors, if you don't owe anything yourself. If, however, you are a debtor, congratulate yourself on also having someone in debt to you, whom you can treat in the way you want to be treated yourself."

Listen to me, and examine yourself, being doubtless among those few upright people who can truthfully pray the Lord's prayer, truthfully say, "Lord, forgive me, as I too forgive." Do this, not dishonestly, not just pretending, but truly from the heart, so that it may truly be done in your case. If the person, after all, who has hurt you, who has sinned against you, asks your pardon, and you say, "Forget it," you are now in a position to say without a qualm, *Forgive us our debts, as we too forgive our debtors*. I mean, if you refuse the one who begs your pardon, you in your turn will be ignored when you beg for pardon. You have slammed the door in the face of someone knocking; you will find it slammed in your face when you knock.[3] Because if you open your heart tenderly to the one who begs you for pardon, God will also open his to you, when you beg him for pardon.

Now, you see, I am addressing those of you who ask their Christian brothers and sisters for pardon, and don't receive it. Look, if you for your part have granted pardon, you will be able to pray without any anxiety. But what about him? If he asked your pardon, and you didn't grant it, how free from anxiety will he be?[4] Whoever you are, though, that may have sinned against another, and not won pardon; don't be afraid, appeal to his God and yours. There are debts at issue; will the servant be able to demand payment of debts which his master has written off? If it so happens, though, that the person who has sinned against you hasn't pleaded with you, if he doesn't pray you to pardon him; if he has injured you, and over and above that is still angry with you, what are you going to do about it? Will you forgive him, or not? Suppose you haven't forgiven him. Why not? Because he didn't ask you to. If the reason you haven't forgiven him is that he didn't ask you to, don't hesitate while saying the Lord's prayer, say it without a qualm, you needn't beat your breast because you haven't forgiven someone who didn't beg you to. So the one who didn't ask for pardon has remained in debt; payment will be required of him, it most certainly will. However, let's hope your charity will be perfect, and that you pray for the one who doesn't pray you to forgive him; because you will be praying for someone who is in great danger.

The example of Christ himself and of Saint Stephen

2. Here and now turn your attention to your master and Lord, not seated on his magisterial chair, but hanging on the tree, gazing all round him at the crowd of his enemies, and saying, *Father, forgive them, because they do not know what they are doing* (Lk 23:34). Observe the master, listen to one who imitated him.[5] The Lord Christ was hardly praying at that moment, was he, for those who had asked him for pardon? No, it was rather for those who were hurling insults at him and putting him to death. Did the physician abandon his duty, because the frenzied patient was raving? After all, he says,[6] *Forgive them because they do not know what they are doing*; they are killing the savior, because they are not seeking salvation. You, on the contrary, are no doubt going to say, "And when can I do what the Lord was able to do?" Why should you say this? Notice where he did this; notice that he did it on the cross, not in heaven. After all he is always God in heaven with the Father; but on the cross he was man for you, where he offered himself as an example to be followed by all. It was for your sake, you see, that he uttered those words, so as to be heard by all. I mean, he could have prayed for them silently, but then there would have been no example for you to follow.

But if the Lord's example is too much for you, don't let the servant's be too much for you. So you are unable to imitate your Lord, are you, when he was hanging on the cross? Pay attention to his servant Stephen, when he was being stoned to death. First he said, as the servant to his Lord, *Lord Jesus, receive my spirit; and after that he knelt down and said, Lord, do not hold this sin against them. And when he had said this, he fell asleep* in the restful arms of love (Acts 7:59-60). He found the most abundant peace, because he desired peace for his enemies. He wasn't praying then either, was he, for those who had prayed him to forgive them? In fact it was for those raging against him, for those who were stoning him and killing him. You have his example; learn from it. Notice how he prayed for himself standing up, and for them he knelt down. Are we to suppose, brothers and sisters, that he loved them more than himself? But he prayed for himself standing up as being a just man, who would readily be listened to; because on behalf of the wicked it was necessary to kneel. So he extended his love even to his enemies who were not[7] asking for his pardon.

So, brothers and sisters, to ensure you can say the Lord's prayer without a qualm, forgive from the heart those who ask you to do so, in order that the Lord may forgive your sins too in this mortal body and in the future forever, etc.[8]

NOTES

1. There is almost universal agreement among the scholars that the authenticity of this sermon is extremely doubtful. Again, most probably, we have in it the work of a patchwork artist; so there are occasional genuine Augustinian touches here and there.

2. That is, has taught you the Prayer, the "Our Father."

3. See Lk 11:9.

4. Reading, as the Maurists suggest, *quomodo securus erit,* instead of the text's . . . *eris,* how free from anxiety will you be. One can readily imagine a somewhat unimaginative copyist changing *erit* to *eris,* but not the other way round.

5. Meaning Stephen, of course. But he won't actually be mentioned for some time; a typical instance of the patchwork artist's faulty technique.

6. Reading *Dicit enim,* instead of the text's *Dic enim,* Say, you see. This is surely out of place here.

7. The "not" is lacking in the text; the Maurists very properly suggest supplying it.

8. A very curious ending; the patchwork artist was in a hurry, perhaps, or even getting a little bored with his work.

SERMON 387

ON THE CORRECTION OF ONE'S NEIGHBOR[1]

On the duty of bishops to correct sinners,
and their own need to be corrected

1. Your graces, dearest brothers and sisters, have frequently heard in the holy scriptures in what great danger bishops[2] are placed, if they are unwilling to carry out what the apostle urges on them: *Preach the word, keep at it in season, out of season; admonish, rebuke, exhort with all patience and positive instruction* (2 Tm 4:2). And because such a heavy weight hangs over our necks,[3] seeing that we are told, *If you do not declare to the wicked man his wickedness, I will require his blood at your hand* (Ez 3:18), we are obliged to take to task, either privately or publicly, those of careless life. But when we reprove someone, if the person we reprove is bad, he fixes his attention on the one he is being reproved by, and happily and more readily acknowledges what has to be put right in his reprover than in himself. And if he can find something true to say against the one who is reproving him, he is delighted. How much better to rejoice about his own healthy condition when he has been put right, than about another person's illness when he is rebuked![4]

Look here, suppose what you say is true; you have found something in the man who was finding fault with you; all the same, through him Truth was speaking to you; through a bad man, a wicked man, Truth was speaking to you. You are looking for something to find fault with in a man; find something, rather, to find fault with in Truth. Whether you like it or not, it is Truth that is your opponent, in whom you will find nothing to accuse her of. Make a friend of her, if you can. Your opponent is the word of God; be it uttered by a sinner, be it uttered by a just man, it's the word of God, it is blameless. There is your opponent for you; *Reach agreement with him while you are with him on the road.* The road is this life; the opponent of all the wicked is the Word of God. Does it mean nothing to you, that while he was abiding in his own most blissful and secluded retreat, he came to you to be with you on the road, and was willing to accompany you, so that while you are still walking along it, and still have it in your power, you may settle your business with him?[5] And when you come to the end of the road, there will be nobody you can settle your business with; and *your opponent will hand you over to the judge, and the judge to the officer, and the officer will put you in prison; you will not get out of there until you have*

397

paid back the very last farthing (Mt 5:25-26). The word of God is with you, like your opponent on the road; you have it in your power; settle with him.

What does this opponent require of you? That you should reach agreement with him. What about, if not your well-being and salvation? He's walking along with his opponents and telling them to reach agreement with him. Let it be done; they haven't got to the end of the road yet. It wasn't done yesterday, let it be done today. You haven't got to the end of the road yet; why wait until you do? When you do, there won't be another road on which you can reach agreement with your opponent. All that remains then is the judge, the officer, and prison. For many people this road, when they have been promising themselves many years on it, has come to an abrupt end. But all right, grant that your road will be a long one, and let your opponent walk along it with you all the time. Aren't you ashamed to be wrangling in disagreement with such an opponent for such a long time?

The Word of God for his part, is your friend; you are the one who make him your opponent. As for him, you see, he is wishing you well, while you on the contrary are wishing yourself ill. He gives the command, "Do not steal"; you do steal. He gives the command, "Do not commit adultery"; you do commit it. He gives the command, "Do not cheat"; you do cheat. He forbids you to swear; you swear false oaths. You do everything against what he tells you, you yourself are making the Word of God into your enemy. And no wonder, when you are yourself your own enemy. *Whoever*, after all, *loves iniquity, hates his own soul* (Ps 11:5, LXX). So if by loving iniquity you hate your own soul, is it any wonder that you hate the Word of God, who wishes your soul well?[6]

We must first reprove ourselves, before reproving a brother or sister

2. So shall we keep quiet, and reprove absolutely nobody at all? Let us administer reproof, surely, but first of all to ourselves. You wish to reprove your neighbor; there is nothing which is a nearer neighbor to you than yourself. Why go far away? You have yourself right there in front of you. What, after all, was it that the Lord said in the scripture? *You shall love your neighbor as yourself* (Mk 12:31; Lv 19:18). So if you don't love yourself, how can you love your neighbor? The rule for loving your neighbor is taken from yourself. "I do love him," you will say to me. That's why I say, first love yourself, and utter the reproof to yourself. But if you really and truly utter it out of love, it's obvious that the word which you utter has done something inside you.[7]

But it is to be feared that you don't love yourself, and that you wish to reprove someone else, and that you do this with hatred. But if you hate your brother, you are objecting to much slighter things in him than you are doing yourself. *Whoever hates his brother is a murderer* (1 Jn 3:15). That's what you heard today, when the letter of John was read. Scripture says it, in case people should ignore what they have inside in their hearts, and blame others for things done outwardly with the body; already *whoever hates his brother*, he said, *is a murderer*. There is no weapon as yet in his hand, he hasn't yet blocked the pass or prepared the ambush, hasn't yet started looking for poison—and is already found guilty in God's eyes because of the hatred he has conceived. The one he's seeking to kill is still alive, and he is already being convicted of killing him. So if you reprove someone with hatred in your heart, it means you have the nerve, as a murderer yourself, to take someone else to task.[8] Or because no human beings are arresting you and taking you before a judge, is that why you don't acknowledge your crime in the eyes of God, the supreme judge? If you are not prepared to acknowledge your crime, you will certainly acknowledge your punishment; he, after all, doesn't spare murderers. "But I do correct myself," you say, "as long as I am on the road." So correct yourself, and then you will be able to reprove your brother. You are objecting to slighter things, committing graver ones; *You can see the speck in your brother's eye, but cannot see the pole in your own eye* (Mt 7:3).[9] The Lord said this, you see, because of people who take others to task with hatred. You take someone to task for being angry, and you are being consumed with hatred? Weigh anger and hatred against each other in the scales of reason. What is anger? A kind of boiling of the spirit. When displayed here and now, it displeases you. But now in you this anger is already chronic, that's why it has produced hatred. Anger is the speck, by growing it is going to become a pole. Just as a speck grows into a pole, you see,[10] in the same way chronic anger becomes hatred. You are now hating, and you're rebuking someone for being angry; already you dislike the speck in him, you still like the pole in yourself. Do you want to know what the difference is?[11] We often find parents being angry with their children; you will have difficulty in finding parents who hate their children. A father can be angry with a son whom he loves; it is possible to say, "He is angry and loves"; it is impossible to say, "He hates and loves." I have said this because of people who punish lesser faults in others, and don't punish graver ones in themselves.

Let us reach agreement with the Word of God
while we are still on the road

3. So then, my dearest brothers and sisters, let us think about these things in a sound and sensible way, and make friends with our opponent while we are on the road with him; that is, let us reach agreement with the Word of God while we are still in this life; because later on, when we pass over from this world, no room will be left for the striking of any bargain or making of amends. All that remains is the judge, and the officer, and prison. So in order that, with the Lord's help, we may carry out all these things, let us love wholeheartedly not only our friends but also our enemies; so that what is written may find its fulfillment in us: *Let the whole law be fulfilled in you in one word: You shall love your neighbor as yourself* (Gal 5:14); and that other text, *Charity covers a multitude of sins* (1 Pt 4:8). May he, the one who is true charity, deign to grant us this, who lives and reigns with the Father and the Holy Spirit forever and ever. Amen.

NOTES

1. This is the heading the Maurists give the sermon, which is also published in the *Corpus Christianorum* series as Sermon 145 of Saint Caesarius, where it is given the cumbersome title, characteristic of that worthy Augustinaster: "Admonition of Saint Augustine on the text, *Reach agreement with your opponent while you are with him on the road;* and about the speck of anger which becomes a pole when nourished on false suspicions." The Maurists remark: "Neither the beginning nor the conclusion suggests Augustine. The matter in between is inelegantly incoherent, and shows a neglect of clarity and gracefulness in the way it is expressed. We consider that we have here a pastiche of Augustine's words or thoughts." So much for poor Saint Caesarius.

2. *Sacerdotes*, priests. But the word was still only applied at this period in the Church's history to bishops, not yet to presbyters, with whom it has since become almost synonymous. It is not, in this kind of context, at all characteristic of Augustine. Hence the observation of the Maurists.

3. The picture seems to be of a rock poised to drop on them—a more rustic version, perhaps, of the sword of Damocles.

4. An instance of the inelegance noted by the Maurists.

5. I here omit a phrase, *et dicas, Quando finiturus es viam?*—may settle your business with him, "and say, When are you going to reach the end of the road?" It seems entirely out of place, and cannot be accounted for even by poor Caesarius' failure in elegance. I can only see it as a marginal doodle by some pre-occupied reader, which found its way into the text.

6. Throughout this section there has been ambiguity about "the word of God"—whether it is that, or "the Word of God," or both.

7. The thought, and the expression of it, is hopelessly confused, though the general idea is clear enough. But the word uttered in this sentence is presumably being thought of as spoken to the neighbor, not to oneself, as in the previous sentence.

8. Treated as a question in the text. I think it makes better sense as a statement.

9. More evidence of the ineptitude of the patchwork artist.

10. Augustine certainly talks several times of anger as the speck and hatred as the pole, and of the one growing into the other; but he never puts this graphically outrageous image quite so ineptly as this—as though specks were always growing into poles in the ordinary course of things.

11. Between reproving simply with anger, and doing so with hatred.

SERMON 388

ON PERFORMING ACTS OF CHARITY

Why Christ only mentioned acts of charity
as the subject of the last judgment

1. This reading, brothers and sisters, which we have just heard from the holy gospel, impresses upon us the importance of performing acts of charity; and it does so in such a way that at the last judgment the Lord attributes to those on the right hand nothing but acts of charity, and to those on the left only the failure to perform them.[2] It's not that people's other actions, good or bad, won't come up for judgment; it's written after all, that everything will come up for judgment.[3] And yet our Lord Jesus Christ did not choose, when telling us in advance about his judgment to come; he did not choose to warn us about anything except solely about acts of charity. Do you imagine those on the right are not to be told, "Because you have lived chastely, because you haven't grabbed other people's property, because you have confessed faith in me to the extent of shedding your blood"? All these good deeds, after all, must necessarily be honored in the judgment of Jesus Christ. Again, do you suppose those on the left are not to be told, "Because you have been shameless, because you have committed fornication, because you have grabbed other people's property, because by your pride and evil morals you have caused my name to be blasphemed"?[4]

Nonetheless our Lord keeps quiet about all the other good deeds of the just, when telling us in advance about his judgment, and only thinks fit to mention acts of charity. He kept quiet about all the evil deeds of the wicked, and decided that they were only to be upbraided for their barrenness in the matter of charity—this only as a warning to us. Why was this so? Because all misdeeds can be redeemed by acts of charity. That's why he praised their abundance on that side, on this side blamed and condemned their dearth.

Acts of charity only cover graver sins if accompanied by a change of
behavior

2. But you mustn't take what you have just heard, that all evil deeds are redeemed by acts of charity, in the way some perverse people take it. Acts of

charity, you see, can indeed avail you for wiping out past sins, if you change your behavior. But if you persist in the same evil practices, you can't bribe the judge with your acts of charity. I'm talking about those misdeeds and crimes which all ought to shun who receive the body and blood of Christ. For the rest, it hasn't escaped my notice that this mortal life, set up in the perishable flesh, cannot be without any sin at all; but those light and daily sins also have their daily wash. That's why we beat our breasts, and say in the prayer to the Lord our God, *Forgive us our debts, as we too forgive our debtors* (Mt 6:12). It's not without reason, after all, that we say this, nor would the heavenly master himself have taught us this prayer, if he hadn't foreseen that we would be sinners. I mean he saw the things we should beware of, and he saw the things it is difficult to be on our guard against.

In fact, the one who judged it impossible for us to be on our guard against everything, was the one who taught this prayer, not just to any Christians you care to think of, but to the rams of the flock, the apostles themselves. Where the apostles have to beat their breasts and say, *Forgive us our debts*, that is, our sins, will any mere little sheep have the nerve to be proud about its justice? Observe what sort of man the apostle John was; he reclined on the Lord's breast,[5] from that deep well of wisdom he drank mysteries. It's from there, you see, that he drank what he burst out with in the gospel, *In the beginning was the Word, and the Word was with God, and the Word was God* (Jn 1:1). And the gospel bears witness time and again that the Lord loved him very particularly.[6] And yet he says, *If we say that we have no sin, we are deceiving ourselves, and the truth is not in us* (1 Jn 1:8).

Nor, because things like that are said, should any murderer feel he has nothing to worry about, if he comes to say, on account of his daily fornications and robberies, *Forgive us our debts*. God, you see, established this to be said every day on account of minor sins; but this man thinks it can serve him in good stead for those grave ones, which he doesn't want to give up, but is keen on continuing with them perpetually. By all means let him beat his breast about these, let him also do acts of charity for them—but after changing his way of life; let him withdraw from that way, turn to this one. But if he says to himself in his heart of hearts, "If I commit robberies every day, if I defile myself with the stench of daily adultery, and if I seek out diviners, sacrifice to idols, consult astrologers, and do not in the least withdraw from such a way of life; nonetheless, by performing daily acts of charity I can extinguish all my sins"—nonetheless you can indeed extinguish them, but when you are extinguished yourself.[7]

Such, you see, will be this evil change you undergo, that there will never be wanting someone to say about you, *And yet a little while, and the sinner will be no more; and you will look for his place, and not find it. I saw the godless lifted high above the cedars of Lebanon; and I passed by, and behold, he was not; and I searched, and his place could not be found* (Ps 37:10.35-36). So your sins will perish, but together with you. After all, you won't be allowed to sin in gehenna; nor, when the eternal fire starts tormenting you, will you go on thinking about satisfying your lusts. So your sins will perish, but together with you. But if you change your manner of life, they perish, and you will be found, and it will be said about you, *He died and has come back to life; he was lost and has been found* (Lk 15:24).

NOTES

1. The Maurists have much the same conviction about this sermon's inauthenticity as they have about the previous two or three. The editors of the Italian edition suggest the author may be Caesarius again. I for once am inclined to support its authenticity—though with occasional misgivings—and I would tentatively suggest a rather late date, say 420.

2. See Mt 25:31-46.

3. See Eccl 12:14.

4. Omitting, as surely the redundant addition of a careless copyist, and also as a phrase impossible to construe in this sentence, "and all the rest he enumerates" (not a relative clause in the Latin, though it sounds like one in the English).

5. See Jn 13:23.

6. See Jn 13:23; 19:26; 20:2; 21:7.20.

7. This language of extinguishing sins and of being extinguished oneself is a point picked on by the Maurists as being distinctly un-Augustinian. I find myself in respectful disagreement.

SERMON 389

ON PERFORMING ACTS OF CHARITY

Date: 410-411[1]

What the heavenly bread is

1. The Lord is instructing me in the reading from the gospel to speak to you on how to obtain the heavenly bread.[2] This earthly bread, you see, is necessary for earth, because our flesh is earth. Now it cannot be the case that our flesh should have its bread, and our souls should not have their own bread. After all, our souls too are in a state of need in this age, needing their own bread just as the flesh does. I mean, who doesn't need bread? God doesn't; so it's only bread[3] that doesn't need bread; he himself, you see, is bread for our souls, and he doesn't need any other bread, but is sufficient for himself and for nourishing us too. And so it's clear what the heavenly bread is that feeds our souls.

Advice on how to obtain this bread

2. But how are we to reach it, in order to take our fill of that bread, from which we can now scarcely gather a few crumbs, to save us from dying of starvation in this desert? So on how we are to attain to a full meal on that bread, of which the Lord says, *Whoever eats this bread will never be hungry, and whoever drinks the drink that I shall give will never be thirsty forever* (Jn 6:52); he's promising us a fullness and repletion to be had without our getting sick and tired of it; so on how we are to attain to that fullness of bread, so far from it do we find ourselves now in this state of famine, we need advice. If we neglect this advice, then we knock on the door for that bread in vain. But no, in fact, if anyone ignores the advice I am going to give you, or rather the advice I am going to remind you of, because it's what I have learned together with you and doesn't come from myself; so if any of you ignore the advice I am going to give you, I don't say that you knock at the door in vain, but that you are simply not knocking on it at all.

What do you suppose, after all, my brothers and sisters—that God really has in material terms a kind of solid door, which he shuts against people, and that is why he told us to knock, so that we should come and hammer on the door, until our knocking reaches the ears of the master of the house, occupied in some private inner sanctum, and he gives orders for it to be opened to us, saying "Who's that knocking? Who's that bursting my eardrums with that din? Give him what he wants, and tell him to go away from here." That's not how it is. But all the same it's something like that. Certainly when you knock on somebody's door, you do it with your hands. There's something you should do with your hands when you knock on the Lord's door. Most certainly do it with your hands, knock with your hands. If you don't do this, I'm not saying that you knock in vain, I'm saying you are simply not knocking at all. That's why you won't be let in, that's why you won't receive anything, because you are not knocking.

"How," you say,[4] "do you want me to knock? Look, I'm praying every day."

That's a good thing you're doing, praying, an excellent thing, because this too is what was said: *Ask, and it will be given you, seek, and you shall find, knock, and the door will be opened to you* (Lk 11:9). All three things are said, Ask, seek, knock. Ask by praying, seek by discussing,[5] knock by giving a helping hand. So don't let the hand be idle.

When we are generous with our acts of charity,
it is nothing to start boasting about

3. When the apostle was reminding a Christian community[6] about being generous with charity, he said, *On this matter I have some advice to give. For this is to your advantage, because you have begun from the previous year not only to act but also to be willing* (2 Cor 8:10). And Daniel had this to say to King Nebuchadnezzar: *Take my advice, O king, and redeem your sins with almsdeeds* (Dn 4:27). So if it's advice that we receive when we are told, or when we are reminded, to give some of what we possess to the needy, let us not grow proud when we give it. After all, if what you have received is advice or counsel, your acting on it is more to your advantage than to that of the person you have given something to. So we shouldn't get conceited about our good works, and pat ourselves on the back for bestowing benefits on those to whom we give anything. People who wish to receive advice are hoping to receive something to their advantage, and those who give advice are considering the interests of their clients. If they give advice, it's to the advantage of those they give it to.

A poor man comes humbly begging, and receives something from you—because if it is unfitting for you to be proud in giving, how much more should he avoid pride in receiving; he receives it humbly, and thanks you for it. You, all the same, should know full well, and never forget, not only what you are giving, but also what you are receiving. If this poor man, you see, were to be given freedom to answer you, if he sensed that you were putting yourself a cut above him, he might say to you, "What are you being so proud about, why so conceited? Because you've given me something? What have you given me? Some bread. If you put this bread aside in your house and forgot about it, it would grow moldy, from being moldy it would get worm-eaten, from being worm-eaten turn into dust; dust would revert to dust. You indeed, when my hand was stretched out to receive, have stretched your hand out to give; but remember what your hand was made from, and what you have placed in mine: dust from dust in dust.[7]

"And then, what do I do with your bread? I eat it. I assuage the pangs of hunger with it. I receive a benefit, I am not ungrateful. You, however, for your part, should think about what the Lord our savior himself reminded you of, that *everything that goes into the mouth passes into the belly, and ends up in the sewer* (Mt 15:17). Again, what did the apostle Paul tell you? *Food for the belly and the belly for food; God, though, will bring to nothing both the one and the other* (1 Cor 6:13). So bread, as I have just said, as earth goes from earth to earth,[8] in order that earth may be sustained, and earth recruit its strength. You are thinking about what you have given, and not thinking at all about what you are going to receive. So just consider whether I am not doing you a bigger favor by receiving than you are doing me by giving. After all, if there wasn't anybody to receive things from you, you wouldn't be handing out earth and buying heaven.[9] I am knocking at your door, and you hear me, and you give orders for me to be handed something in order to relieve my hunger, and stop it causing me this trouble. You've done a good deed.

"Stop hearing me knocking if you dare. If you are not going to beg at all, then ignore the beggar at your door. Ignore me if you have nothing to ask for from the one who made both you and me. If, however, you are going to ask for what you give me,[10] you are ensuring that because you have listened to me, you will be listened to yourself. Thank the one who enabled you to buy something so precious at so cheap a price. You give what perishes with time, you receive what abides forever. You give what you would have to throw away in any case after a little while, if you didn't give it; you receive what you can enjoy forever. You give what appeases the hunger of men, you receive what makes you the companion of angels. You give what ensures a person will not be hungry for a time, though in a short while he is going to experience hunger again; you receive what means that you will never experience starvation, never endure hunger or thirst anymore. So when you realize what you give, what you receive, stop giving if you dare. Let us see who will be stricken with the greater loss; I, to whom you don't give some earth, or you, who fail to reach the one who made heaven and earth."

So if we have received advice and counsel, let us carry it out for our own sakes, and let none of us say we are doing the poor a favor; in fact we are doing ourselves more of a favor than we are doing the poor.

Using the poor as porters to transfer our perishable
worldly wealth to heaven

4. If we think true thoughts, my brothers and sisters, and form our ideas according to the words of the Lord—after all, if we form them otherwise, we are lost—if we don't live by our own counsel and advice but by his, then we really and truly do live. If we have anything which we could give to the poor

and don't give it, then we leave it behind here, or perhaps lose it here while we are still alive. How many people, after all, have suddenly lost all their possessions at a stroke, after hoarding them so carefully! One incursion of the enemy, and all the savings of the wealthy were lost.[11] Nobody said to the enemy, "I'm keeping it for my children."[12] Surely you can see that if they have any faith—we have to talk, after all, of those who suffered these things as Christians; there's no need to mention the others who do not know God; they, you see, lost what they valued in this life, and had no hopes of the other life; darkness outside, darkness inside; poverty in the strongbox, greater want in the conscience; so as I said, there's no need at all to talk about these, but rather about those who have some Christian faith; the reason I said "some," not a full, not a sturdy faith, is that if it had been full and sturdy, they would not have spurned God's advice. Surely, though, dearly beloved, when they saw their houses stripped of everything—or perhaps they were not allowed to see their houses as hollow shells, but were led away captive and on their leaving them their houses went up in smoke; so surely, when they saw themselves stripped of everything, how they must have regretted not having listened to the Lord's advice!

Now what did our Lord Jesus Christ say, what did he say, brothers and sisters,[13] to that rich man who was asking his advice about how to obtain eternal life?[14] What did he say to him? "Lose everything you have"? Certainly, even if he had said, "Lose your temporal possessions, to acquire eternal ones. . . ."[15] All the same, he didn't say to him, "Lose everything you have." He could see, after all, that he was in love with his wealth. He didn't say, "Lose it," but "Transfer it where you won't ever lose it. Are you in love with your treasures? Are you in love with your money? Are you in love with your wealth? Are you in love with your estates? Whatever it is you love, you have it here on earth; you have what you love in a place where you can lose it, and be lost yourself. My advice to you is: transfer it to heaven. If you keep it here, you will lose what you have, and you will perish together with what you lose; but if you keep it there, you haven't lost it, but you will yourself follow what you have sent ahead. So my advice is,[16] *Give to the poor, and you will have treasure in heaven.* You won't be left without any treasure, but what you hold on to so anxiously on earth, you will keep in heaven with nothing to worry about at all. So transfer it. I'm giving you advice on how to keep it, not on how to lose it. *You will have,* he says, *treasure in heaven; and come, follow me* (Mk 10:21), and I will lead you to your treasure; it's not a question of making a loss, but of making a profit.

People should wake up, they should listen; at least if they have experienced what they are afraid of, they should take steps to rid themselves of their fears, they should transfer their assets to heaven. You store your grain in the ground; your friend comes along,[17] who knows about the nature of grain and of ground, and gives your ignorance a lesson: "What have you done? You've stored grain low down in the ground; it's a damp place, what you've stored there will rot, you will lose the fruit of all your work."

So what must I do?

"Transfer it to a higher place, above ground." You listen to your friend giving you advice about your grain, and you ignore God giving you advice about your heart. You are afraid to store your grain in the ground, and you let your heart get spoiled in the ground. Look, here is the Lord your God, when he's giving you advice about your treasure, also giving you some advice about your heart: *For where,* he says, *your treasure is, there will your heart be also* (Mt 6:21). Lift up your heart, he says, to heaven, or it will rot in the earth. It's the advice of one who wishes to preserve you, not to destroy you.

So if that's how it is, how sorry are those people feeling who haven't done this? What are they saying to themselves now? "We would have had in heaven what we have lost on earth." The enemy broke into the house; could he break into heaven? He killed the servant on guard; could he kill the Lord keeping the place *where no thief can get in, nor moth spoil things* (Mt 6:20)? How many must be saying, "We would have had it there, we should have stored our treasures there in that place, where after a short while, without anything to worry about, we would follow them. Why didn't we listen to our Lord? Why[18] did we ignore our father's warning, and so experience the enemy's incursion?" Many people, then, are feeling very sorry for themselves.

Because there was one man—and this really did happen, so it's said—one man, not rich, but all the same fat, on his slender means, with the corpulence of charity, who had sold, as was usual, a gold guinea piece, and from the price he got for it gave instructions for a hundred dollars[19] to be distributed to the poor. It was done. Thereupon that ancient enemy, that is the devil,[20] to ensure that he repented of his good work, and blotted out by his grumbling what he had done rightly by his obedience, sent in a thief and took away the whole sum from which such a petty amount had been given to the poor. The devil was waiting for words of blasphemy, and all he heard was words of praise. He was waiting for the man to stagger, and he found him made stronger in faith than ever. The enemy indeed was hoping he would repent, and repent he did. But notice what of: "Woe is me," he said, "for not giving the whole lot away! I mean I have lost all that I did not give away, because I did not deposit it in the place which no thief can get at."

So[21] if that is the advice we have been given, let us not be slow in following such good advice. If what we possess is to be transferred, let us move it to the place where we can't lose it. What are the poor people we give charity to, but our porters, whom we hire to transfer our assets from earth to heaven? You give the stuff to your porter; he carries what you give him to heaven. "How," you say, "does he carry it to heaven? Look, I see him spending it all on food."

But that's just it; it's by spending it on food, not by keeping it, that he transports it. Or has this slipped your mind: *Come, you blessed of my Father, take possession of the kingdom. For I was hungry and you gave me to eat.* And, *Whenever you did it for one of the least of mine, you did it for me* (Mt 25:34-35.40)? If you haven't ignored the beggar there in front of you, notice who it is that what you have given the beggar has got to. *Whenever you did it for one of the least of mine, you did it for me.* Christ has received what you have given; it has been received by the one who gave you the means to give it; it has been received by the one who at the end will give you himself.

Why it is only generosity to the poor, or the lack of it,
that is mentioned in the last judgment scene

5. I mean, this too, brothers and sisters, is something I have sometimes reminded you of, something which I confess has exercised me no little in God's scriptures, and which I ought regularly to remind you of. I'm asking you to think hard about what our Lord Jesus Christ himself will say at the end of the world, when he comes to judgment; that he will gather all the nations together in his presence, and divide mankind into two parts, placing some on the right hand, others on the left; and that he is going to say to those on the right, *Come, you blessed of my Father, take possession of the kingdom which has been prepared for you from the origin of the world;* while to those on the left he will say, *Go into the eternal fire which has been prepared for the devil and his angels* (Mt 25:34.41). You ask for an explanation of such an enormous reward, or such a stupendous punishment, *Take possession of the kingdom,* and *Go into the eternal fire.* Why are those going to take possession of the kingdom? *Because I was hungry and you gave me to eat.* Why are these going to go into the eternal fire? *Because I was hungry, and you did not give me anything to eat.*

Now what is this, I ask you? I observe about those who are going to take possession of the kingdom that they have been generous in giving, like good and faithful Christians, not ignoring the words of the Lord, and trusting confidently in his promises. They have done this, because if they hadn't, their otherwise good lives would have been rendered unsuitably sterile. After all, they were presumably chaste, not fraudulent, not drunkards, carefully abstaining from evil deeds. But if they hadn't added this, they would have remained sterile. I mean, they would have carried out *Turn away from evil,* and not also, *and do good* (Ps 34:14; 37:27). Nonetheless, he does not say to them as well, "Come, take possession of the kingdom; because you have lived chastely, you have not cheated anybody, you have not oppressed any poor person, you have not encroached on anyone's boundaries, you have not sworn false oaths to anyone. He didn't say that, but *Take possession of the kingdom.* Why? *For I was hungry and you gave me to eat.* How supremely excellent this must be, when the Lord kept quiet about all the rest, and only mentioned this! Again, to those others: *Go into the eternal fire, which has been prepared for the devil and his angels.* How many things he could have said against the godless, if they had asked, "Why are we going into the eternal fire?" Why do you ask, you adulterer you, you murderer, you cheat, you sacrilegious so-and-so, blasphemer, unbeliever? None of that, but simply, *because I was hungry, and you did not give me anything to eat.*

I notice that you too are puzzled and surprised. And indeed it is a very surprising thing. Now I have put together an explanation of this surprising thing as best I could, which I won't hide from you. It's written, *As water does fire, so almsgiving extinguishes sin* (Sir 3:30); again, it's written, *Lock up an almsdeed in a poor man's heart, and it will pray for you to the Lord* (Sir 29:12 Lat). Again, it is written, as I reminded you a short while ago, *Listen to my advice, O king, and redeem your sins with almsdeeds* (Dn 4:27). And there are many other teachings in the divine writings, which show how much almsgiving and deeds of charity avail for extinguishing and wiping out sins. Accordingly, to those whom he is going to condemn—no, first on the contrary to those whom he is going to reward with crowns, he is going to impute nothing but their acts of charity, as though to say, "It would be difficult, if I examined you closely, and weighed you in the balance, and thoroughly scrutinized your deeds, for me not to find reasons to condemn you; but, *Go into the kingdom; for I was hungry and you gave me to eat.* So you are not going into the kingdom because you never sinned, but because you redeemed your sins with almsdeeds."

Again, for the others too: *Go into the eternal fire, which has been prepared for the devil and his angels.* And when would they ever dare, as being guilty and liable from long in the past, to say that they were being undeservedly condemned, that they didn't deserve this sentence being passed on them by so just a judge? Taking a look at their consciences, taking a look at all the wounds they had inflicted on their souls,[22] when would they ever dare to say, "We are being unjustly condemned"? It had already been said about them previously in Wisdom, *Their iniquities will stand up against them to disgrace them* (Wis 4:20); so without a shadow of doubt they will see that they are being justly condemned for their misdeeds and crimes. And it's as though he were saying to them, "It's not for the reasons you think; but *because I was hungry and you never gave me anything to eat;* I mean, if you had turned away from your sins, and turned back to me, and redeemed all those crimes and sins with acts of charity, those very acts of charity would now be setting you free, and absolving you from the guilt of such enormous crimes. *Blessed,* after all, *are the merciful, because mercy will be shown them* (Mt 5:7). But now, as it is, *Go into the eternal fire; for judgment without mercy upon one who has shown no mercy* (Jas 2:13).

Deeds of charity are the proper fruits of repentance

6. This is my recommendation to you, my brothers and sisters; give earthly bread, and knock at the door of the heavenly bread; the Lord is bread. *I,* he said, *am the bread of life* (Jn 6:35). How will he give to you, if you don't give to the person in need? Someone else needs something urgently from you; you need something urgently from someone else. And when you need something from someone else, and another person needs something from you, this person needs something from someone who is also in need of something; because the one you need something from doesn't need anything from anybody. Do what you would like done for you. After all, it's not the way it usually is between friends, competing with each other after a fashion in the favors they do each other: "I've done this for you," and the answer comes, "And I've done this for you." That's not how God wants us to do him favors, because he too has done favors for us; he is in no need of anything at all. That's why he is the real Lord: *I said to the Lord: My God are you, because you have no need of my goods* (Ps 16:2). So while he is the Lord, and the real Lord, and has no need of our goods, all the same, in order that we might do something for him, he was ready to be hungry

in his poor. *I was hungry*, he said, *and you gave me to eat. Lord, when did we see you hungry? Whenever you did it for one of these least of mine, you did it for me.* Again, to the others, *When you failed to do it for one of the least of mine, you failed to do it for me* (Mt 25:35.37.40.45).[23]

In a word, therefore, let us all listen, and seriously reflect what great merit there is in having fed Christ when he was hungry—and what sort of a crime it is to have ignored Christ when he was hungry. Repentance for our sins does indeed change us for the better; but not even that will appear to be of much use to us, if it is barren of the works of mercy. Truth bears witness to this through John, who said to those who came to him, *Generation of vipers, who has shown you how to flee from the wrath to come? Produce fruits, therefore, proper to repentance. And do not say, We have Abraham for our father. For I tell you that God has the power to raise up children for Abraham from these stones. For already the axe has been laid to the roots of the trees. Every tree, therefore, that does not bear good fruit will be cut down, and thrown on the fire* (Lk 3:7-9). This is the fruit, of course, about which he had just said, *Produce fruits proper to repentance.* And so any who haven't produced such fruits have no reason to suppose that by a barren repentance they will earn pardon for their sins.

What these fruits actually are, though, he went on to show. Because after these words of his, *the crowds questioned him, saying: So what shall we do?*; that is, What are these fruits, which you are urging and scaring us to produce? *But he answered and said to them, Whoever has two shirts should give to the one who has none, and whoever has food should do the same* (Lk 3:10-11). What could be clearer, my brothers and sisters, what more certain, more explicit? So what can be the meaning of what he said first: *Every tree that does not bear good fruit will be cut down and thrown on the fire*, but what those on the left are going to hear: *Go into the eternal fire; for I was hungry, and you did not give me anything to eat?* And so it's little enough to give up sinning, if you don't bother to make up for past actions. As it's written, *Son, have you sinned? Do not do it again.* And in case he should imagine that that alone would see him safe, *And about past actions*, he goes on, *pray that they may be forgiven you* (Sir 21:1). But what good will praying do you, if you make yourself unfit to be heard by not bearing fruits proper to repentance, so that like a barren tree you get cut down and thrown on the fire? So if you want to be heard when you pray for your past sins, *Forgive, and you will be forgiven; give and it will be given to you* (Lk 6:37-38).

NOTES

1. I infer this date from section 4, which talks about an incursion by the enemy. I take this as a reference to the sack of Rome by the Goths in 410. See note 11 below. The sermon exists in two forms; that published by the Maurists in the seventeenth century, and a text published in 1948 in the

Revue Bénédictine (RB). This latter is the one translated here, and it includes a whole long portion which the Maurists printed as part of Sermon 60. See that sermon, note 15. The Maurists are satisfied about its authenticity, rightly in my view, though perhaps, given these facts, it was not just one sermon, but two, or more. I give the heading provided by the Maurists; that in the RB text runs, "Treatise on obtaining the heavenly bread, or on performing acts of charity and compassion."

2. See Jn 6:27-35—perhaps, indeed, the rest of the chapter too.

3. Following the Maurists. RB reads "... who doesn't need bread? So God alone, as bread, doesn't need bread."

4. Reading *inquis* instead of *inquit*, he says, with the RB text.

5. So the Maurists; RB has "seek by knocking."

6. *Plebem*, literally, a people.

7. Following the Maurists. RB reads, "but remember what your hand and mine were made from. You have placed dust from dust in dust."

8. Meaning here, from your hand to my hand.

9. So RB. The Maurists have "you wouldn't be handing out earth, and wouldn't receive heaven."

10. An allusion to the petition, "Give us this day our daily bread."

11. I think, if this is a genuine sermon of Augustine's, that this must be an allusion to the sack of Rome in 410.

12. Which is what they invariably said to the bishop when he urged them to give to the poor.

13. This is combining the Maurist and RB texts, a practice usually frowned on by textual critics. The Maurists have, "What did our Lord Jesus Christ say, brothers and sisters?"; RB has, "What did our Lord Jesus Christ, what did he say?"

14. See Mk 10:17-22.

15. He fails to complete the sentence. One old editor did it for him, adding, "it would have been acceptable."

16. Here the Maurist text of Sermon 389 omits the next few paragraphs up to "Why did we ignore our father's warning," referring back to their longer version of Sermon 60, 7.

17. So the Maurists in Sermon 60, 7. RB has "What sort of plan is it for you to have stored grain in the ground? Your friend, who knows . . ."

18. Here the Maurist text of Sermon 389 resumes.

19. He had sold a *solidus*, and ordered 100 *folles* from the price to be distributed to the poor. The Maurists have a long discussion on what he would have sold the *solidus* for, and what proportion of it the 100 *folles* represented. The answer, he goes on to say himself, is tiny, *exiguus*, the equivalent of $100, say, out of $6,000.

20. See Rv 12:9.

21. Here the Maurists refer back once more to Sermon 60, 8 onward, for the rest of the sermon.

22. So the Maurists; RB has "on their consciences."

23. The Maurists omit this last sentence.

SERMON 390

ON ALMSGIVING

Date: 420-425[1]

How to store up treasure in heaven

1. I wish to urge upon your graces, to the extent the Lord enables me to, the importance of giving alms, a practice which with holy and faithful men[2] customarily goes along with fasting, so that what is subtracted from the one who has may be added to the one who has not. This is the way to cheat your soul to your own profit;[3] to place firmly in heaven what you take away from the flesh. That's where you have your granary, where you have your guard. I mean, when people want to place in complete safety what they most love on earth, they hire themselves the securest possible places, and take all the steps they can to keep a place safe for themselves which thieves cannot get at. And while that's what they want, what they try to keep safe, when can this ever really be done on earth? Perhaps the guard will be a thief himself.

The Lord Jesus Christ observed this, what it is that people want, what they strive for when they hope to preserve their possessions on earth, and he has given this advice: "Keep them safe in heaven, entrust them to me." So the one who commanded you to give, did not want you to lose your property, but to transfer it. Let your property go ahead where you are going to follow. What you don't send on ahead you leave behind here,[4] where you are not going to stay very long, where you do not know who will be able to gain possession of what you have saved up after you have gone. So hoist up from here what you love, in case by loving it here you stick here, and by sticking here lose both it and yourself. Your Lord is himself your guard and the guard of your property.[5]

If a family friend of yours were to give you advice, for example about storing grain, you knowing nothing about it, and tell you to hoist it up from the lower to the higher levels, where you would preserve it better; wouldn't you accept his advice? So that's the advice your Lord is giving you; and it's because he doesn't want either you or your possessions to rot. "Deposit them up here," he says,[6] "if you don't want to lose them." Do you want to know how it works?[7] I myself know that nobody can give better advice about this building than the man who put it up. You are saying, "Where am I to lay up my things?"; he

413

answers, "In heaven." This, actually, is what he said: *Store up for yourselves treasure in heaven, where no thief digs through the wall, nor moth spoils things; for where your treasure is, there will your heart be also* (Lk 12:33-34). Take his advice, with the option offered you of such a vast granary, where there is no tariff hung on the door for you, which means you can keep your possessions there forever.

Lend to the Lord; he pays back with incalculable interest

2. You will ask, perhaps, how you can hoist your goods up there. Don't get steamed up about it, and go looking in imagination for ladders or cranes or any such machinery. But do what is habitually done with citizens living abroad; make a mercantile loan.[8] Many people, of course, do this, when they find reliable partners, they do it without hesitation. Your Lord Christ has entered into such a transaction, being rich up above, poor here below. He is hungry here; he asks you for a mercantile loan, he will pay you back on the nail. So why do you hesitate, why do you put off giving? Or isn't he a reliable partner, to be trusted to pay back? Give to the poor, you won't lose it, don't be afraid; you're giving to him, when you give to one of the least of his own. Listen to the gospel; when those placed on the right hand side were amazed, as he recounted a number of needy situations he had been in, they said, *When did we see you in any of these situations?* The Lord replies, *When you did it for one of the least of mine, you did it for me* (Mt 25:37-40). I it was, I'm telling you, who received it whenever poor people received it; it was in them that I was hungry, in them that I was satisfied.

Give without a qualm; it's the Lord who receives, the Lord who is asking. You wouldn't have anything to give him, unless you had first received it from him.[9] If you were lending at interest to human beings, you would be oppressing them; this is not such a debtor as will be oppressed by the rate of interest. "If you want to be a moneylender," God says to you, "be one to me, give to me. I always pay back at a huge rate of interest." Now at last you can perk up, enlarge your avaricious greed. For a single $100 bill,[10] perhaps, you are going to get back not ten, not a hundred, not a thousand, not the earth, but heaven. If you gave a pound of coppers and received a pound of silver, or a pound of silver and received one of gold, you would be delighted at your luck. What you give will certainly be transmuted; it isn't gold, it isn't silver, but eternal life that will come your way. It will be transmuted, because you yourself will be transmuted. All those who have given, will become angels; what they have given will become angelic thrones.

There is no other remedy to deliver us from death but acts of charity. It is difficult for any human being to lead this life without sins. So be generous in giving, my brothers and sisters, distribute your possessions. *Make yourselves purses that do not wear out, treasure that abides in heaven* (Lk 12:33). Listen to the psalm: *Although man walks in the image, yet he is disturbed in vain; he treasures, and does not know for whom he gathers it* (Ps 39:6).[11] *Give, and it will be given to you* (Lk 6:38).

NOTES

1. The Maurists see no reason to doubt the authenticity of this short sermon, and neither do I. They say it is a faulty and much mutilated text. I suspect, however, a rather indifferent stenographer taking it down when it was preached. There is one obvious gap in the text which the Maurists note. But there are a number of other places that suggest to me a rather careless summary or note made by the stenographer. The brevity of the sermon would incline me to put it rather late, 420 to 425 or later, and most probably in Hippo Regius. The manuscripts assign it to the Saturday after the fifth Sunday in Lent, that is the Saturday before Holy Week.

2. *Sanctis et fidelibus viris;* so he is talking to a community of men, it would seem; possibly to the members of his own religious community, possibly to some equivalent in those days of the Saint Vincent de Paul Society. A gross anachronism, no doubt; but who knows whether there were not such groups and associations of pious laypeople in the Churches of those days?

3. I think something is probably missing here; a fuller reference, for example, to Mt 6:25: *Is not your soul more than food, or your body more than clothing?* So it is by fasting that you "cheat your soul," that is your life, of the food that is its normal due.

4. The text lacks the phrase "you leave behind here"; the Maurists suggest adding it: *hic dimittis.*

5. Again, there seems to be something missing between this sentence and the previous one.

6. I have added "he says," to make it clear that, as I understand it, this sentence is the Lord speaking. Again, I think in the next few lines the stenographer has run together what were probably two distinct images or themes; the one we are already embarked on about the best place to store grain, and another about the functions of a building, and who is the right person to consult about them.

7. Or "what should be done"; *quid agatur.*

8. *fac trajectitium.* This was a loan at a very large rate of interest, because it involved the risk of a sea journey. Thus I, a native of Naples say, find myself in Hippo Regius, and in need of money to get home. I borrow from a merchant who trades with Naples, and promise to pay him, or his agent, in that city when I get home—and at a high rate of interest. See Sermons 42,2; 86,11, note 20; 114A, 4.

9. Again, there seems to be a slight hiccup in the sequence of thought.

10. For one *solidus.* A silver one, I presume, not a gold one.

11. Again, I suspect a lapse in the stenographer's attention.

SERMON 391

TO THE YOUTH

Date: 393-396[1]

No age free from temptation, not even infancy

1. My words are for you, young people, in the prime of life, in a time of
spiritual danger. No time indeed, no period of life, while we are carrying this
perishable flesh, can be free from trials and temptations. And as long as good
people are straining in the contest not to be beaten by their opponent, they are
in danger; as long as they are wrestling with him in this mortal life, as on the
sawdust of some stadium. I mean, the moment babies are born in this age, and
proclaim their entry into a life full of misery with tearful cries, prophetic it would
seem of their troubles to come, they can already be tempted; even if not in their
own minds yet, still in the minds of their parents or any other people to whose
hands the task is entrusted of rearing them in their feebleness; through them they
can be snatched away by the devil's tricks, either by abominable amulets and
charms, or the sacrilegious rites of the pagans, or if by any chance death is
imminent, by neglecting to renounce the world through the saving sacrament of
baptism. And to put it in a nutshell, children of that age are subjected to
temptation when they are loved by their families in a worldly way, and neglected
in their relationship with Christ.

They bring with them, you see, the seeds of death, and are rooted in that
deadly wound of sin which the serpent's poisonous fangs inflicted on the first
man, to whom we trace the origin of our corruption.[2] That's why Saint Job says
that nobody is clean, from the filth of sin of course, not even an infant who has
only lived a day on the earth.[3] But why should I speak of one already born, when
David cries out in a voice of woe, and says, *In iniquity was I conceived, and in
sin did my mother conceive me* (Ps 51:5)? The baptism of newly born babies
could well seem superfluous, after all, unless they all died in Adam, and unless
original sin ran along its deadly track through the bodies of parents to bear its
fruit in their offspring. The almighty Lord, for his part, both fashions the human
creature as mortal according to the rules of the order he has established, and also
as the best of fathers by his compassionate grace provides immortality through
renewal.

Old age too has its temptations

2. But if not even the infancy of mortal humanity is free of temptations, because of this chain of corruption, what am I to say about the other stages of life? Or perhaps old age is the exception, is it, when in flesh already close to turning into a corpse the blood and instruments of unlawful lust have grown cold, and the material for temptation has dwindled away from a body that is tired out and as good as dead? On the contrary, however, such in bad old people is the whirlpool of greed, very often, and the insatiable maw of the belly and the palate, that however serene good old people may be in their wisdom, these others simply drown themselves in drunkenness. It's as though the only reason they grow gnarled and withered and sapless, is in order to be restored to their pristine vigor by being watered with a flood of intoxicants. What about avarice, *which is the root of all evils* (1 Tm 6:10)? Aren't frigid old people on fire with it, all the more fiercely set on acquiring things, the nearer they are to leaving behind what they are hoarding? A most extraordinary folly, undoubtedly. They are in a hurry, I mean, to burden themselves with more baggage than ever, now that they are already, as near as makes no difference, at journey's end.

Youth a kind of ulcer inflamed with desire,
swollen with hope, bursting with pleasure

3. So if childhood and old age are not free from temptation, of which the one, that is childhood, has scarcely entered this life, and the other is already departing from it; the one a short while before did not exist, the other a short while later will exist no more; what are we to think, what are we to say, about the fires of youth, which being set in between these other two periods, has already moved away from the feebleness of childhood, and has not yet reached the weariness of old age? It is this period that is tossed about by the most frequent and severe storms of temptation, this that is battered and overwhelmed most often by the tidal waves of the world and this age. Youth is over-confident about its strength, boastful about its handsome appearance, either aims at making a show with the glitter and gloss of temporal possessions, or is delighted at actually doing so. And thus for bad young people, whatever truth has commanded is poison, whatever the devil has suggested is food. But in fact the bitter taste of justice is the right medicine for the ulcer of youth, while the sweet taste of injustice is the bait in the mousetrap to catch its headstrong rashness.

This is what is referred to by the text, *Wounds from a friend are sweeter than the freely offered kisses of an enemy* (Prv 27:6); and also by the thing David said, *The just man will censure me in mercy and rebuke me; but let not the oil of the sinner grease my head* (Ps 141:5). Truth burns, but for all that it heals, while the oil of the sinner, the flattery of the yes-man, is gratifying, but deceitful. Pride, you see, is soothed by it, but life is undermined. The prophet,[4] after all, is speaking in the person of those who are already seeking out the doctor, who bear with the sharp pain his healing hand inflicts, who desire to have their illness cured rather than praised. The ulcer of youth, however, is dangerous, being inflamed with lust, swollen with hope, bursting with pleasure. But this hope is for hopeless things, hope for perishable things, which doesn't release the wretched soul from its passions but inflates them, and makes it intolerant of the touch of truth. The result is that it even despairs of its immortality, and loves to say, loves too those who say to it, *Let us eat and drink, for tomorrow we shall die*, while it hates to say and hear, *Be sober, you just, and do not sin* (1 Cor 15:32.34); loves the pernicious smoothness of the enemy, hates the salutary harshness of the doctor. Such perversity, such madness is what above all else has to be dreaded during youth.

How self-indulgence also breeds cruelty

4. From such mad perversity spring those words of men so abandoned to their shameless pleasures that they go on to violent crimes: *For they said, reasoning unsoundly to themselves, Short and wearisome is the time of our life, and there is no rest at the end for man, and no one is known to have returned from the underworld.* And a little later, *Come, therefore, let us enjoy the good things there are, and use creation with zest as in youth. Let us take our fill of costly wine and ointments* (Wis 2:1.6-7); and the other things which are added in the same place, expressing the self-indulgent words of people who have no hope of eternal life, and place all their hope, so to say, in the sand of the torrent,[5] that is in the temporal, perishable flesh. But from such immoderate lusts, and stinking, worm-ridden shamelessness, see to what misdeeds and what monstrous crimes there is but a short leap. Ruined and drained of all decency by the corrupting effect of their unrestrained foul behavior, and hating the severity of truth that opposes them, *So let us oppress the poor just man*, they say, *and not spare the widow, nor honor the gray hairs and many years of the old. But let our strength be the standard of justice; for what is weak is found to be useless. Let us therefore lay siege to the just man, since he is useless to us, and opposes our activities.* Such were the thoughts the godless Jews had about our Lord Jesus Christ, which becomes clearer in the words that follow. A moment later, you see, they are saying, *He claims to have knowledge of God, and calls himself the Son of God.* Then again, a little later they are saying, *Let us question him with abuse and torture, so that we may know his devotion. Let us condemn him to a shameful death; for from his own words he will be respected.* But notice what a judgment the Holy Spirit passes on them, when he immediately adds, *Such were their thoughts, and they erred; for their wickedness had made them blind* (Wis 2:10-12.13.19-21).

Wine is followed by rage, ointments by torture, roses by blood, enjoyment by anger. By such people was the Lord bound, beaten, slain. Who would suspect that wreaths of flowers could turn into bloodsoaked chains, who foresee the most savage pains issuing from pleasant cups of wine, who foretell from lush meadows the cruel wood of the cross? And yet the only time of life, in this matter of self-indulgence, that has been compared to the time of blossom[6] is the period of youth.

Young men exhorted to follow Daniel's example, and to love wisdom

5. So, young men, it is you in particular that I am warning and urging to be captivated by the beauty of true manly virtue and strength.[7] Do not dream of comparing any earthly loveliness, any glitter of precious metals, any pleasant groves, any brightly colored flowers, any natural or artificial adornment of the body, any sound of violins and flutes, any delightful fragrance, any delicious flavors, any sweet embrace, with the beauty, the inspiration, the delights, the consolations of wisdom. You see, I am only forbidding you things it is a disgrace to love, not love itself. Do you wish to love? Love wisdom, let attaining her be your ambition.

So that the sight of her may not alarm you unduly,[8] bring some order into your inner life. Just as roving, wanton eyes are on the look-out for the embellishments of the body, so is she for those of the heart. And don't imagine you can furnish these embellishments from your own jewel cases, because she hates the proud, and those who are only eager to boast of such things as though they came from themselves. *What, though, do you have that you have not received?* (1 Cor 4:7). So it is she that grants you the means of pleasing her. Only love her, and she will keep you safe; *lay siege to her, and she will exalt you; honor her, and she will embrace you, and will place upon your head a wreath of graces* (Prv 4:8-9). *Wisdom is radiant and never fades, and is easily found by those who love her* (Wis 6:12). Make it your purpose to wed her, sigh for her, be on fire for her, fall head over heels in love with her. Deny yourself to yourself, or you may deny yourself to her, while you are pleasing yourself. *There is no bitterness in her companionship* (Wis 8:16).

If you are lovers, love her; if you are handsome fellows, think of pleasing God; if you are young, overcome the devil.[9] Daniel was called by the angel *a man of desires* (Dn 10:11). What were those desires of his, but ardent longings for the beauty of wisdom? Because in his youth he had trampled on lust, as a prisoner he had crushed the pride of kings, when shut in close he had shut the mouths of lions.

Young women advised to follow the examples of Susanna, Anna, and Mary

6. Nor should you, young women, conclude that this sermon has nothing to do with you. I'm saying these things also to you, after all, not in order to disconcert you, but to advise you as my dearest daughters; shun youthful desires. Think about Susanna if you're married, about Anna if you're widows, about Mary if you're virgins. And don't go around in public, seeking death as a matter of fact in the house of life,[10] in your eagerness to show off the flowers of your grass to the eyes of men. For *all flesh is grass, and the glory of man like the flowers in the grass.* So what will you do when the grass withers, and the flowers droop? But do you imagine that *the Word of the Lord, which abides forever* (Is 40:6-8), and which you now ignore in the proud vigor of your youth, is not easily going to find your ashes?[11] Look, I say it again, I adjure you, shun youthful desires.

If you all[12] listen to this, if you comply, if you take it with respect and fear as the word of God, you will not only be beautiful but also healthy in the eyes of God. But if from these warnings of mine you even, maybe, start making lovers' jokes among yourselves, you will be using the doctor's scalpels to inflict deadly wounds on yourselves. Sure, the Jews who crucified the Lord (when we hear the story we are horrified, and attack them with intense loathing[13]); but still, when they gave thought to their lascivious pleasures, their minds turned to delightful country nooks, and they said, *Let there be no meadow through which we have not passed on our revels* (Wis 2:8 Lat). So how would those people spare Christ, if they found him on earth, who have chosen, not lonely meadows for stimulating their lusts, but his crowded churches as he reigns in heaven? Look, this is the third time I adjure you, and say: Shun youthful desires. Be on fire with the same desires as Daniel. *My children, from your youth up choose instruction, and you will keep finding wisdom until your hairs are gray* (Sir 6:18).

NOTES

1. The older Renaissance editors had their doubts about this sermon, and one of them considered the style to be not unlike that of Ambrose. But the Maurists retort that it is not unlike that of Augustine either, in his early years. I give them the benefit of the doubt, and so assign the sermon an early date; but a very real doubt remains in my mind, especially when I come to the sermon's conclusion.

2. That is, of course, original sin, which is not the sin committed by Adam and Eve, but its consequence, the corruption it has caused in our nature.

3. See Jb 14:4-5, LXX.

4. That is, David, the psalmist.

5. See Ps 124:4.

6. Another inverted genitive; compared, it says, *flori temporis*, to the blossom of time.

7. By just the beauty of *virtus* in the Latin. But this word's basic meaning of manliness is plain to see in the Latin, while it goes totally unobserved in the English "virtue." The preacher is alluding, I think, to Wis 2:11, *let our strength be the standard of justice*.

8. Is he tacitly comparing Wisdom to the Gorgon Medusa?

9. See 1 Jn 2:13.

10. An odd phrase; but I think it is evoking, and as it were parodying, Prv 9:13-18, where the "foolish woman"—the prostitute—sits at the door of her house enticing young men to enter what is in fact "a house of death." See also Prv 7:27.

11. And so bring you to judgment in the resurrection.

12. Now, I think, addressing all the young people, male as well as female; his adjectives are from now on in the masculine gender.

13. He does presumably identify the Jews with the wicked of Wis 2. But the thought occurs to me that this parenthesis is the marginal comment of a medieval copyist, justifying the occasional pogrom. The sentence is left unfinished.

SERMON 392

Date: 420[1]

Concubinage is unlawful, as also marrying divorced persons
while their previous partners are still alive

2. Listen, dearly beloved, members of Christ and children of our Catholic mother. Let the faithful listen to what I am saying to the *competentes;*[2] let the *competentes* listen to what I am saying to the faithful; let the penitents listen to what I am saying to the *competentes* and the faithful; let the catechumens, let everybody listen to what I am saying to the faithful and the *competentes* and the penitents; let all fear, none just ignore me. May your attentive listening be a comfort to me, so that no grief of mine need be a testimony against you.

To the *competentes* I say: You are not allowed to fornicate. You must be satisfied with your wives, or with not having wives; you are not allowed to have concubines. May God hear me, if you people are deaf; may his angels hear me, if you people just ignore me. You are not allowed to have concubines. Even if you haven't got wives, you are not allowed to have concubines, just to send them away later on so that you can marry wives.[3] How much greater will your condemnation be, if you want to have both concubines and wives at the same time!

You are not allowed to take wives whose previous husbands are still alive; nor are you, ladies, allowed to take husbands whose previous wives are still alive. Such unions are adulterous, not by the law of the courts, but by the law of heaven. Not even a woman who has left her husband by formal divorce[4] are you allowed to marry, while her husband is still alive. On account of fornication alone[5] is it permissible for you to put away an adulterous wife; but while she is still alive, you are not permitted to marry another. Nor are you, ladies, permitted to take as husbands those men whose wives have left them by formal divorce; it is not allowed; these are adulterous unions, not marriages. Ignore Augustine if you like; at least fear Christ. Don't imitate the multitude of bad people, of unbelievers, my children; don't follow the wide ways, which lead in the end to destruction.[6] Anyone who is baptized should either make a vow of continence to God, or remain with his wife, or marry a wife if hasn't got one.

421

Sinners in this regard should resort to the keys of the Church

3. Listen to me, you faithful, those of you, that is, who have been baptized. Why will you die, now that you have been reborn? When, after being baptized, you proceed along twisting, slippery, unclean ways, don't you realize that you are lost? You are lost, you perish, my sons,[7] believe me. Don't you want to believe it? What am I to do with you? Those of you who are of the faithful, and are listening to me, if by any chance you have committed such sins, don't add to them; and pray to God to pardon you. If you have been unable, or unwilling, to preserve either conjugal or celibate chastity, and have fallen away from your commitment either to the marriage bond or to a vow of celibacy, show due sorrow and the humility of penance.

I will say it more clearly still, so that none of you can say, "I didn't understand." Those of you that have defiled yourselves with unlawful sexual relations apart from your wives, if besides your wives you have slept with another woman; do penance, as it is done in the Church,[8] so that the Church may pray for you. Nobody should say to himself, "I do it privately, I deal with God privately. God knows, and he will forgive me, because I do penance in my heart." So, was there no point in the Lord saying, *What you loose on earth shall be loosed in heaven* (Mt 18:18; 16:19)? So were the keys given to the Church of God for nothing? Are we to nullify the gospel, nullify the words of Christ? Am I to promise you what he refuses you? Wouldn't I just be deceiving you?

Job says, *If I have been ashamed to confess my sins in the sight of the people* (Jb 31:33). A just man like that, pure gold in God's treasury, tried and tested in such a furnace as he was, says that; and some good-for-nothing son of mine opposes me, and with his stiff-necked pride and twisted mind is ashamed to kneel under God's blessing? It's possible, or rather it cannot be doubted, that that was why God required the emperor Theodosius to do public penance in the sight of the people,[9] especially as his sin could not be hidden. And is a senator ashamed to do what an emperor was not ashamed to do? Is not even a senator, but a mere city councillor to be ashamed, where an emperor was not ashamed? Is a common man or tradesman to be ashamed, where an emperor was not ashamed? What is this pride? Wouldn't it be enough on its own to get you to hell, even if there were no adultery?

Adultery no more excusable in husbands than in wives

4. Finally, my brothers,[10] men are listening to me, women are listening to me; why are you getting angry with me?[11] If only you would do what is written: *Be angry, and do not sin* (Ps 4:4; Eph 4:26). I should be afraid that what happened to the apostle Paul, which you heard, if you were paying attention, when it was read just now, may happen to me: *So have I become your enemy, by proclaiming the truth to you?* (Gal 4:16). And if that's how it is, let it be so. If I have to be your enemy, I prefer being yours, as better than being the enemy of justice. I even commend you to the custody of your wives. They are my daughters, just as you are also my sons. Let them listen to me; they must be jealous of and for

their husbands; they shouldn't cherish for themselves the empty reputation, which married ladies are regularly accorded by their shamelessly unchaste husbands, who praise them for so calmly tolerating their husbands' shameless infidelities. I don't want Christian wives to show that sort of patience; they must definitely be jealous of their husbands; not for their bodies' sake, but for their souls'.

This is my express advice to you, yes, my instructions, yes, my orders; it's the bishop's orders, it's Christ's orders through me. He knows this, the one in whose presence my heart is all afire. I myself, I repeat, am giving you orders: don't allow your husbands to go on fornicating. Bring your complaints against them to the Church. I don't say to the civil judges, to the governor, to the deputy, to the commissioner,[12] to the emperor; but to Christ. In all other respects be the servants of your husbands, obedient and compliant. Don't let any impertinence be found in you, any pride, any shrewish answering back, any disobedience; be in all respects at their service, at their beck and call. But when it comes to the business in which the blessed apostle made you their equals, saying, *Let the husband pay the debt to his wife, and likewise the wife to her husband*; then he added, *The wife does not have authority over her own body, but the husband does*. Why are you so cock-a-hoop, man? Listen to what comes next: *Likewise the husband too does not have authority over his own body, but the wife does* (1 Cor 7:3-4). When it comes to this matter, claim your rights and insist on them.

Your husband has sold your stock of gold coins to meet his own needs; put up with it, woman, put up with it, maidservant; don't quarrel, don't oppose him. Love of your husband means indifference to your stock of gold coins. If he sells your country cottage to meet his needs—which are also, incidentally, yours, because they cannot be his without also being yours, if there is any of the charity in you that there ought to be in a wife—put up with it patiently. And if he hesitates to do so, make the offer yourself. Treat everything as of no account, for love of your husband. But require him to be chaste, fight him over chastity. Accept the loss of your country cottage calmly and patiently; but don't be calmly patient while your husband loses his soul.

Husbands should set wives a good example in this matter

5. I don't have to tell husbands to be jealous of their wives in this matter. I know what they do, yes I know very well. Which of you would ever put up with an adulterous wife? And you bid women put up with adulterous husbands? There's justice for you! Why, I ask you, why?

"Because I, of course, am a man."

You're a man, are you? Let's prove that you're a man, in the matter of courage and strength. So you are a man, eh? Conquer lust. How are you a man, when your wife is the stronger, the braver of the two? You, man, are the head of the woman, it's true.[13] But only where the household is rightly ordered, is the man the head of the woman. If he's the head, he should lead, the wife should follow.[14] If you are the head, take the lead; let her follow her head. But notice where you're going; don't go where you don't want her to follow. Don't go where you're afraid of having her hard on your heels, of your both tumbling together into the pit of adultery, of your teaching her to do what you do. You are sick at heart if you both fall into the pit of adultery together. Be equally sick at heart if you fall in alone. You're jealous, you don't want her to tumble into it; be afraid, don't tumble in yourself.

You, though, chaste and virtuous women, do not for your part imitate your unchaste husbands. Far, far be such a thing from you! Either let them live with you, or let them perish alone. It is not to her unchaste husband that a woman owes her chastity, but it's to God that she owes it, to Christ that she owes it. Let her bear in mind the price that was paid for her, let her reflect on her marriage contract.[15]

Finally, they can think what they like, those people who are perhaps feeling indignant at my bringing up such matters; because I know that those of you who are wise will love me for it; because it is not for nothing that it is written, *Rebuke a wise man, and he will love you; rebuke a fool, and he will continue to hate you* (Prv 9:8). He didn't say "will begin," but *will continue*; because he already hated you. So I know that the wise love me in this connection. Those who know that I know their sins should refrain from communion, in order not to be turned back from the altar rails. As for those whose sins I don't know, I summon them before God's judgment. They too should do penance, and from now on abstain from the filthiness of their fornications.[16]

A word to the penitents and the catechumens

6. A word now to the penitents: what is it that you are doing? You know very well—you are doing nothing! What's the use of your humbling yourselves,[17] if you don't change your behavior? A word to the catechumens: be impatient and on fire in your determination to receive grace.[18] But choose for yourselves the right people in the Church of God to imitate. If you don't find any—woe is me, my God! What am I saying, "If you don't find any"? So is there not a single one among the faithful for you to find? So many years I have been baptizing so many people, and all for nothing, if there are none among them who keep what they have received, and take care of what they have heard. God forbid I should believe that! It would be better for me to stop being your bishop, if that's how it is. But I hope, I believe that there are such people.

All this, however, puts me in the wretched position of being compelled very often to know who the adulterers are, while I cannot know who the chaste people are. What I can rejoice over is hidden and private, what causes me torment is out in the open and public. So then, catechumens, be filled with desire for the grace of God, choose the right people to imitate, to associate with, and to join with in the delightful conversations of charity. Don't listen to malicious gossip. *Malicious conversations corrupt good behavior* (1 Cor 15:33). Live like ears of corn among the weeds; put up with the distresses of this world, like grain on the threshing-floor. The winnower is going to come. Nobody should set up as a thoroughgoing, all-round separator of the two during this age.[19]

NOTES

1. The first section of the Maurists' Sermon 392 has already appeared in this series as Sermon 162B; so there is no point in reproducing it here. In note 1 to that sermon (Sermons, III, 5), I remarked that Sermon 392 "is now generally supposed to be a stitching together of several fragments. Only this one (= section 1), apparently, is definitely authentic." My comment, I regret to say, is wrong on almost all counts, and on what authority I made it, I cannot now remember; but I withdraw it unreservedly. Sermon 392, it is generally agreed, comprises only two sermons; the very short one, 162B, which may indeed be a fragment; and the longer one which we have here, which is also undoubtedly authentic, but possibly lacks its real beginning.

The scholars do not suggest any date. In section 6, however, Augustine talks about his having baptized so many people over so many years, as bishop. So I think it should be put at least twenty years after his ordination as bishop, at least as late, that is, as 416, if not later. So I date it, in round figures, to 420. Clearly it was preached to his own flock in the diocese of Hippo Regius, probably in the principal church of the city, during Lent.

2. Those enrolled to be baptized at the approaching Easter vigil; they were called competentes because they were seeking baptism. There is no equivalent expression in the Church's current practice, even after the introduction of the new Rite of Christian Initiation of Adults; so I keep the Latin term.

3. Which is what Augustine himself had done, or rather what his mother Monica had done for him in Milan, a few months before his conversion. See Confessions VI, 15.

4. per repudium; which looks like the Old Testament bill of divorce, but could also refer to a Roman legal procedure.

5. See Mt 19:9.

6. See Mt 7:13.

7. He is in fact addressing men only, as will become clear in a moment.

8. That is, confess the sin and ask to be admitted to the ranks of the paenitentes, who were barred from communion, and under a distinctly penitential regime, until they were absolved at the end of their allotted penance—provided that during that time they had amended their lives and conducted themselves properly.

9. To be more precise, it was Saint Ambrose who required this of Theodosius in 390, for the massacre of the citizens of Thessalonica, which he had ordered in reprisal for a riot in which soldiers had been killed. The event took place only three years after Augustine's conversion and baptism in the same city of Milan where the emperor was obliged publicly to humble himself.

10. Again, it is primarily the men in the congregation being addressed.

11. Quite simply, in all probability, because their wives were hearing all this too!

12. These dignitaries are, in a literal translation, "the proconsul, the vicar, the count."

13. See 1 Cor 11:2.

14. I have changed the order of these two sentences, which are the other way round in the text. This order seems to me to be the more coherent. In the course of copying and correcting, they could easily be switched round; one of them left out by mistake for instance, and then reinserted in the wrong place.

15. Her tabulae. See, among others, Sermons 9, 18; 37, 7; 51, 22; The City of God, XIV, 18.

16. See Rv 17:4.

17. By taking their place publicly in the ranks of the paenitentes, in the "sin bin."

18. That is, to receive baptism, for which a common name among African Christians was "grace."

19. A parting shot at the Donatists, who were enthusiastic separators.

SERMON 393

TO THE PENITENTS

Date: uncertain[1]

True penance means changing one's mode of life

1. Penitents, penitents, penitents—if, that is, you really are penitents, really are sorry for your sins, and not just treating the whole thing as a joke! Change your mode of life, *be reconciled to God* (2 Cor 5:20). I mean, you are just indulging yourselves, while still in chains.[2]

"What chains?" you ask.

What you bind on earth shall be bound in heaven (Mt 18:18). You hear how you are bound, and you think you can take God in? You perform the penance, you kneel down—and you laugh, and snap your fingers at God's patience? If you're a penitent, repent; if you don't repent, you're not a penitent. So if you do repent, if you're really sorry, why go on doing the bad things you did? If you're sorry for having done them, don't go on doing them. If you still do go on doing them, you're certainly not a real penitent.

Yes, I know, my dearest friends, people are taken ill, they send to the church, or are carried to the church, and are baptized, and are made new, and so will go from here to eternal bliss.[3] But the case of penance is not the same as that. Someone who hasn't yet received baptism hasn't yet violated the sacrament. But those who have violated the sacrament by living evil and abandoned lives, and have therefore been barred from the altar, in case they should *eat and drink judgment upon themselves* (1 Cor 11:29); they must change their way of life and be reconciled while they are still alive and in good health. Are they too expecting confidently to be reconciled when on the point of death? In my experience many have breathed their last while waiting to be reconciled.

Next I will also tell you, in the sight of God, what I'm afraid of, so that you may be afraid too. Those who are not afraid will despise my fears, but to their own undoing. So listen then. I am certain that people who have been baptized, if they live their lives—I dare not say without sin, because who is without sin?—but if they live their lives without serious wrongdoing, and only have such sins on their consciences as are forgiven every day to those who say in the prayer, *Forgive us our debts as we too forgive our debtors* (Mt 6:12); when they come to the end of their days, they do not come to the end of life, but pass from life

426

to life, from a life of toil to a life of rest, from a wretched to a blessed life. Whether they hasten to baptism of their own accord, or are baptized when in serious danger and so depart this life, they go to their Lord, they go to their rest.

Baptized people, though, who are deserters[4] and violators of such a great sacrament, if they repent from the bottom of their hearts, if they repent where God can see, as he saw David's heart, when on being rebuked by the prophet, and very sternly rebuked, he cried out after hearing God's fearsome threats, and said, *I have sinned*; and shortly afterward heard, *God has taken away your sin* (2 Sam 12:13).[5] Such is the effectiveness of three syllables. *I have sinned* is just three syllables; and yet in these three syllables the flames of the heart's sacrifice rose up to heaven. So those who have done genuine penance, and have been absolved from the constraints by which they were bound and cut off from the body of Christ, and have lived good lives after their penance, such as they ought to have lived before penance, and in due course have passed away after being reconciled, why, they too go to God, go to their rest, will not be deprived of the kingdom, will be set apart from the people of the devil. But any who find themselves in the last throes of their illness, and wish to receive penance, and do receive it, and are straightaway reconciled, and so depart this life—I confess to you, we don't deny them what they ask for, but we cannot take for granted that they make a good departure.

I cannot take it for granted; I won't deceive you; I cannot take it for granted. The faithful who lead good lives can depart this life with nothing to worry about. Those baptized at the last minute can depart this life with nothing to worry about. Those who have done penance, and been reconciled while in good health, and after that lead good lives, can depart this life with nothing to worry about. But those who are doing penance to the very last moment, and are then reconciled, whether they have nothing to worry about as they depart this life, I myself cannot be so sure. What I'm sure about, I'm sure about, and I can give you assurances. Where I am not so sure, I can give penance, I cannot give assurances.[6] Pay attention to what I'm saying. I must state it more plainly, so that nobody may get me wrong. Am I saying, "They will be damned"? I am not saying that. But neither am I saying, "They will be saved."

"And what are you saying to me?"

I'm saying I don't know. I'm taking nothing for granted, making no promise. I don't know. Do you want to be rid of the doubt? Do you want to get out of the uncertainty? Do penance while still in good health. You see, if you are doing genuine penance while still in good health, and your last day comes suddenly upon you, hasten to be reconciled. If you do that, you will have nothing to worry about as you depart this life. Why will you have nothing to worry about? Because you have done true penance during the time when you could also have gone on sinning.

But if you only want to do such penance when you are no longer able to sin, then your sins have given up you, not you them.

"But how do you know," you say to me, "whether God may not perhaps forgive me?"

You're right. I don't know. I know that, I don't know this. The reason, after all, why I give you a penance, is that I don't know. Because if I knew it would be no use to you, I wouldn't give it. Again, if I knew for certain it would avail you, I wouldn't be admonishing you now, wouldn't be doing my best to scare you. There are two possibilities; either you're forgiven, or you're not forgiven. Which of these two is going to happen to you, I don't know. So put aside the uncertainty, hold fast to what is certain.

NOTES

1. This sermon, as well as being found in a manuscript collection of 50 sermons of Augustine, also has a place among the works attributed both to Ambrose and to Caesarius. While older editors were skeptical of its authenticity, or simply denied it, the Maurists appear to be non-committal. There is a passage that strikes me as very dubious; but it does not appear in the collection of 50 sermons, and I have relegated it to note 6; the Maurists enclose it in brackets. The rest of the sermon I would accept as authentic. In the text, for some odd reason, it is headed, "About penitents"; but it is manifestly, forcefully addressed *to* the penitents.

2. This is just a guess at the meaning of a very enigmatic statement: *Et vos enim cum catena pascitis*; literally, "For you are feeding yourselves too with a chain." For the institution of public penance, see Sermon 232, 8, note 17 (Sermons, III, 7).

3. Another very succinct phrase: *et felices hinc erunt*. It could mean, "and will be happy from now on." But he is clearly talking about deathbed baptisms, and comparing them with the deathbed reconciliations that the "unrepentant penitents" were no doubt counting on.

4. Baptism was frequently compared to the enrollment of a soldier in the Roman army, when he took an oath of allegiance to the emperor that was precisely called a *sacramentum*, and received the imperial seal or mark, probably branded on his wrist. This was the metaphorical analogy for the Christian doctrine of sacramental character, the mark of Christ branded, so to say, on the souls of the baptized. See Sermon 260A,2, note 7 (Sermons, III, 7).

5. The sentence remains unfinished.

6. Here those manuscripts that ascribe the sermon to Ambrose or Caesarius insert the following:

But someone may say, "Good bishop [*sacerdos*, high priest; a non-Augustinian word in this context], you say you don't know, and can give us no assurance whether those are saved and deserve to come to Christ, who are given a penance as they are dying, and who were unrepentant while they lived, while they were in good health. So instruct us, I beg you, how we ought to live good lives after penance." I say, Abstain from drunkenness, from lust, from slander, from immoderate laughter, from idle words, for which people are going to give an account on the day of judgment (Mt 12:36). Notice how I've mentioned light sins. All, though, are grave and deadly [a distinctly non-Augustinian exaggeration. The manuscript that assigns this sermon to Ambrose reads, "Notice how I've mentioned light sins, and kept quiet about grave ones"]. And there's another thing I will say; it's not only after penance that people should abstain from these vices, but also before penance, while they are in good health; because if they come to the end of their lives, they do not know whether they will be able to receive a penance and confess their sins to God and the priest. There you have why I said that even before penance you should lead good lives, and after penance better ones.

SERMON 394

Some reflections on details of their martyrdom

1. Two jewels have flashed in the Church today, and one brilliant light, because Perpetua and Felicity share one festival; and there can be no doubt about the felicity which enjoys perpetual honor. They were companions in prison, companions also in grace; because there was no discord between them. They sing together in prison, together they come *to meet Christ in the air* (1 Thes 4:17); together they fight with the savage cow, together they will enter their everlasting home. Together they underwent martyrdom; one was suckling a baby, the other was delivered of one. Perpetua said, when she handed over the infant, and removed it from her breast, *Who will separate us from the love of Christ?* (Rom 8:35). Felicity groaned in giving birth, and then hurried fearlessly after her companions; and set free by her groans, what did she say to Christ? *You have broken my chains; to you will I sacrifice the sacrifice of praise* (Ps 116:16-17). And blessed David said, to comfort her in her birthpangs, *May the Lord give you your heart's desire, and support your whole design* (Ps 20:4). There's frailty for you! The powers of darkness were put to flight, and the human condition remained as it was.[2] But the one who has conquered death both delivered Felicity from the dangers of childbirth, and relieved Perpetua of the milk burdening her breasts.

When they climbed the steps of that ladder,[3] you see, and trampled on the neck of the cunning dragon, they came to a green sward of pleasant meadows, and there they found the good shepherd who *lays down his life for his sheep* (Jn 10:11), and who seeks from his flocks a refreshing draft of milk. "He was sitting there," Perpetua said, "a shepherd both young and old, in the prime of life, his hair all white, never knowing old age. His features were bright with youth, because *he is the selfsame, and his years will never fail* (Ps 102:27). His head was hoary, because *the Lord is just and loves justice* (Ps 11:7), and he acknowledged the justice of his martyrs.[4] All round him sheep were lying and resting, and he was milking them with his fingers, and finding plenty of milk in them, that is consciences rich in loving kindness. He was milking them with his fingers, and talking to them in comforting, fatherly tones, telling them about the heavenly promises prepared for them, and saying, *Come, blessed of my Father, take possession of the kingdom which has been prepared for you from the origin of the world*. And he shows them pails of milk frothing[5] from pure hearts through

429

splendid acts of charity, and says, *I was hungry, and you gave me to eat; I was thirsty, and you gave me to drink* (Mt 25:34-35)."

Perpetua received fresh milk from the dear shepherd, before she shed her precious blood. They replied, "Amen," and began to ask for that loving kindness. They were all praying in prison, certain now of their shepherd. "Lord," they said, "may our confession of faith not be fruitless, but may we be found worthy to join your precious flocks, and not be separated from your martyrs." There is set before them in the vision a wrestling ring, on the fine sand of the amphitheatre; enter that Egyptian, who in heaven was Lucifer, the beautiful Morning Star. Coming out to fight, he rolls in the dust, and Perpetua, who would be given a triumph by her Lord and savior, crossed her arms on her breast,[6] having the Lord before her as a young man, her champion. She is accorded a triumph[7] for her victory, and wins the palm with her crown. Let us too offer her our gifts; others at that time offered them visits in prison; let us now offer them the homage of this festivity, so that we may be found worthy of the kingdom together with all the saints.

NOTES

1. For details about the martyrdom of these two saints, see Sermon 280, notes 1 and 4 in particular. Sermons 280—282 (Sermons vol III,8) were preached in their honor. Their feast day is, and presumably was then 7 March, and a full account of their *Acts* may be found under that date in Butler's *Lives of the Saints*. The Maurists consider the authenticity of this sermon very doubtful indeed, and other scholars reject it out of hand.

2. The reference is to Felicity's being prematurely delivered of her child, so that she was able to win the crown of martyrdom together with Perpetua and her other companions.

3. In the vision which Perpetua had in prison.

4. An odd reason for his hair being white. The obvious reason would be that he was "the Ancient of days" of Dn 7:9, and the Christ of Rv 1:14. In both cases, however, it is the divine judge who is seen in the vision, and perhaps his white hairs are taken as representing his judicial character—like the wigs worn by British judges.

5. See Virgil, *Eclogue 5*, 67.

6. *Adjunxit manus in crucem*; literally, joined her hands in a cross. I suppose it could just mean that she grasped a cross in her hands.

7. He has in mind the formal triumph accorded to a victorious Roman general. But I think it is possible that we have some very low Latin here (which would suggest a date about 100 years or more after Augustine; any time before the invasion of North Africa by the Arabs in the 7th century); and that in the two phrases *triumphum de victoria* and *ramum . . . de corona* the preposition *de* means no more than "of," as it would come to mean in French and Spanish. So the two phrases would simply mean "the triumph of victory" and "a sprig of the laurel crown."

SERMON 395

Date: 425[1]

On hope and the thing hoped for[2]

1. Today we are celebrating the Lord's ascension into heaven; let us not hear in vain the words *Up above with your hearts*, and with all our hearts let us ascend together with him, as the apostle teaches us to, when he says, *If you have risen together with Christ, seek the things that are up above, where Christ is, seated at the right hand of God; savor the things up above, not the things on earth* (Col 3:1-2). Let the need for activity be fulfilled on earth, the will to ascend be fixed in heaven. Hope here, the reality there. The time is coming, after all, when the reality there will be ours. But when the reality there is ours, there will be no more hope, either here or there; not because the hope is vain, but because when the reality comes, hope is over and done with. In any case, listen to what the apostle said about hope: *In hope*, he says, *have we been saved. But hope that can be seen is not hope; and why does anyone hope for what he can see? But if we are hoping for what we cannot see, we wait for it with patience* (Rom 8:24-25).

Take a look at ordinary human affairs, and reflect that if someone is hoping to marry a wife, it means he hasn't yet got one. I mean, if he has, why is he hoping for one? So he marries the wife he was hoping for; and now he won't go on hoping. So hope comes happily to an end when the reality comes to pass. Some foreigner is hoping to return to his own country; as long as he's not there, he's hoping; when he gets there, he's no longer hoping, because the reality has replaced the hope. Hope is happily at an end, when what you were hoping for is attained. So now, dearly beloved, that you have heard that we should lift our hearts up above, our very hearts dictate that we should think about that future life. Let us lead good lives here, in order to have that life there.

On our union with Christ our head

2. Just see how great is the consideration our Lord shows us; the one who made us came down to us, because we had fallen away from him. And to come

431

to us he did not fall away himself, but he came down to us. So if he came down to us, he also picked us up. Our head has now picked us up in his body; where he is, the members of his body will follow in due course, because where the head has gone on ahead, the body is bound to follow. He is in heaven, we are on earth. As though he were far away from us, is that it? God forbid! If you question space, he is far away; if you question love, he is with us. I mean if he were not with us, he would not have said in the gospel, *Behold, I am with you until the completion of the age* (Mt 28:20). If he is not with us, then we are lying when we say, *The Lord is with you.*[3] He wouldn't have cried out from heaven to Saul, who was not persecuting him but his saints, his servants, and if I may put it even more intimately, his members: "*Saul, Saul, why are you persecuting me?* (Acts 9:4). Look, here I am in heaven, and you are there on earth, and you are persecuting me.[4] Why me? Because my members; the members through whom I am there. After all, if the foot is trodden on, the tongue doesn't fail to cry out."[5]

So the one, through whom heaven and earth were made, came down to earth for the sake of the one he had made from earth, and lifted earth up from here to heaven. So what has first taken place in him we too should be hoping for at the end. He will pay us what he promised, we can be quite sure of that. He has made out his IOU, he has written the gospel; he will pay us. Much more striking is what he has already spent on us. Can we really suppose, after all, that he is not going to pay us back his life, when he has already disbursed his death on our behalf? The humiliation of his passion, the insults, the abuse, he underwent all those indignities on earth for us; and will he not endow us with the kingdom, with bliss, with immortality, with eternity? He endured our evils, will he not endow us with his goods? Let us walk without anxiety toward this hope, because we have the promise of one who is true and trustworthy. But let us live in such a way that we may say in all honesty, "We have done what you commanded; pay us what you promised."

NOTES

1. The Maurists accept the authenticity of this sermon, and nobody else seems to question it. There is no obvious indication of when or where it was preached. Augustine was not infrequently in Carthage, or on his way there, on Ascension day. But the brevity of the sermon inclines me to date it rather late, perhaps to his last years when his traveling days were almost over. So let us say between between 420 and 429, and at home in Hippo Regius.

2. Or, in Latin, *De spe et re.*

3. This clearly indicates that the greeting *Dominus vobiscum* was taken as an indicative statement, and not as the optative which it has usually been understood to be, "The Lord be with you."

4. The text actually reads ". . . on earth and among persecutors." I am following the suggestion of the Maurists to emend *et in persecutoribus* to *et me persequeris.*

5. Here I think the stenographer must have failed to take down, "You are treading on me," *Calcas me.*

SERMON 396

AT THE FUNERAL OF A BISHOP

Date: 419[1]

This man did not live a short life here, if we consider
his works, instead of his years

1. You, indeed, brothers and sisters, are looking for consolation and comfort from me. But I too need to be comforted and consoled. And no human being can be our consolation, but only the one who makes human beings; since the one who made can make new, and the one who created can create anew. In our weakness we cannot but be filled with sorrow; but we ought to console ourselves with hope. We all want good people to live a long time with us, and we don't want to be abandoned in the harsh conditions of this life by our comrades and companions. But when those who have led good lives go on before us, they encourage us to live in such a way that we eventually come to them, whether we live a long time here, or soon depart this life. Because living here a long time is nothing else but putting up with troubles and vexations for a long time. But to live with God and in God's presence means living without any trouble or vexation, and without any fear that the bliss which has no end may fade away.

Nor ought we to assume that your bishop, my brother, has gone from us all too soon, and that he lived only a short life. There's no question, of course, of talking about a short life over there, where life can scarcely be called long either, because it never ends. Because here too what seems a long life, when it comes to an end, will be reckoned as nothing. All the same this man did not live a short life here, if we consider his works, instead of counting his years. How many others, over many years, have not done half of what he achieved in just a few years? So wishing to hold him here would have been nothing but envying him his everlasting bliss.

Be faithful to his teaching, and you yourselves
will be his memorial chapel

2. On this occasion, of course, we feel sad, as human beings, about a human being. So what can we do, in order not to be human? So as human beings we

are naturally saddened by the departure of one of our number; but didn't we hear the divinely inspired reading, *Being perfected in a short time, he fulfilled long ages* (Wis 4:13)? So let us reckon ages in this case as days are usually reckoned. So then, hold onto whatever he did among you by his encouragement, by his sermons, by the example he set you in praising and worshiping God; and you yourselves will then be his most beautifully adorned memorial chapel. It doesn't mean much to him, after all, to be laid to rest in a marble tomb; but rather to be laid to rest in your hearts. Let him live, when entombed, in living tombs.[2] Your memory of him, you see, is his tomb. He is living in God's presence, and so is blessed; let him live in your presence, so that you too may be blessed.

I could, no doubt, exhort you with many words to be faithful and sensible, except that human grief would scarcely permit me either to speak. Accordingly, because God granted me the favor of being present with the dying man at the time of his death; and as he has also granted me the privilege of conducting his funeral—a service which we owe to charity, but which adds nothing to his felicity; as he has also granted me the consolation of seeing your holinesses and addressing you, to comfort you with what small comfort I can give; you must supply from your own thoughts whatever grief does not allow me to say. And as we cherish the memory of such a great man, even while our spirits are burdened with human sorrow, they are not overwhelmed with the despair that contradicts our faith.

NOTES

1. This date has been carefully argued by O. Perler, *Les Voyages de Saint Augustin*, 352-354. A manuscript published at Monte Casino in 1873 heads the sermon, "Here begins a sermon of Aurelius Augustine, preached in the Florentian Basilica in the city of Bizerta on 17 April, to console the people for the death of a certain bishop." Perler argues cogently that the bishop in question was Augustine's friend Florentius; Augustine had preached at this basilica's dedication some eight years before. He had been bishop, it seems, since 401. Perhaps this is why Lambot disagrees with Perler, and dates the sermon to 412, since it clearly suggests that the dead bishop had only held his see for comparatively few years.

2. One sees what he means; but one cannot help its sounding rather gruesome—perhaps because our modern imaginations are too prone to literalism.

SERMON 397

ON THE SACK OF THE CITY OF ROME

Date: 410-411[1]

On the humility of Daniel

1. Let us take a look at the first reading from the prophet Saint Daniel, where we heard him praying, and were surprised at his confessing not only the sins of the people, but his own as well. Because after the prayer itself—his words indicate that he was confessing as well as praying—so after the prayer itself, *While I was praying*, he said, *and confessing my sins, and the sins of my people to the Lord my God* (Dn 9:20). So can anyone claim to be without sin, when Daniel confesses his own sins? I mean, some proud man or other[2] was asked through the prophet Ezekiel, *Are you wiser than Daniel?* (Ez 28:3). Again, the prophet also placed this Daniel among the three holy men, in whom God signifies the three sorts of human beings he is going to deliver, when *the great tribulation* (Rv 7:14) comes upon the human race, and he said that nobody would be delivered from it except Noah, Daniel and Job.[3] And indeed it's obvious that in these three names God is signifying, as I said, three kinds of human beings. After all, those three men have already fallen asleep long since, and their spirits are with God, and their bodies have dissolved into dust. And they have been placed at God's right hand,[4] and are in no dread of any tribulation from which they are longing to be delivered. So how will Noah, Daniel and Job be delivered from that tribulation? When Ezekiel said all this, Daniel alone was possibly still in the body. Noah and Job had already fallen asleep long before, and been laid in the sleep of death with their fathers. So how could they have been delivered even from the tribulation that was hanging over the people at that time?[5]

But Noah represents good leaders, who govern and direct the Church, just as Noah captained and steered the ark in the flood. Daniel represents the holy celibates, Job represents all the married people who live good and upright lives. It is these three kinds of people,[6] after all, that God will deliver from that tribulation. All the same, Daniel in particular is commended to our veneration, in that he is the only one of the three named[7]—and yet he confesses his sins. So with Daniel confessing his sins, is there anyone whose pride would not start trembling, whose conceit would not be deflated, whose swelling self-importance would not be checked? *Who can boast that he has a chaste heart, or boast that he is pure from sin?* (Prv 20:9).

And people are surprised—and if only they were just surprised, and didn't also blaspheme—when God takes the human race to task, and stirs them up with the rod of fatherly correction, disciplining them before passing judgment; and frequently he doesn't pick out anyone in particular for chastisement, not wishing to find anyone whom he has to condemn. You see, he chastises the just and the unjust together—although who can really be called just, if even Daniel confesses his own sins?

Rome not, in fact, destroyed like Sodom

2. A few days ago we had a reading from the book of Genesis[8] which, if I'm not mistaken, made a great impression on us; where Abraham asks the Lord whether, if he finds fifty just men in the city, he would spare the city for their sake, or destroy the city together with them. And the Lord answered him that if in the city he found fifty just men, he would spare the city. Then Abraham continued with his questioning, and inquired whether, if there were fewer than fifty and only forty-five remained, he would spare it then too. God replied that he would spare it for the sake of forty-five. Why go on? Little by little, by his questions Abraham came down from that number to ten, and inquired of the Lord whether, if he discovered ten just men in the city, he would destroy them together with all the other countless bad men, or whether on account of the ten just men he would not rather spare the city. God replied that for the sake of even ten just men he would rather spare the city.

So what are we to say, brothers and sisters? A very urgent and pressing question occurs to us, after all, one put especially by people who try irreligiously to catch out our scriptures, not by those who search them devoutly. And they say, particularly with reference to the sack of such a great city, "Weren't there fifty just men in Rome? In such a great number of believers, such a great number of nuns and men vowed to chastity, such a great number of the servants of God of both sexes, couldn't even fifty just persons be found, even forty, even thirty, even twenty, even ten? But if it is impossible to believe that, why did God not spare that city for the sake of those fifty, or even of those ten?"

Scripture doesn't mislead us, if we don't mislead ourselves. When one's enquiring about God's justice, and God replies about justice, he is seeking people who are just according to divine, not human, standards.[9] So I can answer straightaway, Either he found that many just people there. and spared the city; or if he didn't spare the city, it means he didn't find the just people.

"But," the answer comes back to me, "it's plain that God didn't spare the city." I reply, On the contrary, it's not plain to me. There was no destruction of the city here, as there was for the inhabitants of Sodom. When Abraham was questioning God, after all, the problem was about the inhabitants of Sodom. Now God said, *I will not destroy the city* (Gn 18:32); he didn't say, "I will not scourge the city." He didn't spare the inhabitants of Sodom, he destroyed

Sodom; he totally consumed Sodom with fire,[10] not deferring this till the day of judgment; he inflicted on that city the punishment which he has reserved for all other wicked people to the day of judgment. Not a single one of Sodom's inhabitants remained alive. Nothing at all was left, of flocks, of people, of houses; the fire swallowed up absolutely everything and everyone. There you have how God destroyed a city. But from the city of Rome, how many people managed to leave and then return, how many remained and escaped unscathed, how many, seeking sanctuary in holy places, could not even be touched!

"But many," they reply, "were led away as captives."

That also happened to Daniel, not as a punishment for him, but as a comfort and support for the others.

"But many," they say, "were killed."

So also were many of the righteous prophets, *from the blood of Abel the just to the blood of Zechariah* (Mt 23:35); so too were all those apostles, so too was the Lord of the prophets and apostles himself.[11]

"But many," they say, "were tortured with a variety of excruciating torments."

Can we suppose that any of them suffered as much as Job?

"Horrific stories have been told us; of destruction, of fires, of rapes, slaughter, people tortured."

It's true, we've heard many things, we've lamented them all, often shed tears, found little to console ourselves with. I don't brush it all aside, I don't deny that we've heard many things, that many bad things were done in that city.

Rome and Job

3. But for all that, my brothers and sisters, would your graces please take note of what I say. We heard the book of holy Job, and how he lost all his goods, lost all his children, and couldn't even keep the good health of his flesh, which was all that remained to him, but was struck with grievous ulcers from head to foot; and how he sat on the dunghill, rotten with his sores, oozing pus, swarming with maggots, tormented with excruciating bitter pains.[12] If we had been told that the whole city endured that kind of thing, that nobody was left there in good health but all were grievously wounded, that the living were rotten with maggots in the same way as corpses rot away—which would be more dreadful, this sort of thing or that war? In my opinion, the fury of steel would be kinder to human flesh than maggots; the flow of blood from wounds would be more tolerable than the oozing of loathsome matter from gangrene. You see a corpse decaying, and you're horrified; but that's why the pain is less, or rather why there's no pain at all, because the soul is absent. But in the case of Job, his soul was present, to feel everything, it was tied there, unable to escape, subjected to all the pain, being provoked to blaspheme.

Job, however, put up with his tribulations, and it was accounted to him as great justice.[13] So you shouldn't pay attention to what people suffer, but to what they do about it. What you suffer, my friend, is not under your control; but as to what you do about it, your will is either guiltless or guilty. Job was suffering, his wife stood there, the only one left to him, not to comfort but to tempt him; not to bring healing, but to suggest blasphemy. *Say something against God*, she said, *and die* (Jb 2:9). You must realize that death would have come as a favor to him, and a favor that nobody was doing him. But in all these things that this holy soul was enduring, his patience was being exercised, his faith proved, his wife put to shame, the devil defeated. A great spectacle, the outstanding beauty of virtue shining in all that filth and squalor! The enemy is behind the scenes of his ruin; the hostile woman is openly prompting him to evil, the devil's assistant, not her husband's. She is another Eve, but he is not another Adam. *Say something against God and die*; extort by blasphemy, what you can't obtain by prayer.[14] *You have spoken like the silly woman you are. If we have received good things from the hand of the Lord, why do we not also put up with bad things?* (Jb 2:10).

Pay attention to the words of this brave believer; pay attention to the words of this man, who was rotting away outwardly, while his inner integrity remained. *You have spoken like the silly woman you are. If we have received good things from the hand of the Lord, why do we not also put up with bad things?* He's a Father; is he to be loved when he coddles us, rejected when he corrects us? Isn't he a Father, who both promises us life, and imposes on us discipline? Has this slipped your memory? *Son, when you enter the service of God, stand in justice and fear, and prepare your soul for trials and temptation. Accept everything that is brought upon you; put up with pain, and also be patient in your humiliation; since gold and silver are tested in the fire, but acceptable men in the furnace of humiliation* (Sir 2:1.4-5). Has this slipped your memory? *For the Lord disciplines the one he loves, while he whips every son whom he receives* (Heb 12:6).

No earthly pains to be compared with those of hell

4. Think about any tortures you like, extend your imagination to any human punishments you can think of; compare them with gehenna, and everything you can think of[15] is trivial. Here they are temporal, there eternal, both the torturer and the tortured. Those people aren't still suffering, are they, who suffered at that time when Rome was sacked? That rich man, though, is still suffering in hell.[16] He was on fire, he is on fire, he will be on fire; he will come to the last judgment; he will get back his flesh, not to his benefit, but to his added punishment. Those are the pains we should fear, if we fear God. Whatever people may suffer here, if they let themselves be corrected by it, it means their improvement; if they are not corrected by it, it means a double condemnation. I mean, they pay the temporal penalty here, and there they will experience the eternal one.

I'm telling your graces, brothers and sisters: we certainly praise the holy martyrs, we reverence their merits, and if we can we imitate them. Great indeed is the glory of the martyrs; but I'm not sure that the glory of holy Job was any less. And yet he wasn't told, "Offer incense to idols, sacrifice to alien gods, deny Christ." What he was told, though, was "Blaspheme God." Nor was this said to him, as though it meant, "If you blaspheme, all this putrescence will vanish, your health will be restored." But, "If you blaspheme," said the mindless, witless woman, "you will die, and by dying you will be done with your torments." As though eternal pain would not be waiting for one who died blaspheming! The silly woman shrank in horror from the distress of the man rotting away there in her presence, and gave not a thought to the eternal flames. He for his part bore with his present pains in order not to fall into those of the world to come. He kept his heart from evil thoughts, his tongue from cursing; he preserved his soul's integrity in the rottenness of his body. He could see what he was avoiding for the future; and that is why he bore with his troubles patiently.[17]

In the same way all Christians, when they are suffering from some bodily or material difficulty, should think about hell, and consider how light in comparison is what they are suffering. They shouldn't grumble against God, shouldn't say, "God, what have I done to you, why am I suffering these things?" On the contrary, they should say what Job said, even though he was a saint: *You have sought out all my sins, and sealed them up as in a bag* (Jb 14:16-17). He didn't dare to say that he was without sin, though he was suffering, not as a punishment, but as a test. Let anyone who suffers say the same.

The just suffer like the poor man at the rich man's gate

5. There were fifty just men in Rome, or rather, if you reckon it by human standards, thousands of just people; if you are looking for the standard of perfection, not a single just person would be found in Rome. Any who have the nerve to call themselves just will hear Truth asking them, "*Are you, then, wiser than Daniel?* (Ez 28:3). So listen to him confessing his sins."[18] Or perhaps when he was confessing he was lying? So by that very fact he had a sin, because he was lying to God about his sins.

But people sometimes argue like this, and say, "Even a just man ought to say to God, 'I am a sinner'; and although he knows that he has no sin, still he should say to God, 'I have sin.'" I wonder if this can be called even sane advice. Who ensured that you have no sin? If you are totally without sin, isn't it because God has healed your soul? If, that is of course, you don't have any sin. I mean, you only have to reflect a little, and you will find not sin but sins. Still, if you really haven't got any sin at all, isn't this a favor done you by the one to whom you have said, *I said: Lord, have mercy on me; heal my soul, since I have sinned against you* (Ps 41:4)? So if your soul is without sin, your soul has been healed in every respect; if your soul has been healed in every respect, why are you ungrateful to the doctor, and saying it still has a wound, when he has restored you totally to health? If you were presenting your body, ill and wounded, to a doctor, and begging him to do all he could to cure you, and he in fact made you well and restored you to complete health, and you still went on telling him that you were not well at all, wouldn't that mean you were not only being ungrateful to the doctor but also insulting him? In the same way, God has healed you, and you still have the nerve to say, "I have a wound"? Aren't you afraid he may answer you, " So I've done nothing, have I, or wasted all I have done? So I don't get my fee, I don't deserve any praise, is that it?" God preserve us from such lunacy, and from such a nonsensical kind of argument. So you should say, "I am a sinner," because you really are a sinner; should say, "I have sin," because you really do have sin. For you are not, if you think you have none, wiser than Daniel.

So then, brothers and sisters, let me now settle that question once and for all. If people are to be called just in the human kind of way in which they are called just, as regards a mode of living among their fellows without blame, then there were many such in Rome, and God spared many on their account, who got away alive. But even those who died were spared by God. After all, they died while leading a good life, in a state of true justice and good faith; so weren't they now rid of all the distress of human affairs, attaining at last to their rest in God? They died after many tribulations, like that poor man at the rich man's gate. But they endured hunger, you say? So did he. They suffered wounds? So did he; perhaps the dogs didn't come and lick theirs. They died, did they? So did he; but listen to how it ended: *It happened that the poor man died, and was carried by angels into Abraham's bosom* (Lk 16:22).

God spared the city in the saints who died there

6. If only we could see the souls of the saints who died in that war, then you would see how God spared the city. Thousands of saints, after all, are now at rest, rejoicing and saying to God, "We thank you, Lord, for snatching us from the distresses and torments of the flesh. We thank you, because now we are not in dread of either barbarians or devil; we are not afraid of famine on earth, or of the enemy; we are not afraid of any persecutor, not afraid of any oppressor. But we died on earth, and are with you, O God, never going to die, safe in your kingdom[19] by your gift, not by our merits." What a city of humble citizens that can say all that!

Or do you suppose, brothers and sisters, that what counts as a city is walls, and not citizens? Finally, if God had said to the inhabitants of Sodom, "Flee, because I am going to set fire to this place," wouldn't we have said that they were people of great merit if they had fled, and fire coming down from heaven had laid waste only towers and walls? Wouldn't that have meant that God did spare the city, because the city had emigrated, and escaped destruction by that fire?

A comparable event at Constantinople

7. Isn't it the case that a few years ago, under the emperor Arcadius[20] at Constantinople—perhaps some people are listening to what I am saying who know about it, and some who were present there at the time are now in this

congregation—God decided to terrify the city and by terror to correct it, by terror to convert it, by terror to cleanse it, by terror to change it; so he came in a revelation to a faithful servant of his, a military man so it's said, and told him that that city was going to perish in fire coming from heaven, and instructed him to tell the bishop? He did so; the bishop didn't make light of it, he addressed the people. The city was converted to mourning and repentance, as once upon a time that Nineveh of old.[21]

However, in case people should suppose that the man who had told them this had been misled by a misunderstanding, or had wished to mislead them deliberately, the day came which God had threatened; everybody was very tense, and in great fear expecting to be destroyed, when at the beginning of the night as the world was already growing dark, a fiery cloud appeared from the east, small at first, and then it gradually grew as it approached over the city, until it hung, terrible and huge, above the whole city.[22] Horrid streamers of fire were seen to hang from the sky, and the stench of sulphur was not lacking either. All took refuge in church, and the place couldn't hold the multitude. Everyone was extorting baptism from anyone they could. Not only in church, but in houses, streets, squares, the saving sacrament was being demanded; in order to escape, obviously, not the present threat, but the wrath to come.

Still, after that *great tribulation* (Rv 7:14), in which God confirmed the truth of his words, and of the revelation made to his servant, the cloud began to diminish just as it had grown, and gradually it disappeared. The people, feeling a little safer now, again heard that they must all quit the city, because it was going to be destroyed the following Saturday. The whole city moved out, together with the emperor; nobody stayed at home, nobody locked his house. They withdrew a good distance from the walls, and looking back at their sweet dwellings,[23] with tearful voices they said farewell to the beloved homes they had left. And when that vast crowd had gone a few miles, stopping together, though, in one place to pour out prayers to God, they suddenly saw a great column of smoke, and cried out with a loud shout to the Lord. At length, when the sky cleared they sent some scouts to bring back news. When the anxious hour foretold had passed, and the messengers reported that the walls of the city and all the houses remained intact, they all returned with great relief and thankfulness. No one lost anything from his house, everybody found his open house just as he had left it.

The example applied to the case of Rome

8. What are we to say? Was this God's wrath, or not rather his mercy? Can anybody doubt that it was the will of the most merciful Father to correct by inspiring terror, rather than to punish, when such an impending, looming disaster in fact did no harm to a single person, a single house, or to any part of the city walls? Clearly, what happened to that city was like when a hand is raised to strike, and then lowered out of pity when the person threatened by it shrinks back in dismay. However, if at that time, when the city was deserted and the

whole population had left, devastation had overtaken the place, and destroyed the whole city like Sodom, with not even any ruins remaining, who even so could doubt that God had spared that city, which being forewarned and terrified had moved out and withdrawn, while only the empty place was consumed with fire?

In the same way it cannot be doubted at all that God did also spare the city of the Romans, who in great numbers had moved out before the enemy set fire to the place. Those who fled had moved out, those who departed more swiftly from the body had moved out and on. Many who remained hid themelves somehow or other, many were preserved alive and safe at the shrines of the saints. So that city was rather chastised than destroyed by the correcting hand of God; just as *the servant who knows his lord's will, and does things that deserve a beating, will be beaten with many strokes* (Lk 12:47.48).

What that whole city suffered, one single man also suffered;
the King of kings and Lord of lords

9. And if only this example availed to induce some fear into the rest of us, so that we restrained our evil desires from thirsting for the world, and from being hell-bent on the most pernicious pleasures! God, after all, is demonstrating in this way how shaky and fleeting are all the vanities and misleading follies of this age. So let us not go on grumbling against the Lord, as we tend to do. There's only one flail, though, experienced by the threshing-floor, both to cut up the straw and to cleanse the grain; there's only one fire experienced by the gold-smith's furnace, both to reduce the straw to ashes and to eliminate the dross from the gold. In the same way Rome endured just one tribulation, in which the godly were either delivered or corrected; while the ungodly were condemned, whether they were snatched from this life to pay even more the justest of penalties, or whether they remained here to go on blaspheming more damnably than ever, or even, out of the unimaginable clemency of God, who knows who are to be saved, to be kept by him for repentance.

So we shouldn't let the hardships of the godly upset us; they are being put through their paces, not being disqualified. Unless of course we are horrified when we observe the grievous and undeserved things suffered on this earth by some just person, and forget what was endured by the Just One and by the Saint of Saints.[24] What that whole city suffered, one man also suffered. But notice who that one man was: *the King of kings and Lord of lords* (Rv 19:16), seized, bound, scourged, treated to all kinds of abuse, hung on a tree and crucified, killed. Weigh up Rome against Christ, weigh up the whole earth against Christ; weigh up heaven and earth against Christ; nothing created can balance the creator, no work be compared with the craftsman. *All things were made through him, and without him was made nothing* (Jn 1:3); and yet by his persecutors he was reckoned as nothing.[25]

So let us bear with whatever God may wish us to bear with, seeing that,[26] like a doctor, he knows what pain is useful for curing and healing us. It's written, isn't it, *Let patience have a perfect work* (Jas 1:4)? But what work will there be for patience to have, if we suffer no adversity? So why should we refuse to endure temporal evils? Do we, perhaps, dread being made perfect? But clearly we should be praying and sighing to the Lord, that he would carry out in our regard what the apostle says: *God is faithful, and will not allow you to be tempted beyond what you are able to bear; but with the temptation he will also provide a way out, so that you may be able to endure it* (1 Cor 10:13).

NOTES

1. The sermon could have been preached any time after August 410; but the indications are that it was soon after the event. Carthage, I think, is the most likely city for it to have been preached in, especially given what he says in his little aside at the beginning of section 7. The sermon is found in two editions; that of the Maurists, and the contemporary one in the series *Corpus Christianorum*, CCL. The text being translated here is the CCL one, but I often prefer the Maurists, and make a note to that effect when I do. I must confess to occasional doubts about the sermon's authenticity; but they are not supported by any of the authorities.

2. The king of Tyre.

3. See Ez 14:12-20. The prophet is making rather a different point, and not giving the passage the eschatological significance which the preacher gives it.

4. As in Mt 25:33, not as in Mk 10:37, or Acts 7:56.

5. The destruction of Jerusalem and the temple in 587 BC, and the subsequent exile in Babylon.

6. In fact, clergy, religious and laity. It is here I begin to have some qualms about the sermon's authenticity - or at least the authenticity of parts of it.

7. In Ez 28:3.

8. Gn 18:16-33.

9. The relevance of this remark escapes me.

10. Gn 19:24.

11. Here the CCL text adds "Jesus."

12. See Jb 1 & 2.

13. See Rom 4:3.

14. That is, the favor of death. Blasphemy would extort it, because it would bring it upon him as the prescribed punishment.

15. So the Maurists; CCL has "everything you suffer."

16. See Lk 16:19-26.

17. Neither Augustine nor any of his contemporary preachers ever seem to have got beyond the first two chapters of the book of Job. Never does he advert, in his references to it, to the problem of innocent suffering which the book wrestles with, nor to Job's very full complaints, the answers given him by his comforters, and the Lord's final reply from the whirlwind. Yes, he does go on in a moment or two to quote from a later chapter; but then he stands the text's actual meaning on its head.

18. In Dn 9:20.

19. This phrase is lacking from the CCL text.

20. Arcadius died in 408. Theodosius the Great had arrranged that after his death the empire should be divided between his two sons; Arcadius to rule the East from Constantinople, Honorius to govern the West from Ravenna. From the aside that follows I infer that Carthage was more likely to be the place where this sermon was preached than Hippo Regius; visitors and traders from Constantinople were more likely to be found in a congregation in the metropolis of Africa.

21. See Jon 3:5-10.

22. I here follow the Maurists, but I also accept an emendation to their text by earlier editors which they turn down. They read *ignis*, fire, which those editors emended to *ingens*, huge. The CCL text reads *ingens timor*, "until a huge fear hung terribly over the city." This strikes me as the weakest of all three variants; it suggests that *timor* was inserted in an "*ingens*" text, because the copyist didn't realize that *ingens* referred to the fiery cloud.

This strange event is related in the *Chronicle* of Ammianus Marcellinus, for the year 396, a year before Saint John Chrysostom was appointed bishop of Constantinople.

23. *dulcia tecta respiciens.* I here suspect a quotation from, or allusion to, Virgil's *Aeneid*; but I cannot trace it.

24. See Acts 3:14; Dn 9:24.

25. So the Maurists; CCL reads, "and yet he was betrayed by his persecutors"—both inaccurate, and feeble in comparison.

26. Again, I follow the Maurists. CCL here inserts, *suum Filium misit*, "he sent his Son for our cure and healing." But it makes the sentence, in fact, grammatically impossible to construe, and has every appearance of being a marginal comment, that was later thrust into the text.

SERMON 398

ON THE CREED TO THE CATECHUMENS

Date: 425[1]

The rule of faith, called the symbol

1. Receive, sons and daughters, the rule of faith, which is called the symbol. And when you have received it, write it on your hearts, and say it to yourselves every day; before you go to sleep, before you go out in the morning, fortify yourselves with your symbol.[2] Nobody writes a symbol for it to be read, but for purposes of recall; to prevent forgetfulness from deleting what carefulness has handed over to you, let your memories be your books. What you are going to hear is what you are going to believe, and what you have believed is also what you are going to give back with your tongues.[3] The apostle says, after all, *With the heart one believes unto justice, but with the mouth one makes confession unto salvation* (Rom 10:10). This, you see, is the symbol which you are going to get by heart and give back.[4]

These words which you have heard are scattered throughout the divine scriptures, but they have been gathered from there and reduced to one short form, so as not to overload the memories of slower minds, and so that all may be able to state, may be able to retain, what they believe. I mean, was it only just now that you heard that God is almighty? But you will begin[5] to have him as your father, when you are born of the Church as your mother.

What it means for God to be almighty

2. So this is what you have already received, and thought about, and held onto after thinking about it, so that you can say, *I believe in God the Father almighty*. God is almighty; and while he is almighty, he is unable to die, unable to be deceived, unable to lie, and as the apostle says, *he cannot deny himself* (2 Tm 2:13). How many things he is unable to do, and he is almighty! And that's why he is almighty, because he cannot do these things. I mean, if he could die, he wouldn't be almighty; if he could lie, could be deceived, could deceive, could act unjustly, he wouldn't be almighty, because if it were in him to do that sort of thing, he wouldn't be fit to be almighty. Of course our almighty Father cannot

445

sin. *He does whatever he wills* (Ps 115:3); that is being almighty, that is omnipotence. He does whatever he wills in a good way, whatever he wills justly; but anything that is done badly, he doesn't will. Nobody can oppose the almighty and stop him doing what he will.

He it is *who made heaven and earth, the sea and all that is in them* (Ps 146:6), things invisible and visible; invisible things such as are in the heavens, thrones, dominations, principalities, powers, archangels, angels[6]—if we live good lives, they are our fellow citizens. He made the visible things in the heavens, the sun, the moon, the stars. He furnished the earth with its own terrestrial animals, he filled the air with those that fly, the earth with those that walk and crawl, the sea with those that swim; he filled everything with its own proper creatures.[7] He also *made man to his own image and likeness* (Gn 1:26) in the mind; that, you see, is where the image of God is to be found. That's why the mind cannot be comprehended even by itself, where the image of God is to be found.

What we were made for was to have dominion over the other creatures;[8] but through sin we fell in the first man, and all came down into the inheritance of death. We became mortal,[9] we were filled with fears, with errors; this as the deserts of sin; with such deserts and guilt every human being is born. That is why, as you can see today, as you know, even babies are breathed upon and exorcised, to drive out of them the hostile power of the devil, which led the man astray in order to gain possession of mankind. So it's not God's creation in the babies that is being blown away and exorcised, but the one under whose dominion all that are in sin are born. And thus it is that, because of the one who fell and sent us all off into death, one without sin was sent who would conduct all who believe in him into life, setting them free from sin.

Jesus Christ equal to the Father; both of them one God

3. That is why we believe *and in his,* that is God the almighty Father's, *only Son, our Lord.* When you hear "the only Son of God," acknowledge him as God. God's only Son, you see, couldn't not be God. The Father begot what he is, even though he is not whom he begot. If he is a true Son, he is what the Father is; if he is not what the Father is, he is not a true Son. Consider mortal and earthly creatures; what each thing is, is what it begets. A human being doesn't beget an ox, a sheep doesn't beget a dog, or a dog a sheep. Whatever the begetter is, that is what it begets. So then, hold staunchly, firmly, faithfully onto this truth, that God the Father begot what he is himself, the almighty. These mortal creatures beget offspring by a process of corruption.[10] Surely God doesn't beget like that, does he? A mortal begets what he is, the immortal begets what he is; corruptible begets corruptible, incorruptible begets incorruptible; corruptible corruptly, incorruptible incorruptly. To this extent does he beget what he is, that the one begets the one, and therefore the only one.

You know that when I was reciting the creed to you, this is what I said, and this is what you must believe: that *we believe in God the Father almighty, and in Jesus Christ his only Son.* As soon as I say "only," you must believe "almighty." It's not the case, surely, that God the Father does whatever he wills, and God the Son doesn't do whatever he wills. Father and Son have one will, because they have one nature. I mean it's quite impossible for the will of the Son to differ in the least degree from the will of the Father. God and God, both one God; almighty and almighty, both one almighty.

The Arians make Father and Son into two gods

4. We don't introduce two gods, as some people do, who say, "The Father is God, and the Son is God, but the Father is a big God, the Son a little God."[11] What are they both together? Two gods? You're ashamed to say it, be ashamed to believe it. You call God the Father Lord, and God the Son Lord; and the Son himself says, *No one can serve two lords* (Mt 6:24). Will it be for us in his household as it is in a big house here, where there is a master and he has a son, so that we too should talk of the big Lord and master, and the little Lord and master?[12] Avert your minds from any such thoughts. If you nurse such ideas in your hearts, you are putting idols in your souls. Get rid of them, lock, stock and barrel. Believe first, understand later. But any of you to whom God grants understanding as soon as you believe, well it's God's gift, not the doing of human frailty. Still, if you don't yet understand, believe: the Father is the one God, Christ, God's Son, is God; both together are what? One God.

And how can both together be called one God? How? You're baffled? In the Acts of the Apostles it says, *And those who believed had one heart and soul* (Acts 4:32). There were many souls, faith had made them all one. So many thousand souls; they loved one another, and the many are one; they loved God with burning charity, and from being a multitude they ended in the loveliness of unity. If it was love that made so many souls into one soul, what sort of love must there be in God, where there is no diversity, but total equality? If on earth and among human beings there could be a love great enough to make one soul out of so many souls, then how, where the Father has always been inseparable from the Son, and the Son from the Father, could they both together be anything but one God? Those souls, however, could be called both many souls and one soul; God, on the other hand, in whom there is supreme and inexpressible affinity, can only be called one God, not two gods.

The Son too is omnipotent

5. The Father does what he wills, the Son does what he wills. You mustn't think that the Father is almighty, and the Son is not. That's an error, get rid of it, don't let it stick in your memories, don't drink it in with your faith; and if by chance any of you have drunk it in, spew it out. The Father is almighty, the Son is almighty. If the almighty did not beget the almighty, he did not beget a true son. After all, brothers and sisters, what are we saying if the big Father begot a little Son? What's being said, after all, "begot"? Yes, a big man begets a little son, it's true; but that's because the first grows old, the second grows up, and

attains to his father's stature at least by growing up. If the Son of God doesn't grow up, because God cannot grow old either, then he was born mature; born mature, so he doesn't grow up, and hasn't remained little; then he is equal.

Well, to show you that he was born almighty of the almighty, listen to what he says himself, the one who is *the Truth* (Jn 14:6). What the Truth says about itself must be true. What does the Truth say? What does the Son say, who is the Truth? *Whatever the Father does, that the Son also does likewise* (Jn 5:19). The Son is almighty, in that he does everything that he has wished to do. I mean, if the Father does some things which the Son doesn't do, the Son was not speaking the truth when he said, *Whatever the Father does, that the Son also does likewise.* But because the Son was speaking the truth, believe that *whatever the Father does, that the Son also does likewise,* and you have believed in the Son as almighty. Even if you didn't use that word in the creed, still you expressed its meaning, when you believed in him, the only Son.[13] Does the Father have anything which the Son doesn't have? That's what the blasphemous Arian heretics say, not what I say. What do I say, then? If the Father has something which the Son does not have, then the Son is lying when he says, *Everything that the Father has is mine* (Jn 16:15). There are innumerable texts to prove that the Son of the Father is true God,[14] and that God the Father begot a true Son as God, and that Father and Son are one God.

Christ's human birth and death

6. But let us see what this only Son of God the Father almighty has done on our account, what he has suffered on our account: *Born of the Holy Spirit and the virgin Mary.* This great God, equal to the Father, was born of the Holy Spirit and the virgin Mary, in humility, as the means by which to heal the proud. Man exalted himself, and fell;[15] God humbled himself, and set him on his feet. What is Christ's humanity?[16] God stretching out his hand to man lying in the dust. We fell, he came down; we were lying there, down and out; he stooped down. Let us grasp the extended hand, and get up, in order not to fall further into the punishment due to us. So this is his stooping down to us: *Born of the Holy Spirit and the virgin Mary.* This human birth too is at once humble and sublime. Why humble? Because he was born a human being of human beings.[17] Why sublime? Because born of a virgin, who conceived him as a virgin, bore him as a virgin, and after giving birth remained a virgin.

7. What next? *Suffered under Pontius Pilate.* This Pontius Pilate was serving as governor, and was the judge when Christ suffered. The time when he suffered is indicated by the judge's name: *suffered under Pontius Pilate,*[18] *was crucified and buried.* Who, what, for whom? Who? The only Son of God, our Lord. What? Was crucified and buried. For whom? For the godless, and for sinners. What unbelievable concern, what marvelous grace! *What return shall I make to the Lord, for all that he has bestowed on me?* (Ps 116:12).

By his birth of the Father he is coeternal with the Father

8. He was born before all times, born before all ages.[19] Born before. Before what, where there is no "before"? You most certainly mustn't think of any time before that birth of Christ by which he was born of the Father—I am talking about that birth by which he is the only Son of almighty God, our Lord; I'm talking about that one first. Don't think about any beginning in time in that birth, don't think about any space of eternity when the Father was and the Son wasn't. From the time when the Father was, the Son was too. And what can that mean, "from the time when," where there is no beginning? So the Father always is, without beginning, the Son always is, without beginning.

"And how," you will be saying, "was he born, if he has no beginning?"

He was born coeternal from the eternal. There was never a moment when the Father was and the Son was not, and yet the Son was begotten of the Father.

What can provide us with some sort of comparison? We find ourselves among things of earth, find ourselves in the visible creation. Let the earth provide me with a comparison; it doesn't. Let the element of the waves provide me with some sort of comparison; it hasn't got the means. Let some animal provide me with a comparison; it can't do it either. Animals indeed reproduce, and what is reproduced is the same as what reproduces;[20] but the father comes first, and the son is born later. Let us find something coeval, and believe in something coeternal. If we can find a father coeval with his son, and a son coeval with his father, we can believe that God the Father is coeternal with his Son, and God the Son coeternal with his Father. On earth we can find something coeval, we can't find anything coeternal. Let us take a look at the coeval, and believe in the coeternal.

Somebody, no doubt, will put you on the alert; he says, "When can you find a father coeval with his son, or a son coeval with his father? For a father to beget, he must come first in age; for a son to be born, he must come later in age. But how can a father here be coeval with his son, or a son with his father?"

Let the thought occur to you of fire as father, its brightness as son; there you are, we've found coevals. From the moment fire begins to be, it straightaway begets brightness; nor is the fire there before the brightness, nor the brightness after the fire. And if we inquire which generates which, fire brightness or brightness fire, the answer occurs to you straightaway by your natural observation, by the common sense built into your minds; you all shout, "Fire brightness, not brightness fire." There you have a father beginning to be, there you have a son simultaneously, neither preceding nor following. So there you have a father beginning to be, a son simultaneously beginning to be.

If I have shown you a father beginning to be, and a son simultaneously beginning to be, believe in a Father who doesn't begin to be, and with him a Son also not beginning to be; the one eternal, the other coeternal. If you're making progress, you will understand; take pains to make progress. You have yet to be born;[21] but you will also have to grow up, because nobody begins from full maturity. The Son of God was free to be born fully mature, because he was born without time, coeternal with the Father, preceding all things, not in time, but in eternity. So he was born coeternal with the Father, and of this begetting the prophet said, *His begetting who will expound?* (Is 53:8). Born of the Father outside time, born of the virgin *in the fullness of time* (Gal 4:4). This last birth had been preceded by times. At the opportune time, when he wished, when he knew it had come, that was when he was born. None of us are born when we wish, and none of us die when we wish; he was born when he wished, died when he wished; born as he wished of the virgin, died as he wished on the cross. Whatever he wished, he did; because he was man in such a way as to remain God in a hidden manner; God taking on man, man taken on by God, one Christ God and man.

The sign of Christ's work, the cross; the reward
of his work, the resurrection

9. About his cross, what am I to say? How can I talk about it? He chose the worst possible kind of death, so that his martyrs might not dread any kind of death. In becoming man he gave us his teaching, in dying on the cross he gave us an example of patience. That was his work, to be crucified; the sign of his work, the cross, the reward of his work, the resurrection. He showed us on the cross what we must be ready to endure; he showed us in the resurrection what we must hope for. Certainly, as the supreme president of the Olympic committee,[22] he said, "Do, and carry off; do the work, and receive the prize; fight in the match, and you will win your laurels." What is the work? Obedience. What is the reward? Resurrection without death. Why did I add "without death"? Because Lazarus also rose again, and is dead; Christ rose again, and *dies no more, death will no longer lord it over him* (Rom 6:9).

The patience of Job

10. Scripture says, *You have heard of the patience of Job, and you have seen the end of the Lord* (Jas 5:11). When the account of all that Job endured is read, we are horrified, terrified, scared out of our wits. And what did he receive? Double what he had lost.[23] So you mustn't be willing to have patience just for the sake of temporal rewards, and start saying to yourself, "Let me put up with losses; God will give me twice the number of children. Job got back twice as much of everything, and he begot the same number of children as he had buried; so it isn't double of everything." It certainly is double of everything, because the first ones too were still living.[24] So you mustn't start saying, "I will bear with evils, and God will pay me back as he paid back Job," so that it's a matter now, not of patience but of avarice. Because if that holy man had not been endowed with patience, he would not have endured so staunchly all those things that happened to him. How would he then have earned the testimonial which the Lord gave him? *Have you noticed,* said the Lord, *my servant Job? There is nobody like him on earth, a man without reproach, a true worshiper of God* (Jb 1:8).

What a testimonial that was, brothers and sisters, which this holy man won from the Lord! And yet his wife wanted to lead him astray with her evil suggestion, playing the same role as the serpent; and as he in paradise led astray the first man made by God,[25] so she now thought she could lead astray, by persuading him to blaspheme, the man who was pleasing to God.[26] How much he suffered, brothers and sisters! Who could ever endure so much, in his property, in his family, in his children, in his very flesh, in this wife of his who had remained to tempt him? But Satan would have taken off long before even the one who remained, had he not been keeping her to assist him, because it was through Eve that he had vanquished the first man. He had kept another Eve for Job. So yes, how much he suffered! He lost everything he had, his house fell down—if only that had been all—and crushed his children. And because patience had played such a great part in his life, listen to the answer he gave: *The Lord has given, the Lord has taken away; as it pleased the Lord, so has it come about; may the Lord's name be blessed* (Jb 1:21). So because he had humbled himself, he was due to be exalted. And the Lord did this in order to make the principle plain to us here below; because in fact he was keeping better things for his servant in heaven. So he exalted Job who had humbled himself, and humbled the devil who had exalted himself; because *this one he humbles, and that one he exalts* (Ps 75:7).

Let none of you, though, my dearest brothers and sisters, expect a reward here when you suffer any afflictions of this sort; for example, if you suffer some losses, don't start saying to yourself, *The Lord has given, the Lord has taken away; as it pleased the Lord, so has it come about; may the Lord's name be blessed*, in order just to receive double. It must be patience that praises[27] the Lord, not avarice. If you are seeking to receive double what you lost, and that's why you are praising the Lord, then you are praising him out of greed or cupidity, not out of love or charity. It's not that holy man's example that has occurred[28] to you; you're deceiving yourself. When Job put up with all his troubles, he wasn't hoping to get back double. And you can confirm what I'm saying both in his first confession when he suffered all those losses and buried his children, and in the second, when he was now suffering the torments of the sores in his flesh. Here are the words of his first confession: *The Lord has given, the Lord has taken away; as it pleased the Lord, so has it come about; may the Lord's name be blessed.* He could have said, "The Lord has given, the Lord has taken away; he can give again what he has taken away, he can bring back more than he has taken." He didn't say that, but, "*as it pleased the Lord,*" he said, "*so has it come about. Because it pleases him, let it also please me; what has pleased the good Lord must not displease his obedient servant; what has pleased the doctor must not displease the patient.*"

Listen to his second confession: *You have spoken*, he says to his wife, *like the silly woman you are. If we have received good things from the hand of the Lord, why will we not endure bad things?* (Jb 2:10). He didn't add, what would have been true enough if he had said it, "The Lord is powerful enough both to restore my flesh to its pristine state, and to multiply what he has taken away from us," in case it should seem that it was with such hopes that he was bearing with those troubles. But it was in order to give us a lesson, that the Lord granted him the things he wasn't hoping for; to teach us that God was with him all the time; because if he hadn't also given him all those things,[29] we would certainly not have been able to see the hidden prize he had in store for him.

And therefore what is it that divine scripture says, by way of encouraging us to be patient, and to hope for a future, not a present, reward? *You have heard of the patience of Job, and seen the end of the Lord* (Jas 5:11). Why, "you have seen the patience of Job" and not "the end of this same Job"? Because in that case you would open your gullet to get double, you would say, "God be thanked; I will endure everything, I shall receive double, just like Job." *The patience of Job, the end of the Lord.* We know the patience of Job, and we know the end of the Lord. Which end of the Lord?[30] *My God, my God, why have you forsaken me?* (Mk 15:34)—that end? They are the words of the Lord as he hung on the cross. As though he had forsaken him as regards present well-being, but not forsaken him as regards eternal immortality. That's where the end of the Lord really is. The Jews arrest him, the Jews revile him, the Jews bind him, crown him with thorns, dishonor him with spittle; they scourge him, heap abuse upon him, hang him on the tree, dig into his side with a lance, finally bury him; he certainly seems forsaken. But by whom?[31] By those who were reviling him. So the reason you must have patience is so that you may rise again and not die, that is, never die, like Christ. That, after all, is what we read: *Christ rising from the dead dies now no more* (Rom 6:9).[32]

He is seated at the right hand of the Father

11. *He ascended into heaven*; believe it. *He is seated at the right hand of the Father*; believe it. By "being seated" or "sitting" you must understand "dwelling"; as we say about some person, "He has been sitting in that country for three years."[33] Scripture also says it: that someone sat in the city for such and such a time;[34] did he just sit, and never stand up? That's why people's dwellings are called their seats. Where they have their seats, they aren't always sitting down, are they? Do they never get up, never walk around, never lie down? And yet their places are called seats. So that's how you must believe that Christ is dwelling at the right hand of the Father; that's where he is.

Don't let your hearts say to you, "What is he doing?" Don't ask what you are not allowed to discover; he's there; that's enough for you. He is blessed, and with the blessedness which is called the right hand of the Father; that's a name for blessedness, the Father's right hand.[35] I mean, if we take it all in a literal sense, because he's sitting on the Father's right, it will mean that the Father's on the left. Can it be fitting that we should arrange them like that, Son on the right, Father on the left? There, everything is on the right, because there no wretchedness[36] is to be found.

12. *From there he will come to judge the living and the dead.* The living, who are still alive on the day; the dead, who have gone before them.[37] It can also be undertood like this: the living, the just; the dead, the unjust. He judges both kinds, after all, giving each what he deserves.[38] To the just he is going to say in judgment, *Come, blessed of my Father, take possession of the kingdom which has been prepared for you from the beginning of the world* (Mt 25:34). Get yourselves ready for this, for this reason live, and live in that kind of way, for this reason believe, for this reason be baptized, to ensure that this can be said to you: *Come, blessed of my Father, take possession of the kingdom which has been prepared for you from the establishment of the world.* To those on the left, what? *Go into the eternal fire, which has been prepared for the devil and his angels* (Mt 25:41). That's how the living and the dead will be judged by Christ.

Christ's first, timeless, birth has been mentioned, Christ's other birth of the virgin in the fullness of time has been mentioned, the passion of Christ has been mentioned, Christ's judgment has been mentioned. Everything has been said which has to be said about Christ, God's only Son, our Lord.[39] But the Trinity is not yet complete.

13. It goes on in the creed, *And in the Holy Spirit.* This Trinity is one God, one nature, one substance, one power, supreme equality, no division, no diversity, perpetual charity. Do you want proof that the Holy Spirit is God? Be baptized, and you will be his temple. The apostle says, *Do you not know that your bodies are the temple of the Holy Spirit in you, whom you have from God?* (1 Cor 6:19). A temple is what God has; because Solomon the king and prophet was ordered to build a temple for God. If he had built a temple for the sun, or the moon, or some star or some angel, wouldn't God have condemned him?[40] So because he built a temple for God, he thereby showed that he worshiped God. And what did he build it out of? Out of wooden beams and stones, because God was pleased to have his servant make him a house on earth where he could be prayed to, where he could be remembered.[41] That's why the blessed Stephen says, *Solomon built him a house; but the Most High does not dwell in temples made with hands* (Acts 7:47-48).

So if our bodies are the temple of the Holy Spirit, what sort of God is it who built a temple for the Holy Spirit? But yes, it is God. You see, if our bodies are the temple of the Holy Spirit, the one who built a temple for the Holy Spirit is the one who also built our bodies. Observe the apostle saying, *God arranged the body, giving greater honor to the part which lacked it* (1 Cor 12:24), when he was speaking of the different parts, so that there should not be divisions within the body. God created our bodies. God created the grass; who created our bodies?[42] How can we prove that God creates the grass? Whoever clothes also creates. Read the gospel: *So if God so clothes the grass of the field which is today, and tomorrow is cast into the oven* (Lk 12:28). So the one who clothes also creates. And the apostle says, *Fool, what you sow is not quickened unless it dies; and as for what you sow, it is not the body that is going to be that you sow, but a bare grain, as it may be of wheat or one of the others. But God gives it a body as he wishes, and to each kind of seed its proper body* (1 Cor 15:36-38).

So if God builds our bodies, if God builds our members, and our bodies are the temple of the Holy Spirit, have no doubts that the Holy Spirit is God. And don't add him as a kind of third God, because Father and Son and Holy Spirit are one God. That is how you must believe.

On the holy Church

14. It goes on, after presenting us with the Trinity, *the holy Church*. God has been pointed out to you, and his temple. *For the temple of God*, says the apostle, *which is what you are, is holy* (1 Cor 3:17). That is the holy Church, the one Church, the true Church, the Catholic Church, fighting against all heresies; it can fight, but it cannot be outfought. All heresies have emerged from it, like useless twigs pruned from a vine, while it remains itself in its root, in its vine, in its love.[43] *The gates of hell shall not defeat it* (Mt 16:18).

On the forgiveness of sins

15. *The forgiveness of sins.* You have the creed complete in yourselves, when you are baptized. None of you must say, "I did this or that, perhaps it can't be forgiven me." What have you done? How serious was it? Tell me some monstrous sin you've committed, as grave as can be, horrific, which it's horrifying even to think about; you've done whatever you like—have you killed Christ? There is nothing worse than that deed, because there's also nothing better than Christ. How impiously wicked it is to kill Christ! Still, the Jews killed him, and many of them later on believed in him, and drank his blood; the sin they had committed had been forgiven them.

When you have been baptized, go on living a good life according to God's commandments, in order to keep your baptism unspoiled to the end.[44] I'm not telling you that you will live here below without sin; but there are venial, or pardonable sins, without which this life cannot be lived. Baptism was introduced on account of all sins; on account of the minor sins, without which we cannot exist here, the prayer was introduced. What does the prayer say? *Forgive us our debts, just as we too forgive our debtors* (Mt 6:12). We are washed just once by baptism, washed daily by the prayer. But don't commit those sins for which you have to be cut off from the body of Christ, which God preserve you from. I mean, those people you can see here doing penance have committed wicked acts, whether adultery or other frightful deeds; that's why they are doing penance. I mean, if their sins were slight, the daily prayer would be sufficient to blot them out.

Three ways in which sins are forgiven

16. So sins are forgiven in the Church in three ways; by baptism, by the prayer, and by the greater humiliation of penance. Still, God only forgives the sins of the baptized. The sins which he first forgives, he only forgives to the baptized. When? When they are baptized. The sins which are forgiven afterward to those who say the prayer, and to the penitents whom he forgives, he forgives those who have been baptized. After all, how can people say *Our Father* (Mt 6:9), when they haven't yet been born? As long as they are catechumens, all their sins remain on them. If that's the case with catechumens, how much more with pagans, how much more with heretics?

But we don't alter baptism for heretics.[45] Why not? Because they already have baptism in the same sort of way as an army deserter has the imperial brand-mark.[46] That's how these also have baptism, but as something to be condemned for, not as something to be rewarded for. And yet if the deserter puts himself right and returns to the colors, does anyone have the audacity to alter the imperial mark?

On the resurrection of the flesh

17. We also believe in *the resurrection of the flesh*, which has already taken place in Christ, so that the body might also hope for what has first taken place with the head. The head of the Church is Christ, the body of Christ is the Church. Our head rose again, ascended into heaven; where the head is, there too are the members. The resurrection of the flesh, in what way? In case anyone should assume it will happen in the same way as it did with Lazarus, to show that that's not how it will be, there is added, *in life everlasting*. May God bring you to new birth; may God preserve and protect you; may God bring you finally to himself, who is himself that very life everlasting. Amen.

NOTES

1. There are two reasons for suggesting this late date. The first is the way in which he warns his hearers against the Arian heresy in sections 4 and 5. But Arianism did not appear in North Africa until the arrival there of the Gothic mercenaries of Count Boniface about 420. The second reason is that he concludes the creed with the article *and life everlasting*. For an explanation of why this indicates a late date, see Sermon 215, note 18. For general comparison see Sermons 212-215. The sermon is found in two editions, that of the Maurists, and the modern one of the *Corpus Christianorum*, CCL.

2. *Symbolum* was a common word for a sign, or a token, or a ticket, and that is the meaning he is playing on here. The creed was seen as the sign of faith, a kind of password, I suppose, to the mysteries, as well as a sort of ticket to heaven. Catechumens were forbidden to write the creed down.

3. See Sermon 212, note 1.

4. Here perhaps the baptismal creed was solemnly recited to the catechumens, it would seem by the bishop himself, and they would repeat it after him, phrase by phrase.

5. Reading *incipietis* instead of the text's *incipitis* you begin.

6. See Col 1:16.

7. See Gn 1:14-25.

8. See Gn 1:28.

9. The text reads *Facti sumus humiles mortales*. The *humiles* seems to overload it; I think it could have been put in by someone copying to dictation and falling behind a little, and conflating *sumus mortales* into *humiles*, thus giving a text, *Facti humiles*. This in turn would be combined by a later copyist with the correct text, *Facti sumus mortales*.

10. *Per corruptionem*. He is thinking of the sexual act as involving a certain destructive violence, *corruptio* in the active sense, as well as of the perishable, ephemeral quality of the semen, *corruptio* in the passive sense.

11. The Arians, being somewhat caricatured. In fact, they denied that the Son is God at all in the strict sense. But they certainly said that he is less than the Father.

12. It would go so much better in Afrikaans, where they regularly talk, on farms, of the *oubaas* and the *kleinbaas*.

13. The text reads, *quando in unicum ipsum Deum credidistis*, when you believed in him, the only God. But they hadn't believed in any such thing—that is, expressed their belief in the words of the creed; they had believed in *Filium ejus unicum* (section 3 above), in his only Son. So I emend the text to *quando in unicum ipsius Filium credidistis*.

14. Again a dubious text, this time overloaded: to prove *quia Filius verus Deus Patris est filius*. I have simply eliminated the first *Filius*. The Maurists keep it and emend *Deus* to *Dei*, which gives the irrelevant sense, "that the Son is the true Son of God the Father."

15. See Gn 3:5-6.

16. I have made so bold as to emend *humilitas*, humility, to *humanitas*; it is Christ's humanity that is like the divine arm stretched out to us.

17. Not, of course, meaning of Mary and Joseph, but of Mary and all those ancestors, right back to Adam, listed in Lk 3:23-37.

18. Here I omit another "when he suffered," surely redundant. The Maurists add "dead" after "crucified."

19. Here he is in fact quoting the Nicene Creed, not the Apostles' Creed.

20. The text actually says, "both what reproduces and what is reproduced," *et quod generat et quod generatur*. I have emended this to *et quod generatur est quod generat*.

21. In baptism.

22. *agonotheta summus*.

23. See Jb 42:10-27.

24. Presumably with life after death. See Jb 1:2; 1:18-19; 42:13. The whole passage here is very muddled and incoherent.

25. See Gn 3:1-6.

26. See Jb 2:9.

27. Reading *laudet* with the Maurists instead of *laudat* with CCL, which makes this a plain statement: It is patience that praises the Lord.

28. This time I read the indicative *occurrit* for the text's subjunctive *occurrat*, don't let his example occur to you.

29. See Jb 42:10-17.

30. Added with the Maurists; CCL omits.

31. Reading *Sed quibus?* with the Maurists instead of CCL's *Sed quid?*, But why/what?—which doesn't fit the context at all. I suspect it is a misreading by a copyist in a hurry of an abbreviation in the text he was copying from.

32. A more muddled, incoherent, badly arranged, badly argued passage than this section, I don't remember coming across in any of the genuine sermons.

33. We don't, of course, in English. See Sermons 213, 5, note 16; and 214, 8, note 20. 34. See 1 Kgs 2:38. The Hebrew *yashabh* means both sit and dwell.

35. See Sermon 214, 8, which concludes by identifying the Father's right hand with "eternal felicity."

36. Signified by the left, the *sinister* side. The translator, being left-handed himself, duly registers his protest at this dextrist language.

37. See 1 Thes 4:16-17.

38. See 2 Cor 5:10.

39. But the resurrection has hardly been mentioned at all; it was rather elbowed out by the long, muddled reflection on the patience of Job. At least, somewhat oddly, he doesn't mention it in this summary.

40. Which indeed he did, because Solomon did; 1 Kgs 11:1-9.

41. So the Maurists, with some manuscripts. Others, followed by CCL, read *ubi moraretur*, where he could stay, instead of *ubi memoraretur*.

42. Now follows a totally pointless digression about God creating grass. The old man (if my dating is right) is letting his stream of consciousness carry him off into side eddies.

43. See Jn 15:1-6.

44. Baptism is not just a sacrament that takes place in a moment; it is a sacramental state that remains, that qualifies baptized persons, so that they are, so to say, visible manifestations of the sacrament all their lives—if they "keep their baptism unspoiled." Even if they don't, the baptismal character remains with them—something he sometimes simply calls baptism. See note 47 below.

45. He means, we don't rebaptize heretics, as the Donatists do. The Donatists were the heretics he chiefly had in mind.

46. Which was called the *character*, a Greek word meaning an engraved or branded mark. It is from this analogy that the concept of sacramental character gets its name.

SERMON 399

SERMON ON CHRISTIAN DISCIPLINE

Date: 400[1]

The Church is the house of discipline

1. The word of God has spoken to us, and it was uttered for our encouragement, with scripture saying, *Accept discipline in the house of discipline* (Sir 51:28.23). "Discipline" comes from *disco*, I learn; the house of discipline is the Church of Christ. So what is learned here, and why is it learned? Who are the ones who learn, and who do they learn from? What is learned is how to live a good life; how to live a good life is learned to enable you to live forever. The ones who learn this are Christians, the one who teaches it is Christ. So be good enough to listen to me saying a few things, as the Lord may grant me, first about what living a good life consists in; next about what the reward of a good life is; thirdly about who are true Christians; fourthly, about who is the true master.

We are all of us in the house of discipline, but there are many people who don't want to accept discipline, and what's even more perverse, they don't want to accept discipline even in the house of discipline. While the reason they ought to accept discipline in the house of discipline is so that they might keep it in their own homes; they, on the contrary, want not only to indulge to give way to indiscipline in their homes, but also to bring it with them even into the house of discipline.[2]

So those of you among whom the word of God is not barren, who link your hearts to your ears, who are not the path, where the seed was eaten by the birds as soon as it fell, who are not the stony ground where the seed cannot have deep roots, and where it springs up for a moment and withers in the heat; who are not the thorny field, where as soon as the seed has sprouted and begun to grow up in the air, it is choked by the dense thorns; but who are the good soil, prepared to receive the seed, and to yield a crop of either a hundred, or sixty, or thirty-fold—you, of course, who have not entered the school of discipline in vain, will realize that I have brought these comparisons to your notice from the gospel;[3] so those of you who are of that sort, please accept what the Lord thinks fit to tell you through me. What am I, after all, since he is doing the sowing? Not much more than the sower's basket; he is good enough to place in me what he wishes to broadcast to you. So don't pay any attention to the cheapness of the basket, but to the high value of the seed and the authority of the sower.

Living a good life means keeping God's commandments

2. So what is the lesson of living a good life that is learned here?[4] There are many commandments in the law, in which this good life is contained, commanded, learned. Many commandments indeed, beyond counting. You could scarcely count the number of pages they take up, how much less the commandments themselves! However, there was something God was willing to do, for the sake of those who might be able to make excuses, such as that they haven't the time to read them all, or that they don't know how to read, or that they find it hard to understand them; he was willing, so that nobody should have any such excuse on the day of judgment, to sum up, as it is written, and to shorten the word on the earth, as the prophet had foretold about him: *A summary and a shortened word will the Lord make upon the earth* (Is 10:23). God didn't want this summary and shortened word to be obscure, either. The reason it's short is in case you haven't the time to read; the reason it's clear is so you can't say, "I wasn't capable of understanding."

The divine scriptures are a vast treasure, containing many wonderful commandments, like so many gems and precious jewels and huge chests, a real gold mine. But who can search through all this treasure, and make use of it, and reach everything to be found there? The Lord gave us this comparison in his gospel, and said, *The kingdom of heaven is like a treasure found in a field*; but in case anyone should say he was not up to searching through this treasure, he immediately gave another comparison: *The kingdom of heaven is like a trader looking for fine pearls, who found one precious pearl, and sold everything he had, and bought it* (Mt 13:44-46); so that if you were reluctant to search through a whole treasure-house, you shouldn't be reluctant to carry one pearl under your tongue, and walk around wherever you like without a worry in the world.[5]

Love your neighbor as yourself; the question is,
how do you love yourself?

3. So what is this summary and shortened word? *You shall love the Lord your God with your whole heart, and with your whole soul, and with your whole mind; and you shall love your neighbor as yourself. On these two commandments depends the whole law, and the prophets* (Mt 22:37.39-40). There you are, that's what's learned in the house of discipline; to love God, to love your neighbor; God as God, your neighbor as yourself. You won't find God's peer, after all, so that you could be told, "Love God as you love that one." About your neighbor a standard has been found for you, because you yourself are found to be your neighbor's peer. You ask how you are to love your neighbor? Look at yourself, and at how you love yourself, and love your neighbor like that. No room for any mistake there. So now I wish to commit your neighbor to you on those terms, that you love him as yourself; that's what I wish, but I still have my qualms about it.

I want to tell you, "Love your neighbor as you love yourself," and I have my qualms; I still wish, you see, to examine how you love yourself. So don't take it ill; you yourself are not to be lightly dismissed, since your neighbor is to be committed to your care; we mustn't deal with you in an offhand manner. You are one person, your neighbors are many. In the first place, you see, you shouldn't understand your neighbor as just being your brother, or relative, or one of your in-laws. Neighbor to every person is every single other person. Father and son, father-in-law and son-in-law are said to be neighbors. Nothing is so near, so much a neighbor, as one human being to another. But if we assume that only those born of the same parents are neighbors, let's turn our attention to Adam and Eve, and we are all brothers and sisters; brothers and sisters, indeed, insofar as we are human—how much more so in that we are Christians? As regards your being human, your one father was Adam, your one mother Eve; as regards your being a Christian, your one father is God, your one mother the Church.

If you love iniquity, you in fact hate yourself

4. So notice, then, how many neighbors one person has. All the people you come across, all those you can associate with, are your neighbors. So how important it is to examine whether you love yourself, since so many neighbors are to be entrusted to you, for you to love them as yourself. So don't be angry, any of you, if I examine how you love yourself. I, to be sure, am doing the examining, but it's you yourself who must do the finding. Why, after all, am I discussing the matter? Because I myself am going to find out? The reason I'm discussing it is so that you should question yourself, should become visible to yourself, should not escape your own notice, not hide from yourself, should place yourself squarely before your eyes, not behind your own back. May you do this while I'm speaking, do it without my knowing the result.

How do you love yourself? Whoever you are, listening to me, or rather whoever you are, listening to God through me in this house of discipline, consider yourself, and how you love yourself. Naturally, I mean, if I ask you whether you love yourself, you will reply that you do. Who, after all, ever hated himself? That's what you're going to say: "Who, after all, ever hated himself?" So you don't love iniquity, if you love yourself. Because if you do love iniquity, it's not me saying it, listen to the psalm: *Whoever loves iniquity hates his own soul* (Ps 11:5, LXX). So if you love iniquity, listen to the truth; the truth not flattering you, but plainly telling you, "You hate yourself." The more you say you love yourself, the more in fact you hate yourself, because *whoever loves iniquity hates his own soul.* What am I to say about the flesh, which is the less valuable part of a human being? If you hate the soul, how can you love the flesh? In any case, those who love iniquity and hate their own souls, perpetrate every kind of infamy through their flesh.

So now, you there who love iniquity, how were you wanting your neighbor to be entrusted to you, for you to love him as yourself? Man, why are you destroying yourself? I mean, if you yourself are loving yourself to your own destruction, that assuredly is how you are also going to be the destruction of the

one you love as yourself. I don't want you to love anybody; at least be alone
when you perish. Either correct your love, or eschew all company.

Lift up your hearts

5. You will be telling me next, "I do love my neighbor as myself." I hear
you, certainly I hear you; you want to get drunk with this man whom you love
as yourself. "Let's have a good time today, let's drink as much as we can."
Notice that that's how you love yourself, and that you are drawing him to
yourself, and inviting him to what you love. Loving him as you love yourself,
you are bound to draw him there to what you also love. All too human man, or
rather bestial man, by loving the same sort of things as the beasts! God, you see,
made the beasts prone in form, with their faces to the ground, looking for their
food from the ground; whereas you he set on your two feet, upright from the
ground. He wanted your face to be looking upward. Don't let your heart contradict your face.

Don't have your face turned upward, and your heart turned downward. On
the contrary, hear what is true and do what is true: "Lift up your hearts"; don't
lie in the house of discipline. After all when your hear this, you answer;[6] but let
what you answer be true. Love yourself in that way, and you will really love
your neighbor as yourself. What, after all, does it mean to have your heart lifted
up, but what you were told first: *You shall love the Lord your God with all your
heart, and with all your soul, and with all your mind* (Mt 22:37)?

So while there are two commandments, wouldn't it have been enough if he
had just given one? Yes, even one is enough, if rightly understood. Because
scripture sometimes speaks in this fashion, like the apostle Paul: *You shall not
commit adultery, you shall not commit murder, you shall not lust, and any other
commandment there may be, is summed up in this saying: You shall love your
neighbor as yourself. Love of neighbor does not work any evil. So charity is the
fulfillment of the law* (Rom 13:9-10). What is charity? It's love. He appears to
have said nothing about the love of God, but he said that love of neighbor alone
was enough to fulfill the law. *Whatever other commandment there may be is
summed up in this saying*, is fulfilled in this saying. In which one? *You shall
love your neighbor as yourself* (Mt 22:39). There you have one. But certainly
there are two commandments on which the whole law depends, and the prophets.

Notice how it has been shortened even more, and still we are so sluggish
about doing it. Look, there were two, they have been reduced to one. Absolutely,
love your neighbor, and it's enough. But love him as you love yourself, not as
you hate yourself. Love your neighbor as yourself; but the first thing is to love
yourself.

It is the Lord, not money, who confers true bliss

6. You're bound to ask how you are to love yourself; and you're bound to
hear, *You shall love the Lord your God with your whole heart, and with your*

whole soul, and with your whole mind (Mt 22:37). You see, just as man was unable to make himself, so he is unable to make himself blessed. It was another thing that made him man, which was not himself; it's another thing, which is not man himself, that is going to make him blessed. And then, when he's going astray he sees for himself that he cannot be blessed by his own means, and he loves something else by which to be blessed. He loves what he thinks will make him blessed. What, are we to suppose, does he love, which he thinks will make him blessed? Money, gold, silver, possessions; in a word, money, or chattels.[7] Everything people possess on earth, you see, everything they are masters of, is called chattels. Be it slaves, utensils, fields, trees, cattle, whichever of these it is, it's called chattels. And why was it first called chattels? The reason we talk of chattels is that the ancients had all their wealth in cattle.[8] The name "chattels" comes from "cattle." We read that the ancients were wealthy cattlemen.

So you love money, Mister, which you think can make you happy; it means plenty of goods and chattels, and you love it very much indeed. You were willing to love your neighbor as yourself; then share your money with him. I was discussing what you really were;[9] you've been found out, been shown up to yourself; you've seen yourself, taken a look at yourself. You are not prepared to share your money with your neighbor. But what answer does kind, friendly avarice give me? How does it answer me? "If I share with him, there will be less both for me and for him. What I love will be diminished, and he won't have the whole of it, nor shall I have the whole of it; but because I love him as myself, my wish and hope for him is that he may have as much, so that what is mine won't grow less, and he is put on a level with me."

Envy and pride, diabolical vices

7. Your wish and hope[10] is to have something you won't lose any of, and if only you were saying this, or wishing this truly and sincerely. You see, I'm afraid that in fact you are being envious. I mean, how can you be sociable and friendly in your prosperity, when someone else's prosperity racks you with envy? Aren't you afraid, when your neighbor begins to grow rich, and begins as it were to rise, and to come after you, aren't you afraid he may follow you, afraid he may pass you? Oh sure, you love your neighbor as yourself. But of course, I'm not speaking to the envious. May God turn away this scourge from the souls of all men and women, not to mention Christians; it's a diabolical vice, the only one[11] the devil is guilty of, and unatonably guilty. The devil, after all, isn't told, when he's condemned, "You committed adultery, you were guilty of theft, you grabbed someone else's estate," but "when you fell, you envied the human race standing firm."[12]

Envy is a devilish vice, but it has its own proper mother. The mother of envy is called pride.[13] Strangle the mother, and you won't be possessed by the daughter. That's why Christ taught us humility. So I'm not speaking to the envious, I'm speaking to those who entertain good wishes and hopes. I'm speaking to those who wish their friends well, who hope they will have as much as they have themselves. They wish the needy well, that they may have as much as they themselves; but they are unwilling to give them any of what they have themselves.

Is that what you pride yourself on, Christian man or woman, that you wish people well? The beggar is better than you are, because he wishes you many more things, and hasn't got anything. You are willing to wish him well, though he gets nothing from you; give something to him for wishing you well. If it's good to wish people well, give him his reward. The poor man wishes you well; why so alarmed? Let me add a point—you are in the house of discipline. Let me add to what I said, "Give to the one who is wishing you well"; it's Christ himself. He's asking you for what he has given you. You should blush for shame. He, though rich, was willing to be poor, so that you could have poor people to give something to. Give something to your brother, give something to your neighbor, give something to your companion. You, after all, are rich, he is poor. This life is a road, you are both walking along it together.

Lighten your load, by giving some of it to the poor to carry

8. But perhaps you'll say, "I'm rich, he's poor."[14]

Are you walking along together, or not? What does it mean, your saying, "I'm rich, he's poor," but "I'm overloaded, he's traveling light." "I'm rich, he's poor." You're mentioning your burden, praising the weight you carry. And what's more serious still, you have strapped your burden to your shoulders; that's why you can't stretch out a hand. Overloaded, tightly strapped up, what are you being so proud of, why are you praising yourself? Undo your straps, decrease your burden. Give some of it to your companion, and you are helping him and giving relief to yourself. Among all these words of yours in praise of your burden, Christ is still asking, and not receiving anything; and you spread the name of family duty over cruel words,[15] and say, "And what am I to keep for my children?" I play Christ against him, he counters by playing his children against me.[16]

Is this, though, such wonderful justice, that your son should have the means of rolling in luxury, while your Lord is in want? *For when you did it for one of the least of mine, you did it for me.* Haven't you read that, haven't you taken any notice of it? *When you failed to do it for one of the least of mine, you failed to do it for me* (Mt 25:40.45). Haven't you read that, hasn't it frightened you? Look who's in want, and you're counting your children! Very well then, count your children, add one more to their number—your Lord. You have one child, let him be the second; you have two, let him be the third; you have three, let him be the fourth. But you don't want any of that. So there you are, that's how you love your neighbor, in such a way as to make him your companion in going to that perdition.

9. What am I to say to you? Do you really love your neighbor? What else are you whispering in his ears, you grasping fellow, but "Son, or brother, or father, it's good for us, while we are living here, that things should go well with us. As much as you have is as much as you will be.[17] Break up the moon, make your fortune soon."[18] These are the things you whisper to your neighbor, things you never learned in the house of discipline, and never heard here.[19] I don't want you to love your neighbor like that. Oh, if only I could ensure that you associated with nobody at all! *Bad conversations*, you see, *corrupt good morals* (1 Cor 15:33). But I can't do it, I can't ensure that you don't associate with anyone, to whom you may whisper these bad things which you don't wish to unlearn, and which indeed you are not only unwilling to be untaught, but are even determined to teach. I don't wish, or rather I do wish, but am unable, to detach you from other people's ears. So let me warn those others, round whose ears you prowl,[20] whose ears you strive to penetrate, into whose hearts you plan to force an entry through their ears.

O you that gladly receive sound doctrine in the house of discipline, *hedge your ears about with thorns* (Sir 28:24, Lat). *Bad conversations corrupt good morals. Hedge your ears about with thorns.* Hedge them about, and with a hedge of thorns, so that the one who presumes to enter inappropriately will be scratched and pricked as well as being driven off. Drive him away from you, and say, "You are a Christian, I am a Christian; this is not what we have received in the house of discipline, not what we have learned in that school where we were enrolled free; not what we learned under that master whose chair is in heaven. Don't say these things to me, and don't come near me again." That, you see, is hedging your ears about with thorns.

10. Let me turn now to that man. You're greedy and grasping, you love money. Do you want to know bliss? Love your God. Money doesn't bring you bliss; you make it into handsome coins, it doesn't make you into a blissful person. But because you love money so much, and I can see that you go in whatever direction greed or cupidity bids you, go instead, idle fellow, in the direction love or charity bids you. Look up, and observe what a difference there is between your money and your God. This sun in the sky is more beautiful than your money, and yet this sun is not your God. Accordingly, if this sunlight is more beautiful than your money, how much more beautiful must he be who made this sunlight? Or perhaps you are ready to compare your money to light? The sun sets, show me your money. It shines brightly, and at night I remove the lamp. Sure, you're rich; show me your riches. Now, if you're deprived of light, now if you haven't got the means of seeing what you have, where are your riches?[21]

And that, all the same, is the way the horrid depths of avarice are hidden from our eyes, while they are seething in our souls. We have even seen blind people who are avaricious. Tell me, please, how blind people, who can't see, can be avaricious. He hasn't even got what he's got, this blind man, and yet he's greedy and grasping. Why? Because he believes he's got the stuff, he's greedy and grasping about it. It's faith that makes him rich; he's rich by believing, not by seeing. How much better it would be if he directed his faith to God! You can't see what you possess, and that is how I preach God to you. You can't yet see him; love him and you will see him. You love money, Mr. Blind Man, which you will never see. You possess it blind, you are going to die blind, you're going to leave behind here what you possess. You didn't really have it while you were alive, because you couldn't see what you had.[22]

Let us at least love divine wisdom as much as we love money

11. What are you told about God? Here is what Wisdom herself says: *Love her like money* (Prv 2:4). It's unfitting, it's insulting, that wisdom should be compared to money, but love is being compared to love. What I see here, after all, is that you all love money in such a way that when love of money gives the order, you undertake hard labor, you put up with starving, you cross the sea, you commit yourselves to wind and wave. I have something to pick on in the matter of what you love, but I have nothing to add to the love with which you love. "Love like that, and I don't want to be loved any more than that," says God. "I'm talking to the riff-raff, I'm speaking to the greedy: You love money; love me just as much. Of course, I'm incomparably better; but I don't want more ample love from you; love me just as much as you love money."

At least let us be ashamed, and confess, and beat our breasts—but not just so as to tamp down a solid floor on top of our sins. I mean if you beat your breast without correcting your way of life, you are just tamping down your sins, not removing them. So let us beat our breasts, and beat ourselves, and be corrected by ourselves, or else the one who is the master here will beat us later on. So we've already said what is to be learned here; now it's time for why it is learned.[23]

Why people go to school to learn their letters

12. Why did you go to school, and get beaten, and run away when taken there by your parents, and get looked for and found, and dragged back again, and laid out on the floor when you were brought back?[24] Why were you beaten? Why did you endure such ghastly evils in your boyhood? To make you learn. Learn what? Your letters. Why? So that you could earn money, or obtain honors, maintain a high social rank.[25] Observe that while you are going to perish, for the sake of a perishable object, you learned this perishable object with such hard effort, driven by such severe punishments, and that the one who dragged you to these punishments did it because he loved you. Yes, it was the one who loved you[26] that dragged you off to receive punishment. He had you beaten out of love for you—so that you would learn, what? Letters. Aren't letters a good thing? Yes, they are.[27]

Yes, I know, you're going to say to me, "Why, what about you bishops?[28] Didn't you study your letters? Why, haven't you used your education in order to study and expound the divine scriptures?" That's so, but that isn't why we learned our letters. I mean, when our parents sent us to school, they didn't say to us, "Learn your letters, so that you may be able to read and study the books of the Lord." Not even Christians say this to their children. But what do they say? "Learn your letters."

Why?

"In order to be a man."

What do you mean? Am I an animal?

"When I say, to be a man, I mean to be eminent among men. Hence the proverb, As much as you have is as much as you will be.[29] In order to have as much as others, or as much as a few others; or more than the rest, or more than the few; as a result to acquire honor, rank, status."

And where will all that be when death comes along? How it disturbs us, this dread of death, how it interrupts and upsets our thoughts! How the very word, when I mentioned it, struck at your hearts! Your groans and sighs testified to your fear, and made it clear enough. I heard, yes, I heard. You sighed and groaned, you are afraid of death. If you're afraid, why don't you take precautions? You're afraid of death; why be afraid? It's going to come; fear it, or fear it not, it's got to come; sooner or later, it's going to come. Even if you're afraid, you will never manage to avert what you are afraid of.

Learn how to die a good death by learning how to live a good life

13. What you should fear instead is what won't happen if you don't want it to. What's that? Sinning. Be afraid of sinning, because if you love your sins, you will tumble into another death, which you would be able to avoid coming to, if you didn't love your sins. But as it is, you are so perverse, that you love death more than life.

"Nonsense," you say. "What human being would ever love death more than life?"

Perhaps I can convince you that you do love death more than life. Look, this is how I will convince you. You love your clothes, you want them to be good ones. You love your villa, you would like it to be a good one. You love your son, you want him to be a good one. You love your friend, you would like him to be a good one. You love your household, you want it to be a good one. What about your also wanting to have a good death? After all, you pray every day that since death is going to come anyway, God may grant you a good death; you say, "May God preserve me from a bad death." So there you are, you love your death more than your life; you're afraid of dying a bad death; you're not afraid of living a bad life. Put right your living a bad life, be afraid of dying a bad death. But no, don't be afraid of that; it's impossible to die a bad death, if you've lived a good life. I can most certainly confirm this, I have the audacity to say: *I have believed, therefore have I spoken* (Ps 116:10; 2 Cor 4:13); it is impossible to die a bad death if you have lived a good life.

Now you're saying to yourelf, "Haven't many just people perished in ship-wrecks? Oh sure, it's impossible to die a bad death, if you've lived a good life. Hasn't the enemy's sword slain many just people? Oh sure, it's impossible to die a bad death, if you've lived a good life. Haven't bandits killed many just people? Haven't wild beasts torn many just people to pieces? Oh sure, it's impossible to die a bad death, if you've lived a good life."

And I reply, "Is that what you think a bad death is? To perish in a shipwreck, to be struck with the sword, to be torn to pieces by wild beasts? Didn't the martyrs undergo such deaths as that, and here we are, celebrating their birth-days?[30] What kind of death did they not undergo? And yet if we are Christians, if we remember that we are in the house of discipline, at least when we are here, at least when we are listening here, if we don't forget it all the moment we go out, if we remember what we hear in this place—don't we call the martyrs blessed? Inquire about the deaths of the martyrs; question the eyes in your head—they died a bad death; question the eyes of faith—*Precious in the eyes of the Lord is the death of his saints* (Ps 116:15). So whatever it is that horrifies you about their death, it won't horrify you at all, if you imitate them.

Take pains to lead a good life, and whatever the occasion is of your departing from this body, you depart to rest, you depart to bliss, which knows no fear and has no end. I mean, it was to all appearances a good death for the man clothed in purple and fine linen; but a bad death for the man so thirsty, and longing for a drop of water amid his torments. It was to all appearances a bad death for the poor man lying at the rich man's gate, among the tongues of dogs, a bad death for him, longing in his hunger and thirst for scraps from the table, a death to be avoided at all costs. But look at the end of it; you're a Christian, open the eye of faith: *It came about that that poor man died, and was carried away by angels into Abraham's bosom* (Lk 16:22). What good did his marble tomb do the rich man thirsty in hell? What harm did his rags, filthy with the pus from his sores, do the poor man at his ease in Abraham's bosom? The rich man, who had ignored him at his gate, saw him at his ease a long way off. Now choose your death; tell me, who died a good death, who a bad one? I rather think it's better for that poor man than for that rich man. Or would you rather be buried in fragrant spices, and thirst for ever in hell? You answer, "God preserve me from that!" Yes, I think that's what you'll say.[31] So you will learn how to die a good death, if you have learned how to live a good life. The reward, after all, of a good life, is eternal life.

The sower sows, regardless of path, stones, and thorns

14. Those who learn this lesson are Christians; those who hear it and don't learn it—what are they to the sower? The hand of the sower is not deterred by the way, not deterred by the stones, not deterred by the thorns; he broadcasts[32] what is his own. Whoever's afraid of the seed falling on bad soil never reaches the good soil. We too, in speaking, are casting the seed, scattering the seed. There are people who ignore us, people who find fault with us, people who mock

us. If we are afraid of them, we are reduced to sowing nothing, we are reduced to going hungry at harvest time. So let the seed reach[33] the good soil. I know that those who hear, and hear well, both fall away and make progress; they fall away from iniquity, make progress in the truth; fall away from the world, make progress in God.

It is Christ who is teaching; his school is his body

15. After all, who is the master that is doing the teaching? Not any sort of man, but the apostle. Clearly the apostle, and yet not the apostle. *Or do you wish,* he says, *to get proof of the one who is speaking in me, Christ?* (2 Cor 13:3). It is Christ who is doing the teaching; he has his chair in heaven, as I said a short while ago. His school is on earth, and his school is his own body. The head is teaching his members, the tongue talking to his feet. It is Christ who is doing the teaching; we hear; let us fear, let us act.

And don't despise Christ, just because for your sake he was born in the flesh, wrapped in the rags of mortality; for your sake felt hunger and thirst; for your sake was tired out and sat at the well;[34] for your sake was weary and went to sleep in the boat;[35] for your sake had unseemly abuse heaped on him, for your sake did not wipe people's spittle off his face; for your sake hung on the tree, for your sake breathed his last, for your sake was laid in the tomb. Perhaps you rather despise all this in Christ? Do you wish to know who he really is? Recall the gospel you just heard: *I and the Father are one* (Jn 10:30).

Concluding prayer

16. Turning to the Lord, let us implore him on our own behalf, and on behalf of all his people standing with us in the courts of his house,[36] that he may be pleased to keep and protect it, through Jesus Christ his Son our Lord, who lives and reigns with him forever and ever. Amen.

NOTES

1. This date is just a guess on my part; but see note 2 for some slight supporting evidence. Van Bavel, in an article in *Augustinian Heritage* (1991, vol 37, 1), "Augustine on Christian Teaching and Life," which is a commentary on this sermon, says it is generally accepted that it was preached about 398. I prefer a slightly later date, because the sermon shows Augustine at the height of his powers, with full confidence in himself as a bishop, and indeed as a representative, in the pulpit, of his fellow bishops. A number of little points suggest that the sermon was preached with other bishops present; see note 28 below; therefore very likely in Carthage, during a meeting of an all-African Council. The sermon is found in two editions, that of the Maurists, and that of the contemporary *Corpus Christianorum*, CCL.

2. The reference is most probably to those who continued to keep up the old custom of venerating

the martyrs at their shrines (the sermon was perhaps being preached at the main shrine of Saint Cyprian) with drunken revels. If this is so, it would support the suggestion of a fairly early date for the sermon.

3. See Mk 4:3-8.

4. So the Maurists. CCL has, "So what is living a good life? What is learned here? . . ." It is just a difference of punctuation, and of reading, at the beginning of the second question, *quid* instead of *quod*.

5. A smuggler's trick?

6. "We have lifted them up to the Lord," *Habemus ad Dominum*. I have emended the text's *responde*, answer, in the imperative, to the indicative *respondes*.

7. Why I am obliged to add "or chattels" will become apparent in a moment. It is the single word *pecunia* being translated, which comes from *pecus*, cattle.

8. As in so much of Africa today, where the so-called bride price, or dowry, is always reckoned in so many head of cattle.

9. Reading *quid esses* with the Maurists. CCL has *quid est*, which makes no translatable sense, and which again I suspect of being a misreading of an abbreviation.

10. Reading *Optas* with the Maurists, instead of CCL's *Opto*, My wish and hope. But this simply does not fit the context; it is, I suggest, a copyist's slip from his eye being caught by the *opto* of the previous sentence.

11. Reading *quo solo diabolus reus est* instead of the text's *quo solus diabolus*, of which the devil alone is guilty—which is palpably untrue.

12. See Wis 2:24.

13. By Augustine himself, *Letters*, 140, 2, 54, and *Exposition of the Psalms*, on Ps 100, 9. But where he gets the saying from I cannot discover.

14. And so, I suppose the implication is, we are not walking together. See Sermon 164,9 for this whole theme.

15. Reading with the Maurists, *et obtendis nomen pietatis crudelibus vocibus*, instead of CCL's *et offendis . . . vocibus*, and you offend against the name of family duty with cruel words.

16. As in a game of draughts (checkers) or chess, I take it. The Latin words are *oppono* and *repono*.

17. See Horace, *Satires*, I,1,62.

18. *Frange lunam, fac fortunam*. It is suggested that this is an old Punic proverb. Van Bavel *(op. cit.* 103) suggests it means "Make your fortune, even if you have to do the impossible" - as good a suggestion as any.

19. Following the Maurists. CCL have "you never heard this."

20. Like the troops of Midian in the hymn by J.M.Neale.

Christian, dost thou see them on the holy ground.

How the troops of Midian prowl and prowl around?

English Hymnal, number 72.

21. If I were this greedy rich man, I would be singularly unimpressed by this argument!

22. Another very unconvincing argument. It's only real point is that if we cannot see God, no more can the rich man, in this case, see his money. Put in a positive way it could be an effective illustration; put in this negative way, it merely irritates.

23. So the Maurists. CCL have a feebler, inconsequential text: "We've already said what is to be learned here, why it is to be learned."

24. He is living over again the horrors of his own school days, graphically described in the *Confessions*, I, 9 (14); 12 (19).

25. The classical education of letters culminated in the course on rhetoric, which Augustine himself had taught, and which was aimed at making you a competent public speaker; hence at fitting you for a career in the law and in public life, as a servant of the state.

26. Your father, like Augustine's father Patrick (Patricius).

27. Again following the Maurists. CCL omit this last phrase, which in Latin is the single word *Bonae*.

28. This suggests that he was preaching in the presence of other bishops assembled in Carthage, no doubt for an African Council.

29. See section 9 above, and note 17.

30. Perhaps they were actually celebrating the feast day of some martyr or martyrs, and possibly with the traditional "indiscipline." See note 2 above.

31. So the Maurists. CCL have "what you'll choose."

32. We have to be aware of the original, proper meaning of this word, before it was ever applied metaphorically to the radio.

33. So the Maurists, *veniat*. CCL have *venit*, the seed reaches.

34. See Jn 4:6.

35. See Mk 4:38.

36. See Ps 134:1. This is an unusual concluding prayer; it seems primarily to be inviting his fellow bishops and clergy to implore the Lord. The Italian edition says that a different prayer is given in the *Patrologia Latina* (PL) text, which reproduces the Maurist text. But in this they are mistaken; my PL text has the same as what is translated here.

SERMON 400

ON THE VALUE OF FASTING

Date: 412[1]

On the hunger and thirst for justice

1. Both God and the season are suggesting that something should be said about the value of fasting.[2] This observance, you see, this strengthening of the spirit, this cheating of the flesh and profiting of the mind is not something that the angels offer to God. Up there, after all, there is total plenty and eternal satiety; and no deficiency for the simple reason that complete sufficiency is found in God. Up there is to be found *the bread of angels* (Ps 78:25), and it was so that human beings might eat the bread of angels that God became a human being. Here below all souls that support some earthly flesh fill their stomachs from the earth; up there the intelligent spirits that preside over the heavenly bodies[3] fill their minds with God. There is both food here below and food there above. But when this food here nourishes, it also diminishes; whereas that food up there both fills its recipients and remains whole and entire. Christ instructed us to hunger for this food, when he said, *Blessed are those who hunger and thirst for justice, since they shall be satisfied* (Mt 5:6).

So it's the business of human beings living this mortal life to hunger and thirst for justice; but to be filled with justice belongs to that other life. The angels have their fill of this bread, this food; human beings, however, in being hungry for it stretch themselves; in stretching themselves they are enlarged; in being enlarged they increase their capacity; through increasing their capacity, they will be filled in due course. So what does this mean? Do those who are hungry and thirsty for justice receive nothing here? They assuredly do receive something; but it's one thing when we are inquiring about their refreshment while they are journeying along the road, and another when we inquire about their perfection when they attain to final bliss.

Listen to the apostle being hungry and thirsty, and for justice of course, insofar as justice can be had, can be practiced in this life. Which of us, after all, would have the nerve to put ourselves on his level, let alone put ourselves before him? But what does he say? *Not that I have already received, or am already perfect* (Phil 3:12). Notice who's talking; *the chosen vessel* (Acts 9:15), and the

471

end, as it were, of the hem of the Lord's garment, but still the thing that cured of her flow of blood the woman who touched it and believed;[4] being the last and the least of the apostles, after all, as he says himself: *I am the last of the apostles*; and, *I am the least of the apostles*; and again, *I am not fit to be called an apostle, because I persecuted the Church of God; but by God's grace I am what I am; and his grace has not been in vain, but I have labored more than them all; not I, though, but the grace of God with me* (1 Cor 15:8-10). You, on hearing this, imagine you are hearing him as one who is complete and perfect. Well, you've heard what he belches out; now hear what he hungers after. *Not that I have already received, or am already perfect*, he says. *Brothers, I do not consider myself to have attained; one thing though, forgetting what lies behind, stretching out to what lies ahead, according to intention I follow on toward the palm of God's calling from above in Christ Jesus* (Phil 3:13-14). He says he is not yet perfect, because he has not yet received, not yet attained; he says he is stretching out, says he is following on to the palm of the calling from above. He is on the way; he's hungry, he wants to be filled, he's busy about it, he longs to arrive, he's simmering with impatience, nothing seems to him to be so long delayed as *his casting off and being with Christ* (Phil 1:23).

The more you delight in the higher life, the more you lay
aside your earthly burden; there you have why we fast

2. So then, dearest friends, while there is earthly food, on which the weakness of the flesh is nourished, there is also heavenly food, on which the loving kindness of the mind is fed. And this earthly food is related to its own kind of life, that other food also to its own kind; this food to human life, that food to the life of angels. But there are faithful human beings, already distinguished in heart from the mass of unbelievers, always looking to God; those who are told, *Lift up your hearts*, who cherish an altogether different hope, and who know that they are *aliens and exiles* (1 Pt 2:11) in this world. They occupy the middle ground; they are to be compared neither with those people who think the only good is to enjoy earthly delights, nor yet awhile with those sublime inhabitants of heaven, whose sole delight is in the bread by which they were created. Those other people are bent down to the ground, seeking nourishment and pleasure for the flesh alone, and so they are compared to the beasts.[5] They are far, far removed from the angels, both in their condition and in their morals; in their condition, because they are mortal, in their morals, because they are self-indulgent.

Between that people of heaven and the people of earth the apostle was, after a fashion, suspended in the middle; he was going there, lifting himself up from here.[6] Still, he wasn't yet with them up there, because then he would have said, "I am already perfect"; nor was he with these others below, sluggish, slothful, languid, half asleep, who assume that there is no reality other than what they can see, and what passes away, and that they were born and are going to die,[7] because if he had been, he would not have said, *I follow on toward the palm of the calling from above* (Phil 3:14).

And so it is that in our fasts we ought to steer a middle course. This is not, as I have already said, an angelic practice; nor on the other hand is it a practice of those people who are slaves to their bellies.[8] It's the business of us in the middle, where our lives are quite distinct from those of the unbelievers, and we are eagerly panting to be joined to the angels. We haven't yet arrived, but we are already on the way; we aren't yet enjoying things there, but we are already sighing for them here. So what good does it do us to abstain a little from the nourishment and the joys of the flesh? The flesh is dragging us down to the earth, the mind is tending upward; it is snatched up by love, but held back by a weight. This is how scripture speaks of this matter: *For the body which is being corrupted weighs down the soul, and the earthly dwelling oppresses the mind thinking many things* (Wis 9:15). So if the flesh, inclining to the earth, is a load on the soul, and a burden weighing down the soul as it tries to fly ahead; the more you delight in your higher life, the more ready you are to lay down your earthly burden. There you have what we are doing when we fast.

The value of fasting; taming the flesh

3. So you mustn't regard it as an unimportant or superfluous matter. Please don't think to yourself, when perhaps you are fasting because it is the Church's custom, don't say to yourself, or listen to the suggestions of the tempter inside you, saying, "What are you doing, you and your fasting?[9] You're cheating your soul, you're not giving it what it takes delight in. You're inflicting punishment on yourself, you have turned into your own torturer and executioner. So does your torturing yourself please God? That means he's cruel, if he enjoys your being punished."

Answer this sort of tempter like this: "Yes, I do hurt myself, so that he may spare me; I do impose my own punishments on myself, so that he may come to my assistance, that I may please his eyes, that I may charm his goodness. I mean, the victim too is hurt, in order to be laid on the altar. In this way my flesh will exert less pressure on my mind." And to someone of this sort trying to dissuade you with bad arguments, reply with this comparison: "Suppose you were going to mount an animal, suppose you were going to ride a horse, and it looked as if it might throw you with its friskiness, wouldn't you make sure of having a safe journey, by cutting the rations of the unruly beast, and taming it with hunger, since you couldn't curb it with the reins? My flesh is my mount. On my journey to Jerusalem it frequently runs away with me, and tries to make me lose my way, and my way is Christ;[10] so as it plays up like that, shouldn't I restrain it with fasting?"

If you see the sense of this argument, you can easily prove the value of fasting by trying it yourself. After all, will this flesh, which is now being tamed, always need to be tamed? While it's being tossed about in time, while it's weighed down by its mortal condition, it manifests that waywardness which is so dangerous to our minds. The flesh, after all, is still subject to corruption, hasn't yet risen again. Well, it won't always be like that. It doesn't yet enjoy the state proper to its home in heaven; we haven't yet, after all, become the equals of God's angels.[11]

4. So your graces mustn't conclude that the flesh is the enemy of the spirit, as though there were one maker of the flesh, and another rival maker of the spirit. Many people, you see, having this idea, have indeed let the flesh run away with them and have lost the way, attributing one maker to the flesh, another to the spirit.[12] Now they support their case with evidence from the apostle, which they don't understand: *The flesh lusts against the spirit, and the spirit against the flesh* (Gal 5:17). That is true; but why don't you pay attention as well to another text: *for nobody ever hates his own flesh; but he nourishes and cherishes it, just as Christ does the Church* (Eph 5:29)? In that first text I quoted there seems to be a kind of struggle between two enemies, the flesh and the spirit, because *the flesh lusts against the spirit, and the spirit against the flesh*. In this other one, though, there is a kind of marriage bond: *for nobody ever hates his own flesh; but he nourishes and cherishes it, just as Christ does the Church*.

Doesn't the comparison frighten you, because *he nourishes and cherishes it*, he says, *just as Christ does the Church*? You think the flesh is a shackle; who ever loves his shackles? *For nobody ever hates his own flesh*. You think the flesh is a prison; who ever loves his prison? *For nobody ever hates his own flesh*. Who doesn't hate his chains? Who doesn't hate his punishment? And yet, *Nobody ever hates his own flesh; but he nourishes and cherishes it, just as Christ does the Church*. So you then, who attribute one maker to the flesh, another to the spirit, are going to attribute one to the Church, another to Christ. If that's your sense, it's nonsense. So everybody loves his own flesh; the apostle says so, and apart from what the apostle says, everybody can prove it by his own experience. However much, after all, you may be a tamer of the flesh, however great the severity you enthusiastically treat it with, I imagine you shut your eye if something or someone is about to hit it.

5. So there is a kind of marriage between flesh and spirit. So how is it that *the flesh lusts against the spirit, and the spirit against the flesh* (Gal 5:17)? It's a result of the punishment which derives from the propagation of death; which is why it was said, *All die in Adam* (1 Cor 15:22), and why the apostle says, *We too were once children of wrath, just like the rest* (Eph 2:3).[13] That man, you see, of whom we are all born, received the punishment of death, and we derive from him something for us to overcome; and that's why we lust against the flesh, in order to subject the flesh to ourselves by taming it, and to constrain it to obey us. So when we wish people to obey us, do we hate them? Everyone in his own home frequently disciplines his wife, and subdues her when she resists; he doesn't pursue her, though, as an enemy. You break in your son, to make him obey you; you don't hate him, do you, don't count him as an enemy? Finally, you both value and chastise your slave, and by chastising him you are making him obedient. On this point you have the clear and full judgment of the apostle himself: *I do not so run*, he says, *as at an uncertain mark; I do not so box as*

though beating the air; but I chastise my body, and reduce it to slavery, lest
perhaps while preaching to others, I myself should turn out to be disqualified
(1 Cor 9:26-27).

So then the flesh, as a result of its condition of mortality, has as it were some
earthly appetites of its own; it's with regard to these that you have been granted
the right of restraint. Let your superior govern you, so that your subject may be
governed by you. Beneath you is your flesh, above you is your God. Since you
wish your flesh to serve you, you are advised how you ought to serve your God.
You pay attention to what is beneath you; pay attention to what is above you.
You only get laws for your subordinate from your superior. You are a servant,
and you have a servant; but your Lord and master has two servants. Your servant
is more under your Lord's authority than under your own.

And so you wish to be obeyed by the flesh. Is it possible in all cases? It
submits to your Lord in all cases; it doesn't in all cases submit to you.

"How's that?" you say.

You're walking, you move your feet, the flesh follows your directives. But
will it go with you as far as you want? It's animated by you,[14] but for as long as
you wish? Is it just when you wish that you feel pain, just when you wish that
you get well? Your Lord, you see, is often using your servant to train and
exercise you, so that because you have often ignored the Lord, you may be
suitably corrected through your servant.

Being moderate and temperate in our pleasures

6. But what precisely is your business? Not to give the flesh its head in the
pursuit of unlawful pleasures, and to rein it in to some extent even from lawful
ones. If you never restrain yourself, you see, from lawful pleasures, you are on
the verge of indulging in unlawful ones. Thus for example, brothers and sisters,
marriage is lawful, adultery is unlawful; and yet temperate men, in order to keep
far away from adultery, will restrain themselves to some extent even from the
lawful use of marriage. Taking one's fill is lawful, getting drunk unlawful; and
yet moderate people, to keep their distance from the disgrace of drunkenness,
will chasten themselves by limiting to some extent their freedom to take their
fill. So then, let us act like that, brothers and sisters; let us be temperate. And as
for what we do, let us be aware of why we do it. Abstain from the joys of the
flesh, and obtain the joys of the mind.

The connection between fasting and our final goal

7. Accordingly, since the purpose of our fasts has to do with the journey we
are on, we have to consider what this journey is, and where we are wending our
way to. After all, even the pagans fast sometimes, and they know nothing of the
region we are wending our way to. And the Jews fast sometimes, and they
haven't taken the way along which we are walking.[15] That's rather like someone
breaking in a horse on which to stray and get lost.

The heretics fast; I can see in what style they are traveling; what I want to know is where they are traveling to. You're fasting, in order please whom?

"To please God," they say.

You asssume, do you, that he will accept the gift? But first see what he says: *Leave your gift, and go first and be reconciled with your brother* (Mt 5:24). Can you be taming your own body correctly, while you are tearing the members of Christ apart?[16]

Your voices are heard, it says, *as a shout, and those who are under your yoke you jab with the goad and beat with your fists. Not such is the fast I have chosen, says the Lord* (Is 58:4-5). So your fast would be repudiated if you showed yourself immoderately severe toward your slave; and will your fast be approved of when you fail to acknowledge your brother? I'm not asking what food you abstain from, but what food you love. Tell me what food you love, so that I may approve of your abstaining from this common food. Do you love justice?

No doubt you will say, "I do."

Let your justice, then, be apparent. I rather think, after all, that it's just you should serve the one who is greater, so that what is less may submit to you. We were talking, you remember, about the flesh, which is less than the spirit, and which has been subjected to being tamed and moderated. You're dealing with it so that it may submit to you, and you deny it food, because you love it when it is subject to you. Acknowledge the one who is greater than you, acknowledge your superior, so that your inferior may rightly give way to you. What if your flesh obeys you, and you don't obey your God? Aren't you condemned by your own flesh, when it submits to you? Doesn't it bear witness against you, precisely by submitting to you?

Preserving the unity of the body of Christ

8. "And to what greater one," he says, "should I submit?"

Look, Christ is talking; you have just said you are a lover of justice. *A new commandment I give you, that you should love one another* (Jn 13:34). So listen to your Lord giving a commandment that we should love one another. While he is making himself a body out of us all, as from his members, a body which has as its one head our Lord and savior, you on the contrary are busy wrenching yourself away from the members of Christ; you have no love for unity. Wouldn't you dread such a thing in your own body? If you had a dislocated finger, wouldn't you hurry off to the doctor to straighten your finger? Certainly your body is then in a good condition when your different parts are in agreement with each other; that's when you are said to be in good health, when you are very well. But if something in your body is disagreeing with the other parts, you look for someone to put it right. So why not seek to be put right yourself, to be fetched back into the community of Christ's members, and to fit harmoniously into his body, yes you too?[17]

Undoubtedly your hair is of less value than the other parts of the body.[18] What is of less value in your body than your hair? What more negligible, more readily discarded? And yet if you get a bad haircut, you are angry with the barber because he hasn't cut it evenly and straight;[19] while you refuse yourself to hold onto the unity of Christ among his members. So what are your fasts, then, or what purpose do they serve? You don't think God is fit to be served in unity by all those who believe in him; and yet you want unity to be preserved among your members, in your body, among the very hairs of your head. Your own bowels are talking to you; your members are giving true testimony against you, while you, for your part, are giving false testimony against the members of Christ.[20]

Even the pagans can teach the schismatics a lesson about unity

9. Have you distinguished your fasting from that of the pagans? That's what you think, and that's why you appear in your own eyes to have nothing to worry about. "I, after all," you say, "fast for Christ, while they do so for idols and demons." I accept what you say, and indeed there's a real difference, I don't deny it. But look; just as your own body's members were bearing witness against you, as I was reminding you a moment ago, in order to admonish you how you ought to take your place among the members of Christ your God; so too let the very pagans, from whom you distinguish your fast, admonish you a little about the unity of Christ your God.[21]

Here you are then; they, with no divisions among them, worship many false gods. Is the reason for which we have discovered the one true God, that we should *not* be united under him? They worship many gods, and false, we the one God and true; and they under their many false gods have no divisions among themselves, while we under the one true God do not maintain any unity. Doesn't it grieve you, don't you groan, don't you blush?

I'll add another point. Not only do the pagans worship many false gods, but most of these are also at loggerheads and hostile to each other. Let's mention some of them, even if we can't do them all; for example, Hercules and Juno were enemies, he being her stepson, she his stepmother.[22] The pagans have built temples to each of them, to both Juno and Hercules. They reverence him, they reverence her; while these two have a grudge against each other, their worshipers are friends. Vulcan and Mars are enemies, and Vulcan has just cause to be so.[23] But give judgment between them who dare![24] The wretched fellow, after all, hates his wife's adultery; yet he doesn't dare to forbid his worshipers to attend the temple of Mars; they give honor simultaneously to both the one and the other. If they imitated their gods, they would quarrel with each other; in fact, they go from the temple of Mars to the temple of Vulcan. What an insult! And yet they are not afraid that the husband will be angry with them, because they come to him straight from the temple of Mars the adulterer. They do have some sense; they know a stone image has no feelings.

There you have them worshiping many, false, diverse, adverse gods; and yet in worshiping them they maintain among themselves some sort of unity. There you are, the very pagans too are bearing witness against you, the pagans from whom you have so carefully distinguished your fasts. So come back to unity, brother. We worship one God; we have never seen the Father and the Son quarreling. And the pagans mustn't get hot under the collar with me, because I've said these things about their gods. Why should they get angry at my words, and not rather at their own literature? Let them eliminate that if they can, or rather if they will. Let the grammarians stop hanging up their curtains for the teaching of it.[25] He's angry with me for mentioning it, and he pays a fee for his son to learn it.

Work for unity a prerequisite for evangelization

10. So, dearly beloved, they do indeed have gods like that, or rather they used to have them. You see, while they were unwilling to abandon their gods, they were abandoned by them. And many did abandon them in fact, and are still doing so. They are pulling down their temples in their hearts. But let us rejoice over them, that they are coming over to unity, not to division. May the pagans find no occasion among us for not wishing to be Christians. Let us be of one mind and heart, brothers and sisters, as we worship the one God, so that we may urge them to abandon their many gods, after a fashion, by our very concord, so that they may come to the peace and unity of worshiping the one God. And if perhaps they should turn up their noses, and find fault with us on this score, that we Christians do not have unity among ourselves, and that's why they are slow and sluggish about coming to salvation,[26] let me address a few words to them, and also tell you what you should say to them.

They mustn't thrust their apparent concord in our faces, mustn't congratulate themselves on what looks like their unity. The fact is, they don't experience the enemy whom we suffer from. He's already in possession of them, even without their indulging in such discord. He sees them adoring false gods; he sees that they are enslaved, and enslaved to demons. What does he gain from their quarreling, or what does he lose from their not quarreling? Even though they are of one mind, though a false and vain one, and in agreement with each other, still that's how he possesses them. But now, when he was abandoned, and many of them came running to the one God, abandoning the devil's sacrilegious rites, demolishing temples, smashing idols, forbidding sacrifices, he saw that he had lost those he used to hold in thrall, he saw that his household had withdrawn from him, had acknowledged the true God. What was he to do? What traps was he to set? He knows that if we are of one heart and mind he cannot gain possession of us, cannot divide up the one God for us, cannot push any false gods onto us. He feels in his bones that love and charity are our life, dissension is our death. So he introduced quarrels among Christians, because he couldn't fabricate many gods for Christians; he multiplied sects, sowed errors, established heresies.

But whatever he has done, he has done it with chaff from the Lord's threshing floor. There you are, that's where our security lies; even though he's raging, even though he is setting his traps and sowing dissension of various kinds among

Christians, if we acknowledge our God, if we hold on to him one in heart and soul, if we keep the faith, we are safe, with nothing to worry about. Brothers and sisters, the grain either doesn't leave the threshing floor, or else comes back to it; the wind of trial and temptation carries off some of the chaff, not to set us on the road to destruction, but to provide us with practice and training. Any chaff, though, that it doesn't carry off outside, is still to be winnowed at the end; and the only place for all the chaff to go to is the fire.[27] So we, my brothers and sisters, while there is still time, ought to be doing our best, with all the powers at our disposal, with all seriousness and dedication, to see both that the chaff returns, if so it can be, while none of the grain gets lost. Right here is a test and proof of our love; the great work of our lives is being set before us. We would never discover how much we love our brothers and sisters, if nobody was ever in peril. How much love goes to the search would never become apparent, if there was nothing caught in the pit of destruction.[28]

The apostles were fishers of men; we have to be hunters of men

11. Let us toil away, brothers and sisters, without ceasing, doing all we can, whatever the sweat, with loving sentiments toward God, toward them, among ourselves. It would never do, after all, for us to create new rifts among ourselves, while wishing to allay their old quarrel. And above all let us be very careful to hold on to the most steadfast love among ourselves. They are frozen stiff in their iniquities; how will you thaw the ice of iniquity in them, if you are not on fire with the flame of charity?

Nor should we worry about appearing to be troublesome to them by driving and prodding them.[29] Let us consider where we are driving them to; that should reassure us. Is it to death, after all, and not rather away from death? Altogether, in whatever ways we can, let us treat these old wounds, but discreetly. And let us take care that the person being treated doesn't pass away in the hands of the doctor. So why should we care that the boy is crying when taken to school? Do we have to bother about the person who's being lanced pushing away the surgeon's hand?

The apostles were fishermen, and the Lord said to them, *I will make you fishers of men* (Mk 1:17). It was said by the prophet, however, that God was first going to send fishers, later on hunters.[30] First he sent fishers, later on he sends hunters. Why fishers, why hunters? Believers were fished with the nets of faith from the bottomless depths of the sea of superstition and idolatry. But where were the hunters sent to? When believers were wandering through mountains and hills,[31] that is through the proud elevations of men, through the swollen elements of different countries. Donatus was one mountain, and Arius another; another mountain was Photinus, another mountain Novatus.[32] These were the mountains they were straying through; their straying, their errors, called for hunters.

And that's why the offices of fishers and hunters were distributed to different times; in case perhaps these people should say to us, "Why did the apostles not apply force or compulsion to anybody?"

Because he's a fisherman, he casts his nets into the sea, hauls in whatever has got caught in it. But the hunter surrounds the woods, beats the thickets, drives animals into the nets by multiplying terror on every side: "Don't let it go this way, don't let it go that way; confront it on this side, beat it on that, frighten it on the other; don't let it get out, don't let it escape."

But our nets mean life; only let love be maintained. And don't consider how irksome you are to him, but how lovable he is to you. What sort of loving care are you showing, if you spare him, and he dies?

The illustration of the old man in a lethargy[33]

12. Brothers and sisters, give a thought to this comparison and illustration; one thing, after all, can have many illustrations. People are born into the situation in which every man wishes to be succeeded by his sons; and surely there is nobody who does not aim at this order in his household, and hope for it, that the begetters of sons give way, and those they have begotten succeed them. Still, if an old father gets sick—I'm not saying if a son does, with his father beside him, looking to him as his heir, longing to have him succeed himself, having begotten him precisely in order that he might remain alive when he himself is dead; I'm not saying that—if an old father gets sick, already on the way out, so close to death, already following the order of nature, no longer having anything further to hope for; still if he gets sick, and his son is dutifully at his bedside, and the doctor sees he is oppressed by a deadly and harmful sleep, the doctor accepts the idea of the old man dying, because he only has a few days left in any case, in which he can live here below.

The son is standing there, anxiously present at his father's bedside. He hears the doctor saying, "This man could be in a lethargic condition, and die from it, if he is permitted to sleep. If you want him to live, don't let him sleep. A harmful sleep is oppressing him, which while being harmful, is also sweet." Now his son, warned by the doctor, is standing there anxiously. He makes himself a nuisance to his father by shaking him, and if shaking him is unsuccessful, he pinches him; and if pinching does no good, he pricks him. He is certainly bothering his father; and he would be wickedly undutiful if he were not bothering him. But the old man, who's looking forward to dying, strikes back with a plaintive look and voice at the son who is bothering him: "Give me a little peace; why are you bothering me so?"

But the doctor says, "Because if you go to sleep, you will die."

And he says, "Leave me alone; I want to die."

The old man says, "I want to die"; and the boy is undutiful and unloving, if he doesn't say, "I don't want you to."

And that life, of course is temporal, and the father won't continue in it forever, whose son is being such a nuisance by waking him up all the time; and nor will the son, who succeeds his father on his decease. Both pass through it, both fly through it in no time; and yet they are undutiful and unloving, unless they take care of each other as regards this temporal life, even when they are a nuisance to each other. So then, do I see my brother oppressed by the sleep of a harmful habit,[34] and not wake him up, because I'm afraid of being a nuisance to him as he sleeps and perishes? Far be it from me to act like that, even if his remaining alive would mean a diminution of our inheritance. But as it is, the inheritance we are going to receive cannot be divided, cannot be diminished by multiple ownership; so am I not going to rouse him, even by being a nuisance, so that he may wake up and, being rid of the sleep of his old, old error, may rejoice with me in the inheritance of unity? Of course, of course, I'm going to do this. If I'm awake I'll do it; if I don't do it, it means I too am asleep.

The Lord's inheritance is not to be divided

13. Dearest friends, when the Lord was talking to the crowds, he was appealed to by a man who said to him, *Lord, tell my brother to divide the inheritance with me. And the Lord said, Tell me, man, who set me up as a divider of the inheritance between you?* (Lk 12:13-14). So he was quite ready to clip the wings of greed, but he was not willing to be made a judge for dividing things. We, though, dearest friends, should not seek him as a judge of such matters, because our inheritance isn't, anyhow, of that kind; with unruffled brow and a good conscience let us appeal to our Lord, and each one of us say to him "Lord, tell my brother, not to divide, but to take possession of the inheritance with me." What, after all, are you wanting to divide, brother? You see, what the Lord has left us cannot be divided. Is it gold, I mean, to have itself divided up on the scales? Is it silver, is it money, is it slaves, is it flocks, is it trees, is it fields? All these things, of course, can be divided up; what cannot be divided up is, *My peace I give you, my peace I leave you* (Jn 14:27).

Finally, even with earthly inheritances, division reduces them. Take two brothers under one father; whatever the father possesses belongs to both of them, all of it to the one, all of it also to the other. Accordingly, if they are questioned about their property, and if you say to one of them, "Whose, for example, is that horse?," he answers, "It's ours." "Whose is that farm, that slave?" In every case he answers, "It's ours." But if they divide it up, you now get another answer: "Whose is that horse?" "Mine." "Whose is this one?" "My brother's." There you have what division has done for you. You haven't acquired one, but lost one.

So even if we had that sort of inheritance which could be divided, we ought not to divide it all the same, or we would diminish our wealth. And certainly there is nothing so inconvenient for sons as to want the inheritance divided while their father is still alive. Anyway, if they attempt to do this, if they throw themselves into disputes and lawsuits, each one laying claim to his own shares, the old man exclaims, "What are you doing? I'm still alive. Wait a little while for my death, and then cut up my house." We, however, have God as our father. Why should we go in for division? Why go in for lawsuits? Certainly, let us wait; if he can die, let us divide up the inheritance.

NOTES

1. The sermon is not only about fasting, but also goes on from that subject to enter a long plea with the Donatists to return to Catholic unity, and with the Catholic faithful to do what they can to encourage their Donatist friends and relatives to do so. Hence a date shortly after the colloquium of Catholic and Donatist bishops in Carthage in 411 is likely; Lent 412, or the September Ember days of 411.

2. God suggests this through one of the scriptural readings they had heard; the season, most likely because it was Lent, but possibly some other fast day like one of the Ember days.

3. Here he is subscribing to the common opinion that the heavenly bodies were controlled by, not animated by, what Aristotle called "subsistent intelligences." Whether this opinion is consistent with that other one which Augustine usually accepted, that angels have very refined or "airy" bodies of their own that they do animate, is debatable.

4. See Mk 5:25-29; also Sermons 63A, 3; 279, 6.

5. See Psalm 49:12.20; 32:9.

6. Following the Maurists. CCL inserts, after "going there," "returning from here, stretching himself out to there." "Returning from here" is quite anomalous and out of place.

7. See Wis 2:2.

8. See Phil 3:19.

9. See Is 58:3.

10. See Jn 14:6.

11. See Lk 20:36.

12. The position of the Manichees, derived ultimately from the Persian dualism of the Zoroastrians, with their two ultimate principles perpetually at war with each other, Ahriman the lord of darkness and matter, Ormuzd the lord of spirit and light. But he goes on to criticize a point of view that was characteristic of the dominant Neoplatonist philosophy and theology, and that already had, and would continue to have an incalculable and lamentable influence on Christian theology and spirituality.

13. In the text of both editions this sentence is presented as three questions, developing the first question, "So how is it. . . ?" That question begins in the Latin with the interrogative adverb *Unde*, and the same word begins the next three clauses; and so the editors, and no doubt their manuscripts, rather heedlessly treat them as questions too. But a little reflection will show that they are not in fact developments of the question, but the answer to it. So I treat the three subsequent *unde*'s as relative, not interrogative, adverbs.

14. Notice how he is assuming the identity of you with your soul, your *anima*, which animates the flesh. He too, of course, was deeply influenced by Neoplatonism; but he was capable, increasingly so as he grew older, of a certain self-criticism in this regard.

15. That is, Christ; Jn 14:6.

16. The heretics he is primarily addressing are the Donatists, whose great sin, in his theology, was destroying, or attempting to destroy, the unity of the Church.

17. Emending the text's *et congruas in ipso corpore et tuo*, to fit harmoniously into his body and yours, to *et congruas in ipso corpore et tu*.

18. See Mt 10:30. The text presents the statement as a question.

19. See Horace, *Epistle*, I, 1, 94.

20. A reference primarily to the original allegations made by the instigators of the Donatist schism against the Catholic Caecilian, elected bishop of Carthage in 310.

21. Emending the text's *de unitate Christi tui*, about the unity of your Christ, to *de unitate Christi Dei tui*.

22. That is, Hercules was one of Jupiter's innumerable bastards, and Juno was nothing if not a jealous wife to the king of the gods. In Africa Hercules really represented the sun god, and Juno the great earth mother goddess.

23. Because Mars committed adultery with Vulcan's wife, Venus.

24. Emending the text's *sed da judicem qui audiat*, but let whoever hears produce a judge, to *sed da judicium qui audet*.

25. Hanging up the curtain means setting up a school. I take it a would-be teacher would hire an alcove in some colonnade round the forum or along a street, and hang up a curtain in front of it, instead of a door. All subjects, of course, from grammar to logic and rhetoric, were taught with reference to the classics. The literature Augustine chiefly has in mind here would have been the epics of Homer and Vergil; but also such works as Ovid's *Metamorphoses*.

26. That is, specifically, to baptism. As "salvation" and "grace" are both names for baptism, so "peace" and "unity" are both names for the Catholic Church.

27. See Mt 3:12; Lk 3:17.

28. He is urging them, after the great conference with the Donatists in 411, to devote all their energies to smoothing the way for their Donatist acquaintances to return to the peace and unity of the Catholic Church.

29. By 411 Augustine had been won over to the imperial policy, supported by all the other Catholic bishops, of coercing the Donatists by heavy fines and confiscations to return to the Catholic Church. See Letters 89 and 93. The text quoted to justify this policy was Lk 14:23, *Compel them to come in.*

30. See Jer 16:16, where it seems to be a rather wrathful fishing and hunting that the Lord has in mind.

31. See Jer 16:16 again; also Ez 34:6.

32. Donatus, the African schismatic, founding a "Church of the saints" with his erroneous ideas about the sacraments; Arius, the Egyptian heretic with his doctrine of the Son being a creature with a beginning in time; both of them living in the first portion of the fourth century; Photinus, the heretical bishop of Sirmium, in modern Hungary, denying the divinity of Christ, and also any real distinction between the divine persons, in the middle of the fourth century. By Novatus Augustine probably means Novatian, a schismatic in Rome in the middle of the third century. But there was a Novatus hovering around about the same time, though he was not important enough to find his way into almost any of the works of reference to which I have had access; however I eventually tracked him down in *The Faith of the Fathers*, volume I, edited by W.A.Jurgens, where I learned that he was a priest of Carthage who fell out with Cyprian, because the latter went into hiding during a persecution. Novatus went to Rome and attached himself to Novatian; hence the confusion. And I was delighted to read in Jurgens' index under Novatus, besides the reference to the information about his being a priest of Carthage, the entry, "For Novatus = Novatian, see under Novatian." So I think my first guess about Augustine's use of the name is correct.

33. We have had this illustration before; see Sermons 40, 6; 87, 15; 359, 8.

34. The habit of being a Donatist. His contention was that most Donatists were not so out of personal conviction, but simply because they had been brought up in the schism, and had got into the habit of it; it was what they were used to, and therefore attached to.

CHRONOLOGICAL TABLE

Abbreviations of Names

(B)	Anne Marie La Bonnardière	(M)	Christine Mohrmann
(Ba)	Tarcisius van Bavel	(Maur)	Maurists
(Be)	Bonifatius Fischer (Beuron)	(Me)	Frits van der Meer
(D)	Michel Denis	(Mo)	Paul Monceau
(DB)	Donatien De Bruyne	(Mor)	Germain Morin
(Ét)	Raymond Étaix	(P)	Othmar Perler
(F)	Georges Folliet	(Po)	Suzanne Poque
(K)	Adalbert Kunzelmann	(V)	Pierre-Patrick Verbraken
(L)	Cyrille Lambot	(W)	André Wilmart

Abbreviations of Works

CCL Corpus Christianorum, Series Latina (Turnhout-Paris, 1953)
CSEL Corpus Scriptorum Ecclesiasticorum Latinorum (Vienna, 1866)
MA *Miscellanea Agostiniana* (2 vols.; Rome, 1930-31). The first volume is *Sermones post Maurinos reperti*, ed. G. Morin
NBA Nuova Biblioteca Agostiniana (Rome: Città Nuova Editrice)
PL Patrologia Latina, ed. J.-P. Migne (Paris, 1878-90)
PLS Patrologiae Latinae Supplementum, ed. A. Hamann (Paris, 1957)
PW *Paulys Realencyklopädie der klassischen Altertumswissenschaft*, new ed. by G. Wissowa et al. (Stuttgart, 1893).
RB *Revue Bénédictine* (Maredsous, 1884).
SC Sources Chrétiennes
SPM Stromata Patristica et Mediaevalia 1 (= C. Lambot, *S. Aurelii Augustini Sermones selecti duodeviginti*) (Utrecht, 1950).

Short Titles of Frequently Cited Works

Borgomeo *L'Eglise* P. Borgomeo, *L'Eglise de ce temps dans la prédication de saint Augustin* (Paris, 1972)
Mohrmann *Études* C. Mohrmann, *Études sur le latin des chrétiens* I (Rome, 1958); II (Rome, 1961)
Mohrmann *Sondersprache* C. Mohrmann, *Die altchristliche Sondersprache in den Sermones des hl. Augustinus* I. *Einfuhrung, Lexikologie, Wortbildung* (Latinitas Christianorum Primaeva 3; Nijmegen, 1932)
Pontet *L'exégèse* M. Pontet, *L'exégèse de saint Augustin prédicateur* (Théologie 7; Paris, 1946)
Poque *Augustin d'Hippone* S. Poque (ed.), *Augustin d'Hippone. Sermons pour la Paque* (SC 116; Paris, 1966)
Verbraken *Études* P.-P. Verbraken, *Études critiques sur les sermons authentiques de saint Augustin* (Instrumenta Patristica 12; Steenbrugge-The Hague, 1976)

Nr.	Theme	Date	Edition
341	Christ, head of the Church	December 12, 418/419	PL 39:1493-1501
341/A	Humility of Jesus		Mai 22 MA 1:314-316 PLS 2:467-469
342	The evening sacrifice Ps 140:2 Jn 1:1-18		PL 39:1501-1504
343	Susan and Joseph, models of chastity	May 6/14, 397(L,B) May 7/13, 397 (P)	PL 39:1504-1512 RB 66 (1956) 28-38
344	Love of God, love of the world	c. 428	PL 39:1512-1517
345	Feast of Martyrs, rejection of the world	411 (P) c. 428 (K,Po,Be) 411, 416 or 428(V)	Frangipane 3 MA 1:201-209 PL 39:1517-1522
346	Our pilgrimage under the sign of faith		PL 39:1522-1524
346/A	Our pilgrimage	December 399 (K, L, Be)	Caillau II, 19 MA 1:265-271 PLS 2:435-441
346/B	Our pilgrimage	393-405 (K, Be)	Mai 12 MA 1:285-287 PLS 2:443-446
346/C	Difficulties of life	c. 410 (K,B,Be)	Caillau II, 92 MA 1:272-274 PLS 2:441-443
347	Fear of God		PL 39:1524-1526
348	Fear of God	425-430 (K, Be)	PL 39:1526-1529
348/A	Prayer	414-415	PL 39:1719-1723 CSEL 9/1:899-903
349	Charity Lk 18:38-42	winter, c. 412(B)	PL 39:1533-1535
350	Charity	425-430 (K, Be)	PL 39:1533-1535
350/A	Charity	c. 399	Mai 14 MA 1, 292-296 PLS 2, 449-452
350/B	Alms		Haffner 1 RB 77 (1967) 326-328
350/C	Riches		Étaix 3 REA 28 (1982) 253-254
351	Penance	391 (K, Be)	PL 39:1535-1549
352	Penance	396-400 (K, Be, Ba)	PL 39:1549-1560
353	To the newly baptized	Sunday, octave of Easter 391-396 (K, Be)	PL 39:1560-1563
354	Exhortations to religious	before 410 (K, Be)	PL 39:1563-1568
354/A	Marriage		PL 39:1732 RB 84 (1974) 253
355	The clerical life	425-426	PL 39:1568-1575 SPM 1:124-131
356	The clerical life	426	PL 39:1575-1581 SPM 1:132-143

Nr.	Theme	Date	Edition
357	Peace	May 411	PL 39:1582-1586
358	Peace and charity	May 411	PL 39:1586-1590
			SPM 1:144-149
358/A	Mercy		Morin 5
			MA 1:606-607
			PLS 2:671-672
359	War and peace	Dedication of a	PL 39:1590-1597
	with the Donatists	basilica 411-412	
359/A	Patience		Lambot 4
	Lk 16:1-9		RB 49 (1937) 258-270
			PLS 2:759-769
360	Conversion of a	Vigil of Saint	PL 39:1598-1599
	Donatist	Maximianus	
		411 (K, Be)	
361	Resurrection of	winter 410-411	PL 39:1599-1611
	the dead		
362	Resurrection of	winter 410-411	PL 39:1611-1634
	the dead		
363	Song of Moses	412-416 (K, Be)	PL 39:1634-1638
	Ex 15:1-21		
364	Samson		PL 39:1638-1643
	Ps 57		CCL 103:491-496
365	Ps 15		PL 39:1643-1646
366	Ps 22		PL 39:1646-1650
367	The rich man		PL 39:1650-1652
	Lk 16:19-31		
368	Jn 12; Eph 5		PL 39:1652-1654
			CCL 104:705-708
369	Birth of Jesus	Christmas 412?	PL 39:1654-1657
	Jn 12:25		RB 79 (1969) 124-128
370	Birth of Jesus	Christmas	PL 39:1657-1659
371	Birth of Jesus		PL 39:1659-1661
372	Birth of Jesus		PL 39:1661-663
373	Epiphany	Epiphany	PL 39:1663-1666
374	Epiphany	Epiphany	PL 39:1666-1668
375	Epiphany	Epiphany	PL 39:1668-1669
375/A	Easter Sacraments	Easter 396-397	Denis 4
			MA 1:21-22
375/B	Christ died for us	Easter	Denis 5
			MA 1:23-29
375/C	Apparition to the	Easter Season 402-404	Mai 95
	apostle Thomas		MA 1:340-346
	Jn 20, 24-31		PLS 2:489-494
376	To the newly	Sunday, octave of	PL 39:1669
	baptized	Easter 410-412 (Po)	
376/A	To the newly		PL 39:1669-1671
	baptized		
377	Ascension	Ascension	PL 39:1671-1673
378	The Holy Spirit	Pentecost	PL 39:1673-1674
	gives charity		
379	Saint John	June 24	Lambot 20
	the Baptist		RB 59 (1949) 62-68
			PL 39:1674-1675
380	Saint John	June 24	PL 39:1675-1683
	the Baptist		

Nr.	Theme	Date	Edition
381	Saints Peter and Paul	June 9	PL 39:1683-1684
382	Saint Stephen		PL 39:1684-1686 RB 80 (1970) 204-207
383	Episc. Ordination	PL 39:1687-1688	
384	The Trinity		PL 39:1689-1690
385	Love of neighbor		PL 39:1690-1695 CCL 103:94-99
386	Love of enemies		PL 39:1695-1697
387	Fraternal correction		PL 39:1697-1700 CCL 104:596-598
388	Almsgiving		PL 39:1700-1701
389	Almsgiving		PL 39:1701-1704 RB 58 (1948) 43-52
390	Almsgiving		PL 39:1705-1706
391	To the youth		PL 39:1706-1709
392	To spouses	Lent	PL 39:1710-1713
393	To penitents		PL 39:1713-1715
394	Saints Perpetua and Felicitas		PL 39:1715-1716
395	Ascension		PL 39:1716-1717
396	Funeral of a bishop	April 18, 412 (L) April 17, 419 (P)	PL 39:1717-1718

For the complete Chronological Table refer to Section III, Volume I, pages 138-163.

INDEX OF SCRIPTURE

(prepared by Matthew Dolan)

(The numbers after the scriptural reference refer to the particular sermon and its section)

Old Testament

Genesis

1:1	342,3; 379,4; 380,3; 380,4
1:2	380,4; 384,3
1:26	398,2
1:27	384,3
2:7	370,1
2:24	341,12; 349,3; 362,16
3:4	341,6
3:18.19	366,6
3:18-19	346C,1
3:19	359,1; 362,16
15:6	363,2
18:32	397,2
39:8-9	359,3
49:9	364,3; 375A,1

Exodus

3:14-16	341,10
15:1	363,2
15:2	363,2
15:3	363,2
15:4	363,2
15:4,LXX	363,2
15:5	363,2
15:6-7	363,2
15:8	363,2
15:9	363,2
15:9.10	363,2
15:10-12	363,2
15:13	363,2; 363,3
15:14-16	363,3
15:17-18	363,3
15:19	363,4
15:21	363,4
20:13.15-16	366,3
32:32	352,4

Numbers

20:12	352,4

Deuteronomy

32:49-50	352,4; 352,5

Joshua

1:5	366,5

Judges

13:25	364,2
14:14	364,2; 364,3
14:18	364,3
14:19-20	364,4
16:2-3	364,5
16:25	364,6
16:30	364,6

2 Samuel

12:13	393,1

Tobit

4:17	361,6
12:19	362,10

Judith

16:3	363,2

Job

1:8	398,10
1:9	385,5
1:21	343,10; 346A,6; 359A,6; 398,10
2:9	397,3
2:9-10	359A,6
2:10	343,10; 397,3; 398,10
7:1	359A,6

Galatians

Ephesians

2 Corinthians

INDEX

(prepared by Joseph Sprug)

499

hate and, 387:2
parents and children, 387:2
animals:
    fight for their lives, 368:4
    friendship in, 385:3
    humans and pleasures of the flesh, 400:2
    humans compared with, 341A:2
    love in, 385:2
    love of their offspring, 349:2
    prone; faces to the ground, 399:5
    sleeping and waking, 361:10
Anna (widow), 370:2; 391:6
Antiochus, 343:2
Apollinarists, 375B:7
apostles:
    Christ chose unlettered fishermen. . .,
        381:1
    fishers of men, 400:11
    light of the world, 379:6
    new covenant, 350A:2
    Pentecost, 352:2; 365:4
    source of learning of, 381:1
    words extend to ends of world,
        359:1; 375A:1
apostolate: hunters of men, 400:11
Arcadius, Emperor, 397:7
Arians, 375B:7
    Father and Son = two gods, 398:4,5
    objection answered, 380:4
    Trinity, 384:1-3
    understanding Christ in scripture,
        341:1-13
    Word of God not created, 380:3
Arius, 364:4; 400:11
ascension:
    Christ, king of glory, 377:1
    confess: he is seated at the right
        hand. . ., 375C:5
    love, he is still with us, 395:2
    real limbs and body, 375C:3
    will fixed in heaven, 395:1
atom (the word), 362:20
Augustine, Saint:
    affairs of community members, 356:3
    anniversary as bishop, 383:1-3
    asks forgiveness from those he
        offended, 383:3
    caught, made a priest, 355:2
    clergy in common life, 356:14
    clothing, 356:13
    confession of faith, 362:5
    debtors pardoned, 383:2
    dread of episcopate, 355:2

monastery in bishop's [his] house,
    355:2
nephew of, 356:3
preaching as service, 355:7
Aurelius of Carthage, Bishop, 355:5
Auses (Jesus Nave), 352:4
avarice, See Greed.

B

Baalim, 365:2
baptism:
    See also Catechumens; Infantes; John
        the Baptist
    birth into new life, 351:3
    buried into death; Red Sea, 363:2
    confessing belief in resurrection,
        362:7
    devil, sins, and the baptized, 363:2
    God as father; Church as mother,
        398:1
    keep unspoiled to the end, 398:15
    life lived in hope, 363:3
    newly born babies, 391:1
    newness of life, 393:1
    panic in Constantinople, 397:7
    passing through the [Red] sea,
        352:3,6
    Red Sea crossing as type, 363:2
    repentance before, 351:2; 352:2
    sacrament violated by doing evil,
        393:1
    spiritual birth, 376A:1
    unveiling of the newly baptized,
        376A:1
    water signed with Christ's cross,
        352:3
Barnabas (priest), 356:15
beasts, See Animals.
beatitudes:
    gifts of the Spirit and, 347:3
    praise of the commandments, 366:3
beauty:
    charity, 365:1
    in God's eye, 391:6
beggar, 367:1
    attitude, 389:3
    bishops and, 355:5
    Christ in, 389:4
    Christ knocking on your door, 389:3
    dreaming of wealth, 345:1
    God treats us as, 350B:1; 350C:1
    wishing people well, 399:7

envy:
    daughter of pride, 354:5,6
    diabolical vice, 399:7
    pride; gives birth to malice, 353:1
Epicureans, 348:3
Epiphany:
    Jews point out Christ to Gentiles,
        374:2
    Magi and the star, 374:1,2
    manifestation of the Lord, 373:1-5;
        374:1-3; 375:1
error:
    defeated by, 358:1
    detest for, 359:5
Esau, 361:16
eternal life:
    See also Heaven
    acquired by faith and loyalty, 344:5
    amazement at prospect of, 342:5
    baptism and, 393:1
    die in hope of, 375B:1
    dwell in house of the Lord, 366:8
    efforts to attain, 368:3
    everlasting wealth vs temporal goods,
        350B:1
    go, sell all you have. . ., 346A:4
    hating one's soul "in this age," 368:2
    hope for; the nativity, 370:1
    kingdom prepared for you. . ., 346:1
    knowing God and Jesus Christ, 365:1
    love of, compared with love of this
        life, 344:5
    need of, 359A:6
    neglecting its worth, 345:2
    only one good (eternal) day, 346C:2
    praise God without ceasing, 362:31
    prepared for, 362:7
    property which cannot be divided,
        359:2
    really deserves name of life, 346:1
    received by some, 351:7
    rest; knowing God and Jesus, 362:30
    reward of a good life, 399:13
    route to, 366:7
    same for married and virginal
        chastity, 343:4
    true health or well-being, 385:8
    whoever hears my word. . ., 362:25
    wishing to have, without dying,
        359A:8
    words of those without hope, 391:4
    yearning for, 359A:2
eucharist:

manna and, 352:3
sacrament of Christ's body, 354:2
separation from bread of heaven,
    351:7
unworthy communion, 351:7; 354:2
evangelists: messengers, 351:8
evangelization: unity and, 400:10
eve, *See* Adam and Eve.
everlasting (the word), 363:3
evil, *See* Goodness; Wickedness.
excommunication: formal judgment,
    351:10
exodus: journey through desert/life, 363:3

F

faith:
    believing is touching, 375C:5
    conviction of things which cannot be
        seen, 359A:4
    evil persuasion; faith is asleep, 361:7
    finding your life/soul in, 344:6
    ground of things hoped for, 359A:3
    heart purified by, 346:2
    hold on to, for sake of eternal life,
        344:5
    hope supports, 359A:4
    life hidden with Christ in God, 346:2
    love while we believe what we
        cannot see, 359A:2
    maturity, 370:4
    no praise for, if Jesus were visibly
        present, 359A:3
    persons presented for baptism, 351:2
    pilgrimage through life, 346:1-2
    pray that it not fail; Pelagian heresy,
        348A:2
    presence of Jesus in all Christians,
        361:7
    resurrection according to the spirit,
        362:25
    resurrection of the dead, 361:2
    rewarded for belief without sight,
        359A:3
    rich by believing, 399:10
    risen again with Christ, 362:15
    see now through a mirror. . ., 346:2
    sluggishness and, 358A:1
    texts on sight and faith, 346:2
    unless I touch him. . ., 375C:2,4
    value; reward for keeping faith, 345:7
    waken Christ abiding in you, 361:15
    walking by; arriving by sight, 346:2

exhortation to, 353:1-2
temptation, 391:1,3
infidelity, 392:3
inheritance:
  coveting, 355:4
  division of, 358:2; 359:3,4
  earthly; lawsuits, 400:13
  Lord is my portion; no litigation,
    359:4
  Lord's is not to be divided, 400:13
  sharing with Donatists, 358:5
iniquity, *See* Wickedness; Wrongdoing.
injustice: insatiable greed, 367:1
innocence:
  boasting of good practices, 351:4
  model of holy infancy, 353:1
interest rate, 390:2
isaiah: gifts of the Spirit, 347:2

J

Jacob, 361:16
Januarius (priest), 355:3; 356:1,11
jars: places set apart, 362:3
jealousy: love, 357:1
Jerusalem:
  Christ the foundation, 362:8
  earthly/eternal, 363:3
  home country, 346B:1
  mother of us all, 346B:1
  spiritual mountain, 347:2
Jesus:
  See also Arians; Incarnation; Son of
    God; Son of Man; Word of God
  alms given to Christ, 359A:11
  ascension, *See* Ascension.
  bridegroom and giant, 372:2
  choosing his apostles, 381:1
  Christ as doctor; healing may be
    painful, 346A:8
  Christ as God; our home country,
    375C:5
  church and, *See* Church.
  commands; promises, 382:1
  creed says all that has to be said,
    398:12
  crucifixion, *See* below: Jesus:
    Crucifixion.
  death taken from us, he gave us life,
    375B:5
  descended into hell, 364:5
  everlasting innocence, 375A:1
  first place in our hearts, 362:9

fraternal concord in, 359:9
from his fullness we have all
  received, 380:7
God and man, at the same time,
  341:3; 371:2,3; 379:2,3
grew, while John the Baptist
  diminished, 380:8
healer; Samaritan, 365:3
healing may be painful, 346A:8
heavenly man (no sin), 362:16
his own people did not receive him,
  342:4
humble in glory, 380:7
humility, 341A:1-3; 375A:1
I will exalt you, Lord, 380:6
Jews and Christians contrasted, 375:1
John and, *See* John, Saint, Apostle;
  John the Baptist.
life-saver in torrent of our lives, 372:3
light of the mind, 366:5
light which enlightens every man. . .,
  380:7
loved more than our dear ones, 349:7
loving and blessing him, 365:1
manna and Christ, 352:3,4
mediator and head of the Church,
  341:1,4
mediator between God and humanity,
  361:16
model: his death and resurrection,
  344:7
mortality assumed to give us
  immortality, 361:16
name; every knee should bow, 380:5
obedient unto death, 354:9
one who descended also ascended,
  362:16
only (!) Son of God, 398:3
parable of the seine, 362:3
parable: rich man and Lazarus,
  367:1-3
parable: unjust steward, 359A:9-10,16
passing by, stopping, standing still,
  349:6
passion, *See* below: Jesus: Passion
  and death.
pastor and provider, 366:3
Paul: God and man, 341:4
physician, 374:3
poor, to make us rich, 375B:1
poor people and, *See* Poor.
praised, to make Christians despair,
  361:15

love people on account of God, 385:4
many souls made into one; early
  church, 398:4
motives, 368:4
multiple roles of, 350:3
mutual love is not enough, 386:1
new commandment, 350:1; 358:4; 400:8
new covenant, 350A:2
objects lower than the person, 368:4
old man, 385:4
order of true charity, 368:5
peace, 357:2
perfect charity casts out fear,
  348:1-2; 385:1
perfected by contemplation, 359A:4
possesses length and breadth of
  scripture, 350:2
poured out in our hearts, 358:4; 378:1
reaching the perfection of, 368:5
right kind must drive out wrong kind,
  368:3
right order; progress, 368:4
road of Christian life, 346B:2
something which you can't see, 385:4
summary and shortened word:
  commandments, 399:3
three sorts of charity, 349:1
two greatest commandments, 350A:1
two paths; one road, 366:4
unlawful human love, 349:3
unlawful; incompatible with divine
  love, 349:4
whoever loves his soul. . ., 368:1-5
whole scripture teaching in one word,
  350:1
wish to love? love wisdom, 391:5
wishing object to be safe and well,
  385:6
love of God:
  bringing love of harlot into your heart
    with, 349:4
  Christ to be loved more than our dear
    ones, 349:7
  divine charity, 349:4
  exhortation to love Christ, 349:5
  fear of God and, 348:1-4
  fight: love of God vs love of the
    world, 344:1
  forsake creator for creature is
    adultery, 385:6
  freely is God to be loved, 385:4,6
  God to be loved more than parents,
    344:2

love me as much as you love money,
  399:11
love one I cannot see, 385:4
only God is loved in other human
  beings, 385:3
pray for this love to be given, 349:5
reward as motive, 385:5
whoever loves father or mother. . .,
  344:2
whole heart, soul, and mind, 348:2
love of neighbor:
  begins with self, 368:4
  concord with Donatists, 359:9
  correct your love, or eschew all
    company, 399:4
  enough for fulfillment of the law,
    399:5
  envy and, 399:7
  hating your brother; not loving
    yourself, 387:2
  if I speak with the tongues . . ., 350:3
  life for one's friend, 385:8
  love of self and, 348:2
  love one another, 385:1-9
  two wings of charity, 352:7
  understanding of term neighbor,
    399:3
  upright kind of love, 348:2
  your neighbor as yourself, 385:1;
    387:2; 399:3-5
Lucifer, 394:1
lust, 343:7; 365:5
  husbands, 392:5
  John the Baptist, 380:8
  trample on; desire eternal life, 346B:4

M

Magi, 373:1-5; 374:1-3; 375:1
Mammon of iniquity, 359A:10-11,13,15
man, *See* human; temple of God
Mani, 364:4
Manichees, 375C:3; 400:4
manna:
  figure of Christ, 352:3,4
  unable to free from death, 352:3
marriage:
  See also Husband and wife
  chastity in, 343:4
  conjugal rights, 354A:1
  continence, 354:4
  lawful love, 385:2
  married couples, 392:1-6

serpent, *See* Devil.
servant:
    authority over, 400:5
    parable of unjust steward, 359A:9-10,16
service of God: prepare for trials and
        temptations, 397:3
Severus, Bishop, 356:3
Severus (deacon), 356:5
sex:
    earthly desire, 362:16
    moderation; married people, 351:5
    unlawful relations, 392:2
shame: love of money, 399:11
shepherd: giving life for his sheep, 366:3
shipwreck: fund to insure against, 355:5
Sicca Venerea, 348A:1
sight and faith, 346:2
silence: God praised by, 341:9
Simeon, 370:2,3,4
sin:
    beginning: gate of hell; pride, 346B:3
    boasting of tamed body, 351:4
    cannot be without, 386:1
    carelessness in avoiding, 351:6
    charity and future sins, 383:1
    children of God do not sin, 351:6
    confessed even by a just man, 397:5
    correct self before judgment day,
        346A:7
    covered by almsgiving, 389:5
    daily repentance, 351:5,6
    daily wash of light sins, 388:2
    deserves death, 361:16
    despair, 352:9
    devil and the baptized, 363:2
    disgraceful for Christians to sin, 371:4
    earthly desires, 362:16
    engulfed in sins, 365:5
    fear of eternal death, 399:13
    fighting for the devil, 363:2
    forgiving, *See* Forgiveness of sin.
    grace and power to avoid; Pelagian,
        348A:3
    grateful for God's healing, 397:5
    grave sins covered by charity; with
        change, 388:2
    guard against, 359:9
    if we say we have no sin. . ., 388:2
    in iniquity was I conceived, 391:1
    knowledge of evil of past sins, 347:3
    love covers multitude of, 387:3
    no dread for past sins, 353:2
    no one is clean in God's sight, 351:2

not allowed in gehenna, 388:2
pagan calumny against the Church,
        352:9
redeemed by almsgiving, 350B:1;
        350C:1
repentance for grave sins, 351:7;
        352:8
Samson and, 364:3
sealed as in a bag (Job), 397:4
shadow of death, 366:5
slavery in Egypt, 352:6; 353:2
soul turned from God by, 366:4
soul without sin, 397:5
venial; life cannot be free of, 398:15
war on God, 365:1
works of the flesh, 351:9
sinners:
    Christ came to save, 381:1
    darkness does not comprehend light,
        342:1
    running away from God's mercy, 381:1
    suffering; blaming God, 341A:3
    threatened, 352:9
skins: suggest death, 362:11
slander: enduring, 357:4
slave(s):
    Augustine's community, 356:3,7
    entrusting gold to, 345:3
    masters and, 361:21
    valued and chastised, 400:5
sleeping: death, 361:10
snakes, 385:2
Sodom: destruction of, 397:2,6,8
Solomon, King, 398:13
    figure of Christ, 358:3
Son of God:
    coeternal with the Father, 398:8
    died and was buried, 375B:6
    Father begot what he himself is, 398:3
    form of a servant, 362:16
    omnipotent, 398:5
Son of Man:
    authority to judge, 362:26
    domicile remains in heaven, 362:16
    less than the Father, 341:6
sons of God, *See* Children of God.
sorrow:
    repentance and, 351:1
    share in, by mercy, 358A:1
soul:
    See also Body and soul
    alive when animated by God, 348:3
    fear of losing, 368:1

cure of the cross, 353:2
devil uses fear or greed, 346B:4
lead bad lives now, 341:6
no age free from, 391:1,3
Pelagian heresy, 348A:1
watch and pray. . ., 348A:2
why devil tempts us, 385:5
terror: God spared city of Constantinople,
397:7
theft: resort to, for giving alms, 359A:13
Theodosius, Emperor, 392:2
Thomas, Saint, Apostle, 361:13;
375C:1,2,4
threshing floor, 364:3; 397:9; 400:10
Thuburbo, women martyred at, 345:1,6
time:
coeternal; coeval, 398:8
divisions, 362:20
tithes: unjust steward, 359A:16
tolerance: necessity of, 359A:5
tombs: dead persons' ashes, 361:12
travel:
journey through life, 346B:1; 378:1
treasure:
found in a field, 399:2
where your heart is, 389:4
tree:
every tree that does not bear. . ., 389:6
full of leaves; full of fruit, 342:4
life cycles, 361:11
wild olive, 342:4
trials: prepare your soul for, 397:3
Trinity:
See also God
Arian heresy, 384:1-3
Christ in, 375C:7
divine unity is three, 384:1
equality in all qualities, 341:8,10
Father and Son glorified, 380:7
inexpressible and boundless, 384:1
procession of Father and Son, 369:2
scriptural texts supporting, 384:3
Son equal to the Father, 341:10
Word in, 375A:2
truth:
enmity from proclaiming, 392:3
finding fault with, 387:1
food in heaven, 362:30
paths of justice, 366:4
victory of, is charity, 358:1
Word of God, 346A:2
turtle-dove finds a nest, 343:1
twelve: totality, 351:8

U

unbelief:
blind Samson, 364:6
darkness is unbelievers, 342:1
death as, 344:6
imitating fathers who ate manna and
died, 352:3
night seeking night (Thomas), 375C:2
resurrection to judgment, 362:26
understanding:
bless the Lord, 365:2,3
commanded to understand, 348A:4
from nature = heresy, 365:2
gift from nature, 365:4,5
gift of grace, 365:2
gift of the Holy Spirit, 365:4
hearts cleansed of false values, 347:3
learning the commandments, 348A:4
seeking and obtaining, 365:5
wisdom reached from, 347:2
ungodliness: conversion, 346A:3
union with Christ: ascension, 395:2
unity:
body of Christ, 400:8
bringing Catholics and Donatists
together, 358:4
brothers in the inheritance, 358:4
early church, 398:4
evangelization and, 400:10
joy in its coming, 357:3
litigation with Donatists, 359:4
pagans and schismatics, 400:9
property; concord between brothers,
359:2
unjust steward (parable), 359A:9-10,16
urbanus, Bishop, 348A:1
usury: mammon of iniquity, 359A:15

V

vale of tears, 347:2
Valerius, 355:2
values:
See also greed; temporal goods;
Wealth
all flesh is grass, 341A:1
inner prosperity, 354:2
inwardly rich, 359A:6
learn to go for true riches, 345:5
love of self, 368:4
turn thoughts from earth to heaven,
350A:4

vanity: improper love, 348:2
vice: chain of effects, 353:1
victoriana, farm at, 356:15
virgin birth:
    desired event, 370:3
    Eve's sin and, 369:3
    sublimity of, 398:6
virginity:
    mind and body, 341:5
    pride and holiness of, 354:9
virgins, dedicated, 355:6
virtue:
    good wives, 343:5
    splendor of, 343:9
vows: holy commitment, 355:6
Vulcan and Mars, 400:9

W

waking up, 361:10
war: horrors, 346C:1
water: rock struck by Moses; figurative
    meaning, 352:4
wealth:
    See also Greed; Money; Rich
    burying in earth; depositing in
        heaven, 345:3
    entrusting gold to slave (God), 345:3
    exclusion from heaven, 346A:6
    expended to live longer, 344:5
    hard labor for love of money, 399:11
    heart is where treasure is, 345:5
    mammon means gold, 359A:13
    overloaded rich man, 399:8
    Psalm 144: true/false riches, 359A:14
    rich man and Lazarus, 367:2; 399:13
    rich will not take it with him, 359:3
    riches sought for sake of life, 345:2
    true wealth vs mammon of iniquity,
        359A:13
    truly rich = rich inwardly, 359A:6
    uncertainty of riches (Paul), 345:1
wickedness:
    bad conversations corrupt morality,
        399:9
    blinded by, 391:4
    Christians become devil's angels,
        376A:3
    duty of correction, 387:1
    loving iniquity = hating yourself, 399:4
    loving your soul in iniquity, 368:2
widow:

two coins bought the whole kingdom,
    359A:12
rejoice; Anna, 370:2
wife, *See* Husband and wife.
will:
    Christ could be tempted, 344:3
    freedom of choice, 348A:3,4
wisdom:
    blessed are the peacemakers, 347:3
    choose instruction, and keep
        finding. . ., 391:6
    disposes all things sweetly, 370:3
    fear of God, 347:1
    found by those who love her, 391:5
    love as much as we love money,
        399:11
    love of; by young men, 391:5
    observe justice, 347:1
    preference for, 343:9
    self-control, 365:3
    unfailing light of the mind, 347:2
witness-bearing:
    confessing from and in the truth,
        362:7
    I will exalt you, Lord, 380:6
    we are proof that gospel is true,
        346B:3
witnesses, *See* False witnesses
women:
    examples for young women, 391:6
    martyred at Thuburbo, 345:1,6
    Susanna, *See* Susanna.
Word of God (second person of the
    Trinity):
    abides forever, 341A:1; 391:6
    agreement with, while in this life, 387:3
    all things were made through him,
        379:4,7
    Arians; not created, 380:3
    everywhere, 341:2
    found truthful in all things, 346A:2
    in the beginning, 341:2,3,4,7;
        341A:1; 371:1; 375A:2;
        375B:4,5; 379:4; 380:2;
        380:3,4,5,6; 388:2
    iniquity as enemy of, 387:1
    leader of Christian pilgrims, 346A:1-8
    life events of Jesus and, 349:6
    no death, no blood, in the Word, 375B:4
    opponent of the wicked, 387:1
    praised by all, 377:1
    suffering, 375B:6
    wholly in the Father; in the womb, 341:2